the world
encyclopedia
of
dogs

the world encyclopedia of DOGS

Associate Editor in America

Arthur F. Jones
Past Editor of *Pure-Bred Dogs, American Kennel Gazette*
the Official Magazine of the American Kennel Club

the world encyclopedia of dogs

edited by
Arthur F. Jones and Ferelith Hamilton

GALAHAD BOOKS · NEW YORK CITY

Copyright © 1971 Walter Parrish International Limited
All rights reserved
Library of Congress Catalog Card Number: 75-7607
ISBN: 0-88365-302-8
Created by Walter Parrish International Limited, London, England
Designed by Robin Hardy
Printed and bound in The United States of America
Published by arrangement with Funk & Wagnalls

Foreword

by Air Commodore J A C Cecil-Wright, AFC, TD,
Chairman, The Kennel Club

The Editor and the Publisher have gained a couple of notable objectives in this book – out of a straightforward and simple concept, they have achieved a comprehensive, accurate and, at the same time, a strikingly handsome book. It is a book which I have no doubt will prosper and serve for many years to come the great and growing interest in dogs in all parts of the world.

There have been, in the past, a number of worthy attempts at compiling comprehensive books on dogs; many of these books were successfully published in their day but, apart from any faults they might have possessed which a modern book might be expected to correct, there is change in the dog world just as there is in any other sphere of life today – new breeds are admitted to the Kennel Club register, obscure breeds achieve greater prominence and popularity; breeds once isolated in some mountain fastness, remote Continental pasture country, or sandy desert have now become favored show dogs; breeds once popular now unaccountably vanished from the face of the earth. Every now and again information on the dog scene must be brought up to date, and this has been done handsomely in this book.

Apart from this necessary light on the dog world as it is today, there is the question of the way in which the material is presented. All too many books, admirable in the extent of their coverage and irreproachable in their standard of writing, have presented their material in a rather confused manner, making it difficult for the reader to find in them the particular piece of information for which he is looking. In this Encyclopedia that particular difficulty should not arise, for great care has been taken to ensure a logical sequence, easy reference and, at the same time, readability.

I am impressed also at how successful the Editor has been, in collaboration with Mr. Arthur F. Jones in America, at making the book as acceptable for readers in America as it is for readers in Britain, and other parts of the English-speaking world. Most of the 120 contributors are British, but many come from America, Australia, Scandinavia and a number of European countries, and include many famous names in the international dog world. The photographs, also, illustrate dogs from many countries.

With registrations of pedigree dogs at the Kennel Club currently running at over 175,000 a year (and over one million with the American Kennel Club), there is a great necessity for a responsible and up-to-date book of reference – for people who are considering their first puppy, for people who already own dogs as pets or for showing, or whose interest is in dogs generally.

This book has a great deal of value to offer them and also to the people who are professionally concerned, the breeders and kennel owners, and also to those devoted amateurs, the show judges, organizers and helpers, and the officers of breed clubs, who serve the dog in that great national structure whose head is the Kennel Club. I unreservedly recommend this book as a much-needed and valuable book of reference and reading on the dog.

Contents

Working Dogs (Sheep, Cattle, etc.)

Other Working and Utility Dogs

Gundogs (Sporting Dogs)

Hounds

Terriers

Toy Dogs

Spitz or Nordic Dogs

Editor's Introduction

To give some idea of the choice of dogs available to suit all purposes of man, whatever the climatic and territorial conditions, we have included descriptions of nearly 280 different breeds in this book. These breeds come from every country in the world. Many of the countries have their own national canine control authorities to look after these breeds. The first of these to come into being was the Kennel Club, belonging to Great Britain. Then came the American Kennel Club. The Scandinavian and European countries, besides their own individual Kennel Clubs, have the Fédération Cynologique Internationale as their overall controlling body.

Many of the breeds exist in small numbers and are confined to a comparatively small locality. Others have spread out beyond the country of their origin, and have become popular in other countries. Dogs have been bred for many purposes, but the one over-riding purpose today is as companion to man, and it is for this reason that most of the distribution of dogs around the world has taken place – the dog has had to possess some other attribute, more widely acceptable, than the one which brought it into being and which possibly had hitherto confined it to one locality. Such breeds were then developed extensively in other countries where they were adopted; and Britain and America have been very much to the fore in this respect.

Never before has the dog been so popular all over the world. Attendance records at dog shows are being broken, many more dogs are being shown, and many more pedigree dogs still are being kept. At this date there are a million dogs registered annually at the American Kennel Club, and over 175,000 at the Kennel Club and nobody knows how many more there are whose owners have not taken the trouble to register.

This book, therefore, is intended to be a useful and practical reference book for anybody at all interested in dogs, whether as show dogs or as pets. Its contents are of necessity condensed, but we have tried to include all the information relevant to its purpose. This information concerns every breed registered with one or more national canine authority, and which exists in sufficient numbers for information about it to be of use outside the limited area which, unfortunately, is the extent of too many obscure breeds which have been accepted for registration in certain countries.

The majority of the breeds included are, naturally, those which are the most popular in Great Britain and America; but this covers breeds which have their origins in many other countries – France, Germany, Belgium, Holland, Sweden, Norway, Finland, Russia, Japan, etc.

The information on the breeds consists either of articles written by well-known authorities on the breeds, or from information supplied by persons delegated by breed clubs in many countries or by national or regional clubs or associations throughout the world. These articles are, for the important and popular breeds, written in the same sequence throughout – history and development, color, care, character and the salient points of the official Standards. But, in an endeavor to maintain readability, we have allowed each expert contributor to express his or her knowledge of the breed in the manner which seemed best to them, subject (for ease of reference) to their keeping to the established sequence. This, although preserving the great knowledge and authority of the writer, has created a certain inconsistency of style throughout the book but, our method is, we believe, very much to the advantage of the reader. In addition to articles on breeds of dog there are a number of articles on complementary aspects of the dog – evolution, anatomy, diseases, nutrition, how to choose and treat a dog etc.

The method of presentation has been to place the breeds in sections according to the standard grouping adopted by most countries – gundogs, working dogs, other working and utility dogs, toy dogs, terriers, hounds and Spitz or Nordic dogs. Within these groups the breeds appear in alphabetical order. Obviously these groupings will not please everyone, as each country has different ideas. For example, in the U.S.A. the Toy Poodle appears in the toy group. In this book we have followed the British method and kept it with the Poodles under Utility. We have purposely included the words "other working and utility breeds" because so many of these breeds, called non-sporting in some parts of the world, are in fact extremely sporting and have as much claim to be among the working breeds as those which come under this heading. In other words "non-sporting" is a misnomer, and used only to split up what would otherwise be an unwieldy group. For the Basenji we have followed the Scandinavian classification which puts the breed under the Spitz group.

We had the same problem in using correctly the word "champion". If a dog has the letters Ch. before its name, it signifies that it has won its title in its own country. An American champion which has not at the time of publishing won its title in Britain is described as American Champion. Likewise a British Champion which has to date not obtained its title in America.

Where a breed is known under a different name in English-speaking countries, we have cross referenced the names, but have placed the relevant article under the name by which the breed is known in Great Britain (thus the reader referring to the German Shepherd Dog will be referred back to Alsatian). There are several anomalies here. In the U.S.A. the breed in Britain called the Cocker Spaniel is known as the English Cocker Spaniel, whereas the States' Cocker Spaniel is called in Britain the American Cocker Spaniel. In the case of the Pointer, Britain calls its own breed simply the Pointer while other countries define it as the English Pointer. The Contents Page will indicate the groups and the individual breeds included in them, and the Index will additionally indicate the page numbers of all breeds.

There are over 1,100 illustrations (mainly photographic) in this book to illustrate as many types of dog as possible. A note on the captions is necessary; we have composed them as far as possible to explain the points concerning each dog, but also we have included names of dogs, their performance, and the names of their breeders and owners. This is because for the most part, these are the names which are significant in the breed, in pedigrees and important blood-lines. The general policy with regard to illustration has been to display the development of each breed, and to portray the salient points (and sometimes bad points) in photographs of male and female animals, usually champions, and puppies at the age when they are likely to be purchased. In addition we have illustrated as many as possible of the breeds with head studies, front and side views, of leading pedigree dogs.

The Notes on Contributors provide basic information about them. This section has necessarily been highly condensed, and much that could have been said has perforce been omitted. Where dogs' names have been included, again it is because they have had a significant effect on the breed. The Bibliography introduces the reader to the famous old books on dogs but, more usefully perhaps, it indicates which are the most useful current books dealing at greater length with dogs as a whole, or on individual breeds or aspects of dogs. We believe that all of these books can be obtained from book-stores or from libraries.

The Index gives the page numbers of all breeds, whether of the articles concerning them or of reference to them in other articles. Also given are the page numbers of references to extinct breeds, ancestor to existing ones. Apart from this the complementary articles are fully indexed but the breed articles are only referenced in the index where they contain references which are important and have a more general significance. References which are peculiar to the individual breeds are not indexed since they can readily be found in the breed article concerned.

Finally, I must express my deep gratitude to the many persons, all over the world, for the great interest they have shown in the book and the trouble they have taken to provide material for it on the breeds to which they have, in most cases, devoted a lifetime. Especially I must mention the expert help and advice I have received from Mr. Arthur F. Jones, who has ensured that the text throughout is properly representative of the American canine scene and has himself contributed a number of the articles; to Mr. Clifford Hubbard who, apart from contributing some of the articles, has advised on the rarer breeds and has provided a number of the photographs; to Mrs. Barbara Burrows of Thomas Fall, whose photographs are more abundant in this book than those of any other photographer, and who has been unfailingly willing to provide them. My thanks are also due, for the help they have given me in respect of Continental breeds, to M. Jean Servier of the Club du Braque Français; Dr. Antonio Cabral, past President of the F.C.I. and the Club Portugues de Canicultura; Mr. Heinrich Reitzel of Bad Sachsa, Germany; Mrs. A. Gondrexon-Ives Browne of Rhenen, Holland; Mme. Leemans of the F.C.I.; and Dr. Zoltan Balassy of Gödöllo, Hungary. Special help has also been provided by Mr. E. Pellikka regarding Finnish and Russian breeds, and by Miss Margaret Osborne. Invaluable advice has been given by many international bodies, particularly the Kennel Club of London and the American Kennel Club, who have allowed the use of quotations from their official Standards, the Fédération Cynologique Internationale, and many other national bodies and breed clubs.

I would also like to thank the many contributors to this Encyclopedia, who have written articles, and who have also provided photographs from their own collections and, finally, my thanks are due to the staff of *Dog World* who have good-naturedly given so much help and advice on the breeds and matters within each of their own spheres.

Ferelith Hamilton, London.

Acknowledgments

Photograph Credits

The photographs in this book have been obtained from many sources. Largely selected by the contributors themselves, they are nevertheless frequently the work of some of the most famous dog photographers in the world. Not only do the Publishers express their gratitude for the photographs but also for the information about the individual subjects, and for much advice during the preparation of the book.

So many photographs are included that there is not sufficient space for us to credit each individual picture to the photographer whose work it is, and we have therefore listed them, initially in the order of the magnitude of each photographer's contribution, and subsequently in alphabetical order.

The major contributor of photographs is Mrs. Barbara Burrows of Thomas Fall, of Stanmore, England. Nearly 25% of the total illustration has been provided by Thomas Fall, over 250 photographs, including the color pictures in the cover design. Another well-known British dog photographer, Mr. C. M. Cooke of C. M. Cooke & Sons of Uxbridge, England provided 100 photographs; Animal Photography Limited (Sally Ann Thompson) of London, 45; Mr. Ake Wintzill of Sweden, 36; Clifford Hubbard, apart from his two valuable articles and much other help, contributed nearly 30 photographs from his collection. Miss Evelyn Shafer, one of the outstanding dog photographers of America, provided 33, and Miss Diane Pearce of Dunstable, England, also 33. Miss Anne Roslin-Williams of Sedbergh, England, provided 19. Photographs were also contributed by Stg Ahlberg of Sweden; Alexander Photo of Dallas, Texas; Andreas Foto of Sweden; Angel Photographic of Bicester, England; Anning of Ilkley, England; Edgar Bradshaw of Padiham, England; William Brown, Long Island, N.Y.; Peter Basden of Redhill, England; Beaverbrook Newspapers of London; Bo Bengtson of Sweden; J. Bradley of the Working Kelpie Council, Australia; Michael Charity of Cheltenham, England; Anthony Clarke of Luton, England; Cliffords of Darwen, England; Ann Cumbers of Reigate, England; The Daily Mirror of London; The Daily Telegraph of London; Davidson of Norwich, England; Dog's Life of Maidenhead, England; The Evening News of London; Fox Photos of London; The Frasie Studio of Chicago; William P. Gilbert of Somerville, New Jersey; H. J. Goater of London; Kenneth Graham of Alnwick, England; Grierson of Ayr, Scotland; Hedges of Lytham, England; Hellemaa of Finland; Hemel Hempstead Echo & Post, England; Hodgman of St. Leonard's, England; The Hungarian News Service; Jason of Liverpool, England; The Kent Messenger, England; Keystone of London; A. Vaughan Kimber of Rye, England; Stephen Klein of New York; Constance Stuart Larrabee of Chestertown, Maryland; Frank Longmore of Victoria, Australia; Ludwig of New York; Johnnie McMillan of Oakland, California; Hugh F. Meaden of Wincanton, England; Frank H. Meads of Hatfield, England; Monty of Birmingham, England; Nordisk Pressefoto of Copenhagen, Denmark; Bernice

B. Perry of Wilton, New Hampshire; Monika Peters of Hagen, Germany; H. Francis Pilgrim of Bledlow Ridge, England; D. Pitt of Stourport, England; Polmont of St. Helens, England; John Ross of Baton Rouge, La; A. J. Rowell of Hove, England; Ryslip Shipping Company of Bracknell, England; Simms of Windsor, England; The Sport & General Agency Ltd of London; Studio D of Blackpool, England; Suschitzky of London; Tauskey of New York; Westcombe Motion Pictures of St. Mary's, New South Wales, Australia; Thomas A. Wilkie of Guildford, England; O. W. Wilmot of Petersfield, England; Wyant Studios of Birmingham, England; Lionel Young of Bristol, England; The Zoological Society of London.

Photographs have also been provided by the following, to whom the Editor's gratitude for their other contributions is expressed in her Introduction – The Club du Griffon Vendéen (M. Hubert Dessamy), The Rallye Kereol, the Club Suisse de Chien Courant (Dr. G. Riat), Mr. Heinrich Reitzel, M. Jean Servier, Dr. Antonio Cabral, Mrs. A. Gondrexon-Ives Browne, Mr. E. Pellikka.

The photographs of the Japanese Spitz breeds were obtained from a source in Tokyo.

The drawings and diagrams in the article on Basic Canine Anatomy, and for the endpaper design, were done by Miss M. Davidson of Sydney, Australia.

Evolution of the Dog

The early history of the dog is a most fascinating study, and one which despite its having no finality is nevertheless intensely rewarding. Ever since I wrote forty years ago on "The Peculiarities of the Cape Hunting Dog" for a leading magazine in the English dog world, indeed ever since I was a kennel boy, I have never failed to be thrilled at the discoveries which from time to time confirm or confound earlier findings in the realm of cynological evolution.

When a new breed appears at Cruft's or Westminster, inevitably someone of the canine cognoscenti will observe that there stands yet another example of mutton dressed as lamb, an old defunct breed resuscitated in new guise; or a newly discovered race of breeding purity until now preserved in the fastnesses of some shangri-la. These observations, and others which may cynically suppose the newcomer at the show to be a cross between a bear and a racoon, or something like that, may surprisingly have a good many grains of truth in them; for it is quite true that if we go back far enough in cynological history we find that there was a kinship between even the most outlandish creatures . . . if as I say we go back far enough!

Avoiding the use of too technical jargon, (autochthonic chondrodystrophic forms and so on) on the one hand, and the pitiable ambiguities of the venerable savants of yesteryear ("it is an animal of a lumpish shape") on the other hand, I will try and present the story straightforwardly as I see it. To begin with let us forget all about what happened to one breed when its club was formed say in 1885, or what the captain did for the other breed back in 1851, for these events are so recent they are but leaf rustlings of a twiglet of the family tree of the dog . . . forget the breeds, the groups and even the divisions for the moment and reach back to the essence, the very stuff of which dog was made. Therefore, let us first locate our tree in this morass of the early animal kingdom, and having found it let us examine it with an open mind.

Its roots certainly do go back, even to the time-phase between the Eocene and the Oligocene periods, some thirty-five to forty million years ago – or even to fifty million years back, as elastic as that. To a time when carnivorous mammals were few, and in fact all mammals were in a transitional stage of development, being much smaller than their counterparts of today. For instance the hippopotamus was barely the size of a large pig, while the horse was as small as a Welsh mountain sheep. There was certainly no dog on earth then as we know a dog today; but there was a creature known as *Miacis*, which was the forerunner of several forms from which the true dog evolved. This animal was arboreal, long-bodied and short-legged, with an elongated tail like that of a polecat . . . in fact *Miacis* was rather like a polecat of today.

From *Miacis* evolved three main lines: the weasel trunk (retaining much

The Miacis *was rather like a polecat of today.*

Wolf (Canis lupus)

Canis lupus – the Wooly Wolf.

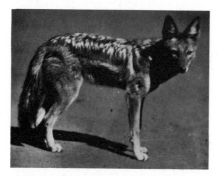

Jackal (Canis aureus)

Fox (Vulpes vulpes)

of the aboriginal form); and the cynodictine branch with which we are concerned. The form known as *Cynodictis* evolved from *Miacis* in the latter half of the Oligocene period, some fifteen to twenty million years ago, still reminiscent of its parent but having what in the dog world we would call more "substance" altogether – not unlike a primitive sort of Cardiganshire Corgi. Then from *Cynodictis* two sub-branches sprang from which evolved racoons on the one hand and bears on the other, while the main growth of this cynodictine trunk flowed on to dogs proper, significantly between the bears and the racoons. This trunk-line was transitional and flowed through two intermediate forms, the Miocene *Cynodesmus* (of around twelve to fifteen million years ago) and the Pliocene form *Tomarctus* (of about ten million years ago). By the Pleistocene era of about one million years ago the dog had become larger and, now established as *Canis*, was already diversifying into the forms we now know as wolves, jackals and coyotes, with some parallel aberrant forms like the so-called wild dogs.

In the meantime a primate creature, a *sort* of man, was emerging, until by about half a million years ago, or even less, it developed into *Homo sapiens*. This being we see, then, is quite a recent one . . . indeed its length of life on earth compared with even that of the dog is as short as the reign of the dog tribe compared with those of the earlier dinosaurs and reptiles generally. Briefly, then, that is the journey dog has taken to arrive with us in its present form – the Family Tree will illustrate this admirably. But while we indulge in this reach-back to the "lost world" of *Tomarctus* and its own ancestor *Cynodictis* let us not dismiss them as being slow-moving and slow-thinking animals, for they were quite intelligent hunters and the very foundation from which all the predatory dog-like runners sprang. But it is time to take a closer look at the family *Canidae* and see its members for what they were and are.

The family *Canidae* embraces the true dog (*Canis familiaris*), the wolf (*C. lupus*), the jackal (*C. aureus*), and various other forms. These true members of the dog tribe are structurally similar, with skeletal and dental kinship, and will breed one with another – they are each species of the one genus *Canis*. It is possible, of course, that with an advance of knowledge it may be agreed to promote the jackal, and perhaps the coyote (*C. latrans*), to generic rank as the sum total of likeness may no longer be held to warrant their inclusion as sub-generic relatives – as happened to the fox, which suddenly ceased to be *C. vulpes* and was, possibly prematurely, recognized as a distinct genus and renamed *Vulpes vulpes*. Moreover the coyote has an established dozen or so variant forms which together indicate a need for taxonomical revision at some future date, not necessarily involving total divorce from the group. In any study of the dog it is impossible not to devote considerable attention to the wolf . . . and therein to my mind lies the principal progenitor of all modern breeds. A lot of work has already gone into wolf study, by Pocock and his assistant Dolman, Osgood, Anthony, Young and Goldman, R. and A. Fiennes, and from other approaches perhaps Konrad Lorenz and Farley Mowat: and the more I assess their work the more convinced I am that the three or four dominant wolf strains have together been responsible for the bulk of today's canine breeds. Man has himself been responsible for dreaming up and breeding specifically for the retention of various fancy points and so-called desiderata in these breeds over the past century – indeed to such

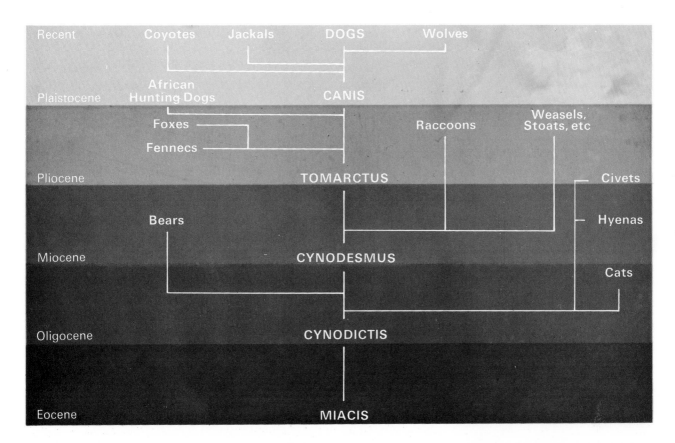

an extent that these very points have from time to time in this or that breed had a number of near tragic sequelae, plainly through his overdoing things! (And we must remember that differentiations in skull formations between breeds manufactured by man himself are far more striking than the natural differences between the various wolves and jackals). Nevertheless although man has taken licence with the canine form generally it is to the wolf the older credit goes for the biological balance, the constitution, the intelligence and the social behavior of the dog.

Special mention should also be given to the Dingo (*C. dingo*) for here we have, albeit a wild animal, a true dog. I regard the Dingo as a basic type of the family *Canidae*; probably a domestic or semi-domesticated dog of wolf extraction gone wild or reverted to type through the course of its history and travels to Australia via the chain of island stepping-stones from its original Asiatic home. I have studied many dogs in New Guinea and Papua identical with the Dingo, as have other observers right up through the early migration routes of the Aborigines. However, there exist also a number of forms which in the recent sense are unrelated to *Canis*. There is the fox already mentioned, and more remotely the hyena, the thylacine, and the host of so-called wild dogs of both the Old World and the New World.

The hyena has several species, one of which, *Hyaena spelea*, was in the days of very early association between man and dog-like forms, found in caves in South Wales. Three common species of today are the brown hyena (*H. brunneau*), the striped hyena (*H. striata*) and the spotted hyena (*H. crocuta*). The thylacine (*Thylacinus cynocephalus*) is the almost extinct creature of Tasmania which in some ways is reminiscent of the primitive *Cynodictis* – certainly far removed from the image of dog as we accept it today.

Dingo (Canis dingo)

Hyena striata – the Striped Hyena.

19

African Wild Dog (Lycaon tricolor venaticus)

Indian Wild Dog (Cyon deccanensis)

Siberian Wild Dog (Cyon alpinus)

Then there are the myriad "wild dogs": animals which at first glance, from hunting methods, from diet, and from behavior patterns, seem to be wild dogs but which on closer observation are revealed as aberrant types differing in skeletal, cranial and dental features from the true dog. These are the members of the widely scattered genera, *Cyonidae, Lycaonidae, Chrysocyonidae, Dusicyonidae* and others. These are distributed for the most part in South America and the New World generally, with strong representation in Asia and a few forms in Africa.

Of these additional genera the *Lycaonidae*, the African Wild Dogs, have attracted much attention; certainly the best recent study is the book *Innocent Killers* (Collins) by van Lawick-Goodall, whose work is both reliable and sympathetic. Even so although possibly resembling dogs more than hyenas superficially, these African Wild Dogs (Cape Hunting Dogs, or Hyena-dogs, call them what you may) are indisputably non-relatives. And so too are all the peculiar things in South America; one of which, the Bush Dog (*Speothos*) was mistakenly accepted in the London Zoo as a badger – so the renowned naturalist Reginald Innes Pocock told me years ago when I spent much of my time in the workrooms of the Natural History Museum, London.

As many cynological students still appear to take an intense interest in wild dogs generally I give here a Table of the principal forms, taken from my *The Complete Dog Breeders' Manual* 1954 – the Latin nomenclature which follows each common name in parentheses is, on repetition, abbreviated to the initial letter of the genus or species concerned.

WILD DOGS OTHER THAN FOXES
Old World

Africa:	African Wild Dog *(Lycaon tricolor venaticus)*
	Somali Wild Dog *(L.t. somalicus)*
Asia:	Buansuah *(Cyon primaevis)*
	Indian Wild Dog (Dhole) *(C. deccanensis)*
	Ceylon Wild Dog *(C. ceylanicus)*
	Malay Wild Dog *(C. rutilans)*
	Siberian Wild Dog *(C. alpinus)*
	Racoon-like Dog *(Nyctereutes procyonides)*
Australia:	Dingo *(Canis dingo)*

New World

N. America:	Coyote *(Canis latrans)*
	Indian Territory Coyote *(C. frustror)*
	Mexican Coyote *(C. microdon)*
	Gray "Fox" *(Urocyon cinereoargenteus)*
S. America:	Bush dog *(Speothos venaticus)*
	Panaman Bush Dog *(S. panamensis)*
	Santa Catherina Bush Dog *(S. wingei)*
	Tyra Bush Dog *(S.w. lacarrei)*
	Colpeo *(Dusicyon culpaeus)*
	Andean Colpeo *(D.c. andinus)*
	Tierra del Fuego Dog *(D. lycoides)*
	Falkland Islands Dog *(D. australis)*
	Aguarachay (Azara's Dog) *(D. gymnocercus)*
	Ai (Arecuna Hunting Dog) *(D. silvestris)*
	Short-eared (Sclater's) Dog *(D. microtis)*

Peruvian Wild Dog (*D. sechurae*)
Chilla (*D. griseus gracilis*)
Aguara-Guaza (Maned Dog) (*Chrysocyon brachyurus*)
Crab-eating Dog (*D. (Cerdocyon) thous*)
Cayenne Wild Dog (*D. (C.) t. cayenensis*)
Small-toothed Dog (*D. (Lycalopex) vetulus*)

Coyote (Canis latrans)

This list not only omits foxes and fennecs and things, but the Dingo and Pariah also, for the two latter are true dogs. And when the observations carried out some years ago by R. and R. Manzel have been properly evaluated and the more recent studies embraced, then the full influence of this type on the diversification of domestic breeds of dogs in the Near East will prove to be part of the answer to the development of the seven basic dog groups we have today. To my mind, the various Pariah types are so intimately linked in essence to certain dogs (including the Dingo) that a full study of the types and their habitat should prove richly rewarding.

Crab-eating Dog (Dusicyon) (Cerdocyon) thous)

domestication

We know how man himself improved upon his way of life through successive cultures following the Ice Age, and discovered how to fashion tools for tree felling and crude agriculture, and learned to erect hutments for communal living and make dug-out canoes from tree-trunks. By the Neolithic Era, he had tamed the most useful kinds of dogs then around him and as communications with other societies improved, used them as barter goods, or changed them for other dogs discovered along his trade routes. There had already been a considerable period of association between man and dog, ever since dogs were not only allowed but encouraged to scavenge the middens or refuse tips of the early settlements. Their presence in and around the camps had so often proved useful when barking at the approach of strangers that they were then given a rudimentary sort of training as guard dogs.

Bush Dog (speothos venaticus)

In time, the most tractable were subjected to more intensive training; the heavier types as hunters of forest game, the speedier and lighter dogs for hunting in the open, and some as herders of the small flocks of sheep and cattle then being domesticated. Later on the guardians, the herders and the hunters were subdivided into more specialized types. Their importance to the community was paramount; hunting dogs for example had a high value set upon them; and while certain of them have become defunct because their special prey died out, and so the need to continue their breeding no longer obtained, others became the ancestors of some of the most prized breeds of today. The chase of wild beasts was originally essential in order to obtain food and skins, but it later descended to a form of sport.

Short-eared (Sclater's) Dog (Dusicyon microtis)

Sport and work diverted the various types of dogs of even a thousand years ago into two main channels, sporting and working; and into these divisions most modern breeds still appear to fit. Sporting breeds like Pointers, Retrievers and Setters did not, of course, exist under these names at that time but their Group ancestor, the Spaniel, certainly did. In fact, the Spaniel of the year 920 A.D. had a high value set upon it in the Welsh Laws codified by Hywel Dda (King Howell the Good). These laws (which embraced the best of the enactments brought into Britain by the Romans as well as the age-old Brythonic social codes) even graded the values of each breed of dog according to the degree of training it had received . . . leaving no doubt that dogs had their place in British culture. Incidentally, the thousand-year-old penny, now thrown out from British currency, was worth in its beginning an untrained puppy; as was the pound itself of equal value to a fully-trained royal Spaniel.

As property, the dog had had a value from the very beginning of its domestication, and legal worths had also been included in the ancient Germanic laws and those of the Chinese before them. By Elizabethan times the officer appointed as Master of Game was able to keep precise accounts of his packs, and value to the penny the cost of their maintenance, as would a modern Master of Foxhounds. These accounts often appeared in commonplace and house books and rolls throughout Europe, together with the details of game killed during successive seasons. Some great hunters like the Pharaohs, the Khans, Assurbanipal, Emperor Maximilian, King John and Charles IX had all their pursuits recorded, and themselves wrote a number of most valuable historical records. A manuscript of this type was that written by Gaston de Foix, which as the *Livre de la Chasse*, 1387, was translated and added to by Edward, second Duke of York, as something to do when he was under house arrest at Pevensey Castle for having plotted against his uncle. His book was actually called *The Master of Game*, and although written between 1406 and 1413, it was never published until 1904, when W. Baillie-Grohman rescued it and issued it under his own editorship.

Once the merits of British and foreign breeds became better known through the copying of these early treatises on hunting and training there naturally followed a considerable exchange of dogs from one country to another; and with the influx of foreign breeds into Britain some native dogs were more or less improved by cross-breeding with the importations. And with the arrival of more and more distinct breeds and varieties from abroad, it was time to compile lists and classify them.

breeds

Dogs always seemed to come and go – and for every breed that died out there was surely a score of new types coming in. Breed catalogues lengthened decade by decade. Indeed the 800-odd breeds of which I wrote myself ten years ago are already short of the full mark today! Of classification proper the Romans were first to produce a serious effort; their list was of six recognized groups. Then the old Brythonic laws took the lists a stage further, and by Elizabethan times there were at least a score of defined breeds well above the degree of common cur.

One of the quaintest of catalogues was that of Dame Juliana Berners, which was published in the *Boke of St. Albans* in 1486 (the first privately printed dog book?). I quote part here *(verb.lit.punc.)*:

> This be the namys of houndes. First ther is a Grehound a Bastard. a Mengrell. a Mastyfe. a Lemor. a Spanyell. Raches. Kenettys. Teroures. Bocheris houndes. Myddying dogges. Tryndeltayles. and Prikherid curris. and smale ladies popis that beere a way the flees and dyveris smale fawlis.

What the small fowls, which puppies conveniently removed from milady's person, were we can only guess (ach y fi!); there were plenty of fleas, of course, as the dogs were washed even less often than their owners. Anyway, Dame Berners' superior list was accepted as authentic for we find it used by Shakespeare himself in 1605; modifying it to his own style in *King Lear* he gives us

    Mastiff, greyhound, mongrel grim,
    Hound or spaniel, brach or lym;
    Or bobtail tike or trundle-tail.

And note that these old dogs are still with us.

Johannes Caius, Physician-in-Chief to Queen Elizabeth I and cofounder of Caius College, Cambridge, published in 1570 his *De Canibus Britannicis*, a now excessively rare work which tabled sixteen breeds. Poor Caius has suffered a lot of nonsense written about him in recent dog books, and in order to keep the record straight, I do beg would-be copyists either to consult his original work or my *Literature of British Dogs*, 1949, before quoting him in detail. We have no opportunity here to analyze his table but, in modern spelling, his list ran as follows: the Harrier, the Terrier, the Bloodhound, the Gazehound, The Greyhound, the Lyemmer, the Tumbler, the Stealer, the Setter, and the Spaniel, being breeds for finding game on land and water; then came his Spaniel Gentle or Comforter, Sheepdog, Mastiff, Wapp, Turnspit, and Dancer, being used for other purposes.

Two centuries later Carl von Linné recognized thirty-five distinct breeds. By 1874, the English Kennel Club was officially recognizing forty breeds, which have since then grown to a hundred and fifty or so varieties, and grouped them according to the design of Rawdon Lee into an unscientific but administratively simple scheme. By 1945, I had published my little *Observer's Book of Dogs*, which dealt with no less than three hundred varieties, and now we see that even that total falls short of the full mark. Finally, a few notes on the classification of all these breeds, whether bred in this country or that, for work or for pleasure, or for mansion or maisonette. We have seen that various convenient forms of division of all known breeds were devised from time to time, and that although they each seemed to differ, more appeared to be based on sporting proclivities than on natural features. Hence none of the early systems has proved dependable on closer testing. (Henry Pye's notion was surely the most absurd, for in 1778 he divided all dogs into four categories; white, black, gray and yellow, these in order of value and beauty!) However, as one studies the arrangements of old Buffon, Bell, Beilby, Goldsmith, Cuvier, Walsh, Baron, Martin, Youatt and a veritable host of others, one sees the number of divisions growing as each strove to solve the problems of inclusion and exclusion. I have written fully on this very subject in *The Complete Dog Breeders' Manual*, 1954, so we shall not elaborate here; let it perhaps suffice to say that, after very many years of study over the schemes produced by scores of naturalists, cynologists and canine governing bodies the world over, I found that practically all varieties fitted into seven basic groups, the Greyhounds, the Mastiffs, the Spitz, the Sheepdogs, the Spaniels, the Terriers and the Hounds. These groupings were first published in 1948; and so far have proved serviceable. They have also won the acclamation of leading British and foreign taxonomists – indeed Vesey-Fitzgerald in his *The Domestic Dog*, 1957, reported that he found my system as great an advance upon a classification by E. C. Ash as was that of Ash himself upon all earlier ones. Very briefly then, let us see these seven groups at closer quarters.

Greyhounds are mostly coursing dogs, with the group readily recognized by its deep, roomy chest, well tucked-up loins, long legs, sharp-pointed muzzle and streamlined build. Except for the bred-down diminutives raised as pets, the group has generally been used in the chase of fast-moving quarry, hunting by sight rather than by scent.

Mastiffs are characterized by the group's large square head, well defined stop, short and square muzzle, and heavy weight and build generally. Employment has for centuries been mainly that of guard-dog for person, property and stock, not forgetting its use as a heavy battle dog in even earlier years.

Spitz form a remarkably tidy and constant family, with a rather broad skull having a sharp-pointed muzzle, small and sharp-pointed ears carried erect and enjoying extreme mobility. The coat is generally one with stand-off hair of medium length, more often forming a frill around the neck; and a generous brush to the tail, which is carried curled over the back. This group has a marked independence of character, and is normally confined to the Artic belt and near latitudes, where it is widely used for sledge hauling, pack carrying, herding and hunting – altogether a very versatile group.

Sheepdogs reveal more variation than any other division in the system, for physical, climatic and social influences of the many countries in which they work the sheep, cattle, goats and swine, all play their parts in moulding character and form within the group. They all agree, however, in equal powers of sight and scent, with good hearing, great intelligence, and great hardihood and adaptability. The head is powerful with fairly long muzzle and a negligible stop; fairly long back, with good angulation allowing a tireless gait; and the tail set low, thick and carried low.

Spaniels proper form the base of this group but it also embraces Pointers, Retrievers and Setters. The rather broad skull is generally convex with either the typical dome or an occipital ridge, a well defined stop, fairly thick, long and pendant ears, loose lips, and rather full round eyes. The body is lithe and muscular, with the back slightly sloping to the set-on and the legs of substantial but not coarse bone, with fairly large feet. The tail is natural, tapering, and flagged with long fine hair, while the coat is soft, of medium length, and well feathered.

Terriers represent a large yet recently manufactured group on the whole. Small to medium in size, and the most square in design. This type has a tightly-knit and very robust frame, with a rough weather-proof coat. Keen vermin hunters, many members of the group still retain the inclination to go to earth after fox and badger. In temperament the Terrier is excitable and vociferous, and makes an excellent house-dog.

Hounds are generally medium to large in size, hunt principally by scent, and are renowned for their musical voice when giving tongue. The skull of good breadth with a long foreface, usually slightly domed on the top, with low-set and long, broad pendant ears. The body is medium to long with a deep chest, with heavily boned and well muscled legs, having rather large feet. The tail is of full natural length, thick at the root, tapering, and carried gaily.

Basic Canine Anatomy

The study of anatomy of all species of animals, including man, is an intense and complex one, taking some years at Technical College or University level to complete. This applies also to the anatomy of the dog. It is not the purpose of this encyclopedia to delve too deeply into the intricate details of canine anatomy – there are a number of excellent specialized text books which do just that – but rather to offer some elementary knowledge on the subject of special interest to dog owners, dog breeders and dog lovers in general.

At Veterinary School level the subject of anatomy usually is divided and taught under the following headings:

1 *Skeleton* – the entire bony structure, the identification and description of the individual bones making up the whole and the various joints or articulations formed by the inter-relationships of individual bony components.

2 *Muscles and Accessory Structures* – muscles, tendons, ligaments, fasciae, etc.

3 *Digestive System* – those organs which play a part in the prehension and digestion etc. of food.

4 *Respiratory System* – those structures involved in the process of respiration, e.g. nasal cavity, larynx, windpipe, lungs, etc.

5 *Urogenital System* – the urinary system on the one hand and the genital organs, male and female, on the other. The reason for combining these two systems for study purposes is that some anatomical structures are shared. The kidneys, ureters, bladder, urethra, testicles, accessory sex glands, penis, ovaries, uterus and external female sex organs all come under this heading.

6 *Blood Vascular System* – the organs of circulation, commencing with the heart and following the arterial circulation through to that of venous return. The lymphatic system is dealt with also under this heading.

7 *Nervous System* – including the brain, spinal cord and related structures.

From the average dog owner's point of view the greatest interest in the field of canine anatomy lies in the skeletal section. It is with this subject that this article is concerned primarily. Discussion of the subject material will take place under two separate main headings, namely:

(A) Skeletal Anatomy: reference is made to the bony skeleton, identifying its various component parts and studying briefly the joints or structures formed by their relationships to or with one another.

(B) Topographical Anatomy: the external appearance of the dog, correlating it to the underlying structures. Mention is made of the terminology employed to describe the various regions, parts and/or points. This material is dealt with mainly in illustrative form.

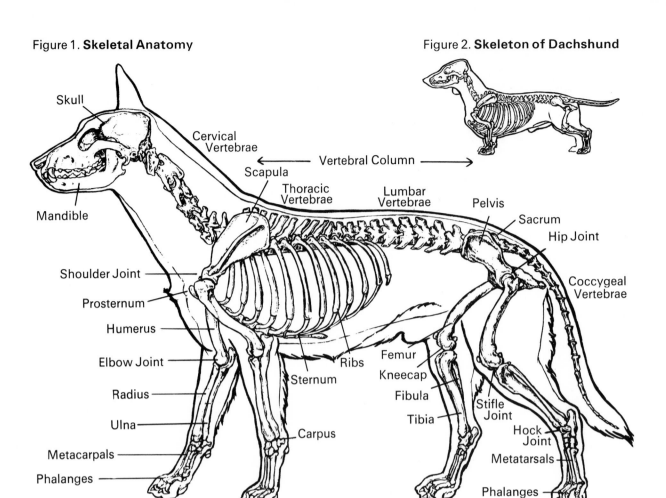

Figure 1. **Skeletal Anatomy**

Figure 2. **Skeleton of Dachshund**

Skull

Cervical Vertebrae

Vertebral Column

Scapula

Thoracic Vertebrae

Lumbar Vertebrae

Pelvis

Sacrum

Hip Joint

Mandible

Coccygeal Vertebrae

Shoulder Joint

Prosternum

Humerus

Elbow Joint

Radius

Ulna

Metacarpals

Phalanges

Ribs

Sternum

Carpus

Femur

Kneecap

Fibula

Tibia

Stifle Joint

Hock Joint

Metatarsals

Phalanges

Forequarters

Hindquarters

(A) Skeletal Anatomy

The skeleton of the dog is made up of a series of single bones held together by ligaments, tendons and muscles. The most common method of anatomical division of the skeleton is into five parts, namely: (i) Head and Neck, (ii) Chest Cavity or Thorax, (iii) Abdominal Cavity, (iv) Forequarters or Thoracic limb, (v) Hindquarters or Pelvic limb.

Diagrams 1 and 2 depict the complete skeleton of a dog, with the various parts clearly identified and labelled. The first diagram shows the skeleton of an Alsatian (or German Shepherd Dog) and inset is that of a Dachshund for comparison. In this way it is possible to demonstrate that, despite the great variation in external appearance of these two breeds or any others, the skeletal components are identical in number, if not in shape or size.

(i) *Head and Neck:* The head of the dog is made up of a series of individual bones, joined by soft cartilagenous tissues at birth. With developing maturity solid bony fusion takes place, the actual time depending on the breed (i.e. more rapidly in small breeds than in the larger ones).

From the practical view point the head of the dog is divided into two separate portions, the Skull and the Lower Jaws or Mandibles. No movement takes place between the bony components of the skull itself, nor is any possible between the two mandibles which are fused in the centre line at the mandibular symphysis.

26

The only actual movement which occurs in the head is that of the mandibles as a whole in relation to the fused bones of the skull. This takes place at the mandibular notch, where the condyles of the mandibles articulate at either side of the head with the temporal bones. The movement of the lower jaw is mainly up and down, although some side to side motion is possible. This allows for the picking up of food and its mastication prior to swallowing. Figures 3, 4, 5 and 6 illustrate clearly the structure of the canine skull.

Although the number of bony components of the head is identical in all breeds, there is nevertheless great divergence in shapes, due to variations of the individual bones. Long narrow skulled breeds e.g. Borzoi, Collie, etc. are termed dolichocephalic, while the opposite, very broad and short skulls e.g. Pug, Pekingese, etc. are designated as brachycephalic. The intermediate forms are referred to as mesaticephalic. The Fox Terrier, Dachshund, are good examples of this type.

The drawings show some extreme variations in skull shapes, yet the actual bony components are identical in number.

The teeth of the dog are situated both in the upper, as well as in the lower jaw. Four types of teeth occur. These are Incisors, Canines, Premolars and Molars.

The Incisor teeth are placed in front and are fairly small in size. They are used to pick up food. There are twelve incisors in all, six both in the upper and in the lower jaw.

At each side of the Incisor teeth is a large, deeply rooted Canine tooth, used for tearing purposes.

Back along the sides, just past the Canines on both upper and lower jaws, are the Premolar teeth. These number four on each side of the upper jaw, and four on each side in the lower jaw. Finally, at the back, and following on the Premolars, there are two Molar teeth on the top and three on the bottom on each side of the jaws. This situation is depicted in Figures 6, 10 and 11.

In summation, the full adult complement of teeth is forty two. This number is made up of twelve incisors (six in the upper and six in the lower jaw), four canine teeth (two each in the upper and lower jaw), sixteen premolars (eight each in both the upper and lower jaw) and ten molar teeth (four in the upper and six in the lower jaw).

To confuse the picture further, dogs develop two sets of teeth. The first is deciduous, occurs during puppyhood and early life and is followed by a permanent set later on. Although eruption and replacement times tend to vary somewhat with individual breeds, environment and nutrition, the following table will serve as a guide:

Teeth	Age of eruption (temporary)	Age of replacement (permanent)
Incisors	4 – 6 weeks	3 – 5 months
Canines	3 – 5 weeks	5 – 7 months
Premolar (1)	Not present	4 – 5 months
Premolar (2 – 4)	5 – 6 weeks	5 – 6 months
Molars (1)	Not present	4 – 5 months
Molars (2)	Not present	5 – 6 months
Molars (3)	Not present	6 – 7 months

Skull Types

Figure 7.
Dolichocephalic

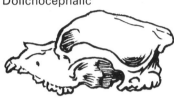

Figure 8.
Brachycephalic

Figure 9.
Mesaticephalic

Figure 3. **Skull—Lateral View**

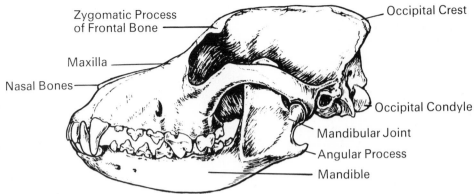

Zygomatic Process of Frontal Bone

Maxilla

Nasal Bones

Occipital Crest

Occipital Condyle

Mandibular Joint

Angular Process

Mandible

Figure 4. **Skull—Dorsal View**

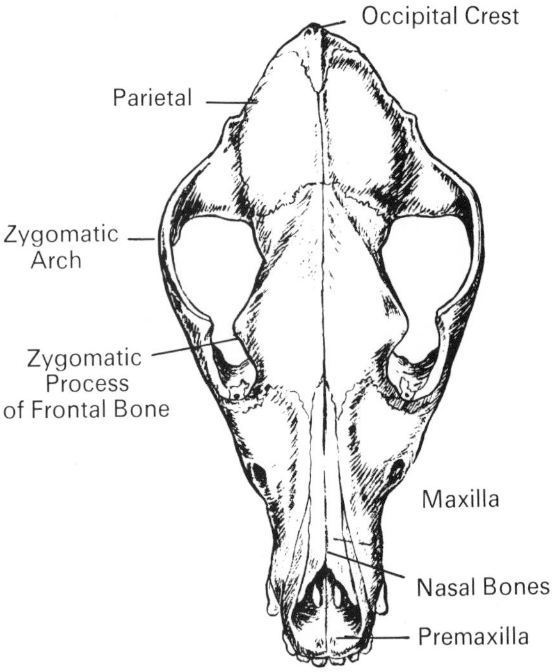

Occipital Crest

Parietal

Zygomatic Arch

Zygomatic Process of Frontal Bone

Maxilla

Nasal Bones

Premaxilla

Figure 5. **Skull—Ventral View**

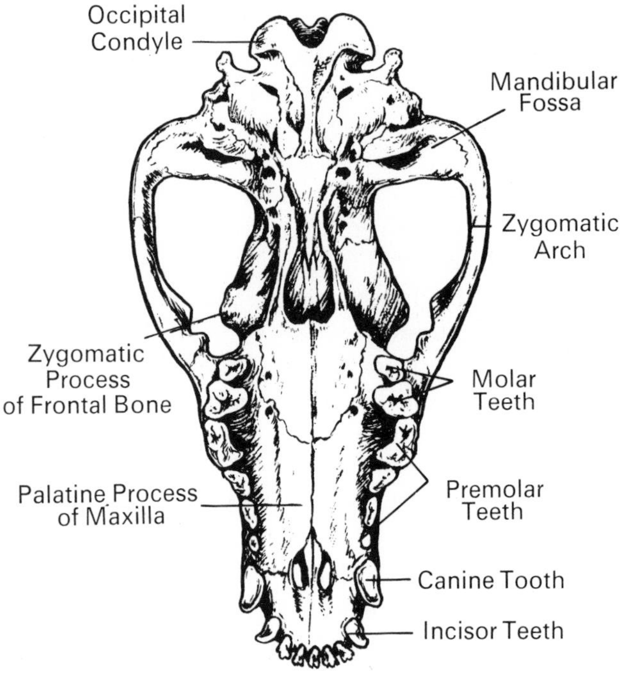

Occipital Condyle

Mandibular Fossa

Zygomatic Arch

Zygomatic Process of Frontal Bone

Palatine Process of Maxilla

Molar Teeth

Premolar Teeth

Canine Tooth

Incisor Teeth

Figure 6. **Mandibles**

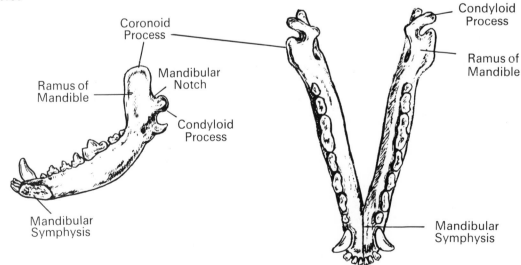

Coronoid Process

Ramus of Mandible

Mandibular Notch

Condyloid Process

Mandibular Symphysis

Condyloid Process

Ramus of Mandible

Mandibular Symphysis

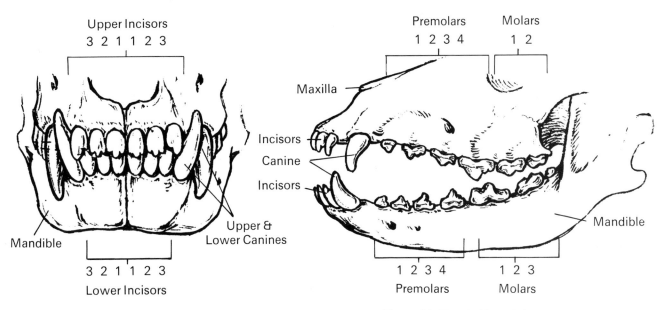

Upper Incisors
3 2 1 1 2 3

Premolars
1 2 3 4

Molars
1 2

Maxilla

Mandible

Incisors

Canine

Incisors

Upper &
Lower Canines

Mandible

3 2 1 1 2 3
Lower Incisors

1 2 3 4
Premolars

1 2 3
Molars

Figure 10. **Teeth (Front View)**

Figure 11. **Teeth (Side View)**

The head is joined to the rest of the body by the spinal column. This is made up of a series of small bones called vertebrae. Each vertebra consists of a central portion or body from which processes arise, both dorsally as well as laterally – it is through holes in the centre of the vertebral bodies that the spinal cord runs to transmit nervous impulses to and from the brain. In this way maximum bony protection is afforded the spinal cord. The spinal column itself is divided into five sections. The first of these is termed the *cervical* or *neck* portion. It is followed, in turn, by the thoracic, lumbar, sacral and coccygeal sections, as illustrated in Figure 12.

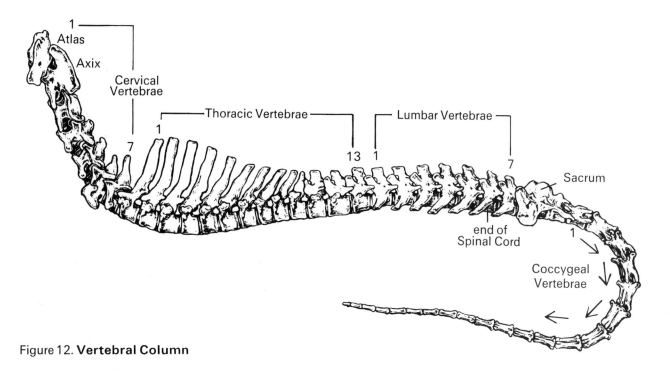

1
Atlas

Axix

Cervical
Vertebrae

Thoracic Vertebrae

Lumbar Vertebrae

1

7

13 1

7

Sacrum

end of
Spinal Cord

1

Coccygeal
Vertebrae

Figure 12. **Vertebral Column**

Once again, despite the great variations which occur in the shapes and lengths of the bodies of the various breeds of dogs, the numbers of vertebrae remain constant in each anatomical section, as does, more or less, their relative individual design – it is only in the length, width and depth of vertebral bodies as well as the processes, that differences occur.

Some detailed, yet brief, explanation of the divisions of the canine spinal column is necessary at this point:

(a) Cervical vertebrae – these join the head to the body and are seven in number. The first two, the atlas and axis, are highly specialized, so as to allow for maximal rotary movement of the head.

(b) Thoracic vertebrae – these form the dorsal components of the chest cavity and from their sides the ribs arise. The thoracic vertebrae number thirteen.

(c) Lumbar vertebrae – there are seven of these and they form the back region of the abdomen

(d) Sacral vertebrae – this section is composed of three relatively small individual bones, fused together so that little or no movement can take place between them. The sides of the pelvic girdle from which the hindlimbs arise, are attached to the lateral portions of the sacral vertebral bodies – this will be dealt with in some detail later.

(e) Coccygeal vertebrae – sometimes called caudal vertebrae, these form the tail. They vary in number from breed to breed.

(ii) *Thorax*: This is the chest cavity. It is bordered by the thirteen thoracic vertebrae above and the breast bone or sternum below; this latter bone is made up of a series of eight small bones, called sternebrae.

The sides of the chest are formed by the ribs. As already mentioned, these arise from the thoracic vertebrae and, like them, number thirteen. The ribs, at first, run outwards, then downwards and inwards to join the sternum in cartilagenous union.

It is important to note that, while the first front nine ribs are joined below directly to the breast bone, ribs ten – twelve are joined by way of cartilage to the ninth rib only. The last (thirteenth) rib remains completely unattached ventrally – for this reason it is referred to often as the floating rib. This arrangement allows for maximum side to side movement in the posterior portion of the chest cavity, permitting great lung expansion in that region.

The chest cavity contains a number of vital structures including the lungs and heart, both of which are concerned intimately with exercise tolerance, speed and stamina. It is of some importance therefore that the dimensions of the chest be adequate in all three directions, namely depth, length and width, so as to allow for maximal development of these organs and that it affords them adequate protection.

Frontwards the chest emerges with the region of the neck. Posteriorly it blends into the abdomen, from which it is separated by a strong muscular/ligamentous sheath, the diaphragm. In breathing piston-like contractions of the diaphragm into the abdominal cavity produce inhaling efforts, the opposite movement results in exhalation. At rest and during mild exercise breathing is carried out mainly by diaphragmatic pumping action, coupled with some activity of the intercostal muscles situated between the ribs. During violent exertion and severe stress other muscles also come into play. It is only then that actual side to side movement of the chest wall becomes pronounced.

For clearer understanding of the structure of the chest cavity see Figure 1.

(iii) *Abdomen:* The only bony component of the abdomen is the lumbar portion of the vertebral column, which makes up the dorsal section. The walls and floor of the abdominal cavity consist entirely of muscle and tendinous sheaths. In front the abdomen is separated from the chest by the diaphragm, while posteriorly it ends with the body of the dog.

Inside the abdomen are housed a large number of vital soft tissue organs, such as stomach, liver, intestines, spleen, kidneys, bladder, etc. So as to afford adequate protection to these structures it is essential that the development of the abdominal muscles be as strong as possible.

Figure 13 shows, in their respective positions, some of the organs enclosed in the thoracic and abdominal cavities.

From the last lumbar vertebra arises the sacral portion of the spinal column. This has been dealt with previously to some degree. It is to the sides of the sacral vertebrae that the bones of the pelvis are attached and from these, in turn, originate the hind or pelvic limbs (See Figure 1).

Figure 13. **Viscera of Dog (female) showing position of main organs**

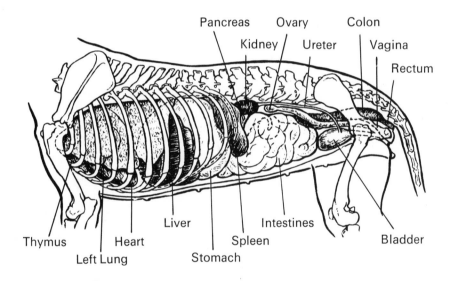

(iv) *Forequarters or Thoracic Limb:* The first bone of the thoracic limb is the shoulder blade or scapula; this is a relatively long and narrow bone, roughly triangular in outline. It is attached to the side of the chest wall by means of muscles, ligaments and tendons and lies in the region of the first four ribs; thus it is capable of great movement. A bony ridge, termed the spine of the scapula, runs downwards, roughly in the center line, and is palpable in the live specimen.

Figures 14 and 15 illustrate the skeletal components of the forelimb.

The scapula runs in a downward and forward direction and ends just in front of the sternal end of the fourth rib by forming the shoulder joint in articulation with the bone of the upper arm, the humerus. This is a relatively long bone, rather slender and has a slight spiral twist along its length. It runs downwards and backwards, ending at the elbow joint, which it forms in articulation with the radius and ulna.

31

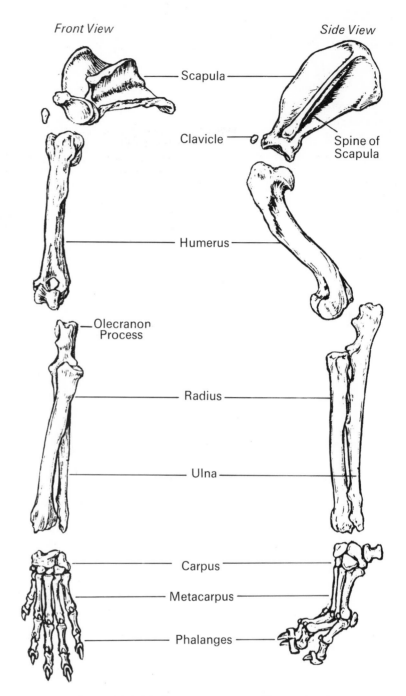

Front View　　　　　　　　　　*Side View*

Scapula

Clavicle

Spine of
Scapula

Humerus

Olecranon
Process

Radius

Ulna

Carpus

Metacarpus

Phalanges

Figure 14 & 15. **Forequarters or Thoracic Limb**

These two bones, firmly fused to each other both above and below, form the region of the forearm. Their fixed union allows only little interaction between them and, for all practical purposes, they move as a single bone. Running downwards in a more or less vertical direction the radius and ulna terminate by forming the carpus or wrist joint with seven small carpal bones.

From the carpal bones arise five metacarpal bones. The first one is vestigial only and is referred to as the dew-claw. The other four, numbered two to five, are fully functional and form the pastern region. They end in articula-

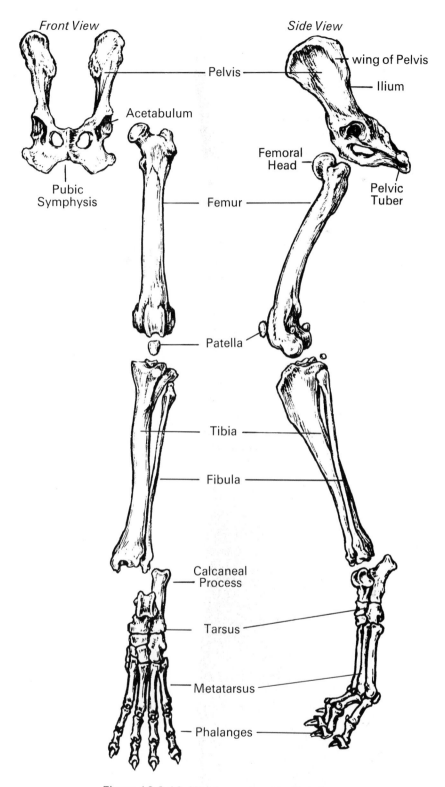

Front View

Side View

Pelvis — wing of Pelvis

— Ilium

Acetabulum

Femoral
Head

Pubic
Symphysis

Pelvic
Tuber

Femur

Patella

Tibia

Fibula

Calcaneal
Process

Tarsus

Metatarsus

Phalanges

Figure 18 & 19. **Hindquarters or Pelvic Limb**

tion with the bones of the foot, termed the phalanges. The first digit has two phalanges only, while each of the other four has three, as illustrated below. A toenail emerges from the end of each third phalanx to complete formation of the foot. Each toe has a thick individual toepad, with a large communal pad behind. Once again the diagram helps in interpretation.

Figure 20. **Stifle Joint in Profile**

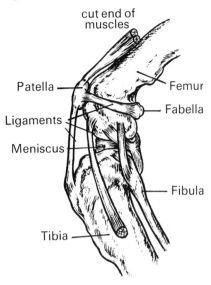

cut end of muscles

Patella

Femur

Ligaments

Fabella

Meniscus

Fibula

Tibia

Figure 16. **Forefoot-Dorsal View**

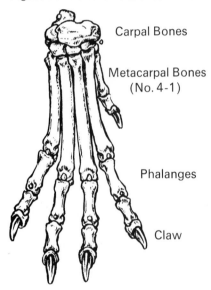

Carpal Bones

Metacarpal Bones (No. 4-1)

Phalanges

Claw

Figure 17. **Forefoot-Palmar View**

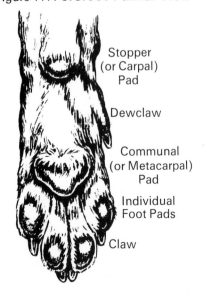

Stopper (or Carpal) Pad

Dewclaw

Communal (or Metacarpal) Pad

Individual Foot Pads

Claw

(v) *Hindquarters or Pelvic Limb:* The first bony component of the hind limb is the pelvic girdle. It is made up of two sections, fused at the rear at the pubic symphysis.

The anterior portion of the pelvic bone, termed the ilium, forms itself into a wing-like projection, which is attached at its medial surface to both sides of the lateral parts of the sacral vertebral bodies.

The most rearward section of the pelvis is referred to as the ischial tuber. The hip joint is situated between the pelvic wing and tuber of the ischium, at a distance approximately twice as far from the wing than from the ischial tuber. Both the pelvic wing and ischial tuber are palpable in the live specimen. It is possible therefore, by manual examination, to plot the location of the acetabulum which forms the socket portion of the hip joint. From this region arises the thigh bone or femur. This is the longest and strongest single bone in the canine skeleton. It runs downwards and forwards to form the knee or stifle joint at its lower end in articulation with the tibia and fibula below, and the knee cap in front.

Although it is difficult to explain the construction of the pelvic limb verbally, the accompanying drawings will assist in demonstration.

The uppermost portion of the femur, the femoral head, fits snugly into the acetabulum of the pelvis. It is held there by a short, elastic, round ligament, supported by the adjoining muscle groups. The muscles surrounding the thighbone form the region of the upper thigh, which ends at the stifle joint. The tibia and fibula originate there to form the lower thigh.

The actual stifle joint then is made up of the lower portion of the thighbone above, the upper extremities of the tibia and fibula below and the kneecap in front. The kneecap or patella is a small, relatively long and narrow bone which runs in a groove, termed the trochlea, in the lower end of the femur. It is kept in this position by bony ridges on either side of the femoral trochlea, supported by a series of ligaments. A detailed illustration explains the anatomical composition of the stifle joint.

The bones of the lower thigh are two in number. The tibia in front is a relatively large bone, approximately equal in length to the femur. It is joined both above and below by a much thinner bone, the fibula. Similarly to the position of the radius and ulna, this fusion of tibia and fibula permits their use as a single structure. The tibia and fibula run downwards and slightly backwards to end in articulation with seven small tarsal bones, thus forming the tarsus or hock joint. The fourth tarsal bone bears special mention.

It is fairly large and forms a prismatic projection, easily seen and palpated. Onto this bone attaches the achilles tendon, by means of which some groups of strong thigh muscles exert their action on the hind leg.

From the tarsus downward, the construction of the rear pastern and foot is remarkably like that of the front leg. Five metatarsal bones are present; the first however, is often either quite small or absent entirely.

The digits of the hind foot arise by way of three individual phalanges from each of the metatarsal bones, resembling those of the thoracic limb in all respects. This statement holds true also for the toe and communal foot pads.

Figures 16 and 17 show this in some detail.

Having completed discussion on the subject of skeletal anatomy of the dog within the permitted limits of space, it now remains only to touch briefly on the second portion of the topic, namely:

(B) Topographical Anatomy

This topic refers to the recognition and identification of the external areas, portions and points of the living dog in relation to the underlying skeletal structures and the terms used in description.

Descriptive topographical anatomy is best dealt with in illustration. By considering the above drawing together with illustration 1, it is possible to locate, recognize and define the skeletal structures lying beneath the skin.

It is not practicable, in an article of this length, to deal with the other fields of anatomy, mentioned in the introductory paragraph. Further information can be obtained from any of the references noted in the Bibliography.

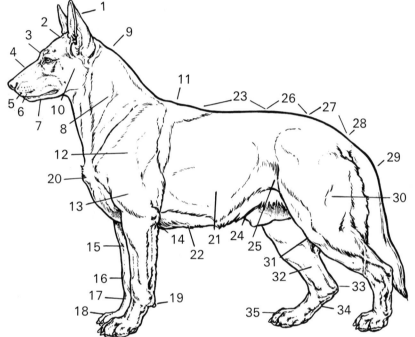

Figure 21. **Topographical Anatomy**

Legend for Topographical Anatomy.

1. Ear.	19. Stopper pad.
2. Skull.	20. Prosternum.
3. Stop.	21. Ribcage or
4. Foreface.	chest.
5. Muzzle.	22. Sternum.
6. Top lip.	23. Back.
7. Bottom lip.	24. Belly.
8. Neck.	25. Flank.
9. Crest of neck.	26. Loin.
10. Cheek.	27. Croup.
11. Withers.	28. Set on of tail.
12. Shoulder.	29. Tail or brush.
13. Upper arm.	30. Upper thigh.
14. Elbow.	31. Stifle joint.
15. Forearm.	32. Lower thigh.
16. Wrist.	33. Hock.
17. Pastern.	34. Rear pastern.
18. Forefoot.	35. Hind foot.

35

The Dog
in the Home

Thinking of Having a Puppy: When buying a puppy for a special reason, that is to say if you wish to have a dog that can do a particular job of work, the choice is comparatively easy for you. If you wish your dog to herd sheep or cattle, you wouldn't be looking for a Pekingese. If it is a guard dog for your country estate you would more than likely be on the look out for a Dobermann, an Alsatian (German Shepherd) or a Boxer, than a dog like a small terrier bred for ratting or rabbiting. The choice of a pet, however, is different and advice taken by a family about to take a dog for a companion for the first time can be extremely helpful. Let us take first things first.

The cost of purchasing and of the upkeep of the pet is of primary importance. For the family of moderate means living in an appartment, that is if pets are permitted at all, it would be silly to suggest a large breed like a Great Dane or an Irish Wolfhound. Though if you were asked to help choose a breed for a large home in the country these are two breeds you might suggest. What must you expect to pay for a well bred and well reared pedigree puppy? The choice of breed will, of course, determine the price, but for a puppy that before the last war would have cost you from £5 to £10 ($12. to $24.) it would be reasonable in Britain to expect to have to pay £15 to £25, and in the U.S.A. a minimum of about $100. If one is only going in for a puppy whose birth is an accident, then the cost will, or should be, considerably less. But beware of the pitfalls in buying a mongrel or crossbreed.

To ascertain the parentage of all puppies is most important, with a mongrel or crossbreed the necessity is ten-fold. I have seen a small bundle of joy and mischief, supposedly to be the product of a Pekingese Cavalier association, grow into an animal the size that could eat small children for breakfast. Furthermore, don't let anyone be persuaded by the dog expert next door that a mongrel has greater powers to resist disease than a pure bred.

With the breeding, planning and out-crossing that go into dog breeding to-day, without doubt the pedigree dog is far tougher in constitution. There are over 120 breeds registered at the English Kennel Club and 116 in America, and most of them are suitable and will make excellent pets. Smaller dogs of course are more suitable for the life in town. It doesn't require a lot of intelligence to realize that life in a multi-storey flat would be little joy with a Pyrenean Mountain Dog (Great Pyrenees) weighing between 100 and 125 pounds. Obviously a flat dweller would be better with a Chihuahua, under six pounds, or the Griffon, with its amusing little ways.

Dogs of the terrier size are adaptable in the town house, and the Cocker Spaniel usually makes a gay little companion. Along the same lines, and about the same size, is the Corgi, not at all the nipper that he is given the credit for being. All these can, if properly brought up, be most affectionate and great companions for young children.

Retrievers and Dalmatians, though larger in size, are also good tempered animals, and again great with children. However, the final choice is yours and your family's. Just one other point to keep in mind. There are flat coats, long coats, wiry coats and wavy coats; we have hard coats, fluffy coats and hard to groom coats. Some dogs, like the Poodles and most terriers, need to be trimmed by an expert, and some breeds shed their coats on your clothes and furniture a couple of times a year. Back to the shaggy dog – the Old English Sheepdog, sometimes known as the Bobtail, or the massive coated Afghan – I would not like to suggest, unless at least one of your family enjoys spending a good deal of time grooming.

Buying a Puppy: Though thousands of puppies are bought and sold each year, it is not always easy to locate one of the breed you have made up your mind to own. I would like to go on record as having said when purchasing all livestock, cut out, if possible, the middleman. Though there are many pet shops and dealers that can be relied on for a good square deal, there are many, however, that are only interested in making a quick sale. Only the breeder is in a position to know a puppy's correct age, and a sound purchase can only be made when the correct age is known.

From reputable journals devoted to pedigree dogs, you will be able to find advertized, puppies and young stock of almost any breed or variety, usually to be seen at reputable kennels open for your inspection. At these establishments you will be able to choose from a litter, and it should be possible for you to see and handle the parents. Buyers beware of choosing the little waif that looks at you in such a pathetic way and just asks to be taken into your heart and home. The death rate of these litter runts is very high indeed, and I only wish that some control could be placed upon the selling of young, and sometimes too young, puppies.

You have made your choice, and you are not going to take the puppy away until it is properly weaned, at least eight weeks old for most breeds. You have seen to it that you have put your deposit on a bright eyed little chap or Miss that came welcoming towards you, not the one that backed away into the furthest corner. You have seen that the kennels in general, and particularly the place where your baby is living is clean and well disinfected. See to it that although at this stage, possibly the dam of the puppies is on the lean side, she is in good health, bright of eye and not nervous. A good well run kennel will give you a diet sheet that will tell you how the puppy should be fed when weaned, and it is always a good idea to stick to this way of feeding as closely as possible for at least a month or so after you have the little fellow home.

When the time comes for you to take the pup home it is also a good idea to let your veterinary surgeon examine him, the same day if possible. At the same time let it be known to the breeder that this is your intention. I have known breeders and dealers on knowing you intend to do this, stop the sale, surely a pointer to the fact that all is not well. On receiving a clean bill of health from your veterinary surgeon, ask his advice on inoculations, and then of course, take his advice. If you buy from a reputable breeder your puppy will already have had his initial wormings.

Later on, if your pet loses condition, or shows any signs of having worms, ask your veterinary surgeon for a recommended preparation.

Introducing the Puppy into the Home: Put yourself into the place of a young puppy. If not just that very morning taken away from his mother, he has been whisked from his brothers and sisters for the first time, and on arrival, what does he see? All strange faces and a place he never dreamed existed.

Your family has been looking forward to his arrival for days, maybe months, but this is not the time for you to allow your children to give him a party. A saucer of milk, a soft word and that is all that is needed until he has for himself explored your home and the place that he has not yet accepted as *his* home. Already a bowl of cold, clean drinking water should be in place. A large enough dog bed slightly raised from the ground and out of the draughts should also be in place. If you take him to bed with you for the first few nights because he is alone and crying downstairs, that will be the place he will expect to sleep every night for the rest of his natural life.

Don't let your dog develop bad habits, be firm from the start. Making him house clean is the simplest job imaginable. Choose a place in the garden that is easily accessible and disinfected, and after a meal, or each time he makes a puddle or a mess on your kitchen floor, quietly but firmly take him out and put him down on the place you have chosen. In a very short time your puppy will be scratching and whining at the door to get out when nature calls. First thing in the morning on being wakened, your puppy or even the fully grown dog will want to relieve him or herself, and the same after a feed. Put him outside without delay.

Keeping a pet clean in an upstairs flat is, of course, a slightly different matter, but the same rule applies. They must be taught to be clean and to go to a flat box or tray, or even just newspapers spread on the floor in a convenient out of the way place. Even at eight or ten weeks old five minutes grooming a day will not be out of place. Left until six or more months and it could just be more of a full staged wrestling contest.

Bathing: How often must we bath our dog is a question asked all the time by pet owners. Generally speaking it is not a simple question to answer. With a long haired and low to the ground dog living in the country and taking its exercize off the lead, the answer is more than likely to be frequently. With a short coated dog, longer on the leg and living a town life, possibly hardly at all. With regular grooming and an occasional dry shampoo, it is possible to keep these dogs healthy and sweet smelling with only the occasional tubbing. Simply, the answer to this all important question is – bath your dog when it is medically and socially required to do so. I would sincerely hope that no bathing will have to be done until the puppy is at least fourteen to sixteen weeks old, if then. We have some wonderful sweet smelling insecticide and germicide shampoos on the market these days. When preparing the bath the water should never be more than warm. A good soaking, a good rubbing, a good rinsing and a good towelling. Keep him out of the wind and draughts until thoroughly dry. The longer coated dogs will, of course, require combing out after the bath. But, remember, only warm water. Shield the eyes from the shampoo. Don't bath too young, nor would I recommend bathing a bitch in whelp after she is over three or four weeks pregnant.

Nails: It is a common mis-belief that dogs who have plenty of exercize on hard ground require little or no attention in the way of nail cutting. Just in the same way as some of us have soft nails, so does the dog. A dog with hard nails will require cutting shorter from time to time even though he spends his time running the streets. Nail cutters, or nail clippers are designed to pass easily between the toes, and a good quality tool is noiseless and therefore causes the animal little or no panic. One should never attempt to cut a dog's nails with ordinary scissors. To do this would split the nail. Great care must be taken not to cut the nail too short and so pass through the quick. With the white or light colored nail this is no problem, as the quick can be clearly seen as a dark shaded line within the nail itself. Care must be taken not to snip off the nail closer than a good sixteenth of an inch from the quick. With the black colored nail one must be very careful, taking a little off at a time.

Dew-Claws: While on the subject of nails, I think it would be worthwhile if a special mention was made of the dew-claw, on the inside of the front legs, and with some breeds on the hindlegs as well. These claws will at times grow back into the leg and cause considerable pain and lameness. It is possible, however, that your dog has had them removed just after birth.

Care of the Teeth: A puppy is born with no teeth, but by the time he is about seven weeks old he will have twenty-eight. These are his first set, his puppy teeth. When he reaches about four months, a puppy (this does not include most toy breeds) will begin to lose the puppy teeth and by the time he is five to five and a half months old, he should have his permanent set of forty-two to forty-four. Toy breeds usually take a little longer. A hard biscuit or a marrow bone helps this change of teeth. Puppy teeth which are not cast should be extracted at the time the second teeth begin to come through. Unless these first teeth are very loose and one is able to pull them out with the fingers, they are very brittle and I would like to suggest the job is left again to a veterinary surgeon or experienced breeder. Sloppy food is not only bad for the dog's digestion, it is very bad for the animal's teeth. Dogs will get that yellow/brown tartar on their teeth very early in life if continually fed on soft food and never given anything hard to eat. This will affect both teeth and gums. The gums will become swollen and tender and eventually the teeth will become loose. From an early age a dog should have a hard biscuit and/or a chew at a good strong marrow bone daily. Once the tartar has been allowed to form on the teeth nothing but a regular scraping will remove it, three or four times a year.

Ears: Ear trouble in dogs would be very rare if it were not for their owners' neglect. There is a lot of loose talk about ear canker, but in fact a very small percentage of ear trouble in dogs is caused by canker.
Home treatment: First see to it that all the growth of hair is removed from around and a way into the ear. Next, putting the dog's head on one side, holding firmly and gently at the same time so as not to cause the

animal to panic, with the aid of a *slightly* heated teaspoon pop in as far down into the ear as possible a few drops of either almond or olive oil. Work the oil well into the ear cavity by massaging at the base of the ear. If you were born with three hands, so much the better. When the oil has been given a little time to soften the wax and the dirt formation, dip some cottonwool swabs or cottonwool buds into a mild solution of surgical spirit and spend a little time removing the filth as it softens and comes with the massage more towards the surface. Care must of course be taken as you would with a child's ear, not to poke too far down into the cavity and so cause injury. When all or most of the wax and dirt is removed, then, and only then, is the time to bring ear powder into play. There are a number of ear powders on the market, but it must be thoroughly understood that the instructions must be followed to the letter. If this treatment does not work out, please do not hesitate to take your dog to a veterinary surgeon, as it is very likely that the trouble is more deeply rooted.

Anal Glands: The cleaning and emptying of the anal glands is a very simple little routine job, that can in the animal's later life save a lot of trouble. We have all seen a dog drag its backside along the ground, or suddenly tuck the tail in as if something was pricking him from behind. This is more than likely a congestion of the anal gland due to an accumulation of a secretion. If this duty is not neglected, it is only a matter of squeezing the gland and so removing the contents. In some cases the glands will require attention every month or six weeks. In the first place, let your veterinary surgeon or the breeder to the job, by watching him you will realize how very simple it is to perform.

Training: A dog that is properly trained is not only a pet that you yourself can be proud of, he will be a source of pleasure to others. All that is required with most puppies of average intelligence is a little time, a little patience and firmness. A puppy at first has only a very short memory, which means that you can only hope to have any success by repetition. Training periods must be short, only a few minutes at first, and if possible given every day. Repetition; patting; scolding; and an occasional titbit. When your puppy does as he is told, a friendly word, a pat, and at times, though not all the time, a titbit. When he has done wrong or is fooling around, the slight punishment must be immediately following the mistake. A rather harsh voice saying "Bad dog" or "Bad dog Rover" and a sharp slap across the buttocks is all that is necessary. We all like to be appreciated, and remember, so does your pet. A verbal scolding is the best, no screaming or loss of temper. From the start of training use the same words. The words you use are really of no importance, but the tone of the voice is. "Sit" (sharply), "Stay" should be "staaay", "bad dog" (in a deep voice) "Bad dog, gurr!!" etc.

Collar and lead work: Start your puppy wearing a collar at an early age. A light one at first, and not too tight. At this age his neck thickens almost daily. At first he will scratch and try to get it off. Once used to the collar, the next step is the lead. Gently does it at first; you must get him used to the slight pull very gradually. He will more than likely sit down on you at first. With the lead under his chin a slight pressure will soon bring him along. All the time using a reassuring voice.

The first and most important thing to teach a dog is to sit. With the dog on your left side, hold his head up with your right hand, and then press him down into the sitting position with your left hand. At the same time say "sit" in a sharp commanding voice. Hold him in this position until you feel him relax. Gradually leave go. If he makes a move to get up, and at first he will, push him down again and at the same time say "SIT". Then in exactly the same way he should be taught to lie down, and the command is "DOWN". In the same position as with the "Sit", pull his front legs forward until he is lying down. From now on it is only a matter of repetition for you to get him to sit and lie when not on the lead and from a distance.

Do not allow your pet to become a nuisance at meal times. At his feeding time it is not a bad idea to bring this "sit" training into play. Make him sit and not touch his food without a "go on", "go get it" from you. When training, praise followed immediately after success cannot be overdone. From the sitting or down position walk away, only a very short distance at first, with a happy voice call "COME". Right from the start put no thought in his mind that this coming lark is anything but a very pleasant experience to be enjoyed.

Pulling on the lead and jumping up against you and others is possibly one of the worst torments of dog ownership. If your puppy, or grown dog will insist on pulling on the lead, unless with a very small dog or puppy, a choke chain is the answer. Use your "SIT" to start off the walk. Many people are not in favor of a choke chain or lead, but take it from me it is the best tool for making a dog walk to heel. There are two ways of attaching the choker, and you know the two ways. The correct way is when used in the left hand the ring comes upwards to tighten and drops down and slackens. "HEEL" is the command you must continue saying and with a rolled up newspaper in your right hand for a smart whack across the chest when he tries to get ahead. The paper will make quite a clap of noise, but no harm done. A gentle tug is no good at all. A sharp jerk is necessary and then release immediately.

Working Dogs

Cruft's Supreme Champion 1971, the Alsatian (German Shepherd Dog) Ch. Ramacon Swashbuckler, a perfect example of this famous Working breed.

Alsatian
(German Shepherd Dog)

Ch. Fenton of Kentwood, supreme best in show at Cruft's in 1967. This beautiful dog is the result of over a dozen generations of careful line breeding in his home kennel, and is easily recognizable as "Kentwood type". Bred and owned by Miss Sonnica Godden.

history and development

Despite the enormous popularity of this breed and the fact that it has topped the Kennel Club registrations in Britain for several years past (nearly 17,000 in 1969), the general public remains, by and large, in complete ignorance of the origin and purpose of this magnificent dog.

It is in all respects a normal dog, no trimming or preparation being required for the show ring or to enhance its great natural beauty.

Along with many other herding and working breeds, the German Shepherd Dog was certainly a dog which came side by side with man from the cave-dwelling days of pre-history. The development and refinement into the noble animal we know today, is largely due to the work of Rittmeister von Stephanitz; the first stud books date back only to the end of the 19th century. So, in this respect, it is still considered as a "new" breed.

A well-developed ten-weeks bitch puppy with her lovely construction, easily assuming show stance and showing one of the stages of ear development.

Two long world wars involving the country of its origin have done much to obscure the correct nature and purpose of the dog, the greatest impediment being the distortion of its true name – German Shepherd Dog – by which it is known in almost every country in the world, except Britain, where it began its show career classed as a "Foreign Sheep Dog", then as the Alsatian Wolf Dog, which did much to foster the stupid supposition that it is closely related to the wolf and, therefore untrustworthy – neither being true. Not until the middle thirties did the Kennel Club agree to have the title changed to Alsatian (German Shepherd Dog); and responsible breeders look forward to the day when "Alsatian" is dropped and the

The supreme champion at Cruft's in London, 1971 – the Alsatian (German Shepherd Dog) Ch. Ramacon Swashbuckler, owned by Prince Ahmed Husain, handled and presented at Cruft's by Mr. & Mrs. E. White and bred by Mr. W. Rankin.

Lothar of Jugoland, a striking example of how successfully the best German and British blood lines blend when intelligently planned

simple "German Shepherd Dog" will be used, thus bringing the name into line with the rest of the world. In Britain this will assuredly help more than any other single factor to dispel the bad publicity the breed suffers when one dog commits, as members of all other breeds do (no more and rather less), a misdemeanor.

Rittmeister von Stephanitz was also the founder of the world renowned Verein Für Deutsche Schäferhunde, known as the S.V., which is the parent club of this breed and has its headquarters in Augsburg, Germany. This club closely controls the breed in Germany, and through its qualified S.V. judges influences and guides breeders all over the world. The main object is to keep the working qualities of the Shepherd Dog and to see that its construction and stamina are maintained to equal its extraordinary intelligence. The membership of the S.V. numbers some 43,000; and with an entry at its Siegerschau of nearly 700 animals (200 in the open dog class!) it may clearly be seen that the origin and purpose of the breed is safeguarded, as all exhibits must pass stiff tests for character, and only those with a working qualification may be entered in the open classes.

In most European countries, the Police in rural areas work with a German Shepherd Dog – in rural Switzerland the proportion is one dog to each man. In the British Isles it grows steadily in popularity with the Forces;

and the stories of its courage and tenacity would fill a large book. In the African countries its reliability as a tracking dog over vast territories, together with its stamina, make it a firm favorite everywhere. Used as a customs patrol dog in the mountainous frontier regions of many countries it is a splendid guard to its handler, a keen tracker after smugglers and an excellent messenger dog, covering long distances over rough territory with its surefooted and tireless gait. In "man" work its control, application and courage are second to none. As guide to a blind person, its sensitive performance stirs all hearts, although it is sometimes passed-by for other breeds less expensive to feed.

The German Shepherd Dog, like Paris, can "be all things to all men". Its great versatility has raised it to the top position wherever it is established. It has a fantastic record in crime detection and in the control of crowds and even mobs. It is an ideal demonstration dog in the displays of the Armed Forces, not only for its great training potential but by reason of its impressive beauty of form and movement. Farmers use it in increasing numbers, and even consider it an excellent gundog for rough shooting, since it is an un-flustered retreiver. Its courage and devotion will always make it, above all, the very best of family and companion dogs.

This is Ch. Jugoland Afstan Lulabelle, of German descent, bred by Mrs. P. Stanley in 1962; a lovely black and gold daughter of Lorenz of Charavigne.

Twin sisters interested in a flight of birds. At three months their ear carriage is fully developed.

color

Colors may be black and tan (golden to fawn), golden sable, gray sable or all black. Pigmentation is important, dark eyes and points being desirable while color-paling should be penalized. White dogs or albinos are not permitted by any Standard.

care

This most natural dog requires no trimming, only to be kept clean by vigorous and daily grooming. Good condition depends mostly on its feeding, ample freedom and exercise. Plenty of fresh raw meat, wholemeal rusk or kibble, seaweed powder, and calcium (when a puppy) will develop and maintain its strong construction and muscles. Soft, dainty or minced foods are detrimental to the highly desired firmness. Slow to mature it must be brought carefully through its first twelve months.

character

Certainly a sensitive dog, but never fearful or cringing, it is watchful to the point of suspicion and ever ready to defend its master and his property, and should thus be treated with the respect due to any guardian. Extremely keen senses make it both an excellent herding dog and companion, while its devotion and gentleness are unsurpassed. It learns very fast, even as a small puppy; and the ease with which it can be trained makes it a popular choice for obedience and working trials enthusiasts. It is an independent thinker, yet has a strong desire to please its owner. Usually strongly protective to children and small animals, which is normal in a herding breed.

standards

The German Shepherd Dog impresses immediately with its strong bone and powerful muscles, its proud head carriage and its well angulated (but never exaggerated) shoulders and hindquarters, which enable it to cover the ground with a typical effortless stride and to turn swiftly, as befits a herding breed. The broad thighs give its action strong propulsion, and with an outreaching front movement, allow it to cover the ground with an economy of stride and great smoothness.

The back must be particularly strong, and contrary to some opinions, is fairly short, the length of the body overall being measured from the point of the prosternum to the rump. In the AKC Standard the ideal proportion of length to height is 10 to $8\frac{1}{2}$; i.e. height is eighty-five per cent of length. The withers are high, with the backline sloping down to the croup without any dipping or other sign of weakness. The croup is well moulded and in harmony with the powerful, but not heavy, hindquarters. The tail is set fairly low and must be straight, with a gentle turn up (often called a sabre tail) at the tip. Ring tail and corkscrew tail are ugly faults; and while the tail may be lifted in movement or excitement it should never curl over the back or be carried above the backline.

The body is deep and roomy with a solid appearance, yet shapely and not clumsy or heavy, the bitch being allowed rather more spring of ribs than the dog. The belly, or underline, is clean and firm but not tucked up in loin to give a Greyhound appearance. The chest is deep and well developed, and the depth of ribs should be carried down to the breastbone, which is ideally on a level with the elbows.

(Opposite) The head of a champion of champions – Ch. Ramacon Swashbuckler.

Miss Z. Pearce's black and tan bitch, Ch. Lucille of Keyna, born in 1966, is one of many champions sired by Ch. Ludwig of Charavigne, described as one of the truly great stud dogs of all time. Ludwig has done a great deal to combat color paling.

One of the breed's "greats" and a popular winner for nearly nine years in the ring, maintaining his beauty and action to the end. Mr. R. Hall and Mrs. M. J. Pilling's English and Irish Ch. Gorsefield Granit was several times qualified "excellent" by visiting S.V. judges, and was winner of twenty-three C.C.s.

49

A police dog demonstrates the man work exercise.

This picture of Ch. Leo of Llanyravon, bred by Mrs. Nancy Evans, shows natural method of posing an Alsatian in the show ring.

The legs are perfectly straight with strong "dry" bone, and the pasterns gently sloping but not overlong or weak. The hocks are well let down, and the bone must not be heavy or clumsy. The feet are those of a working breed, the pads being deep, thick and hard so that they grip the ground well. The claws should be strong and short, and preferably dark colored. Thin and spreading feet are a definite fault, as are weak and overlong pasterns and cow hocks.

The breed shows great nobility of bearing, with a broad skull, erect ears well used to show the dog's alertness, and an almond-shaped eye of great depth and warmth, showing no fear or tension, and immensely wise and keen in expression. A dark brown eye is preferred; but an eye the color of the surrounding coat is allowed, though it must never be yellow or pale. The lips must not be loose. The nose should be dark in color. A full dentition is particularly required. Missing teeth are strongly hereditary and prevent the dog from exercising his powerful grip, which is so highly desired in his "criminal" work: in Germany, a dog with more than one of the small premolars missing cannot be given a Class I certificate for breeding, while three or more missing teeth preclude the animal from entry in the Stud book.

The double coat, with its soft, downy undercoat and firm, closely held guard-hairs or top coat, makes the dog very hardy and enables it to endure severe climates without detriment to health.

Height of a dog is 24″ to 26″ and a bitch, 22″ to 24″. The A.K.C. Standard cites 25″ as ideal for a male and 23″ for a bitch.

Two keen herding dogs which have charge of a valuable herd of Jersey cows.

Alentejo Herder

The Rafeiro do Alentejo, an ancient Portuguese breed is found mainly in the Province of Alentejo, south of Lisbon. It is a strongly built, hardy dog, used for herding livestock and guarding farms and has a reputation for being especially alert during the night.

The head resembles that of a bear; wide skull; neither frontal furrow nor occiput being very noticeable; small oval-shaped eyes and small ears, triangular in shape and hanging folded over. The muzzle is shorter in length than the skull and is level, not very wide and the stop is slight. Jaws meet in a level bite.

The short, strong neck is straight and has a dewlap, the brisket, wide and deep; slightly arched ribs; long and level back; croup slightly inclined and the loins, which are medium sized, are straight, wide and arched. The thick tail is slightly curved and sometimes curls when the dog is in action. Quarters are strong, straight and well-muscled.

The coat may be short but hair of medium length is preferred; coarse, smooth and dense. Colors are black, wolf-gray, fawn or yellow with white markings, or white marked with these colors, striped, brindle or tiger-marked.

The height at the withers varies from 26″ to 29″ in a dog and from 25″ to 27½″ in a bitch.

A typical specimen of this Portuguese working dog.

Anatolian Sheepdog
(Karabash)

The Karabash are descended from the mastiff dogs existing in the Middle East over 3,000 years ago; a likeness may be seen in Babylonian terra cottas in the British Museum, and in the Louvre in Paris. They are still used as guard dogs by Anatolian shepherds to protect their flocks of sheep from wolves, and as protection have their ears cropped and wear massive iron spiked collars.

Pockets of well-bred dogs may be found in many sheep rearing districts of Anatolia in Turkey; large numbers of typical dogs exist in the provinces of Konya and Sivas. Strict selection for working qualities, type and strength have ensured that the breed is immensely tough and has great stamina. A pair were first introduced to Britain in 1965 by Charmian Steele; there are now approximately twenty examples in the country. The Anatolian Karabash Dog Club was formed in 1968.

The following description comes from a Standard now being drawn up: A large, powerfully built dog with short, dense coat. The head large with broad skull, eyes medium sized, set well apart and golden brown. Ears V-shaped and pendant. The back long and powerful, loins slightly arched; chest deep and broad. The tail long, carried low, the end curled over but when in action carried high over the back. The color is cream to fawn or striped brindle with black mask and ears. Height 26″ to 30″, less in some countries, dogs considerably larger than bitches. Weight from 90 to 150 lbs. Not known in the U.S.A.

Mrs. Charmian Steele's dog, Gazi of Bakirtollukőyu, demonstrates the desired heavy head and front compared with the lighter hindquarters.

Armant

(Egyptian Sheepdog)

Boy of Armant, a pre-war dog owned by Dr. Hassan Nachat Pasha. Face, head and ears well-covered with long hair, but the eyes are visible.

This is a breed not known to any extent outside Egypt. It is thought to have resulted from crossing local dogs with the French dogs which accompanied Napoleon's army in the Egyptian Campaign in 1798.

It is strongly built, compact and used as a guard dog, although it has also been used as a sheepdog and for sporting purposes.

The not too long but narrow head with skull of medium length has a long and somewhat snipey muzzle. It has a pronounced moustache and a definite stop. Nose, black and round. Eyes, medium-sized and brown, often hidden by the hair of the forehead. The Armant is disposed to be fierce and can show a belligerent expression.

Color: dark gray and all shades of gray, also grayish yellow, with a darker mask.

Height at shoulder: 22".

Australian Cattle Dog

Mr. and Mrs. Walters's Ch. Wooleston Blue Jack began to dominate his class in the show ring in 1966. He was top Australian working dog in New South Wales in 1968, his daughter winning in 1969.

A dog bred for hard work, the breed has been known by many names, Blue Heeler, Queensland Heeler, Cattle Dog, Australian Heeler, but now the dog has both a breed name and a universally accepted Standard of Points. As with other Australian breeds it is obvious that many breeds have a part in the development of the Australian Cattle Dog – the Black Bob-Tail, the Smithfield Blue, the Dalmatian, the Scottish Collie, and the native Dingo, but only the best working animals were used to further the breed, and ruthless culling of inferior workers, quite apart from the appearance factor, have produced the finest cattle working dog in the world.

Records of around 1830 in Australia show that the breed had begun to emerge, and at the turn of the century the late Robert Kaleski drew up a Standard which was published in the *Agricultural Gazette* of New South Wales. Obviously required to be a dog of tremendous stamina, and obedient and intelligent withal, the Australian Cattle Dog should have strong jaws and a perfect mouth. It should have the sound feet and legs and the well-ribbed body of the active working dog.

Its colors are red or blue speckled (mottled) with tan markings, and dogs should weigh 35 lbs. and stand 20" to shoulder.

Belgian Sheepdog
(Groenendael, Laekenois, Malinois, Tervueren)

The Tervueren in typical stance

Much more popular in America than in the United Kingdom, these handsome Belgian working dogs have developed into four breeds, or types, the Groenendael, Laekenois, Malinois and Tervueren.

Basically, they are the same, roughly like the German Shepherd Dog (Alsatian) in appearance, differing from each other in coat and coloration. In Belgium the interests of the Belgian Sheepdogs are watched over by the national canine society, La Société Royale Saint-Hubert.

In the U.S.A. only the Groenendael is called Belgian Sheepdog. The Malinois and Tervueren are registered under those names. The Laekenois is not recognized in the U.S.A.

The Standard in Belgium recommends that they should be medium-sized dogs, well proportioned, intelligent, robust, used to an open-air life, and of a physique resistant to the weather extremes of the Belgian

53

climate. They should give an impression of elegance and durability, an impression of pride in their work, for they are most definitely bred and developed for a specific task; and the well-proportioned body and the high head carriage do indeed give this impression.

These sheepdogs have an instinct for guarding sheep, but the guarding instinct has a wider application in Belgium today, the breed is used also as a general guard dog, and is especially vigilant and protective of family and property.

standards

The Standards common to all four breed types require that the head should be well moulded, fairly long and lean. The muzzle should be very slightly longer than the skull, the whole presenting a balanced effect. A strong jaw, scissors bite and the lips having a blackish pigmentation. There should be a slight but definite stop, the face narrowing towards the nose but not so long as to be snipey. The ears are triangular in shape, the outsides well rounded at the base.

The neck is muscular, widening into the shoulders, longish and with a slight arch at the nape. The forelegs should be straight, well-boned and should move in a direction exactly parallel to the axis of the body length. The shoulder-blades should be long and oblique, attached flat, allowing free play to the elbows; the forearms long and muscular, and the front feet round, with close, curved toes and thick, dark claws. The body is powerful without being heavy, and the length from shoulder to haunches is approximately equal to the height at withers, but the female is slightly longer. As with all animals noted for their endurance, the chest is very deep, although not very wide. The top-line is straight, broad and powerful, and the belly is neither low hung, nor cut up like a Greyhound.

The croup slopes gently to a strong tail, of medium length, with the tip slightly curved upwards at the level of the "knee", this curve is accentuated when the dog is moving.

The hind-legs are muscular, not heavy, and very powerful, moving in the same planes as the forelegs, and angled perpendicularly to the ground. The thighs are broad and the stifle joint is approximately perpendicular to the haunches. Feet slightly oval. Apart from the general pleasing balance and good proportions of the breed, the gait and freedom of action provides a clue to its tirelessness. This is an athlete of a dog whose every movement proclaims the ease with which it is performed; it can go all day without flagging or losing its look of grace and power.

All four breed types have the same size specifications, $24\frac{1}{2}''$ for males; $23''$ for females, with a tolerance margin of $\frac{3}{4}''$ less/$1''$ more.

The Standard height is $24\frac{1}{2}''$, equal to length of body from shoulder to haunches. The A.K.C. requires $24''$ to $26''$ for males, $22''$ to $24''$ for bitches. The Standards so far are common to all breeds, but coat and color vary for the different types.

Groenendael and **Tervueren** are long-haired dogs, with shorter hair on the head, outside the ears, lower part of legs, except for the lower part of the forelegs, which are trimmed from elbow to wrist with long hair called fringes. The body hair is long and sleek, longer and more abundant around the neck and on the breast, where it forms a ruff, and on the haunches, where it forms the "breeches". The tail has long hair, forming a plume. The Groenendael is self-colored black, while the Tervueren is

A typical example of this Belgian sheepdog the Tervueren.

54

A typical Groenendael, Viroflay Nightingale

fawn, a warm color, with shadings of black, and a black mask.

The coat hair varies from type to type in direction of growth and appearance and this is the main difference between them, but in all varieties the hair should be abundant, whether long, short or coarse-haired, and there should be a definite undercoat.

In the long-haired varieties it is faulty when the hair is wooly, curly or wavy, or is not long enough. The Groenendael should not have red tints, nor black covering, nor gray breeches. The Tervueren should not depart in any way from jet black.

The Malinois is short-haired, the only one of the four. The hair is very short on the head, outside the ears and on lower limbs. Over the rest of the body it is short, although it thickens at the tail and round the neck, where it forms a deep collar; and the edge of the haunches is fringed with longer hairs.

It is generally fawn in color, with dark tips to the hairs on back and sides, giving a "blackened" or shaded effect, and with a black mask. Color imperfections are a washed-out looking fawn, or putty-gray, complete absence of black, or on the contrary, black in patches instead of the specified "blackened" effect on the fawn coat. Excessive black is unwanted. **The Laekenois** is a coarse-haired variety; rough, dry hair, with a tousled appearance. The hair is the same length over all the body, about $2\frac{1}{2}''$ long, although the hairs around the eyes and over the muzzle are longer. The muzzle hair must be present. The tail does not form a plume, and the coat should not be too long or silky, curly or wavy, and neither should the tail be thick.

The Laekenois color is fawn, with traces of blackening, mainly in the muzzle and tail.

Mrs. A. O'Shea and Mr. E. C. Irvine's Quentin de la Baraque de Planches won best of breed at Cruft's 1971, the first time Challenge Certificates had been on offer for Groenendaels in Britain.

Bergamaschi Herder

This is a large, hardy breed from Italy, classified there as a working dog – "cane da pastore". It is descended from the ancient herding types originating with the Romans and used throughout the succeeding centuries in roughly the same parts of Italy in which they were first used – the mountains of Northern Italy.

The characteristic coat is thick, long and hangs in matted shanks to the ground; rough on the back and sides of the body, wooly underneath – a perfect insulation against high altitude cold. It is a large dog, measuring some 22″ to 25″, with a body of medium length. The head is large, with broad skull and pronounced stop; the muzzle is somewhat blunt. The ears are semi-erect, set-on high and well feathered. The shaggy coat conceals a strong, agile body. The back is straight, the loins broad and muscular. The chest is broad and deep, the shoulders sloping and well muscled.

The forelegs are straight, with short pasterns. The thighs well muscled, second thighs long, and hocks well bent and well let down. The dew-claws remain on the hind feet. The limbs are well covered with profuse hair.

The Bergamaschi can be gray, self-colored or in shadings, or pied in white, isabella or fawn. Whole-white is not permissible.

Bouvier des Ardennes

This cattle dog of the Belgian Ardennes is, next to the Bouvier de Flandres, the most popular with cattle farmers. There are two sizes, bred for the hard work of controlling bovine stock, it is tough, hostile to strangers, but an intelligent affectionate companion to its master.

The large head is rather short but heavily boned, with a wide, flat skull. The muzzle is wide and short, with bushy hair forming moustaches and beard and falling over the forehead. The uncropped, preferably erect ears must not be flat; straight ears with a pointed fold in the front and slightly folded in the back are acceptable. The medium-sized eyes are dark. The nose is large, bulbous and black. The neck is short and thick and set tightly to the body and the back is broad, straight, of medium length and powerful. The wide chest reaches the elbow. The tail is docked completely or very short.

The coat, which may be of any color, must not be too long or too flat – about 2″ long on the body but shorter on the head and legs. The dense winter undercoat thins out during the summer.

The medium sized dog should stand up to 24″ at the withers, and the large size over 24″, bitches being slightly shorter.

Faults are flat ears, yellow or varicolored eyes, dew-claws on rear legs.

Bouvier de Flandres

The fierce expression of this Belgian working dog is emphasized by the cropped ears.

The Bouvier des Flandres is a shaggy dog, bred from a multiplicity of working types in Belgium over many years. He is not large, ideally 24″ high, but he is rather fierce, with a somewhat menacing mien; he looks like a large dog. He is covered with longish, shaggy hair, from head to foot, and on the Continent his appearance has been "improved upon" by cropping his ears so that his appearance would daunt any potential foe. Nevertheless, he is as responsive to training, and to persuasion, rather than harsh coercion, as any breed. He can become a trusted pet, he can be a natural guardian of children, and he most decidedly is a one-man dog. His natural job is to do all those things any farm dog does all over the world, herding, some work as a draught dog, guarding herds and flocks, and possibly aiding in a bit of rough shooting. And for this he was bred in the great farmlands of Flanders, in between the valley of the River Lys and the coast.

A formidable guard dog, the Bouvier de Flandres

Ch. Deewal Grand Prix, an American dog, owned by Dr. Murray Horowitz.

Up to about 1910 dogs existed in this region to perform all of these tasks, but in no case was there a pedigree, and neither was it thought necessary to select the desirable characteristics by careful breeding. Elements of the present-day Flanders Bouvier are undoubtedly the Mastiff, the Sheepdog and probably also the Spaniel, but none of these was used deliberately.

M. F. E. Verbanck, the leading expert on the breed in Belgium today, has protested that the first Standard to be compiled for the breed was modeled upon specimens selected from the heterogeneous mass of mongrel dogs working in the farms at that time. His contention is that the Standard should have been of the ideal to be aimed at, and that breeding should thereafter have aimed at achieving this ideal. The selected specimens were not thoroughbreds, and their choice to represent "a breed in the making" contradicted what M. Verbanck states is the aim of a Standard – the description of an ideal which one will strive to attain, or at best approach, but not the portrait of an already existing subject.

Two Flanders Bouviers were indeed shown in Belgium prior to the Standard, a dog, Rex, and a bitch, Nelly; and although these animals have often been quoted in subsequent writings as being representative of the breed, it is significant that there is no trace of them in present Bouvier pedigrees.

A meeting in 1912 to discuss and form Standards for the Bouviers of the Rouliers-Courtrai-Ypres region was not decisive, but it produced two possible Standards. The First World War, however, entirely disrupted progress and indeed lessened the number of Bouvier working dogs in Flanders.

After the War, selective breeding began towards a Standard devised in 1922 by the Club National Belge du Bouvier des Flandres. Breeders avoided one trap in their search for a true-bred Bouvier type, they went for type, not for color. Gradually the type became established and the Bouvier we know today emerged – a stocky "square" dog, with a large head furnished with moustache and beard and a short tail set-on high and carried gaily. Legs with strong bone, and straight. A well-boned frame, rather massive for its size, and a well-balanced gait and an eager bearing. The coat is rough, slightly ruffled, a factor which proved difficult to breed-in for consistence and, since this factor was more important to fix than coat color, color remained a lesser consideration so long as it came within the wide range accepted by the Standard, ranging from fawn through to black with all the possible shades and tones between. As well as these physical qualities the breeders were at pains to preserve those characteristics which were thought to be most desirable – trustworthiness, affection, the guarding and herding instinct; and the Bouvier has to a marked degree retained the best of these qualities, and is kept as a pet or a house dog all over Belgium, and in many countries abroad.

The breed has continued to improve, although much of the improvement has taken place in other countries. Numbers, however, have not increased, possibly because many litters contain throwbacks to earlier days of indiscriminate breeding.

Canaan Dog

There are two types of Canaan Dog, the Collie type and the Dingo type. Both have certain characteristics in common – they are medium-sized, around 20″ to 24″, weighing around 40 to 55 lbs. The differences lie in their outward appearance. Both are used as working dogs, for guarding and herding sheep and cattle; and they have proved teachable and useful as guide dogs for the blind and, in war, in mine detecting.

It is descended from the Pariah Dogs; dogs of dubious parenthood, apparently ownerless, which are still quite common in the Orient and are also to be found in parts of North Africa and the East Mediterranean countries. The Canaan Dog has however bred true for many generations. It is a rather lightly built, well proportioned breed with a strong body, a short, straight back, and a well tucked-up belly. The tail is set-on high, bushy, and carried curled over the back when excited.

The coat hair is medium-long, straight and harsh, with an undercoat becoming more evident in the winter. Smooth, long hair is allowed, but not desirable. The legs should be well feathered and the tail plumed. Males are preferred with a noticeable mane.

Colors are sandy to a reddish brown, white or black. Large white markings are preferred on all colors, and harlequin patterns and white masks are permitted. Markings are frequently like those of a Boston Terrier.

The Canaan Dog – typical body shape, tail and markings

Catalonian Sheepdog

This dog, the Perro de Pastor Catalan, a native of Catalonia, is in two varieties. The Long-haired variety is known in Catalonia as Gos d'Atura cerda and the Smooth-haired as Gos d'Atura.

Sheepdogs of distinction, these animals are extensively used to herd, drive and round-up sheep under the control of the shepherd. They are also used as watch-dogs and by the police and military.

The head is round with a definite stop, and domed to a pronounced occiput with a straight, rather short muzzle with strong jaws. Wide, expressive eyes, dark amber in color with eyelids edged in black. The ears are set high and are rather short, thin and pointed; close-lying with long tufts. The massive, short, muscular neck is set on sloping shoulders; all being very flexible. A well-developed chest with lightly sprung ribs; a level back of medium length, broad but short loins with the rump slightly raised and the belly slightly tucked-up.

The tail is usually long and curved, sometimes short and occasionally lacking altogether. The legs are lean, strong, straight with oval paws, well-feathered between the toes; the dew-claws remain.

The coat is either smooth or slightly curly, on legs and paws long and silky; on the rest of the body, considerably longer and coarse, almost wiry, especially on the rump and spine.

Colors: Legs and paws fawn to tan; on rest of body black and white; tan, gray and white marks are not allowed.

Height in dogs is 18″ to 20″ and bitches 1″ less.

Collie, Bearded

Two lovely true to type Bearded Collies, Ch. Benjie and Ch. Bravo, both of Bothkennar, owned by Mrs. G. O. Willison.

history and development

Large dogs used as guard dogs have been known from very early times. Discovery of bones of the type in North-Western Europe place the date at about 400 B.C., and from the climate of the region it can be deduced that they were probably shaggy.

It is from the 9th century that the Lowland Polish Sheepdog has been known as a pure-bred type, and at about the year 1514, when the Poles were beginning to trade with other countries, there is a record of a ship trading from Gdansk to Scotland, with grain to exchange for Scottish sheep. The trader is recorded as having exchanged two Polish Lowland Sheepdog bitches and one dog for a ram and a ewe. Thus the Polish animal was introduced into Scotland, and became the progenitor of the present-day Bearded Collie.

So far as we know we are indebted for the first reference to the sheepdog in Britain to the Welsh king Howel Dda, who reigned early in the 10th century. He wrote "whosoever possesses a cur, though it be the king, its value is fourpence. A herd dog that goes before the herd in the morning and follows them home at night is worth the best ox".

Had the Beardie been owned exclusively by the noblemen and gentlemen of the country, as were the Bloodhound and Greyhound of olden times, records of his ancient history would be numerous and our knowledge of him more positive. But he was the hill herdsman's humble worker, and no records or pedigrees have been kept.

The Beardie was first pictured in a painting by Philip Reinagle (1749–1833), which is captioned "Old English Sheepdog". This dog is a long, lean animal, brown, with a tail, and looking like a half-starved Bearded Collie, certainly quite unlike the Old English Sheepdog as it is known today. Even the present-day Beardie has a much heavier coat, for the tendency is towards breeding for very heavy coats, regrettable to my mind, as this seems to be foreign to the Beardie's character.

The well-known Beardie fancier, the late Mr. Jimmy Garrow, commented

A typical puppy of four months old.

Collie
(Rough, Smooth)

Besides being a particularly good dog himself, Ch. Ramsey of Rokeby, owned by Mr. and Mrs. Jack Eglin, proved a good sire with four champions to his credit by the time he was four years old.

history and development

It is reasonable to assume that sheepdogs of one type or another came to Britain at the time of the Roman invasion. Rarely, if ever, did an army travel without its dogs. Later, when the Picts and the Scots invaded northern England, the dogs were probably captured and taken back over the Border. While this is only conjecture, the fact remains that the Collie was bred as a really intelligent, hardy sheep-herding dog. Type, except possibly for good, dense, weather-resistant coat, would hardly have entered into the earliest selection of all. It was not until the mid-19th century, and the coming of the dog show, that the looks of the dog were first considered.

Although shepherd dogs, in great variety, were known world-wide, it has always been accepted that Scotland was the birth-place of the Rough Collie. He is still, erroneously, often called the Scotch Collie. Gradually the Collie spread throughout the British Isles and so throughout the world. At the end of the last century, and the beginning of this, the breed became very well known on the Continent, some of the very best specimens being found in the Low Countries. In the early part of this century the breed made a strong impact in the United States where, today, it is one of the numerically strongest breeds. Similarly in Britain, the breed is regularly found in the top ten (generally 7th or 8th) in the annual Kennel Club list of registrations.

Lost to us is any authority for the name of our breed. A variety of possibilities has been put forward, and each individual can but choose which

The correct front with good, straight legs, with quality (not heavy) bone, and oval (not round or spread) feet, is demonstrated by Set Free from Shiel, owned by Miss Osborne. Note also the good head.

explanation he considers the most likely to be valid. The history of the word "Collie" is every bit as obscure as that of the dog itself! The word has been spelt differently at different times: "Coll", "Colley", "Coally", "Coaly", "Coley" to mention just a few. The most generally accepted theory is that the Anglo-Saxon word "col" meant black and that the dogs were so called, either after the black-faced sheep which were so common in Scotland, or else because the dogs themselves were black.

In the Canterbury Tales, published at the end of the 14th century, in the *Nonnes Priores Tale*, Chaucer says "Ran Coll, our dogge". If this is used as the name of the dog, then one may assume that the dog was black, but since the verse continues "Ran Coll, our dogge and Talbot and Gerlond", Talbot may well have been a hound, and if this is so, all three words more probably describe types of dogs, than their three call-names. If so, then we have our earliest certain reference to the breed of Collie.

Be that as it may, by the end of the 18th century, this sheepdog was sufficiently well established to have been given a name, and that name was "Collie", however it may have been spelt.

A blue, a tricolor and a sable-and-white pose for the camera. From the left, Westcarrs Blue Mistral, a blue merle; Geoffdon Imagination, a tricolor; and Westcarrs Whacko, a sable-and-white, all owned by Miss C. Molony.

color

The introduction of dog shows brought together those people who applied themselves to breeding for points of beauty in the dog, rather than concentrating on their working ability. This lovely breed already existed in a variety of colors; sable and white, that is to say, any shade from pale gold to rich mahogany, with a white collar, shirt front, possibly a blaze on the forehead or skull; white legs, either entirely or in part, and also a white tip to the tail. (Such markings are known as the "Collie color pattern", and are found, to a greater or lesser degree, no matter what color the dog). Tricolor, that is black, with tan markings on cheeks, over the eyes, inside the legs if they are black, and under the flanks and tail. Also blue-merle; silvery blue, scattered with small black patches. Each of these colors also carries the white markings. These lovely colors made it a breed of great attraction, and one which lent itself to the art of the gifted breeder. In order to improve certain points, such as color of tan, and length of head, judicious and, alas, sometimes injudicious matings were carried out.

care

No special care is required for this breed. Regular exercise is, however, necessary for a dog bred to work and keep constantly on the move.

character

Falling into the "medium size" group, the Collie adapts himself rapidly and extremely well to family life. Doubtless the inherited instinct of guardian of the flock makes him the perfect family dog. He has a great sense of propriety, of helpfulness and loyalty. He is, possibly, the most faithful of all breeds, with a gentle, sweet disposition, extremely intelligent, affectionate and biddable, with a brain which seems to reason almost as does our own.

He does not readily make friends with strangers, holding himself somewhat aloof until he decides whether to accept or reject the newcomer. He is a dog which, while very amenable with his own kind, thrives on human companionship, and a Collie, lacking this, is truly sad. Having most of the attributes of a big dog, he is not one, and only looks so on

(Opposite)
Blue merles provide an extra challenge for Collie breeders, because of the difficulty of producing correct markings and a good color. Silva Gale from Shiel was not only a lovely merle but certainly lost no points in head. Look at the perfectly balanced skull and muzzle, set off by good ears well-placed, a well-set eye, and even markings.

Miss M. Osborne's Such a Struggle from Shiel and Ch. Swagman from Shiel provide a comparison between the Rough Collie and the Shetland Sheepdog.

account of his big coat. He suits any size of house, is gentle, clean and kind. His loyalty, unselfishness and understanding make him a perfect companion.

standards

The first Standard of the breed was drawn up in 1881, revised in 1898, 1910 and 1950 and then, once again, in 1969. Certainly the establishment of a Standard helped to define type in the breed, and at the dates when the Standard was revised, it does not appear to have been done to "make the Standard fit the dog".

Almost all the countries of the world have adopted the Collie, and most of them have adopted also the Standard of the breed of its country of origin. However, U.S.A. has made certain alterations to the Standard, and whether or not this is a good thing often gives rise to discussion when Collie folk meet. The main differences are that, in the U.S.A., the color white is permitted, while in Britain an all-white dog is unacceptable. Again, in size: the British Standard says dogs 22″ to 24″ at the shoulder, bitches 20″ to 22″, while the U.S.A. Standard puts the height up 2″ for each sex, starting where the British Standard leaves off. This, to many Britons, seems undesirable, since surely a dog of this large size is not really properly constructed for his work?

Once the Standard was established the breed went ahead with great rapidity, and a far greater unity of type was apparent but, even after all these years, there is still much to be done, and the breed still presents a challenge to its addicts. To enable the Collie to fulfil a natural bent for sheepdog work, its physical structure should be on the lines of strength and activity, free from cloddiness and without any trace of coarseness. Expression, one of the main points when considering relative values, is obtained by the perfect balance and combination of skull and foreface; size, shape, color and placement of eye; also the correct position and carriage of the ears.

Mr. and Mrs. Eglin's Ch. Romney of Rokeby had a sensational puppy career, gaining her title at a very young age. She went on to prove her worth in another direction, producing three champions in her only litter – Ch. Ramsey, Ch. Rosalinda and Int. Ch. Romaine, all of Rokeby.

In general appearance, the Collie should instantly appeal as a dog of great beauty, standing with impassive dignity, with no part out of proportion to the whole.

When viewed from both front and in profile, the head bears a general resemblance to a well-blunted, clean wedge, being smooth in outline. The sides should taper gradually and smoothly from the ears to the end of the nose, without prominent cheek-bones or pinched muzzle.

The eyes, which are an important feature in the breed, should give a sweet expression, be of medium size, set somewhat obliquely, of almond shape and dark brown in color, except in the case of blue merles, when the eyes are frequently blue or blue-flecked.

Movement is a distinct characteristic of the breed. A sound dog is never out at elbow, although it moves with its front feet comparatively close together. Plaiting, crossing or rolling are highly undesirable. The hind legs, from the hock to the ground should be parallel when viewed from the rear, and powerful. A reasonably long, smooth and light stride which

An outstanding example of a Smooth Collie is provided by Joyce Beddow's American Ch. Maries Ridge Riffling Water.

69

A lovely study of Sirko de Ronceval at fifteen months old. The breeder is Madame Robigo of France.

should be effortless. The tail should be long with the bone reaching at least to the hock joint, carried low when the dog is quiet; it may be carried gaily when the dog is excited, but not over the back.

The Rough Collie is still gaining in strength throughout the world, and it seems as if this trend will continue. Unfortunately this is not true of the Smooth Collie. This variety is, according to the Standard, exactly the same as his Rough brother, except for the coat, which should be dense of under-coat, but with the top coat short, harsh and smooth. The Smooth Collie has always been a great deal less popular than the long-coated variety, and in recent years, especially in Britain, the numbers are very low indeed, and for many years, the quality has not been particularly high either. The first classes for this variety were scheduled in 1877, and although, from time to time, there have been quite outstanding specimens, which have held their own in the fiercest competition against all breeds, it is a long time now since we have seen this happen in the British show ring. The situation is rather different in the U.S.A., where some quite exceptional specimens exist.

Croatian Sheepdog

The Croatian Sheepdog, a Yugoslavian breed, known locally as Hrvatski Ovcar, is at the lower end of the scale of medium-sized dogs, being between 16″ to 20″ high at the withers. It is a quiet dog but lively and very hardy. Its instinct for herding and guarding the flock is extremely well-developed and it makes an excellent watchdog, being alert and with keen sight and hearing.

The V-shaped head is fairly small and about 8″ long, the line of the forehead being continued down the muzzle. The nose is always black and does not stand out above the line of the face. The stop is minimal.

Almond-shaped eyes which are chestnut to black in color, lively in expression and of medium size with dark eyelids.

The erect ears are triangular in shape, of medium length and set slightly to the side. Cropping is not permitted.

The back is short and muscular. The bushy tail, set fairly high, is carried below the back-line when at rest but above the horizontal when working. Puppies are sometimes born without tails or they may be docked to $1\frac{1}{2}$″.

The coat is long on the back (3″ to 5″) and short on the head and feet: of silky texture, wavy or curly it must not be wooly; with a fine dense undercoat.

The background color is black; white markings are allowed on throat, croup and underbelly.

Dutch Shepherd Dog

As with many dogs bred for a specific purpose, the Dutch Shepherd Dog is perhaps more often seen these days as a house dog, a pet or a guard dog, than as a true sheep herding dog. It is true to say that some breeds are more amenable to training and change than others, and because it has this characteristic to a marked degree this breed has, over the years, diversified successfully. Rarely seen outside Holland it is nevertheless a popular dog in that country.

The breed has three varieties, short-haired, long-haired and wire-haired. The short and long-haired varieties have gold or silver colored coats, both with streaks of black. The short-haired has a collar and breeches of longer hair. The wire-haired coat is blue-black or gray-black, the hard outer coat molting twice a year, when it should be plucked with finger and thumb.

It is a medium sized breed (dogs 23″ to 25″; bitches 21½″ to 24½″), with watchful expression, prick-eared. Nowadays it is used in Holland for police work, as a guard dog, a guide dog for the blind, and in sport, as a retriever and as a destroyer of vermin – mice, rats etc.

The Dutch Shepherd Dog, which comes in three coat varieties, short, wire and long-haired, is illustrated by the wire-haired, Ch. Ben.

Estrela Mountain Dog

The Cao Serra da Estrela takes its name from the Estrela Mountains where the breed has been known for many centuries. It has long been pure and is prominent in dog shows in Portugal. Although it is primarily a sheep herding dog, an activity at which it excels, it is also used to haul carts.

The Portuguese Sheepdog is an animal of very considerable power, able to withstand the rigors of climate and mountainous terrain over long periods. It has a most independent and truculent nature, but can be trained to obedience.

The fairly massive head is broad and moderately long and has a slightly domed skull, with a well-defined stop and a strong muzzle with level teeth. It has almond-shaped, dark eyes and wide-set, small ears which are folded back.

The body is somewhat rectangular in overall shape with a broad, short, firm, muscular back, deep chest and slightly raised loins. It has straight, strong legs and the long tail is carried low.

It may be long or short-haired, thick, rather coarse, smooth or slightly wavy, with undercoat.

Colors are gray, tawny and red, red or light tan with white points, black and tan, black and white, red and tan and grizzle. Height is 23″ to 27″, weight 90 to 110 lbs. for males, bitches considerably less.

A working dog of the Portuguese Estrela Mountains, bred and still maintained for work with sheep, and at protection. The Mastiff influence can be seen quite strongly.

French Sheepdog
(Beauceron, Briard, Picardy, Pyrenean)

Ch. Quassus d'el Pastir, a Briard belonging to Monsieur Seron, who displays all the best points of this breed.

Outstanding among Pyrenean Sheepdogs is M. Mansencal's Guagnotte de l'Estaube, best of breed at Paris in 1969 and Poitiers in 1970, where he won the Grand Prix of the President of the Republic.

The history of the Sheepdogs of France, in common with that of most other nations, is very ancient. Throughout the centuries several varieties of Sheepdog have come and gone, all, in their turn, being local breeds bred for the different kinds of terrain on which they worked. Today there remain but four distinct sheep herding breeds, in four different areas of France. The Beauceron, the Briard, the Picardy and the Pyrenean. These are the only four breeds actually recognized by the Société Centrale Canine. The earliest of the French Sheepdogs undoubtedly were dual purpose dogs and so they mostly remain today, as shepherds or guardians of the flocks, and watch dogs for the family and farm. However, with the possible exception of the little Pyrenean, the breeds have also, it is fairly certain, been used in the past as hunting dogs, especially in the hunt for wild-boar. **The Beauceron** is the largest. He is well-built, with short hair, and his most usual color is black with rich tan markings on legs, face and under the tail. For this reason, he is familiarly known as the "Bas-rouge" (red

72

stockings). However, it is possible to have other colors, and the Standard admits a harlequin or a gray black with tan (tricolor), i.e. he can be gray, with black patches, and with tan in the same places as the "Bas-rouge". This excellent Sheepdog should be 25″ to 27½″ for dogs; 24″ to 27″ for bitches, the minimum changing in 1972 to 26½″ dogs and 25½″ bitches. The first Standard was drawn up about the end of the last century and, from then until the First World War, the breed made good progress. On the cessation of hostilities the Club des Amis du Beauceron reviewed the Standard, and it is on this revised Standard that the breed is judged today. In France the breed is second only to the Briard in numbers.

The Briard is the most popular; he has the most charming, gentle nature, adapting himself to his work on the farm and equally well as family pet. He is probably the most ancient of the Sheepdogs, although the name Briard was only used for the first time in 1809. He is a dog of the plains, used to herd and guard sheep. In 1863, at the first dog show in Paris, a bitch, Charmante, greatly resembling today's Briards, was placed first of all the Sheepdogs exhibited. In the last century there were two distinct types of Briard, one with silky hair, the other with a coarse, rough and "goat-like" coat, and it is the latter type which exists today. He is about 26″ in height, with the female rather smaller, strong and muscular. The A.K.C. Standard specifies 23″ to 27″ for dogs; 22″ to 25½″ for bitches.

Today, the Briard is more elegant than he used to be. His development has been in the hands of devoted breeders who, while making of him a dog which is not too shaggy and too big, have yet retained all his original characteristics, especially his alert expression and his biddable temperament, together with his rough coat which is, however, so easy to keep in good condition and which, because of its "self-cleaning" nature, makes this dog a most acceptable companion in the home.

The Briard is a self-colored dog, the darker the better.

A head study of M. Seron's French and international Champion Briard, Java du Val de Multien.

The Picardy Sheepdog is again of very ancient origin; in the opinion of many authors, this dog came to France in the great Celtic invasion of the 9th century. Many breeds of similar type are to be found throughout Germany and the Low Countries. Despite this, the breed seems to have been ignored by writers of more or less modern times, and even at the end of the last century when the French Sheepdog Club was founded, the Picardy was not mentioned. At the show in Amiens in 1899 twelve Picardys were entered, but the judge, President of the French Sheepdog Club, refused to recognize them, despite the fact that many examples of this breed were shown in other parts of France. The breed was decimated by the 1914–18 War, many of the best specimens being taken to Germany, while others died as it was impossible to find food for them. The breed revived in the 1920's but less than twenty years later, was ravaged by another Great War.

But by the early 1950's excellent specimens were again seen. Today, the breed is steadily gaining recognition all over France. The Picardy is a rugged dog and a superb worker with sheep and cattle. His great devotion to children makes a strong contrast with his guarding abilities. Of medium height, 23″ to 25″ for dogs; 21″ to 23″ for bitches, he is a strong, well-muscled dog, with harsh coat of fawn to dark gray in color.

The Pyrenean is the smallest, and impresses one forcibly with his great vigor. Always alert, with an expression both cunning and suspicious, and great speed in every movement, he is different in character and appearance

Milord du Grand Tarsac, a Picardy of high quality, owned and bred by M. and Mme. Senecal. Tarsac won the C.A.C. – C.A.C. I'B. at Paris in 1966.

73

A young bitch of the Pyrenees type, Oulettes, owned by M. Mansencal.

from any other breed. His origins are not known but the breed has been known since the beginning of this century. He exists in a fairly confined geographical area, between the Pyrenees and the Black Mountains. He is certainly not, as has been suggested, a miniature Briard. Before the 1914–18 War, the breed was very little known outside its own area, but in 1916 the head of the French Service of War Dogs obtained a number of the breed to be trained as messenger dogs and to accompany patrols. Since 1926 the breed has been recognized by the French Ministry of Agriculture and it was at the Paris show in that year that this little breed really stood out as different from all the other Sheepdogs of France.

His coat is fairly long, abundant, straight or slightly wavy, with featherings on the hind legs, and fairly harsh. There are in fact two varieties, the one with shortish muzzle, covered with short hair, standing off forwards. The other with a slightly longer muzzle, the head covered in short, fine hair, and with body hair rather shorter than that of the first variety, and the legs covered with short hair with only very slight featherings.

His wicked "gamin" look is an outstanding feature, and he is an enchanting little dog, with a most unusual personality. He is quite tiny for a Sheepdog, only 16″ to 20″ high for a dog, bitches smaller, and in color he is usually fawn, but this may be mixed with black hairs. Sometimes gray specimens are encountered and all colors are allowed with white markings on chest, head, legs and feet. Even the harlequin pattern is tolerated, and may be of shadings of gray, black or fawn with white.

Kelpie

Ch. Meson Brandy and his offspring Navajo Buntijo, both best in show winners at the Australian Kelpie Club.

German Shepherd Dog
See page 45

Great Pyrenees
See page 86

An Australian breed developed for hard work on the sheep ranges where conditions are different from anywhere else in the world, and this dog, in all its stages of development has been essential to the establishment of the industry. Kelpies were bred back in the early days of settlement from the Collie type dogs which came to Australia with the early farmers.

The very restricted inter-mixing of the strain in the early days helped to stabilize it. It is recorded that in 1870 a pair of Collies produced a pup, Caesar, which later was mated to a famous bitch called Kelpie. The mating produced the famous King's Kelpie, which won the first sheep-dog trial ever staged in Australia, in 1872. The Australian Kelpie of today is a light-footed, fast-moving animal, capable of withstanding extremes of heat, and untiring in his work – largely indifferent to the flinty ground and thorny bush of the country where sheep are farmed, nevertheless he sometimes has to wear boots, when the ground is too rough.

In Australia shows are held by the Australian Kelpie Club, of which the writer is Patron, and there are also the sheep-dog trials conducted by the Sheepdog Workers Association throughout Australia.

The Kelpie is alert, intelligent, obedient and will run along the backs of the sheep to the head of a mob. Tail swinging, cat-footed and fast, he will make a wide cast and pick up sheep with uncanny speed. He can also go without water for long periods.

Colors are black-and-tan, red, black or blue. He weighs 30 lbs. and measures 18″ to 20″ to shoulder. The coat is short and smooth. The ears are pricked.

Komondor

"King of Hungarian Sheepdogs", the Komondor is commanding in appearance likely to cause fear in the beholder, and is a fearless intelligent animal. Legend has it that as the Magyars migrated through the steppes of Russia, they bred the Komondor from the large, heavily coated Aftscharka. The unique coat of the Komondor labels him as close cousin to the Puli. The Komondor was brought to Hungary over 1,000 years ago, and the name may be found in literature as far back as 1544, in the *History of King Astiagis* by Peter Kakony.

Imposing size, strength and profuse coat enable him to withstand severe Hungarian winters, long hot summers, and protect sheep and cattle from wolves and other predators. Introduced to the United States in the early thirties, and recognised by the A.K.C. in 1938. The Komondor is not known in Britain.

The coat is white and consists of long, wavy, coarser outer hair, and a short, dense, wooly undercoat. These combine to form ribbon-like cords or tassels. Never combed, this special coat structure is found only on the Komondor and the Puli. Easily trained, he is happy when accepted and respected as a member of the family. He is affectionate and gentle with children, and adapts well to city life.

The Komondor's height often exceeds 30″ and a weight of 110 lbs. is common. The A.K.C. Standard allows a minimum of 25″ for males; 23½″ for bitches. A large, strong-boned, muscular dog, he is fast and agile, alert and courageous, stable in temperament and of superior intelligence.

Oscar Beregi's Ch. Hattyu, the first Komondor champion in America.

Kuvasz

The Kuvasz was the first of the ancient Hungarian breeds to become adapted to domesticity and modern living. The name is basically Sumerian, the ancient Mesopotamian culture which had reached an advanced state of civilization by 3,000 B.C. The history of the breed has been traced by Dr. Palfalvy of the Alabama Academy of Science, back to its establishment in Hungary centuries ago. It spread out to India, Tibet and China, and to Turkey giving rise to the erroneous theory that the Kuvasz was Turkish. The Kuvasz was recognized by the American Kennel Club in 1931. The Kuvasz Club of America was formed in 1966. So far it has not been recognized in Britain.

The Kuvasz is spirited, intelligent and courageous. Primarily a one family dog, quietly devoted and gentle with children, and excellent as a guard dog, he has also hunted large game. He is a working dog, large, sturdily built, graceful and well-proportioned. The impression of strength and agility shows, even in repose, and he moves freely and often at great speed. His coat is white, or ivory white; wavy to straight, never curly. Outer coat medium coarse, under coat fine.

The neck carries a mane extending to and covering the chest; tail is set low, reaching to the hocks. The head is a most distinctive and beautiful feature, of perfect proportions, his kindly look adding expressiveness. Height for dogs is 28″ to 29½″; bitches 26″ to 27½″. The A.K.C. Standard specifies approximately 26″ for dogs; bitches slightly less.

Ch. Hamralvi Demost Happy Fella, a lovely young Kuvasz owned by Dr. and Mrs. Z. Alvi, gained his American title in June 1969 at fourteen months old. Within another fifteen months he had achieved thirty-two best of breed awards and one group placing.

Maremma

A typical example of a strong, well-grown Maremma in good coat – Mr. and Mrs. Spears's Ammeram Pietro Rossano, best of breed at the Birmingham show in England 1969.

The Maremma Sheepdog was first mentioned by Columella in his book on Roman rural affairs 2,000 years ago. It is believed that it was introduced to the mountains of Northern Italy as a guard dog by Magyars migrating from Asia.

The first record of an importation into Britain was in 1872, but no British-bred litter was recorded until 1936. There are now 140 in Britain, and no less than 1,000 are known in Italy.

Still used as a working sheepdog in Italy, the Maremma has retained great hardiness, but in the home is affectionate, loyal and intelligent, and is a magnificent guard dog. The Maremma is a large, strongly built, but agile dog, with a stately head, and ears smaller in proportion to its size. It has a magnificent long, white coat, slightly wavy, thick round the neck and flanks, but thinning out on the undercarriage, occasionally with light fawn markings. The tail is heavily feathered and carried low, except when excited, or in fast motion. The thick undercoat enables it to withstand cold and wet, and little dirt can penetrate. In the worst of conditions they are well able to keep themselves scrupulously clean. The eyes are brown or ochre, with eyelids, nose and lips black. Dogs stand 25″ to 28″; weight 75 to 100 lbs. Bitches 23″ to 26″; weight 65 to 85 lbs.

Mudi

A trustworthy and experienced Hungarian sheepdog, the Mudi.

This is a medium-sized herding breed which originated in Hungary either at the end of the 19th century or the beginning of the 20th.

Its energetic, intelligent and fearless nature, together with its natural aptitude for herding, make it particularly suitable for work with large cattle as well as with sheep and goats. It is a ruthless destroyer of rats and other rodent vermin and in some areas it is used for blood sports. Having very keen and alert hearing it is extensively used as a watchdog; frequently kept in the house for this purpose.

It has a long tapering head which is clean in line with a negligible stop. The pointed muzzle is narrow, and the jaws deep and well-muscled, with regular, strong teeth meeting evenly. Ears are erect. The eyes, set slightly obliquely, are dark brown in color.

The neck is slightly arched and muscular. Shoulders are sloping and the forelegs, which are of moderate length, are nearly vertical. The shoulders are well developed with a short straight back, sloping slightly downwards towards the rump, with the loins moderately tucked up. The tail which is set at medium height, points downwards and is short or docked to 2″ or 3″. Colors are white or black also white and black interspersed with spots of more or less equal size.

Height at shoulder 14″ to 18″.

Old English Sheepdog

Mr. C. and Mr. E. B. Riddiough's Ch. Pendleford Prince Hal was the top winning dog in the working group in Britain in 1970, with a best-in-show win at the Three Counties show, reserve BIS at Dumfries and group wins at Windsor and West of England Ladies K.S.

history and development

The Old English Sheepdog has been known as a distinct variety in Britain for at least two hundred years. The Old English is quite unlike the Collie varieties of sheepdog, with the exception of the Bearded Collie, with which breed it seems certain it shares a common origin, and possibly the Russian Owtcharka. In general shape, he is not unlike some other European and Asiatic sheep herding breeds, notably the French Berger de Brie or Briard, but nothing is definitely known to link him with these breeds. When the wolf and other large predators lived in England, there was need of a strongly built, heavy, herdsman's dog capable of defending flocks and herds from attack. Later, as times changed, the Old English Sheepdog, or Bobtail as it is commonly known, was employed more as a drover's dog with cattle, but has never lost its ability to work with sheep though, in modern times, far more of the breed are kept as companions and for show than for work on the farms.

The first club for the breed, The Old English Sheepdog Club, was formed in 1888 and the type has remained substantially unaltered over the years, although perhaps the modern dog is a little more compact and the coat more profuse than it used to be. In recent years, the breed has increased vastly in popularity and is in great demand abroad, particularly in

This head study of Loakespark's Shaggy Wonder Samson was taken when he was in quarantine at thirteen months old. Imported into England from Belgium he was by Belgian and Int. Ch. Bobtail Acres Shaggy Wonder Snowman ex Int. Ch. Shaggy Wonder Personal Jewel.

One of the many lovely Old English Sheepdogs being shown in the sixties. Mr. and Mrs. S. E. Fisher's Ch. Rollingsea Ringleader, bred by Mrs. J. R. Gould, was a consistent winner in Britain over several years.

America, with a very large number going to California.

color

Color is an important aspect of the show Bobtail. The body color is any shade of blue-gray; pigeon blue is preferred by some but grizzle is equally acceptable by the Standard. Any shade of brown or sable is very objectionable.

Although the Standard does not demand it, white markings on the head and face are greatly preferred. In recent times, a wholly white head has come to be accepted as ideal, especially in America, though many good dogs are still marked on the ears and eyes. Very often there is a white shirt-front and a white neck and white forelegs are also preferred. Hind legs must be colored, but white on the feet is not objected to. White splashes on the body are regarded as mismarked and in large litters such puppies are destroyed.

Puppies are born black and white, the blue-gray coloring beginning to appear at about four months old. The break, starting round the eyes and on the hocks, takes some months to clear completely.

care

Bobtails fit readily into a household routine even in town, and do not need an undue amount of attention apart from half-an-hour's exercise twice a day and regular grooming. For this, use a good-sized whalebone brush and a steel comb with widely spaced teeth so that too much coat is not pulled out during grooming. Brush daily for five minutes as a puppy and comb through once a week. Continue regular grooming throughout the growing period and when adult, brush regularly right down to the skin all over. The hair must be brushed from the roots out to the tip, not dabbed at from the surface. Mats must be avoided at all costs. Tease out with the finger and complete with the comb, used gently to part the hair,

Two Old English Sheepdog puppies.

not to pull it out. Wire brushes should never be used on the breed.

When grooming for show, powder the white and the gray parts, and brush out all over. For the ring, brush the hair on the loins and hindquarters – where it grows more profusely than anywhere else – forward towards the dog's head and on its forelegs and chest brush it downwards. The head is brushed out to cover the eyes and face, the topknot is brushed forward from early puppyhood. Only the white parts of a Bobtail need to be washed for show. Ears must be watched for canker and the feet for felting with dead hair, which can cause lameness.

They are best kennelled in pairs on wheat straw bedding.

The puppies require to be docked at four days old, very short, with no stump being left.

character

The breed is tough, hardy, workmanlike and even-tempered, easy to keep in health and will put up with a simple diet and strenuous exercise without harm to its constitution. It makes an excellent companion, is good with children and is a vigilant guard. It is a one-man type of dog and not given to wandering. In temperament they are very steady and sensible. They mix well with other dogs and are not aggressive.

A unique feature of the breed is its bark, described in the Standard as Pot Casse, which means low pitched but loud and ringing.

standards

The breed presents a thick-set, burly, square appearance with nothing leggy or rakish about them. Despite the heavy appearance imparted by the profuse coat, the breed is built on strong, active lines, and must be able to gallop freely at some speed. They are strongly built, compact with heavy bone, good straight legs and neat feet, with well-laid shoulders, a good length of neck, well rounded ribs and a deep brisket. Hindquarters

Mrs. A. Davis's Ch. Reculver Little Rascal, bred by Mr. and Mrs. A. G. Wilkinson, in addition to being top winning Old English Sheepdog in 1965, was Joint No. 2 and top scoring bitch in the Woffle competition for all breeds. She won thirteen C.C.s and was best bitch in show at the Three Counties, and reserve best-in-show at Birmingham National championship shows, both in 1965.

A winner of the early thirties, Miss C. M. Ashford's Ch. Hammerwood Hurly Burly.

are especially important; they must be substantial, well angulated at hock and stifle, but not exaggerated, and freedom of action in the hind legs is very essential, much of the power in movement coming from the strong, gently arched loins. At slow speeds the breed has a characteristic ambling gait.

The skull should be large and square, the top skull slightly rounded and the length equal to the width in the mature dog. The foreface is strong with good width and depth of under-jaw, the mouth level, scissor bite, with big teeth. There is a marked stop between the skull and foreface. The ears are small and held flat to the head, the coat mingling with the top-knot. Nose large and black. Lips should be clean and either black or pink. Eyes may be dark or wall eyes – blue, a dog may have one eye of each color or both of the same color.

A great beauty of the breed is the coat, which should be very profuse with the blue-gray contrasting strongly with the pure white. In texture, the top coat is hard, harsh to the touch and weather-proof with a soft water-proof pile underneath of the same color as the top coat. The coat must not be straight but shaggy and free from curl, about 6″ long in the adult. A slight wave in the top coat is not objected to.

The Standard recommends 22″ at the shoulder as a good height for the dogs, and 20″ for bitches, but many exceed this. However, type, symmetry and character supersede size in importance.

Polish Sheepdog
(Owczarek Podhalanski, Owczarek Nizinny)

There are two varieties of the Polish Sheepdog, both strong, vigilant guards and sheep herders, requiring little in the way of care and sustenance, and very resistant to weather extremes. The breeds have changed little from the time of Hunsa, who first introduced them into Poland.

A full-grown Podhalanski sheepdog from the Tatra Mountains.

The Lowlands type of Polish Sheep-dog, the Owczarek Nizinny.

Tatra Mountain Sheepdog (Owczarek Podhalanski): This is a large dog, docile and good-natured, measuring at least 26″ at the shoulder, the bitch somewhat smaller. It is rectangular in form. The head well-proportioned, with short muzzle, black nose and large nostrils. The eyes of medium size, slightly oblique, brown in color, and expressive. The ears thick, triangular and hanging close against the cheeks. The body long and massive; back broad; straight, powerful quarters. The coat short on the head, long elsewhere – thick, straight or wavy, hard to the touch; white, and sometimes has cream-colored markings.

Lowlands Shepherd Dog (Owczarek Nizinny): This is perhaps the livelier of the two breeds. It is of medium size (16″ to 20″ high), the body being a little longer than the height, with a free gait.

The head should not be too heavy; the muzzle slightly shorter than the skull, the nose big, black, with large nostrils. The eyes of average size, oval, with alert expression. The ears medium-sized, heart-shaped, hanging against the cheeks, and very mobile.

The quarters are straight when viewed from any direction; the tail either missing or docked very short. The coat long and heavy; the hair of the head covering the eyes. All colors are permissible.

The Nizinny is lively, intelligent and docile; and has an excellent memory.

Portuguese Sheepdog
(Serra de Aires, Castro Laboreiro)

Castro Laboreiro: One of the two main types of sheepdog in Portugal, comes from the North of the country, in the area between Mounts Peneda and Suajo, north of the River Douro. It is described as of the mastiff type, and tends towards the watchdog rather than the herder. It is a devoted breed; trained to be vigilant, it is hardy, agile and very handsome.

The body is short, with a level back, strong loin, with a full-size tail, thick at the set-on, and slightly curved. The head has a slightly pronounced stop and a long, strong muzzle, and drop ears held close to the head. The coat is thick, rough and short, even shorter on head and legs.

The colors are wolf-gray, dark fawn and brindle.

Height for dogs 22″ to 24″; bitches are one inch less.

This dog displays the major points, straight back, straight legs, and the drop ears – this specimen is not cropped.

Serra de Aires: The other type of Portuguese Sheepdog, old-established, exceptionally intelligent and, by training and instinct, a herding type of dog, driving and guiding flocks.

It is a medium-sized dog with a longish body, straight, with short, wide loin, sloping croup, and tail set-on high. The tail is pointed, slightly curved with an upward curl at the tip when at rest, standing up curled in movement. The quarters are strong.

The coat is long, goat-like in its rough texture, stiff and tending to wave. The beard, whiskers and bushy eyebrows make up a well-furnished head; the eyes should be visible.

Colors are yellow, brown, gray, fawn, wolf-gray and black. Tan markings are accepted, but never white spots or markings.

Height for dogs 17″ to 19″; bitches one inch less.

The Castro Laboreiro gives a strong impression of self-reliance and hardiness. A typical dog whose purpose is still to work.

Puli

A fine example of the Puli in America, Ch. Skysyl November Leaf, bred and owned by Mrs. Sylvia Owens, on this occasion going best in show at the Eastern Dog Club at Boston, Mass. in 1967. He was whelped in 1963.

Ch. Skysyl Question Being Is It, winner of two all-breed best in show awards in America.

history and development

The Magyar tribes, which inhabited the eastern Urals, moved down to the open grassland to the west where they intermingled with the Turki peoples and later, at the end of the 9th century, occupied the central Danube area. With them, they brought the Puli.

Whether it originated east of the Urals or whether it is of Turkish origin is not known. However, for many centuries, it has been used to herd sheep on the edge of the puszta, the Hungarian plains, and is well-known to travelers in the countryside. Excellent as a sheep-dog, it is also used as a police dog in many towns, but was not shown to any extent until after the Second World War.

It has been exported to most European countries and to the United States, where in 1935, it was imported by the Department of Agriculture at Beltsville, Maryland, to improve the breeding of cattle herding and sheep dogs. Although the war defeated this project, the Puli's versatility, courage and working ability became well-known and the A.K.C. recognized the breed in 1936. The Puli earned an enviable position in the working group, and continues to gain popularity and success as show winner, obedience title holder, watchdog and, of course, as a field worker.

color

The Puli's coat color is black, various shades of gray or pure white, which is somewhat rare. It must be of one solid color; nose, flews and eyelids should be black. Hungarian herdsmen and shepherds prefer working with black or gray Pulis, because white dogs are not so easily seen at a distance.

care

The Puli is an easy whelper and excellent mother. Puppies are unusually hardy, vigorous and not prone to sickness. They can be trained at a very early age and what is learned is never likely to be forgotten. All Puli puppies, except the white ones, are born jet black, smooth-haired and with the sheen of a retriever or labrador puppy and so, distinguishing mature coat color at birth is impossible. After a while, those destined to become gray show a distinctive pale gray shading on their paw pads; so faint, it could be mistaken for white down. Gradually gray appears around eyes and muzzle, also under the tail, eventually extending to all four legs. It is not unusual for a gray Puli not to turn into a solid gray until two years old, after which the coat shade may vary yearly at shedding time or, in the case of a bitch, after whelping. The coat, like that of all long-haired dogs, requires constant care with brush, comb and conditioning spray, the only part requiring scissoring is around all four feet to give a neat look to the paws.

character

The Puli's devotion, loyalty and high intelligence make him a very special dog of great personality. Observing the intensity of his vigilance, one has the feeling this little dog knows more than most people would suspect and, likely or not, in many instances, this proved to be true. The Department of Agriculture experiment showed his intelligence I.Q. chart topped an all breeds high average, but being of a very independent mind the Puli can also be stubborn at times. Like all sheepdogs, the Puli is likely

This is probably how you would see working Pulis in their native Hungary; a black bitch with her white puppy.

Another product of Mrs. Owens's Skysyl Kennels in New Canaan, New Hampshire, Ch. Skysyl Sketch in Shaded Gray, whose lovely coat is, as her name implies, black, almost gray.

to remain a one-man, one-family dog with a certain stand-off aloof attitude towards strangers. To overcome this trait is essential for a show dog, and today in the U.S.A., the only difference between those shown some thirty years ago and present winners is their confidence and friendly outgiving temperament. Although very active, the Puli readily adapts to our way of life in the city or country with or without a lot of exercise. He is not a roamer nor a fighter and is very obedient, always close at hand, willing to please. Puppies are easily house-broken being naturally very clean. They are extremely fond of each other, being very clannish dogs.

standards

The Puli is a dog of lower medium size, vigorous, alert and extremely active. The head is of medium size in proportion to the body. The skull is slightly domed and not too broad. Stop clearly defined but not abrupt, neither dished nor downfaced, with a strong muzzle of medium length ending in a nose of good size. Teeth strong, comparatively large; the bite either level or scissors. Flews tight.

Ears – hanging and set fairly high, medium size, and V-shaped.

Eyes – deep-set and rather large, should be dark brown, but lighter color is not a serious fault.

Neck – strong and muscular, of medium length, and free of throatiness. Shoulders clean-cut and sloping, with elbows close. The chest is deep and fairly broad with ribs well sprung. Back of medium length, straight and level, the rump sloping moderately. Fairly broad across the loins and well tucked up.

Occasionally born bobtail, which is acceptable, but the tail is never cut. Carried curled over the back when alert, and low with the end curled up when at rest. Characteristic of the breed is the dense, weather-resisting double coat. The outer coat, long and of medium texture, is never silky. It may be straight, wavy, or slightly curly. The corded coat may be shown either combed or uncombed.

Height: males about 17″, and should not exceed 19″. Females about 16″ and should not exceed 18″.

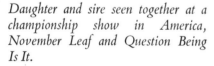

Daughter and sire seen together at a championship show in America, November Leaf and Question Being Is It.

Pumi

The Pumi Kutya or Hungarian Cattle Dog seems to have evolved from a crossing of the Puli and an unidentified dog, probably a German sheep-herding Poodle type, several centuries ago. In earlier times it was used as a sheepdog, but is now mainly employed in herding cattle and pigs and is of considerable importance in the rural communities of Hungary.

Although not a large dog, it is used as a guard. Its strong jaw and noisy bark, coupled with its ability to move quickly and intelligently, make it a considerable deterrent to an intruder. Although not very striking in looks, it is a likeable dog with a considerable sense of fun.

It has a rather narrow and long head with a slight stop; a strong well-bearded muzzle and good, level teeth. The eyes are coffee-colored, and the semi-erect, smallish ears tend to give a bright, intelligent expression. The body is muscular and compact with a deep but not barrelled chest. The straight legs are well-muscled but not heavily boned. The coat, which is harsh-textured, long on the hindquarters but of medium length else-where (except for the forelock which is soft and very pronounced), is usually reddish black, but dark and light gray are fairly common. White is an objectionable color.

Height about 19″.

A young Pumi

Mountain Dog Pyrenean
(Great Pyrenees)

Bergerie Knur, Mr. and Mrs. S. F. Prince's beautiful young all white dog which was best in show all breeds at Cruft's in 1970, thus realising for his owners the ambition of every breeder. Bergerie Knur's outstanding conformation and free movement, coupled with intense quality and superb presentation and fitness made this a most popular award.

Ch. Generale de Fontenay, owned and bred by Madame J. Harper Trois Fontaines and sired by the celebrated Kop de Careil, one of Madame's first importations when she re-introduced the breed to Britain between the wars. This dog was the winner of many C.C.s and sired six champions.

history and development

Tibetan Mastiffs, used as guard dogs in China more than 1,000 years B.C., became the forebears of the great Molossian Hounds, the Roman War Dogs and of the Pyrenean Mountain Dogs, officially known as the Great Pyrenees in the U.S.A.

It is thought that the Romans may have brought the Pyrenean to Spain and that the breed also spread across the mountain ranges of Asia and Europe before establishing itself in the Pyrenees, where, for some unaccountable reason, it remained isolated for over a thousand years. From earliest times, Pyreneans were used to guard sheep. They ran in pairs, wearing spiked iron collars to protect their throats and they were truly formidable adversaries of all predators, including human marauders. In the middle ages in France, the Pyrenean Mountain Dog was used for guarding fortresses from surprise attack and to prevent the escape of prisoners. In the 18th century Madame de Maintenon and the Dauphin took one back with them to the court of Louis XIV where they were soon in great demand. By the beginning of the 20th century, however, the breed had declined until only a few ill-assorted specimens could be found, mostly in the Basque country. Later Pyrenean shepherds began to sell poorly bred puppies to delighted tourists, who saw these magnificent

Mountain Dogs for the first time. By this means a few Pyreneans reached England and other countries during the early part of the present century and quite a number were registered at the Kennel Club at that time. Interest in Britain declined but remnants of the breed in France were preserved, enabling English and American breeders to restart in the early 1930's. New kennels were established between the wars in France, Holland and Belgium, but these were depleted during the occupation.

In 1931, when Pyrenean breeding began in America, Miss G. Perry and later Mrs. F. Crane's Basquaerie Kennel imported the best obtainable stock from France, while soon afterwards Madame Harper Trois Fontaines established the de Fontenay kennel in England. The early foundation stocks naturally included some of the original Mountain Dogs which were generally very large, rather coarse animals with markings of badger, lemon or tan on head and body. The all-white show type has, alas, evolved only too often at the expense of the great size and characteristic majesty of the original dog of the mountains. Pigment also generally deteriorates in the mating of white to white dogs, and for these reasons breeding back to the original mountain type still remains a recurring necessity.

In 1965, the breed's first Supreme Champion, Bergerie Charlemagne de Bedous was made best in show at the West of England Ladies Kennel Society championship show, followed in 1968 by the reserve best in show at Cruft's by Ch. Bergerie Diable. Finally in 1970, with 8,000 dogs of all breeds competing, the top honor in the world of dogs, Cruft's supreme best in show was won by Bergerie Knur. At present, Australia, New Zealand, Denmark, Sweden, Italy and Spain, and many other European countries, all have their Pyrenean breeders and the breed is now known in practically all parts of the world. In America, breed clubs exist in places as far apart as Alaska and Maryland, and in Great Britain both Ireland and Scotland now have their separate breed clubs.

Ch. Bedat de Mondà, a Pyrenean of the so-called "mountain type", was presented to Field Marshal Lord Alanbrooke by the people of Bagneres de Bigore, where he was born. Ch. Bedat later became an important sire in the breed.

color

The assumption that the pure bred Pyrenean must be white is erroneous. The permitted colors are all-white or mainly white with markings of badger, gray or varying shades of tan, mainly on the head, or at the root of the tail. Badger, or blaireau, as it is called, is an admixture of brown, black, gray and white hairs and is common in puppies, but generally fades on maturity. Patches of pure black are not admitted in the show ring, although black and white dogs sometimes appear in correctly color-bred litters. The desired jet black nose, lips and eye rims still cannot be maintained in successive generations of all-white dogs without breeding back to the colored mountain type. It is noticeable that not only pigment but increased size and vigor become apparent when color is introduced into the all-white strain, and in spite of the lack of scientific support for the fact, all-white breeding also tends to produce progressively smaller Pyreneans.

care

The Pyrenean is an exceptionally hardy and healthy dog and he is unlikely to require very much veterinary attention. During the growing period he needs highly specialized feeding if he is to achieve full development, but once maturity is reached, contrary to popular belief, his appetite is com-

Bergerie Knur shown with his young, blaireau marked son. This photograph illustrates the elegance and dignity of the Pyrenean at its best.

Typical Bergerie puppies

A lovely head study of Ch. Generale de Fontenay.

paratively small. He does well on a very wide variety of foods and these are sometimes necessary to maintain him in top condition.

The general conviction that a big dog needs to live in a large house in the country is erroneous. The Pyrenean, because his double coat makes him appear much larger than he really is, takes up surprisingly little space, even in the smallest room. He is never clumsy and he seldom sits in front of the fire, preferring to curl up in a corner with his back to the wall. The Pyrenean is not particularly active, although exercise requirements vary with age and individual temperament, and will take long or short walks with equal enjoyment. In town and country, the Pyrenean must be controlled and unless a garden is dog-proof, he should be provided with a strongly fenced-in area where he can stay for reasonably short periods when not in the house or out walking. It is of primary importance to train all puppies of the giant breeds, from the earliest age, not to jump up, pull on the lead or chase moving objects, since large dogs out of control are considerably more of an embarrassment than small ones.

In spite of his immense size and thick white double coat, the Pyrenean keeps himself surprisingly clean, and except when shown, bathing is not necessary. He needs a thorough grooming not less than once a week to keep his coat in good condition and to look for fleas or skin eruptions. For the young puppy, grooming serves a double purpose and should be given daily for two very important reasons – getting the youngster used to being handled, and keeping him clean. At grooming times, his mouth should be inspected and his rear parts accustomed to the brush. Calluses on the elbows may also need attention if the dog customarily lies on hard surfaces. It is important that the double dew-claws, which are a distinguishing feature of the breed, should not be removed, and the nails growing out of them need to be trimmed occasionally if they tend to grow round into the flesh.

character

By instinct the Pyrenean is a guard dog and it is therefore to be expected that, however gentle either sex may be, it will surely guard if the need arises. The Pyrenean is a one-family rather than a one-man dog. Although not usually demonstrative towards strangers, the majority show great affection for children and are tolerant of their most exacting demands.

A certain independence, more pronounced in the male, is characteristic of the breed. The Pyrenean learns quickly, but being more intelligent than the average, he may not be particularly easy to train. He will respond the more readily if rewarded rather than corrected and, when it becomes necessary, correction should be sharply decisive and used with discretion. Although a Pyrenean does not fully mature either physically or temperamentally until he is well over two years old, he grows very rapidly when a puppy and simple obedience training should be completed by the time he is six months old.

Standing up to a maximum of 32″ at the shoulder, the Pyrenean is a deceptively fast mover and should the boisterous, virile male, approaching sexual maturity, cause management problems, there is a strong case for castration. The Pyrenean seldom bothers to fight other dogs and gets on well with most animals. As a rule he is exceptionally clean in the house and astonishingly adaptable to his owner's circumstances. His greatest enemy is boredom and he is never happier than when he has a job to do.

standards

The first Pyrenean Standard to be generally accepted was laid down by the Reunion des Amateurs de Chiens Pyrenéens, shortly after the First World War. When breeding began in America in the early 1930's, the French Standard was translated and accepted as it stood, but in 1935 it was replaced by a new one which contained a significant number of omissions and alterations, one of which, to the detriment of the breed, lowered the minimum height by 2 cms. Another alteration included the head, with the shorter muzzle favored in England and America, but which is not acceptable in France, where the longer foreface is considered correct. It was the American Standard which, a few years later, was adopted in its entirety by the Pyrenean Mountain Dog Club of Great Britain, apparently without further reference to the original French translation. Essentially, however, all the Standards call for a dog of great size (27″ to 32″ for dogs, 25″ to 29″ for bitches), strongly built, but with a certain elegance and a kindly disposition. He should have a thick double coat, with a fine white undercoat and a long, flat outer coat of a coarser hair. Black on nose and eyerims and an unbroken black mouth line are also necessary. In the all-white dog good pigment would ideally be linked with black pads, nails and palate. Double dew-claws on the hind legs are a distinguishing feature, and their removal constitutes disqualification in the show ring.

Mrs. B. Lord's Ch. Laudley Prettilie Natalie, a superb example of the female of the breed, winner of twenty-five C.C.s and considered to be the outstanding bitch of her time. Natalie's feminine lines are in sharp contrast to the masculinity of the dogs, and yet she shows no lack of substance.

The massive head of Ch. Tartuffe of Oloron.

Mrs. Passini Birkett's Ch. Pondtail Zborowski, another grandson of Ch. Bedat de Monda, with a great winning record.

When Mr. and Mrs. Prince's Ch. Bergerie Diable, pictured here, won reserve best in show at Cruft's in 1968.

Russian Sheepdog

(Mid-Asiatic, North Caucasian Steppe, South Russian, Transcaucasian)

Transcaucasian Owtcharka

The Owtcharki are found in a wide area across European and Asiatic Russia and arose from the needs of the localities in which they were bred. In the Caucasus Mountains for example, the need was for a dog of good herding ability and of sufficient size and fierceness to protect flocks and herds from wolves and robbers. This seems to have been satisfied by crossing Mastiff-type dogs with sheep-herding Spitz, thus producing a breed which was resistant to the cold; fierce, strong and with herding ability; rather like the Old English Sheepdog, with long shaggy coat which gives warmth in the cold winter climate of the Steppes, and with long hair over the eyes.

These dogs are relatively slow workers, but are nevertheless efficient and, with training, make excellent guard dogs, often being used in this role to protect remotely placed camps and military installations. There are four main types of the Russian Sheepdog and although they are almost unknown in the West, exceptionally large specimens have been exhibited at German dog shows. Although they are reputed to be reasonably easy to train, the old Russian saying "Troublesome as a Caucasian" seems to apply to these dogs as much as to their masters!

Transcaucasian Owtcharka: which has a height of 26″ at the withers, is a large, powerful, thick-haired dog with small, hanging ears and the tail is docked. It has a massive head with a blunt nose and small, oval-shaped eyes. Its neck is strong and short; its body, sturdy and powerful and the quarters are straight and only slightly angulated. The coat is long, dense, and rough. Colors are gray, reddish, white, yellowish or spotted.

A South Russian Owtcharka

Mid-Asiatic Owtcharka: almost as large. It has a coarse appearance with small, hanging ears, docked tail, and heavy coat. The size varies according to the area. In the desert regions, the dog is usually of lighter build and has a less heavy coat. The average height is 24″-26″ at the shoulder. The skull is broad, muzzle blunt, and the eyes small, round in shape, and placed far apart. The body is muscular and roundish in shape. The front legs are short and straight; the hind legs well-angulated and powerful.
The coat is hard and straight. Color ranges between black and white.

Steppenowtcharka: found in the desert (steppe) regions of North-Caucasia and the lowlands around the Caspian Sea. It is a squarely-built dog with small ears and the tail is usually docked. It is somewhat smaller than the other two already described and its head is a little longer and cleaner.
The coat also is a little shorter. Colors are usually gray or white, but may also be brindle or spotted.

South-Russian Owtcharka: bred in the Crimean area as well as the Ukrain. It is a medium-sized dog (20″ at the shoulder) with long hair, hanging ears, and a curly tail. The head is longish, the muzzle long and sharp, and the triangular ears, which hang on the cheeks, are on the small side. Its body is strong and muscular, and the legs are strong and straight. The tail, which reaches the hocks, is particularly long-haired. The coat is extremely long, and colored white with or without yellow markings, ashen gray, or gray with white spots or patches.
In character the South-Russian Owtcharka is the most docile of the four.

The Transcaucasian – a fully grown specimen.

Ch. Altai, a Mid-Asiatic Owtcharka

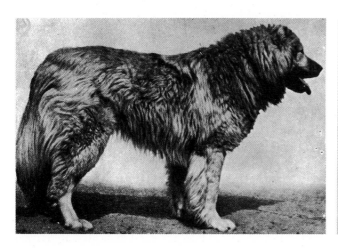

Rumanian Sheepdog

This dog is suggestive of the descendants of the Greek *Simocyon* which, in turn, is related to the Roman Mollossus. It is, as its name implies, used extensively as a Sheepdog and it was recognized as a distinct breed by the Rumanian Kennel Club in 1937.

It is large, heavy dog with a massive head, rather like that of the St. Bernard. There is a distinct stop and the skull is slightly domed. It has medium-sized eyes which are slightly sunken, and dark amber in color. The somewhat small ears are set wide apart and rather low, and are folded backwards.

The tail is usually left undocked but sometimes docked very short. The soft, smooth, medium length coat is wavy and longer on the flanks and hindquarters than on the head.

This is a vigorous, loyal and strong breed; able to tackle wolf or bear.

Accepted colors are tricolor, sable with darker head-points, black-and-tan and various brindles.

Its height is from 24″ to 26″ at the shoulder and it weighs some 110 lbs.

The heavy coat of the Rumanian Sheepdog is not carried through to the skull and foreface.

Schapendoes

Another Dutch sheepdog, bred when sheep were one of the staple farm products and now used as a house dog, and for guard duties, but still occasionally for sheep. Its ancestry contains, among other breeds, infusions of Puli, Bearded Collie, Bergamasco and the Briard. The Schapendoes had been established in the 1800's and had appeared at agricultural shows but, for some reason unknown, virtually disappeared after that until around the time of the German occupation when efforts were made to re-establish the breed in its former character and appearance. The Schapendoes is now a very popular dog in Holland. It was accepted by the F.C.I. in 1970.

It is lightly boned, with profuse, long hair, and very lively. The head is broad, muzzle of medium length, covered with long hair which has the effect of making the skull look broader than it really is. The eye is an important characteristic; it should be round and rather large and dark, but not bulging nor deep set. The jaws have scissor bite, the ears are pendant, set-on high. The head is carried high. The body is longer than its height, with well sprung ribs and deep chest. The front legs are straight; hind legs well muscled, feet rather large. The tail is long and set-on low. The coat is long, about three inches, and harsh and shaggy, with a soft undercoat. Height for bitches 15″; dogs 21″.

A typical example of a young Schapendoes.

Saint Bernard

More champions than one cares to count have carried the Corna Garth prefix, owned by Mr. A. K. Gaunt. The 1970 representative was Ch. Corna Garth He's Grand.

history and development

It is believed that the breed was first introduced at the Hospice of St. Bernard in the Swiss Alps between the years 1660 and 1670 and that it was originally used as a watch dog. They are said to be descendants of the old Roman Molossian dogs. Due to their very good sense of direction and their excellent path-finding ability in fog and snow, the monks took the St. Bernard through the mountains on long trips of service. This association developed into a wonderful combination of man and beast in the service of life-saving in the snow. The renowned Barry, who is credited with having saved forty lives between 1800 and 1810, and whose mounted likeness is now in the Berne Natural History Museum, is representative of the older type of St. Bernard.

The first St. Bernard was introduced into England from Switzerland in 1810. This dog, called Lion, was comparatively large, standing 32″ to 33″ at the shoulder. The first exhibition showing of a St. Bernard took place in 1863. In 1823, the writer Daniel Wilson first spoke in Britain of the so-called St. Bernard but it was not until 1880 that the name was officially recognized. Previous to 1830, all St. Bernards were short-haired but, in that year, in an attempt to give added size and new vitality to the breed, they were crossed with Newfoundlands. As a result, the first long-haired St. Bernards appeared. Schumacher, who in 1884 arranged for the first collection of the Swiss Kennel Club records to be published, is also to be

Ch. Abbotspass Friar was a top winner of his day, winning fourteen C.C.s in 1932, '33, '34, and '35. He was bred by Mrs. E. K. Staines.

Side and front head views — the Saint Bernard.

Two promising young puppies.

It is difficult to breed a St. Bernard sound enough, and at the same time excelling in breed points, to compete successfully with the top dogs of other breeds — and a group win at a championship show is thus rare. But in 1969 Mrs. and Miss Muggleton's Ch. Bernmont Warlord achieved this at Bath championship show in England.

thanked for the first systematic breeding to be carried on outside the Hospice. He idealized the old Barry type and many such dogs were sold in England. By 1887, a new type, neither English, German nor Swiss, had come into being and a congress was held in Berne in that year, at which an international Standard was set up.

Between 1875 and 1885, America had come under the spell of this giant dog and in 1888, the St. Bernard Club of America was formed and it adopted the international Standard set up at the Berne congress.

At the present time, there are two St. Bernard Clubs in England; the English St. Bernard Club and the United St. Bernard Club. There is also the St. Bernard Club of Scotland. The breed is now very popular and the standard of type and quality is very high. Really good sizes have been achieved; up to 36″ at the shoulder for a dog and 33″ for a bitch. In the U.S.A. the Standard sets a minimum of $27\frac{1}{2}$″ for a dog and $25\frac{1}{2}$″ for a bitch. Gorgeous heads are to be seen, with good strength of muzzle, diamond-shaped eye and benevolent expression; altogether portraying dignity, kindness and affection.

color

Orange, mahogany-brindle, red-brindle; white with patches on the body of any of the above-named colors. There should be a white blaze up the face, white muzzle, chest, legs and tip of tail, and a white collar round the neck. Black shadings on the face and ears give the dog a very attractive appearance and are greatly appreciated. Fawn or self-colored are faults.

care

The chief factors in raising a St. Bernard are regularity in diet, time of feeding, exercise, sleeping and the administration of such medicines and health aids as one proves by success. A puppy of two to four months should be fed four times a day; four to six months, three times a day; six to twelve months, twice a day. After twelve months, one meal a day is sufficient. Much harm can be done by giving a St. Bernard puppy too much exercise. Short frequent walks are far better than long, tiring ones. Care of the coat is very important and a daily grooming will keep it clean and lovely. Care must be taken to ensure that the dog is kept free from worms as these pests derange the system and cause the coat to fall.

character

The St. Bernard normally has a wonderful disposition. Its grace, dignity and especially its devotion to children, make it a highly popular breed to many dog-lovers. It is easy to train and has a wonderful brain. It is a stalwart and faithful companion at all times.

standards

The British Standard varies a little from that of other countries. In America, size is not so great as in Britain and the Standard stipulates that dew-claws may be removed by surgery. In Britain, they are removed when only a few days old. Italy and Germany also produce lovely dogs but they do not seem to possess the softness of expression and side wrinkle of the British-bred dogs. They usually have round eyes instead of the diamond shape which is essential in Britain. However, most of the basic characteristics are common to the breed the world over.

The coat is long or short according to whether the dog is rough or smooth-coated. The smooth-coated specimen should have a dense, close, hound-like, tough coat, but it should not be rough to the touch. The thighs should be slightly feathered. The rough-coated dog should have moderately long, flat hair; not curly or shaggy. The hair should be longer on the neck and the tail should be bushy but never rolled.

The large and massive head and skull should in circumference be rather more than double the length of the head from nose to occiput. Muzzle short, full in front of the eye and square at nose end. Cheeks flat, with great depth from eye to lower jaw. Lips deep but not too pendulous. From nose to stop, perfectly straight and broad. Well defined stop. Broad skull, slightly rounded at the top and with a somewhat prominent brow. Nose large and black. The eyes should be rather small and deepset and dark in color, the lower lid drooping to show a fair amount of haw at the inner corner. It should have good body and bone portraying power and endurance and it should have a free and easy movement.

Daphnydene Karro vom Birkenkopf, owned by Mrs. D. Ayckbourn, is one of a number of German imports brought into Britain to strengthen the existing bloodlines. Karro, bred by Mr. O. Ulrich, became the first German import to win a C.C., and later a second at Richmond championship show in 1970 when only nineteen months old.

Shetland Sheepdog

history and development

Shetland Sheepdog, Shetland Collie, Miniature Collie, Shetland, Sheltie, Toonie or Peerie – at some time or other the Sheltie has answered to all these names. On the Kennel Club register they are officially Shetland sheepdogs, but it is by their pet name of Sheltie that the general public knows them. Incidentally, the word "Sheepdog" is rather misleading as they can be confused with Old English Sheepdogs.

The Sheltie must always have been on the Islands of Scotland. They were known as Toonie dogs, the Toon being the local name for farm. As all-purpose dogs, they were supreme; whether keeping livestock away from the cultivated land (since there were no fences), helping with the sheep, ponies and hens, or keeping an eye on the children. They were members of the household and their long association with man has made them the lovable, companionable dogs they are today.

There must have been working Collie blood from the Scottish mainland in their makeup, as well as blood from the Yakki or Iceland dogs, which were on the whalers calling in at the Islands. It is also reputed that a black-and-tan King Charles Spaniel left behind by a yacht played a part in their ancestry; this is borne out by the number of black-and-tans registered in the first Island Club register and also in the color inheritance. The breed was not recognized until 1909, though some were benched at Cruft's in 1906. In that year the Shetland Sheepdog Club was formed, followed by the formation of the Scottish Shetland Sheepdog Club in

A very early Sheltie of 1911. Thule Norna was a tricolor bitch bred and owned by Mr. W. J. Greig.

96

1909. The English Shetland Sheepdog Club was not started until 1914 and in that year the Sheltie received a separate classification in the Kennel Club register. The name Shetland Collie was the first choice but the Collie Clubs objected so strongly that the Kennel Club would not allow it and "Sheepdog" had to be used instead.

The Shetland Sheepdog owes a lot to the British Navy. Before the First World War, the Fleet used to visit the Scottish Islands on manoeuvres and sailors would take puppies home. The Islanders found that there was a ready sale for the small, fluffy puppies and a lot of indiscriminate breeding went on. The formation of the Clubs however helped to stop this.

In 1908 the Shetland Sheepdog Club Standard said that the points shall be similar to the Rough Collie in miniature, height not to exceed 15″. In 1909 the Scottish Shetland Sheepdog Club said "height about 12″" and in 1914 the English Shetland Sheepdog Club agreed on 12″. In 1923 however, the height was increased to 15″, a much more realistic size. In the U.S.A., the Standard specifies 13″ to 16″.

The first Challenge Certificate was awarded in 1915 and in 1917 the first champion achieved his title. This dog was Ch. Woodvold, whose dam was a small Collie. A good deal of Collie crossing went on "sub rosa"; the late Miss Humphries, Mr. J. Saunders and Mr. Pierce made Collie crosses quite openly and this did help to improve type. It also led to a great divergence in size however, as it was possible to produce in one litter dogs varying between 13″ and 17″. The question of size is still not entirely resolved.

color

One of the most fascinating things about the Sheltie is the enormous variety of colors possible. Starting with pale wheaten it ranges through all shades of gold and red sable, to the dark shaded mahogany. All these colors have white markings. Then there is the tricolor – black with tan and white markings, black-and-white (known as bi-colors in America) and the very rare black-and-tan with no white markings. Finally, there is the blue-merle. This is really an interloper, as blue-merle has never been known on the Islands. All the present-day blue-merles owe their color to the Collie crosses, and there are also sable-merles, which cannot be shown and which are the result of breeding blues to shaded sables. Although this is considered unorthodox, in the right hands it can nevertheless produce the most lovely colored blue-merles. Another interesting point about color-breeding is that two tricolors can produce a pure golden-sable. This has never been known to happen in Collies. It will be remembered in the history of the breed that a black-and-tan King Charles Spaniel was reputed to have been used on the Islands and, since a black-and-tan King Charles can produce the ruby color, this is further confirmation of King Charles blood in the Sheltie. Two sables can also produce black-and-white offspring and it is possible to breed two blue-merles together, yet produce only tricolor puppies. If, by any chance, a pure white puppy should be produced from such a mating, it must be destroyed at once as it will be both deaf and blind. The color permutations are endless in Sheltie breeding and it is impossible to be dictatorial about color inheritance.

care

Beyond a good brushing with a stiff-bristled brush once or twice a week, the Sheltie requires little grooming although a comb may occasionally be

Ch. Riverhill Rufus (1935) who is considered to have the best head in the breed. This photograph is used as an illustration in the Club's Standard.

Ch. Tilford Tontine, the most successful pre-war bitch, and the dam of four champions. She was whelped in 1929.

Ch. Riverhill Rogue, owned by the Misses Rogers; an outstanding blue merle dog, who is the only Sheltie ever to have won two C.C.s at Cruft's. This he did in 1959 and 1960.

used, especially to prevent tangles forming in the soft, fluffy hair behind the ears. If excessive, some of this hair can be plucked out with finger and thumb to give a neater effect. Once a year or, in the case of a bitch, after a litter, the coat will come out and then a comb must certainly be used as the undercoat rises like a fleece and just falls out. When it has all come away, a bath is advisable. Frequent bathing is, however, quite unnecessary, for the correct (harsh) coat has a wonderful way of shedding mud and dirt. A dog may return from a long country walk caked with mud, yet as soon as he is dry again he will look fresh and clean with coat gleaming. City grime is, of course, more clinging, and if a town-dwelling Sheltie is to remain spotless, his white markings will need a little more attention than those of his country cousin.

The Sheltie is very fastidious and will keep his feet and legs immaculate, licking them like a cat.

Ch. Lothario of Exford, owned by Mrs. F. P. B. Sangster, was the first tricolor dog to sire champions of all colors. He was born in 1952.

If the dog does not go on hard ground it may be necessary to cut the toenails occasionally to keep the feet in good shape. The pricked ear is a very common fault. In a pet dog, this does not matter and, in fact, some people think it looks better but, in the case of a show-dog, this is the one fault any judge can see. It is very important never to let the ears go up, no matter how young a puppy may be. A little grease rubbed into the eartips keeps them supple and soft. Ears often go up when a puppy is teething and, in the case of a bitch, when she comes in heat.

Ch. Riverhill Rare Gold (front) with her four champion daughters. She also had a C.C.-winning son. No bitch in the breed has either won so much herself or bred so many winners. Her descendants have now reached the third and fourth generation. Left to right – Ch. R. Ready Cash (1958), Ch. R. Real Gold (1956), Ch. R. Rather Rich (1959) and Ch. Rarity of Glenmist (1961, owned by Mr. F. L. Mitchell).

character

The Shetland Sheepdog has the true Sheepdog character; wanting to help and be with his master. He has initiative and is very responsive to his owner's wishes, for his owner's business is his own. He often has an uncanny built-in radar system telling him when his master gets within a mile or two of home. This may sound far-fetched but has been proved again and again, and it is not just a matter of acute hearing, although the Sheltie has this too.

Shelties also have the Sheepdog dislike of being touched by strangers; they like to make their own advances.

House-training presents no problems and obedience work comes easily to them. The larger ones still make good sheepdogs, for this instinct has not been bred out.

If started as young puppies, they make the most wonderful companions for children. They are very adaptable, will follow a horse, go for a steady walk, or just run about in the garden. As long as a Sheltie is with his master or mistress that is all that matters to him. These are not dogs to keep in large numbers. To thrive and develop their brains, they must have human companionship. Remember, they have lived as members of families for a great many years.

standards

There is now only one Standard in the British Isles.

Formerly each Club had its own Standard, but this led to a diversity of type in different parts of the country. The Kennel Club put a stop to this

Sheltie puppies

by instructing the Clubs to agree on one Standard, which is now official. Size is about the only difference between the British and American Standards; the British Standard says "The ideal size is 14″ for bitches and 14½″ for dogs". The American Standard says "Size between 13″ and 16″ at the shoulder. Disqualification: heights above or below the desired size range". There is no disqualification for size in the British Standard.

It should always be remembered that the Sheltie is a working breed and should be lithe and active with jumping power great for its size. The Sheltie's expression is one of its great charms, conveying sweet, alert, gentle intelligence. This is brought about by the balance of head, ear-set and placement and shape of the eyes. Factors that ruin the expression are an overlong foreface, receding skull, roman nose, round eyes, very small piggy eyes, ears set wide or pricked.

The head should be refined and, when viewed from top and side, is a long, blunt wedge, tapering from ear to nose. Strong and clean jaws with well-developed underjaw. Tight lips and sound and level teeth. The eyes should be brown, but blue is permissible in a merle. Small ears, moderately spaced, placed fairly close together at the top of the skull. Forelegs straight when viewed from in front. Level back with a graceful sweep to the loins. A broad and muscular thigh, clean-cut hockjoint and low-set tail. The Sheltie should be free from exaggeration, and balanced all through, looking as if he could do a day's work.

A beautiful head. The Misses Rogers's Ch. Riverhill Richman, the top Sheltie dog of 1969.

Swiss Mountain Dog
(Appenzell, Bernese, Entlebuch, Great Swiss)

A Bernese Mountain Dog at work delivering dairy produce.

There are four varieties of the Sennenhunde, or Swiss Mountain Dogs – the Appenzeller, the Bernese, the Entlebucher and the Great Swiss, all but the last being named for the Swiss regions in which they were bred and used. Their particular strength lies in their sagacity and their power to endure in the difficult mountain regions of the Alps.

Although they vary in size their inheritance of Mastiff characteristics is evident, and their capacity for work in mountainous country probably derives from Molossian ancestry, for it is remarkable how adaptable for mountain work are dogs of this descent.

We know that large dogs of the Molossian type accompanied the Romans through Europe, the Middle East and North Africa. On their passages through Switzerland many such dogs must have been left behind, to breed through the succeeding centuries and to develop into as many different kinds as there were isolated communities in which they were used. Until the late 1800's little difference was noted between any of these proliferating mountain dog breeds, until Professor Dr. A. Heim undertook a course of research which led him to identify the four types which we know today. This work was done in collaboration with the Swiss Kennel Club and, in at least one case, with the assistance of the Canton authority.

Each breed now has a separate registration and a Standard defining its required points, and they are all known, to lesser or greater extents, in other parts of the world. These dogs have been important to the livelihoods of Swiss farming communities, herding, droving, guarding, hauling,

Int. Ch. Jungzar v Grimmeustein, a fine, sturdy, healthy specimen of the breed.

with a remarkable responsiveness to any task required of them. This importance is not so great today, and the breeds have come into their own in the show world, by virtue of their outstanding physical qualities and appearance.

Bernese: Switzerland has bred many fine dogs and the Bernese is possibly one of the finest; certainly it is the most popular of the four types, and the best known in other countries, standing comparison with any other of the world's working dogs. Apart from sheep and cattle herding, droving and guarding (rigorous tasks in this part of the world) the Bernese has been much used as a draught dog, hauling loads of baskets to market for its weaver owners in the canton of Berne.

The virtues of the Bernese had been evident for some time during the 1800's but, up to the time they were rediscovered by Dr. Heim, an influx of other breeds had tended to obscure them, and they were somewhat neglected. At one time they could be found only in the valleys of the lower Alps. It was here that Dr. Heim found them, and, with the official assistance of the Canton authorities, he assumed the responsibility of promoting a renewed interest in them in Switzerland, and in Europe at large. Perhaps the most tangible expression of Dr. Heim's efforts was in the Durrbach area, where some especially fine specimens were found, giving to the breed the name "Durrbachler". As ownership of these Bernese dogs spread, the name changed to what it is today, and the breed is now under the sponsorship of the Klub fur Bernersennenhunde. There are societies of fanciers in Germany, Holland and Scandinavia, where breeding is successfully carried on.

The Bernese Mountain Dog is an animal of imposing appearance and size – dogs stand $24\frac{1}{2}''$ to $27''$, bitches $23''$ to $24''$ – and they have an ideal temperament for discipline and training. They are not noisy, are friendly and compatible with other dogs and animals and do not need a great deal of exercise. Although showing a keen spirit and courage as watchdogs they can become lovable, affectionate family pets, appealing as much for their intelligence as for their great beauty.

Their coloring is striking. A dog in good condition has a soft, smooth coat, long and slightly waved, but not curled; and it is gleaming black, with bright tan brands on the haws, above the eyes and on all four legs. It has a white blaze on the head and a white chest, with white paws and end of tail. The tail is shaggy, straight and hangs slightly below the horizontal.

The coat needs regular grooming and the diet is standard for dogs in this size range. The dew-claws should be removed as a puppy.

Despite its size the body is compact, with a broad, strong chest and powerful hindquarters. The head is held proudly and the neck has a prominent ruff, or collar. The female is decidedly smaller.

Appenzell Mountain Dog: The Appenzell is descended from the Asian Mastiffs of the Greeks and Phoenicians. In 1906, at a meeting in Appenzell, a decision was taken to develop the special qualities of this typically Swiss mountain breed. This meeting was virtually the beginning of the important Appenzell Sheepdog Club. The breed is now fully established and specimens have been exported to many countries.

The Appenzell is the ideal farm dog, adapting himself by instinct to all tasks on a farm. It is a rugged dog, very resistant to weather extremes, intelligent and easy to train, especially the bitches, and is unequalled as a

An Appenzell Mountain Dog of the Swiss herding group.

herding dog, and as a guard dog for sheep.

As to his food, although he is happy with pigfood or milk, this diet is often too high in carbohydrates and lacking in protein; and many become fat and heavy with age. To keep him fit, he must have his daily ration of meat – and plenty of exercise.

As a pet the Appenzell becomes a natural part of the family. The myth that the prick-eared breeds are the most intelligent is erroneous; the drop-eared dog is more submissive and useful.

The Appenzell is black with tan and white regular markings, and medium-sized (maximum 22″ to 23″). Special features are the tan spots over the eyes, and the white on breast and throat, and touching muzzle, paws and tip of tail.

Entlebuch Mountain Dog: The smallest of the four Swiss Sennenhunde, named after the town of Entlebuch and the river of the same name which runs into Lake Lucerne.

Used for herding, it is very compact and sturdy, standing some 16″ to 20″ high, and is found fairly extensively in the rural areas around Lucerne and in the Bernese Emmenthal.

It has a broad head, ears set-on high and rounded at the tips. The body is very compact and the back is firm and level. The chest is deep and the hindquarters strong, with a tail either short at birth or docked.

The coat is smooth and short and the colors are tricolor, black, tan and white.

Great Swiss Mountain Dog: This is the largest of the four, very well suited to haul the light carts carrying farm produce to remoter dwellings in the valleys. It is a very gentle and safe breed with children but nevertheless is an extremely good watchdog, with a reputation for protecting its owner and family and for securing property. It also has been successfully trained as an avalanche dog, being able to carry a heavy load, due to its robust physique.

It is a compact, very powerful dog, but without coarseness in its build. Well-boned, straight, muscular legs and strong hindquarters provide the extraordinary power for hauling carts. The tail is carried low.

The large head is flat on top with a moderate stop and a foreface of medium length; the ears are high-set and are carried folded and pointing downwards.

The height is 26″ to 27″ for the dog and one inch less for the bitch.

A front view of the Entlebuch Sennenhund, showing the typical broad head, with ears set-on high and rounded at the tips.

A typical Entlebuch Sennenhund.

Two of these hard-working Swiss Mountain Dogs at rest.

Baldo v. Breitenegg, the Great Swiss Mountain Dog, owned by A. Kobelt, who was the Schweizer-Sieger winner in 1963 and 1964.

Welsh Corgi, Cardigan

Mrs. J. H. Jones's Eng. and Am. Ch. Dilwel Maggie, top brood bitch in 1967 and the dam of two champion bitches. A lovely red/white, she excels particularly in head and expression. Note the more rounded and larger ears than those of the Pembroke Corgi.

history and development

The Cardigan Corgi is one of two types of working cattle dogs, known to have been kept in South Wales since the time of the Domesday Book. In A.D. 990 Wales was governed by a ruler named Howell Dda, many of whose laws are incorporated in the laws of Great Britain today. He placed a value upon every domestic animal, and equated the value of "a cattle dog" with that of "a steer". The Corgi is the indigenous dog of Wales and probably existed in the time of Howell Dda. The Pembrokeshire type Corgi has always been smaller, more compact, more foxy in expression and livelier in temperament. Students of history think there is a strong possibility that there is spitz-type blood behind it, whereas the Cardigans differ in several respects. Used for precisely the same work – the driving and herding of wild steers, dairy cows and mountain ponies – the Cardigan is a larger, longer-bodied dog. Equally low to ground and short legged, it has a triangular head with larger, rather rounded, ears. Coat texture is similar but tends to be smoother and harder to the touch though in no way harsh or wiry.

There is absolutely nothing about the Cardigan to suggest a "spitz" ancestry. Rather its supporters think it may have much in common with the old English turn-spit dog. This was a short-legged, long-bodied dog used in private kitchens, inns and hostelries, to turn the spits on which the huge joints of meat roasted beside the open fires. While opinions differ as to the precise meaning of the word "Corgi", it is commonly supposed to have its basis in the word "Cor" – to collect, to gather, and "Gi" meaning dog. In parts of Cardiganshire the dogs are referred to as "Ci-llathed", the "Yard-long dog"; for the original Cardigan Corgis were supposed to measure a Welsh yard (which is slightly longer than an English yard) from the tip of the nose to the tip of the tail.

There are some fascinating references to the Cardigans in Welsh folk-lore. For instance, old people (many of whom, even today, speak only Welsh) in remote country districts, believe that the blue merles were never bred; the fairies brought them one dark night! As long ago as the 16th century, a Welsh writer referred to the sharp bark of the Corgi as "tuning-keys for the harp".

Cardigan Corgi puppies

The Cardigan Corgis of today are much the same as their earliest recorded ancestors. Type, although stabilized, has changed very little, although quality is higher and size and general conformation more even. In character and disposition the "Cardie", as he is often called, is the same. Still the sturdy, stalwart, farmer's friend, keen to work, keen to play, incorruptible, full of fun – the fairy dog of Wales.

The Cardigan Corgi entered the show ring in Britain about 1925, at the same time as his Pembroke brother received official Kennel Club recognition. Numerically, however, this unusual and attractive breed has not become so well-known or so popular and this is difficult to understand, as it possesses all the same excellent characteristics. While Pembroke registrations run well over the 4,000 mark, Kennel Club figures show less than 300 Cardigans registered in a year. Nevertheless, entries at shows are on the increase and Cardigans continue to increase in numbers.

color

Cardigans come in a far greater variety of colors. Reds, reddish-browns, sables, light reds or fawns, usually marked with white on legs, chest, head, neck – and tail tip, for the Cardigan has a long, thick brush like a fox and

The City of Birmingham championship show in 1965 where Mrs. D. Albin (centre) awarded the C.C.s to Mrs. T. Gray's blue/merle bitch, Ch. Rozavel Blue Tinsel (left) and Mr. D. Jones's brindle/white dog, Ch. Pantyblaidd Pip (right). Pip has an impressive show record with ten C.C.s, and three times best of breed at Cruft's, the only Cardigan Corgi to do so; he has also sired champions in the U.S.A.

A beautiful blue merle bitch, Mrs. T. Gray's Ch. Rozavel Blue Rosette, who has won nine C.C.s and five reserve C.C.s. Note the shape of her feet, round and rather large, quite different from those of the Pembroke Corgi.

the tail is never docked. These are popular color combinations, as are the tricolors – blacks marked with rich bright tan, and with the acceptable white marks. The most distinctive, typical Cardigan colors, however, are the brindles and the blue merles, all, as above, marked with white.

Heads of the Cardigan Welsh Corgi

care

They are tireless, built to run up and down the hillsides for hours on end, and are strong and healthy, rarely ill when properly fed and exercized. They have one bugbear, however; Progressive Retinal Atrophy, which has been discovered in a number of breeds, exists in Cardigans. Happily, this has been tackled and is well on the way to being eliminated; some strains are notably free of this eye affliction. If P.R.A. is suspected advice should be sought from a veterinarian.

character

The Cardigan is a quieter, more placid dog than the Pembroke and often less bold. He is a faithful and devoted companion and a good watch dog. As a family dog he has few equals, having a natural fondness for children. The years of working on Welsh farmsteads, on open hill country, through wild winters and wet springs have left their heritage; Cardigans are rugged, tough, hardy dogs. They have large, rather flat, round feet because they walk in marshy places. Their short front legs are slightly bowed to encompass the wide, deep chests and to help them to duck down quickly to avoid kicks from the cattle and horses.

standards

The Cardigan should have an alert expression, "as foxy as possible". The Standards follow the "Ci-llathed" definition – it should still be 36″ from nose to tail tip. The A.K.C. Standard allows up to 44″. The head is foxy in shape, with a three-inch muzzle, and erect ears which are rather large and prominent. The body is fairly long and strong, with a broad chest with prominent breast bone. It has short, strong legs, with the round, well-padded feet, and no dew-claws, which should have been removed.

The tail is moderately long, undocked, set in line with the body. It should not curl over the back.

It should measure around 12″ at the shoulder and dogs should weigh 22 to 26 lbs. and bitches 20 to 24 lbs.

Welsh Corgi, Pembroke

history and development

The Corgi was widely kept and bred in parts of South Wales for hundreds of years by farmers who found these dogs invaluable for herding and driving cattle and mountain ponies. The breed developed on two distinct lines in Pembrokeshire and Cardiganshire, and while a limited amount of inter-breeding took place, in the main the two types were kept separate. The origin of the Corgi is obscure – but a Welsh cattle dog is mentioned in the Domesday Book, the economic survey of Britain prepared by William the Conqueror in the 11th century, and was even then a highly prized animal. There is a breed in Sweden, used for herding work, called the Vastgötaspets which bears a marked resemblance to the Pembroke type Corgi. This coincidence is thought to have arisen in the past from trade with horses between Wales and Scandinavia when the dogs were introduced from one country to the other. It is not certain which was the country of origin; most people think it was Wales, but we can never be sure that the little Welsh heelers had ancestors from Sweden, or if the Vastergötland herding dogs came from Welsh forebears.

It was not until 1925 that Corgis were exhibited at shows in Britain, and at that time pedigrees were scrappy or non-existent, and type varied. The

Pembroke Corgi puppies

character and intelligence of the breed, coupled with its medium size, short hair and attractive appearance brought it rising popularity, accelerated when King George VI became the owner of a succession of Corgis of the Pembrokeshire type. It is still a favorite of Queen Elizabeth II, who has known the breed since her childhood.

At the same time intelligent breeders were concentrating on improving their stock, and gradually some very beautiful specimens began to appear. Overseas visitors fell for the Corgi which was soon firmly established in the U.S.A., Australia, New Zealand and South Africa, not to mention several Continental countries.

Unless one has seen the Corgi at work, one may wonder why a dog so small should be designed to tackle beasts weighing the best part of 1,000 lbs. on the hoof.

The size, and the shortness of leg, are essential requirements to enable the dog to duck down when the animals kick, the flying hooves lash out harmlessly over the head of the dog, and where a larger heeler might easily be severely injured or killed, the Corgi continues to dart to and fro, barking, nipping, running from one side of the road to the other, or rounding up the stragglers into the mass. The ability of the Corgi was most neatly summed up, many years ago when the breed was just becoming popular. A visitor to Pembrokeshire saw a particularly nice specimen bringing in the cows for milking in a remote country district. She approached the old farmer and asked if the Corgi was for sale, adding that she would be prepared to pay a good price. The old man gave her a quizzical look. "Lady", he said "if I was to sell that little bitch there, I'd

Mrs. G. Rainbow's Ch. Caswell Duskie Knight, in 1970 the new C.C.-record holder. At seven years old he beat Ch. Zephyr's record – up-to-date he has won over thirty C.C.s Apart from being a superb showman this dark sable/white dog is also an outstanding sire, and was leading stud dog in 1966 to 1969.

Lack of stop gives this dog a faulty expression. His back is too short, and his chest needs to be deeper.

Mrs. L. Moore's Ch. Kaytop Marshall. Born in 1967 this beautifully colored, deep red/white dog, who has had a most successful show career in Britain to date, is also making a name for himself as a stud force.

have to pay a boy to do her work around the farm!" and that was final. No money would tempt him to part with his devoted "assistant".

The Corgi's natural work also explains why a flattish, triangular head is a breed point – a round skull would be more vulnerable to kicks. One has to admit that there appears to be no very good reason for the prick ears excepting that sometimes such ears enable a dog to be especially sharp of hearing, and the herding breeds must be on the *qui vive* for a distant shout or a whistle. Corgis still work on lonely farms, though not so frequently as in the past. Cattle, once driven mile upon mile to market, are packed into trucks and taken by road, though often the Corgi helps to round them up for loading. Generations of Corgis kept for breeding, showing or as pets, have never seen a steer or a pony. Yet the old instincts die hard and there have been fascinating cases where puppies, introduced to farm stock, have immediately started to heel and to round them up.

Corgis are essentially a "natural" breed. No detrimental fancy show points have been imposed on them, they remain today, though greatly improved in type and quality, what they have always been – super-intelligent, hardy dogs, easily trained to be satisfying and often exceptionally long-lived, companions.

Time and time again, families lose an old and valued Corgi friend at up to seventeen years of age, and invariably come back for another – nothing but another Corgi will do, they say, after so many years of happy dog-owning.

For the past few years, annual registrations at the Kennel Club in Britain have fluctuated between 4,000 and 5,000, and the A.K.C. registers some 2,000 a year.

color

The Corgi is predominantly a reddish brown, red, sable, or fawn dog, popularly marked with white on chest and legs, sometimes on head and neck. Very heavy, predominant white markings are faulty, and the smokey-gray color sometimes encountered is disliked. There are also black-tan-and-white Corgis which are most attractive, and occasionally black-and-tans without white on them, these being less eye-catching.

care

A Corgi is a tough, hardy dog, not subject to any particular ailment and when properly fed and exercized, seldom ill. The coat is weather-resistant, and easily sheds mud and grime although a brisk brush-down daily keeps it smooth and shiny and removes any dead hair that might sift out on to carpets and furniture. Thoroughly adaptable, a Corgi can keep fit with one or two short walks daily provided it has plenty of freedom about the house and garden or in a spacious enclosure. At the same time these little dogs are virtually tireless and can follow a pony or keep going longer than any companion on foot can hope to do.

character

The Corgi has been bred to snap at the heels of the animals it drives. Consequently, since instincts die hard, young puppies sometimes "heel up" human beings! This habit should be discouraged in early life since, while it may be good-humored, it may be misunderstood and has indeed earned many a Corgi a reputation for being bad-tempered – something that is normally quite foreign to this breed. A Corgi is an exceptionally intelligent dog. As such, it is quick to take advantage of its owner's weaknesses, and if it finds it can get away with mischief and misdeeds it will certainly become disobedient. Because it is so brainy, it is most easily trained, naturally clean and fastidious and very faithful. It merely needs to have these splendid qualities – by no means found in every breed of dog – channelled into the right direction. Kindness to a dog does not mean spoiling. Love and affection it must have – these are as essential as food and water, but let the Corgi understand that "No" means "No". He will respect you for it.

The average Corgi is a wonderful guard and defender for its size; gentle and tolerant with children, and particularly appeals to a public who, preferring big dogs, are prevented by circumstances from keeping them.

standards

The Pembrokeshire Corgi is a small to medium sized dog, the preferred size not exceeding 12″ at the withers, bitches weighing 20 to 22 lbs. and dogs 22 to 24 lbs. The A.K.C. allows 10″ to 12″; 18 to 22 lbs. for bitches,

The typical Pembroke Corgi's head – Miss Hewan's Ch. Stormerbanks Sabre Flash.

Frontal head view of a typical Pembroke Corgi.

A grand-son and grand-daughter of Ch. Kaytop Marshall, at ten weeks old. Note the slightly heavier bone, bolder outlook and masculine head of the dog puppy (left).

111

Mrs. K. Butler's Int. Ch. Gayelord of Wey, the sire of four champions in England before he was exported to South Africa. Gayelord is particularly noted for his very beautiful head and expression.

20 to 24 lbs. for dogs. As a matter of fact the breed as a whole has increased in size since the British Standard of Points was drawn up, perhaps because this was founded on the more slightly-built working dogs. Present-day show dogs are lavishly fed from birth onwards, the tough little heelers on the hills of Wales more often than not had to scrounge for food for themselves. The majority of show dogs and bitches probably weigh closer to 30 lbs.

The distinctive head is foxy, with ears neither very pointed nor very rounded, and always carried erect. The body is medium length, short backs being bad faults. Legs are short, thick, fairly straight, and feet tight, thick and neat, neither round nor narrow but with the two center toes slightly protruding. The tail is either short or non-existent. Some Corgis are born without tails; the rest are docked within a few days of birth. The coat is short, smooth, and should be almost glassy in texture with a dense, wooly undercoat close to the skin. A very short coat without undercoat, or a coarse, long, or wooly coat are all serious faults. Eyes are hazel in color, neither black nor yellow but usually a warm brown. Although the legs are short, the well-made Corgi is a smart mover. Well-placed shoulders enable the front legs to reach well forward with every step, while the hind legs provide plenty of thrust. A restricted, "pottering" gait is undesirable, especially in what is designed to be an active working dog capable of great endurance.

Yugoslavian Sheepdog

Caruga, a typical Yugoslavian Sheepdog.

This is one of the oldest established of the Yugoslavian working dog breeds. The Sar Planina is used in mountainous districts where he has over centuries become adapted to the most difficult type of work. It is said that it does not bark, but gives voice in a cry, rather like a howl. It is not a breed which is especially shown, but it has been a point of pride among Yugoslavian farmers to breed only from the best specimens, and the breed has thus remained strong and pure.

Strebel, writing in 1901, puts forward the theory that the Sar Planina is a link in the development from the ancient Molossus to the modern European sheepdogs.

It is a medium-sized dog, very strong, some 22″ to 23″ in height and weighing 55 to 75 lbs. The back is of medium length, straight, and the withers are high and long. The loins are broad and well muscled, the chest deep, broad, with well-sprung ribs. The forelegs are vertical, pasterns slightly sloping. The upper thighs are long, muscles powerful; hindlegs long and straight, hocks slightly bent; feet are round and close.

The tail is moderately long, set-on high, with an upward curve. Docking is permissible.

The head has a broad forehead, slightly domed, slight stop. The muzzle is broad and deep, nose large, ears moderately long and pendant, eyes dark, almond shaped.

The coat is fairly long and thick, of equal length over all the body, the undercoat not thick. The color is iron-gray, with a little white allowed on legs and chest.

Other Working and Utility Dogs

The winner of the Non-Sporting group at Westminster 1971, the Miniature Poodle, Ch. Tally Ho Tiffany, in perfect show form.

Boston Terrier

history and development

The Boston Terrier was accepted by the American Kennel Club in 1893, after some forty breeders from around Boston organized a club in 1891 and application was made for membership. The original name (American Bull Terrier) was not acceptable because of objections from other bull terrier clubs, but a noted writer and authority (James Watson) suggested that the dog was not a bull terrier and, having been bred in and around Boston, U.S.A., why not name the breed "Boston Terrier". Another name by which it had been known was "Round-head".

The breed actually was started about 1865, when the coachmen, who worked for the wealthy people living on Beacon Hill, congregated on their evenings off at Cotter's Tavern on Charles Street, and they wondered what might come of breeding the fine imported dogs owned by their employers, one breed to another. There is no question that it was highly selective breeding, for they selected the pedigreed dogs, mostly imported, and since the dogs were kept in the care of the stable men, it was possible for a cross mating between a Bulldog and an English Terrier and, at some time later, another cross in of the French Bulldog. In 1865, these breeds looked unlike the dogs we know today, and neither did the

Int. Ch. Payson's Miss Patricia GG, by Ch. Hayes Diplomat ex Payson's G-G Girl, had 107 best of breed wins, sixty-two times first in group, twenty-one times second and thirty best in show awards. She was owned by Charles D. Cline of Los Angeles.

early Boston Terrier, but by the time the breed was recognized by the American Kennel Club, a Standard had been set up, which was not unlike that of today. However, little attention was paid to the colors of the early dogs, pied or splash markings were of less importance than size. It was not until the early part of the twentieth century that color and marking became important, and a "must" for show-ring dogs.

Early breeding had to be kept secret, marking the early Boston Terrier as the stableman's or barber's dog, and frowned on by the owners of pedigreed stock. When enough stock had been bred from the cross matings, pedigrees were kept and, by this time, the breed was fairly established.

color

Brindle with white markings, the brindle to be evenly distributed and distinct. Black with white markings permissible. White muzzle, even with white blaze over head, collar, breast, part or whole of forelegs and hind legs below hocks. Disqualifications: solid black, black-and-tan, liver or mouse colors. Faults: preponderance of white on body, lack of proper proportion of brindle and white on head.

care

Like all other dogs, Boston Terriers are susceptible to the common diseases of dogs. The eyes of the Boston Terrier need to be watched carefully, because of their size and location. They should not sit in a car where the wind can hit them, nor be exercized near rose bushes or other thorny shrubs where the eyes might be injured. In whelping, Caesarian section must be considered in Boston Terriers, especially those of smaller weight. The large heads of the puppies are one factor, but mostly a narrow cervical canal is the reason for most Caesarian sections. The Veterinarian should always be alerted of the due date of an expected whelping although, in fact, many whelpings are normal.

In some countries, it is against the law to trim, or crop, ears, but in many

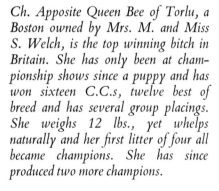

Ch. Apposite Queen Bee of Torlu, a Boston owned by Mrs. M. and Miss S. Welch, is the top winning bitch in Britain. She has only been at championship shows since a puppy and has won sixteen C.C.s, twelve best of breed and has several group placings. She weighs 12 lbs., yet whelps naturally and her first litter of four all became champions. She has since produced two more champions.

States of the U.S.A. where it is allowed, a Boston Terrier is seldom seen untrimmed, and all show entries are trimmed. The best time for ear trimming is between seven and eight months, after the teething period, but never during a time when the puppy is ill or weak. Having inherited the bat ears from their ancestors, most Boston Terriers hold their ears erect, and many pet owners just leave them that way.

character

The combination of size, disposition and adaptability make it a fine companion and its obedience makes it an excellent house dog. The short thick coat of the Boston is lacking any strong doggie odor, and is very easy to keep clean. This breed cannot endure living outside, although daily outside exercise should be provided for, either in a fenced-in yard or exercise run. A walk on leash is fine, although it is not common for a Boston Terrier to be lazy. These fellows love toys, and are full of play. Soft rubber balls or other rubber toys should be used so as not to injure the teeth, which are not strong because of the short muzzle. Care must, of course, be taken to ensure that they do not chew up and swallow any rubber, which can be fatal.

Puppies – Boston Terrier

standards

The general appearance of the Boston Terrier should be that of a lively, highly intelligent, smooth-coated, short-headed, compactly built, short-tailed, well balanced dog of medium size. The head should indicate a high degree of intelligence, and should be in proportion to the size of the dog; the body rather short and well knit, the limbs strong and neatly turned; tail short; and no feature be so prominent that the dog appears badly proportioned. The dog should convey an impression of determination, strength and activity, with style of high order; carriage easy and graceful. The ideal Boston Terrier expression indicates a high degree of intelligence. Skull – square, flat on top, free from wrinkles; cheeks flat; brow abrupt, stop well defined. Eyes – wide apart, large, round, dark in color, expression alert but kind and intelligent. The eyes should set square in the skull, and the outside corners should be on a line with the cheeks as viewed from the front. Muzzle – short, square, wide and deep, and in proportion to skull; free from wrinkles; shorter in length than in width and depth, not exceeding in length approximately one-third of length of skull; width and depth carried out well to end; the muzzle from stop to end of nose on a line parallel to the top of the skull; nose black and wide, with well-defined line between nostrils. The jaws broad and square, with short,

American Ch. Apposite Montecalvo's Little Whiz II was advertised for sale by Mr. Frank Montecalvo at a time when the British breeders were seriously in need of new blood lines. His record was already known in Britain. He was purchased in New York by Miss Welch and, up to the end of 1970, he sired eighteen champions in the U.K. and Europe – but equally important, he did not sire one splash-marked puppy!

Frontal head view of the Boston Terrier.

regular teeth. Bite even or sufficiently undershot to square muzzle. The chops of good depth but not pendulous, completely covering the teeth when mouth is closed. Ears – carried erect, either cropped to conform to the shape of the head, or (compulsory in Britain) natural bat-shaped, situated as near the corners of the skull as possible. Neck – of fair length, slightly arched and carrying the head gracefully; setting neatly into shoulders.

Body – deep with good width of chest; shoulders sloping; back short; ribs deep and well sprung, carried well back to loins; loins short and muscular; rump curving slightly to set-on of tail; flank very slightly cut-up. The body should appear short but not chunky. (Top line should be level). Elbows – standing neither in nor out. Forelegs – set moderately wide apart and on a line with the point of the shoulders; straight in bone and well muscled; pasterns short and strong. Hindlegs – set true; bent at the stifles, short from hocks to feet; hocks turning neither in nor out; thighs strong and well muscled. Feet – round, small, and compact and turned neither in nor out; toes well arched.

Gait – the gait of the Boston Terrier is that of a sure-footed, straight-gaited dog, forelegs and hindlegs moving straight ahead in line with perfect rhythm, each step indicating grace with power. Tail – set-on low; short, fine and tapering; straight or screw, devoid of fringe or coarse hair, and not carried above horizontal. (Natural short tail, never docked.) Coat – short, smooth, bright and fine in texture.

Weight – not exceeding 25 lbs., divided by classes as follows:—lightweight, under 15 lbs., middleweight, 15 and under 20 lbs., heavyweight, 20 and not exceeding 25 lbs.

Faults would be anything other than the Standard calls for. Disqualifications – in the U.S.A., in addition to color, faults already mentioned include dudley nose and docked tail.

118

Boxer

Owned and bred by Mrs. M. Fairbrother; Ch. Summerdale Walk Tall, a Sirocco grandson.

history and development

Many historians of dog breeds have gone to considerable length to link the Boxer and England's Bulldog, but aside from the fact that both have undershot jaws most so-called similarities are shared by a number of other breeds. Bull-baiting, the original use of the Bulldog, was not exclusive to England. It was known throughout Continental Europe. As a consequence those who bred dogs for this so-called sport were prone to favor the undershot or protruding lower jaw. Indeed even today when the great majority of breed Standards call for a level meeting of the teeth, occasional undershot specimens show up. (The undershot lower jaw, of course, gives a leverage similar to that of the plumber's Stilson wrench; once contact is made it cannot be broken; a pull just makes it tighter.)

Lacking even the slim documentary evidence left by Herr Dobermann and Capt. von Stephanitz in the cases of the Doberman Pinscher and the German Shepherd (Alsatian) we can only analyze the present-day Boxer and judge him part by part. Basically he is a descendant of the Molossus or Mastiff-type, heavy-boned dog that is the progenitor of so many of the world's big, powerful breeds. Many varieties of this dog were known in Rome and when the Romans swept across the Alps many such dogs came with them to move the "beef on the hoof" needed to feed their hungry legions. Thus it would seem that the Boxer is closer in ancestry to the Rottweiler than it is to England's Bulldog. It must be remembered that the Boxer emerged in the decade between 1890 and 1900. True the automobile was being invented in that same period, but travel was still mostly by steam train or horse and buggy.

The first Boxer was registered by the American Kennel Club in 1904 but

Who could resist this pair of thoughtful-looking Gremlin puppies?

Ch. Arriba's Prima Donna, the magnificent Boxer bitch owned by Dr. and Mrs. P. J. Pagano and Dr. T. Fickes. Prima Donna went best in show all breeds at Westminster, New York, in 1970.

it was not until 1915 that the first championship was recorded for the breed. This was the imported German Sieger, Dampf von Dom, a brindle, marked with white on the chest and white feet, brought to the U.S.A. by the late Herbert H. Lehman, who was later to become Governor of New York State. It is of some interest that Mr. Lehman continued as a breeder and exhibitor for more than a decade.

To return to the early German history of the breed, among the names most prominent in the beginning were Friedrich Roberth of Munich, Elard Konig, and R. Hopner. They were breeding dogs and encouraging others to breed. They were mainly responsible for putting on the first class for the breed in Munich in 1895, judged during the St. Bernard Club's show. The first Boxer specialty took place the following year with twenty entries judged by Mr. Konig, and it is said that the Standard was drawn with the top dog, Flock St. Salvator, as a model. Actually type was not completely set at that time. Each breeder was following his own conception of what was wanted in the breed. It was not until the late 1920's that standardization began to emerge. There was even divergence of type in the early 1930's. For instance the first bitch champion finished in the U.S.A., Ch. Dodi v.d. Stoeckersburg was not in the classic mold of the breed. Still, in 1933 when Dodi completed her points she was outstanding in her sex.

The American Boxer fancy got its greatest boost in 1932 when the Cirrol Kennels of Marcia and Joseph Fennessy imported the current German Sieger, Check von Hunnenstein, a dog of striking presence. He was a dog that commanded attention; so much so that he scored a first for the breed by going all the way to best in show at the big Greenwich K.C. all-breed. It was his first big one of many more triumphs to come. More importantly it turned the attention of the show-minded to the possibilities

Mr. and Mrs. Wilson-Wiley's Ch. Wardrobes Miss Mink, one of the greatest winning British Boxers of all time.

in this breed that had been almost overlooked for three decades. Check was by Carsar v. Deutenkofen ex Dina v. Hunnenstein, wh. March 3rd, 1927 br. Alfred Liebold. This well-balanced male continued to win with regularity in the summer and fall of 1932, finishing his championship undefeated. He was entered with high hopes in February of 1933 at the great Westminster show of that year, and justified them by going best of breed under the noted all-rounder, Enno Meyer. It seemed almost certain that Check would do well at the 1934 Garden event, but time was starting to catch up with him and another great all-rounder of the past, Vinton P. Breese gave the nod for best of breed to that outstanding bitch, Ch. Dodi v.d. Stoeckersburg, then owned by the Barmere Kennels of the late Mrs. Miriam Hostetter Young.

Top winning Boxer in Britain 1968, 1969 and 1970, Ch. Wardrobes Clair de Lune, owned by Mr. and Mrs. Wilson-Wiley.

Although then almost eight years old, Cirrol Kennels still had confidence in Check and entered him at the Westminster show under Alva Rosenberg, the man who had started him on the road to fame. But Mrs. Young, then in the process of building her Barmere Kennels into one of the greatest forces in the American branch of the Boxer breed, had imported the male that had practically walked through to two notable Sieger titles in Germany and also in Austria, Ch. Sigurd von Dom, perhaps the greatest Boxer sire the world has ever known, bred by F. M. Stockmann. Sigurd took best of breed with no trouble, then moved into the Non-Sporting Group (Boxers were mistakenly kept in this Group until 1936 when they were shifted to their proper spot, the Working Group) where he met some immortals of other breeds. William L. McCandlish, the then famous English all-rounder, placed Sigurd in third place behind that champion of five countries, the Standard Poodle, Ch. Nunsoe Duc de la Terrace of Blakeen, owned by Mrs. Sherman R. Hoyt, that was later named best in show, and one of America's all-time great Chow Chows, Ch. Far Land

A very well-known American star, Dr. and Mrs. R. C. Harris's Ch. Bang Away of Sirrah Crest.

121

Thundergust, and defeated another immortal, the Boston Terrier, Ch. Grand Slam, which took fourth.

Before he finished his competitive career in the U.S.A. Sigurd had added another best in show triumph to one he had scored in California before coming to the Garden. He continued to sire outstanding sons and daughters in America just as he had in Germany. It was the writer's pleasure to get his hands on Sigurd at the Barmere Kennels. He was good from muzzle to stern, put together smoothly but powerfully; his bone was the greatest; his head was classic. He moved effortlessly. In his arched neck one could see basis for some authorities' claims that the Boxer has some Great Dane ancestry. At the time of my visit to Barmere Sigurd was the leading stud of the kennel but seldom shown anymore at close to seven years. For the record he was by Iwein v. Dom ex Belinoe Hassia, wh. July 14th, 1929.

Perhaps his greatest sons sired in Germany were Ch. Xerxes v. Dom and Ch. Zorn v. Dom. In 1933 Frau Thekla Schneider raised a litter sired by Ch. Xerxes v. Dom ex her Saxonias Andl that included a pup that was later to become Ch. Dorian v. Marienhof of Mazelaine. He was imported by John Phelps Wagner to become the top stud of his Mazelaine Kennels. Dorian was a big winner, but it seemed to me when I visited the Wagner establishment that he had lost some of the powerful look of his grandsire, Sigurd. He was lighter in bone. Dorian was best of breed at Westminster in 1936, and again in 1937 when he made history for the breed at the Garden by topping the Working Group under that all-time great judge, Oliver C. Harriman. He lost out for best in show to a Wire Fox Terrier. In 1938 at Westminster, a monster entry of 103 Boxers was judged by Philip Stockmann, who chose as best of breed, Ch. Lustig v. Dom of Tulgey Wood, owned by the Tulgey Wood Kennels of Erwin Freund. Lustig was just two months past his fifth birthday and in his prime. It is too bad that it was his luck to come before a judge noted as a Cocker Spaniel breeder in the Working Group. Lustig did not even place. When the writer visited the Tulgey Wood Kennels this dog impressed him as a worthy bearer of the Sigurd majesty.

Boxers were well on their way to a dominant place on the show scene. The studs mentioned, plus many other good lines, gave the U.S.A. an even greater reservoir of bloodlines than in the breed's native Germany. Then came the Second World War, which meant curtailment of breeding in Germany. The American Boxer breeders had a great opportunity and made the most of it. In the years from 1947 to 1951, they scored three best in show triumphs at Westminster. The first was Ch. Warlord of Mazelaine, owned by Mr. and Mrs. Richard C. Kettles, but bred by John Phelps Wagner, sired by Ch. Utz v. Dom; in 1949, Ch. Mazelaine Zazaarac Brandy, bred and owned by the Wagners; and 1951, Ch. Bang Away of Sirrah Crest, bred and owned by Dr. and Mrs. R. C. Harris. Bang Away, a dog with great ring presence, was campaigned extensively, first in California by the late Harry Sangster, and then in the East by Nate Levine. He scored some 129 best in show triumphs, more than any other dog of any breed up to that time.

For a time the Boxer seemed destined to be the No. 1 dog in registrations, but it never got to the top. It went as high as fourth place before the bubble burst, mostly due to indiscriminate breeding to meet demands of the pet market. Still it remained for a new breed record to be made at the

Top winning Boxer in Scandinavia, Int. Ch. Queen v. Letzten Hafen, with eighteen C.A.C.I.B's to her credit.

Rainey-Lane Sirocco, an American-bred dog, who was purchased by Mrs. M. Fairbrother (with Mr. M. Summers) for $6,000 at ten months of age. The sire of fifteen champions, he has had the greatest impact on the breed of any dog ever imported to England.

(opposite)
A magnificent head study of the American bitch, Terndon's Kiss Me Kate.

123

Ch. Witherford Hot Chestnut, bred in England by Mrs. Pat Withers and exported to Germany to become one of the top siring stud dogs of late years. He is owned by Mrs. Karin Rezewski.

1970 Westminster Show when Ch. Arriba's Prima Donna, owned by Dr. and Mrs. P. J. Pagano and Dr. Theodore S. Fickes, handled by Mrs. Jane Forsyth, went best in show at Westminster. The judge was Miss Anna K. Nicholas. Prima Donna was the first Boxer bitch to take it all. The source of the breed name "Boxer" has been the cause of speculation. Some have tried to link it to certain contributing breeds, but many claim it is so-called because it has a tendency to use its front paws fighting.

color

Fawn and brindle; the fawn in various shades from light tan to dark deer red or mahogany. The brindle should be clearly defined black stripes on fawn background. White markings on fawn or brindle dogs are not to be rejected and are often very attractive but must be limited to one third of the ground color and are not desirable on the back of the torso proper. On the face, white may replace a part of the otherwise essential black mask. It is desirable to have an even distribution of head markings.

character

Although the Boxer qualified as a "working breed" through service with the armed forces and the police of various nations, he has found his most congenial niche as a companion and home guard. He is alert and playful and loves the companionship of people.

standards

The essential difference between the Standard approved by the American Kennel Club and England's is that Boxers in the U.S.A. are shown with cropped ears. It is a medium-sized breed, the male required to stand 22½" to 25" at the withers (in Britain 22" to 24"); a bitch, 21" to 23½" (21" to 23" in Britain). Males must not go under the minimum nor females over the maximum. It should be sturdily built. Its length should equal its height. Developed to serve the multiple purposes of guard, working and escort dog, it must combine elegance with substance and power; at highest efficiency it must never be plump or heavy. (Some modern breeders seem to have misinterpreted this to produce some specimens that seem very light – much lighter than the greats of the past.)

The head is the unique feature of the breed. It must be in perfect proportion to the body; never small in comparison to the over-all picture. The muzzle should always appear powerful. Normally undershot, the lower jaw protrudes beyond the upper and curves slightly upward. The upper jaw is broad where attached to the skull and maintains this breadth except for a slight tapering to the front. The lips should meet evenly.

The top of the skull is slightly arched, not rotund, flat nor noticeably broad, and the occiput not too pronounced. The forehead forms a distinct stop with the topline of the muzzle, which must not be forced back into the forehead like that of a Bulldog.

The brisket is deep, reaching down to the elbows; the depth of the body at the lowest point of the brisket equals half the height of the dog at the withers. The ribs are well arched but not barrel-shaped. The withers should be clearly defined as the highest point of the back. The hindquarters should be strongly muscled with angulation in balance with that of forequarters; croup slightly sloped.

Coat, short, shiny, lying smooth and tight to the body.

Born in 1965 this brindle/white dog, Ch. Witherford Stingray, has proved to be an influential stud dog.

Bulldog

Mrs. V. M. May's Ch. Walvra Sans Souci, a high quality female. Note the good head points, fine wrinkles and dark, intelligent eye. A massive underjaw for a bitch and beautiful balance throughout. The front and feet are exceptionally good; straight legs with the desired "turn of forearm" showing on the outside of the forelegs.

history and development

The Bulldog is named for the rather grim sport for which it was bred, bull-baiting. The story goes that in the year 1204 Lord Stamford of Lincolnshire, in England, saw dogs belonging to some butchers chasing and tormenting a bull. He found this extremely entertaining and he offered the use of a suitable field in which the canine "gladiators" could fight the bulls, provided the butchers would set up one bull per year. Thus bull-baiting tournaments came into being and the sport became so popular that

125

soon dogs were being bred specially for it. The horns of the bulls were covered with leather sheaths to save the dog from being gored and, should he be tossed into the air, the owners would gather round to catch him before he hit the ground. At a later date, there were several so-called "pits" in different parts of England – where dog fought dog, not a bull, but it was also used in ratting contests – a very famous one was the Westminster Pit; another the Gentleman's Subscription Pit in West Smithfield, and the Tottenham Court Road Pit, all in London, and there were a number in the outlying districts.

The first specialist club for the Bulldog was the Bulldog Club Incorporated, formed in London in 1875 and now the oldest specialist breed club in the world, and the foremost Club in Britain at present. Another breed club was formed in 1891, the London Bulldog Society, then known as the South London Bulldog Society, to be followed closely by the British Bulldog Club, with no fixed headquarters, operating in the North of England; this Club now holds its annual meeting at Cruft's Show, a convenient time when most fanciers can attend.

Bull-baiting was prohibited by law in Britain in 1835, and this necessary measure led for a time to a lessening in popularity for the Bulldog. It is largely due to the faith and pride of a handful of working-man fanciers that the breed survived at this time. Slowly the Bulldog came to be accepted in its own right, as a handsome animal, well suited for showing and, with breeders attempting improvements for this purpose, the size and shape of the dog began to change. Since that time the changes have been many – the skull is larger, the forelegs are bigger boned, he has a more rounded body shape, and is altogether a much heavier dog. In fact there was a danger at one time that he would become too big. But this tendency to be over-sized was controlled, and the size of today's dogs is very good. The Standard originally laid down by the Bulldog Club Incorporated is regarded as ideal but, in my opinion, the top dogs of today are not so good as those of thirty or forty years back, although the majority in the middle range are better.

Mr. A. Westlake's Ch. Tinka of Westframcott, a Standard weight dog (50 lbs.), showing the desired roach back and wide underjaw.

color

The unacceptable colors are black, black and white, and black and tan. Dudley noses are also considered unacceptable (one old breeder used to say that dudleys could be avoided by never mating a red to a fawn, but I do not concur with this theory).

At present fawns are very much in evidence, and the fallow pied is very much favored. A good white, with what is known as a silver coat, is easy to keep clean and always looks good in the show ring. The brindle is still quite popular, but this color, unless relieved with a little white on the head, is difficult to assess and a judge needs a keen eye to spot a good one. A red brindle is most attractive. A fawn looks best if it has a dark muzzle, otherwise it is apt to look a little too mild, instead of having the sour expression a Bulldog should have.

care

A Bulldog is not trimmed, and his shape cannot be improved by this means. His faults thus cannot be covered up, or camouflaged, as can those of some other breeds, and the owner must therefore pay heed to other means of presenting him in the best possible condition. He needs exercise

Three stages of growth and development of the Bulldog are shown on this page. The owner must have faith that a promising puppy will finish well, even though he goes through a plain stage, when his early promise appears to vanish.

Mr. N. Pitts's Ch. Walvra Red Ensign won the championship at Cruft's three years running, twice with best of breed. A great-headed dog, extremely sound and active. Note: the hind feet are closer together than the forefeet, indicating the lighter hindquarters required by the Standard.

The late Mrs. E. E. Smith's Ch. Leodride Beau Son, a great dog of the post-World War II period. Very few Bulldogs show the fire and dominant outlook of Beau Son, and he had one of the best heads ever seen.

(opposite)
Mr. and Mrs. John Barnard's Ch. Noways Chuckles, a magnificent bitch of substance and quality who crowned a great winning career by winning best in show at Cruft's in 1952. It is extremely rare to combine such excellent type and sound construction in the same animal.

on hard ground, as well as on grass; his feet will give no trouble under this treatment. He carries heavy bone and he should be fed with this in mind, but, with an eye to the future, it is also important that the dam in whelp should be well fed before the pups are born, so that they will have good, straight bone to start with. The young Bulldog grows heavy quickly, and pre-natal and early feeding is most necessary if he is to bear the adult weight.

I believe in daily exercise – at first a very short distance, increasing as the dog grows older. In summer weather or in hot climates, this exercise should be given early in the morning, or when the heat of the day is over. It is not necessary to bathe too often; a good, hard brush, followed by a rub with a damp chamois leather, and then with a clean towel, is sufficient. Lastly, a rub up with the palms of the hands is the best polisher I know.

The ears should be inspected daily, and also the eyes and wrinkles.

character

It is difficult to describe the character of a Bulldog; they all have a number of characteristics in common, but each one differs from his fellows in many individual traits. There are many misconceptions concerning the breed; he is not slow or sluggish. I once had an eight year old bitch which was being teased by a neighbor's black cat, rubbing itself around my legs. The Bulldog set it off, and I have seldom seen such a turn of speed. The cat darted off, but only just escaped losing its tail altogether. The dog returned to me with a suspicion of a black moustache, but the cat escaped injury. Another dog, my very first as it happens, used to adore riding in my open car, solemnly sitting upright, wearing a pair of goggles and earflaps, all of which he submitted to, but nobody showed their amusement; a Bulldog will laugh *with* you, but you must not laugh *at* him.

Bulldogs are capable of thinking things out for themselves, and they are very good-tempered with children, but let anyone lift a finger against those they love, and they will wish they had not. If you will talk to your Bulldog puppy for the first six months of his life and teach him all you want him to do, he will never, for the rest of his life, forget the lessons he has learned. Force is not necessary, but you must be persistent in your teaching. This is most important, for the Bulldog can be a very obstinate creature, and will only do what you want if you persuade him, and encourage his inherent desire to please.

128

A head study of Ch. Broomwick Blytholme Bumble Bee.

The late Mrs. E. E. Smith's home bred Ch. Leodride Poppet, a great winning bitch in Britain.

The Bulldog's apparent stolidity, stemming from his somewhat forbidding exterior, covers many sterling qualities – abundant affection, kindliness, especially to children, reluctance to fight, but courageous and steadfast if he has to, unparalleled loyalty, coupled with an unfailing sense of humor.

standards

The British and American Standards are almost identical; the differences are minor.

In general appearance he should be thick-set, rather low in stature, broad, powerful and compact. The head strikingly massive and large in proportion to his size.

The body is short, well knit, with stout and muscular limbs. His hindquarters rather lighter than the heavily made foreparts. He should convey an impression of determination, strength and activity.

The peculiar formation of the Bulldog, his heavy front quarters, his large head and his comparatively lighter hindquarters, give him a rather odd motion. All his weight is "up front" so to speak, and he walks without raising his feet very high, seeming to skim over the ground. When he runs, he keeps his right shoulder forward, only slightly, but very noticeably. But as we have seen, this does not prevent him from being extraordinarily speedy.

The skull is large, the larger the better, with flat forehead, with the skin on it, and on the head, very loose and well wrinkled. The nose is broad, large and black – not liver colored or brown - with large, wide nostrils. The flews are thick, broad and hanging deep, completely over the lower jaw at the sides, but not in front. The jaws are broad, massive and square, the lower jaw projecting considerably and turned up. Eyes are situated low down, as far from the ears as possible; and the ears are set high on the head; small, thin, and folded inwards at the back. "Rose ears" they call them. I have described the head Standard at length because the head is the most distinctive feature of the Bulldog, that and his characteristic front.

The late Dr. E. M. Vardon's home-bred American Ch. Vardona Frosty Snowman, a dog of superb all-round type and quality, one of the greatest winners the breed has known. A noted sire of remarkable quality and balance.

The chest is wide, round and deep, and he looks a little bow-legged as a result, certainly his well muscled legs look shorter than they really are. His back has a slight fall just behind his shoulders, and then it rises again to the top of the loins at a point which should be higher than the shoulders, and curving down suddenly to the tail. This is another characteristic of the Bulldog (it has far more "characteristics" than any other dog), called a "roach" back. His tail, after all this, is fairly short, smooth, straight and tending slightly downwards.

The desirable weights are 55 lbs. for a dog and 50 lbs. for a bitch. The A.K.C. Standard says about 50 lbs. for a mature dog; a mature bitch about 40 lbs.

Bulldog, Mallorcan

The Perro de Presa Mallorquin, stemming originally from Mallorca in the Balearic Islands, is a powerfully built dog of medium height and a fearless nature. It is a guard dog of considerable reputation.

Its head is large in proportion to its body and the skull is massive, broad and square in outline, carried above the body line, having a very marked frontal furrow and a prominent stop. The rose ears are set-on high and are lean. The dark, protruding, oval-shaped eyes are obliquely set. The neck, which is long and very strong, is as broad at the head as it is at the base. The back is of medium length, the loins are short and the brisket is round and deep, broad and long and the belly well tucked up. The tail, which is thick, reaches to the hocks, is carried low, rising in a curve to the level of the spine. Fore and hindquarters are straight, vertical and strong with the elbows turned slightly outwards to make room for the wide chest, but the elbows do not stick out. The feet have thick toes which are well separated and round and the dew-claws remain.

The coat is short, smooth-haired and striped like a tiger, but the less white hair shown, the better. Height is 23″.

Bullmastiff

This lovely fawn champion bitch, owned by Mr. and Mrs. Short, is called Ch. Bullstaff Topsy. Note her correctly masked head, width of chest and the impression of strength and solidity which she conveys so well.

history and development

The English Kennel Club recognized the Bullmastiff as a separate breed as recently as 1924, following some admirable work by Mr. S. F. Mosely and his friends in which they bred mastiffs to bulldogs until they had produced a type sufficiently stable to be accepted by the Kennel Club as a true type, and which they named Bullmastiff. They deliberately worked for an animal which was sixty per cent mastiff and forty per cent bulldog. But the name was not entirely new. It had been used before, by "Stonehenge" (John Henry Walsh, 1810–1888) who referred to "bull-mastiff", and we also find paintings, apparently of Bullmastiffs, by Morland (1763–1801) and others. Why was this? We know that mastiffs are associated with the Romans when they arrived in Britain in the first century and we know that a few centuries after this, a dog known as the "lesser" mastiff was kept, as a working edition of the original animal. Were these "lesser" mastiffs the result of selective breeding of the smaller dogs from mastiff litters, inter-bred to produce smaller, handier guard dogs? And, later still, when this kind of dog was used by royal foresters to guard the king's deer, were they bred especially for the work, because the larger, slower mastiff was far too obvious? These "lesser" mastiffs came to be known as keepers' dogs, or specifically, Keepers' Night Dogs.

Emily Brontë painted a picture of their dog, Keeper, and his companions, and in 1847 her sister, Charlotte Bronte, in her novel *Shirley*, referred to a dog as "Tarter . . . a rather large dog, strong and fierce-looking, of a breed between mastiff and bulldog . . . black muzzled and tawny".

It was thus no novel idea of Mr. Mosely's to cross-breed the two types.

Bullmastiff

The inference is also strong of common origin between an ancient French breed and the Bullmastiff. Go to any large championship show on the Continent and visit the Dogues de Bordeaux, and there you will see a striking likeness to the Bullmastiff.

We know that in the 19th century the keepers attached to the large estates in England were given charge of the so-called night-dogs. They had an evil reputation for savagery, unsafe unless muzzled, and kept by day in pens; and yet Charlotte Brontë described her fictional "Tartar" as "loving his mistress, yet indifferent to the rest of the world unless struck or threatened". We can surmise that breeding at this time was not as discriminating as it later became and it must certainly have been necessary for Mr. Mosely and his friends to stabilize the breed, to start again with the mastiff and to return to the original type by introducing the bulldog, to

George Morland painted this picture in 1801. There are noticeable differences between the dog in the foreground and today's Bullmastiff, but the likeness is strong. (Below) A little later, around 1835–1845, an unknown artist painted this picture of playful dogs of undoubted Bullmastiff origins.

lessen the size and to tighten up the dog to make it more active than the larger mastiff could be expected to be. So there we have it; a working dog, a guard dog, and a one-time fighting dog, and yet withal, now a family dog – a Bullmastiff.

color

When Charlotte Brontë described her mastiff-bulldog type as "black masked and tawny" she could have been writing of a Bullmastiff of today. The mask is an essential, and the color "tawny" is, presumably, meant to be of reddish hue. Today's dogs can vary from a light fawn to a deeper fawn, from a light red to a rich deer-red, and they can be brindled with a background color of any of these shades.

Black plays an important part. The muzzle must be black (or very dark) and this should reach to within an inch or so of the black eye-patches. These eye-patches should also fade away, and not reach over the forehead, but the darker color should be repeated on the ears and in the toe nails. But slight variations from this need not prevent the dog from being shown. Some puppies are born with over-much black which, in some cases, takes several months to clear. One rarely finds an *under*-marked puppy developing his mask and the other required pigmentation later in puppy-hood. The only permitted white is a little on the chest, but preferably there should be none at all. The white chest is forbidden in America and, while a few non-black toe nails are accepted in Britain, they are frowned on in America and Canada.

care

This short-haired, though comparatively massive dog needs little in the way of special grooming; brushing regularly, especially when help is needed to assist the moult, and routine inspection of eyes, ears and under tail. Such a heavy dog would tend to get fat if he lacked exercize, and this must be given daily, but he is not all that active and does not need much exercize free of the leash. He should be walked, particularly on hard ground, for the sake of his toe nails, and to keep his paws from splaying. Remember he has a heavy body to support. Puppies should not be allowed to exhaust themselves; heavy bodies on tender young bones often need rest as they develop. Feeding must be calculated according to his individual needs, and according to his weight. Meat and biscuit meal, once a day, for an adult dog – 1½ lbs. to 2 lbs. of meat, with gravy and vege-tables, with occasionally an admixture of cod-liver oil and proteins to keep a balance to his diet. Puppies get more frequent feeding, little and often, three times a day, raw or lightly cooked minced meat, with puppy meal, and gravy and vegetables as a main meal; and lighter meals, eggs, milk and protein foods which help him to build bone structure and body.

King, a typical sound puppy of seven weeks old.

character

Little is seen nowadays in the Bullmastiff to remind one of his fierce origins. Indeed he looks rather sad, as if ashamed of his past, and will often try to climb on to your lap, big as he is, as if to claim consolation for the sins of his fathers. But they are a playful breed, as you will find out in a painful way if you encourage them to be too boisterous; it takes a strong man to keep upright against the full weight of a playful Bullmastiff, and a child could not possibly withstand his weight.

There is no vice inherent in the Bullmastiff. He is especially good with children, who can do almost anything with him, and as a guard dog he has two valuable attributes, one his great size and menacing mien, and the other his readiness to guard and warn with his deep baying note.

standards

The head, the most important point of a Bullmastiff, must be square; in fact the whole picture should represent a square imposed on another square, since the muzzle also should be square.

This squareness is in some danger of being lost at the present time since far too many exhibits are being approved despite round skulls with the ears coming out at eye level – ears should follow the straight, flat line across the skull, and be folded forward so that the tips are at eye level when the dog shows interest.

The ears should be "flown" but should never be "rose" as in the bulldog. For many years a great many exhibits lacked stop and wrinkle. This wrinkle should really only be present when the dog is interested, but these lines of "interest" do eventually form nice creases. The dewlaps, or lip-line, should not fall beneath the jaw-line, and thus we get a clean line of mouth, helping to create the necessary square. There should be adequate cheek development yet not so much that its roundness breaks the suggested square of the skull. The length of the muzzle should be approximately one-third of the whole head. As for the rest of his make-up, the chest should be wide and deep and the shoulders powerful and sloping into a short, straight back. The hind-legs should be strong but not cumbersome and the forelegs powerful and straight. The feet, large, cat-like, with rounded toes. The tail is set high and carried either straight or curved. The coat should lie flat to the body and should be short and hard, not silky or wooly.

Dogs should be 25″ to 27″, weighing 110 lbs. to 130 lbs., with bitches 24″ to 26″, and 90 lbs. to 110 lbs.

Two brindles belonging to Mrs. Warren's Harbex kennels, who have kept this color going through its days of unpopularity and so ensuring the brindle a place in the breed today. These are Brindled Taurus of Harbex and litter sister Twinklebrin of Harbex.

One of the more recent top winning bitches in England, Mr. H. Colliass's Ch. Oldwell Queen Gwenevive of Mureken.

135

Dalmatian

Queen of the breed, Ch. Fanhill Faune, who won best in show at Cruft's in 1968. Her owner, Mrs. Woodgate, then retired her. Her record stood at twenty C.C.s, all won under different judges, nineteen best of breed awards, eight groups, four best in show awards and four reserve best in show awards. She was top winning bitch of all breeds in 1967. Proving that she was to be as successful as a brood she bred a champion in her first litter.

history and development

Arising from painstaking research and investigation, the most likely theory about the origins of the Dalmatian we know today seems to be that the breed was developed as a mid-European hunting dog. The name would seem to imply that they came from Dalmatia, now part of Yugoslavia; there is little evidence to support this, but we do know that a spotted dog very much resembling the Dalmatian has been widely distributed throughout Europe for the last four hundred years or more. The evidence for this comes largely from the many paintings housed in galleries all over the world; the Dalmatian is one of the most easily recognised dogs and this visual evidence is more credible than it would be for the majority of breeds.

One famous work, painted by Jan Fyt, the Flemish animal painter (1611–1661), for the Emperor Maximilian, called The Hunting Party, shows a rather heavily built but most obvious Dalmatian, among other types of hunting dogs. There are several pictures in Holland, where there are many enthusiastic breeders today, and many handsome dogs. Another picture called A Musical Party, by the Dutch master Pieter de Hooch (*c*.1650), noted for his quiet paintings of domestic scenes, shows a patched Dalmatian romping in the foreground; and in the Mauritshuis at the Hague a charming 17th century picture shows a more elegant Dalmatian appearing from under a table, both paintings giving evidence perhaps that the Dalmatian was not always consigned to the stable yard, even in those days. In Germany the breed is shown in such paintings as The Hawking Party, said to be by a Genoese, Castiglione Francesco, in 1716, and in France and Italy there are many more, one surprising painting now in

Venice is by Federigo Zuccari (1543–1609) better known as portrait painter of Queen Elizabeth and Mary Stuart, and constructor of the Zuccari Palace in Venice.

In England there are many examples of paintings and engravings in galleries and in the collections of lovers of the breed. The National Gallery has one, a painting of the signing of the peace after the Thirty Years War in 1648; it is by Gerard Ter Borch and is called the Signing of the Treaty of Munster. The Kennel Club in London, as you would expect, owns a number of paintings of dogs of all breeds. Among them is one by the 17th century artist Pieter Boel, showing a Dalmatian with heavy black ears. Another painting, by S. Mercier (1689–1760), hangs in the Temple Newsam Gallery in Leeds; it is a portrait of Lady Jenkinson with her Dalmatian, a more lightly built animal but still with the heavy ears, and again obviously a pet.

In most people's minds the Dalmatian is linked with the horse, and it is from records of the 18th and early to mid-19th centuries that we first learn of this affinity. These records show that the Dalmatian was used as a running dog and as a carriage dog. A picture by William Bariaud, The Carriage Horse, shows a very modern type dog except that his ears are cropped. An engraving from a painting by the famous English sporting artist, Alken, shows a horse and a liver-spotted Dalmatian, also cropped, "after performing the distance of sixteen miles in one hour". The horse is very distressed but the dog is quite fresh and has his tail in the air! A painting of about the same period (early 19th century) by H. B. Chalon shows a good-colored liver, stocky Dalmatian; the spots are small, which has been the case until fairly recently with dogs of the liver coloration. This particular dog is wearing a heavy brass collar, probably as a guard dog for his master's menagerie.

color

The basic color is pure white on which appear spots of either black or liver, in no case should combinations of spots of both colors show, it is either black or liver.

These spots should be separate and distinct, round and well-defined, the size of a dime to half dollar (sixpence to florin), and well distributed over the body.

In a puppy the spots are not apparent, he is pure white when born, and it is impossible then to determine whether he will be black or liver.

care

The Dalmatian is a very active dog and needs plenty of exercize. If he can

Thirty years and two continents separate these two dogs. Left is Miss I. B. Clay's liver spotted Ch. Lucky James, born in 1930, showing great presence and correct make up despite being only eleven months old; and right is American Ch. Dottidale Jo Jo, over seven years old, a great winning American dog owned by Miss Amy S. Lipschutz. The type remains similar.

137

This eighteen-weeks-old youngster was to fashion Dalmatian history by producing one of the great dogs of post-war times. Colonsay Lady Anne was the dam of Ch. Colonsay April Jest, bred by Mrs. A. Marshall and owned firstly by the late Miss Macfie and then by the Gatheral family. Not only was he a top winner in the show ring but was stud dog of the year in 1967, 1968 and 1969. Included among his progeny is Ch. Fanhill Faune.

(opposite)
A beautiful head study of the liver spotted Ch. Tantivvey Sowest Mystic, showing a prettily spotted face and bright, keen eye. She is owned by Miss I. B. Clay.

138

be exercized with a companion and they can be allowed to run free, he will exercize himself, otherwise a good, daily, lead walk is necessary. It is unfair to the animal if it is kept where facilities for exercize off the lead do not exist. He loves his comfort and needs a warm, dry bed, free from draughts. He has a disposition to feel that his proper place is on your lap and, if once this is allowed, it is difficult to persuade him otherwise. Normally the Dalmatian is a healthy, strong dog and, if fed correctly, will remain fit and his coat will keep in good, glowing condition. He needs a short, daily grooming and frequently his ears, teeth, anal gland etc. should be inspected. He should be given a bath only occasionally, when it is obvious that he needs one, but most of them are like cats in the way in which they keep themselves clean.

Most Dalmatians are natural "show-offs" and take a great interest in all around them, and are most anxious to please. These traits need to be harnessed if the dog is to be shown in the ring, and he must be taught natural free-standing and moving on a loose lead. Preparation for showing needs only a bath and a good grooming, while at the show a rub down with a silk or velvet cloth or wash leather gives the final polish.

character

In the 19th century, the Dalmatian was often kennelled in the stable yard, with little human companionship. Some relief was given by reason of his running powers, and his handsome appearance – he ran with the horses, and with the carriage. Being comparatively isolated from intimate human society may have made him seem stolid and unresponsive, and this may have led to the view that the Dalmatian was a rather stupid dog. But in *The Book of the Dog*, published in England around 1880, this idea was refuted on behalf of at least one member of the breed, "some few years back" it said, "when the Holborn Amphitheatre was open, there was a wonderfully clever troupe of performing dogs among the attractions there. Among these was a rather good Dalmatian who was entrusted with the role of clown, and it was really surprising to see the intelligence he displayed in burlesquing the tricks of the members of the troupe". The Dalmatian is still a clever clown, and his amiable grin is one of his most attractive characteristics.

His distinctive and striking markings and clean active appearance have marked him out for many unusual uses down the years, but today there is no need for many of these tasks and his place is mainly in the home and on the show bench. He gives endless gratification to all his owners; he is a delight to look at, graceful, fastidious, active and anxious to please. Although he appreciates comfort he will endure a great deal of discomfort to be with his owner under any circumstances. He is particularly good with children; his kind of dignity is not lost whatever games they get up to with him.

The delight in the breed shown by all its owners is conveyed by Miss Dodie Smith in her famous book *A Hundred and One Dalmatians* and in another less well-known, *Starlight Barking*. The author is obviously a Dalmatian owner, and has made a close study of her dogs.

This capacity to become a friend and companion must have been latent in the Dalmatian, even in the days of its banishment to the stable yard, and now that the dog in general is admitted so completely to human companionship, he has truly come into his own as a dog better suited to

Typical Dalmatian puppies.

that role than the vast majority of other breeds; his character to that end is still developing, and bonds of loyalty and devotion between dog and owner are still being strengthened. Breeders not only select for elegant types but try to keep and improve on this heaven sent adaptability and identification with man.

standards

The first official Standard for the breed was drawn up in 1890 by the Dalmatian Club in England, which was founded in that year. In 1950 the Kennel Club in London published an up-to-date Standard which became binding, as with all such Standards, on the breed as a whole and the various clubs existing in its interest. The present American Standard was approved in 1962. Many Dalmatian Clubs all over the world have based their Standards on the version adopted by the English Kennel Club. This Standard was modified a little in 1968, in stressing the need for a "balanced, strong, muscular, active dog", and a paragraph on gait was introduced. The Standard indeed requires an athletic animal.

The ideal height in Britain ranges from 22″ to 24″, differing very little from the measurement of a dog at the Birmingham Show in 1862! The Standard in America gives the low limit as 19″ and the tallest measurement as 23″, saying "any dog or bitch over 24″ is to be disqualified".

He should have a flat skull with moderate stop, entirely free from wrinkles. The nose should be black or liver colored according to the color of the spots.

His other main points are a deep capacious chest, moderately well sprung ribs, powerful back, with loins slightly arched. Straight forelegs from moderately oblique, clean shoulders, and with cat feet. The tail tapers and is carried with a slight upwards curve, never curled; it should for

A pre-war championship best in show winner, Ch. Cabaret Copyright, a liver spotted dog owned by Miss Monkhouse. Although shown for only eighteen months prior to the outbreak of war, he won fifteen C.C.s, was reserve best in show at Blackpool and Manchester championship shows, best dog all breeds at Leeds, non-sporting group winner and fourth best in show at the Kennel Club show and, finally, best in show all breeds at Harrogate, his last show. Little used at stud he yet sired Mr. E. Davies's Ch. Turpins Shadow, one of the top winners immediately after the war.

140

Note the lovely, clear spotting, good depth of brisket and lovely clean lines of Dr. and Mrs. Piper's Ch. Greenmount Grace Darling, who won twelve C.C.s and eleven reserve C.C.s at a time when Ch. Fanhill Faune also was showing.

preference be spotted. The coat should be quite dense, and short and hard, and appear rather sleek and glossy.

It should always be remembered that although spots are the Dalmatian's main characteristic and so are important, the correct structure of the dog must come first.

Mrs. F. C. Gore's Ch. Duxfordham Neptune demonstrates quality, substance and keenness. Born in 1955 he was a popular winner of his day and will go down in history as the sire of Ch. Duxfordham Prince Tarquin, one of Jest's great rivals.

Dobermann
(Doberman Pinscher)

Ch. Acclamation of Tavey, the record-holding sire of the breed in Britain. Note particularly the elegant top and under lines portrayed by this dog at twelve months old. Owned by Mrs. Julia Curnow.

history and development

Following its origin in Germany towards the end of the last century, the Dobermann has spread to most other countries in the world, in particular into the United States, where it has become one of the more popular breeds. Other European countries, notably Holland, Switzerland and Sweden adopted the breed in the 1920's but it was not until 1947 that some imports were made into Britain. Since then, Britain has become the second largest producer of Dobermanns, registering about 1,500 puppies each year. Type varies from country to country, the Europeans in the main producing what might be termed the working class of dog, while in the United States and in most of Britain a more elegant and refined animal is bred and preferred. The original Dobermanns were bred mainly as guard dogs and they performed their task with the utmost fidelity, but in other countries, primarily in America and Great Britain, while the guarding instinct is still appreciated, concentration has been on breeding towards a dog of better conformation and one that is more tractable to handle. During the 1880's Herr Louis Dobermann, of Apolda, in Thuringia, Germany, decided to evolve a dog after his own ideas. He wanted a medium-sized dog of sharp character, full of alertness and watchfulness, able to guard him while acting as tax-collector. In those days, taxes were collected by calling from house to house, so it was a simple matter for Herr Dobermann also to undertake the job of dog-catcher. This enabled him to collect the various breeds he needed, and it is assumed that "Dobermann's dogs" were the outcome of the Rottweiler which gave stamina and tracking skill, the old German Pinscher which gave sharp alertness, and the Manchester Terrier which gave the coloring and perhaps a little towards outline.

Pointer and Greyhound blood may also have been used in the evolution of this dog to give us the elegant animal we now know, which differs greatly from the smaller, cloddier animal first recognized as a Dobermann. The fact that this dog has come so far so quickly is a great tribute to his, even then, inherent qualities, his great watchfulness and alertness, his loyalty to and fidelity to his family, his aloofness to outsiders, his braininess and his regard for property.

It was in 1899 that Otto Goeller organized the National Dobermann Pinscher Club in Germany and one year later the breed was given official recognition and a Standard drawn up. In 1908, Dobermanns were imported into America where the breed has since notably been improved. At the same time, the Dutch, Scandinavians and Swiss took the Dobermann to their hearts and today are producing some excellent specimens.

It was not until 1948 that serious importations into Britain began. During that year, twenty-four keen admirers, among whom are some of the most respected judges, formed the Dobermann Pinscher Club, which almost immediately received the recognition of the Kennel Club. In most cases, the imported bitches were mated before leaving their native countries but, unfortunately, almost all litters were lost in quarantine.

Fortunately, two enthusiasts were very discerning in their choice of animals and wisely selected descendants of such internationally famous dogs as Troll v. d. Engelsburg, Graf Dagobert van Neerlands Stamm, Artus v. Furstenlager, Jessey v. d. Sonnenhohe, Waldo v. d. Wachtparade, Rancho Dobes Storm and Rustic Adagio, all champions which have left their stamp on their progeny.

Many people have reported that their first introduction to the breed was made while they were engaged on active service in the Middle East in the Second World War, and it was in this particular theater of war that Dobermanns were extensively used for tracking and police work.

An informal shot of Mrs. Joan Barrett's Ch. Weichardt's A-Go-Go, C.D. while in competition in the Working Group at Westminster in 1970. By mid-1970 she had fifty-six best of breed awards, sixteen group firsts and for the half year was among the top working dogs in America. In addition she finished her Companion Dog degree with scores averaging over 190 out of a possible 200 points.

color

Although the majority of Dobermanns are black with tan markings the recognized Standard all over the world allows for brown-and-tan and blue-and-tan. Recently, in the United States, after several years of discussion between the American Kennel Club and the Dobermann Pinscher Club of America, another color, which is known as Isabella, has been recognized and accepted. Isabella is almost the color of parchment, and is derived from the story that when Queen Isabella of Spain was besieged in her castle a few centuries ago, she swore not to change her linen until her capital was relieved. As this war went on for a couple of years, one can easily imagine the shade of Queen Isabella's linen, which gave her name to animals and articles of light fawn or parchment color.

Ch. Elegant of Tavey, owned by Mrs. Curnow. The first Dobermann champion in Britain, Elegant won the first eight bitch Challenge Certificates on offer in the breed in 1952.

care

Being a short-coated dog, the Dobermann needs little care in that respect,

143

apart from a daily grooming with a piece of Turkish towelling or wash leather to remove any loose hairs, especially when moulting.

Bodily, however, great care is essential to keep the dog in good, muscular condition. It is not essential to exercise a Dobermann for more than one hour or so each day and experience has shown that, if a dog is walked on hard roads or on a sidewalk for twenty or thirty minutes morning and evening, plus being allowed a five or ten minute gallop in a park or over fields, he will remain in excellent condition for the whole of his life.

This breed loves warmth and sunshine and, if living in the house, will lie up close to the fire or radiator during the winter and will select a sunny spot for his rest period during the summer. However, should the dog live or sleep outdoors, it is essential that warm, draught-proof quarters are provided.

character

Perhaps the most dominant characteristic in a Dobermann is alertness. His eyes, his mind, his action and appearance are all full of this quality, and there is no better sight than a top-grade Dobermann waiting to welcome you home.

When Dobermanns were first introduced into Britain, the "know-alls" described the dog as vicious and unsafe, and while this may be partly true of a small percentage of the breed in Continental European countries, it

Contrast these two lovely head studies. On the right is Ch. Iceberg of Tavey, Britain's top winning Dobermann, owned by Mrs. Curnow and on the left Ch. Weichardt's A-Go-Go. Cropping is not allowed in Britain, the ears are left to lie naturally against the head, in contrast with the smart finish provided by the cropped ears of A-Go-Go.

is obvious that any instability has been bred out of the modern British Dobermann. Fortunately, this has been accomplished without decreasing his strength, brain power, alertness and courage.

Dobermann owners already know of the fanatical loyalty which is inherent in the breed, which asset is apparent from the moment the puppy enters your home. He loves to ride in your car, to sleep on your hearth, run in your garden and he is playmate and guardian of your children. At least, that is what you think about it! Actually, it is you who rides in *his* car, he allows you to enjoy *his* home, he romps in *his* own garden and he plays with and protects *his* youngsters. It is this sense of ownership which endears the Dobermann to his family, making him into the best guard in the world, and quite candidly most humans are sufficiently egoistic to like the idea of being owned by a Dobermann.

A Dobermann is not a bully, neither does he have a mean character, but should he be attacked by another dog, or some foolhardy human, then his fighting spirit is immediately aroused, usually with sad results for his opponent. He stands aloof from those outside his circle and will accept them into the home only if accompanied by one of the family, but even then will invariably keep one eye on the visitor just to make sure that nothing untoward occurs. Tremendous power is built into a Dobermann which, together with his intelligence and skill at tracking, makes him the ideal guard and police dog.

Every line of this top winning American champion's body portrays to perfection the alertness required in a Dobermann.

A boxful of promising youngsters. Notice the strong jaws and heavily boned legs.

Ch. Tavey's Stormy Achievement, owned by Mrs. Curnow, was the first Dobermann to win best in show at a championship show in Britain, at Hove in 1960.

standards

The Dobermann is a dog of medium size with well-set body, muscular and elegant. It has a proud carriage and a bold, alert temperament. Pride and alertness are absolutely essential, but these qualities are not to be confused with viciousness, which is a fault.

The head resembles a blunt wedge, when viewed from the side and above, with a slight stop. Eyes should be almond shaped, not round, moderately deep-set, with a vigorous, energetic expression. Ears must be set high, as small as possible – erect or dropped, the former preferred; in Britain ears are not cropped but cropping is allowed in America, Germany and some other countries. Because much of the Dobermann's character is seen in its head, long, pendulous, heavy and low-set ears are not desirable, whereas small, high-set, well-used ears add much to an alert expression. The British Standard allows for a naturally erect ear and, although it is the wish of every breeder to produce puppies with this asset, it is doubtful whether it will ever be attained.

Teeth should be well-developed with a scissor bite. A graceful, long and slightly arched neck flowing into the top-line of the body in one rhythmic sweep is not only pleasing to the eye but proves correct shoulder placement.

The body should be square, height measured vertically from the ground to the highest point of the withers, equalling the length measured horizontally from the fore-chest to the rear projection of the upper thigh. The ideal height at the withers is 27″ in males and 25½″ in females. The loins should be fairly well tucked up, slightly higher than quarters, to give a sloping top-line. Ribs should be deep and well sprung, reaching to the elbow. The shoulder blade and upper arm should meet at an angle of ninety degrees.

The legs, seen from the front and the side, are perfectly straight and parallel to each other from elbow to pastern, muscled and sinewy, with round bone proportionate to body structure. In the hindquarters, the accent is again on muscular formation, hard yet supple muscles easily visible to the eye, well developed but not cloddy, will enable the Dobermann to work all day. When the dog is standing naturally, the hocks should be perpendicular to the ground, and here particular notice should be taken whether the hocks are too long. If they are, the dog will look unbalanced, mainly because the long hocks so often go with short and straight stifles.

Much emphasis should be placed on correct movement, because invariably an incorrect gait means that the dog is faulty in at least one part of his body formation. Ribs which are barrelled right to the bottom of the brisket will cause the dog to plait, as will also badly angulated shoulder blades and upper arm. Weak elbows or pasterns give a peculiar paddling action, while splay feet compel the dog to flop along in a most ungainly fashion. Cow hocks will cause weaving in the hind legs, as will also those hindquarters which are bandy. The front legs should reach well forward when the dog is in motion, but with no semblance of a high-stepping action and the hind legs, which are, after all, the driving power, should move with a cycling movement. The whole action of a Dobermann when seen from front, rear or side must give the impression of rhythmic power.

A full view of Ch. Iceberg of Tavey, showing his gleaming coat and alert expression.

Dogue de Bordeaux

Having a great likeness to the Bull-mastiff, this Dogue de Bordeaux is resident in Germany.

The Dogue de Bordeaux, the national watch-dog of France, is one of the oldest known dogs. Introduced into the Bassin Aquitain by the Romans, it is descended from the Tibetan Mastiff. Raised and bred in different conditions it became the Dogue de Bordeaux in France, the Dogue de Burgos in Spain, and the Matin di Napoli in Italy. In later years the breed was established in Germany as the Danish dog, or German dog, while in England and America it became the Mastiff, with which it has much in common. In France the Dogue de Bordeaux has been used against the bear and the wolf. Later it became a fighting dog and, until the turn of the century, there were dog fights in Bordeaux which drew crowds just as bull fights do today. Nowadays this dog leads a far quieter life, as a vigilant watch-dog, faithful to masters who, realizing its great strength, make sparing use of it.

In France it should weigh between 55 to 65 kgs, 120 lbs. to 145 lbs., and measure $27\frac{1}{2}''$ to $30''$ at the withers, according to sex. Its massive head should have a circumference which equals its height.

Its colors should be apricot, silver, fawn or dark fawn-brindle, with muzzle, ears and nose black.

It is calm in temperament, affectionate, and easy with children, and is an admirable watch-dog.

Fila Brasileire

A large, brindle Mastiff-type dog, originating in the Iberian Peninsula.

Introduced from Spain and Portugal into Central America at the time of the Conquistadores, the Mastiff-type dogs, originally used for guarding, herding and tracking, have developed little since that time. The Fila Brasiliere retains its Mastiff appearance, and it is still used in Brazil as guard, drover and tracker, and also as a sporting dog. It is registered at the F.C.I. as a Brazilian breed.

It is a large dog, around $26''$ high, with powerful back and strong loins. The chest is broad and deep, shoulders sloping, forelegs with strong bone; hindquarters a little higher than the forequarters, hind-legs less heavily boned, with well-bent stifles and hocks.

The tail is thick at the set-on and tapers to a point.

The head is large and massive, with broad skull and well-defined occiput. The muzzle square and broad. The eyes dark, almond-shaped and deep set. Ears large, drop, V-shaped and placed well back on the skull.

This is a smooth-coated dog, dense, short and soft; the throat hair a little longer than elsewhere. The colors are any self-color or brindle; white is permitted on the feet and tip of tail.

French Bulldog

Bomlitz Koko, a junior warrant and reserve C.C. winner, was in the author's opinion the best French Bulldog she has bred and owned. He was tragically denied a show career through an ear injury at two years old. His son, Tucki V. Schubinsdorf, made a major impact on German breeding in recent years.

history and development

A careful study of the best available authorities leaves little room for doubt that the origins of the French Bulldog are to be found in England. In the middle of the 19th century numbers of lace-workers went from Nottingham to France, where new factories were springing up. Nottingham was a great center for the breeding of Bulldogs at that time, so many of the emigrants took their Bulldogs with them when they crossed the Channel. These included a small stamp of dog weighing between 16 and 25 lbs.

The French were quickly attracted by these little dogs, especially those whose ears were erect – a common fault with Bulldogs at that time. Realising that there was a market for this type, two London dealers visited Nottingham and bought stock for export. It is perhaps hardly surprising that the size of the small Bulldogs and their clown-like appearance enormously attracted the demi-monde in Paris, so that they soon became the rage of the capital. Every cocotte wanted to own one and the name French Bulldog was given to them at this time.

For the next forty years, small backyard breeders in France strove to perfect the erect ear carriage which is such a characteristic of the breed. That the quaintness of the French Bulldog also caught the imagination of French artists and writers of the period is reflected in the sketches of Toulouse Lautrec and Degas, while an early photograph of Collette shows her with one. Perhaps this was the Toby-dog immortalized in her *Dialogues des Bêtes* written in 1904? Influences of this sort brought the breed from the stews and backstreets to the comfortable homes of the rich and fashionable.

Ch. Bomlitz Schnucki, daughter of the imported Bomlitz Mix V. Schubinsdorf, was the only particolored bitch champion since the early twenties.

An internationally famous stud dog, Ch. Bomlitz Edward Bear displays a particularly fine head in this frontal view.

In the 1890's some Americans, attracted by the breed during visits to Paris, began to buy them in and founded the French Bulldog Club of America. At the same time, a man named Hartenstein began to breed French Bulldogs in Germany, while others are known to have found their way to Belgium and Russia. The American influence was the most important of all in the early development of the breed. Haphazard breeding by the French had produced wide variations in type. By selective buying and breeding, the Americans developed the massive-headed, square-jawed, compact dog that we now know and which contrasts with the dome-headed, rather weak-jawed type originally favored by the French.

The breed had an unhappy start in England. In 1898 certain Bulldog owners imported some indifferent French Bulldogs in an effort to resuscitate the old Toy Bulldog. French Bulldogs were not then recognized as a breed and these Toy Bulldog fanciers made every effort to thwart the efforts of a small but determined group of breeders who were trying to get the Frenchman established.

Despite opposition, the French Bulldog Club of England was formed in 1902 and was soon on solid ground. In 1905 the Kennel Club gave official recognition to the breed. Initially, they insisted on the title "Bouldogue Francais" and classified it as a sub-variety of Foreign Dogs.

Meanwhile, the Americans made great strides in the perfection of their type. From 1913 onwards, various excellent American dogs were introduced into England, with great benefit to the British stock. Today, French Bulldogs may be found in most countries of the world, but are only found in small numbers outside Europe. They flourish particularly in England and Sweden, while some good specimens are to be seen in Germany. Sadly, for a variety of reasons, far fewer are to be found in America than in the past, although efforts are being made to build up the numbers once more.

color

Brindle, fawn, white and pied (or a mixture of brindle and white in which white predominates) are all correct, although fawn is not recognized in Europe, except in England. Black, without brindle, is to be avoided.

care

French Bulldogs are generally active and enjoy a good walk daily, but are less dependent upon exercize than some larger breeds. They need warm, comfortable quarters. However, being adaptable, they will fit into most surroundings in town or country. Human companionship plays a big part in their development. A daily brush, eyes kept clean and care to keep the folds of the face free from soreness (a little Vaseline will do this), is all they need. Routine checks of ears, nails and teeth are as for any other dogs.

character

The deeply affectionate, gentle, clown-like qualities of the French Bulldog, combined with great sturdiness and agility, quickly win him a place in his owner's heart. He has considerable strength of character but this can be affected seriously by ill treatment.

standards

The Standard for the breed is now almost universal. Inevitably there are minor differences of preference or emphasis in different countries, particularly in relation to size and color. The French Bulldog is essentially a sturdy, compact little dog, ideally weighing between 24 and 28 lbs., but in the U.S.A. the minimum is 22 lbs. Soundness must not be sacrificed for smallness. He has a broad, flat skull and a square powerful turned-up muzzle. The bat-ears must be carried upright and the coat must be smooth and soft. Shoulders are laid-in to a deep, well-developed rib-cage and support straight legs on compact feet. His chest is broad and square. The short back is roached and the body pear-shaped, tapering to fine but well muscled loins, with a good cut-up. He has a small tail, set below the backline. Above all, a French Bulldog must be well-balanced and move easily. Exaggerations which destroy balance are to be deplored.

Ch. Chasewood Crème Brulée is still the only fawn bitch champion in the breed in England.

A charming study of an eight-weeks-old litter of French Bulldogs.

151

Great Dane

Great size and commanding appearance are two most important points in the Dane. Mrs. E. A. Danby's Bencaross Beau Brummel illustrates them to perfection, his beautiful head and neck are a pattern for the breed. Note also the high withers, firm backline and well turned stifles. He is a best in show winner at championship shows.

history and development

It is impossible to pin-point the origin of the Great Dane. One can only say that, from a study of wood-carvings, paintings, parchments etc., it is a breed that has been known from earliest times. A Grecian coin dating from the 5th century B.C. in the Royal Museum of Munich, shows a dog resembling a Great Dane, proving that this type of dog existed in those early days. On the oldest Egyptian monuments, dating back to *circa* 3000 B.C., dogs of the Great Dane type are carved. They appeared on a tapestry worked in 1609. They are described in the writings of Ware (1554); Holinshed (1560); Camden (1568); Evelyn (1670) and Ray (1697). Alexander Goldsmith, in 1770, mentioned the Great Dane by name.

From all this we conclude that the Great Dane has been a native of the British Isles for many centuries. Ancestors of the present-day Great Dane were imported by the Romans, from the British Isles, and used as fighting dogs in the circus, along with the Molossian dog, which took its name from an ancient Greek city, and Tibetan Mastiffs. All these probably played a part in the development of the Great Dane.

The Great Dane's earliest uses were as war dogs, by Attila the Hun; and the Roman legions; as fighting dogs in the arenas of Rome; and as hunting dogs in the pursuit of wild boar which, in the Middle Ages, were plentiful in the huge forests of Europe. A dog of great courage, size and agility was required to hunt this ferocious quarry. The Great Dane was carefully bred in the courts of Royalty throughout Europe, to partake in this sport. Old records tell us of the numbers of boar, and the prowess of the Great Dane, when we read that the pack owned by Earl Phillip of Hessen accounted for 2,572 boars in 1563. Great Danes were also very numerous in those times; we read that the Duke of Braunschweig arrived at a hunt in 1592 with a pack of 600 male Great Danes!

It is thought that ear-cropping began at this time, to prevent the boar from slashing the dog's ears. There are many graphic paintings and engravings which show boar hunts. One, by Benno Adam, entitled "At Bay" shows a pack of dogs very like Great Danes. Even today a Dane will playfully take your whole hand into its mouth and gently hold on. It is thought that this trait stems from pulling the boar to the ground by its ear.

Few breeds have been accorded such a variety of names as the Great Dane. Ulmer Doggen, Danish Dog, Hatzruden, Grosse Doggen, Grand Danois, Boarhund, English Dogge, and more recently Deutsche Dogge and Great Dane. While the most poetic title of all is the unofficial one, Apollo of Dogdom.

The Great Dane first appeared at a show in Hamburg in 1863. Although there were fifteen of them present they were announced as two different breeds, Ulmer Doggen and Danish Doggen. In 1876 show judges decided to bring them all under the same heading. They became known as Deutsche Dogge. German dog-lovers then chose this as the national dog of Germany. However, the name Deutsche Dogge did not become official until 1880, when German breeders, under the leadership of Dr. Bodisius, banned all other names for the breed. In 1888 the first German specialist club for the breed was formed, The Deutsche Doggen Klub.

Six years earlier, in England, the Great Dane Club had been formed. This club is still functioning today. In 1884 the Great Dane was accorded a place in the Kennel Club Stud Book, and breed classes were scheduled for them at Birmingham show.

Blendon, owned by Miss H. M. Osborn, is one of the oldest established kennels in the breed, with a particularly strong male line. Ch. Sherelake Stormcrest of Blendon is the fourth consecutive generation of champions; his sire, grandsire and great-grandsire in the male line were all champions bearing the Blendon prefix and owned by Miss Osborn.

Good blacks are rare in Britain. Mrs. G. LE' Coyne's Ch. Kaptain of Kilcroney was the first black champion dog for many years. Note the head with the dropped ears, compared with the black American dog whose ears are cropped.

153

Mrs. J. Kelly's Ch. Surice of Leesthorphill, a top winner and brood bitch, is a splendid example of the black and white harlequin Great Dane, possessing size and substance along with great elegance. Especially notable are her well knuckled feet and the white neck, a point that is much sought after in America and on the Continent.

Blues of sufficiently high standard to become champions are very rare. Mr. and Mrs. B. Craig's Ch. Sarzec Blue Baron is one of the best of his color to be seen in Britain for many years.

color

There are five recognised colors of Great Dane – brindle, fawn, blue, black and harlequin.

Brindles must be striped. The ground color may vary from the lightest yellow to the deepest orange. The stripes must always be black. A brindle that is marked with numerous well-defined stripes on both sides of the

154

body makes a far better picture than one with a few oddly placed stripes. Fawns may vary from the lightest yellow to the deepest orange. In England, a shading of black around the muzzle, the ears, and eyes, is usually preferred by most breeders, but is not essential. However, in America it is considered a fault for a fawn to be without a black mask.

Blacks are blacks.

Blues may vary from light gray to deep slate. The American Standard calls for nothing less than pure steel-blue.

On all four colors white is admissible, but not desirable, on the chest and toes. Eyes and nails should be dark. The nose is always black, except that blues may have a black or a blue nose.

Harlequins should have a predominating pure-white background, with clearly defined and irregularly torn patches of either black or blue, preferably all black or all blue on an individual dog, distributed to give a harmonious and pleasing appearance. America prefers a pure-white neck. Wall-eyes, pink noses or butterfly noses are not faults in this color.

It is not unusual to see at a show which is being held outdoors when the sun is hot, black and blue Great Danes covered with towels. This is to prevent the sun from causing a rusty tinge to appear on the dog's coat. Of course, this tinge will also appear when the dog is changing coats and a judge should make allowance for this condition.

Great Danes, with ears uncropped.

care

Being smooth and short-coated, a Great Dane does not require the hard work that must be put into the care of some breeds. It is not a hard task to keep a Great Dane in top condition. All that is needed is a good hound-glove or a brush. A body-brush, as used for horses, is ideal. The whole coat should be brushed daily with this. The ears should be kept clean with a cotton-wool swab dipped in alcohol. The nails should be

Puppies – Great Dane

kept short, which will keep the feet tight. Each day check teeth, gums, ears and feet. At times a Dane will develop a bloody tip to its tail, caused by excessive wagging, or knocking against furniture etc. If treated promptly it is no serious problem, and a good thing to use in the treatment is a ladies' plastic hair-roller. About four inches long is ideal; slipped over the end of the tail and held in place with sticking-plaster this will prevent the dog from splitting the tip while healing is taking place.

As a puppy, do not over-exercise your Dane, allow bone and muscle to form before subjecting him to strenuous effort. A puppy should be allowed to dictate his own exercise routine, being allowed to go until tired. An adult Great Dane will be happy to go as long as you want him to, and go where ever you wish to take him. Steady exercise on a hard surface will ensure the cat-like feet that a Dane should have. Lack of exercise, or constantly being on a soft surface, such as grass, will cause the feet to spread. Many people consider steady trotting beside a bicycle as the ideal form of keeping a Dane in show condition. If given daily attention, there is little extra to do on show days, just trim off the whiskers and rub a little oil on the nails.

character

Great Danes have the character that will fit most types of home. They can be happy, if well-exercised, to live in a flat or a mansion. They are dogs of courage and devotion, and are not given to fighting. They will get along with most other animals and are happy to have a small dog, or even a cat, as a companion, and there are no better friends than a child and a Dane that have grown up together. They tend to be one-family dogs as opposed to one-man dogs. They are easy to train and eager to please, once taught they do not forget. It is usually enough to reprimand them once for any wrong-doing, and then merely by saying "No". If you want

This fawn bitch, owned by the Yarrabrook kennels, is a well-known Australian champion called Brindayne Estelle. She won challenges in Melbourne and Sydney, finishing her championship career in 1966 at Melbourne Royal.

to sit and read, a Dane will be happy to lie at your feet. If you want to play games, a Dane will join in. A word of advice, never play rough games with a Dane puppy. Remember that one day he will be far too big for such games, and will not understand when you want to break off. A Great Dane conducts himself with the dignity that comes with his noble bearing. He is slow to anger, but will not be found wanting.

standards

A great Dane should have symmetry that pleases the eye, along with the powerful muscular build that will carry him through a long day in the hunting field. Size and substance are a must. Height should not be sought at the expense of substance. An adult dog should stand over 30″ at the shoulder and weigh over 120 lbs. An adult bitch should stand over 28″ and weigh over 100 lbs. A Great Dane should move freely with a lithe, springy action, head held high, tail curved sabre-like behind, in line with the back. A good head on a long well-arched neck, free from any loose skin, nicely moulded into the shoulders. Correct angulation of the shoulder and stifle. A broad, deep, chest with well-sprung ribs, neither narrow nor round. There must be an elegance and grace in the outline, briskness in movement, alertness of expression, and "a look of dash and daring".

There are many who feel that the abolition of ear-cropping in England took something away from the "look of dash and daring". Ear-cropping was outlawed in Great Britain in 1895. It is still practised almost universally in America and in Germany. A portion of the ear-flap is cut away, causing the ear, after training by taping, to stand erect. There are short crops and long crops, and there is no doubt that a long, elegant crop adds to alertness of expression. Most of today's cropping is done by attaching a clamp to the ear and cutting around it, removing the unwanted portion. But some cropping is done free-hand. Breeders have their own preference of style and operation. Cropped-ears or dropped ears, a Great Dane still is a GREAT dog, and to see a good specimen is to want to own him.

Contrast these two Great Danes, both winners in America. The black dog on the left at only ten months old shows exceptional quality, beautiful balance and substance, combined with elegance. This is Leland O. Kew's Auburn Hill Illya. On the right is a beautifully marked brindle, but showing some weaknesses of conformation, particularly in hind-quarters and top-line.

Hovawart

The Hovawart, like the Leonberger, arose from the work done by breeders in the Württemburg area during the latter part of the 19th century to produce a handsome, intelligent utility dog. Closely related to the Leonberger, by the middle of this century it had become more popular than the Leonberger at shows.

The name comes from Hofewart – estate dog or watch dog – protected by law in the Middle Ages. Its function today, apart from that of companion, is to guard, and the name Hovawart has appropriately been given to this breed of comparatively recent creation.

It is large to medium sized (25″ to 27″ high; 65 to 90 lbs. in weight, bitches somewhat less), long coated, in deep golden, black and gold or entirely black apart from a suggestion of white at tail tip.

A large, wise-looking dog, the Hovawart.

Leonberger

This breed is basically a cross between the St. Bernard and the Newfoundland. In 1855, Herr Essig of Leonberg, crossed a St. Bernard (not at that time completely stabilized) with Landseer, Newfoundlands and Pyrenean Sheepdogs. Later, other blood was added to the breed including Sennen hund, Pyrenean Mountain Dog (Great Pyrenees), Wallis Sheepdog, Kuvasz and possibly Austrian Jagdgriffon. The popularity of the Leonberger increased and by 1872 other breeders were competing with similar crosses to obtain large, handsome utility dogs, often of a golden color.

By the end of the 19th century the breed had become stable and officially recognized by the canine societies of France, Germany and Holland. In Western Germany, the Netherlands and Belgium it is used as a draught dog, and also for protecting livestock, an activity for which it has shown considerable aptitude.

The moderately sized head is neither so wide nor as high as that of the St. Bernard and the skull is flat across the top. The stop is halfway between the occiput and the nose and there is a slight median furrow. The eyes are dark in color and the ears, high set and fairly wide apart, hang close to the cheeks. The muzzle is powerful with strong even teeth. The fairly long body has a deep chest, firm, level back and muscular loins and the legs are heavily boned and straight. The fairly long coat lies flat to the body and colors vary; gray and fawn predominating, with saddle markings in tan or black.

Height is usually about 27″ to 28″, but some are 30″. It is currently unknown in the U.S.A.

A beautifully coated specimen of the Leonberger.

Mastiff

Mrs. L. Scheerboom's Ch. Hotspot of Havengore, born in Britain in 1958, winner of ten C.C.s, two reserve C.C.s and ten best of breeds, up to date. Note the massive head and tremendously powerful chest and forequarters.

history and development

The origin of the Mastiff has been the subject of much supposition, many erroneously believing that the dog was found in the British Isles at the time of the first Roman invasion in 55 B.C. It is possible that such dogs could have been in Britain at this time, but what the Romans certainly found were broad-mouthed, courageous dogs which they called "canis pugnaces". Whether these dogs evolved from a type indigenous to Britain or whether, as some suggest, they were introduced by Phoenician traders from Babylon-type dogs cannot be proven. My own theory is that from the canis pugnaces there evolved two types of the same family, the rudimentary bulldog, and the equally rudimentary mastiff, and that it is only of comparatively recent times that the two breeds have been so dissimilar.

Mastiff types appear on the Bayeux tapestry, and Caius (*c.* 1550) wrote that "the mastyne or bandogge is vast, huge, stubborne, ougly, of a heuy and burthenous body". In 1575 in *The Four books of Husbandry*, the mastiff is described as "the mastie which keepeth the house".

In Shapespeare's *Henry V* a Frenchman says "That Island of England breeds very valiant creatures. Their mastiffs are of unmatchable courage". Shakespeare obviously knew the story of how the wounded Sir Peers Leigh was guarded at Agincourt by his mastiff bitch. Sir Peers died of his battle wounds but his body returned to Lyme Hall, Cheshire accompanied by the mastiff, who was in whelp. It was alleged that this bitch founded the Lyme Hall strain of mastiffs, which were kept at the old residence, from Agincourt to the outbreak of the 1914 war.

Van Dyck's painting of the children of Charles I shows a very different mastiff from today's specimens. Here is a decidedly boarhound type with

This is a portrait, done in loving admiration, of Eng. and Am. Ch. Falcon of Blackroc. Falcon is the epitome of the Mastiff type, massive and strong, yet eager and well-balanced.

Mastiff; the front head of a British specimen.

a white stripe running up the foreface. This stripe is seen on many mastiff pictures up to early 19th century. Howitt shows many mastiffs of distinctly bulldog type, and often pied or particolored.

Factual mastiff history can be traced from early 19th century when Bill George kept his "Canine Castle", an exclusive London dog-dealing establishment. He supplied a number of mastiffs which became the foundation of successful kennels, but these mastiffs were often of foreign extraction, a fact which he in no way disguised. Lukey, and later Thompson, were successful breeders and helped in establishing type, but one of the greatest sculptors was Rev. W. B. Wynn author of the classic *The History of the Mastiff* (1886), who laid down that the true mastiff should be a short-headed, truncated-muzzled dog. It was probably the desire for the short head which caused the indiscriminate use at stud of Ch. Crown Prince (*c.* 1880), a dudley-muzzled, yellow-eyed dog with particularly poor hindquarters. The latter defect, according to E. G. Oliver, he passed on as "damnosa hereditas" to all mastiffs. Towards the end of the 19th century, and the beginning of the 20th, interest in the breed was at a low ebb, and it was extremely difficult to find a mastiff that was not descended from Ch. Crown Prince.

A census taken after the Second World War suggested that there were only eight mastiffs in Britain of an age suitable for breeding. There had been little breeding during the war, and mortality had been high. Only one puppy born during the war could be traced. Some specimens were imported, but stock was difficult to obtain; the position of the breed in America was almost as serious as in Britain. Mrs. Mellish in Canada kindly supplied a pair of puppies to the Old English Mastiff Club, and the Kennel Club took the unprecedented step of allowing the Club, as breeders, to register the puppies with the prefix O.E.M.C. Gradually the tide turned, numbers increased, and at present there is a great deal of interest in this fine breed.

color

Brindle, apricot, fawn, silver fawn. The muzzle, ears and nose to be black, with black round the orbits, and extending upwards between them. Brindle is the dominant color.

care

Mastiff puppies and their dam.

There is a need for quality food, in quantity while the puppy is growing. Good exercizing spaces, dry quarters and a real need for regular, steady walking exercise to build the muscles. Dogs of this size should be conditioned as athletes by gradual building up of muscles. Puppies are better for being kept in a hard condition until the joints and bones are well-formed. This is best achieved not by reducing food intake, but by reducing the carbohydrate (biscuit) and increasing the protein (milk-meat-eggs). Growth continues well into the second year in many specimens.

character

This breed develops personality from human contact. It is quiet, a combination of grandeur and good nature with extreme loyalty, intelligence and courage. Its abilities as a guard are superb. It is hoped that breeders will never lose sight of the Mastiff's function as a working guard dog, nor of the need for the Standard squareness of skull. If a Mastiff has height

without breadth, it is robbed of the breed's chief characteristic.

standards

The breed should be very large, but its size must be balanced by soundness. The head is large and square when viewed from all angles, with great breadth. The muzzle broad, strong and cut off square, and of great depth from the point of the nose to the under-jaws. Ears thin to the touch and small, set widely apart at the highest points of the side of the skull so as to continue the outline across the summit.

The body is massive with great breadth especially between the forelegs, causing these to be set wide apart. The deep ribs should be well set back, and the body girth should be more than one-third greater than the height at the shoulder. There should be great depth of flanks. The A.K.C. Standard sets a minimum height of 30″ at the shoulder for dogs, and 27½″ for bitches.

Mrs. A. Davies's bitch, Mab Myfanwy o' Nantymynydd, well-balanced and sound, showing the typically square muzzle and the regular outline across the skull, carried on by the ears.

161

Mastiff, Neapolitan or Italian

Italy's native mastiff, and probably descended from the Roman Molossus which accompanied troops in their northerly conquests. The breed is of easily recognized mastiff type.

The coat is short and can be black, gray, or brindled. The head large and powerful with flat skull, the upper line of the skull being parallel with that of the muzzle. The upper lip is pendulous, the bite scissors, the eyes fairly large, brown in color and with lively expression. The neck is of medium length, running well into the shoulders with much loose skin and dewlap. The body square, straight back, and on strong legs. The tail reaches to the hocks, and in its native country the breed normally has cropped ears. Dogs stand 25″ to 29″ at the shoulder, bitches 23″ to 27″; and the broad, short, truncated muzzle gives this mastiff an appearance of great power.

The guarding instinct is present to a major degree, and the breed has been used as a service, guard, or escort dog. It is alleged to be of very reliable temperament unless ordered to attack.

Great power is evident in every line of this Mastiff.

Mastiff, Pyrenean

The Mastin de los Pirineos should not be confused with the Pyrenean Mountain Dog. It is an intelligent, strong dog of imposing appearance which is used mainly to protect flocks in the high mountains. Although the ears can be cropped and the tail can be docked, this is not advised.

The head is big, broad and strong with a broad skull and convex, prominent occiput, flat forehead, wide muzzle, small, dark eyes with the lower eye-lid showing some haw, and with short, pointed, pendant ears. The neck is slender, flexible and strong, with double dewlap. The body has a deep and ample brisket and the thick flexible tail hangs in a slight curve, stands up when active but is never carried over the back. The back is level and inclined towards the withers and slightly hollow.

The fore and hindquarters are strong, with plenty of bone; muscular and straight. Feet showing the toes and phalanges well developed and there are double dew-claws.

The coat is not over-long but it is thick and wiry. The body color most frequently seen is white, with markings, either grayish or yellow, on the cheeks and the neck. These colors are sometimes seen on the body, as also are markings of black or jasper, but always the body color is white. The Pyrenean Mastiff is a tall dog, around 27″ to 32″ high.

Mastiff, Spanish

The Mastin Español is a breed of great strength and stamina, bred and used for guarding farms, cattle and flocks, and also in the hunt for wild boar and other large game. Today, the breed has many other uses, apart from being a house-dog – in war it has been used as guard, and for mountain communication work.

It is a stocky, compact dog, well-balanced and agile. It stands 26" to 28", and its coat is not long, but fine and dense, soft to the touch, and with a strong tail, well feathered. The tail and ears (which normally are small with the points folded) are often cut, a custom dating from the Mastiff's use as a fighting dog, but now much deplored, since the tail, in particular, is a striking feature of this distinctive breed.

The head is large, with pronounced stop, and long, powerful muzzle. The neck is short, with a double dewlap; the back sloping and slightly hollow. The quarters are straight and strong, the feet having well-defined toes and double dew-claws.

Colors are varied; most frequent are wolf-gray, brindle, white and black, white and golden yellow, and white and gray.

Mastiff, Tibetan

When Marco Polo travelled in the Far East in the mid 13th century, he is reported to have made specific mention of native Mastiffs "as large as asses". Whether these words were his own, or his biographer's, is not known, but a type of Mastiff has existed in the East for centuries, although in many ways it differs from European types.

The Tibetan Mastiff can still be found in the Central Asian Steppes, and the foothills of the Himalayas where it is much used by the nomadic shepherds as a guardian for their flocks. The breed type has remained constant, not so much by planned breeding programs where type is considered, but by the necessity to produce good size, and sound working abilities. In its native land, the Tibetan Mastiff can be as large as a St. Bernard and most impressive, dogs standing 27½" at the shoulder. The small drop ears are set low on a broad skull which is usually well wrinkled. The deep-set eyes are protected by a heavy brow, and the lips are usually pendulous. The long outer, and thick under coat plus the bushy tail carried curled over the back, give the animal a Chow-like appearance. Colors are usually black and tan, with tan markings over the eyes, but there are all blacks and some golden specimens.

An excellent example of the true Tibetan type. Below – the broad skull, and sagacious look, of the Tibetan Mastiff.

163

Newfoundland

Ch. Cherry of Littlegrange, owned by Mrs. Warren, shows the great strength, good bone and deep chest so necessary in the Newfoundland. Note also the good coat – even from a photograph you can see how dense it is; ideal for resisting water.

Note the breadth of skull, the short, clean-cut muzzle and the small, deeply set eyes of this Newfoundland, Ch. Harlingen Sand Piper.

history and development

The origin of the Newfoundland is a very debatable matter. Although the dog has been in existence for many, many years, its owners and breeders through all this time have not recorded the history of their canine companions; even Cabot, the explorer, whose name is so closely connected with Newfoundland, never mentioned the dogs. One explorer has recorded that he expected to find there a dog differing from any other breed, but he found dogs which had mostly an obvious cross of the Mastiff. The theory mostly accepted among experts is that the Newfoundland dog descends from the Tibetan Mastiff, and that in Newfoundland a type developed and was bred in numbers, which was adapted to the rugged conditions there, and that dog is now known as the Newfoundland – black, good size, with a massive head formation, a strong swimmer, with an oily coat and webbed feet, which enables him to stay in the water longer than most breeds. At a later stage came the Landseer, which must have bred with the Pyrenean sheep dogs, but this type was later thought to be of European origin, although many people prominent in the dog world believe that the Newfoundland descended from the Pyrenean Mountain Dog (called Great Pyrenees in America).

The breed was named around 1775 by George Cartwright, when he gave to his own dog the name of the island, the dog he used to draw his Esquimaux sled. In 1779 a well-known English naturalist described a very fine specimen in Northumberland, England, and this dog was later identified as a Landseer.

The Newfoundlands throve in England, but they were being exported in quantity from the country of their naming, and also Governor Edwards, in 1780, proclaimed that ownership of more than one dog per family was prohibited, and the Newfoundland had difficulty in surviving. Its aptitude for work proved its salvation.

In 1860 the Birmingham Dog Show included an entry of six Newfoundlands, and two years later entries at another show numbered forty-one. A fine black of the time was called Cato, and yet another, Leo – and modern pedigrees can be traced back to these dogs.

The first Newfoundland Breed Club was established in England in 1886, the writer's father being one of the founder members, and the Club formed the Standard of Points, which has not since been changed, and which has been adopted by the United States and most European countries. Prominent among exhibitors, whose activities have led to the excellence of the breed today, was Miss Goodall, whose black dogs, Ch. Gipsy Duke and Ch. Gipsy Duchess, were winning before the First World War. The breed was hit badly in Britain during this period but, subsequently, regained its strength, due to the efforts, among others, of Mr. Bland, with his Ch. Suki and two good bitches, and Mr. Horsfield, who still had his famous stud dog, Ch. Ferrol Neptune.

Another blow to the development of the breed was dealt by the Second World War; at the end of that war there were only about a dozen Newfoundlands in England. The American Newfoundland Club presented the writer with a bitch in whelp, which produced five puppies. Later the bitch was mated to an English dog, and had thirteen. Mrs. Bennet also imported a bitch in whelp from Holland, and these imports helped to revive Newfoundlands again in Britain. Three more were imported from Finland, and a number came in from the United States. Recovery seems now to be complete; registrations in ten years rose from twenty in 1960 to 117 in 1969.

color

The most popular colors are all black, and the Landseers, which are white and black. There are a few browns, but these are mostly seen in Holland with a few in Finland; I have never seen one on the show bench in England. Some Newfoundlands have a gray undercoat; Judith van de Negerhut, imported from Holland, was one such, but she always bred all-black puppies.

care

A Newfoundland nearly always sheds its coat completely in the summer, and it is most important to keep the coat well combed out, or the dog is likely to develop skin trouble. The undercoat is very oily, thus preventing water penetrating to its skin when it is swimming. When it comes out of the water and shakes itself, it is quite dry about an inch from the skin. Keep the hair well combed out behind the ears, and keep the ears clean

A lovely well-balanced black in show bloom, Merikarhun Fay of Sigroc, imported into England from Finland and owned by Miss Davies, was best of sex at Cruft's in 1970.

Taaran Taru, another Finnish dog, owned by Mrs. C. Roberts in England, is a typical example of the Landseer Newfoundland.

Mrs. Hamilton Gould's Ch. Harlingen Sandpiper is the only post-war Landseer Champion. Although not quite so heavily built as the blacks, the dog shows the good shoulders, straight topline and correct tail set of the typical Newfoundland.

Notice the good bone, legs and feet of Ch. Sigroc King Neptune, owned by Miss Davies. He is obviously a dog of great strength and substance with good, dense coat.

inside. Brush generally with a good hard brush for a few minutes each day.

Newfoundlands do not require a great deal of exercize, but road work is necessary to strengthen their muscles. They should be hard, not soft, and not over-fat.

character

The Newfoundland has an equable temperament, and a noble, rather grand bearing. It is gentle and patient with children, and paternal towards little dogs. It is a good guard dog, without being ferocious, except when provoked.

standards

The Newfoundland should look strong and active. It should move freely with perhaps a slight roll in the gait. Its head should be broad and massive, very little stop, with the muzzle short, clean cut and rather square. Eyes brown, deep set, wide apart. Ears small, set well back, lying close to the head. The coat should be dense, coarsish, and oily, and the body well ribbed, broad back, with neck well set on to the shoulders. Forelegs straight, feathered all down; hind-legs very strong, with a little feather. The chest deep, fairly broad. Bone massive throughout, but not too heavy. The feet should be large and well-shaped; tail of moderate length, reaching a little below the hocks, and broad and strong at the base. The height for a dog should be 28″ and for a bitch 26″, and weight for dogs 140 lbs. to 150 lbs., bitches 110 lbs. to 120 lbs.

Pinscher

An alert specimen of the Pinscher, beautifully conditioned.

This breed, of German origin, officially recognized in 1879, has many of the characteristics of the Schnauzer. A stylish, heavy-set, muscular dog; sturdily built and square in the proportion of body length to height, it is extremely active and agile, lively and attentive. In spite of its playful character, it is rather distrustful of strangers and makes a very good watch-dog and guard for the house, farm or automobile, which duties it takes very seriously. Because of its clean, neat, short-haired coat it is suitable for apartment living and it needs comparatively little food.

The head is long and sharp with a slight groove down the forehead. The top of the head is flat. The ears are placed high and always cropped. The deep-colored eyes are moderately large and oval. The chest should be well-developed and deep. The tail, which is high-set, is docked and carried vertically.

The coat is thick, smooth, flat and glossy and colors are black with tan or deep red, whole black, chestnut, chocolate, gray-blue with red or yellowish tan markings, salt and pepper.

The youthful elegance of the Pinscher with its rippling muscles and graceful short coat, give it an extremely noble appearance.

Height about 15½″ for a bitch and 18½″ for a dog.

Pinscher, Austrian

In general appearance, the Osterreichische Kurzhaarige Pinscher is a small to medium-sized dog, 13½″ to 19½″, with a very small body. It is fearless and alert and has a lively personality. Its ears may be button, drop, rose (seldom) or prick; the button ear is preferred and breeders tend to select for this.

The tail is set high and, if not docked, carried well forward over the back, rather rough-haired with a slight brush.

There is a great size range in this breed from 13″ to 19″ possibly because type is not set.

The coat is short, either tufted or of even texture, and has an undercoat similar to that of a smooth-haired terrier.

color:

Generally flaxen-yellow, fawn, yellow-brown, deer red, black and tan, often with streaks. In most cases there is a fine display of white self-markings on muzzle, collar, throat and chest, and from the feet to various heights on the legs. The prominent blaze should be pure white. Dappled, spotted or patched and pure white are not desirable.

Pinscher, Harlequin

This medium-sized Pinscher, the Harlekinpinscher from Germany, averages 13″ at the withers. Kept principally as a pet or companion dog, it has frequently proved itself a general utility dog in the rural areas, gaining praise as a watchdog and ratter.

It is a squarish, slightly stocky dog with a hard, well-muscled, flexible body. Agile and alert in bearing. The ears are small, pricked and tilted. Nose black.

The tail, which is carried high and slightly forward, is very straight and is generally docked short.

The name Harlequin comes from the checkered coloration of a white, gray or light colored background, with black or dark irregular markings, streaked, with or without a red patch.

The coat is short, smooth and dense, and covers the body evenly, with a marked sheen.

Poodle
(Miniature, Standard, Toy)

history and development

There is a saying that the more classical the object, the less it needs to be changed. Fundamentally one can apply this very markedly to the Poodle as a breed. It is certainly true that breeders have now successfully evolved three individual sizes and various colors, which are becoming the more firmly established as years pass. Each size has its individual charm and appeal, depending on whether you 'live in a home with generous space around it or a compact city apartment. For the owner of a Poodle as a companion, there can be few breeds to equal it. Firstly, it comes to you in a wide range of colors – dense black, various shades of brown from a deep rich chocolate to soft café au lait, hazy pastel silver, glowing peach or deep apricot, sparkling white or the color of whipped Cornish cream. Its coat never moults, a boon to the houseproud; if a door is left open, it is never off roaming for hours, a boon to the busy, and provided it is brought up sensibly and trained to be left alone when necessary, it has the sincere faithfulness of a dog, coupled with the sophistication and

Poodle puppies of any age or size have tremendous appeal. These white Standards, owned by Miss M. Willis, were sired by Ch. Bibelot's Polar de la Fontaine of Springett, a white dog imported into Britain from Canada. He later had a successful stud career.

Although the Standard in Britain specifies 11" as the upper limit for Toy Poodles many are bred to go under the 10" measure – the size of Toys in America. Mrs. S. Barratt's International Ch. Great Westwood Monmartre Maria is one of these, but her diminutive size did not prevent her from winning twenty-one C.C.s, several groups and best in show at championship shows.

humor of an amusing (but not always sincere) human being! If one wants a majestic "broth of a lad" the choice is a Standard Poodle; if your space is more limited, the Toy makes a charming companion. If you prefer happy mediums, but at the same time, a good country walk, then the Miniature is your choice. In any instance, with sensible regular maintenance, you have made yourself an unforgettable friend and companion. The Poodle is a breed of considerable antiquity. Roman coins show upon them a medium sized dog with a lion-like mane and long tail on which is a large tuft of hair. It was first recorded coming from Russia (but its name is from the German word "Pudel", to splash) and finding its way, probably by following troops during wars and sieges, into France, which country concentrated on developing it as a retrieving and water dog, characteristics its contemporary counterpart still strangely retains. Hence always the necessity to have a thick curly coat as a protection against cold water and the elements. At this time the average animal was neither as large as some present-day Standard Poodles, but at the same time approximately 4" to 6" taller than the present-day ideal Miniature size of under 15" to the shoulder. It is the French who claim the present-day Poodle to be a direct descendant of their breed, the Bichon. In the early part of the 19th century, the Corded Poodle was to be found. Not a breed any one would much want to foster in these days as the long cords had to be oiled and tied up with rag to retain the heavy coils of hair.

Broadly, whether it be the early French engravings of the pet dogs in the courts of the Louis or those of Corded Poodles or Poodles retrieving duck from the marshes at this time, although the art of presentation has become of a brilliantly high standard in these days, there is really very little change in this delightful and most classical of breeds.

color

I have touched briefly on color in my first paragraph, but to take this more fully, I think it fair to say that each color has its particular characteristic. The type of the blacks, especially in Miniatures and Toys, is more clearly fixed than the other shades. There has been great work and advancement on the part of persevering breeders in the Miniature and Toy whites which are now taller on the leg, more refined in head and freer in hind action than immediately after the war when championship shows recommenced. In silvers, we have now a clear pastel blue color, or a deeper, even shade of pewter with no traces of brown tinge, or small, white "mis-marks" on chest or feet, as sometimes used to be the case. The apricots now retain their depth of color for many years, and in this color Miniatures have become more refined in head and shorter in body and, in the instance of apricot Toy and Standard Poodles, there has been spectacular improvement; both of these sizes in this color having been capable of winning best in show awards at major championship shows, including Cruft's, in the last few years, a great credit to the conscientious Poodle breeder. Blacks, also, are denser in pigment with many less white hairs in the coat, eyes have darkened, while still retaining the soft gentle expression but, at the same time, that "twinkle of humor" which is so much part of the breed's charm. Most important of all, the intelligent breeder is more than ever aware, other than in the most exceptional instances of breeding, of the necessity of breeding color-to-color and not intermixing them.

care

Here one does touch on a rather sensitive subject as few breeds can look so spectacular when beautifully maintained, nor as dismally depressing when neglected or badly turned out. For this reason, there has sprung up, throughout the world, probably in these enlightened days of travel, an army of professional Poodle trimmers whether for pet clip or the lion clip which is insisted upon for the show ring. You can, of course, teach yourself the fundamentals of keeping your Poodle well turned out and clipped, but pet owners are best advised to leave this to the skill of the neighborhood professional. A wire-pin pneumatic brush and a wire-toothed metal comb are all that is necessary for everyday grooming, making sure you go thoroughly through the coat without raking out handfuls of it. Regular shampooing is also essential as the dirtier the coat

Next to blacks perhaps whites are the most popular and successful in Poodles of all sizes. Mr. and Mrs. Price's Ch. Tophill White Lord of Montfleuri, bred by Mrs. Strawson, is a splendid example of a white in full show coat and bloom. He shows a particularly exquisite head and eye and excellent pigmentation.

171

"Well, as I was saying – these owners!". A conversation piece between two delightful silver Miniature Poodles owned by Miss C. Seidler. Their coats have been cut down to a manageable length.

becomes, the more difficult it is to keep it under control and tangle-free which, in view of the fact that the natural characteristic of the coat is to curl, must always be borne in mind.

character
Summed up in two words "unique and charming". Many Poodles have been the beloved companions of children, but I would nevertheless not describe them as being the ideal children's pet. Adult yes, when they are

A study of Ch. Montfleuri of Longnor with her seven-weeks-old sons.

not suddenly seized or subjected to sudden shuffling footsteps, or un-expected commotion. Perhaps as a sensitive breed the best is brought out in them by someone who transmits a sense of calm assurance – noisy people tend to create noisy children and noisy dogs as well! As a breed they have a wonderful sense of fun – I always remember a large white Standard Poodle whose joy it was to sneak into his owner's dining room when a dinner party had been laid and, with a twinkle in his eye, go round to each place-setting and gently carry off the cone-rolled napkin until he had collected the lot; or a Miniature who would jump into a basket specially made for him on the back of the motor bicycle his master rode during the period of the war!

One very important characteristic of the Poodle, especially the two larger sizes, is its great response to obedience training, and where it compares so favorably with the other breeds which immediately spring to mind in this particular activity. The great difference, certainly to the onlooker, is that the Poodle is so obviously enjoying carrying out its routine, jumping and retrieving, as if it were its favorite game, rather more than a routine it has been "instructed" to execute.

In the pre-war days of the Crystal Palace Shows in London, King Leo of Piperscroft, a performing Standard Poodle, would bring down the house in comparison to the rather more staid German Shepherd Dogs (Alsatians) and Great Danes working with him.

Ch. Montfleuri Sarah of Longnor, owned by Mr. and Mrs. Price and bred by Mrs. Worrall, was a great show bitch and also a successful brood, producing in her first litter Ch. Tarka of Montfleuri.

Standard Poodles have attained a very high level of quality in America. American Ch. Alekai Marlaine is an outstanding white bitch with a tremendous winning record.

Now that the wave of commercialism has passed over the breed, we have not only better looking Poodles on our sidewalks, but also more sensible ones, and it is up to serious breeders and new owners to keep it this way.

standards

The Standard in Britain and the United States is broadly the same. One major difference is that, in America, to be shown, a Toy Poodle must be 10″ or under at the shoulder, and in Britain another 1″ grace is allowed in this variety. To have brought the breed size down from an average of 20″ to such a diminutive size is a very major breeding achievement. The introduction and insistence on the use of the 11″ or 15″ measure at shows has brought about a much more even size in these two smaller varieties. From the aspect of those requiring a pet, a slightly oversize Toy or Miniature is no deterrent, and as a result one may often be able to purchase

174

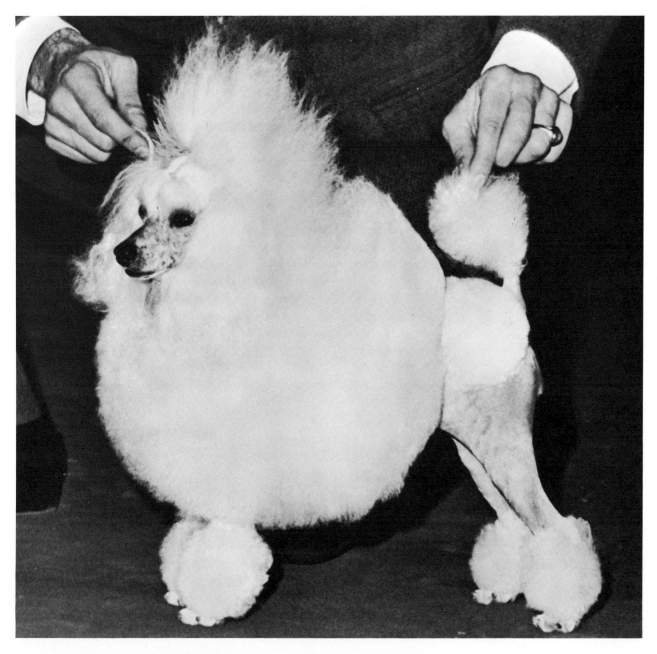

A difference of one inch in the Standards of Toy Poodles in America and Britain presents problems for judges when judging in both countries. This is American Ch. Arundel Brazen L'il Raisin, best Toy Poodle at Westminster, New York in 1967. The handler is Frank T. Sabella, one of the top handlers in the U.S.A.

Three beautiful head studies. Even-ness of type is very evident in this trio of Montfleuri champions. From left to right they are Ch. Lorna Doone, Ch. Moensfarm Mascot and Ch. Rioletta.

175

a very good specimen of the breed for a very reasonable price.

It is equally important to retain size in the Standard Poodle, which should not be a small dog. I always think that the most important phrase in the Standard is "A Poodle should be a very active intelligent dog carrying himself proudly"; for this sums up the instant impression one should always have when seeing a good example of the breed.

It should be a compact dog with a long neck enabling it always to hold its head high; its tail, which is docked as a puppy, also should be carried proudly, but never curling over its back.

A Poodle's head is of the greatest importance; it should be in perfect balance to its size with delicate bone structure, neither snipy, nor Greyhoundlike.

Its nose should always be black, except in the case of the browns or creams. Eyes always as dark as possible, oval and full of fire and intelligence; again neither round and full nor mean and beady. Its coat cannot be too profuse or thick in texture; it should be curly and dense in whatever color it may be. Its feet should be tight and arched, with thick pads; never thin and spread like a chicken's. Its action, one of the great features of the breed should be in the nature of a hackney pony, at the same time covering the ground.

Mrs. A. D. Jenkins's Ch. Rudolph of Piperscroft, top sire in the breed in Britain, and Mrs. Austen Smith's Ch. Braeval Black Nylons, at Richmond championship show in 1953, when Mr. Howard Price (centre) judged. Both of these kennels have had a profound influence on the Miniature Poodle.

Rottweiler

history and development

The Rottweiler takes his name from the town of Rottweil in Württemberg, West Germany, and was formerly known as the Rottweiler Metzgerhund (Rottweil butcher's dog).

The breed is of great antiquity, probably deriving in part from the large Molossian hounds. Certain other large breeds found in the same area, such as the St. Bernard and the Leonberger, may have a similar origin.

The Rottweiler is first heard of as a distinct breed in the Middle Ages when they were used extensively for boar hunting. Large kennels were kept, and heavy fines were imposed for killing or stealing them. Indeed so highly were they valued that they were sometimes provided with coats of iron mail to protect them against the sharp tusks of the wild boar. Later still, they were used as cattle dogs, and it is in this role that they are best known. The work was arduous, demanding fitness, courage and devotion to duty, for the dog had to guard the herd by night, prevent any cattle from straying, drive them long distances by day, and often carry the master's purse round his neck, for few would venture to molest him. The strong constitution and firm temperament established in this way were invaluable when planned breeding was started in the early years of this century.

The butchers and cattle dealers also used the Rottweiler as a draught dog to pull their small carts. This was the only occupation left to him – when the driving of cattle on the hoof was forbidden by law with the coming of the railways in the 19th century – until 1910 when he became one of the four breeds used for police work (the others were the Alsatian (German Shepherd Dog), the Dobermann and the Airedale). Since then

The Rottweiler, side head, and front.

Int. Ch., German Federal Ch. (Bundessieger 1960/'61/'62) and Am. Ch. Harras v. Sofienbusch, Sch. H 1, owned by Mr. P. G. Rademacher and Mr. R. F. Klem, of Wheaton, Illinois. An outstanding German-bred dog who has sired fifteen U.S. champions, and has many champion grandchildren.

the future of the breed has been assured.

With the formation in 1907 in Heidelberg of the first club devoted solely to the breed, planned breeding was started and records began to be kept. The present club, Allgemeiner Deutscher Rottweiler Klub (A.D.R.K.) was formed in 1921 and, since that time, has assiduously promoted the development of the breed, first for work and second for beauty. Its slogan is "Rottweiler breeding is working dog breeding".

World War II exacted a heavy toll on the breed: breeding inevitably declined and a substantial part of the breeding population was lost. After the war, the A.D.R.K. made sterling efforts to put the breed on a sound footing again, and their success is shown by the very high standard of the present-day dogs.

In West Germany breeding is supervised carefully by breed wardens who are appointed by the breed club to cover specific districts throughout the country, and they in turn are supervised by a chief breed warden. It is the task of these wardens to examine litters soon after birth and decide which puppies should be put down and which should be retained by the breeder. Not more than six puppies are reared in each litter, preferably fewer in the first one. Before dogs and bitches are permitted to be used for breeding, they must pass the Club's Test of Suitability for Breeding in which attention is paid not only to general appearance, but also to movement, teeth and temperament. Nervousness, insufficient guarding instinct, faulty bite, monorchidism or cryptorchidism are just some of the faults which prevent an animal from passing the test. Thus only the best stock is bred from.

The pioneer of the breed in Britain was Mrs. Thelma Gray of the famous Rozavel Kennels who imported the first specimens from Germany in 1936. Several more importations followed, litters were born, classes were scheduled at shows and public interest was aroused. When World War II intervened, however, breeding and showing activities were again suspended, and by the time the holocaust was over, the stock which remained in the country was too old for breeding, no puppies having been born during the War.

It is to a young veterinary surgeon serving with the Army of Occupation in Germany, Captain Roy-Smith, that the breed owes its re-introduction to Britain, for he brought over a breeding pair, and since then the breed has enjoyed a steady growth in popularity.

One very considerable advantage which the Rottweiler enjoys is that he has been little affected by passing fads and fancies; he remains a working dog of great intelligence, with no exaggerated physical features. It is these qualities which will continue to assure him of a steady and devoted circle of admirers.

color

In the early years of this century Rottweilers of colors other than black were seen: the first Standard laid down in 1901 allowed "black stripes on an ash-gray background with yellow markings; plain red with a black nose; dark wolf-gray with black head and saddle, but always with yellow markings". But when the A.D.R.K. was formed in 1921, a new Standard was drawn up which debarred all colors except black-and-tan, and so it has remained. The white chest markings which used occasionally to be seen are now rare.

care

A Rottweiler puppy has a great deal of growing to do in a short period and if he is to become a strong, healthy, happy dog, it is essential that he should be reared well; fed a proper diet with supplements; not exercized too much too soon; and given early socialization. Without this care, the best of puppies will not realise his potential. Owing to the strong constitution of the breed as a whole, an adult dog needs only a modicum of care to keep him fit: a daily grooming, walks, and especially companionship. No trimming is required except that the tail hairs may be trimmed, if desired, to give a tidy appearance. It cannot be stressed too strongly that the Rottweiler is not a dog to be kept on a chain.

character

In a working dog character is extremely important: a nervous animal, besides being untypical and unsatisfactory to own, can be a liability if it is a "fear-biter"; conversely, it is not desirable to have one which is too sharp.

The Rottweiler's best quality is his character: his intelligence is high; his devotion to his family is absolute; his working ability is considerable; and he is a formidable guard without being excitable or given to barking without cause, nor is his reaction to outside events hasty. He is adaptable and easy to live with, given proper care and training.

In Germany, Rottweilers are used by the Police, Customs and the Army; in Denmark and Austria mainly for police duties; in Norway some are used for mountain rescue work, for which they are well fitted by reason of their excellent noses, hardiness and agility; and in Finland, which has a large population of Rottweilers, they often pull sleighs in winter. In England and in the United States, they are valued highly as companions/guards, mostly living with families, although some are successfully

Top winning American Rottweiler, Am. Ch. Rodsdens Kurt v.d.Harque, owned by Mrs. L. Putman, showing a beautiful head with lovely markings of rich tan.

Typical Rottweiler puppies at seven-and-a-half weeks, bred in England by Mrs. M. Macphail. In Germany one of these puppies would have to be destroyed in compliance with the strict breeding regulations of the German Kennel Club.

Rintelna the Bombadier, C.Dex, U.Dex, owned by Mrs. Macphail. Note the tremendous spring for such a heavy dog, derived from the typically powerful hindquarters.

employed with the police and in security work.

standards

After the start of planned breeding, the appearance of the Rottweiler underwent some changes, and the compact, sturdy dogs of today are certainly an improvement upon the early specimens. His appearance was always distinctive – his size, fearless gaze and calm, confident manner compelling attention. He is above medium size, with a strong compact body, indicative of great strength. His coat is short, coarse and flat, always black with well-defined rich tan markings on the legs, chest, muzzle and above both eyes. The head is broad with pendant ears and a strong muzzle. The tail is always docked short, although pups are occasionally born with tails too short to need docking.

In height, dogs should be between 25″ and 27″ at the shoulder, and bitches 23″ to 25″ (the A.K.C. Standard specifies $23\frac{3}{4}''$ to 27″ for males; $21\frac{3}{4}''$ to $25\frac{3}{4}''$ for bitches), but the height should always be considered in relation to the general appearance and conformation of the dog. Nothing is laid down in the Standard concerning weight, but a fair estimate of average weights is: dogs, from 115 to 125 lbs; bitches, from 90 to 108 lbs. There are slight variations between Standards in various countries though they are basically similar, and it is the hope of the German Club that all countries will ultimately adopt the same Standard. The present German Standard is extremely comprehensive with a lengthy section on character and explicit directions as to which animals may be used for breeding.

Schipperke

The Schipperke silhouette – Ch. Sequin of Schippland, a lovely bitch who has won twelve C.C.s and has been many times best of breed.

A Schipperke who has made history. Ch. Cracker of Schippland is the first and only Schipperke to win a group at a championship show in Britain. In 1970 he became a champion, was three times best of breed, and won the utility group at a championship show while still a puppy. Cracker was best of breed at Cruft's in 1971.

history and development

The Schipperke is a Belgian dog, originating in the Flemish Provinces. It is sometimes said to be a Dutch dog, but this is an error, probably due to the fact that Belgium and Holland were united at times before 1832. It is certain that the breed has been in existence for well over 100 years, and some say 200, but definite conclusive evidence as to its origin is lacking. Some cynologists classify Schipperkes as members of the Spitz family. Others are of the opinion that they come from a Terrier/Pomeranian cross, while there is an important body of expert Belgian opinion that they are a diminutive version of the black Belgian Sheepdog. This body of opinion maintains that both the Schipperke and the Groenendael have descended from this common ancestor.

The Schipperke first appears in the records of the Kennel Club in 1887, but there is good evidence that some came to England in various ways before that date. The word "Schipperke" means "little skipper" and he is often referred to as a "barge dog", and it is certain that many Schipperkes were used as guards on canal boats.

Unquestionably the Schipperke has been greatly improved since its arrival in England. The breed went through a very bad period in the 1920's and 1930's when there was a great deal of breeding to mistaken standards. There was a cult for breeding a hard terrier-type coat, which is quite wrong, and this resulted in the loss of the characteristic and essential ruff and cullotte without which the dog is not really a Schipperke at all. This can be seen very clearly from photographs of Schipperkes of that period.

Father and son. Ch. Schippland Skipsgreen Filmstar is the sire of eight champions and was twice best of breed at Cruft's. The puppy is his son, Ch. The Raven of Schippland also twice best of breed at Cruft's.

Mrs. Carlton Jones's May-He-Co K's team of American Schipperkes.

A Continental Schipperke, showing rather racier lines.

An American best in show winner.

Today, through the efforts of breeders the ruff and cullotte have been restored and the conformation and soundness of the dog raised to a higher standard than ever before. The "all-rounder" judges deserve much of the credit for this improvement

color

Typically and traditionally the Schipperke is a black dog, though in England and South Africa other colors are now accepted, but not in Belgium, his country of origin, the U.S.A. or most European countries.

character

He is an excellent guard dog as one would expect from his function on barges. He is active, inquisitive and alert. He does not bark without reason, but can really give tongue when there is need. Very affectionate, loyal, and intelligent, he is devoted to his owner or family, but is slow to accept strangers, for he is not a dog who likes to be taken for granted or fussed or handled by those he does not know. He is very active, and can keep going after his owner has stopped, but also he can adapt himself to his circumstances, and where there is little ground can be virtually self-exercizing.

He is an individual, and needs interest and affection. Every Schipperke would like to be a pet. He does not thrive in a large kennel among other dogs because he needs individual attention, and to belong to some one person. He will be very much what you make him. Give him affection and talk to him, and you will have an ideal dog who will live for you. He is a dignified little dog, so never tease him or laugh at him. If you do he cannot trust you and that will be the end, for he needs someone he can trust absolutely. He will travel with you happily in your car or caravan. He is an ideal dog for this present age if made a friend and companion,

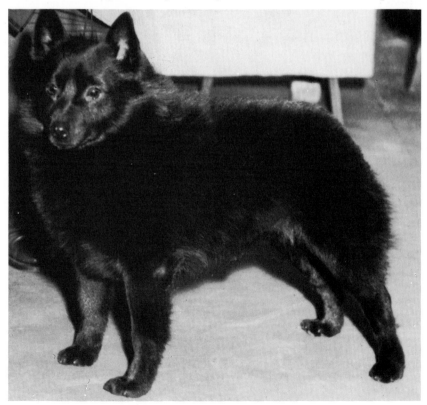

A Schippland Schipperke puppy.

Ch. The Raven of Schippland, winner of nine best of breed awards, including Cruft's 1965 and 1966.

and quickly becomes part of the life of his owner and family.

standards

The Schipperke is unique in appearance, for he has a silhouette quite different from that of any other dog. Once you have seen a Schipperke you can never mistake him for any other breed. He has a very distinctive character too.

What is he like? The photographs are the best answer, but in words, he is a small, alert, tail-less, short-backed dog, with a foxy head and fully erect pointed ears which give him a smart appearance. He has small dark eyes more oval than round and full of expression. He must have a large ruff or mane, which is essential, a cullotte, and a dense coat. The chest should be broad with a deep brisket, and the back short, straight and strong. The neck is strong, short, broad at the shoulders and slightly arched. The shoulders should be muscular and sloping. The forelegs should be straight, the thighs muscular and the hocks well let down. The feet should be small and cat-like. The hindquarters are finer than the fore, and the rump is well rounded.

His weight should be between 12-16 lbs., dogs being heavier than bitches.

Ch. Mottram Be Friendly, owned by Mrs. E. Jackson; a notable winner, including best of breed at Cruft's in 1970.

183

Schnauzer
(Giant, Miniature, Standard)

This beautiful Standard Schnauzer, Ch. Stone Pine Nickel, owned in America by the late Mrs. Nancy Aronstam, provides a worthy subject to head this chapter. Perfectly balanced and full of quality, she continued winning when most dogs were dreaming of lying by the fireside.

The well-furnished head of the Schnauzer, Dondeau Hornito.

history and development

There are three varieties of Schnauzers – Giant, Standard and Miniature. They originated in South Germany.

The oldest of these three varieties, and the prototype, is the Standard Schnauzer whose long history dates back to the 15th and 16th centuries. Rembrandt and Sir Joshua Reynolds were among the famous painters in whose works the Schnauzer appears. Albrecht Dürer, one of the greatest German painters, owned one for at least twelve years and the earliest portrayal of the breed is featured in his painting, Madonna with the Many Animals, painted in 1492.

The Crown of Thorns, a 16th century tapestry by Lucas Cranach the Elder, contains the likeness of a Standard Schnauzer. At Mechlinburg, in Germany, in the market place there is a statue of a hunter dating from the 14th century, with a Schnauzer crouching at his feet, which conforms closely to the present day show Standard. So, we have proof that the breed is long established.

The German word "schnauzer" means snout, so emphasized because of the heavy, wiry beard, the name was given to the breed because of its characteristic and conspicuous whiskers, which drew attention to the

184

muzzle. Or perhaps it was that the breed derived its name from a dog called "Schnauzer" – who was aptly named – and who won first prize at the third German International Show in Hanover in 1879 where they were first exhibited as Wire Haired Pinschers. The Standard Schnauzer was bred from Black Poodles, Wolf Spitz and Wire Haired Pinscher stock. To uphold this theory, it is said that from the Pinscher element the tendency to fawn colored undercoat can be attributed, the pepper and salt color and its harsh wiry texture comes from the Wolf Spitz. Solid black specimens are still fairly common in Germany and the rest of Europe, but relatively uncommon in the U.S.A.

The Standard of the breed was first published in Germany in 1880. In 1890 the first Specialty Show was held in Stuttgart with an entry of ninety-three dogs. In 1895 the Pinscher Club was founded in Cologne and the Bavarian Schnauzer Club in Munich in 1907. These two clubs united in 1918 to become the official representative of the breed in the German Kennel Club.

The Miniature Schnauzer was derived from the Standard Schnauzer and was produced by the selective matings of small specimens – it is said these were crossed with Affenpinschers. They were exhibited as a distinct breed as early as 1899.

The Giant Schnauzer is reputed to come from Southern Bavaria and in Germany the Giants are known as Riesenschnauzers. It is believed the crosses used to develop the Giant Schnauzer were probably smooth-coated drover dogs, rough-coated shepherd dogs, black Great Danes and Bouvier des Flandres. These crosses produced a robust, agile dog with a deep chest and hard wiry coat of black or salt and pepper.

The Giants were originally cattle driving dogs, then guard dogs. In Germany they have been known to show-fanciers since 1900. Hardiness, intelligence and courage make them one of the principal breeds used for police and security work in Europe. All Schnauzers in Germany are cropped. Cropping in America is governed by the separate laws of the different states and now both cropped and natural ears are permitted in the show ring. Between 1927 and 1930 American anti-cropping laws cut down entries at the shows. Most people were showing cropped dogs from Germany and there was a conflict between those who favored the English position against cropping while others preferred to crop and not show. Rules were changed in 1933 to permit showing of both.

Miniature Schnauzer registrations in America have leaped up in post war years until they are fifth among all breeds with 36,000 and in Britain there are over 500. The Standard Schnauzers have not enjoyed such a spectacular increase and are still under the hundred in England, but have more than 1,100 a year in the U.S.A. Giants are still quite rare, but register some 200 a year in America.

It is interesting to note that although the Miniatures are enjoying a new found popularity the greatest number exhibited at Cruft's in post war years is only about fifty.

There can be no doubt that American imports have greatly affected the Miniature Schnauzers in Britain and the Wilkern and Sternroc strains were among those who played a great part in this evolution in the 1950's and 60's.

Concurrently Dondeau exports to Italy in the 1950's were prevalent in the pedigrees of subsequent Italian champions and later Eastwight played

The Continent is rich in beautiful Schnauzers of all sizes. This black Miniature, owned in Italy by Mr. Filippo Pozzi, Niks mei Diavolineri, is a champion in Italy, Austria, Czechoslovakia and Germany.

One of the most successful Miniatures of recent years in Britain is Mrs. D. Crowe's Ch. Deltone Pinchpenny Luke of Gayterry, imported from America. He was top-winning dog in the breed at Cruft's two years running and has headed the Utility Group at a British championship show.

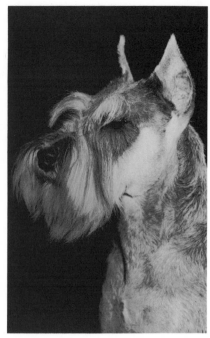

Compare these two head studies of Miniature dogs, both sires of many winners. On the right is Mrs. P. Cross-Stern's American Ch. Sternroc Sticky Wicket, with cropped ears. On the left, Mr. D. Becker's Dondeau Heureux, with his ears hanging naturally.

an important part. So, from American imports to Britain, carrying Dorem, Handful, and Marienhof bloodlines, the Dondeau line was reinforced and passed its strength on to the Italian line. Gosmore exports to Australia strengthened the breed in that country and Deltone, too, has played a major part in strengthening Miniature Schnauzers all over the world. Giants are more prevalent on the Continent with thirty-three pepper and salt and seventy-three blacks registered in Holland in 1969; sixty-five Standard pepper and salt and twenty-seven Standard black for the same period and seventy-two Miniature salt and pepper and sixty-two black.

Sweden shows registrations of 225 Miniatures in 1969 nearly doubling their 1962 figures, 137 Standards and 158 Giants. Unfortunately, the figures for Germany are not available, but in 1970 the Pinscher Schnauzer Club held its 75th Anniversary Show which was attended by representatives from all over the world. In Germany breeders are required to cull their litters to six puppies.

Standard Pepper and Salt Schnauzers appeared in Italy before 1914 when they were imported from Austria. Giants arrived after 1945. All three varieties are well represented there now. There can be no doubt that a lot has been done in America to improve Standard and Miniature Schnauzers both in conformation and presentation. Certainly a lot of refinement has come into the Standards since Ch. Claus v Furstenwall won best of breed in 1927 and they are shown with more furnishings and better presentation.

In 1933 the American Kennel Club made separate breeds of Standards and Miniatures with separate registrations. During the 1920's interbreeding between the two sizes had taken place as the Americans considered this necessary for the development of the Miniature.

Giant Schnauzers were first imported into America in 1925, but not registered until 1930. South Africa, too, shows an interest in Miniature Schnauzers with a registration which has nearly doubled in the two years from 1967 to 1969 when it stood at forty-four.

The Standard Schnauzer, Ch. Pavo de la Steingasse, owned by Mrs. Margaret Smith; best working dog, Westminster, 1971.

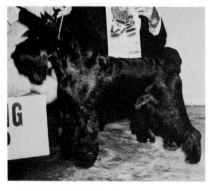

The first Schnauzer, Standard as we now know it, was imported into England by the Duchess of Montrose who exhibited it at Cruft's in 1928. The breed was recognized by the Kennel Club in 1930.

Schnauzers have proved themselves excellent obedience dogs and in England the famous obedience test-winning Schnauzer, Brenda of Ashways, shown from 1934 to 1939 had a run of twelve firsts at Open and Championship Shows. She won the first Gold Star Dog Tournament held in Wembley in 1935. One of the biggest changes since the war is that current obedience winners include some breed class winners too. This also holds true in America. Giant Schnauzers are more popular in America than Britain and Ch. Le Dauphin della Breteche CDX was the first Giant to win both titles – this dog won both titles on the same day in 1969, a great feat.

In Britain and the Continent, the Schnauzer is regarded as a working dog. Originally used as rat-catchers in Germany – ratting trials are still in evidence there to ensure the dogs do not lose their original characteristics. In Britain both Standards and Miniatures are classified as Non-Sporting. In 1905 the first Standard Schnauzer (termed Wire-haired Pinscher) was imported into America and at that time shown in the Terrier Group.

Present classes and Groups of the A.K.C. began in 1924. In 1945 the breed was properly put in the Working Group, where it remains. The Miniature Schnauzer, however, is shown in the Terrier Group in America.

An Australian champion in 1965, owned by Mr. Kevin Brown, Ch. Casa Verde Zipper.

color

Both forms of Schnauzer can come in all colors of pepper and salt, the contributing colors being in roughly equal proportions, and it can come in pure black. In America the addition of tan with black is accepted.

care

The Schnauzer coat is one of the most distinctive attributes of the breed. Only a serrated stripping comb, or finger and thumb should be used to pluck out the dead hair – clipping or razoring ruins the texture of the coat. The undercoat is a different color from the top coat and care must be taken not to make the undercoat look "moth eaten" when stripping out the dead top coat. Scissors are used to trim the eyebrows, leg hair and round the feet.

The beard and legs should be washed frequently, but constant washing of the body coat only softens the hair. Harsh Schnauzer coats stay clean

When Mrs. Cross-Stern brought back to Britain her American Ch. Sternroc Sticky Wicket she certainly started something – a cricket team! This team of delightful puppies, all carrying the Gosmore prefix, owned by Mrs. A. Dallison, is named after terms used in the British game of cricket – Missed in the Slips, No Ball, Ch. Hat Trick, Maiden Over, Ch. Wicket Keeper, How's That, Spinner's Wicket, Mid-on, Mid-off, Ch. LBW, Bring Back the Ashes. All sired by Sticky Wicket or his sire, American Ch. Nicomur Chasseur.

Following the success of his Dondeau Standards and Miniatures, Mr. Donald Becker imported this Giant Schnauzer, Risengardens King of Putszamerges, one of the few Giants in Britain.

(on the right) Continental and Scandinavian shows make a big feature of their team classes and this team of Italian black Miniature Schnauzer champions would certainly catch the eye anywhere in the world. Mr. Filippo Pozzi holds Malya Gunther, Malya Quiz, Worl Niks mei Diavolineri and Malya Ivette.

and the dogs seldom require bathing.

Daily grooming with a wire glove on the body (except immediately after stripping) keeps the coat in good shape. Whiskers, eyebrows and legs should be combed and care taken to see that the eyes and ears are kept clean. Regular exercise on hard surfaces usually keeps the nails well worn down.

character

Schnauzers are fearless, sagacious, hardy and tough. They are certainly versatile dogs and the larger varieties were used by the Army in war as dispatch carriers and red cross aids. They are used in police work and as guide dogs for the blind. The Standards and Giants are slow maturing and normally do not reach their prime until they are three years old.

The Miniatures are compact, muscular dogs that adapt happily to life in town or country – their size makes them perfect pets for the city flat dweller and, although they do not need as much exercise as their larger "brothers", they are game little dogs and can take a ten-mile hike in their stride. Amenable to training, with a wonderful sense of humor, they are slightly suspicious of strangers, which makes them admirable guards; they are not fighters but, if provoked, can give a good account of themselves. The Miniatures mature earlier than the two other varieties and usually reach full maturity by the time they are a year old.

Schnauzers enjoy longevity and one old stalwart, Ch. Sir Toby of Langwood, a Standard, won four Challenge Certificates in Britain at eleven years of age.

standards

This is a powerfully built, robust dog, presenting a nearly square appearance, that is, the length of his body to root of tail, should equal his height at the shoulders. He is high spirited, reliable and vigorous. The color, or other points of purely aesthetic quality, are less important than correct formation. The head is strong and long, narrowing from

eyes to the ears (which are V-shaped, set-on high, and drop forward) and through to the tip of the nose. The powerful muzzle should end in a fairly blunt line, with a bristly, stubby moustache and whiskers on the chin. The neck is moderately long, set cleanly on the shoulders, which are flat and sloping. The forelegs are straight from any viewpoint; the thighs slant and are flat, and the feet are short, round, compact with close-arched toes. The tail is set-on and carried high, and docked at the third joint up.

The coat is hard and wiry, and fairly short, and with a good undercoat.

In Britain the ideal height is 18″ for bitches, 19″ for dogs; in the U.S.A., half an inch more is preferred.

The Miniature Schnauzer has exactly the same specifications except that the bitch should only be 13″ high, and the dog 14″; in America it is 12″ to 14″.

Descended from Ch. Gosmore Opening Batsman this Miniature, Ch. Rownham's Batsman, is himself a top sire, winning the progeny stakes at Windsor championship show in 1970. Owned by Miss P. Morrison-Bell and Miss R. E. Ashworth.

Shih Tzu

Ch. Soong of Llakang, a ten lb. bitch owned by Mrs. L. G. Widdrington, is an outstanding specimen of the smaller type.

International Ch. Golden Peregrine of Elfann, bred by Miss E. Evans, gained his British title when owned by Mr. and Mrs. Leadbitter, and was later exported to Italy where he is now owned by Mrs. M. Belli. Peregrine left behind him some notable stock.

history and development

Although the Shih Tzu gained its name (Shih Tzu Kou, meaning "Lion-dog") and present form in ancient China, its ancestors are known to have originated in Tibet, and existed in that country as prized "holy dogs" from Tibet's first recorded history in the 7th century A.D.

It was not until the Chinese Ch'ing (Manchu) Dynasty (1642–1912), that the Tibetan "lion-dog" really came into vogue. Dogs were sent to all the Ch'ing monarchs down to 1908, when the Dalai Lama visited Tzu-hsi, last Empress of China (who was particularly interested in dog-breeding) shortly before her death in 1908, and presented her with several specimens. The Shih Tzu and Pekingese were occasionally interbred in China, for mutual benefit. The lion-dog appears on an infinite variety of objects in Chinese art – from massive beasts carved from stone guarding a temple to delicate silken embroideries. There are lion-dogs (or kylins) in silver and gold, bronze, jade, ivory and alabaster, fashioned in pottery or exquisite paintings on porcelain. The Shih Tzu type can be differentiated from the Pekingese type by the beard and whiskers and often with bumps on the head denoting a top-knot (Pien-ji).

Although Shih Tzus existed in the Imperial Palace under the puppet Emperor, Pu-yi, as late as 1928, breeding to type really languished after the death of the old Empress, Tzu-hsi in 1908. Stock became scattered abroad – smuggled out of the Palace and sold by the eunuchs to Chinese noblemen or presented as gifts to important foreign visitors. After this time, and up till the end of the 1930's, much confusion arose as to the correct form and name of these dogs. Outside the Palace, the Shih Tzu and Apso types, existing in China at that time, were all lumped together. The China Kennel Club, Shanghai, was formed in 1923, but it was not until 1930 that the first class was scheduled for this type of dog, under the name of Lhassa Terrier or Tibetan Poodle. In 1934 the Peking Kennel Club was formed and a class scheduled for "Lhassa Lion Dogs". A Standard now existed, but the exhibits were said to deviate greatly from it, especially in size. In 1935 the Lhassa Lion Dog proved one of the most popular in the show, an amazing number of ribbons being won by Mrs. Kun Chin's small black and white bitch.

Luckily by the time the Communists took over in China, the Shih Tzu was becoming well-established in the Western world. The first three specimens were introduced into England by General Sir Douglas and Lady Brownrigg in 1930. At first all importations were classed together under the name of "Apso" which meant "shaggy or goat-like". But when they and their offspring appeared together in the show ring in Britain for the first time in 1934, they differed so much in appearance that it was decided to divide into two quite separate breeds; those with longer noses and legs were named "Lhassa Apso". and those which came from Peking and had there developed shorter, rounder heads and shorter legs, were called "Shih Tzu" by which name they had been known colloquially in China. From this time on the two breeds drew steadily apart, although to this day an occasional specimen is seen in the show ring which resembles the other. In 1934, the Shih Tzu was recognized in the Non-Sporting Group in "Any Other Variety", and Lady Brownrigg was granted permission to register a club under the title of "The Shih Tzu Club", under the presidency of the Countess of Essex.

By the end of 1938 well over a hundred Shih Tzus had been registered by the English Kennel Club. Championship status was granted in 1940, but this lapsed during the years of the Second World War. It was not until June 1949 that Lady Brownrigg's beautiful bitch, Ta-Chi of Taishan became first breed champion at Blackpool Championship Show.

In 1952, a Pekingese-cross was introduced into English stock to improve various points. This was done under Kennel Club control and each generation published in the Kennel Gazette until the fourth and "pure-bred" generation was reached, which was eligible for the breed register. A small dog of this line, Fu-ling of Clystvale, was exported to Sweden in 1959 where it produced numerous champions. This line proved very popular and is now in all English kennels. A somewhat smaller type of Shih Tzu

The face of the Shih Tzu

Ch. Ta-Chi of Taishan, a bitch owned and bred in Britain by Lady Brownrigg, became the breed's first British champion in 1949.

191

Yangtse of Taishan, born in quarantine in Britain from the original pair Hibou and Shu-Ssa in 1930, became a pillar of the breed.

was thriving on the Continent where they were classified in the Toy Group. During the 1960's the breed started to popularize sensationally in U.S.A., and in the latter part of the decade there was a rapid increase in exports from Great Britain to U.S.A. The American Shih Tzu Club was founded in 1957 in Philadelphia, but it was not until September 1969 that the breed finally gained official recognition and was granted championship status by the American Kennel Club, classified in the Toy Group.

color

All colors permissible, but a white blaze on the forehead and a white tip to the tail are highly prized. Dogs with liver markings may have dark liver noses and slightly lighter eyes. Pigmentation on muzzle as unbroken as possible.

care

The coat of the adult Shih Tzu grows long and is like human hair. It needs daily grooming otherwise it will get matted and be very painful to comb out, and can cause the dog to become overheated. If a long coat is desired, brush very carefully to avoid breaking the coat, and only comb about once a week. A pure bristle brush with rubber cushion, and a wide-pronged metal comb are best. Tangles should be parted first with finger and thumb. Sponge round eyes and muzzle after evening meal. A male should also be sponged underneath. If found more convenient, the dog can be kept in a "puppy-clip", i.e. the hair cut all over to 1½"–2" Spring and Fall. But this is not permissible for show. Anal glands need squeezing occasionally. Ask your vet to show you how. If left they may become ulcerated. Nails and dew-claws need trimming about twice a year. If neglected the latter may grow in a circle and cut into the flesh. Ears should be inspected regularly and kept clear of matted hair and wax. When the top-knot grows long it should be tied up with a small rubber band to keep the hair out of the eyes.

character

The Shih Tzu should be kept as a house-dog as it is highly intelligent and

A charming study of two four-months-old puppies from the Chasmu kennel, owned by Mrs. A. Fowler, which specializes in honey and golden shades.

Mr. and Mrs. Rawling's Ch. Ya Yung of Antarctica, who made a sensational show debut as a puppy and became a top winner in the breed in 1970.

craves human companionship. It needs freedom to develop its amusing and independent character and to take part in the daily life of its owner. Hardy and adaptable, it is equally suitable for town and country, providing it is not shut up alone in a flat all day. Like all dogs it should be given daily exercise to keep fit – a walk of about two miles per day would be adequate.

standards

General Appearance – very active, lively and alert, with a distinctly arrogant carriage. The Shih Tzu is neither a terrier nor a toy.

Head and Skull – head broad and round; wide between the eyes. Shock-headed with hair falling well over the eyes. Good beard and whiskers; the hair growing upwards on the nose gives a distinctly chrysanthemum-like effect. Muzzle square and short, but not wrinkled like a Pekingese; flat and hairy. Nose black for preference and about one inch from tip to stop.

Eyes – large, dark and round but not prominent.

Ears – large, with long leathers, and carried drooping. Set slightly below the crown of the skull; so heavily coated that they appear to blend with the hair of the neck. Mouth – level or slightly underhung.

Forequarters – legs short and muscular with ample bone. The legs should look massive on account of the wealth of hair.

Body – body between withers and root of tail should be longer than height at withers; well-coupled and sturdy; chest broad and deep, shoulders firm, back level.

Hindquarters – legs short and muscular with ample bone. They should look straight when viewed from the rear. Thighs well-rounded and muscular. Legs should look massive on account of the wealth of hair; the feet, firm and well-padded, also should look big for the same reason.

A somewhat stylized painting of three generations of golden Shih-Tzu, showing how suitable is the breed for the decorative themes of Far Eastern art.

Tail – heavily-plumed and curled well over back; carried gaily, set-on high.

Coat – long and dense, but not curly, with good undercoat.

Weight and size – 10–18 lbs. Ideal weight 10–16 lbs. Height at withers not more than $10\frac{1}{2}''$.

Type and breed characteristics are of the utmost importance and on no account to be sacrificed to size alone. Faults – narrow heads, pig-jaws, snipeyness, pale-pink noses and eye-rims, small or light eyes, legginess, sparse coats.

193

Tibetan Breeds
(Lhasa Apso, Spaniel, Terrier)

Robert D. Stamp's American and Bermudan Ch. Kyi-Chu Friar Tuck, is the greatest winning Lhasa Apso in America, with a tremendous record behind him. The outstanding condition in which he is shown shows the importance of presentation and showmanship in America.

Tibet has produced a number of breeds, four of which have reached the world outside Tibet. Through their intrinsic merits, three of these have become recognized as valuable additions to those breeds kept in the pure state by dog fanciers for companionship and exhibition. The fourth, and largest, is the Tibetan Mastiff, which is described elsewhere.

The three smaller Tibetan breeds, the Tibetan Spaniel, the Lhasa Apso and the Tibetan Terrier have certain characteristics in common. All are gay and fearless, structurally sound and chary of strangers, though not aggressive. All are now well established despite wartime set-backs, enjoying separate registers at the Kennel Club in London. In America, the Apso is very strong and is the only one registered by the A.K.C., and it is hoped that the Terrier and the Spaniel will be in due course.

Resemblances between the Tibetan Terrier and the Lhasa Apso and between the latter and the Chinese breed, the Shih Tzu, have on occasion given rise to considerable confusion. However, each has definite characteristics which clearly differentiate it from the others.

The Tibetan Terrier's skull and muzzle are equal in length, while in the Apso, the muzzle, about 1½″ long, is only half the length of the skull. In the Shih Tzu, the nose is shorter still, approximately one-fifth of the total length of nose and skull together, and the nose is placed higher than in either the Tibetan Terrier or the Lhasa Apso. In the latter, the ridge of the nose should be in line with the bottom of the eye and in the Terrier a little lower still.

Each of these breeds also varies in body proportions; the Tibetan Terrier is decidedly taller than the other two and somewhat shorter in back. The length from the withers to the root of the tail in the Terrier should equal the height at shoulder whereas, in the Apso and the Shih Tzu, the body should be appreciably longer than the height at shoulder; the Apso being somewhat more lightly built in body and less deep in brisket than its Chinese rival.

Tibetan Spaniel: This is a small, hardy, cheerful breed, mostly bred in the valleys bordering Tibet and China, popular in monasteries, but not for any religious purpose.

In Europe and America it has become a charming pet, a good town dweller as well as taking active part in country life. Capable of following a horse, it also has an excellent nose, and will find a bird, but not retrieve it. Though independent by nature, it responds readily to obedience training. It has acquired popularity rapidly since a resurgence of interest in the fifties, and is now catered for by most of the major shows in Britain and America.

Points to be specially noted are a slightly undershot jaw with good, large, evenly placed teeth. The nose should be straight and come directly from between the eyes, a substantial muzzle, never snipey. A scowl is characteristic and also a slight lift of the ears away from the skull which should be slightly domed, but never apple headed. A well coupled body, not too long, with clean, laid back shoulders and tight elbows, slightly bowed forelegs, firm straight pasterns with hare-shaped feet, with feathering

Compare this Tibetan Spaniel, Seu of Ladkok, with the type being shown today, as represented by Ch. Lotus Bud. Seu, owned by Mrs. A. R. Greig, was being shown pre-war.

Relative positions of eyes and nose, full face, contribute subtly and distinctively to the typical expression of a breed; (a) the straight foreface of the Lhasa Apso has the tip of the nose scarcely below the lower rim of the eyes; (b) the Tibetan Terrier's more down-face "natural" head, with slightly longer muzzle, has the nose below eye level; (c) the Shih Tzu has a definitely Chinese air, round eyes giving an owl-like look accentuated by the nose-tip being placed higher than the Apso's; (d) in the Pekingese can be seen the true Oriental head, the shortened and "folded-up" nasal structure taking the nose high up between the wide-spaced eyes.

Ch. Braeduke Lotus Bud of Szufung, bred by Mrs. D. M. Battson, was by one of the first champions of the breed in Britain, Ch. Khan Dee of Cur-wenna, ex Ch. Yaso of Szufung. Owned by Mrs. E. J. B. Wynyard, she won five C.C.s, including best of breed at Cruft's in 1968, where she was in the last five in the utility group. Later, owned by Mrs. C. Jeary, she won further successes, and was also an outstanding brood.

between the toes. The neck and shoulders should be covered by a shawl delineated with black hairs. Hind legs well feathered, and the tail profusely plumed; action should be light and easy.

Correct colors in the Tibetan Spaniel range through white, cream, fawn, red, dark sable or sable-and-black, all with white, black-and-tan, and tricolor. A black nose is preferred but brown or liver is permissible. Eyes should be dark brown, bright, expressive; set fairly wide apart, never full or prominent. Coats are double, soft and silky, rather flat-lying except in the cape. Any resemblance to the Pekingese is deprecated. Height at shoulder up to 11″ for dogs, 9½″ for bitches. The ideal weight for a dog in top condition is 11 lbs.

Lhasa Apso: Altogether, a more solid and substantial breed than the Tibetan Spaniel, the Lhasa Apso was originally kept in the monasteries and private houses, where it acted as companion and guard. It seems likely that both the Apso and Tibetan Terrier are descended from a long-haired, herding type of dog known to have lived in Asia many centuries ago. The word "Apso" is believed to be derived from the Tibetan word "Rapso", meaning "goat-like", the long-haired Apso in an unkempt state

196

Miss B. Harding's Brackenbury Lhotse, the foundation bitch of this very successful kennel. Lhotse is behind a large proportion of the Apsos in Britain as well as in Canada and Sweden. Her show career took place before C.C.s were allotted to Apsos, but she was many times best of breed, and is the dam of the redoubtable Ch. Brackenbury Chigi-Gyemo.

bearing a strong resemblance to the small Tibetan goats.

When the breeds first arrived in the Western world, around the turn of the present century, brought back by travelers and diplomats, both Apsos and Terriers were known as one breed, dubbed Lhasa Terriers. There was confusion over the various Eastern breeds until, in 1934, the British Kennel Club requested the formation of the Tibetan Breeds Association to clarify the situation. In 1933, the breed got away to a good start in America with stock presented by the Dalai Llama, although here again they were at first registered as Lhasa Terriers. The Apso is gay and assertive; chary of strangers. It has a free and jaunty movement. The skull is moderately narrow, falling away behind the eyes – in contrast to the

Miss M. Wild has owned Lhasa Apsos since the early years of the century. This picture of her four Apsos, taken in 1934, shows how little the type has changed. Left to right, they are Satru (golden), Chora (silver-gray), Sona (golden) and Tarcum (red). Miss Wild's Apsos now carry the Cotsvale prefix.

International Ch. Fo de l'Annapurna, winner of twenty-four excellent, twenty-two C.A.C. and eight C.A.C.I.B. Although not in full coat it is clear that this modern dog is very similar in type to the Apsos of the thirties.

Ch. Brackenbury Chigi-Gyemo, a Lhasa Apso owned by Miss B. Harding.

Tibetan Terrier in which the skull tapers in the opposite direction. The muzzle is blunt and straight but not broad or heavy. The proportions of muzzle to skull are of vital importance to preserve this type. There is a slight stop, sloping gently to the rear.

Ears are set well back at about eye level – no higher, and the leather should hang close to the head and reach down to the lower jaw. Eyes are dark, and large enough to give a sweet expression neither full nor deep sunk.

Developed to cope with a rigorous climate at high altitude, the Apso is physically tough with tremendous lung power and has a lithe, strongly coupled body, agile and enduring, adapted to the rough terrain. Ideal height at the shoulder is given as 9″ to 10″, with a somewhat greater length of body. Improved feeding in the West often produces Apsos of greater size than this (the A.K.C. Standard says about 10″ or 11″ for dogs; bitches slightly less). The body is well ribbed back and ribs must be well sprung but not unduly deep or broad.

The tail, profusely feathered, should be equally well carried over the back, a trailing tail is a sorry sight in the naturally jaunty Apso. A level top-line and a high tail set are essential. An Apso's coat must be double, heavy, straight, hard, not wooly or silky, of good length and very profuse, with a good fall of hair over the eyes. The dense undercoat can be cast in hot weather. Long and profuse coats as carried by the Apso call for adequate care and attention.

Colors are golden, sandy, honey, dark grizzle, slate, smoke, particolor white, black or brown. In Tibet the golden color was preferred, hence the name by which the breed was known in Tibet – Lion Dog. Dark tips to the ears are a desirable point.

Highly intelligent, adaptable and long-lived, the Apso is good with children; an excellent housedog and intensely loyal.

Tibetan Terrier: To have described this breed as a Terrier was an unfortunate beginning, as it is devoid of all terrier characteristics; it does however resemble some terrier breeds in its square build and lively action. It is alert, intelligent and game, not fierce nor pugnacious. Unlike the Spaniel and Apso, the Tibetan Terrier is a herding type of dog, used on the farms as a general utility dog and by traders on their caravans. Not having received the same recognition and protection as the Spaniel and the Apso, it is a genuinely hardy "natural" breed with no fancy points or frills. Its progress was much slower than that of the other Tibetan varieties and, although Challenge Certificates were available to the Terrier before either Apsos or Spaniels, it fell into very low water and for many years was in extremely few hands in Britain, and was equally little known in America. It is not registered by the A.K.C.

Early in the sixties there was a revival of interest, and it now has a strong following in many parts of the U.K. and is becoming more popular in the New World and in Europe.

The head is well balanced, with a slight stop; the whole covered with long hair falling forward covering the eyes, with a slight beard on the lower jaw. The skull is of medium width, the nose always black. The large dark eyes are set wide apart with dark rims. Ears are V-shaped, lying close to the head and heavily feathered. The square body is compact and strong. The tail is set-on high and carried gaily over the back with profuse

Typical head of the Tibetan Terrier.

Buttons of Ladkok, owned by Mrs. A. R. Greig, was the type of Tibetan Terrier being shown pre-war.

Tibetan Terrier puppies

199

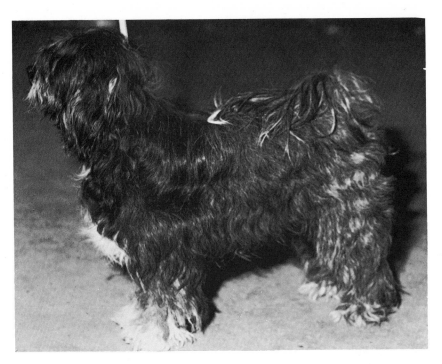

feathering; often, as in the Apso, with a kink near the tip. The coat is double with an undercoat of fine wool, the top coat fine but not silky or wooly; long and straight or wavy.

Height at shoulder is 14″ to 17″.

Colors are white, golden, cream, gray or smoke, black particolor and tricolor. Chocolate is not approved.

Tosa

Strongly harnessed, the Japanese Fighting Dog, the Tosa.

The Tosa, or Japanese Fighting Dog, was bred specially for the dog fights which became very popular in Japan during the Meiji period (1868–1912). Basically of native blood, it was interbred with Bulldog, Bull Terrier, St. Bernard and Great Dane. It gets its name from the area in which it was bred, Tosa, on the island of Shikoku. When dog-fighting was made illegal in Japan, the Tosa found itself in a new role, that of companion and guard. Still retaining its fearless courage, it is, nevertheless, a patient and cautious dog and makes a good guard as well as a family pet. It is a large dog (over $23\frac{1}{2}$″ high) of the Mastiff type, and powerfully built.

It has a large skull with a definite stop, but without exaggeration, a muzzle of moderate length, and a straight forehead. The nose is large and black.

The ears are relatively small, set high and extending along the cheeks, and lie close to the side of the head.

The eyes, somewhat small, are russet brown in color and have a sharp expression. The dewlapped neck is muscular and the withers are high and well developed. The back is horizontal and straight and the loins large and powerful. The tail, which is set-on high, tapers towards the tip and lies close to the hocks.

The coat is close and dense, hard to the touch.

Colors: all tan, or tan markings on white or on a base of a different shade of tan.

Gun Dogs
(Sporting Dogs)

Supreme at Westminster, 1971, the English Springer Spaniel, Ch. Chinoe's Adament James.

This elegant dog, English Setter, Sh. Ch. Trodgers Scot's Oat won the Gundog group at Cruft's, 1971.

Barbet

This ancient and long-established breed seems to be included among the ancestors of many other breeds, be it those with wooly coats like the Poodle, or those with wire-haired coats. The wooly coat of the Barbet has been a factor in the breeding-in of wire hair more or less deliberately by crossing with short-haired dogs. One finds traces of it in all the Griffons and modern short-hairs, like the German Drahthaar, the Poodle Pointer, a number of French hounds, the Spinone, the Korthals, and numerous other varieties, including the water dogs of Portugal. Apart from its physical characteristics the Barbet has bequeathed to its descendants, even those also containing other blood-lines, an amiable temperament, intelligence, and a passionate love for being in water, even icy water.

That the breed has changed little over the many years of its existence is shown by the fact that those Barbets which were shown at the Marseilles Dog Show in 1970 bore a close resemblance to the descriptions of the breed written in the 16th century.

The Barbet is not only a faithful companion, but it is also a water retriever of extraordinary capability; it points, and is also used to flush game.

It is of medium height, between 18″ and 22″; weight 55 lbs. The body is strong, the chest broad, round and deep, arched over the kidneys; the tail set low and carried high, sometimes curved at the extremity.

The feet are characteristic; palmate, allowing the dog to swim and dive. The legs are not well angulated, and this gives the dog a rather stilted gait. The muzzle is broad and short, the ears outstanding and set low, with thick leathers.

The coat is wooly, long and thick, with a tendency to knot if not kept well groomed.

Colors are gray-black, café au lait, dirty white and brown, and white and black.

The Barbet, an old established French gundog

Bracco Italiano

The white and tan Bracco Italiano

Like its wire-haired brother, the Spinone, the Bracco, in its shape and structure, seems to be mid-way between the modern Pointer and the Hound; and some sheepdog characteristics might also be detected in it. Records seem to prove that the breed was already established in the 18th century and, unlike most of its contemporaries, has changed very little.

The Bracco's head has a resemblance to that of the Continental hound, and the line of the lower body has similarities to the old hound breeds from Southern France. On the other hand it has neither the nervousness of the Pointer nor the independent spirit of the Hound.

The Bracco is the only Italian Pointer breed having short hair. It stands between 21½″ and 26″. The head is long, dignified, the stop not too pronounced, the muzzle half as long as the entire head. The ears should be long enough to reach the nose, with the ends rounded. The chest is broad, the upper profile of the trunk is one of the important breed characteristics. It consists of a straight incline towards the withers at the eleventh vertebrae, becoming a curve, slightly inclining to the hindquarters. Many Italian breeders leave the dew-claw.

The tail is docked to leave between 6″ and 10″.

The colors are white, white and orange, or white and brown; or white speckled with orange or brown. A self-color is a fault. Coats with black, or tricolors are not acceptable.

Drentse Partrijshond

The name means partridge dog from Drente, a province in the North-east of Holland.

It is a pointing dog, used a good deal in Holland as an all-round gundog. The breed has a kindly nature, very affectionate and obedient, and its qualities for working with the gun on various kinds of game are good. It is ideal for rough shooting in the smaller shooting fields.

Rather sturdy, medium-sized dogs with a shoulder height of 21½″ to 22¾″. The coat, never curly, is not really long but there is long feathering on the ears and on the fore and hind-legs, breech and tail.

The color is white, clear or with spots, and nearly always liver-colored patches, although orange is permitted.

Dogs which are dark all over the back and body are not favored. As a working breed the Partrijshond is not trimmed for show.

Note the definite markings and the feathered tail of this Dutch bird dog.

The Drentse Partrijshond, wild fowler par excellence

Griffon, Pointing, Wire-hair

The rough coat of this Korthals masks the athletic lines but, as can be seen in the next photograph, this breed is as keen and alert as any other type of Pointer.

history and development

This dog, popularly known as Korthals, is named after Edward Karel Korthals who was a brilliant breeder, born in Amsterdam (Holland) and who lived in Germany in the household of the Prince of Solms; between 1880 and 1900 the Wire-haired Pointing Griffon in its present form was bred by Korthals.

It originated almost exclusively from the French Griffon Pointers already existing in France, and which were probably the result of a cross between the French Braque and the Barbet or duck dog, which bequeathed the very wiry hair and beard. From the point of view of working qualities, the result was equally extraordinary. The Barbet contributed its ability for working in water, its docility and its extreme intelligence, and the French Braque, the Pointer's ancestor, its proverbial qualities on dry land. Korthals' outstanding achievement was in not resorting to hound blood, thus avoiding the physical and temperamental disadvantages of hound/pointer cross breeds.

Several early outcrosses were abandoned as failures. To produce his eight great sires, who founded the present breed, Korthals used selection by type and natural qualities only from the French Griffons. This is the main reason for the decision of the F.C.I. to classify the Wire-haired Pointing Griffon as French.

The Korthals is very different in build from the German Drahthaar and the Italian Spinone, the two breeds which are most like it. The Drahthaar has a square body with long limbs, whereas the Korthals has a much longer body and stands closer to the ground, with well-bent limbs. The skull of the Drahthaar is not so sculptured as that of the Korthals, with its stop and lines more convergent than divergent. Another enormous difference from the Drahthaar is in the coat. Whereas the Drahthaar's coat is single, usually quite short and close, that of the Korthals is double with the long, wiry top coat covering a softer, shorter undercoat which makes the top coat more stand-offish. As a result, the Korthals is very hardy in bad weather, particularly icy water, in which it can work for prolonged periods.

The Italian Spinone resembles the old French Hound and is clearly very different from the Korthals; the rare crosses with the Spinone have produced rather discouraging results.

color

The colors preferred are particolor white and tan (the latter predominating) in big patches, or an effect of steel gray made of a close mixture of white with very dark tan. Black is not allowed. Pied coats, white and tan and white and orange are allowed but not desirable.

care

The coat should not be too vigorously groomed so as not to damage the undercoat, nor should it give the trimmed appearance of a Terrier or Schnauzer, but a slight trimming may be given to prevent excessive under-hair and to give the head a more pleasing, cared-for, appearance. No traces of cutting instruments (clippers, razor or scissors) should be left on the coat. The tail is docked by about a third.

The Korthals on point. With great control the dog remains in rigid pointing stance while indicating the presence of game.

character

It is an extremely good worker and is valued by those sportsmen who are only able to keep a single dog. It has proverbial courage and enthusiasm, hunting in all weathers and fearing neither thicket, heat, cold nor water. In spite of its eagerness it is quite compatible with its kennel companions.

standards

One of the most important points of the breed's Standard is the size. In theory, a bitch should be between $19\frac{1}{2}''$ and $21\frac{1}{2}''$ at the withers, but we have seen some excellent bitches of 23". On the other hand, dogs should be between $21\frac{1}{2}''$ and $23\frac{1}{2}''$.

The very sloping shoulders give an elegant silhouette with a beautiful neck and, as a result, an elegant gait, with good head carriage. The average weight is about 50 lbs., but there are lovely bitches weighing less than 45 lbs. and powerful males of about 55 lbs.

Griffon, Pointing, Long-coat

This Griffon, the Boulet Griffon, after its breeder, Emmanuel Boulet, was really only established in the second half of the 19th century. Boulet was an industrialist from Northern France, who was advised in this matter by the great canine authority, Leon Vernier. The breed would appear to be intermediate between the Barbet and the Korthals. The Boulet has the physique, and the head, of the modern Pointer, but it has wooly textured hair, like the Barbet; but the hair is not curly, rather it is almost like silk, smooth and comparable to the Afghan's hair. This coat results from the crossing of the French Pointer and the chestnut-colored Barbet.

Ten years after their beginning, in 1882, Boulet produced two magnificent and famous specimens called Marco and Myra, who were successful in many international competitions; and are the foundation of all of today's Long-coated Griffons. There is something of a resurgence of interest in the breed today; a wonderful specimen was awarded the French Certificate of Aptitude in the 1970 International championships, held in Marseilles.

The Boulet stands between $21\frac{1}{2}''$ and $23\frac{1}{2}''$ (two inches less for bitches), exactly the same size as the Korthals, although its body is not so low slung, and is longer. The rather long neck joins a back which is powerful and straight, with strong and slightly arched loins. The chest is broad. The tail is slightly docked.

The head is powerful and nicely formed, muzzle long and large and well-whiskered. The eye intelligent, with heavy brows. The ears low-set, pendant.

The color is usually dead-leaf, a grayish brown.

Hungarian Vizsla

The Vizsla is a close-coated dog, of unique copper red coloring and there is no better sight than this Hungarian Pointer in good condition.

Mrs. M. Foster's Kinford Zuszie, top winner in the breed in Britain in 1970.

At present this Hungarian Pointer has achieved a great deal of success outside its country of origin, largely owing to its attractive self-colored coat. It is particularly attractive to ladies, both hunting and non-hunting alike. The aim of its breeders was to produce an all-purpose hunting dog in the manner of the breeds which were having such a success in Germany; the Vizsla was produced entirely in Hungary.

Apart from its other attributes the Hungarian breeders wished for a dog with skill at tracking, and this was attempted with a cross of one of the self-colored hounds from Central Europe. This now quite long-established breed, the Hungarian Vizsla, was already fixed in the 18th century, with an elegant, noble and light conformation, with a minimum of loose skin, lip and dewlap, closely resembling the Segucio Italiano. It is believed by some people that the Vizsla came from the Turkish Yellow Dog, but it is more likely that its origin was the old European Pointer, mainly from Württemberg, Swabia and Bavaria.

Despite its bold temperament and love of hunting, careful breeding has made of the Vizsla a dog with good nature, generally easy to train and to work. It loves hunting in marshy country, and it is a good swimmer and a good retriever. It is especially good at tracking, and loves to follow ground game; it would be difficult to find a more skilful hunter of hare and deer. The Vizsla has a lively, elegant and graceful gait.

It is a lean dog, well-muscled, and with good but light bones. The tendons and feet should be strong – the shape being that of a fast galloper, not a trotter, with sloping shoulders and well let-down and angular hocks. The back is short and well-muscled, often slightly arched. The breast bone is visible, the chest long, rather let down, the sides slightly arched. The belly is rather like the Greyhound's.

The tail is set-on low, docked by about a third, generally carried horizontally, and should not be too gay when working. The head is large with little occipital bump, and only a slight stop. The muzzle should not be too pointed, the lips should not be pendant, and the ears are longer and heavier and set-on lower than, for example, those of the Kurzhaar, and without being fleshy. The eyes are brown.

The size is that of a large Pointer and the Vizsla stands around 21″ to 24″ for bitches; 22½″ to 25½″ for dogs. The AKC Standard specifies 22″ to 24″ for dogs and 21″ to 23″ for bitches; weights, dogs 45 to 60 lbs., bitches 40 to 55 lbs. The coat is short and close, dark yellow in color, often giving a reddish reflection. Colored or spotted coats or white feet are bad faults.

Kooikerhondje

The Kooiker dog is a spaniel type which, in the past, was used in duck-decoys in Holland. Its name means "dog belonging to the 'Kooiker'", the man who worked the duck-decoy. After the Second World War the pure breeding of this old national breed was seriously taken in hand.

In the duck-decoys these dogs are used to entice the duck. For that purpose, they are trained to walk in and out of low reed fences placed obliquely along the banks of a dyke, by which behavior they are visible in short glimpses. The duck, being curious, are thereby enticed up the dyke to investigate and, when enough of them have moved up the narrowing dyke, it is closed.

The dog used for this work must therefore be visible from afar, and the Kooiker dog is a clear white with red.

It has a long coat and tail, both well feathered. The shoulder height is about 15″. There are only a few dogs still used in the duck-decoys; they are lively but not excitable, affectionate and intelligent little dogs. For show only, the feet are trimmed slightly.

Munsterlander

While the great black and white Munsterländer is gradually falling out of favor with sportsmen in Germany, the small Munsterländer is thriving. Generally known as the Heidewachtel, it must not be confused with the German Spaniel, the Wachtelhund. Although the Munsterländer would seem to have come from the white and chestnut Breton Spaniel, it has little of the Breton's "softness". It is an aggressive hunter, courageous in thicket and water and will kill small red deer, seize game and return with it still living, and it is a keen and persistent follower of a scent. The ideal size is between 19″ and 20″, but it sometimes reaches 21½″.

The muzzle is longer than that of the Breton and more like that of the French Spaniel but with less depth of the jaw and lips. The tail is long, like the French Spaniel, but carried slightly higher when in action. The hair is longer than the Breton's and although the Standard allows several colors, black is never seen. The most common colors are white and chestnut particolor, and roan. This breed is of considerable interest to the modern sportsman as it combines good hunting ability with retrieving and is small in size. Many believe that it is the only breed among German gundogs which can compete successfully with the popular Kurzhaar and Langhaar in the major shows in Germany.

The smaller Munsterlander.

A typically marked Munsterlander, with standard marking.

Pointer

Mr. F. R. Duke's Sh. Ch. Dalric Fern, a lovely example of a quality, well balanced, black and white Pointer bitch.

history and development

Much of what we know about the Pointer's early history comes from the first recorder of the breed, William Arkwright of Sutton Scarsdale, near Chesterfield in England, whose work during the period 1890–1919 gave us a book on early Pointer history which is the Bible of the breed today.

The Pointer appears to be of Continental origin. Most countries of Europe seem to have contributed, but the first definition and early improvement would appear to have been made by English breeders selecting for added speed on the advent of the sporting gun. The present Standard is basically the same as it was in Arkwright's time. It was formally adopted in 1936 by the newly formed Setter and Pointer Club, and reassessed and confirmed in 1970 by the present Pointer Club.

In the 19th century the breed was increasing in popularity as a working Pointer, used on large estates, on moorland shoots, and when shows came to be a major concern of dog breeders, the Pointer became one of the most prominent of all breeds consistently shown, strengthening the appeal of the breed and bringing to the fore some famous personalities whose Pointers were making breed history. Of the earlier strains which played such a large part in the development of the breed, the most influential were the Lunesdales (Mr. and Mrs. Horner), the Mallwyds (Mr. Steadman) and the Ferndales (Mr. Davies). Such powerful representatives were produced as Ch. Lunesdale Wagg, Ch. Lurgan Loyalty and, outstandingly, Ch. Lune Prince, owned by Mr. T. Moorby, said to be the most outstanding winner of all time, with seven hundred firsts and thirty-three Challenge Certificates. The Pointer Club has a model of Prince as one of its trophies.

In the 1920's the Ardagh prefix (Mr. and Mrs. Whitwell), the Pennines (Mr. Eggleston, and later his sons), and the Stylish Kennel (Mr. Isaac Sharp) produced some outstanding Pointers, many of whose descendants figure in present-day pedigrees.

With the passing of ownership largely into individual hands the kennels are now much smaller. But there is nevertheless much activity in the breed, both for show and for work. Influential names today include Mr. Neville Christie, Mrs. Badenach Nicholson, Lady Jean Fford, Mr. D. McGarry and the late Mr. W. Edmondson, now succeeded in this field by his wife and daughter, Mrs. C. Robertshaw, with their show Pointers.

Immediately before the last war Banchory Spey (first registered as Stylish Spey) was one of the famous field trial Pointers. He was a lemon and white dog, bred by Isaac Sharp in 1938 at his Stylish kennels and owned by Lorna Countess Howe.

color

Various Standard colors are allowed. Liver and' white, black and white, lemon and white. The all-black pointer, or the tricolor, are now rarely seen, except in Scandinavian countries.

care

The Pointer is a large, active dog and it should be exercized where freedom is unrestricted, as these galloping dogs must develop strong, muscular bodies, legs and feet, and free-moving hindquarters. Such exercise must be given two or three times a week. The old saying that a Derby winner is never trained in the stable yard is also the rule for Pointers.

Feeding is not difficult. There are good proprietary foods now available and these, with added meat, cooked or raw, will keep the dog in good condition. Rules regarding quantities cannot be made, some like a lot to eat, and some do not. Good feeding is a matter of carefully observing how much a dog eats, and how he responds to given amounts. Dogs cannot

A brace of Pointers on point. Crookrise Vogue is backing Crookrise Sensation. Both are bench winners, owned by Mrs. Edmondson.

The Pointer head is the hallmark of the breed, and great importance should be attached to it. These three line drawings show the correct head (top) and the other two show deviations which are most often seen.

The Pointer.

The type of Pointer depicted in this drawing is far from perfection, look at the poor neck-line, the straight stifles and the straight pasterns.

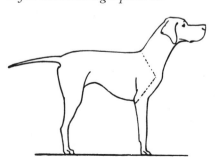

work if over-fat. Dogs having work and regular exercise will eat well, and do well.

Puppies, say from eight to sixteen weeks, should be all feed, sleep and play. Feed them four times a day with three basic milk foods and one meat and cereal and vitamins. At sixteen to twenty weeks the lead can be introduced for walking exercise, with short gallops, increasing as he grows stronger, but here again, careful observation will control development.

character

The Pointer is a very adaptable dog, easy to manage, in the main obedient and eager to please. He is undoubtedly the aristocrat of the gundog breeds, the epitome of canine beauty, whether in the show ring or hard at work on some expanse of moorland.

In field trials he has an instinct for natural performance, and is steady and obedient. He possesses bird sense, searching upwind and locating the quarry quickly and accurately. His pointing attitude, with the body rigid, is marked by his accurate orientation to game when quartering; with his head held high, receiving body scent through the air through quivering nostrils – the Pointer at work is a noble sight, and there can be nothing finer in the entire canine world.

standards

The head is the most important part of the Pointer and should have special attention in any breeding plan. It is the hallmark of the breed. A true Pointer head should have the dished face, well defined stop, raised brow, with bright, kindly but intelligent eye, looking straight ahead, not down the nose. Wide, soft nostrils; ears set-on high, lying close to the head, of medium length and with pointed tips, on a skull of medium width, and in proportion with the strength of foreface; skull and foreface equal in length. By stressing the head, I do not wish to undervalue the other important factors; a body with well sprung ribs, well laid shoulders long and sloping; brisket well let down on level with the elbows; strong, short, muscular loin, slightly arched; and the neck long, slightly arched and with no throatiness. The whole a series of graceful curves, giving a strong, lissom appearance.

Forelegs straight and firm, pasterns long and sloping and very resilient. Behind, he should have a good expanse of thigh, very muscular, as with the under thigh, well bent stifles and short hocks, oval feet, well knit, arched toes, well cushioned beneath.

The tail should be of medium length, thick at the root, set-on high and carried level, not upward; and it should lash from side to side when he is moving.

The coat should be fine and short and with a distinct sheen. Long-haired

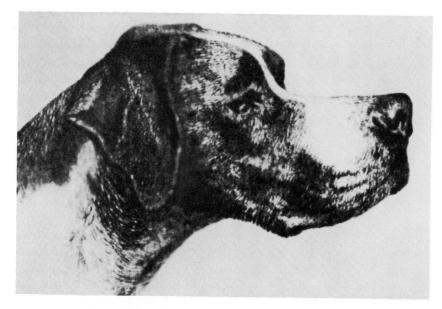

The perfectly formed head of Sh. Ch. Dalric Fern.

A profile of a Pointer dog which embodies all that is good in the ideal Pointer.

coats are undesirable, and are said to throw back to early hound crosses. However, there is no doubt that the "Pointers" having the correct head and all that this implies to the dogs or bitches having them, places them away ahead of any others and brings out other great characteristics in their make-up, which go to make the true champion.

Pointer, Auvergne

The Auvergne Pointer today is a handsome dog, breeding true to type. There have been numerous hypothetical fantasies on the subject of its possible origin, but I believe that the only tenable theory is that it is based on a cross between the Old Pyrenean Braque and the Gascony Pointer.

The original Auvergne Pointers were bred in France, South of Toulouse, and by the end of the 18th century, the type was firmly established. The new breed was particularly well adapted to the mountainous regions of the Massif Central and Cantal. Very quickly the Auvergne spread throughout France, and then to Europe. It is a handsome dog, unexcitable, and not too fast.

Color: White, long-haired coats with black ears, and spattered "blue-black" markings. Tan markings are a disqualification. Another color allowed is "charcoal", a dark color.

Short-haired, longish ears, docked tail – the Auvergne Pointer.

The Auvergne is a large dog, distinguished in appearance. The head is long, held high, with a faint stop; the heavy pendulous lips give a square shape to the muzzle. The eyes have a lovely deep color in the iris. Ears are very elegant and fairly long, springing from the level of the eyes.

The tail should be docked to about 6″ to 8″ in length.

During the past forty years a lighter, more elegant dog has been evolving with less pendulous lips.

Height: 21″ to 25″. Weight: from 53 lbs. to 71 lbs.; the dog should be powerful without being heavy.

Pointer, French

An athletically built French Pointer bitch of good quality. Note the powerful quarters and the docked tail following the line of the hindquarters.

history and development

The catalogue of the championship exhibition in Paris gave my definition of the French Pointer, or Braque Francais – "Undoubtedly the oldest breed of pointer in the world. It has been the origin of nearly all the continental and British short-haired 'setters'. It has kept its qualities as an intelligent, balanced, unruffled, hardy hunting dog, with a powerful nose even in hot and dry weather". This is a highly compressed description of the ancestry of the Braque. The word "Braque" seems most likely to have come from the old French "braquer" – (to aim). The words Braque and Pointer, therefore, have the same derivation, and they have been used for dogs who point themselves, in a rigid stance, in the direction of the game. The word should not be confused with the German "Bracke", which is applied to hounds.

There are two varieties of the French Pointer; the larger, Braque Francais, and the smaller, Braque Francais de Petite Taille. The Braques seem to have originated in the region of the Pyrenees and to have spread over large parts of Continental Europe. These primitive Pointers seem to have been of medium size, energetic, fast and completely different from the hounds which then existed, hunting exclusively by scent. Environment and selective breeding caused diversification of the original stock. Some early breeders crossed them with local hounds, such as the old Bleu de Gascogne, and some were crossed with herding dogs or mastiff breeds. This fanning out of the old European Braques resulted in the Portuguese Pointer, and those of Burgos, Navarre, Bearn, the Garonne valley, Auvergne and Württemberg, the latter being the basis of the modern German Pointer.

This Pointer expresses interest in every line of its body.

The two closely related varieties of the present French Pointer each have separate Standards. The large French Pointer stands about 24″ at the withers and weighs some 60 lbs. The small Braque Francais de Petite Taille (not to be confused with Braque Francais léger) being about 20½" high and weighing 42 lbs. The Braque should not be too heavy, fleshy, or with very loose skin, and ears that are too large; these characteristics probably denote a throwback to the hound infusion.

Many modern sportsmen, living in town, have taken unreservedly to the smaller dogs. They find in them all the qualities of a brilliant game dog, and their smaller size makes them much more convenient for apartment living and smaller automobiles.

The small variety usually shows some divergences from the general conformation of the large. Ears are shorter and set higher; the dewlap is minimal and may be entirely absent; the muzzle proportion shorter and the tan color more widespread, even going as far as an almost self color.

The fine head of the smaller French Pointer.

color

The colors most sought after are white and tan with tan or cinnamon flecking. Equally roans and red speckled are very much in demand. Black is not permitted in the coat but many breeders prefer some traces of flame markings in the muzzle and on the limbs.

care

Apart from regular food and grooming, this breed requires no special attention but, bred as a gundog, needs a reasonable amount of exercise to keep it fit and well.

character

It is a most interesting and intelligent dog, instinctively able and requiring little training. Its working abilities are apparent at a very early age and from its very first outing with the gun. Its poise in movement allows it to work for long periods without tiring and its excellent nose enables it to work under difficult, dry conditions. It is not quarrelsome in the kennel and is very gentle with children.

standards

A dog of noble appearance, powerful but without excessive weight, robust and with strong quarters.

The head should not be too heavy but, nevertheless, be of imposing appearance with the skull almost flat or very slightly rounded. The ears of moderate length are set at the level of the eyes, and not too wide at the set-on. The tail is usually docked and follows the line of the hindquarters. The coat is coarse and thick; somewhat softer on the head and ears.

Pointer, German Long-hair

Can this breed, the Deutsche-Langhaar, or Long-hair, only be considered a simple long-haired variety of the short-haired German Pointer (Deutsche-Kurzhaar) with the same title as the Drahthaar, which is a variety of German Pointer with rough hair?

Almost a century ago, the majority of German sportsmen favored the Gordon Setter, a dog which adapted itself very well to the temperament of its master and the general conditions in Germany. Its energetic character was most pleasing, as was its discreet coloring for forest hunting.

Unfortunately, the Standard of the Gordon Setter requires such precise coloring that it was very difficult for the German huntsman to adapt it to his personal tastes by selective breeding for the desired characteristics, when seen only from the utilitarian point of view. The Gordon Setter undoubtedly plays an important part in the creation of the Langhaar. It has given it, temperamentally, its passionate love of the hunt, its capacity for working in water and its loyalty to its master; and, physically, it has bequeathed its bulk, stature, its beautiful pigmentation, health and staying power.

The coat color of the Langhaar, basically chestnut, was certainly acquired by the crossing of German varieties like the Württemberg Bracke and some varieties of Dutch and French Spaniels.

In its physique, it resembles a large Spaniel, rather elegant, since the Standard condemns all massive types "reminiscent of a bear". It stands 24″ to 25″ at shoulder. The presence of the colors red and black is strictly penalized, the coat most often being one color, a quite light brown or dead leaf. The tail has less hair than the Setters and is perhaps shorter by a few centimeters at the most.

The Langhaar's development seems to have stopped completely. Only occasional survivors are to be seen, victims of the invading tide of the Drahthaar (Rough-hair) and the German Bracke.

An enquiring stance, typical of the German Long-hair.

Pointer, German Rough-hair

The Stichelhaar, or German Rough-haired Pointer, was a great favorite in Germany towards the end of the 19th century, but has been displaced by the great increase in favor of the Wire-hair, the Drahthaar. The Stichelhaar has now largely disappeared. It is basically a breed deriving from the old stock of the Barbes-Sales from Hesse. The Stichelhaar was known and used in the 16th century but it was not until around 1865 that a Frankfurt cattle breeder, named Bontant, brought it into prominence by introducing a cross of Continental Pointers, especially the Württemberg variety. The body structure of the Stichelhaar then become more or less like that of the Korthals, but shorter, the skull less shapely and the undercoat less abundant.

These Pointers were excellent hunting dogs, very obedient and biddable; less obstinate than today's Drahthaars.

The head is long, softly shaped, with brown, almond-shaped eyes and with ears set-on lower and less flat than those of the Drahthaar, and they should not be folded.

The chest is not large, low-slung, the sides nicely rounded. The tail is docked to leave two thirds of its original length.

The coat hair is coarse, about $1\frac{1}{2}''$ long and, although there is an undercoat, it is not very noticeable. The whiskers are definite and the hair is short on the top of the head.

The colors are not definite, rather they are a grayish-brown – a white base mixed with chestnut, with an occasional speck of clear chestnut. Too much white is not approved, and neither is black nor traces of flame color.

Pointer, German Short-hair

A self-colored German Pointer.

(opposite)
Mrs. C. Bede Maxwell with American champion, Ch. Able von Eltz, on exhibition at the Del Monte Kennel Club, Pebble Beach, California in 1960. Already a field trial champion, he was on his way to becoming a dual champion.

history and development

The Deutscher Kurzhaarigen Vorstehhund, or Kurzhaar, is a breed which has taken a position of considerable and growing importance in Germany and, since 1946, interest in the breed has intensified abroad. The old German Pointer was the result of crossing the Spanish Pointer with the Bloodhound to produce a dog which would not only point but would also trail by scent. At the end of the 18th century, these old German Pointers were well-established in Baden Württemberg and in the surrounding area of the Black Forest, and these were the ancestors of the Württemberg Pointer. Their tricolor coats with "flame" markings, suggested the infusion of Bleu de Gascogne blood introduced by sportsmen from the Black Forest area who, from their travels in Gascony, brought back some of the largest and best-built French Braques. The Württemberg Pointer was held in high esteem for its calm nature and its ability to track wounded game. It did not require great speed as game was abundant and not easily startled.

Since the end of the First World War, there has been a persistent effort to evolve, from this Pointer of South-west Germany, an ultra-modern gun dog to compete successfully with foreign competition from the point of view of efficiency, speed and temperament. By concentrating on the useful qualities desired, the new generation of sportsmen-breeders achieved magnificent results. To breed specimens which had the speed necessary for success in field trials, the breed has been continually infused with the blood of English Pointers and other dogs chosen for their speed from Scandinavia.

In addition to speed in open country, other, almost opposite, characteristics were demanded. Retrieving under the most difficult conditions such as from deep water, tracking with precision over long periods, giving voice when on a blood trail, sufficiently good jaws to kill a fox and the strength to bring it back over obstacles, and to raise game and to stay when this is

The beautiful head of a champion German Short-hair, Sh. Ch. Patrick of Malahide, best of breed at Cruft's in 1968.

The Pointer breeds generally are instinctively alert to any manifestation of wild life. This dog adopts the pose common to all Pointers when their suspicions are aroused.

achieved. Physically, evolution has been rapid and successful. Heaviness in body, ears and excess skin have been eliminated. The articulating joints have been transformed to allow a rapid galloping movement permitted by the very sloping shoulders and sharply angled stifles.

The eyes are dark, thanks to the pigmentation of the English stud, but what mysterious sire gave them their rather harsh expression? Do they have, as many have said, an ancestor in common with the Dobermann? The German Club (Deutsche-Kurzhaar Verband) has persisted in the search for the best working dog; show championships can only be awarded in the trials class. An example of the Club's scorn for "color-mania" is its recent decision to allow the previously forbidden black coat.

color

White and tan or white with black; some traces of "flame" markings are allowed, especially on the muzzle. The self-tan is fashionable, but the mixed and dark coats are sought after by the real rural sportsmen. The English and American Standards call for solid liver, liver and white spotted, liver and white spotted and ticked, and liver roan. Any other colors than liver and white (gray white) are not permitted by the American Standard but the English Standard permits black and white.

care

Good feeding, plenty of exercise and moderate grooming are all that this hardy breed requires to keep them fit and well.

standards

A noble, steady dog showing power, endurance and speed, giving the immediate impression of an alert and energetic (not nervous) dog, whose movements are well co-ordinated. Neither unduly small nor conspicuously large, but of medium size and, like the hunter, "with a short back stands over plenty of ground".

Grace of outline, clean outlines of head, sloping, long shoulders, deep chest, short back and powerful hindquarters, good bone composition, adequate muscle, well-carried tail and taut coat giving a thoroughbred appearance. The skin should not fit loosely or fold. The coat is short, flat and hard to the touch, slightly longer under the tail. The tail is set-on high and docked to medium length. When the dog is quiet, the tail should be carried down and, when moving, horizontally. It is never held high over the back or bent, but is violently waved when on the search. The head should be clean-cut, the skull reasonably broad, without a definite stop as in the English Pointer, but when viewed from the side there is a well-defined stop effect due to the position of the eye-brows. The ears are broad and set high, hanging close to the head, with no pronounced fold. The eyes should be medium-sized, soft and intelligent, and varying in shades of brown to tone with the coat. Light yellow, China or "bird of prey" eyes are not desirable.

A dog well-balanced in all points is preferable to one with some outstanding qualities and some defects. A smooth, light gait is most desirable. Height for a dog 23″ to 25″ and 21″ to 23″ for a bitch.

A well-known winning British bitch at the end of the sixties – Ch. Inchmarlo Cora, owned by Mr. I. E. T. Sladden.

Pointer, German Wire-hair

This rough-coated variety of the German Pointer is a fairly new breed, created early this century. One might say that the Drahthaar was "made to order"; German hunters in general prefer a dog with a lot of spirit and aggressiveness, and their breeders set out to supply just such a dog.

The Old German dogs had already been refined and improved with many outcrosses to the English Pointer, particularly those of solid tan color. This lighter, more elegant dog was then crossed with the Pudel Pointer for its temperament, intelligence, love of water, and the rough texture of its coat. Then the Airedale came into the picture, increasing the wiry character of the hair, shortening the ears, and reinforcing the belligerent character so admired by gamekeepers. This particular cross left its mark also in the shape of the eye and feet.

A strong-looking Drahthaar.

The results were extraordinary; the Wire-haired outdistanced the other Rough and Long-haired dogs in the field, being equalled only by the Smooth-haired Pointer. Indeed, it is generally acknowledged to be superior in the forest, in water, and hunting bigger game, especially when the quarry is dangerous or aggressive. On the other hand, its "nose" is admittedly less powerful.

I must repeat here the excellent advice offered by one of our great dog-lovers, Alban de Lamothe: "The breeding of the Wire-haired Pointer, and its enormous success in the field, should be a lesson to those who regard the secondary and conventional characteristics as immutable dogma. They are in danger of forgetting that our hunting dogs belong to working breeds, not the category of domestic pets".

Although not too long established in America it stands about 73rd among all breeds, and registers some 400 a year.

The breed has a wide range of coat color. The shades are similar to those found on the English Pointer, with this one practical exception; white fronts are not highly regarded by the German hunters, as they prefer that their dogs are not easily glimpsed from afar, by game or poachers.

A well-marked male.

The temperament of the Drahthaar has been as carefully considered as its physical attributes; the rough, wiry coat matches its character. Punishment inflicted by an over-eager trainer is endured more equably, and it will lie quietly for hours at the foot of a deerhide, or follow silently at heel during a big-game chase. Often at the disposition of game-keepers, it makes a good patrol dog, killing the wild-cats which prey on the game. The Standards make it quite clear that practical application in the hunting field has been the main consideration.

The head is very similar to the German Braque; the muzzle must be extremely powerful – long, wide and strong. The eye, small and lively; the ears, short and carried jauntily forward; the nose, slightly convex (Roman). The hocks are let down, well bent, with cat feet. The tail must be docked to about a third of its natural length; short enough so that it is less likely to be injured in the forest, or make noise which will flush the game; long enough to allow the animal to express its feelings, and protect its genitals if necessary. A male should stand 24″ to 26″ at the withers, a bitch less, but not less than 22″.

Pointer, Old Danish

The Old Danish Pointer; note the deep head and comparatively short muzzle.

The Old Danish Pointer (Gamal Dansk Honsehund) is a breed which originally came to Denmark from Spain some 300 years ago. Thanks to the exhaustive researches of Mr. Johannes Matzen it was shown in Sweden, Germany and France, and has since been recognized by the Danish Kennel Club in 1962. Slightly heavier than most pointers it is particularly suitable for hunting in the Danish countryside.

A rectangular shaped, solid looking dog, substantially built, its head is deep and fairly short with a wide skull showing a pronounced occiput. There is no definite stop and the nose has large nostrils which indicate its keen scenting powers. The nose varies in color from light to dark liver. The lips are not overhung and the teeth meet in a scissor bite. The medium-sized eyes, which may show a little haw, are from light to dark brown in color. Long, wide ears, with the tips slightly rounded, are set-on fairly low and carried with the inner sides close to the cheek. A strong neck on which loose skin is favored, particularly on dogs, and a strong body with a muscular back and a deep, wide chest. The tail, which is of medium length, is thick at the root and tapers to a point, set fairly high and carried almost horizontally when still and slightly more raised when moving. It has muscular shoulders and strong pasterns and the hindquarters have wide thighs, well muscled; and well bent stifles. It moves with a free, easy motion. The short, dense, smooth coat is straight and has a decided sheen. Color: White, with light to dark brown markings.

Height of a dog is about 22″ and a bitch, about 1½″ smaller.

Pointer, Poodle

A highly intelligent breed from Germany, descended from the Pointer and the old European Hunting Poodle.

It would be much too naive to imagine that a Poodle Pointer could be produced by crossing an English Pointer with a Poodle. The breed which, although most attractive, has become very rare, was founded by crossing the Barbet Pointer, a very old wooly-haired breed, with some short-haired gundogs: Württemberg Braques, French Braques and, in particular, Pointer. These last two breeds passed on the typical skull shape, especially the pronounced stop, which distinguishes them from other Pointers. Gradually the Pudelpointer has been improved with infusions of English Pointer blood.

Unfortunately this interesting breed has not developed as expected and has become gradually merged with the Drahthaar. It is not uncommon to see excellent examples, having an almost perfect Poodle Pointer appearance, being presented with a Drahthaar pedigree. The rare Poodle Pointers that one still comes across in exhibitions have the appearance of a large and very elegant dog (over 24″ to the withers, weight about 58 lbs.). They appear generally in a dead-leaf-colored self coat with quite wiry hair – but not too thick, though the Standard requires very harsh, thick hair.

The Standard insists equally on a dished muzzle like the old Pointer, but it is difficult to find sires with this characteristic, without having the undesirable very short forehead.

The gradual disappearance of this appealing breed is sad, for it offers advantages which the Drahthaar does not generally have; more docility and suppleness, often a better nose, and it is adaptable to all uses.

Pointer, St. Germain

The breed arose early in the 19th century from a cross between a white and orange hound bitch, named Miss, brought to France by the Count of Giradin, and a French Pointer called Zamor, owned by the Count of Aigle. Miss was of a type between the Porcelaine hound and the modern English Pointer, and Zamor had the reputation of a superb hunter, with the capability of bequeathing this instinct to his offspring. The result of this cross was excellent in every respect.

Since the pedigree was already known the type quickly became established. The original cross had taken place in the Forest of Compiègne and the subsequent breeding was conducted by the foresters who, around 1850, took several of these dogs with them to St. Germain en Laye, from which place the breed took its present name. Further French Pointer crosses were introduced, and, later the modern English Pointer. A comparison with the Pointer shows that the St. Germain has a less sporty look, is slower, and the general outline of body and head is not so clean cut. The texture of its coat is less smooth, the hair not so thick, and the tail less bushy at the root, and lower set. There are other differences. The St. Germain is a strong dog, well adapted to the hunting conditions of the plains, and for larger game.

Dogs stand between 22″ and 24″; bitches 21″ to 23″.

Colors: white with orange spots or patches; some ticking of orange is allowed, but the bolder marking is preferred.

This light-colored dog is easy to see in close undergrowth and in open country, an advantage in certain sporting conditions.

Pointer, Spanish

The Perdiguero de Burgos is one of the oldest of Spanish gundogs, strong, easily trained, with a keen nose. It is an excellent retriever, working in all kinds of country and with all kinds of small game. The breed has remained pure, far more so than other Spanish breeds, and is possibly the most popular with sportsmen.

This is a large breed, $25\frac{1}{2}$″ to $29\frac{1}{2}$″ in height, with a long, straight back, and loin, and a tail thick at the set-on and docked by one third of its length. The head is large with an arched skull, slight stop, large, long ears set-on high, folded, and with pointed tips.

The quarters are muscular, with prominent joints, speed being sacrificed for strength.

The coat is smooth and short. Two colors only are allowed – white with patches and/or flecks of liver, and liver speckled with white.

Portuguese Perdigeiro

Note the large head of this Pointer, and the pronounced stop; this specimen also shows the length of tail left after docking.

In Portugal, this breed is most popular as a gundog, but is also found in cities where it flourishes as a pet. It is a reliable Pointer, very active and with considerable stamina.

It derives its name from "perdiz", cartridge, and was early on used with the gun. Although related to, and possibly a descendant of, the Spanish Navarro and Burgos Pointers, it is lighter and more agile in movement than they are and, in action, more closely resembles the Hungarian Vizsla. The rather broad head is flat across the skull and has a pronounced stop, the muzzle being moderately short and blunt. The oval eyes are large and colored dark hazel or brown. It has thin ears, medium-sized, very wide where they join the head; folded downwards and hanging close to the side of the head.

The rather long neck is powerful and thick, while the body gives an overall appearance of power and agility, with its muscular loins and deep chest.

Legs are well-boned and the sinews, which are visible under the skin, are strong. The tail is set-on in line with the back, docked by about one-third and carried horizontally.

The short, wiry coat is yellowish brown in color with darker (usually reddish tan) head, ears and mask.

Height at shoulder is 24″ to 25″.

Portuguese Water Dog

A dog in typical show trim.

The Portuguese Water Dog, or Cao d'Agua, has been bred for retrieving fish, nets and other tackle from the sea for the fishing vessels on which it is carried, virtually as part of the crew. Used also as guard and as a means of communication between boats and sometimes for sea rescue work, it is an exceptionally fine swimmer with very great powers of endurance. Once very common in all the fishing ports of the Iberian Peninsula, it is now found chiefly in the Algarve region.

There are two varieties of the breed; one Long-coated and the other with a shorter, curly coat: there is no under-coat. The photograph illustrates a typical Long-coat trim. Since both varieties differ only in the coat, there is only one Standard for the breed.

The head, although appearing disproportionately large due to its topknot, is nevertheless fairly large with prominent occiput, and a distinct stop. The dark brown or black eyes are round and medium-sized. Ears, triangular in shape, are set fairly high and carried folded close to the head. The tapering muzzle is without snipeyness and the jaws are powerful. A short, well-muscled neck, short level back, broad deep chest and strong, straight legs, all indicate an exceedingly active dog. Its interdigital webs assist it in swimming and its tail is set in line with the back, and curls over; and is of full natural length.

Colors are black, black and white, deep brown, deep brown and white, dark gray, light gray and all white.

Height for a dog is 20″ to 22½″.

Retriever, Chesapeake Bay

A Chesapeake in action, retrieving a shot bird from water. The coat on the back retains its curl, despite the recent immersion.

Sharland Clipper, one of the comparatively few British specimens.

history and development

Unlike so many of the world's breeds, the origin of the Chesapeake Bay Retriever has been pinpointed to the year 1807 when an English brig was shipwrecked off the coast of Maryland. An American vessel, the *Canton*, rescued the crew and two puppies; one a male already named Sailor and a young bitch that was forthwith renamed Canton in honor of the rescuing ship. Both pups were presented to the families that gave shelter to the English sailors. The male was a dingy red and the bitch black. They were of the Newfoundland breed. Both puppies were trained as duck retrievers, and both were eventually bred to the various breeds then in use for that work in the Chesapeake Bay area.

There is no record that Sailor ever sired a litter out of Canton. It has been suggested that the Curly-coated and the Flat-coated Retrievers were early used as crosses but, although color could come from either breed, coat texture could result only from the use of the Curly-coated.

From the beginning, the Chesapeake dog was developed as a working breed and even today only a handful of its breeders take an interest in dog shows.

With the obvious attributes of the Chesapeake, it seems puzzling why it is only third in A.K.C. registrations of retrievers, but his loyal supporters explain that they do not want to make him just a pet-owner's breed, as the others are becoming; that they do not mind his oily coat which strictly pet-owners sometimes term offensively smelly; and, additionally, his aficionados say that he has been over-shadowed in the Retriever Trials because the tests are too simple at these formal events to give a true index to his abilities.

Notable advocates of the Chesapeake are August Belmont, a grandson and namesake of the famous sportsman who was president of the American Kennel Club longer than any other (27 years).

The current August Belmont, delegate of the American Chesapeake Club, presently a Director of the A.K.C., trains and handles this breed in trials. Also Mrs. Daniel Horn of Maryland who has trained many of her Chesapeakes and handled them to their show championships as well as obedience degrees.

For some years the writer attended many trials of the American Chesapeake Club in the mid-thirties when its then young president, Anthony A. Bliss, was bending every effort to bring the breed into greater prominence. I wrote detailed reports on the performance of every dog in competition. It was hard not to note how well the breed marked the fall of a duck. However, if any competitor failed to locate the bird, a judge would turn to Harry T. Conklin and ask him to send "the Skipper" out. The Skipper was Field Champion Skipper Bob. He would always come back with the "lost" duck. It is of note that the breed's first registration was that of a dog named Sunday, owned by G. W. Kierstead of Laporte, Indiana. It was whelped in October 1875.

color

Color may range from a dark brown to a faded tan or, deadgrass. The idea of course is to breed dogs that blend with surroundings when they are working. The deadgrass coat came from the Mid-West, to which the breed had spread shortly after the Civil War.

care

This rugged breed needs little or no special care, just an ample supply of food and clean dry quarters.

character

Some claim the breed to be rather hard to train due to its hard-headedness and propensity to fighting; others would deny this. An overall explanation is that the aggressiveness of the Chesapeake is what makes it a really great retriever.

The Chesapeake Bay Retriever's tight wavy outer coat plus his dense soft undercoat and very active oil glands enable him to withstand any degree of cold. He loves the water and at trials when given the word to go he races forward and plunges far out. Sometimes before he can start swimming he has to break through the shoreline ice. With his weight of sometimes up to 80 lbs., this is no great problem.

Four generations of Chesapeake Bay Retrievers; beautiful specimens from America.

standards

The A.K.C. Standard specifies 65 to 75 lbs. for males and 55 to 65 lbs. for females. The heights are 23″ to 26″ for males, and 21″ to 24″ for females.

Retriever, Curly-coated

Ch. Banworth Orenda, owned by Mrs. C. Easton, was one of the only three full champions alive in 1970. A lovely, typical Curly whose balance and good construction are obvious in this picture.

history and development

The one genetically distinctive characteristic in this breed is its curly coat; whatever sorts of dogs were crossed with whatever sorts of bitches, the curly coat is the main clue from which the investigator could work. A strong case can obviously be made out for the water dog or water spaniel, which have been recognized canine variations for several centuries; as far back at least as the 17th century, writers were praising the sagacity, fondness for water, the retrieving power and quality of endurance of this kind of dog. It is not easy to determine what other breeds occurred in its development but it is possible to discern the Old English and the Irish Water Spaniels, the Poodle, one or more breeds of Setter, and the small Newfoundland. It would seem that the balance of evidence shows that these breeds, crossed from time to time with the unidentified and now unknown water dog, produced the Curly-coated Retriever we know today.

Curly-coated Retriever.

The Curly was probably the first breed to be used seriously as a retriever in England; a dog approximating to it in size and coat can be seen in sporting prints of the late 18th and 19th centuries. The Curly-coat first appeared in shows in England in 1860, and separate classes were given to it at the Islington International Show in London, and at Birmingham in 1864. As other retriever breeds began to expand around 1914 the Curly-coats waned in popularity. Numbers have fluctuated since then, and as late as 1969 only ninety-three dogs were registered at the Kennel Club in London.

In Australia the record of breeding goes back to 1930 when Curlies were bred from dogs taken out early in the century by immigrants and settlers. In the past twenty years only six Curlies have been imported into Australia, but they are now becoming more popular, and up to seventeen of them have been exhibited at one time at the Melbourne Royal Show, the vast majority being bred in the country. Curlies have been imported from Britain to Germany, Holland, Canada, America, Australia, India and the Scandinavian countries.

color

There are only two recognized colors, black and liver, both self colors. There were one or two distinct yellow or golden colored animals bred many years ago but these were never popular. Blacks are numerically stronger than livers, although the latter were considered useful in Norfolk, England, on account of the color being less conspicuous than the usual black, and thus more useful in the field.

As well as being different in body color, the livers are also a little lighter in eye and nose than the blacks.

care

As with all largish dogs the Curly needs a fair amount of exercise to keep him in good, hard condition, and for show purposes needs a certain amount of road work.

The coat needs to be regularly dampened with water and massaged with the flat, bare hand in a circular movement – this helps to keep the coat

Ch. Darelyn Dellah, owned by Mr. and Mrs. F. Till, won the C.C. and best of breed at her first show in 1959 and in 1966, at eight and a half years of age, she ended her career by winning best of breed and best bitch in show at the United Retriever Club show in England. After the age of two she was unbeaten in the breed with nineteen C.C.s and twenty-three best of breed awards.

228

Ch. Pamika Gypsy Moth, owned by Miss V. Richardson, was Curly of the year in Australia in 1968 and 1969. She has numerous group and best in show wins.

Sh. Ch. Banworth Sunflower of Siccawei, owned by Mrs. C. Halford, holds the breed record with twenty-eight C.C.s. She was best of breed at Cruft's, London, in 1966, 1968, 1969 and 1970.

clean and tight. On no account should a brush and comb be used; the coat is trimmed lightly, removing the too prominent curls on body and head, and trimming a little closer on the tail, which is lightly done so as to show the shape, and the taper from root to tip. The ears should be trimmed around the edges, and the legs should be tidy.

character

The Curly's usefulness as a sporting dog comes from a combination of pace, endurance, intelligence and a good nose. With his size and strength he is able to retrieve almost anything shot for him. He has an excellent nose, especially on runners, and he retrieves quickly to hand. One of his outstanding characteristics is his ability to mark down and memorize the fall of the bird; this is especially useful when shooting over rough marshes offering no direct line of approach to the shot bird. Different country conditions provide different uses for the Curly, and he adapts readily to most of them. For example, in Australia he is occasionally used to track down kangaroos.

One of the reasons advanced for the decline in his use in the field was his reputation for being hard-mouthed, and it is remarkable how faults displayed by one or two individuals are speedily attributed to the breed as a whole. Nowadays there is no sign of this tendency to be hard-mouthed, if it ever existed. Curlies make excellent guard dogs. They do not bark unnecessarily but they let you know immediately if anything is wrong.

standards

The English Standard is adopted in both America and Australia, and the first registrations in the American stud book appeared in 1924. The Curly is the tallest of the retriever breeds, standing 25″ to 27″ to shoulder, and weighing 70 lbs. to 80 lbs. He differs from the Golden and the Labrador in that his head is long and wedge-shaped. He has strong jaws, free from lippiness and throatiness. His main feature is the coat, which must be a mass of close, crisp curls from the occiput bone to the tip of his tail, and the tail must be carried straight, any gaiety in this respect is undesirable.

Retriever, Flat-coated

Ch. Fenrivers Golden Rod, a dog who impressed not only in his breed but also in variety competition. A beautifully balanced and well put together dog he was particularly sound, with good coat and always full of vitality, as this picture shows. He is also a worker! Owned by Mr. Read Flowers.

The Flat-coated Retriever, front head view.

history and development

During the 19th century, with the improvement of firearms and ammunition, and the more widespread adoption of the art of "shooting flying", sportsmen began to discover the need of a specialist dog to retrieve their bag and especially to find wounded birds, instead of, as hitherto, leaving the work to their Setters and Pointers.

The basic ingredients for this new type of gundog seem to have been the Lesser Newfoundland or Labrador (a great water dog which was imported in some numbers by the cod fishermen and sailors on the timber boats), the larger Spaniels and the Setters and Pointers.

By crossing and selection, improved retrieving performance was obtained. One variety, then known as the Wavy-coated Retriever, became very popular, and with its Curly cousin was widely used both by gamekeepers and sporting men. These Wavy-coats were the progenitors of the modern Flat-coat.

It is likely that Collie blood was introduced around the 1890's to produce the flatter coats which were becoming fashionable. The efforts of Mr. Shirley, of Ettington Park, Warwickshire, and other shooting men developed the Flat-coat into a breed of such known excellence that it was quite the most popular variety of Retriever in Britain from around 1890 up to the First World War. When breeding resumed after the war, the position had altered. Labradors and Goldens had become recognized varieties and their popularity grew as that of the Flat-coat waned, until the mid-1950's, since when the position is much improved. Today the breed, although not numerous, is gaining in numbers and supporters annually.

color

The Standard colors are black and liver. The most popular has always been black, and a good dog of this color, in full coat, is a fine sight. Livers appear from time to time in litters of black ancestry, also some kennels specialize in this color, which may be preferred for some specialist duties such as wildfowling. A liver dog is more easily hidden than a black by day or night upon an open marsh. The writer recently saw a magnificent golden Flat-coat, bred from "pure" black parents.

care

The Flat-coat must indeed be one of the hardiest of British breeds, having for years largely been bred and kept by gamekeepers, whose demands upon their dogs are often more exacting than many realize. Like a shepherd's, a keeper's dog is a tool of his trade, and must if, necessary be able to work hard day after day.

The puppies are easy to rear and do well on an ordinary sensible diet. Exercise should be liberal according to their age, if the youngsters are to develop their full potential. Like many gundogs, adults must not be allowed to become overfat, which they do easily.

Another prolific winner on both show bench and field was Mrs. Hutton's Ch. Pewcroft Prop of Yarlaw. Bred in 1957 by Mrs. K. O'Neill, she was owned by Air-Commodore W. H. Hutton, and won her first C.C. in 1958, and her ninth in 1963.

A group of Flat-coats owned by Mrs. Kearsley in 1951. From left to right: Black Lion Rex of Ibaden, Ch. Flash of Ibaden and Ch. Lili Marlene.

One of the Flat-coats' most distinctive features is its head. Claverdon Rhapsody, owned and bred by Dr. Nancy Laughton, portrays the correct type.

A bitch who also scored in variety competition was Mrs. P. J. Robertson's Sh. Ch. Stolford Wychmere Blackseal, who won the group at the Scottish Kennel Club championship show in 1969.

A keen wildfowler myself, I often have my dogs out in frost and in ice-cold water. After such a jaunt, immediately upon reaching home I give them a good drink of warm, milky, well-sweetened tea, which they love, and which I believe helps them to get warm and dry quickly.

When working on heavy soils the dog's feet should be looked at to ensure that balls of soil have not collected between the toes. If these are allowed to remain and harden, lameness will follow. For showing the dog should be in good condition, regularly groomed with a little tidying of the coat around the ears, feet and tail.

character

A typical present-day Flat-coat is, when properly educated, at home in any capacity. Though large, he is easily disciplined to be a quiet and sensible housedog and is good with children, and a delightful companion. He will be found to enjoy the atmosphere of a show, and his reaction to encouragement usually makes it possible to persuade him to look his best. His greatest joy, however, is to accompany his owner as servant to the gun and at this, his natural duty, he is hard to beat. Though of course, like all gundogs, he must be taught discipline and obedience, it is seldom necessary to teach him much about his work; retrieving comes naturally. He will face the densest covert and coldest water in quest of his game with delight, and his good coat sees that he seldom comes to any harm thereby. If required, he can easily be taught to hunt unshot game, and to point, although I believe that this aspect of his training is best left until he is thoroughly experienced and steady at his proper duty, retrieving.

standards

This is a blueprint for a working animal, which was the intention when the present Standard was written in 1923.

"Power without lumber, and raciness without weediness" aptly describes a typical Flat-coat when fully fit. There must be no exaggeration of any kind; soundness, activity and balance are all-important.

The Flat-coat's head and coat are the breed's two most distinctive and attractive features. The coat should be as straight as possible, dense and not too soft and thick on the underparts of the body, which are particularly vulnerable in low covert. When in full coat, the limbs and tail should be well feathered.

The head also should be well-filled-in between, in front of, and below the eyes, thus giving a very gradual taper all round from the skull, which should be only moderately broad, to the muzzle. The eyebrows, if somewhat raised and mobile, give life to the expression, which must always be kindly.

Retriever, Golden

history and development

The origin of the Golden Retriever as a breed goes back to the middle of the 19th century, when there were long-coated Retrievers known as Flat- or Wavy-coated Retrievers. These were mostly black, but occasionally "sports" of liver, brown or yellow cropped up from black parents.

At the same time, there were various types of water-dogs or water-spaniels. One type of water-spaniel was bred and used off the coast of the Border Country of England and Scotland and known as the Tweed water-spaniel, and in this type light liver color or yellow was the most common, and it carried a very closely curled coat, and was "retrieverish" in type.

I give an outline of these early yellow flat – or wavy – coated retrievers and Tweed water-spaniels as it is from the union of one of each of these two breeds that the Golden Retriever as we know it today was evolved. One was the yellow retriever Nous (whelped June 1864) and purchased by the first Lord Tweedmouth in 1868 and recorded in his stud book as bred by Lord Chichester. The other was the Tweed water-spaniel Belle entered as of Ladykirk breeding and born in 1863.

Lord Tweedmouth's stud book (1868–1890) is now preserved in the Kennel Club Library in London and shows his extensive line-breeding to this original mating, with the judicious introduction in the early years of other black retrievers, another Tweed water-spaniel (Tweed), a red setter and a sandy-colored Bloodhound. From some of the early pictures taken at Guisachan (Lord Tweedmouth's Scottish home) it is seen how little the breed has changed in a century, and how true to type they bred even then. The origin of the breed was in doubt until 1952, when the first Lord

Golden Retriever owners have not forgotten the working side. Here is a Golden retrieving teal from the water.

233

A side head view of Ch. Boltby Skylon, an important sire in the North of England.

Golden Retriever – front head view.

Tweedmouth's great-nephew, the sixth Lord Ilchester, brought his uncle's records to light. Together with Mrs. Elma Stonex (who spent many years researching into the subject) in 1960 he produced all the evidence necessary to get this officially recognized by the British Kennel Club as the true origin of the breed throughout the world. Here I quote Mrs. Stonex, from whom so much of our knowledge stems, "the first Lord Tweedmouth thoughtfully planned matings on a foundation of yellow retriever of unknown antecedents (Nous) and two Tweed water-spaniels (Belle and Tweed). The roots of the breed lie in Scotland and the Border Country."

It was not until 1913 that Goldens were given a separate register by the Kennel Club, and became known as Retrievers (Golden or Yellow). Until then they were called Flat- or Wavy-coated Retrievers, only identifiable by their color. In 1920 the Yellow was dropped and they became Retrievers (Golden). One of the early enthusiasts of the breed was Mrs. W. M. Charlesworth, who founded the Golden Retriever Club in Britain, which drew up the Standard of Points, and this, with very few exceptions, is the same today. This lady produced the first Champion in the breed, Ch. Noranby Campfire, and was still exhibiting and running her Goldens in field trials after the Second World War. She was a great advocate of keeping the breed's working instincts to the fore, and did much to popularise the breed in field trials, and with the ordinary shooting man. Her outspoken attitude on the matter of "show bench loungers" may not have won her popularity with the primarily show-minded, but it must have intimidated many into gun-training their Goldens, and thus helping to preserve their reputation as first-class gun dogs.

A mere handful of Goldens were shown before the First World War, but, during the 1920's and 1930's, their good looks and sagacity helped to win them popularity in various parts of the world, so that the restriction on breeding brought about by the Second World War did not mean that the breed's characteristics were lost, and there was a nucleus of good stock left with which to continue in the 1940's.

Since then the breed's popularity has continued to rise. Show-wise, the entries are extremely high and keep on rising, until they are within the four highest of all breeds at most Championship shows in England – the

Mrs. Tudor's Ch. Camrose Lucius, winner of eleven Challenge Certificates. Note the kind expression, and the permissible wavy coat.

average number of entries being about 200. Indeed at some shows, such as the annual Golden Retriever Club's Championship, entries are well over 400. During 1950 there were nearly 2,500 Goldens registered with the British Kennel Club; now, twenty years later, the numbers registered each year are still rising, and there were nearly 3,500 registered during 1969, and in the U.S.A. there were 9,535.

All over the world Goldens are on the increase, and though type varies in some countries, all were evolved from the same original stock.

Puppies – Golden Retriever.

color

The original Golden Retriever Club Standard did not include the color cream. However, it was found that some outstanding dogs, both on the show bench and in the field, were being excluded, so in England in 1936, the Standard was amended to include cream-colored dogs, and the wording is still the same today, i.e. "Any shade of gold or cream, but neither red nor mahogany".

From this it will be seen what a wide range of shades are permissible – any shade of gold or any shade of cream covers a variety of beautiful colors and it really is delightful at shows to see a ringful of dogs with all these variations of color. One sometimes sees a show critique which says "Correct color". This is very confusing to the novice owner, who then turns up the Standard and is left in a state of doubt, for there is no one correct color – variations can be from the palest of creams to the darkest shade of gold, but not as dark as setter red (mahogany). In the U.S.A. and Canada, however, cream is still excluded from the Standard.

Usually the feathering on the tail, stomach and hindquarters is of a lighter shade than the rest of the coat.

Puppies' coats can be shades lighter than their adult coats, and a fairly safe guide to the final color of a puppy is that of its ears, for the coat usually finishes up somewhat similar to the ear coloring. So it is possible that a cream-coloured puppy can finish up quite a dark golden adult.

care

Goldens are usually very healthy dogs and, if well-cared for, have few

Record holder with the most Challenge Certificates in the breed in England, Ch. Alresford Advertiser, owned by Mrs. L. Pilkington. Note the proud head carriage and true Golden expression.

235

A lovely example of a cream, Camrose Cabus Christopher, at nine months old he qualified for the Junior Warrant twice over.

Compare this puppy with Cabus Christopher. He will never be a show prospect, with his big ears, bad topline, low tail set and weak pasterns.

ailments. They need a good nourishing, balanced diet of protein and carbohydrates. The average amounts for an adult dog kept as a family companion should be about 1 lb. meat (tinned or fresh) and $\frac{1}{2}$ lb. biscuit a day. If the dog is being regularly worked then the quantities should be increased. Where several dogs are kept they will probably be kennelled. Goldens are friendly dogs and I think it cruel to keep one Golden kennelled alone – he needs a companion. The space required for the sleeping kennel of two Goldens is at least 4 feet × 6 feet. If kept indoors then the dog needs a warm bed (about 3 feet × 2 feet), which should be out of all draughts.

A Golden should have at least one hour's exercise a day, some of which should be on the leash on hard roads, and the rest free running on grass. Other than these requirements he asks little more of his owner than his companionship and affection.

character

As his name implies, the Golden Retriever was evolved to retrieve game for his master while out shooting, and his popularity for this sport is ever increasing, as the accounts of his exploits in the shooting field are related and observed. He is a highly intelligent dog, easy to train, with a will to please, great courage in facing the thickest of cover, and with much perseverance and drive. He has an excellent nose to scent out lost game, and has a soft mouth. He also loves water, so in addition to being a great asset to the organized shoot, he is an excellent wild-fowler's dog. Mostly used as a "non-slip" retriever, he can easily be trained to be an all-purpose gun-dog, and used with the beaters in the locating, and putting up, of game for the guns.

So well-instilled is his retrieving instinct that one very seldom finds one who does not at some time or other produce a "present" for his owner. Indoors he will greet one with a "toy", his greatest joy of all being to carry a shoe or slipper around. Handbags, purses, cushions, shoes, gloves – all these are greatly prized objects to be presented to the returning owner, and, so soft is his mouth, that none will show any mark of his carrying.

236

A beautiful, feminine Golden bitch, Mrs. Tudor's Ch. Camrose Wistura, winner of seven Challenge Certificates in the U.K. Her very bearing demonstrates a sensible, reliable and kindly character.

Being such an intelligent dog his manners in the house are soon learned, and once learned, never forgotten. This makes him a delightful creature to have as a family companion. He is unobtrusive in the house, and can curl up into a small corner, but is always ready for a romp or a game with any member of the family – including the smallest child. Gentle, biddable, affectionate, clean in his habits – no dog can be more suited to sharing one's home. His nature is such that nothing ruffles him and he can be trusted in any circumstances. It is alien to a Golden's nature to be aggressive with other dogs, and his regard for humans is so high that he will accept any treatment, whether good or bad, without question or anger.

standards

The Golden Retriever Standard adopted by the British Kennel Club is accepted the world over, except in U.S.A. and Canada, where a Golden is somewhat larger than in Britain and the cream color is still not allowable, but otherwise is basically the same. He should be a powerfully built dog of medium size, the largest being 24″ at the withers. He must have plenty of substance to enable him to work all day without tiring, yet he must not be too heavily built or cloddy. He should present a well-balanced appearance, with all the parts in symmetry – the length of his body should be in proportion to his length of leg, so that he looks neither too short nor too long on the leg. His neck should be fairly long, and fit into well-laid shoulders. His front legs should be well-boned and straight, and his feet catlike. He should have well-sprung ribs with good depth through the brisket, a short, strong loin, very powerful hindquarters with well-bent stifles and well-muscled thighs and second thighs. His back should be level from withers to croup, and his tail set on almost level with his back. The tail, when in action, should not be carried too high, but roughly in line with his back. His head should be broad across the skull, have a well-defined stop, and a broad, deep foreface of the same length as his skull. Above all he should have dark, appealing eyes and a very kindly, yet alert expression.

This Golden has nice legs and feet, and a good top-line but has a weak head and straight stifles.

Retriever, Labrador

Irish field trial Ch. Ballyfrema Lou, a beautiful bitch of dual purpose type, owned by Mrs. Ruth Tenison. Note the excellent expression, perfect coat, and the correct "otter" tail.

history and development

It is generally accepted that the Labrador originated in Newfoundland as an active, fast-running, short-coated, black water-dog, bred to swim from boat to shore on various errands, even being reported as towing-in small boats. That great sportsman Colonel Peter Hawker saw it in Newfoundland in 1814 and described it exactly, calling it the St. John's Newfoundland, which no doubt should be its proper name. The Labrador was bred as a general utility and hunting dog to supplement the monotonous diet of fish, with game and an occasional wounded deer, and to pull sledges carrying provisions, under terrible icy conditions. All these instincts survive; the Labrador is still a hardy, active dog, strong in bone and pulling power, a powerful swimmer, sensible in temperament and build, and ready for any job. Its true work today differs little from that of those early days, i.e. retrieving game that could not otherwise be picked up. The Labrador is still required to work on land and in water, in all weather conditions, the only difference being that game and wildfowl are now picked instead of fish (although many Labradors still help by retrieving fish, and love to do it). Apart from this change of quarry, their job is identical to that of those far-off days on the cod-banks.

Thought to have been introduced into Britain in the 1830's, crossing on the cod-boats from Newfoundland, the breed was not finally established until the 1870's, when a few sportsmen, notably the Earl of Malmesbury, Lord John Scott, the Duke of Buccleuch, and others, bred various Labradors

(left) The Duke of Buccleuch's Avon, 1885, the ancestor of every Labrador. (right) Mr. K. Thompson's Midge, 1965, showing that the type, style and beautiful head and expression have not changed in the intervening eighty years.

together, incorporating other retrieving dogs into their strains. From the few resulting Labradors the present-day breed descends. There were later additions, but every Labrador of today descends from Lord Malmesbury's dog Tramp, through the Duke of Buccleuch's bitch Avon, mated in 1885. The breed was recognized by the British Kennel Club in 1903.

In 1899, the Yellows appeared, one of this color, Ben of Hyde, being whelped in a litter of blacks from two black parents. From this dog descend all the Yellows. The color Liver, sometimes called Chocolate, was never a true Labrador color but stemmed from various crosses, although good breeding has now confirmed Liver as a Labrador color; the present-day Livers being equally as good as the other colors.

A prime figure in the development of the breed was the Hon. A. Holland-Hibbert, his Munden prefix being behind every dog today, as is Major Twyford's Whitmore strain, these being the forerunners of the supreme Labrador kennel of all time, the Banchory Labradors of Lorna, Countess Howe. Lady Howe will always be remembered as the greatest breeder of the dual-purpose dog, capable of winning supreme honors both in the field and on the show-bench, her wonderful Labradors giving us the strong foundation on which the breed stands today.

Its popularity is attested by 21,611 A.K.C. registrations in 1969, placing it ninth among 116 breeds.

The frontal head view of a Labrador.

color

The Labrador is a self-colored dog, generally either black or yellow, covering all shades from near-white, cream and golden to dark red. Other whole colors are permissible; liver or chocolate are gradually gaining favor. The term "Golden Labrador", so often heard, is incorrect; by direction of the British Kennel Club, the color is always "yellow". This is to avoid confusion between yellow Labradors and Golden Retrievers, only the latter breed now being allowed to be termed "Golden".

In Labradors, the color should be whole, i.e. not black-and-tan, nor yellow-with-white markings. A small white spot on the chest is allowed, and no adverse notice is taken if the white undercoat shows between the pads or in the hollow of the heels, this being taken to indicate the good, dense, typical water-coat. There is also a very old variant of the blacks, when the coat is covered all over with tiny, white spots, known as the "hailstorm" Labrador. These dogs are now seldom seen and, except under the older judges, would probably be penalized for not being self-colored, as required by the official Standard. Black is dominant to yellow; thus two blacks, both carrying the gene for yellow, may produce some yellows in the litter, but two yellows never produce blacks, with the extremely

Head profile – Labrador Retriever.

Ch. Cookridge Tango, the very first liver colored champion, owned and bred by Mrs. Pauling.

unlikely exception of a genetical mutation. In practical breeding it can be taken as certain that, while two blacks will produce yellows, two yellows never produce blacks, any deviation from this rule being extremely suspect. Liver is a more complicated color to pin down. It appears to be dominant to yellow and recessive to black, i.e. you can get litters containing all three colors, as well as litters containing a majority of livers with a couple of yellows, thus mirroring the black-yellow ratio. Apart from this such genetical knowledge is inconclusive.

Yellow puppies owned and bred by Mrs. Lidster, by Ch. Reanacre Twister ex Lidcoats Chrystabel. The kindly, intelligent expression is already there, while still in the nest.

240

care

Labradors are hardy dogs, requiring little special care. A good, dry bed, free from draughts, plenty of water at all times, somewhere to let off steam galloping about, a kind word and one square meal a day, and they are happy. If you can teach them a job of any sort, to make them feel important, then they are your slaves for life. The coat is easily cared for, a good brush and rub-down being all that is required. The routine of dusting with insecticide, worming and keeping an eye on their ears and anal glands is the same as for all other dogs.

Compared with the starvation diet of early Labradors modern living is very affluent. If fed too richly or too much, they can become fat and their coats become staring. The diet should be kept plain, biscuit meal with meat, fish, eggs and vegetables, according to the needs of each dog.

A puppy, however, must have the best food and plenty of it. At least four meals a day when tiny, gradually reducing the number of feeds but not the quality, until about six months old, when they are down to two meals a day. After that, they soon attain their normal life-routine of one meal a day. Heating is not required in the adult kennel, although it may be necessary in sickness, or when the litter is new-born.

character

The Labrador is a most reliable, good-humored dog, very obedient and easy to deal with. Boisterous sometimes as youngsters, they must be made aware from the very first of who is the master and a firm "No!" is usually sufficient to stop any trouble. Once they realize you mean what you say, they become the most reliable, stable characters, willing, obedient and trustworthy. One of their greatest assets is their fondness for children. They become besotted with their "own" children and adore others, which can be very embarrassing when a smiling black muzzle is lovingly thrust into a completely strange pram! Yet they are remarkably safe with children, standing any amount of teasing. They are also ideal for such jobs as guiding the blind, for which purpose large numbers are trained.

Mrs. Ruth Tenison's Ballyfrema Teal, jumping into deep water off the top of a high bank.

International Swedish, Finnish and Norwegian Ch. Kamrats Spader, an outstanding Labrador.

The qualities required of them in the field are the same as those previously mentioned; a sensible, good-tempered obedience, plus good nose and eyes, soundness and activity coupled with strength of build and an ability and willingness to try to understand and to carry out an order. Add to these, speed and the strong retrieving instinct, with a very great love of water, and you have the ideal non-slip retriever, invaluable for present-day shooting and hunting.

standards

The Labrador is medium-sized; in England the height for bitches is 21½" to 22", dogs 22" to 22½". The A.K.C. Standard now permits 21½" to 23½" for bitches; 22½" to 24½" for males.

Because it was bred entirely as a sporting dog, the Standard was drawn up to maintain the necessary qualities, producing a specification of a useful dog, able to act in any weather or terrain. Great stress is laid on strength of build coupled with great activity.

The orthodox work of the Labrador is either to sit quietly in a "stand" or blind, or to walk to heel equally quietly until the game is shot. Whereupon, on command, he goes to the "fall" either finding the dead bird or hunting the foot and blood scent until he locates the wounded game. He then picks it up and retrieves it tenderly, right up to hand. This is the job for which the Labrador is bred, although the retrieve may be from either land or water. Other methods of working a Labrador may be used, but its orthodox work is to move on command, after the game is shot. Strength and activity with enough speed is required to overcome obstacles, face thick

Ch. Midnight of Mansergh in the line at a field trial, the photograph being taken immediately after a water test, showing the effect of water on a good Labrador double coat. Notice the lack of any sign of discomfort or bedragglement.

covert, steep banks and heavy tides, and also to carry in his mouth over these obstacles anything from tiny snipe to a heavy goose.

While speed is useful, stamina is even more important, so the Standard calls for a short-coupled, thick-set dog with deep, well-sprung ribs, legs straight and strong-boned with good pasterns; round compact feet, with well-arched toes and well-developed pads. The chest, ribs and loin must be broad, deep and strong, as must be the hindquarters. The head is broad, with plenty of brain room, the eyes any shade of brown or hazel.

The coat is all-important for working in icy water and cold winds. Short, dense and free from feather, and top coat giving a fairly hard feeling to the hand, the whole dog should be covered with the dense weather-proof undercoat which is such a feature of the breed and so necessary for its work. We are, unfortunately, in great danger of losing this undercoat, as the Labrador becomes more popular as a house-dog. If this does happen, one of the most valuable and unique features of the breed will have disappeared, one that is essential to its well-being when working.

Another notable feature of the breed is its tail; broad at the base, tapering to a point and reaching not lower than the hock, being clothed all round with the short, dense double-coat. This gives it the peculiar rounded appearance known as the ottertail. It is used as a rudder and to balance in the water, particularly when carrying a heavy bird in its mouth, when the Labrador adjusts his tail action to prevent his head going under. Thus, the three key-points in a Labrador are his broad head, his dense weather-resisting double-coat and his otter-tail.

Reanacre Sandylands Tarmac swimming in deep water, showing the tail being used as a rudder, to help him turn in his own length.

Some of the Mansergh Labradors at play in the water, their favorite occupation – left to right, Groucho, Ch. Damson, Black Spice and Dillettante, all "of Mansergh".

Setter, English

Mrs. Williams's Sh. Ch. Silbury Soames of Madavale, a blue belton and tan, born 1959, was not only a top post-war winner with twenty-four C.C.'s but also a top winner of all breeds, winning supreme best in show at Cruft's in 1964 and reserve best in show 1961 and 1963.

history and development

The English Setter is one of the oldest breeds of gundog. He has been mentioned in European literature since the 14th century as a setting dog, and has been defined and registered at the Kennel Club in London since 1873. The breed had become established for its purpose, and its type, for many years before this; many noble families in Britain kept their own kennels of Setters for their private hunting and shooting. Famous kennels include the Featherstones, the Edmond Castles, Lord Lovat's breed, the Earl of Southesk's, the Earl of Seafield's, the Earl of Derby's and the Welsh or Llandiloes setter.

The first recorded breeder of English setters, who initiated tabulated pedigrees much as we know them today, was Mr. Edward Laverack, whose pedigrees go back to about 1860, seventeen years before the Kennel Club was founded in England. One of the founders of the Kennel Club, and later its Chairman, and another English Setter enthusiast, was Mr. S. E. Shirley. Following in the line of great early breeders of English Setters was Mr. R. Purcell Llewellin, who purchased his original stock from Laverack and introduced various outcrosses, most of which were, however, unsuccessful.

Although Laverack and Llewellin aimed to produce their individual ideals of English Setters for show and work combined, they each had a different way of working towards this goal; Laverack practised inbreeding within his own strain, and Llewellin used various other strains mixed with his original Laveracks. These differing methods of breeding led in later years to the main division in the breed as we know it today, between show dogs and working dogs; although it must be remembered that both types originated with the Laveracks. Edward Laverack indeed produced the first book on the breed, *The Setter*, published about 1875, and the Standard which he then compiled for the breed is the one used, in almost identical words, to the present day.

color

One of the chief attractions of the breed is the variety of permissible colors; blue belton (black and white), orange or lemon belton (orange or lemon and white), blue belton and tan (black, white and tan, or tricolor) and liver belton. The origin of the word "belton" comes straight from Laverack's book, which describes the ticking, or roan, which varies from light to dark, so giving the light or dark blue beltons, and the other combinations of this "color". Belton is the name of a village in Northumberland, England, one of the many places where Laverack rented shooting land.

Puppies are usually born white except for those with solid black, orange or liver patches, which are generally less popular in the show ring, although they are most attractive to look at.

care

Being a particularly affectionate and gregarious breed, English Setters thrive best in human company as family companions, or kennelled with other dogs, never alone. They are not difficult to rear and feed providing they receive ample food of good quality. Adults need 1 lb. to 1½ lbs. of meat daily, and biscuits with wholemeal flour. Puppies need best quality

An extremely rare photograph of the late Robert Llewellin, taken in 1909, with one of the breed he did so much to establish.

An engraving of Mr. Purcell-Llewellyn's Laverack Setter, Countess, born in 1869, and the first dual champion in history.

minced meat, milk, cereal, vitamins and calcium from about three to four weeks old in addition to the mother's milk. When they are weaned at about seven to eight weeks, they need five meals a day, graduallydecreasing by about nine months old to one or two meals a day. If English Setters are kennelled, good straw beds and plenty of sawdust on the floor will keep them clean, warm and content. If kept in the house, they must have a bed or rug of their own where they know they can rest. Water must be provided at all times from the age of four weeks. Road work and free exercise are essential for such an active dog, every day from about three to four months old, when ten minutes twice a day is enough, but an hour or more when adult is really needed to keep a dog in show form. It is very dangerous to exercise for long periods at a time when the dog is not used to it – there is as much harm done in over-exercizing as under-exercizing. It is still possible to train English Setters to the gun provided they are handled carefully and live in adequate game-country from an early age.

For the show ring and to a lesser extent to keep them tidy in the home, trimming is necessary, with a fine steel comb, finger and thumb and thinning scissors, used down the sides and front of the neck, on top of the ears, to display the outline to its best advantage. The feet should be tidied with scissors on top of the toes, underneath the pads and round the edges of the feet, but hair must be left between the toes, to give the effect of close, compact feet. All straggly hair should be plucked from the body, at root of tail etc. before going into the ring. Daily grooming with a coarse steel comb and stiff brush is essential to keep the coat in good condition, not forgetting to be especially careful to comb out the feathering on legs and tail very carefully to discourage knotting. Before a show it is necessary to bath the English Setter and before it is quite dry the coat should be combed flat and the dog wrapped in a coat or towel, to give the appearance, when dry, of a slightly wavy, long and silky coat. In America show dogs are much more heavily trimmed, with clippers, than they are in Britain.

The English Setter, with its gentle, affectionate and patient nature, is an

The Crombie prefix, first owned by Prof. L. Turton Price and later by Mr. G. Crawford, appears time and again in the history of the English Setter. This is the lemon belton, Rufus of Crombie, born in 1930 and the sire of two champions and three show champions. He came from Mr. D. K. Steadman's Maesydd kennels.

Mrs. K. Broadheads' beautiful lemon belton bitch, Ch. Ernford Evening Flight. Born in 1951, she won five C.C.s.

Mr. and Mrs. W. Foss's Sh. Ch. Elswood Renmark Baronet, a blue belton born in 1963, was a great winner of his time with eleven C.C.s. He was also a long-lasting dog, still winning in 1970.

ideal family dog, but like other large active breeds it is full of spirits and liveliness, so ownership imposes a duty which should not be undertaken lightly, and attention to the needs of the animal must be given at all times.

standards

The English Setter Standard is international, with minor variations. It is comprehensive which should help all interested in the breed to recognize good and faulty points. The head should be long and reasonably lean, with well-defined stop. The skull oval-shaped from ear to ear. The muzzle moderately deep and fairly square; from the stop to the point of the nose should equal the length of skull from occiput to eyes; the nostrils should be wide and the jaws of nearly equal length; flews should not be too pendulous. The eyes should be bright, mild and intelligent, of dark hazel color, the darker the better. Ears of moderate length, set-on low and hanging in neat folds close to the cheek. Mouth to be level. The neck should be rather long, muscular and lean, slightly arched at the crest, not throaty or pendulous below the throat, but elegant in appearance. The body should be of moderate length, the back short and level, with good round, widely-sprung ribs and deep in the back ribs, i.e. well ribbed-up. The hindquarters should be wide, slightly arched, strong and muscular, with defined second thigh. Stifles well bent, thighs long from hip to hock. The shoulders should be well set back or oblique; the chest should be deep and of good depth and width between the shoulder blades. Pasterns short, muscular, round and straight. Feet close and compact.

The tail should be set-on almost in a line with the back, to be slightly curved but with no tendency to turn upwards. The feathering should commence slightly below the root and increase in length to the middle and then gradually taper off towards the tip. The coat should be slightly wavy, long and silky, but not curly. Those without heavy patches of color on the body, but flecked all over, are preferred.

The British Standard says that weight and size should be, dogs, 60 to 66 lbs., $25\frac{1}{2}''$ to $27''$. Bitches, 56 to 62 lbs., $24''$ to $25\frac{1}{2}''$; the American simply calls for dogs to be about $25''$, bitches $24''$. Among the faults are: coarse shoulders, short foreface, tapering muzzle, lack of stop, obliquely-set eyes, high ear placement, loose elbows from bad shoulder-placement, flat ribs, too long loin, lightness of bone, wide feet, weak pasterns, straight stifles, narrow quarters, gay tail, mouth undershot or overshot, lacking freedom of action.

Miss M. E. Jarry's Sh. Ch. Ripleygae Mallory was born just after the Second World War. This blue belton was a great winner of his day, with sixteen C.C.s. He also sired two champions and six show champions.

Setter, Gordon

Mrs. M. M. C. Rowe's Sh. Ch. Vanity of Cairlie, who among her many other wins was best of breed at Cruft's in 1965. Here she is pictured in typical show stance. She was by Salters Billy Budd ex Ch. Quality of Cairlie.

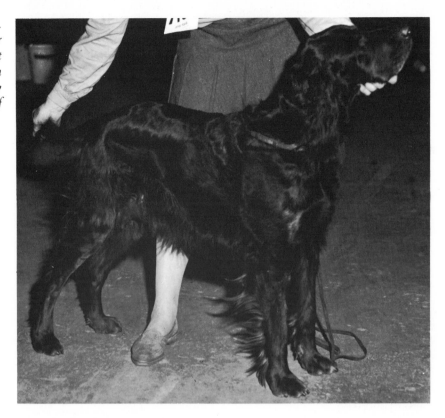

An expression of sagacity and faithfulness in the head of Ch. Elegance of Cairlie.

history and development

Although it is fairly certain that there were black-and-tan setters in Scotland as long ago as the year 1600, the breed of Gordon Setters really came into being with the 4th Duke of Gordon, in late 1770's and early 1800's, and were called the Gordon Castle Setters. (The Gordon remains the only gundog native to Scottish breeds.)

On the death of the 5th Duke of Gordon in 1835, the kennel was sold and the title passed to a cousin, the Duke of Richmond, who built up the breed again at Gordon Castle, and Gordon Setters began to appear in England. A dog and a bitch were exported to America in 1842, probably the earliest exports of the breed. In the early 1800's little attention was paid to looks but a great deal to working ability and soundness, and the Gordons were highly thought of as quick scenting and hard-working gundogs. In fact, in 1863 at Southill's first field trial three Gordons took the first three places. When shows commenced in the middle 1800's there immediately developed a divergence of type. Show people wanted a large heavy dog quite different from the stylish, racy setter so well established for work with the guns, and a great deal of harm was done to the breed as a whole until, in 1875, Mr. Robert Chapman of the, later, famous Heather prefix succeeded in getting back, to a great extent, the lost qualities. He bred very many most beautiful dogs, all of whom worked and were shown with great success. Since World War II, the breed has gradually increased in numbers for exhibition, possibly the middle '50's and early '60's provided the greatest competition in the breed's

history, many open shows including Gordon classes, and more championship shows in Britain offering Challenge Certificates than today. Sadly the interest in the breed in Britain for working and field trials has declined over the last decade mainly due to the use of the all purpose Labrador.

color

In the early days of Gordons the colors differed very much. At Gordon Castle many were black and tan, black, white and tan, even lemon and white, black and white and liver and white appeared quite usual. Gradually, the black and tan became fully established, a little white permissible if appearing in very small amounts on chest and feet. White on the head and behind the collar is a serious fault and is very rarely found today.

When dog shows began the Gordon color was often either of the very light straw color tan or of very dark, shaded tan, but about 1928 Mr. W. Murray Stewart established the Bydand strain of beautiful Gordons, carrying a lovely bright chestnut tan. Today very few pedigrees are without a Bydand ancestor.

The breed Standard is for a coat of deep, shining, coal black with tan markings of a rich chestnut red; in fact the color of a ripe horse-chestnut when taken from its shell. Tan should appear as two clear spots over the eyes about three-quarters of an inch in diameter; on the sides of the muzzle but not reaching above the base of the nose, resembling a stripe around the end of the muzzle from one side to the other; on the throat; two large clear spots on the chest; on the inside of the hind legs and inside the thighs showing down the front of the stifle and broadening out to the outside of the hind legs from the hocks to the toes – it must not completely eliminate the black on the back of the hind legs; on the forelegs, up to the elbows behind and to the knees or a little above in front. Black pencilling is allowed on the toes and also a black streak under the jaw.

care

From the time of weaning the Gordon needs plenty of meat and a good nourishing and consistent diet, for he is going to grow very fast and make a fairly heavy frame to carry his adult weight of about 70 lbs. (dog) and 60 lbs. bitch. In the U.S.A. dogs may be 55 to 80 lbs., bitches 45 to 70 lbs. As a puppy and up to six or eight months his exercise must of necessity be restricted to free play in his own run or garden; after which he can start on some on-lead road walking with a brief free gallop if possible on open fields. All this can be increased very gradually. To take a heavy Gordon puppy for long walks before he is twelve months old may, and probably will, do him irrevocable harm although he is only too willing to go. As a growing puppy he needs three meals a day to at least six months, and always two good daily meals of one-third meat two-thirds biscuit meal will be needed to keep him fit and strong, with plenty of "rest" periods.

As a puppy little brushing is needed but as his coat grows it will need regular attention; ears, eyes and feet need checking and nails kept short by a monthly clipping.

character

The Gordon is above all a gundog, take him in open country and he will show you where he is at his best and happiest. He has a strong will and very definite ideas on what is best for himself. But he is not a difficult dog and a firm kind attitude and understanding by his owner will make him into the most wonderful companion in whatever field he is required. As a showdog he is rarely at his best, only putting up with all the fuss to please his owner, so that it becomes most necessary to apply extra efforts in his training and in his presentation in the show-ring.

He is a marvellous housedog and, although fairly big, manages to take up very little space indoors, preferably the best armchair, and will also be quite at home in a warm comfortable kennel.

standards

The English Standard says the Gordon should be "a stylish dog, built on galloping lines, having a thoroughbred appearance consistent with its build which can be compared to a weight-carrying hunter". Add to this his height of 25″ to 26″ (in the U.S.A. the heights are: males, 24″ to 27″ females, 23″ to 26″), his deep muscular, short-coupled body, black silky coat, rich chestnut tan markings, and arching neck and well laid shoulders, well feathered legs and waving tail, charming expression and bright intelligent eyes, and the picture is complete. The only drawback surely is the difficulty to reproduce perfection. No one has done it yet. We strive for it and in doing that we can best serve our chosen hobby in the most rewarding way.

A lovely group of show champions, left to right: Sh. Ch. Yeoman of Cairlie, Sh. Ch. Vanity of Cairlie, Sh. Ch. Unity of Cairlie and Sh. Ch. Xella of Cairlie.

Setter, Irish

Mr. and Mrs. Brook Emory's Ch. Phantom Brook's Brian Boru, the best possible example of the type winning in the U.S.A. in the late fifties.

history and development

Much about the Setter of Ireland must be rated conjecture rather than knowledge. Knowledgeable conjecture, however, filled with fairly solid reasons for belief.

In Ireland, as elsewhere, most men loved to hunt, or lived to hunt. Especially desired were upland game birds, partridge, quail, pheasant. The hunters had fine little "spaniels" to help find them. The fastest workers among these were bred to those with keenest noses. By the end of the 16th century, Irish shooting dogs were very good indeed.

Some time during the next century, the greatest smelling mechanism of all, that of the Bloodhound, was almost surely introduced and with splendid result. The intensified scenting powers caused these new spaniels to creep still more cautiously in the presence of even far-off game, crouching low, halting, and often "setting" right down. The biggest of these, usually white with reddish patches, were the easiest to keep in sight. Somebody then heard of a strain of black pointers in Iberia, tall, with fast flying legs to carry them across its barren soil at a tremendous clip. Little doubt exists about this importation since, in certain districts, the pigmenting among new longer-legged setting spaniels – Setters – darkened dramatically.

By the 18th century, red-and-white setters of Ireland had achieved a reasonable degree of uniformity – type. Occasionally a black or largely black whelp appeared, ascribed later on to an admixture of blood from the Duke of Gordon's black-and-tan setters of Scotland and, probably, the sporadic English Setter with patches of varying color, or an Irish Water Spaniel. But the greatest influence may still have been that of the

The head of Sh. Ch. Wendover Caskey, winner of two best in shows and seven C.C.s, and still going strong.

253

Ch. Palmerston, bred by Mr. Cecil Moore of County Tyrone, Ireland, could be looked on as the corner-stone of the modern Irish Setter as a distinct and genetically reliable variety; such was his prepotency as a sire.

Spanish Pointer. Whichever was responsible, outcrossings of the Irish Setter with any other breed to this day often "throw" black.

Later in that century, numerous important fanciers of the red-and-white dog began favoring a solid dark red one. White areas on the animals shrank and narrowed until, around the middle eighteen-hundreds, the self-colored Irishman predominated, often being called the Irish Red Setter, all a deep chestnut or mahogany red with, at most, a dash of white on head, chest or toes only. He is that way today.

In 1862 (it is believed), a puppy was produced by a Mr. Cecil Moore of County Tyrone which would affect the breed ever afterward. Ch. Palmerston was to prove so unbelievably prepotent, and be used so much, that his birth might be said to mark the advent of the Irish Setter as a distinct and genetically reliable variety.

The period of Palmerston's coming was not unqualifiedly favorable. He paralleled, without precisely causing, a most alarming deterioration. The culprit was an entirely new idea: the dog show. Up to then, the leading enthusiasts, all men, had bred "meat dogs". But the Irish Setter now become excessively beautiful, was a "natural" for the fast mushrooming exhibitions, an instant success in them. They brought him low. Suddenly breeders everywhere, breeding and inter-breeding for glamor and newspaper notices, virtually wrecked the red Irish breed. America was perhaps the worst. There, in the 1920's, you sometimes saw a fourth of the competitors in a show ring slinking around terrified, tails down. or trembling too hard to stand.

It took a second half century to rebuild. The idea of the "dual type" Irishman quickly waxed, especially in America, the aim being to retain the beauty while recapturing the sound sense and hunting abilities of old. Palmerston himself, as well as many of his more immediate successors, had still been fine dogs afield, and their blood flowed in the veins of most every strain in both hemispheres, producing often the narrow white centered streak on the head, vestiges of which pop out even today and are still called the "Palmerston Blaze".

Although the red dog never regained full pre-eminence in the field trials, he did become once more a worthy competitor in them in Britain, the Continent and throughout North America. Among the very many dedicating themselves to this challenge, Mrs. F. Nagle and her Sulham-steads in Britain deserve special mention, Mr. E. Berolsheimer's O'Cloisters in the U.S.A. (Elias Vail training), and Mr. H. Dean's Canadian Ardees. The recovered soundness of the product further demonstrated itself in obedience work. This new concept, launched in Europe, spread quickly to America. There, in 1935, England's Mrs. Whitehouse Walker held the first small U.S. Obedience Class in Westchester County, New York, an Irish Setter taking part. The breed is still actively engaged, and is usually among the higher scorers.

In Britain, post-Palmerston, three giants linked to dominate the breed worldwide for a full century. Reverend Robert O'Callaghan had been quick to spot, and exploit for his Brandeston Kennels, Suffolk, Palmerston's uncanny power. A parade of excitingly beautiful champions (which could still hunt) streamed from his establishment throughout the eighteen seventies, eighties, nineties – Shandon, Shandon II, Aveline ("The Beautiful"), Aveline II, Geraldine, Geraldine II, Fingal III, Winifred. When at last the vicar's strength waned, it was, amazingly for those days,

Mrs. Cheever Porter's Ch. Milson O'Boy, a son of the great sire Ch. Higgins Redcoat, one of the greatest show-dogs of his time. Whelped in 1932, in a five-year period he won eleven best in shows, forty-six group firsts and 103 best of breed awards. He was also a key sire.

a girl who took over. With his Lady Honora and Winifred, young Mrs. N. Ingle Bepler of Tottenham started off her magnificent Rheolas – and a dominance of eighty years by two women breeders; forty for Rheola, followed by a second forty of (largely Rheola) Hartsbournes. From the Rheola yard unnumbered choice bitches, Didona, Dione, Daphne, Bryndona, on and on, to the standout Norna; with companioning males, four of them singularly prepotent, Toby, Bryn, Boniface, Benedict.

Irish Setter puppies.

Then from the pens of Mrs. Eileen K. Walker, Stanmore Common, Benedict's daughter emerged as Champion Hartsbourne Vanity in 1930 to lead off the second forty years of continuous supremacy. The Rheola flag in effect still flew at Mrs. Walker's death, while visiting U.S.A., 20th May 1970. On that date her final favorite, Sh. Ch. Hartsbourne Starlight, was busy delivering for her absent mistress the last Hartsbourne litter.

While the Rheola/Hartsbourne did maintain their leadership, it was not without constant and capable bombardment from all sides, usually, but not always, by bloodlines partly derived from them; the most puissant attacker – Boyne:

Mr. A. Ashworth (Halcana)   Mrs. G. E. Leighton (O'Murrell)
Mrs. E. M. Baker (Gadeland)   Miss S. Lennox (Brackenfield)
Mr. J. H. J. Braddon (Ide)   Mrs. M. Ogden (Borrowdale)
Mr. J. H. Carbery (Boyne)   Mr. W. W. Poole (O'Kilner)
Mr. & Mrs. Cucksey (Maydorwill)   Mr. W. J. Rasbridge (Watendlath)
Mr. R. N. Foote (Beorcham)   Mrs. J. M. Roberts (Corneven)
Mrs. Ray Furness (Raycroft)   Mrs. P. Selwyn (Matsonhouse)
Mrs. Holt (O'Moy)   Mrs. M. Stokes (Marrona)
Mr. & Mrs. L. C. James   Mr. J. A. L. Wenger (Rattlin)
   (Wendover)   Mr. J. Whittaker (Gaelge)
Mrs. E. F. Leighton-Boyce   Mrs. H. E. Whitwell (Ardagh)
   (Norlan)   Mr. & Mrs. Yeoward (Cymran)

Show Ch. Hartsbourne O'Mara, a good example of the type produced by Mrs. Eileen K. Walker in her English kennel.

A bitch significant in the development of the breed in the 1920's, Mrs. Margery Ogden's Ch. Norna.

America from early on bought consistently Britain's best; then, ever the mass producer, soon outstripped her, quantity-wise. Fresh importations continuously had their strong say through bloods of leading sires – Punchestown Chieftain, Hutchinson's Bob, Finglass, Plunket, and numerous others. But in 1875 stark coincidence provided a major face-lift. Two fine setters, Charlie and Nell, had a litter in Ireland while awaiting shipment to a Mr. Oppenheimer of St. Petersburg, Russia. "One of the puppies", wrote R. A. Greenfield, in charge, "is the best, at a year, in my training experience". Hearing of this, Mr. C. H. Turner and his St. Louis (Missouri) Kennel Club brought the yearling over; Elcho! He was used unceasingly. Among reported matings to 51 females, Elcho was put nine times to Palmerston's daughter, Rose; five to grand-daughter, Noreen; both imported. He imprinted his excellent type solidly and permanently upon the breed. No wonder the alert O'Callaghan, looking across, would write, "I have no hesitancy in saying that I have found the Elcho blood, crossed on Palmerston, to be the most successful, both in field and on bench".

Benefitting were to be all the great American kennels, coast to coast; L. Contoit, New York (St. Cloud); J. S. & T. Wall, Brooklyn (Lismore); Mrs. A. E. Sturdee, Albany (Glencho); W. McRoberts, Illinois (Culbertson); Otto Pohl, Nebraska; Nancy Lee Nannetti, California (Shagstone). If the Boynes failed to dislodge Rheola in England, maybe they could do it in America. Paddy of Boyne took ship ca. 1923 to Mr. W. W. Higgins, New Jersey, making at once an arch nick with a local lass, Craigie Lea

Mona. They produced more champions than non-champs., among them, in a repeat mating (1927), Ch. Higgins Red Coat, a scintillating sire who would get used as much as, or more than, Elcho. He was put forward by Mr. H. Hartnett, professional handler supreme, manager and later owner of Milson Kennels, Harrison, New York. Again the Rheolas came alive. A Connecticut kennels, Kinvarra, began concentrating on them, delivering up shortly Ch. Kinvarra Kermit, an instant threat to the Red Coats only twenty miles away. A Montague, Capulet feud ensued:

Ch. Caldene Ailene comes from a line based on a fusion of Milson and Jordan Farm blood-lines, which had a lasting effect on breed type in America.

In the Boyce/Milson camp:
J. P. Knight (Knightscroft)
E. Levering (Ruxton)
J.W. Calhoon (Caldene)
C. F. Neilson (Rosecroft)
Mrs. C. Porter
  (numerous top campaigners)

In the Rheola/Kinvarra camp:
E. I. Eldredge (Tirvelda)
J. A. Spear (Tyronne Farm)
H. & J. Wilson (End O'Maine)
Mr. & Mrs. G. Brodie (Seaforth)
A. & J. Nilsen (Thenderin)

The feud lasted 15 years, neither family clearly winning. Red Coat had produced 30 champions, Kermit only 29. But Kermit's came from far fewer bitches, and their progeny arrived late enough to have to campaign during World War II with its many limitations. Meanwhile, intermarrying had become so common that neither side could claim blood "uncontaminated" by the other, and the battle fell apart.

The Irish Setter continued a mainly British/American institution, as these statistics show (based on official registrations): 1969 England, 2,679, all-breed ranking 20; United States, 16,631, ranking 13. Canada registered 456 Irish Setters (1968). These probably the top three. Nevertheless,

Show Ch. Wendover Nancy (right) is one of the many top-winning Irish Setters to come from Mr. and Mrs. L. C. Jane's kennel. Shown at ten championship shows in 1965 she won best of breed at them all and had several group wins as well. On the left is Mrs. A. M. and Miss J. M. Gibson's well-known Sh. Ch. Cornevon Snowstorm, with judge Mrs. L. M. Daly in the center.

A scintillating sire was Ch. Higgins Red Coat, who himself produced thirty champions.

A beautiful Irish Setter bitch, Int. Ch. Wildair Visionary Hour was bred in Canada.

numerous other countries have shown great and increasing interest. It seems reasonable to list several of them, with one or two fanciers in each who devoted major portions of their lives to thoughtful worthwhile work in the breed:

In Norway – Col. C. Schilbred (Erin); Mr. J. Borge (Montebello).

In Sweden – Capt. & Mrs. B. Engelbrecht (Holmsund); Mr. L. Borg (Evadal).

In Holland – Col. G. Verwey (Of Sutherland).

In Australia – Mr. & Mrs. A. Thor and Miss M. Deane (Tatlow).

In New Zealand – Mr. & Mrs. Newman (Korere); Mrs. R. Cummings (Red River).

In Canada – Mrs. Gertrude W. Drew's Wildaire reigned supreme.

color; character; standards

A technical Standard of perfection was drawn up by the Irish Setter Association (English) soon adopted almost verbatim (*circa* 1892) by the Irish Setter Club of America. Carefully studied wordings aimed to picture (to paraphrase in part a much later description published by I.S.C.A. in 1960) a medium sized sporting-dog of streamlined substance, graceful and very spirited.

He has a long molded head, on a long clean neck fitting smoothly into sloping shoulders fine at the top; low-set ears, medium to dark eyes, very soft in expression and sweet – above all, the sweetness, written unmistakably in each warm, chiseled line of the face – with, however, just a little neat touch of Irish wit and mischief to flavor. Viewed from above or in profile, planes of muzzle and skull, equal in length, are parallel but with a defined stop.

The whole dog done up in a flat, stove-shiny top coat of deep rich chestnut or an even darker mahogany red, ending in long, feathery fringes on back of the legs, below brisket, and the pennant-like tail, carried level or a trifle above. Legs are four-square throughout. Angulated stifles and hocks deliver a rhythmic drive with much push and power for eagerly reaching forelegs to pull in the ground, whether in gallop or trot. The body is deep, a fraction longer than high, back sloping slightly downward from the withers. Prominent overall is the balance and fit of each part. A dog of distinction.

In the middle 1800's a British male stood around 23″ at the withers. Within one century this height would increase about 15%. But in America, to the despair of many, the rise reached fully 25% despite I.S.C.A.'s officially published recommendation: Males: 27″, 70 lbs. Females: 25″, 60 lbs.

Mr. Albert M. Greenfield Jnr's Ch. Major O'Shannon, one of the top winning dogs of all breeds in the U.S.A. during the latter part of the sixties.

Ch. Kinvarra Kermit, whelped in 1937, produced twenty-nine champions. He was by Ch. Kinvarra Craig ex Ch. Kinvarra Mollie of Gadeland, an imported bitch.

Spaniel, Cocker
(American)

In both 1969 and 1970 the top winning Cocker Spaniel in America was the striking particolor Ch. Burson's Blarney, owned by Silver Maple Kennels and Oren Q. Jones. Color patterns in American Cockers are quite different from the English Cocker, and the sloping topline with the exaggerated hind angulation are much desired points.

history and development

The development of the American Cocker Spaniel (now called "Cocker Spaniel" in America) as a separate Spaniel breed began about 1880 with the advent of the black Cocker Spaniel, Obo 2d, A.K.C. No. 4911. He came from English imports and was first shown at Manchester, New Hampshire, in September of 1883. Greater development came when the American Kennel Club permitted the breed to be divided into two varieties. At this time there was a definite upturn in the breeding and showing of the American Cocker Spaniel.

A great change in the type and general outline of the Cocker Spaniel began about 1920. During this period, they began to show more height at the shoulder, a longer stretch of neck and a distinct change in head type. Skulls became a little more rounded, a bit narrower, and muzzles a little shorter. This was the beginning of the shorter back and sloping topline that became the popular outline in vogue today.

During the last thirty years there has been a gradual increase in the amount of coat seen on the American Cocker Spaniel; until today, in the opinion of many judges as well as the average pet owner, the coat is entirely too profuse as it requires so much care to keep it properly groomed and trimmed. However, regardless of the opinion of some, the show Cocker is still very heavily coated and it is impossible to win in the show ring today with a sparsely coated Cocker Spaniel.

The Spaniel, from which family the Cocker came, is one of the oldest

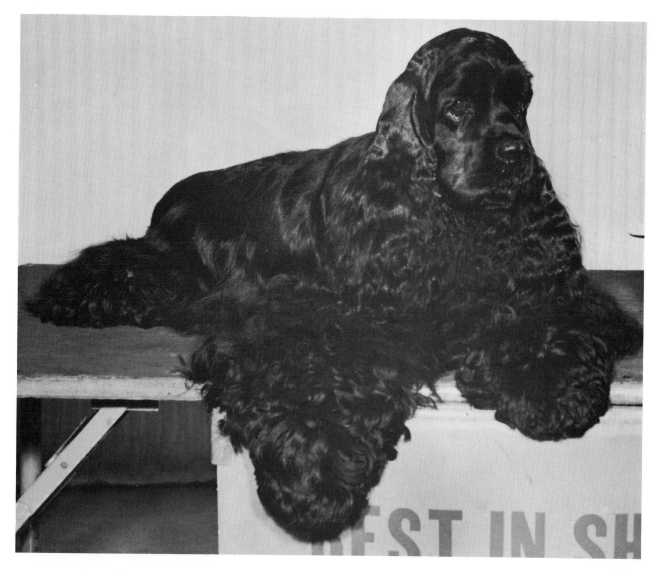

An unusual pose for American Ch. Har-Dees Hell Bender II, best in show winner at the Marion, Ohio, Kennel Club show in 1961. Note the tremendous coat on the front legs.

breeds known. Ancient models showing resemblance to the Spaniel were uncovered in some of the old Egyptian tombs. Because of the name, it is assumed by some that the origin of the Cocker Spaniel was in Spain, but there is nothing to discount the idea that his ancestors could have been dogs brought into Spain during the early migration from the East. The Spaniel is mentioned in English literature as early as 1340 in Chaucer's Wif of Bathe's Prologue in which is written "For as a Spaynel she wol on him lepe". This is proof that the breed was well-known in England six centuries ago.

There are indications also that the Spaniel was known in Southern France as early as 1387 as shown in the writings of the French Count, Gaston de Foix, and since his vast estates were close to the borders of Spain, it is assumed by some that the name "Spaniel" originated there. He wrote much of the nature of the breed and his book was translated into English by the Duke of York about 1410.

The first division of varieties of Spaniels came in those early days when they were designated as land or water Spaniels. There was some out-crossing of breeds during that period and even the Setter originated through a cross of the Spaniel with the Spanish Pointer. After that period, the terms Springer, Springing Spaniel, Cocker, Cocking Spaniel and

A key import for Britain was Miss J. Macmillan's American Ch. Lochranza Evdon's Escort, a black and tan who was the first American Cocker dog to win a group at a championship show in Britain – Windsor, 1969. He is also a good sire. Already British breeders are mastering the difficult art of presenting the American Cocker coat in all its profusion.

Britain was slow to recognize the American Cocker, but once it was introduced – the first specimens were imported from Holland – it caught on immediately and quickly gained considerable popularity. Challenge Certificates were made available for the first time in 1970, and the first champion was the black dog, Messrs Hull and Horn's Sh. Ch. Lochranza News Flash.

William J. Laffoon, Jr. and Mrs. Rose Robbins's Ch. Pinetops Fancy Parade, shown winning the sporting group at Westminster, New York, in 1960. A very typical black and tan American Cocker who had a great career.

Cock Flusher seem to have been applied to Spaniels of all sizes. The term "Cocker" was given to the smallest, most compact of this family and it came from their use in woodcock hunting.

The English Spaniel, developed about 1837, was probably the type ancestor of our Cocker Spaniel. In 1866, the Spaniel classes were divided into Large Size and Small Size, which included the Cocker. By 1874, the Cocker, no longer a separate breed, was entered in the classes as a Field Spaniel.

About this time the founders of the American Spaniel Club were becoming actively interested in the Cocker, which was not yet recognized as a separate breed of sporting Spaniel. A weight division was established between the smaller and the larger Field Spaniels, in both of which the type was identical. The Cocker came from the smaller class although at that time, because of his size, not much headway was made. When, in 1901, the American Spaniel Club abolished this limitation in size, more uniformity in type was seen, and the progress of the Cocker has gone ahead rapidly ever since.

Later, when the American Kennel Club rules were changed to allow two varieties, there was a definite upturn in the breeding and showing of Cocker Spaniels.

By 1920, the popularity of the Cocker was growing. Specialty clubs were being formed and entries were on the upgrade, both in quality and quantity. In 1917 the first National Specialty Show was held in New York City by the American Spaniel Club. The Futurity Stake was introduced in 1923 and has continued ever since.

During the years 1940–1956 the popularity of the American Cocker Spaniel reached its peak, and it led registrations in the American Kennel Club for all breeds; a record for popularity of any breed. Since then they have remained in the top ten in American Kennel Club registrations, and registrations in 1970 showed a decided upturn. In 1942, the English Cocker Spaniel was recognized by the American Spaniel Club, not as a separate breed, but as a variety of the Cocker Spaniel. Until the ASCOB variety (any solid color other than black to include black-and-tans) was given a separate variety, three Cockers appeared in the groups – solid, particolor and English. Following the recognition of the ASCOB variety, four Cockers were sent into the group – Black, ASCOB, particolor and English. In 1946, the American Spaniel Club dropped their jurisdiction over the English Cocker Spaniel, and the Cocker Spaniel, English type, was designated as the English Cocker Spaniel, while the Cocker Spaniel, American type, was designated as the Cocker Spaniel.

color

There is a wide variation in colors in Cocker Spaniels – black, black-and-tan, buffs from the very lightest shade, often termed silver, to the very darkest red, and liver. The particolors come in black-and-white, red-and-white with the red appearing in all shades from the very light to the very dark, and tricolors – black-and-white with tan markings similar to the tan markings on the black-and-tans. Mis-marks are those solid colors with white anywhere other than a small amount on the chest and throat, which is penalized but not subject to disqualification. In particolors, the contrasting color must be ten per cent or more and broken markings on the back are desirable.

care

The present day Cocker Spaniel needs grooming often to prevent matting of the coat or an unkempt look. Professional trimming and bathing every two months will keep the Cocker looking clean, typy and stylish in appearance. Proper trimming of the Cocker Spaniel consists of cleaning the skull and muzzle and trimming about two inches down on the ears with an electric clipper. The neck and shoulders and the body should be carefully scissored with thinning scissors to give an outline to the dog that closely resembles a top show dog in appearance. Leave all feathering on the legs, ears and underneath the dog. The bottom of the feet should be trimmed with straight scissors, the nails cut and the feet neatly rounded to give the appearance of a large fluffy paw.

character

The Cocker Spaniel was originally a hunting dog and could still be if those characteristics were developed.

He has great intelligence and is willing to obey. To sportsmen he is known as a "close hunter" which means he should never hunt out of gun range which is approximately thirty yards. His purpose in hunting is to find game and flush it or make it rise for the shot, then go out and retrieve the bird. While the Cocker may not be used as extensively as a hunting dog as some of the larger breeds, he is extremely popular with those who do use him. Many feel that he has a better nose than many other breeds and seldom does he miss locating a wounded or running game bird.

The Cocker Spaniel is popular as a pet because he is adaptable. He adjusts himself to any surroundings – whether it be an apartment, a country estate, a farm, or an automobile. He is an ideal family dog. He is a wonderful companion, ready for a walk in the woods or for an evening at your feet in front of the fire. He much prefers the companionship of humans to that of his own kind. He has a great record in obedience work.

Undoubtedly, the amazing popularity of the Cocker Spaniel and the

American Cockers come in all Spaniel colors, and a few peculiar to themselves. In this charming picture four blacks flank a buff puppy – sometimes described as blond.

Top winning Cocker Spaniel in America in 1967 was Mr. and Mrs. Norman Juelich's Ch. Dream Echo Magic Touch. His gleaming black coat is groomed to perfection.

fact that he set an all time record by remaining at the top in registrations of the American Kennel Club for over sixteen years, is due to many things that go to make up this wonderful breed. His wonderful disposition, his desire to socialize with the human race, his love for the outdoors and hunting, his wish to please his master and to obey his every command, his beauty, his lovely expressive eyes, and many more lovable traits make the Cocker Spaniel the ideal breed for all.

standards

The present Standard of the Cocker Spaniel was approved by the American Spaniel Club and by the American Kennel Club in 1957. The greatest change made at this time was to include a different requirement for size. Previously, weight was the size control. This called for a minimum of 22 lbs. and a maximum of 28 lbs. for both sexes.

The present requirement is based on height. Males are given a maximum of $15\frac{1}{2}''$ at the withers and females $14\frac{1}{2}''$. Any dog or bitch exceeding these maximums is subject to disqualification. Since the new Standard has been in effect, there has been a definite improvement in uniformity in both dog and bitch classes at the shows. Although there is no minimum requirement, there are very few extremely small individuals seen in the shows.

The Standard gives a detailed description of every part of the Cocker Spaniel but a summation of it all is well described in the paragraph titled "General Description" included in the Standard: "Embodying the foregoing, we have a serviceable looking dog with a refinedly chiseled head, standing on straight legs and well up at the shoulder; of compact body and wide, muscular quarters. The Cocker Spaniel's sturdy body, powerful quarters and strong, well-boned legs, show him to be a dog capable of considerable speed combined with great endurance. Above all, he must be free and merry, sound, well-balanced throughout, and in action show a keen inclination to work; equable in temperament with no suggestion of timidity".

This blond American Cocker, Ch. Pah-Mars Jack Frost, owned by the Silver Maple Kennels, illustrates the characteristic and very individual head of the breed, shorter in muzzle, deeper in the stop, and more chiseled than any other of the Spaniel breeds. The low set ears and profuse feathering of the legs are also clearly seen.

Spaniel, American Water

The close curled coat of the American Water Spaniel.

When the American Kennel Club admitted the American Water Spaniel to registration in 1940, it seemingly did little or no research into the early history of the breed. As a matter of fact, it had not then set up a formula by which new breeds were to be admitted. A so-called national breed club then in existence could come up with only the visual evidence that it was descended from either/or the Irish Water Spaniel and Curly-coated Retriever. For good measure the sponsors threw in reference to the long defunct English Water Spaniel. It is doubtful that anyone living on the North American Continent within the last 100 years ever saw a specimen of the last named breed. For the rest, only the Irish Water and the Curly Retriever could have passed down the tightly curled coat in the liver or dark chocolate colors. No conjecture was made as to how the breed got a size smaller than either of its obvious ancestors, other than to tack the name "Spaniel" on to a small retriever. It does, however, work like a spaniel in upland hunting.

The group that petitioned the A.K.C. to accept the American Water Spaniel as a distinct breed came mainly from the Mid-West and the North-East, but there is evidence that this is the same breed that was known since before the Civil War (1861–65) as the Boykin Spaniel. Indeed, in many parts of the United States that name is still in everyday use. Over the years, the Information Service of the A.K.C. has received countless inquiries on the Boykin. Pursuing this line the Service has traced the breed to Boykin, South Carolina. Furthermore, it has on file a rather poor photograph that is still good enough to identify both the Boykin's size and coat as being identical with that of the American Water Spaniel. One of the foremost breeders was a Whit Boykin. And as late as 1953, one of the prominent breeders was Mrs. William A. Boykin, Wannah Plantation, Boykin, S.C. Undoubtedly, one of the smaller spaniels, possibly the American Cocker, played a major role in developing the American Water Spaniel, which is among the smaller of the medium-sized breeds. It stands 15″ to 18″ at the shoulder. A male should weigh 28 to 45 lbs. and the bitch 25 to 40 lbs.

It is said to be very efficient on grouse, quail, woodcock, snipe, rabbits and even pheasant. On water, he can even manage duck, for he is a strong swimmer.

The breed has a head moderate in length, skull broad and full, stop moderately defined; short, smooth hair on forehead. Fairly wide nose to insure good scenting; even bite; well-developed body; not too compactly coupled; shoulders sloping; strong loins, lightly arched and well furnished; deep brisket but not excessively broad; well-sprung ribs. Legs are of medium length and well-boned; forelegs powerful; hindlegs with suitably bent stifles; tail moderate in length, carried slightly below level of back, tapered and covered with hair.

The American Water Spaniel is still principally a working gun dog. Not too many are seen at the shows. Registrations are now close to 300 a year, the breed standing about 80th among 116.

The alert, inquisitive expression of a typical American Water Spaniel.

267

Spaniel, Brittany

A beautiful specimen of the Brittany Spaniel, working in America.

A Brittany Spaniel in the field in France.

history and development

"A maximum of quality in a minimum size!" That most admirable description of the Brittany Spaniel was written by one of the most distinguished experts of the dog world, Gaston Pouchain, President of the Kennel Club of France, and the Brittany Spaniel Club of France.

The growth of this delightful breed has been amazing; during the present century its popularity has spread not only in Europe, but all over the world, and particularly in the United States. This is all the more surprising when we consider that they were not breeding true to type until around 1907, so that in the space of sixty years or so, a local breed from the provinces of France has caught the imagination and affection of dog-lovers everywhere.

One reason for this growth may be the common-sense used to protect and improve the basic stock; sound utilitarian principles have always been followed, and these have not been debased by purely aesthetic considerations which might have weakened and debilitated the original strain.

The first Brittany Spaniels were not exported to America until 1931; by 1934 there were already enough pure-bred dogs available for showing to qualify for American Kennel Club registration. The number increased steadily throughout the following decades, and by the end of 1969 the

Brittany had climbed to 20th place amongst the 116 breeds in the A.K.C. book, with a yearly registration of almost 11,000 specimens.

The ancestral history of these dogs is much harder to establish with any certainty; there are very few records of individual breeds and out-crosses during the early years of Western civilization. At the time of the first Crusades, dogs and horses traveled all over the known world with their masters; English, French, Spanish and Arab animals inter-bred for centuries. Some Spanish influence is indicated by the name, but by the Middle Ages the "Espaigneul" had become so popular in France that we call this common ancestor of all hunting spaniels the Old French Spaniel. Tapestries and paintings throughout the mediaeval period show hundreds of such dogs as hunting and domestic companions.

The northern region of Brittany was already known for its "cobby" stock in both dogs and horses; through various genetic influences the spaniel of the north adapted itself to the new climate and environment. It grew smaller and more square-bodied than its southern relatives; its ears were shorter, and a natural instinct for hunting found ample exercise in the thick forests full of woodcock and other game.

No doubt at some time during this long period Celtic huntsmen brought

A Continental Brittany Spaniel.

269

A Brittany Spaniel out on a shoot in France.

Welsh Springers across the Channel, and perhaps the ancestor of today's mahogany-red Irish Setter as well. Somehow the little Breton dog absorbed all these influences, but it was not until the 19th century that the Brittany really emerges from the mists and confusion of conjecture.

A Breton Count lived, at the beginning of that century, in Pontou, a small community in the Valley of Douran. Like so many local sportsmen, he hunted woodcock, and for that purpose kept a number of smallish, red-and-white setters, thought to be of British origin. It seems that one of these dogs mated with a local bitch; her litter included two short-tailed puppies, and this was the beginning of the Brittany Spaniel. The little female proved to be the dominating influence, and most of the setter characteristics disappeared, except for increased scenting powers, excellent health, and a refined and well-bred appearance. In addition, the coat color retained the vivid red splotches of the sire, adding to the breed's appeal.

Since that time, constant improvement has resulted in a type that is almost in a class of its own.

color

The original coat color was orange or red on a white base; each of these types had a pinky-beige nose. In 1933, the Brittany Spaniel Club of France changed the Standards to include black and white coats, with tobacco-brown noses. At the outset, many protests were heard from the purists, but the Club felt that it was becoming increasingly difficult to breed light-colored coats with healthy pigmentation. In America the black and white is not yet considered on a par with the red or orange-white coats.

The various markings may be in large spots, or speckled all over the coat. If the coat is orange-and-white, some tan speckling around the edges of the orange markings is permitted. In any case, there should be no speckling on the nose. Washed-out or faded colors are not desirable.

character

A courageous, almost reckless hunter with an excellent nose, the Brittany is very fast, very strong, and afraid of nothing; the brambles and impenetrable thickets, which form the autumn and winter home of the woodcock, will never discourage it. A natural talent for "pointing" has been well developed, and a Brittany will never flush or start the birds until his master is within easy range. Great intelligence and a deep affection for his owner will make the dog shrink from any harsh treatment; kindness is the most important word in the training vocabulary. The Brittany may be tempted by the scents of other game animals while hunting; this tendency can easily be curbed with a firm, but kind, hand.

standards

The Brittany stands somewhere between the spaniels and the setters. A square-shaped body is matched with well-rounded sides. Bone structure is solid and powerful, but should never become so heavy that the dog is out of proportion. A well-built Brittany can sustain its characteristic energetic gallop over long periods of time, and even over rough and difficult terrain. The silhouette, especially when tracking, shows a distinctive thrust of the neck, and good head carriage.

The skull formation is unusual; well-rounded, with a good stop, although the slope is fairly gentle. Broad at the stop, the head narrows towards the nose, although never enough to give a wolfish shape. The middle furrow is lightly marked, but the occipital bump is small compared to the English Setter.

Perfectly trained Brittany Spaniels – four American National field champions.

271

The muzzle is fairly short. Dark amber eyes have a lively, expressive look; the color of the nose may vary from pinky-beige to tobacco brown, as indicated above. No speckling is permitted on the nose or the eyelids. Ears are very important, being set high on the skull; they should be flat and fairly short.

In addition to the general outline given above, the Brittany should have good sloping shoulders, and powerful legs. Height at the withers should be about the same as the length of the back.

The tail may be missing altogether, naturally short, or artificially docked; in any case, it must not exceed four inches in length.

The coat is not as thick as the English Setter; the texture is fairly silky and straight, or with a slight wave. Feathering occurs on the throat, under the stomach, on the legs and tail.

Height is 17½″ to 20½″ at the shoulder; weight 33 to 44 lbs.
The American Standard is slightly lighter in weight (30 to 40 lbs.).

A sturdy specimen of the breed.

Spaniel, Clumber

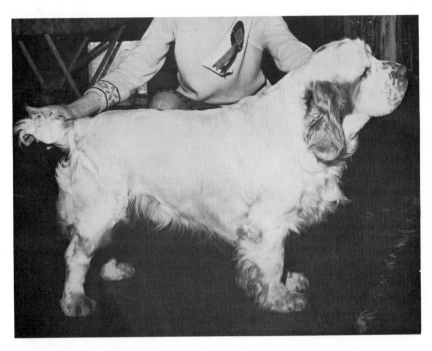

Mr. and Mrs. F. Stanley's Ch. Frastan Anchorfield Bardolph, winner of eight C.C.s and fifty best of breed awards. He won the gundog group at Birmingham National championship show in England, and reserve in the gundog group at Cruft's in 1968: and reserve in the gundog group at Birmingham in 1969. He was the first Clumber Spaniel to qualify as a full champion for many years.

history and development

These great dogs, the heaviest of the Spaniel family, are said to have their origin in France. It is believed they were derived from a cross between the now extinct Alpine Spaniel and a Basset Hound about two centuries ago. They were fostered and bred by the Duc de Noailles before the French Revolution and were much prized for their work in the field, where they were used as beaters and retrievers. When troubled times came to France the Duc removed his famous kennel to England, to the care of the Duke of Newcastle at Clumber Park and so they got the name Clumber Spaniels. The Duc de Noailles returned to France and was killed in the Revolution, and the Spaniels remained in England.

The first class for Clumbers in England was at Birmingham in 1859 and the breed was first registered in the United States in 1878. They gained in popularity. Foremost among their owners was King George V and from his great Sandringham Kennels he worked and showed them. Unfortunately, during the First World War, and afterwards, they declined in numbers but they have been built up again to a fine standard by a band of devoted breeders.

Among the many wins of Mr. and Mrs. G. Foreman-Brown's Sh. Ch. Vence of Hamrik was best of breed at Cruft's in 1970.

color

Plain white, with lemon markings; orange permissible, but not desirable; slight head markings and freckled muzzle, with white body preferred. The fewer markings on the body, the better.

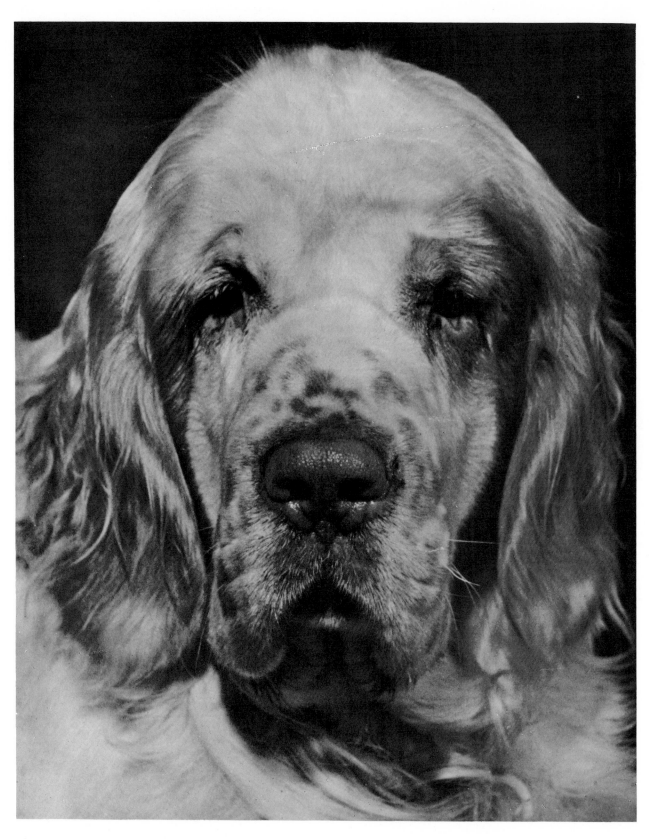

This head study of Bardolph shows how well he represents the breed Standard. Note the great breadth of skull and the intelligent, thoughtful expression.

care

Regular feeding and an availability of fresh water at all times are basic requirements of any dog including the Clumber, together with normal exercise routines and coat care.

character

This is a great-hearted dog who works patiently and well; he is much used for rough shooting, working silently through the thickest cover. A very willing dog and, although rather slow, is a sure finder and a splendid retriever when trained.

standards

The Clumbers are square, massive, very heavy dogs with a kind and thoughtful aspect. They weigh about 55 to 70 lbs. and several working together are a most impressive sight. They have a rich creamy white coat, straight, thick and silky.

The head is square and massive, broad across the top, with heavy brows and a distinct stop. The muzzle is heavy with well-developed flews, the jaws are level, the nose square and flesh colored. The eyes are dark amber and slightly sunken; the ears, large and vine-leaf shaped, are covered with straight hair and are carried forward.

The neck is fairly long, thick, muscular and well feathered below. The shoulders are long and sloping, the chest deep and ribs well sprung. The front legs are short, strong, straight and thick.

The body is long and heavy, near the ground, wide and powerful. The hindquarters and hindlegs are strong, muscular and wide. The stifles are well bent and hocks low. The tail is set low, is well-feathered and level with the back. The feet are rounded and large.

Sh. Ch. Oldholbans Flare, best of breed at Cruft's in 1969, has also proved a good brood. Note her great depth of brisket and chest, with big rib development.

Sh. Ch. Eastway Lion, owned by Mr. and Mrs. Foreman-Brown, top winner in his breed and best in show at all-breed championship shows.

Spaniel, Cocker
(English)

Miss Joan Macmillan's black Sh. Ch. Lochranza Strollaway, winner of eighteen C.C.s and seventeen best-of-breed awards before being exported to the Argentine. The best of his many top wins was reserve best in show, all breeds, at Cruft's in 1969.

history and development

The Cocker Spaniel (known in the U.S.A. today as the English Cocker Spaniel) can claim to be one of the oldest and most popular varieties of the Spaniel family, whose ancient lineage can be traced back to the 14th century. Although popularly believed to have originated in Spain, records show that these early Spaniels were widely used in many parts of the world in the sport of falconry, where, presumably the Spaniel was used to flush game for the hawks. This cannot have been the most efficient means of filling the larder, which is no doubt why we find reference to the practise of netting, with the aid of Spaniels to drive the game into the nets.

Basically, the Spaniel's work is the same the world over, but the game and the terrain, which he was required to work, differed greatly, resulting in a gradual evolution in type and size which became apparent between Spaniels from one country or district and another. As a result of this evolution, the Spaniel became subdivided into the different types which go to make up the numerous varieties known today.

In the early 19th century, the term "Cocking Spaniel" or "Cocker" (said to have originated through his aptitude for use on woodcock) was used to describe a small Spaniel, particularly popular in Devon and Wales, being, on account of its size, thoroughly adapted to the low and thick covert prevailing in these areas.

It was not, however, until 1892 that the Cocker was recognized by the Kennel Club in England and entered in the Stud Book under its now official title of Cocker Spaniel. In the years since the first dog show in

1859, the Cocker had competed under the classification of "Field Spaniel of 25 lbs. and under" (the term Field Spaniel did not refer to the breed that we recognize as such today but to all Spaniels used in the field). Ridiculous as it may seem today, the Cocker could, at that time, change his breed by eating a hearty meal and become a "Field or Springer Spaniel". Worse still, dogs born to the same parents could belong to different breeds; a situation which caused untold complications when the Kennel Club came to separate the varieties and record pedigrees.

In 1901 the weight limit, which had so hampered the progress of the Cocker, was abolished. From then on, uniformity in type was established; quality made rapid improvement and many good strains were established which were to become the foundations of the modern Cocker.

One of the most successful kennels of almost a century ago was that of Mr. James Farrow, whose great dog, Obo, founded a strain which was to prove the basis of many of our Cockers today.

While the Cocker continued to improve and draw increased entries at shows under the guidance of such breeders as Mr. R. Lloyd, founder of the Of Ware suffix, and father of the late Mr. H. S. Lloyd (often called the Wizard of Ware because of his phenomenal successes as a handler), others were achieving equal successes at field trials. One who had perhaps most influence in developing the working side of the Cocker was Mr. C. A. Phillips, whose Rivington Cockers won no less than 38 single stakes between 1919 and 1939.

Today, breeders tend to support either the shows or the field trials – seldom both – a pity perhaps, but understandable in this hurried age when the cost of both is so high.

The Cocker today is still the smallest of the British Spaniels in the Gundog Group, but by no means the least significant as he tops the Spaniel

Demonstrating that show dogs also have the ability to work is Miss J. Macmillan's Ch. Lochranza Latchkey, a popular winner in Britain in the late forties and early fifties.

F. T. Ch. Goldspan Jet Adore, owned by Mrs. P. Leigh, who had twenty-five field trial awards to his credit. He was second in the K.C. Championship in 1965 and third in 1969.

Miss Pat Nielson with the red bitch, Sh. Ch. Noslien Naughty Nineties, and the black dog, Sh. Ch. Noslien Nathaniel, who both won C.C.s at Cruft's in 1966.

registrations by a considerable margin (a position he has held for many years) with 6,465 registrations being recorded with the Kennel Club in 1969 proving him to be the most popular of all the Spaniels in Britain.

color

With no less than fourteen possible variations, the Cocker can boast a profusion of colors enjoyed by no other breed or variety. These can, however, be divided into two sections i.e. solids, and any other color.

Solids are self-colors; black, red, golden (a misnomer often applied to a red, but an uncommon color these days, and a much paler shade); and liver (another rare color, at one time common, particularly among the Devon Cockers of long ago). In solids, a small amount of white, although undesirable, is allowed on the chest but penalized elsewhere, for which reason it is unwise to risk mating a solid to anything but another solid, for fear of producing mismarked puppies.

Particolor and tricolor are those with an intermingling of the above colors with white, singly or in combination; flecked, ticked or patterned; creating a variety of combinations which is almost bewildering.

Another color is the black and tan, which is gaining popularity at the moment. These are born of solid color parents which carry the tan gene. This color does not compete with the solid section in this country as in the United States, but in the any other color section.

Most of the colors known today can be traced back to those early ancestors of the breed, with the exception of the blue roan of which no early mention is made.

care

The Cocker is remarkably hardy and, if fit, can work tirelessly to the end of the day, in all weathers, without suffering any ill-effects, provided he is dried well on his return.

A well-balanced diet will keep him in good shape, but beware of those pleading eyes and do not allow constant tit-bits or he may develop a figure of which you will be ashamed and he will be uncomfortable.

Regular exercise is essential, and a country walk is his greatest pleasure, but train him well in his youth to come to heel on command or he may chase off after a rabbit.

Although he will happily suffer the greatest discomfort for the pleasure of accompanying the family on any excursion, he will object strongly to lying on a hard, draughty floor and will choose the softest chair and the warmest spot in front of the fire, if his master is so uncivilized as to neglect to provide a warm comfortable box or basket of his own.

The Cocker's coat is one of his attractions but regular grooming is essential for his comfort. The amount of coat varies between individual dogs, but most require to be trimmed every three to six months, largely depending on the efficiency of routine grooming. This is a job for the Spaniel expert as Spaniel-trimming requires more skill than, say, Poodle clipping.

character

The passing years have seen changes in the shape and size of the Cocker, but his character, the very essence of the "Merry Little Cocker", remains as always; no man having found it wanting nor having envisaged any possible improvement.

(opposite)
A black and white bitch with a lovely head, English and South African Ch. Craigleith Sweet Charity, bred by Mrs. Mollie Robinson.

A promising puppy—Mr. Wm. A. Mathew's Ardnamurchan Mac.

Although Mrs. Doxford has made champions in both solids and particolors, undoubtedly her reds have proved the most successful. Ch. Broomleaf Bonny Lad of Shillwater was a top show dog and sire in Britain in the late forties and early fifties.

History records the faithful, loving nature of the Spaniel, none of which has greater affection for his master than the Cocker. He may not win a place in the prize-lists at Cruft's, or at a field trial, but win a place in your heart he most certainly will.

His desire for constant human companionship, combined with a happy, gentle nature makes him an ideal family pet. Adaptable and willing to participate in all the doings of the family, he is equally happy sitting by the fire, romping on the floor with the children or pottering about the garden. He can be taught to employ his natural instincts to retrieve in many ways in fetching and carrying and is a professional in the nursery game of Hunt the Slipper. In training a young Cocker, it should be remembered that his desire for the approval of his master is paramount – the voice, not the hand, is usually all that is necessary to chastise the Cocker.

The Cocker is, however, really in his element working with the gun and it is here perhaps that one really appreciates him. The joyous busy little figure, with ever-wagging tail – the hall-mark of the Cocker – will quarter the ground at speed, pausing to nose out a sitting rabbit; becoming as if rooted to the spot as the rabbit bolts and is dropped by the gun; then on to push out another; ignoring, but not forgetting, the first.

At a trial, a judge may require the dog to pick the last rabbit first; scent may be bad and the dog may not have been in a position to see where it was dropped – at the same time he may have marked the first and the inclination will be to go for this one. It is here we see the complete obedience and understanding which exists between dog and handler; in this' case he must rely almost entirely on his handler to guide him by whistle and hand signs.

If any owner of a Cocker has the opportunity to watch at a Spaniel trial, he will most certainly return with a greater respect and understanding of the true nature of the Cocker.

standards

In modern times, the Cocker is seen in greater numbers in the show ring than in the field; it should be remembered, however, that the Cocker is, by tradition, instinct and origin, a gundog and the Standard (little altered from the original drawn up nearly a century ago by those with considerable experience of the working Cocker) by which a judge assesses the merits of an exhibit, is based entirely on working essentials.

From time to time controversy arises between those whose sole interest is in the field trial and those mainly concerned with exhibition. The former contending that the show Cocker is in danger of losing his working instincts through lack of usage and the latter making the counter charge that many of today's working Cockers do not conform to the Standard. In Britain a working Cocker can become a field trial champion without ever having to compete at a show; in the same way a show Cocker can become a show champion without having to prove his working ability, although in his case he can, and often does, run at a trial to gain a qualifying certificate which entitles him to drop from his title the restricting prefix "show".

In some countries, the working Cocker has to come up to a reasonable Standard in appearance before he is allowed breed registration, and the show Cocker is expected to prove some ability in the field.

No doubt controversy will continue as long as Cocker continue to be bred but no Cocker can be the worse for being as near as possible in appearance to the ideal as visualized by the official Standard.

The Cocker should be well-balanced and compact, and measure about the same from withers to the ground as from the withers to the root of the tail. A good square muzzle with a distinct stop mid-way between nose-tip and occiput; a well-developed, cleanly chiseled skull; full but not prominent eyes should be brown or dark brown, never light; lobular ears set-on low should extend to the nose-tip; quarters well-boned; tail set-on slightly lower than back level, carried in line with back and not docked too long or too short.

The coat should be flat and silky in texture, never wiry or wavy, with sufficient feather.

Height about 15½″ to 16″ for dogs; bitches about ½″ less. In the U.S.A. it is 16″ to 17″ for males; one inch less for bitches.

Mr. A. S. Mansfield's Ch. Lucklena Musical Maid, born in 1955, won eighteen C.C.s between 1956 and 1961 and was one of the few Cockers ever to beat Ch. Colinwood Silver Lariot – perhaps it was poetic justice that she bred three champions, all to Lariot.

Ch. Colinwood Silver Lariot, a blue roan owned by Mr. A. W. Collins, is the breed record holder in Britain, with fifty-seven C.C.s won under fifty-three judges. He was also nine times best in show at all-breed championship shows, and ten times reserve.

Spaniel, English Springer

Ch. Alexander of Stubham, owned by Mrs. F. Oughtred Till, was son of a famous sire, Boxer of Bramhope, and had a great show record in the fifties. He won twenty-three C.C.s and was best in show twenty-four times. At the ages of three and ten years he was best of breed at Cruft's. A big dog with great style and show presence Alexander proved a most successful ambassador for the breed in post-war England.

Most of the big winning English Springers have been liver and whites. A notable exception is the lovely black and white, Ch. Swallowtail of Shipden, owned by Mr. and Mrs. C. Muirhead. Not only a multiple C.C. winner, he also scored in championship show group competitions in 1969.

history and development

The English Springer is the oldest of the sporting spaniels and is thought to be the origin of all the land spaniel varieties, Clumbers excepted.

It was originally used for springing game for the net, falcon or greyhound, methods of hunting followed before the use of shotguns. The earliest reference to the name Springer was used in England by Dr. Caius who wrote on dogs about 1570 and he used the term for land spaniels. About 1800 the Boughey family of Aqualate developed a distinct variety of land spaniel and maintained a stud book for their strain from the year 1813. In 1903 Sir Thomas Boughey bred Field Trial Champion Velox Powder, winner of twenty field trial stakes, whose pedigree extended back to a bitch whelped in 1812. The family retained its interest in the breed until the 1930's and many of today's bench and field trial winners are in direct descent from this strain. The Norfolk family also kept a distinct strain of Springing Spaniel but before the year 1900 these had become known as Springer Spaniels.

The first field trial organized by the Sporting Spaniel Club was held in 1899 at Sutton Scarsdale in England. The Spaniel Club, founded in 1885, organized its first field trial in 1900. At the second trial in 1901 a Springer won the open stake; this was Mr. Gardner's Tring. In 1902 the Kennel Club gave separate classification for Springers and the first champions on

The best in show winner at West-minster, 1971, English Springer Spaniel Am. Ch. Chinoe's Adament James.

English Springer Spaniel – side and front head views.

the bench were the dog, Beechgrove Will, and the bitch, Fansom. The first field trial champion was Rivington Sam. The English Springer Spaniel Club was formed in 1921 with a strong committee of show and field trial owners. The Club has continued to flourish and organizes its own championship show and field trials on an annual basis.

color

Any land spaniel color is acceptable with the exception of the red/white of the Welsh Springer. The most usual and generally exhibited colors are liver/white, black/white, liver/white/tan and black/white/tan. There is no rule as to the proportion of dark color to white. Heavily or lightly marked animals are both accepted.

care

Generally speaking, this is not a breed for a town house or flat unless one has access to open country or common land. A Springer needs a fair amount of exercise and is a very active dog. He will benefit from daily grooming and it is wise to check on eyes and ears after work in thick cover. It is also a good thing to dry out the inside of the ears after swimming.

character

The English Springer is extremely easy to house train and makes an excellent companion but it is as a gundog that he excels. As a breed they really enjoy work and although it is difficult for many Springer owners to find enough work for their dogs during the shooting season, they can be trained for ordinary obedience work or gundog working tests. The latter provide a great deal of fun for both dog and owner. They are loyal and affectionate to man but they have a great love for their own kind.

standards

The general appearance of the English Springer is that of a symmetrical, compact, strong, upstanding, merry and active dog, built for endurance and activity. He is the highest on the leg and raciest of build of all British land spaniels.

The head is of medium length, fairly broad and slightly rounded. There should be a definite stop divided by a fluting between the eyes and gradually dying away along the forehead. Eyes should be of medium size, not showing haw, and should be dark hazel in color. The ear should be lobular in shape, set in line with the eye and carrying feather. The neck should be strong and muscular and well set in the shoulders; the body strong and of medium length with well sprung ribs and muscular quarters. The tail should be set low and never carried above the level of the back, well feathered and with a lively action. Forelegs should be straight and well feathered; the feet well rounded, tight and compact with full pads. Stifles and hocks should be moderately bent. The coat should be close, straight and weather resisting. The approximate height at the shoulder should be 20″ and the approximate weight 50 lbs. The American Standard gives 20″ at withers as the ideal for a dog, an inch less for a bitch.

Unfortunately, there is some divergence of type between the show bench dog and its field trial counterpart. The show dog being bigger, in some cases over the Standard height and the working dog being considerably smaller

Mrs. M. Scott's Boxer of Bramhope, key sire of the breed in the post-war period, but with a rooted dislike of the show-ring.

The greatest winning English Springer after the Second World War in Britain, Mr. Ernest Froggatt's Ch. Moorcliff Dougal of Truelindale has twice been best in show at general championship shows in Britain, has won twenty-two C.C.s, and has also qualified in the field.

(opposite)
Mrs. J. A. Hancock and Mr. J. Cudworth's Sh. Ch. Slayleigh Paulina, noted especially for her beautiful neck and shoulders and excellent hindquarters.

Mrs. D. Dobson's Ch. Teesview Titus. A working show dog, this is a slightly different type from the other English Springers illustrated here, but is nevertheless a descendant of the great Boxer of Bramhope.

English Springer Spaniel puppies.

than the Standard. However, there is a small but enthusiastic following for the working show dog and it is from these breeders that most of the Springers in Europe descend. In France, for example, a dog must be passed as a typical specimen of its breed before it is issued a pedigree. As the average field trial dog does not conform to the accepted Standard, it is seldom passed. Therefore most of the dogs in France are working show bred. To become a full champion in France the dog has not only to win its C.A.C. (equivalent of the British Challenge Certificates) at the annual Paris Show but it must win at a field trial as well. Similar standards are required in Italy and Sweden.

In America only bench wins are required for a championship, and field trial wins for a field trial champion. At present there is a good demand for the breed in both Europe and America. To become a show champion in Britain a dog requires to win three Challenge Certificates under three different judges. To become a field trial champion the dog is required to win two open stakes at a championship trial. To become a full champion, a dog must win three Challenge Certificates under three different judges plus a Qualifying Certificate at a field trial or a Qualifying Certificate at the special qualifying trial for Spaniels which is held annually. It is now possible for first prize winners at a championship show to be entered for the Qualifying Certificate at the annual trial. Challenge Certificate winners are still able to run at this trial or at a championship field trial.

Mrs. F. H. Gasow's American Ch. Salilyn's Aristocrat, pictured here winning the group at Westminster, America's greatest dog show. The similarity in type and the different style of trimming between the British and the American Springer is very apparent. Aristocrat has an impressive record both on the bench and as a sire.

Spaniel, Field

Captain and Mrs. Jones have played an important part in the revival of the Field Spaniel and this black bitch, Elmbury Morwena of Rhiwlas, has contributed much to their success.

history and development

The Field Spaniel and the Cocker Spaniel had a similar origin and these breeds were not separated until 1892. Up to that time they were known as "Field Spaniels Under 25 lbs." and "Field Spaniels Over 25 lbs.". However, with the separation into two separate breeds, a great change came about. The Cocker Spaniel, improving in type and appearance, went from strength to strength, whereas the Field Spaniel went through many vicissitudes. It became grossly exaggerated, being very long in the body and very short on the leg. There was a famous dog in 1900 that stood 12″ high and weighed 40 lbs. It was this exaggeration that nearly finished the breed and it is wonderful that it has been rescued and re-modelled in the way that it has. The Field Spaniel Society was re-formed in 1948. Much enthusiastic work has been done by a handful of people and a shapely, useful, intelligent dog has been evolved, which has become fixed in type, and which is breeding true. This is indeed a triumph.

In the United States, considerable difficulty was experienced as the Springer–Cocker crosses, which were introduced to eliminate the earlier exaggerations, were ineligible for registration by the American Kennel Club. However, although the breed is now firmly established and accepted, only nine specimens were registered with the A.K.C. in 1969, and one only in 1968.

It can be seen from this head study that Little Corporal of Mittina has the true Field Spaniel head and expression.

color

The Field Spaniel should be a self-colored dog: black, liver, golden liver, mahogany red, roan, or any of these colors with tan over the eyes, on the cheeks, feet and pasterns. Other colors such as black and white, liver and white, red or orange and white etc. are a fault.

care
No special care is necessary with this breed.

character
Level-headed and intelligent, it field-trains well and is easy to handle. It makes a most affectionate companion, and has a reliable temperament and is very docile.

standards
The general appearance should be that of a well-balanced, noble, upstanding sporting dog; built for activity and endurance; a combination of utility and beauty. The head is the very stamp of the Field Spaniel and should at once convey the impression of high breeding and character; and it should be of good contour, slightly domed. The well-developed skull has a distinct occipital protuberance. Not too wide across the muzzle, long and lean, neither snipey nor square cut and, in profile, curving gradually from nose to throat; lean beneath the eyes (any thickness here gives coarseness to the whole head). The great length of muzzle has made for free development of the greatest possible scenting powers. The ears should be moderately long and wide, set-on low with ample feather.

The neck is long and muscular, set into long well-laid shoulders. The body, not too long, is slightly longer than the height, the chest is deep, the quarters strong. The forelegs are straight and have good bone and hind-legs are muscular, firm and well turned. The tail must always be carried low, be constantly moving and must not get up too high. The coat is dense and silky, feathering must be moderate.

Dogs stand between 18″ at the shoulder and weigh between 35 lbs. and 50 lbs.

Spaniel, French

This French Pointing Spaniel is the mainspring of all other breeds of long-haired Pointers, commonly called "Spaniels". It is interesting to note at this point that the word "Spaniel" does not derive from "Spanish", but from the old French term "s'espanir", meaning "to flatten oneself" or "to lie down", a meaning somewhat akin to the English "to span". The long-haired hunting dogs had existed in large numbers for very many years in France, although they were never bred to any extent in Spain, due probably to the climate, which does not favor long-haired dogs.

Imported from England since the 14th century the French Spaniels were the very prototype of the "setting" dogs, specially gifted for pointing, and having little of the hound in their blood, contrary to the French Pointer. The two breeds, long-haired and short-haired, were at the end of the Middle Ages called Oysel Dogs, not only because they were originally bird dogs but also because they were used as an ancillary to the falcon (synonymous with Oysel). The term was especially reserved for the Spaniel, or pointing dog with long hair, adapted to hunting with a snare, creeping along and standing still when he smelled feathers.

It is relevant to say that when the English Setter was evolved it retained this quality of creeping and setting. The foreign Spaniels, on the other hand, did not achieve this capacity to the same degree. Physically the French Spaniel is very like the English Springer Spaniel and the Dutch Drentse Partrijshond, especially in the coat and shape of head. The very bushy tail is never docked, and the coat is smooth, the hair on ears and sides of the body being slightly wavy. The body is not so long as the English Setter, and lower.

Dogs over 23½" in height are preferred, and bitches over 21"; the weight is generally between 44 and 59 lbs. The preferred colors are white and tan, specks of tan are allowed on the white so long as they are not too numerous and do not give the impression that the dog is marked in this way. The tan is quite different from the liver of the English Setter.

Typical coat and coloration of the French Spaniel.

Spaniel, German

This is Hajduk, bred in Yugoslavia in 1938 by the Conte Marin Pavlovic and owned by Edvard Gregoric.

The Wachtelhund is similar to the English Springer Spaniel in its use, size and coat, but it is reputed to be hardier and has a strong bite when used against game. Its temperament is better suited to German conditions and methods than the British breed.

Although the Wachtelhund is well behaved in the kennel it does not have the gentle character, say, of the Cocker Spaniel. One wonders why this interesting breed is so little known outside Germany, where it is renowned as a retriever and an outstanding gundog.

It has an impressive appearance, standing some 18″ to 20″ high. It is bred for hard work, being very well muscled and boned.

The head is lean, the crown and muzzle long, with a slight occipital bump, and the stop hardly visible. The ears are set-on high, broad and flat (unlike the Cocker). The nose brown, mobile, with large, open nostrils.

The neck is strong, no dewlap, the chest ample and deep, the body a little longer than its height at the withers. The tail set high, docked, and carried energetically. The back legs well angled, rather long pasterns. Good quarters, well angled.

The thick coat is shiny, but not silky in texture, slightly wavy, fuller at the neck and forelock. The legs and tail well feathered.

Colors are dark brown, often with white marks on chest and toes. The coat can also be white, or white and brown, or white with brown spots.

The Wachtelhund, or German Spaniel.

Spaniel, Irish Water

history and development

This is an ancient breed which goes back in history for over 1,000 years. Drawings of dogs looking very like the Irish Water Spaniel of today can be seen in old manuscripts. Two different strains of Irish Water Spaniel appear to have existed before 1859; the South Country and the North Country. From the distinctive color and conformation of the South Country variety, it appears that it played the larger part in forming the breed as it exists today. Its likeness to the Standard Poodle is striking and is shown not only in its general outline and structure but in the texture of coat; crisp, harsh and of the non-moulting type; also by the smooth short hair on the face, neck and legs, now so rarely seen in the untrimmed Poodle but produced still in their show presentation.

Head profile of an Irish Water Spaniel.

color

This Spaniel is always a rich liver puce in color, and should have no white on it.

care

The coat with its crisp curls and dense undercoat does not present the problem that might be expected. It should be thoroughly combed through at least once a week using a steel comb to prevent felting. The old discolored hair should be removed with a stripping comb. The feet should be trimmed round, but not between the toes. When cleared of tangles, a good swim will instantly bring back the curl and give the rugged finish to this handsome dog.

character

This powerful breed is well suited to all the hard work it can be given. It is easy to train, deeply affectionate and reliable in temperament. It is strongly built and intelligent. Ideal for all kinds of shooting, especially wild-fowling and work in water. Biddable and loyal, it will show great courage and face the thickest cover. It has an excellent nose, quarters ceaselessly and retrieves tenderly to hand. It always works as a spaniel, not as a retriever.

standards

It is the tallest of the Spaniel family standing about 21″ to 23″ at the shoulder in the dog, 20″ to 22″ in the bitch. It has a gait, peculiar to the

In America Ch. Kalibank's Water Gate Wandrer was handled by Joseph Baker through to best in the sporting group at Westminster in 1959.

breed, which differs from that of any other variety of Spaniel.

The coat is dense, covered all over with crisp curls except on the face, front of the neck, front of the hind-legs and the far three-quarters of the tail, all of which are covered with short smooth hair. The face and muzzle is smooth, but the hair on the head is long and curled forming a pronounced top-knot coming down between the eyes into a widow's peak. The head is strong, high in dome and of good length with a well marked stop midway between the nose and the occiput. The muzzle is long, strong and square; the nose well developed and liver in color with wide nostrils. The eyes, light in puppies, darken with maturity to a dark brown. They are alert and kindly in expression and have tight rims. The ears are long, low-set and covered with twisted curls. The mouth has strong, regular teeth which meet in a scissor bite.

The neck is strong, muscular and arched and carries the head majestically above the level of the back. It is well set into powerful, sloping shoulders, the chest is wide and deep, the ribs well sprung and carried well back into short powerful loins. The forelegs are straight and well-boned with strong pasterns and large, well-rounded feet. The back is short, broad and level, well coupled with wide, powerful hindquarters. The hind-legs are well-boned, muscular, with well bent stifles and low-set hocks. The characteristic tail, which should reach to just above the hock, is undocked and has a wide base, well covered with hair, which quickly thins into the typical "rat-tail" for three-quarters of its length. It acts as a powerful rudder in the water.

Spaniel, Picardy

The Picardy Spaniel is an old breed coming from the North of France, mainly from Picardy. Bred for the hunt in this region, which is partly marshland and partly plains, dotted with small woods, the Picardy Spaniel is a subtle blend of guile, agility and endurance, enabling it to hunt for whole days.

The breed reached perfection in the 19th century, and figured successfully in the first dog shows in Paris in 1882.

The general public first became aware of the Picardy Spaniel through articles in the *Chasseur Francais* in 1908, and since then interest in it has spread in France and abroad.

It is an elegant dog, broad backed, 22″ to 24″ – the female about one inch less – to the withers, and well developed in the forequarters. The coat is speckled gray i.e. blue-roan and tan, with brown chestnut colored marks on various parts of the body; usually reddish colored on head and paws. Except on the head where it is fine, the coat is thick, and slightly wavy; different in this respect from other Spaniel breeds.

There is another variety, the Blue Picardy Spaniel, having the same features, but with black markings rather than brown. Neither variety has been brought to the U.S.A.

The Picardy Spaniel is an intelligent, faithful and obedient dog, and makes a very pleasing companion.

An excellent example of a Picardy Spaniel, Ch. Iole de Villers-le-Sec.

Spaniel, Pont Audener

Now only occasionally to be seen in France, the Pont-Audemer Spaniel is still used with the gun in parts of Normandy.

This long-haired French pointing spaniel lives particularly in Normandy and is adapted for marsh hunting. This breed, numerous at the beginning of this century around Pont-Audemer, has now almost disappeared.

As a breed, the Pont-Audemer began in the second half of the 18th century when the French Spaniel, its probable progenitor, was, undeniably, the oldest and most widespread breed of long-haired Pointer, but several other varieties had begun to emerge, more or less specialized according to conditions, doubtless due to many out-crosses. It is thought, however, that a powerful influence was a stud brought to Normandy at that time – a cross between an Irish Setter and a Greyhound type. It seems this half-breed was extraordinary at hunting game in water and resembled the present-day Pont-Audemer, which could well have inherited from it the large forelock or topknot and the tapering forehead with its elegant curve.

The Pont-Audemer is a stocky and vigorous dog measuring to the withers $20\frac{1}{2}''$ to 23″. Its head, elegant and characteristic, has a slight stop; the muzzle is snipey with a roman nose, and a large waved and drooping forelock at the top of the head gives it an amusing and appealing appearance. The ears are long and well furnished with long, very wavy, silken hair. The tail is generally docked to about a third of its length. The coat is wavy but not curled as in the Irish Water Spaniel. The color is tan with a moiré effect due to white or gray hairs with tints of dead leaf.

The Pont-Audemer is a very useful dog for hunting woodcock, snipe and duck. It resists cold and damp. Very keen in searching out game, it is at times a little independent, but stops spontaneously and has no tendency to mouth the game as some spaniels do.

Spaniel, Sussex

This long established Spaniel breed has a most characteristic head and expression, very well illustrated here by Dr. Esther Rickards's Sh. Ch. Hornshill Elizabeth, a Sussex Spaniel of character and quality.

history and development

Sussex Spaniels have been known in southern England, particularly in the county of Sussex, for over 100 years. They were originated as a recognized breed by Mr. Fuller in 1795 at Rosehill and once established, were owned by many farmers and countryfolk throughout Sussex, thereby gaining their name. They were much bigger in those early days than they are now. Later, another strain, the Harvieston, was developed. This was bigger, more the size of a Clumber and with the look of a Bloodhound. Even now an occasional puppy turns up with a definitely "houndy" look.

The breed has had its ups and downs over the years. Specimens competed in the Crystal Palace show of 1862, but its continued survival is due to the devoted care and wise breeding of Mrs. Freer of the Fourclovers Kennels who, during and between the two World Wars, kept her strain going and thus provided stock for all the kennels of the present day.

About 1954, in order to bring fresh blood into the breed, a cross was made

Head profile of a Sussex Spaniel.

Willing and eager workers in the densest cover, these two Sussex Spaniels, owned by Mrs. Joyce Munday, have also been successful on the show bench. They are Sharland Sussex Keg, a C.C. winner, and Sharland Chesara Joyful.

Type runs strongly in the families of this breed, as shown by Hornshill Elizabeth and her son, Sh. Ch. Kingfisher of Tarbay, owned by Dr. Rickards, who has worked so hard to preserve blood-lines in many of the rarer Spaniel breeds.

with the Clumber Spaniel and by the fourth generation the improved size, better bone and improved temperament have shown how valuable an experiment it was.

color

Its most striking characteristic is its coat. The color is a rich liver brown which has a golden glint. This is brought about by each hair having a tip of gold thus giving the wonderful golden sheen so strikingly distinctive of the breed. This beautiful color is maintained if the dog lives out-of-doors but it has been noticed that the coat becomes darker if the dog lives indoors.

care

No special points of care are necessary with this breed but as they are bred for an active working life in the field, they need plenty of outdoor exercise.

character

A very active and alert breed which, though not so fast as some other Spaniels, trains very well and will work tirelessly all day. They have a very good nose and when hunting tend to give tongue, which is accepted generally. They are devoted companions and give themselves to one person.

standards

The Sussex Spaniel is a sturdy, heavily boned dog standing 16″ at the shoulder and weighing about 40 to 45 lbs. It appears rather longer in the body than its height. It is not, in fact, a square dog and has a distinctive, longer loin than is usually found in Spaniels. It is because of this that it moves with a characteristic rolling gait, quite unique to this breed. Nevertheless it is a sound, well-moving dog, most active and tireless. There is a dense undercoat and the golden-tipped main coat is of long, silken hair, flat, with good feathering on the legs and ears.

The head is broad, slightly domed with a marked occiput and well-defined stop not quite midway in the length of the head; that is to say the muzzle is slightly shorter than the skull. The muzzle is deep and wide and the lip square. The nostrils are wide and well developed; the nose liver in color. The jaws are strong and level and the teeth even, meeting in a scissor bite. The eyes are large and deep set under heavy brows. They are dark hazel in color and have a kindly, benevolent expression. The ears have long fine leathers, they are set low and covered with long silky hair.

The neck is moderately long, muscular and arched. There must be no throatiness but a well-marked frill. The chest is deep and wide with well-sprung ribs carried well back. The loin must be strong, sufficiently long and muscular. The hindquarters must be wide, powerful, well-muscled with good second thighs and well-bent stifles and hocks. It is a serious fault if the body tends to tail off into weak hindquarters. The tail should have a long dock. It should be thick, set-on low and never be carried above the stern. It should wag gaily especially when working. Both fore and hind legs are very heavily boned with strong pasterns. The strong deep rounded feet should be well-feathered between the toes.

Spaniel, Welsh Springer

At eleven-and-a-half months old Mr. G. H. Pattinson's Tidemarsh Tidemark not only won the C.C. and best of breed at Birmingham City Championship Show in England in September 1970, but was best gundog in show, and won the trophy presented to the best Spaniel by the Netherlands Spaniel Club in honor of the European Spaniel Conference held the same weekend. Tidemark had his junior warrant and had qualified in the field by the age of thirteen months. He was bred by Mrs. Russen.

history and development

A dog which can be identified as the Welsh Springer Spaniel is mentioned in the earliest extant records of the Laws of Wales (c. A.D. 1300). It seems certain that for many centuries before that time, the breed, a white spaniel with red spots, had been indigenous to the Principality. Almost certainly it had an early shared ancestry with the Brittany Spaniel, for they are so similar in their structural essentials and their great ability as gundogs.

The development of the two breeds is slightly different in that the Brittanies are higher on the leg, lighter in bone and paler in color of coat, eyes and nose. It is possible that in the early days of the Gauls there was a migration from Brittany to Cornwall and South Wales, and that these dogs were taken with their masters. They are too alike to have no common origin. In more recent times the breed spread to Scotland and England, and many have been exported to America, India, Australia and other areas in the Far East.

color

Rich-red and white only.

care

No special care is necessary for this breed; just normal feeding and grooming.

1970 was an important year for the breed, for another Welsh, Mrs. D. M. Perkins's Sh. Ch. Bruce of Brent, handled by Mr. Perkins, won best in show all breeds at the Ladies Kennel Association championship show in England.

A basketful of Welsh Springer puppies makes an appealing picture.

character

The Welsh Springer Spaniel is an excellent water dog, being assisted by his flat and even coat with its soft undercoat. A very tough, hard worker; faithful and willing. A well-trained Welsh Springer makes a first-class gundog. Its excellent nose, which is such an asset in this direction, can also be a fault if the animal is not trained, since it is inclined to become a lone hunter. However, early training, at about six months, in obedience and retrieving should control this tendency.

standards

The Welsh Springer is a compact, symmetrical, powerfully built and very active dog, with great drive and endurance. It stands about 18″ to 19″ in height at the shoulder, the bitch being slightly shorter than the dog and weighing 45 lbs. Thus it comes between the Cocker and English Springer Spaniel in order of size and gives the impression of an active, bustling alert dog; not stilty and obviously built for hard work and endurance; quick and active in movement, displaying considerable drive.

The head is of moderate length slightly domed and broad between the ears but never coarse. There is a well defined stop and good chiseling below the eyes. The muzzle is medium in length, wide and fairly square, but it must not be exaggerated and there should not be a heavy jowl. The nose is dark, though a flesh-colored one is not penalized and the nostrils must be wide. The mouth has strong jaws and even teeth which meet in a scissor bite. The eyes are hazel or dark brown, and are medium in size, never prominent; the rims must be tight. The ears are short and are quite typical of the breed; they are set fairly low, hanging close to the cheek and should be the size of a vine leaf. They taper to a point and are covered with short feathering.

The neck, which must not be throaty, is of moderate length and fits cleanly into long, sloping shoulders. The forelegs are straight, well boned

The head of the Welsh Springer Spaniel.

Sire of Tidemark and a big winner himself, Ch. Tidemarsh Rip, owned by Mr. Pattinson, is seen here at eighteen months old. By the age of sixteen months he had won his junior warrant and qualified in the field.

and only lightly feathered; the pasterns are strong and the feet small, firm and catlike. The body, which is wide and compact, should be as long from the withers to the stern as the height is at the shoulders. The ribs are well-sprung and deep; the loin short, well coupled and muscular and should be slightly arched. The hindquarters are strong, muscular and wide, giving the impression of great strength and drive. The hindlegs are muscular with well developed second thighs, a good bend of stifle and a low-set hock. They should be lightly feathered to the hock. The tail docked by one third is low-set and, though merry, it should never be carried higher than the back.

The coat is quite remarkable and one of the chief characteristics of the breed. Always a deep rich red and pearly white, it is dense, flat and silky. It has a "keep clean" quality which is probably due to its oilyness, for when the mud dries on it, it is thrown off and no stain is left.

This Spaniel goes with a great swing, bustling merrily through its work and moving its hindquarters with a swagger. They are great workers, training easily at an early age and are tireless at work. They live to a great age and are robust dogs. The Welsh Springer is little known in the U.S.A.

Spinone

The Spinone is a coarse-haired Pointer from Italy, very long-established, thought to have originated in France, in the region of Bresse, near Lyons, spreading later to the Piedmont in Northern Italy. Its main progenitors were probably the French Pointer, the Porcelaine and the Barbet, with occasional cross-breeding with the French Griffon hound. More recent cross-breeding with the German Rough-haired Pointer, Korthals and the German Wire-haired Pointer was not successful in improving type; all were dark-colored, without dew-claw, and the type bred from the Korthals had too long a body; but hunting quality was improved.

The Spinone is a very old-established Italian gundog.

Today the Spinone is well-established, and is much favored by Italian sportsmen, especially for use in marshy country (where it seems to work best) and in woods. It is an excellent retriever, with a soft mouth.

It is an affectionate dog, attached to its master, and it is very hardy, withstanding cold water and weather extremes. It is at its best when used for water fowl.

The back is rather short and a little concave; the shoulders long and sloping, the tail docked and low slung; long tails and no tails at all are faults. The head is long and narrow, the skull softly curved with a noticeable occipital bump, and a scarcely visible stop. The ears are set-on level with the eyes, which are yellow or dark brown.

The coat is coarse and wiry, some $1\frac{1}{2}''$ thick, without undercoat (a characteristic shared by the Korthals).

Colors are white, or white with spots of orange, chestnut and liver roan. Tricolor dogs with black and tan in their coloration are not approved. The lighter colors of the Spinone are in contrast to the coats of the two other breeds most like it, the Korthals and the Drahthaar.

Stabyhoun

A typical Stabyhoun, Dutch Ch. Elske fen't Hounehiem.

Rarely seen outside Holland, the Stabyhoun is nevertheless one of the most popular of the native Dutch breeds. Bred in the Friesland region originally to combat vermin, it has an aptitude for water and is used as a dog to accompany the gun. Recorded as far back as 1800, it was officially accepted in the Netherlands in 1942. Registrations currently number 300 to 400, and it is most commonly used as a house dog.

The Stabyhoun is medium sized (dogs up to $19\frac{1}{2}''$ at withers; bitches smaller), somewhat longer than its height, sturdily built, free from lippiness and throatiness. Its coat is long and straight over the rump, in particolors – black, blue, brown and orange, all with white. Dark brown eyes go with black and blue; lighter brown with other colors.

The head is close-coated, the skull longer than it is wide, muzzle strong and gradually tapering to the nose, but not pointed. The ears are set on low and close to the head. The short, round neck makes an obtuse angle with the back, which is straight and rather long with a long tail, not set-on high, with long tufted hair, and reaching down to the feet. The Stabyhoun is affectionate and amenable to human companionship, is easily trained, a good guard dog, without vice.

Wetterhoun

Alwin, owned by Mej Th. Wedding, is a young winning son of Dutch Ch. Nicolaas fen de Alde Slûs ex Fenna fen de Alde Slûs.

Perhaps a hundred years covers the known history of the Wetterhoun (Dutch Water Spaniel). The breed was officially recognized in the Netherlands in 1942, and there are perhaps no more than 100 of them in the country today. It is rare outside Holland. Although its present use is mainly as a house dog, the Wetterhoun has developed in the sport of otter-hunting. It is a sturdy animal but not ungraceful, larger than its compatriot, the Stabyhoun, ($21\frac{1}{2}''$ high); it is also more compact. There is another difference – it has a much more aggressive nature and is commonly used as a watch-dog.

The body is strong, with a straight short back and strong hindquarters. The tail is long and curled over the croup in a characteristic manner (see photograph). The coat, apart from the head, has close, firm curls, coarse and somewhat greasy (as a water dog's coat should be) – in self-colored black, brown or bluish-gray.

The head has a slightly arched skull, appearing broader than it is long, the ears set-on low, close to the head, and the eyes slightly slanting, dark brown for the black and gray dogs; lighter brown for the brown. There is only a slight stop and the muzzle is strong, tapering slightly to the nose.

Weimaraner

Sh. Ch. Ace of Acomb, owned by Dr. A. W. Mucklow, was one of the top winning Weimaraners of his day. He was one of the important offspring of Sandrock Admiral, who can be found in the pedigree of nearly every winner today.

history and development

There have been theories of the relationship of the Weimaraner to German Short-haired Pointers, Spanish Pointers and the Bloodhound. Major Herber published the theory in 1939 that the Weimaraner, named for the German city of Weimar, was a mutation from the now extinct black St. Hubertus Brachen, but today the Weimaraner shows very consistent breed type, litter by litter.

The early use of the Weimaraner was as a tracking dog for deer and boar. They later became more specialised as "bird" dogs and now hunt by quartering ground in advance of the guns, point live game, flush and retrieve from land or water, in and through any cover and under all weather conditions.

The Weimaraner reached America after World War I but did not become well known in the United Kingdom until around 1952. There has been a steady trickle of stock since then from America, including one imported by Miss Monkhouse (Cabaret), and from Rhodesia. There are probably 1,000–1,500 in the U.K. now. Registrations are running at between 140–200 a year with a good growth trend.

Quality-wise, the American and British Weimaraners are probably the best in the world. There is no marked difference between the breed in different countries but a bigger dog was, until recently, more acceptable in the U.S.A. than in Britain and on the Continent.

Mrs. E. Hackett's Sh. Ch. Ballina of Merse-Side, whose many wins at variety shows, including best in show, have done so much to popularize the breed. She was Weimaraner of the year in 1968 in Britain, when very young, and was just beaten the following year by Ritter.

color

The color is one of the most striking features of the Weimaraner. At birth

Mrs. J. Matuszewska's Sh. Ch. Monroe's Nexus who, although still only a young dog in 1970, had already had a great influence in the breed, both in the ring and at stud.

the whelps are striped. This effect disappears within about ten days and the color should then be a pale silvery gray. At maturity, the preferred color is still silver-gray but shades of mouse or roe-gray, or even iron-gray do occur. The roe-gray type has a pinkish base color but the whole coat should give an appearance of a metallic sheen. Small white marks are common and acceptable, but on the chest only. Occasionally, puppies are born with tan markings, generally on the legs, but this is not acceptable. The color should generally be free from brownish tinges, whether tan or liver. The pale eyes are amber or blue-gray, the blue shades frequently persisting until full maturity. The eye color tones in with the coat. The skin is pale, the nails are unpigmented but the nose is most commonly

Two real dual purpose champions. Lying down is Gunmetal Guy, C.D. ex, U.D. ex, a multiple winner in working trials and obedience, who also won in the show-ring. Sitting is Waidman Giselle who, beside her Challenge Certificate win in the show-ring has the working qualification C.D. ex.

quite a rich shade of chocolate or deep gray.

care

The Weimaraner thrives living in the house. Whether in the house or kennelled, he needs a draught-free warm bed. As a thin-coated dog of considerable weight, he needs a resilient or padded surface to prevent the formation of callouses. He does best if fed, and fed well, twice a day. His ears should be kept gently clean, teeth descaled from time to time and front nails kept short. If wet when brought in, he should be dried off but there is no need to worry about him out in the rain, providing he is not kept waiting about. There is no real need to brush him at all. If the dog is in good health and properly fed, the coat will be sleek and shining without it. Dirt simply drops off the coat and they frequently groom themselves, like cats. There is no nuisance from shed hair in the house.

character

The Weimaraner is fearless, friendly, protective and obedient – to a firm handler who has trained him properly and indicated clearly that he too

Mr. and Mrs. A. Burgoin's Sh. Ch. Ragstone Ritter, one of the top winning gun dogs of 1970, not only winning best in show at open shows but also scoring group placements at championship events.

Sh. Ch. Coninvale Paul of Acombdale, owned by Dr. Alex Mucklow.

Weimaraner, typical head studies.

has a strong personality! The dog is full of drive to hunt and general zest for living. Because he is just that little bit sharper than the average gundog, he makes a good police dog. The bitches particularly are very sweet and devoted.

One of the most valuable characteristics of the Weimaraner is its adaptability. It can take city life in its stride five days a week and take to the stubbles, roots, bracken and marshes gratefully at the week-end. It is a breed of many parts. But it should always receive training and have some useful role to play.

standards

In 1971, in the official Standard for the United Kingdom, the height was raised from 23″ to 25″ for dogs to 24″ to 27″, and for bitches from 22″ to 24″ 22″ to 25″. This merely places the U.K. Standard closer to the International and American ones and recognizes the sizes which actually occur and win in championship shows. The critical overall requirement is that the dog should present a picture of great driving power, stamina, alertness and balance. Above all, the dog should be constructed to work hard in the field. The brisket should drop to the elbows. Forequarters and hindquarters show moderate angulation. Legs should be strong and sound. The feet are rather large, but should be firm and well arched. The tail is docked.

Any unsoundness of temperament i.e. shyness or viciousness, structural unsoundness or color or markings not specified in the Standard constitute faults. Breeding stock should conform closely to the Standard.

The breed is fortunately relatively free from the incidence of serious defects. Currently, only sub-clinical hip dysplasia requires care but almost all breeding stock is X-rayed and the less good hips not bred from.

Hounds

A great American champion, Kentucky Lake Big Red, an American Foxhound.

Afghan Hound

Ch. Horningsea Tiger's Eye, owned by Mrs. M. Dods, is a fine example of an unusual color, a blue/gray brindle. In addition to winning eleven C.C.s he was best in show at the British Hound Association championship show in 1969. His breeding is interesting; his sire is by a well-known American champion, Chinah of Grandeur while his dam is by Ch. Horningsea Khanabad Suraraj, a multiple best in show winner in Britain.

history and development

For several centuries at least, the Afghan Hound has been the hunting dog of the royal family and the nobility in Afghanistan. It is conjectural whether the breed represents the original coursing hound as it was developed several thousand years ago, probably in Central Asia, and that other coursing hound breeds, such as the Saluki, are descended from it; or whether it was developed at a much later date in Afghanistan from the Saluki, with possibly an admixture of spitz-type shepherd or working dogs.

Regardless of the place and time of its first appearance, the Afghan Hound, underneath its coat, is a relatively sturdy coursing hound of the type commonly used in Egyptian and other early cultures. The coat, however, does seem to be particularly suited to a high-altitude climate such as that of Afghanistan.

Although it was "discovered" by the Western world in the latter half of the 19th century by British soldiers on the border between India and Afghanistan, it was not until 1907, when an exceptionally impressive dog named Zardin was imported to England and widely exhibited, that the Afghan Hound attracted any serious attention and following. Even then, the interest proved to be short-lived. All the progeny of Zardin and other early imports vanished from the scene in the course of World War 1, and the true start of the breed in the West, and as we know it today, came with two groups of Afghan Hounds brought to Britain in the 1920's.

The first of these groups was acquired in Baluchistan and taken to Scotland in 1921 by Major and Mrs. Bell-Murray and Miss Jean Manson. The

Mrs. Molly Sharpe's Chaman hounds had a tremendous influence in Britain between the wars and in the early years after the Second World War. This is Ch. Taj Amrit of Chaman, a top winner in 1953 and an important sire.

American and Canadian Ch. Crown Crest Mr. Universe, a great winner in America, taking one hundred hound groups and thirty-five breed B.I.S. awards. Mr. Universe was owned by Kay Finch and the late Charles Costabile.

(opposite)
Mrs. Holden's Ch. Ranjitsinjhi of Jagai, a black-masked golden, shows his paces. This dog had a most successful career, winning groups at championship shows in Britain in 1968, 1969 and 1970.

The black-and-tan, Canadian Ch. Ahmed Khan Tajallu, moves easily, with his head and tail held in the correct position.

second group, bearing the kennel name Ghazni, was acquired in the area around Kabul and brought to England by Mrs. Mary Amps in 1925. All of the Bell-Murray breedings were based on just eight individuals, and Ghazni on nine. These seventeen hounds, plus less than a dozen other imports to Britain or the United States from Afghanistan and India prior to the Second World War, represent almost the total foundation for the thousands of Afghan Hounds now being registered every year – although there have been a few later imports, usually via the Continent and usually found only well back on British or American pedigrees.

The Ghazni dogs from the mountains of north eastern Afghanistan and the Bell-Murray dogs from the desert and plains south of Afghanistan differed considerably in type, amount of coat, colors etc., and for a number of years were maintained as separate strains. The combining of bloodlines and the blending of traits was inevitable, however, and although partisanship for one type or the other persisted for a great many years, to most fanciers today the ideal Afghan Hound embodies the best of both types. Although some Afghan Hounds may have made their way to the United States much earlier, the first American Kennel Club registrations date to 1926. As in Britain two decades before, this proved to be a false start. The permanent establishment of the breed in America began in 1931 when Zeppo Marx and his wife acquired Asra of Ghazni and Westmill Omar in England and brought them to California, from where they went eventually to the Massachusetts kennels of Q. A. Shaw McKean. In 1934 McKean also obtained a young English champion, Badshah of Ainsdart, and his "Prides Hill" breedings based on these three – Asra, Omar and Badshah – became the foundation for the breed in the United States, even though supplemented within the next six years by dozens of imports from Britain and four from Afghanistan and India.

Due in part to the fact that the Afghan Hound has proved to be the show dog *par excellence,* the growth of the breed's popularity over the years and throughout the world has been steady and, at times, spectacular. Annual registrations with the A.K.C. rose from a level of 200 or less in

Braden and Kay Finch with a group of Crown Crest hounds at Corona del Mar, California, in 1960.

Miss Sams poses her Ch. Bondor Azim Khan for the camera. This lovely quality, well-balanced dog, with his good head carriage and spectacular coat, is litter brother to Ch. Bondor Dera Ghazi Khan. They were bred in 1966 by Messrs. Brooks and Swallow, with Int. Ch. Moonraker of Moonswift as sire and Ch. Bondor Serenade as dam.

(opposite)
Mr. and Mrs. R. G. Elmore's Ch. Bondor Kumari Khanum provides a particularly fine subject for a head study.

the early 1940's to more than 6,000 in 1970.

color

Probably no other breed comes in as many different colors, color combinations and shadings as the Afghan Hound. All are permissible although, white markings on the head or extensive white markings elsewhere are considered undesirable. Commonly seen are all solid colors from near-white through black, with the exception of liver and chocolate brown hues, but including blue and various shades of gray. Black masks, sometimes in combination with black ear-fringes and even with black on the tail or feet, are frequent and popular markings, with red, fawn, silver and other body colors. Both gray and red brindles and the bicolor patterns of black and tan, blue and silver etc. are prevalent. Generally, the basic color of an Afghan Hound is considered to be that of the short-haired saddle area, which tends to be darker than that of the long coat.

care

Afghan Hounds are hardy, and adapt well to a wide variety of climates and living conditions. They require no special care other than in the maintenance of their coat, which they do not shed but, because the coat is so thick and fine, dead hair tends to form mats. To prevent this, regular grooming is necessary – preferably daily by brushing out the coat, layer by layer, sweeping the brush from the skin outward on each layer. The Afghan Hound coat should not be trimmed, clipped or otherwise barbered.

Although the more regular exercise the better, the breed is adaptable. Many have lived long and healthy lives in urban environments where their exercise was limited to a few short strolls each day.

Almost any well-balanced canine diet will meet its nutritional needs, although many consume somewhat less food than is normally prescribed for dogs of their size.Whatever its appetite, an Afghan Hound should never be fat or heavy; in top condition, it will have some flesh on its ribs but its hip bones and two or three vertebrae will still be sharply evident.

character

The "true" Afghan Hound temperament is commonly described as dignified, proud, and aloof – all in perfect keeping with the regal appearance and background of the breed. Yet it is a king who also delights in playing the court jester – cavorting like a kitten, lolling in ridiculous poses and indulging in wily pranks and whimsical jokes. Along with this sense of humor and a high degree of intelligence, most Afghan Hounds possess a strong spirit of independence.

The most common trait of the breed as a whole is an insistence on being treated as an individual and with intelligence and humor equal to its own.

standards

Head – long, lean, combining strength and refinement. Prominent occiput, slight stop, profile falling away below the eyes and rising slightly over the nasal bone. The head is surmounted by a topknot of long, silky hair. The eye opening is almond shaped (almost triangular) and slants slightly upward. The ears are long, set well back at about the same level as the outer corner of the eye, carried close to the head and covered with

Owned by the Soroya Kennels of Wisconsin, Ch. Sahadi Shikari, a most impressive American Afghan.

long, silky hair.

Body – the neck is long and strong, running in a curve to the shoulders, which are sloping and well laid back. From the shoulder to the prominent hip bones, the back is level, then falls away slightly to the stern. The chest is deep and not too wide between the forelegs, curving into a distinct tuck up at the flanks. The length of the body should be about equal to the height of the dog at the shoulder.

Feet and legs – the forelegs are straight and strong with great length from elbow to pastern. The forefeet are very large, with well-arched toes and covered with long, thick hair. Hindquarters are powerful, muscular and well-angulated, with great length from hip to hock and short from hock to foot. Viewed from the rear, the hind legs appear slightly bowed. Hindfeet are long but not as broad as the forefeet and covered with long hair.

Tail – long, slender, ending in a ring or curl and only sparsely feathered.

Coat – hindquarters, sides, forequarters, legs, feet, top skull and ears, well covered with thick, long, silky hair, very fine in texture. On the foreface and from the shoulders back along the saddle to the croup and tail, the hair should be short and close in the mature Afghan Hound. Short hair on the pasterns is also permissible. In all cases the coat must be allowed to develop naturally, and is not clipped or trimmed.

Size – dogs about 27″ to 28″ at the shoulder and 60 lbs. in weight; bitches about 25″ to 26″ and 50 lbs.; an inch less in either sex is not penalized.

General Appearance – the Afghan Hound should be aloof and dignified yet gay and stylish. He should move with an extremely smooth and springy gait. Moving or standing, he should bear himself proudly and give an overall impression of strength combined with great speed and agility. Any coarseness, sharpness or shyness is a serious fault.

Mr. and Mrs. Harris's Ch. Bondor Dera Ghazi Khan in natural pose. He is one of an outstanding litter, containing also, among others, Ch. Bondor Kumari Khanum and Ch. Bondor Azim Khan. A large, impressive-looking dog, Ghazi was best in show all breeds at Bournemouth, England, championship show in 1968.

Ariegeois

Ariège is one of the provinces of France which borders Spain. The region provides circumstances for the hunt which are different from those obtaining elsewhere in France and the Ariègeois was developed to satisfy the peculiar requirements of the region – the hilly uplands where strength, agility and, above all, a very powerful scenting mechanism, were of greater importance than speed and keen sight. The hare is its main quarry, but it is occasionally used for larger game.

The breed arises from the old Briquet crossed with the large "chien d'ordre" of Saintonge and the Gascogne.

The coat is smooth, fine and close; the colors are white and black, or mottled. Red occasionally occurs, and is permitted, and patches of pale blue sometimes occur on the cheeks and above the eyes.

It is a medium sized hound, standing some 22″ to 24″ for dogs, one inch less for bitches.

The head is long, with moderately long ears, set-on rather low, and hanging against the cheeks. The skull is narrow, the occiput pronounced. The back is straight and long, and the loins are fairly broad and straight. The tail tapers, sickle-shaped, carried gaily.

Austrian Hound

The Oesterreichische Bracke or Brandlbracke (so-called because of the sharply defined red "fire marks" on the black-coated dog) is of medium height, 18″ to 20½″ at the withers, and of a strong yet classic build. The body is somewhat long and the head held high.

The tail is long and moderately thick at the root, gradually thinning towards the tip. Normally it is carried low, with a slight upward flourish at its tip, but held high when the dog is hunting or excited. The hair on the tail is rougher and forms a modest brush.

The coat is thick and full, smooth and with a silky texture, and short on the muzzle and cheeks.

Colors—black with red "fire marks", and red.

The Austrian Hound is not a pack hound. It has been bred for work in the mountains where its keen nose, tracking sense and agility combine to make a purposeful hunter.

Balkan Hound

Hunting has a long tradition in South East Europe, where horses and hounds have been bred and trained for centuries for the particular requirements of the region. The Balkan Hound is a breed, one of a number, which has arisen from the old Austro-Hungarian Empire, when it was used as a pack hound for fox and hare. It is a well-disciplined dog, docile, good-natured, and industrious.

It is medium-sized, 18″ to 21″ at the shoulder, with a broad skull, narrowing evenly to the nose. The ears are set-on high and hang close to the cheeks, and the eyes are large and dark.

The body is a few inches longer than its height; the back is broad and straight, the quarters strong and well-angulated, and the tail straight or lightly curved, just reaching the hock joint.

The coat is dense and thick, but short, and the colors are deep reddish-tan with a black saddle reaching up to the back of the head, and two black marks over the eyes.

Basset, Artesien-Normand

Basset Artesien Normand – a bitch of the breed.

Of ancient French origin and descended from the old French Bloodhound and the St. Hubert Hound, this breed was used by the nobility for trailing deer and small game.

The dome-shaped head is medium sized with the bone structure apparent through the skin, giving a lean appearance to the whole head. Deep wrinkles provide well formed cheeks. Black nose, of medium length, with wide nostrils. There is a well defined stop and the occiput is sometimes quite marked. Large dark eyes impart a calm and serious look, the red of the lower eyelid sometimes noticeable. The ears, set as low as possible but never above the line of the eye, are narrow at the base and very long, reaching to the end of the muzzle, and end in a point. The rounded, strong, short, well-muscled shoulders support a fairly long neck, without excessive throatiness.

The forelegs are short, heavily boned, crooked or half-crooked with wrinkles on the pastern, and the feet are large.

The breast-bone protrudes and the chest is moderately let down but wide and rounded. The back is wide and well ribbed-up, with slightly harp-shaped loins and deep; full flanks. The thighs are very fleshy and muscular, forming with the croup, an almost spherical mass. The tail is well set on and strong at the root; rather long and tapering. It is carried gaily in hound fashion but never falling on to the back and is never docked. The coat is close, short and smooth, but not fine.

Colors are white or white and orange. A tricolor dog must be widely marked with tan on the head, with a mantle of specks of either black or badger color. Height: 10″ to 14″.

314

Basset Hound

Ch. Balleroy Chestnut, a red and white owned by Mrs. P. Moncur. A strong stallion hound, he demonstrates the scope and length looked for in the British show ring.

A typical Basset head.

history and development

It is exceedingly difficult to pinpoint the exact period when the Basset evolved. Short-legged dogs which could be called "basset-type" were shown on wall paintings in Egyptian tombs around 2,000 B.C., and from that era until the Middle Ages various chroniclers have mentioned low-set, long-bodied dogs. However, one cannot be certain that these were Bassets. The first recorded mention of the word "Basset" is found in Jacques du Fouilloux's *Venerie de Jacques du Fouilloux* published in France in 1585. Therefore if this date is accepted as the beginning of the modern Basset, and if the earlier recordings of low-bodied dogs are dismissed as not relating to true Bassets, then the breed is undoubtedly of ancient origin. Not many breeds have four centuries of authenticated history behind them. Du Fouilloux writes of the breed being employed as badger dogs and of them going to earth in the style of terriers. He draws attention to two types of Basset, the rough-haired variety and the smooth-coated type, and states that they originated in Artois and Flanders. Modern canine historians do not disagree with this opinion and are unanimous in considering the northern French departments as the homeland of the breed. The two French hound authorities Leon Verrier and Alain Bourbon, whose works on the Basset remain classics, support the theory that the first Basset appeared in a litter of normal-sized hounds; to all intents and purposes, a freak. By retaining the Bassets (French for dwarf, or low-set) and breeding from them, the French hound men eventually established a standardized type of dwarf hound. They corresponded in all points to the parent breed except, of course, in length of leg. It should be pointed out

A Basset Hound pack sets off to work.

that the reverse procedure has occurred where a normal-sized hound has been born into a litter of Bassets.

In du Fouilloux's time the Basset was being used as a terrier, but in the 17th century it was held in high esteem as a gun-dog. The low stature of the breed allowed it to penetrate dense cover and flush out game. The Basset's conformation was such that they were unable to pursue the game with speed and therefore being unhurried the flushed game presented an easy target for the waiting sportsmen and their unwieldy weapons. Hare, rabbits, deer, fox and occasionally wild boar were the Basset's quarry at that time and it is still the same in France today.

The Bassets of various types (i.e. Artois-Normands, Gascons, Vendéens and Fauve de Bretagnes, dealt with elsewhere in this book) rapidly gained favor in France and the surrounding countries as a dependable sporting dog, and were also docile enough to be recommended as an ideal breed for the fair sex. The Basset was eventually imported into England in 1866 and there it became known as the Basset Hound. They were described as being "long, low hounds shaped much like a Dachshund, with crooked forelegs at the knees and with much more bone and longer heads than on Beagles. They were not the dark tan color of Dachshunds but the color of Foxhounds with a certain amount of white about them". Two hounds, Basset and Belle, were imported by Lord Galway and it is from this pair of tricolor hounds that the breed in Britain is descended. Sir Everett Millais was another early importer and it was he who experimented with the Basset-Bloodhound cross and thus established a distinctly

British type of Basset. The infusion of Bloodhound gave the Basset Hound substance of body, more bone and developed a wrinkled skull and deep-set eye thus evolving the sad reposeful expression which is the hallmark of the breed to the layman.

color

Bassets come in many colors. The tricolors are in varying patterns of black, white and tan; on some the white is splashed with black mottles or spots. The bicolors range from pale lemon and white through to mahogany red and white. Sensibly there is no rigid ruling for color and therefore "no good hound can be a bad color".

care

Opportunity for exercize, ample living space and firm but sympathetic handling are needed if one's hounds are to be happy. If the hound is to grow and mature into a healthy Basset then the diet also must be adequate and correct in content. The breed when developing is almost a contradiction, Basset puppies grow at an enormous rate and are massive animals at six to eight months, and yet it is true to say that the breed is slow to reach maturity, continuing to develop for at least two years. Therefore, this rapid and sustained period of growth must be assisted by a diet rich in protein and vitamins. Only the best quality meat and meal should be used and the diet can be varied by using fish and feeding liberal quantities of eggs, honey and all the other dietary additives associated with growing livestock – cod liver oil, calcium plus vitamin D, iron etc. On reaching maturity the Basset Hound is quite content with one good meal daily. Of course, in-whelp or nursing bitches need additional meals containing extra protein and vitamins. Bassets usually are good mothers and produce about eight puppies per litter.

The signs of correct feeding are readily apparent, the coat is glossy and clean, eyes sparkle and the hound is alert and ready for food or exercize. The smooth coat of the Basset needs little attention other than a daily brush and comb, and seldom needs washing. Despite the length of ear

Two Basset Hound puppies, Syke-moor Papyrus and Sykemoor Pascal, at twelve weeks old. Note the large feet, folded leather and soft, wise expression of the true Basset.

Basset Hound: A tricolor, Ch. Dower-wood Soames.

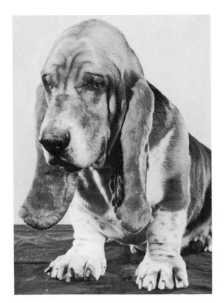

Mrs. Lyle Cain's Santana Mandeville's Claude, a lovely head study of an American champion.

the breed is not prone to ear-disorders, but they should be kept clean, and like eyes and nails, checked regularly. The Basset puppy should not be exercized or allowed to run up and down steps or stairs; strains and dislocations of the front legs are the chief dangers to the immature youngster. Properly supervized exercize can commence at six or eight months.

character

The Basset Hound is today one of the most popular of all hound breeds, never before in its history has the breed been so popular. Many are kept as companions, but it must never be overlooked that they are true hounds in every sense of the word. In Britain their role is hare-hunting and this instinct for the chase is far from latent. Consequently, the pet hound must be catered for with this in mind. The Basset should never be kept in cramped quarters or confined to the house, and ample exercize for the adult hound is a prime necessity. It is cruelty to enforce a life of inactivity on any sporting breed. Some patience is needed in house-training Bassets, for one must allow time for commands to penetrate and be mulled over awhile inside that unique skull. The Basset seldom obeys commands immediately in the way a terrier or gundog will. I think it is true to say that they are happiest and easiest managed when in the company of other hounds.

standards

The Basset Hound rapidly settled into the mould cast by Millais and the breed in Britain gradually became different in some points, especially size and weight, from its French ancestors. In France today the nearest equivalent of the Basset Hound is the Basset Artesien-Normand, and both are regarded there as different breeds. To emphasize the differences the ruling body for European canine affairs, the Federation Cynologique Internationale, has adopted the American Standard for Basset Hounds.

A trio of Basset Hounds, Bundeseiger Sykemoor Khartoum in the center, showing the correct Basset front with the brisket nicely filling the crook.

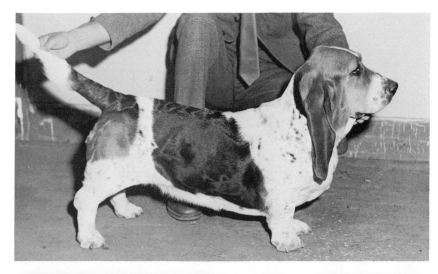

Like a good horse, a Basset Hound cannot be a bad color, and the breed comes in a variety of shades. Sykemoor Miriam, owned and bred by Mr. G. I. Johnston, shows the attractiveness of a mottled tricolor bitch.

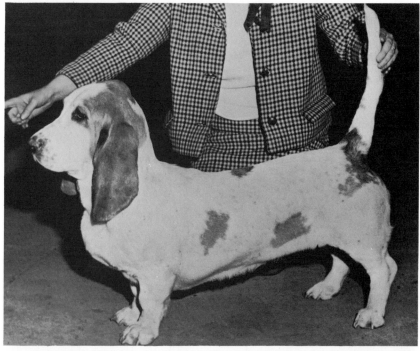

Ch. Rollinhills Wingjays Fabric, owned by Mrs. B. White, is a lovely example of a lemon and white bitch. Tragically she was lost before being bred from.

Ch. Santana Mandeville's Ella, a tricolor bitch, owned by Mrs. Lyle Cain Jnr., demonstrates the American Basset Hound. Contrast this smart, compact, deep-bodied hound with her British counterpart.

319

Mrs. Nixon's bitch Brackenacre Anna-bella, a fine representative of the British type.

This calls for a heavier type of hound than does the official British Standard. In general the Basset in America is much bulkier and deeper in the chest than the type favored in Britain, and also the American Standard does not insist on such points as crooked fronts and fine textured and inward curling ears as do the British and French. But despite these differences the Basset remains basically the same – a low and long-bodied hound.

To many people the Basset has a comic, sorrowful head and a bizarre body, but lovers of Basset Hounds see them only as aristocratic hounds with a somewhat superior appearance. The skull, being of medium width, and with some dome and the occipital bone developed, is handsome enough without the long low-set ears and the kind, deep-set, dark expressive eyes. As a whole the headpiece of the Basset is one of the finest in the canine world. The neck is long and muscular, and the dewlap on the throat should be apparent. Understandably, the stature of the breed must be low, never exceeding 15″ at the shoulder. The low-set body, descending well in the chest is substantial and strong, well rounded in the ribs, firm over the loins and well endowed with muscle especially in the hindquarters. A mature hound weighs on average 55 lbs., and it is essential that this weight is supported on sound and strong legs and feet, therefore heavy bone and firm pads are required. Any unsoundness in the limbs and feet is penalized. The Basset Hound is not a gay dog and when mobile should move at a steady and determined pace with the tail carried up in true hound fashion. Balance is important in any breed but in a Basset it is essential. In a breed which verges on the abnormal it is easy to over-emphasize certain features, be it skull or length or size. This must be avoided and undue exaggeration of any point is a bad fault.

Bavarian Schweisshund

Dark, short-haired coat and large ears – the Bavarian Schweisshund.

The Bayrischer Gebirgsschweisshund is a medium sized hound with a light, agile yet muscular appearance. Dogs should not be over 20″, nor bitches over 18″ at the withers. The body, which is somewhat elongated, rises slightly towards the hindquarters while the legs should not be too long.

The ears are heavy, set high and wide apart, and drooping.

The tail, which is of medium length and thinly tapering, is carried horizontally or drooping. It has thicker hair on the underside. The coat is thick and lies flat and smooth. On the head and ears, the hair is fine and short, and on the belly and hindquarters, it is rougher and longer.

Colors are deep red, deer red, reddish brown, ochre yellow and fawn to flaxen, and red-gray like the winter coat of foxes and other red wild animals; most colorings can be dark stippled, particularly on the muzzle, ears, back and tail, and in red-colored dogs the basic color is more intense on the back.

Beagle

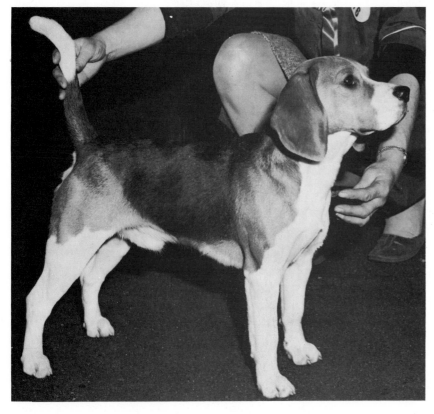

Ch. Southcourt Wembury Merryboy, pictured here winning best of breed as a junior in 1968, went on to become one of the top Beagles in Britain in 1969 and 1970. Merryboy was bred by Mrs. Hastie and was later owned by Mrs. H. Priestley.

history and development

Like so much of what is now regarded as English, the ancestors of the Beagle seem to have come to England with William the Conqueror. The Talbot hounds which he brought with him were the progenitors of the Southern hound which, in turn gave rise to the Beagle.

Hunting dogs which relied on scent rather than sight were well-known in England as early as the beginning of the 16th century and one of the first references to this breed, by name, appears in the Privy Accounts of Henry VIII where payment is recorded to a Robert Shere, the "Keeper of the Beagles". The deforestation of the 17th and 18th centuries provided more open country for horse-riding and greatly reduced the number of deer, leaving the fox and hare as the main objectives for sportsmen on horse-back. The second Duke of Buckingham (1687) was one of the first to keep a genuine pack of foxhounds.

By the beginning of the 19th century, Beagles were said to exist in several sizes. Reinagle, in the *Sportsmans Cabinet* in 1804 says: "They are the smaller of the hound race in this country, are exquisite in the scent of the hare and indefatigably vigilant in their pursuit of her". He also says "Though wonderfully inferior in point of speed yet equally energetic in persevering pursuit, they follow her through all her windings, unravel all her mazes, explore her labyrinths and by scent alone trace and retrace her footsteps to a degree of admiration that must be seen to be properly understood, during which the soft melodious tone of their emulous

Top Beagle bitch during 1970 was Mrs. Sutton's Ch. Rossut Bobbin who became her owner's eleventh champion in the breed in the United Kingdom. She was full sister, in a later litter, to another Rossut champion, Nutmeg, who was exported to Italy.

321

Top winning Beagle dog in Britain is Mrs. C. G. Sutton's Ch. Rossut Triumphant, winner of twenty-three C.C.s, all under different judges. He was best dog in show at a British championship show, and is a great showman, full of Beagle type.

vociferation seems to be the most predominant inducement to the well-known ecstatic pleasure of the chase".

An artist, J. F. Herring, painted a picture of Prince Albert, the Prince Consort of Queen Victoria, together with his Beagles. Prince Albert acquired his Beagles in 1841 when about a dozen were kept at Cumberland Lodge. The painting was executed at about this time, and is not the only one which portrays the devotion to the breed of the British Royal family at that time – another was painted about ten years after, of Queen Victoria's Beagles, descendants no doubt of those Beagles shown in the Herring portrait of 1841. In both paintings the dogs are very small.

These Pocket Beagles were hunted on foot but had considerable difficulty in traversing ploughed fields and in clambering up the banks of streams or drains and they frequently required assistance to prevent them from drowning. Small though they were (often only 9″ high) they were nevertheless models of symmetry and power, working well even in bad scenting conditions and able to keep up their work through thick furze brakes, for five hours at a stretch.

About 1880, a number of Beagles from the Royal Rock pack, were imported from England into the United States and these had a good deal of influence on the development of American Beagles. The National Beagle Club was formed in America in 1888 and the Beagle Club in the United Kingdom in 1890. Breeding to a set show standard has been more widely practised in the United States than in England and furthermore, the American Beagle breeds extremely true to type, a somewhat different type from the British, although some American Beagles have been imported and successfully integrated into British bloodlines.

Whereas the hunting Beagle has not altered, except in size, in recent years, the show Beagle has become shorter-coupled and more compact, better in skull, foreface and expression and improved in reach of neck and lay-back of shoulder.

Many packs are still hunted under the Rules of the Association of Masters of Harriers and Beagles which was founded in 1891; the main U.K. Show for these pack Beagles is at Peterborough.

Over the last few years the Beagle has gained tremendously in popularity. In 1945 only one was registered with the English Kennel Club but in the first seven months of 1970, 1,875 were registered. After the Cocker Spaniel (American) it was No. 1 in the U.S.A. but gave way to the Poodle. Presently fourth it registers some 65,000 a year. Individual hunting with Beagles is practised by thousands in the United States and, in addition, many packs are regularly hunted.

color

Both the U.K. and U.S.A. Standards provide that any true hound color is acceptable but the tricolors attract much preference, particularly the "black blanket" coloration – an all-black back and the head, sides of neck, flanks, shoulders and top of the legs and the greater part of the stern are all of tan; the lower part of the legs and feet, the chest and tip of the tail are white. An interesting fact about the tricolors is that they are whelped almost black and white, the tan coming through as they grow on.

Pieds are not quite so popular as the tricolor but are very attractive, with their basic white marked with various shades of lemon, tan and sable (badger). Liver, white and tan is not very common; almost always they

(opposite)
A promising three-months-old Beagle puppy, Barvac Rota, who later became a C.C. winner. Note the good bone and the desired sweet expression.

have yellow eyes and this rather unattractive feature may account for their relative unpopularity.

Mottles, that is dogs with white portions flecked heavily with blue or tan, have always been popular in hunting Beagles but are not often seen in those bred for showing.

care

A pack or a single dog needs a regular, and well-balanced routine. The program should include plenty of controlled exercise both on and off the leash, proper regular feeding and periods of rest. Beagles need no peculiar additions to the normal diet for a more-than-usually active hound. Although trencher feeding is usual with pack hounds, show hounds are individually fed in order to ensure that each dog gets its fair share of food and so is maintained in top condition.

character

One may ask what has caused this sudden increase in the number of these merry little hounds with big hearts; I would say attractive qualities, a disposition different from any other hound, adaptability to indoor or outdoor life, they are not aggressive and are very easy to take around, taking up very little room in a car or public conveyance. They are especially good with children and as house dogs are easy to keep clean, their fine close coats need no trimming and have the advantage of hardly bringing any dirt into the house. They can switch in an instant from being a lovable pet to an out-door dog, all-a-quiver and full of go. As there is no difference in the temperament of the sexes a dog hound makes an ideal companion for the whole family.

One of the many lovely Beagle bitches exhibited in 1970 was Ch. Webline Holly, owned by Mr. David Webster, secretary of the British Beagle Club, together with Mr. and Mrs. D. George.

standards

The preference in the U.S.A. for a smaller dog is shown in the Standards–the height limit in the U.S.A. is 15″ and in the U.K. 16″. In America there is a smaller type of Beagle under 13″ which competes separately from those under 15″. In other details there is little difference between the two Standards. The U.S. Standard however calls for a moderately defined stop and the U.K. for a well defined stop. In general appearance it should be a compactly built hound without coarseness, conveying the impression of great stamina and an ability to keep going.

The head is a hound head with drooping ears and long leathers. The skull domed, moderately wide with an indication of peak. The muzzle, of medium length should not be snipey and while flews are required by the English Standard they are not by the American. The nose is black, broad and the keenly scenting nostrils well expanded. The eyes have a mild, gentle expression.

The throat shows some dewlap but although the American Standard says that the throat should be free from folds of skin it allows a slight wrinkle below the angle of the jaw. The shoulders should be clean and slightly sloping with the forelegs quite straight, well under the dog and of good substance and round in bone.

Short between the couplings, the body is well let down in chest, ribs fairly well ribbed up. Loins powerful but not tucked up. The hindquarters are very muscular about the thighs; stifles and hocks well bent and hocks well let down. Feet are round, well knuckled up and strongly padded. The tail is of moderate length set-on high ("moderately high" in U.S. Standard) and carried gaily but not curled over back.

The coat of the smooth variety is not too fine or short but, as with the rough variety, very dense.

This splendid trio of Beagles represent three generations of Barvae stock bred by Mrs. G. M. Clayton. Notably English in type with well-marked stop and complete absence of wrinkle, the good, round bone and excellent feet are typical of this Lincolnshire breeder's old-established strain.

Billy

The Billy emerged in 1880 from a series of crosses performed by M. Gaston Hublot du Rivault at his home in Billy, Haut-Poitou, France. The origins of this dog can be clearly traced back to the Great White Hound of Louis XII of France, (which it greatly resembles), and result from a cross between the Montemboeuf and the Ceris, while an infusion of blood of the Poitevin-Larrye may also be found.

In France there are ten packs of Billys, all staghounds, excepting one pack which hunts wild boar. The breed is recognized by the Societé de Venerie, which has drawn up the official Standard.

The Standard calls for a well-built dog, elegant, strong, yet light, with forequarters slightly heavier than hindquarters. The dog should stand 23½″ to 27½″ to shoulder. The head is fairly fine, of medium length, with a rather square muzzle; nose black or liver, slight plume or crest on neck. The Billy's coat is completely white or cream, occasionally showing patches or saddle of orange, but this orange color must never approach red. The hair should be short, sometimes rather coarse. Its well-muscled thighs and strong hocks enable the Billy to run with great ease and lightness. Disqualifications: black or red hairs in the coat; a forehead too short, long or thin.

The Billy.

325

Bleu de Gascogne
(Basset, Grand, Petit, Petit Basset)

A typical specimen of the male Bleu de Gascogne Grand.

Bleu de Gascogne Grand: According to the well-known French authorities on hunting and hounds, Count le Couteulx and Count de Chabot, the Chien de Gascogne derives from the black variety of the Chien de Saint Hubert (Bloodhound); it is certainly one of the oldest of French hound breeds. It has always excelled in a very fine nose, and in olden times was preferably used for hunting wolves. The name derives from the district of Gascogne in Southwest France. Although Count le Couteulx in his *Manuel de Venerie Francaise,* 1902, describes them as very large with a shoulder height of 25″ to 29¾″ or even more, the modern Standard prescribes a shoulder height of 24¾″ to 27¼″ for dogs and 23½″ to 24½″ for bitches.

Henry IV (1553–1610) had a pack of very beautiful Chiens de Gascogne, and it is one of the few large French hounds still in existence. The Standard demands a strong, long head, with thin, curled, low-set-on ears, a sturdy body with a deep chest, a rather long, strong back and a long tail which is sometimes a little bristly on the underside. The coat should not be too short and is white, with so many small black spots as to give the dog a blue-mottled appearance. Black patches may be on the body and are always evident on the head, enveloping the eye and ear tan markings.

Of later date are the following varieties:

Two examples of the Bleu de Gascogne Petit.

Bleu de Gascogne Petit: With a shoulder height of 19″ to 22″ and some slight deviations in its Standard compared with that of the Grand.

Bleu de Gascogne Basset: The difference in appearance is more marked in the Basset, whose short legs may be either straight, half-crooked or wholly crooked, although the latter is the least desirable. The shoulder height is 12″ to 15″. In other respects the Standard is almost the same as that of the Grand.

These hounds are never seen at shows outside France, and in their country of origin they are usually seen as packs at country shows.

Bleu de Gascogne Petit Griffon: Now extremely rare, the Petit Griffon differs in having a shorter and less curled ear; and the coat should not be too long or woolly but be hard and dry, and standing 17″ to 20½″.

A bitch, with the characteristic markings.

Bloodhound

The ability to gallop on with a free, swinging stride is essential in the Bloodhound. This black and tan bitch, Mrs. Y. Oldman's Ch. Barsheen Rosita, gives the impression of being built to do this, and at the same time shows excellent breed type and quality.

One of the most famous prefixes in Bloodhounds, covering the period of two world wars, is "Brighton". Today the founder, Mr. F. Hylden, shares it with his daughter and son-in-law, Mr. and Mrs. Ickeringill. Here Mrs. Ickeringill is seen with Ch. Freesia of Brighton, just one of many champions to carry this suffix.

history and development

Bloodhounds are believed to have been brought into England in 1066 by William the Conqueror, and it is doubtful if they existed in Britain before that time. They were used extensively in the Ardennes for deer hunting, and must for ever be associated with the Flemish monastery of St. Hubert, where both the black and the white colored hounds were kept, the latter being the Talbot hounds and a color not in existence today. The name Bloodhound is thought to have originated in the same way as a thoroughbred horse is called a blood horse, thereby a thoroughbred hound, a Bloodhound, not a blood-thirsty hound as might be imagined.

During the Second World War the breed nearly became extinct in Britain and it was only due to Mr. F. Hylden of the Brighton prefix and Mrs. Elms of the Reynalton prefix, who struggled to keep approximately a dozen hounds between them, that the breed managed to survive at all. Before the war Kennel Club registrations were about 140 Bloodhounds yearly; during the war ten a year only were registered, and there were twenty-one in 1945, fourteen in 1946 and twenty-one in 1947. These puppies were very in-bred and delicate, and in 1947 and '48 there was a great danger of their becoming extinct altogether. However after re-forming the Association of Bloodhound Breeders three members were appointed to decide what could be done, and Sir John Buchanan-Jardine, Master of the Dumfriesshire hounds, provided a cross-bred Foxhound/Bloodhound bitch to help form outcross blood. Then in 1949 the first of the many imports arrived in from Canada, and so started the great come-back of Bloodhounds in England.

The Bloodhound has been developed in America since the mid 1800's and has been represented at dog shows almost from the beginning. During the two world wars, when the severe food rationing in Europe made it difficult to maintain large dogs, they continued to be bred in the U.S. and many were used in the Armed Forces, especially for tracking in densely forested areas. Their use for police work in America has been very widespread and the achievements claimed for individual dogs almost beyond belief, but there can be no doubt that a good Bloodhound can follow the faintest of scent trails, quite undetectable by any other dog.

color

The colors are black and tan, liver and tan (i.e. red and tan) and self-colored red. The darker colors sometimes being interspersed with lighter or badger-colored hair and sometimes flecked with white. A small amount of white is permissible on chest, feet and tip of stern, but white is not permitted on face or head.

care

Bloodhounds are a country breed and need plenty of space and a lot of exercise as, contrary to their sedate appearance, they are quite boisterous, and although they can be kept in towns, the wide open spaces are more to their liking. They need generous feeding, and a growing puppy will require up to four lbs. of meat daily and about three pints of milk at approximately five months of age, in order to attain maximum size, bone and body. An adult hound will require about three lbs. when fully grown, but this can include cooked offal. Two smaller feeds daily are better than one large one for as in several of the big hound breeds, bloat is an ever-present danger. Two important points to remember are never to allow water for two hours after food, and never to exercise immediately after a meal.

Their short coats are easy to keep clean, and a good daily grooming with a

Mr. and Mrs. D. E. Porter's Ch. Sherlock Sea Serpent, a tall and active black-and-tan hound showing the ground-covering stance the Standard requests. Note the very good top-line and depth of brisket, rib and bone.

Head points are regarded as being very important in Bloodhounds, the heavy wrinkle adds greatly to the sagacious expression typical of the breed. Mrs. J. Rawle's Barnspark Dilemma is well endowed in this respect.

329

hound glove and an occasional dry shampoo is all the cleaning required. Ears need regular attention. Nails might need trimming if not regularly exercised on hard surfaces. Most Bloodhounds prefer the cold to extreme heat although extremes of both should be avoided.

character

A sensitive breed, harsh treatment or teasing can easily ruin their normally affectionate and delightful temperament. They are easily controlled by voice and quickly learn to differentiate between praise and correction. They are very much one-man dogs and do not take kindly to a change of owner after puppyhood.

Despite the tendency to treat the Bloodhound as a show dog, they still have the ability for tracking the cold boot, and if trained for this work can follow a human trail for many miles.

standards

In general appearance it is very powerful and stands over more ground than is usual with a hound of other breeds. The skin must be thin and extremely loose, this being especially noticeable about the head and neck where it hangs in deep folds. The expression is noble and dignified and characterized by solemnity, wisdom and power. The gait is elastic, swinging and free, and the hound should really cover the ground when moving.

The head is narrow in proportion to its length and long in proportion to the body, tapering but slightly from the temples to the muzzle. The skull is long and narrow with the occipital peak very pronounced. The brows are not prominent although owing to the deepset eyes, they may have that appearance. The head is furnished with an amount of loose skin, which in nearly every position appears super-abundant, but more particularly so when the head is carried low; the skin then falls into loose, pendulous ridges and folds, especially over the forehead and sides of the face. The nostrils are large and open. In front the lips fall squarely, making a right angle with the upperline of the foreface; while behind they form deep hanging flews, and, being continued into the pendant folds of loose skin about the neck, constitute the dewlap, which is very pronounced.

The eyes are deeply sunk in the orbits, the lids assuming a lozenge or diamond shape, in consequence of the lower lids being dragged down and everted by the heavy flews. The eyes correspond with the general color of the animal, varying from deep hazel to yellow. The hazel color is, however, to be preferred, although very seldom seen in liver and tan (i.e. red and tan) hounds.

The ears are thin and soft to the touch, extremely long, set-on very low, and fall in graceful folds, the lower parts curling inwards and backwards.

The stern is long and thick, tapering to a point, set-on high with a moderate amount of hair underneath. It should be carried scimitar fashion but not curled over the back or corkscrew at any time.

The average height of adult dogs is 26" and bitches 24". Dogs usually vary from 25" to 27" and bitches from 23" to 25". The average weight of adult dogs in fair condition is 90 lbs. and of adult bitches 80 lbs. Dogs attain 110 lbs. and bitches 100 lbs.

Hounds of the maximum height and weight are preferred providing always that quality, proportion and balance combine.

A typical ten-weeks-old puppy, with ample bone and plenty of wrinkle. Bloodhound puppies of this age appear to possess all the wisdom of the ages.

Borzoi

Breed record holder Ch. Zomahli Chernila, who won twenty–two C.C.s under twenty-two different judges. He is owned by L. Pearson and K. Prior.

Creator of one of the seven types of Borzoi (see text) Col. Nicolai Dmitrievitch Tchelitcheff with two of his dogs in the early 1890's.

history and development

From time immemorial, the bojary (noblemen) and princes of Imperial Russia kept tall, swift hounds for the sport of coursing the wolf. In the 15th and 16th centuries these were crossed with different shepherd dogs of this vast country, to obtain more strength. Later, the blood of Crimean Hounds was introduced for speed and agility. By the end of the 18th century a small group of breeders set out to develop from the few pure lines left the Borzoi such as we know him today. Half-way through last century there were seven distinct types of Borzoi, varying according to height, coat, color, and temperament. Of these, the Perchino-type of the Grand Duke Nicolai Nicolayevitch was the most uniform, and our present-day dogs are mainly descended from this variety.

Decades of careful, selective breeding produced an animal fast and courageous yet beautiful and intelligent. When hunting, a pack of Russian Hounds or Russian Particolored Hounds drove up the wolf, and a hunter followed them on horseback, with a pair of Borzoi on the leash. When the wolf was sighted, he released his Borzoi, who caught the beast and forced it down, holding it until the hunter arrived. This sport demanded extreme speed and accuracy from the hounds, for if they did not strike simultaneously, the wolf would have had time either to shake them off and escape or to turn round and fight.

This most aristocratic of all hounds was introduced to Britain in the late 19th century. The breed enjoyed the patronage of dedicated and knowledgeable breeders from the very beginning, and fortunately never became excessively popular numerically. Thus when supplies from the country of origin were drastically cut off in 1917, the breeders had to be careful with

332

the bloodlines they had built up by 1920, as true outcrosses were increasingly difficult to obtain.

Present-day breeders are also acutely aware of this problem, as the situation has not improved much over the last fifty years. There are some pure outcross bloodlines on the Continent, but these are not always obtainable. And as far as the American imports are concerned, many descend from British-bred hounds and thus do not give the breed a real outcross in the true sense of the word.

Nowadays, of course, there is no possibility of allowing the Borzoi to do his original work, but still this beautiful breed should not be allowed to deteriorate into a mere companion dog. In this, the Continental breeders are one up on the British, as they race their Borzoi on the tracks, thus allowing these magnificent animals the exercise they need. In Russia, there is still one yearly wolf-coursing trial, and to this the hounds are selected from regional trials, which are mainly held on foxes. Some half-hearted attempts have been made to arrange Borzoi coursing in England, but it has never developed.

This side view shows a good length of neck, excellent shoulder placement and smooth arch of back. Finnish and Swedish Ch. Igor of Iochum, owned by Mr. E. Pellikka, is of Continental-British breeding.

color

The British and American Standards allow all colors. Color has never been a subject of controversy although the self-blacks often seem to have that extra little bit of quality. Most common colors are white with red, brown, black, or lemon markings; self-white, black, or red. Gray and brindle-colored hounds are rarer, and a true blue has not been seen since the 1940's. On the Continent, however, the color of the Borzoi is controversial. The Germans led the way here by specifying that the lighter the dog the better. They were also inclined to view black as a minor fault and that most attractive combination, black and tan – with or without white – as a disqualifying fault. France, Holland, and Belgium followed suit, so to a lesser degree did Switzerland and Sweden. This has been the cause of many a good pup being put down under the illusion that he was of a wrong or

Borzoi puppies.

Typical feminine Borzoi bitch of outstanding quality, Ch. Angelola of Enolam. Winner of fourteen C.C.s, she is owned by Mrs. J. Bennett-Heard.

333

A really typical Borzoi head. Note the dark eye, fine, small ear and beautiful outline. Int. Ch. Frimodts Frappant, owner M. L. Wallner, is all Continental breeding.

Typical Borzoi heads.

"bad" color. However, the present F.C.I. Standard accepts all colors, even though there still is in some countries a tendency to favor lighter-colored dogs.

character

The Borzoi is cool and peaceful, reserved and suspicious of strangers. This aloofness in the breed must not be considered as shyness; the true Borzoi is always superbly self-composed and in command of any given situation, never shy or vicious. He is affectionate to those he accepts on his own terms, and a very clean and intelligent house dog. His temperament does not always make him the best of playmates for young children, for although gentle, he wants to preserve his dignity even when playing. He needs plenty of free exercize to keep him in hard, fit condition.

standards

The Borzoi is a very large hound of aristocratic bearing and noble appearance. The height of a male is upwards of 30″ at the shoulder, often reaching 32″ or 33″, the female somewhat smaller. His back is gracefully curved and the gait springy and light.

The head is long and narrow, finely chiselled with a large, always black nose. The mouth has a scissors bite. The eyes are of medium size, somewhat slanting, preferably dark, and never round or bulging. The forehead has no perceptible stop, the outline of the skull flows smoothly from nose to pronounced occiput. Exaggerated Roman nose is to be avoided. The face is well filled below the eyes, the jaws powerful and the muzzle never looking snipey. The ears are small, fine, and high placed; carried pressed flat back on his neck, in excitement raised upright like a horse.

The neck is fairly long and smoothly curving to join the sloping shoulders. The bone of the foreleg should be bladed, never round. The feet are long and arched, "hare-feet", with plenty of hair in between the toes.

The body is deep and very slightly rounded at the sides, never barrel-shaped. The belly is tucked up like that of a Greyhound. The arch of the back starts behind the withers and continues in an unbroken curve over the loin. The profusely feathered tail is long, sickle-shaped and carried low. It should not deviate to either side, nor ever be raised above the back level. The hindquarters are powerfully muscled and well angulated in stifle and hock, which latter is placed very low. The movement is true, front and back, the forelegs must not show any tendency to crossing when moving. Viewed from the front or behind, the legs must be perfectly straight and parallel.

The coat is long, silky, flat or wavy but not curly. It is shorter on the head and on the front side of the legs, longer on the neck, body, and behind the legs. It is profuse but must not be over-heavy. This coat needs surprisingly little care, one of the Borzoi's special characteristics being the tendency to keep clean and unmatted with the minimum of daily attention.

Coonhound, Black and Tan

The lay visitor to a dog show might well confuse the Black and Tan Coonhound with one of his close-up ancestors, the Bloodhound, for these two breeds are identical in size and often in color. However, there are differences that any knowledgeable dogman could point out. The Coonhound is missing the almost excessive wrinkling of head that is the hallmark of the Bloodhound. The "cooner" has a clean profile with no hint of wrinkle. He is never anything except black and tan, while the Bloodhound may also be red and tan, or tawny.

The Black and Tan Coonhound probably goes back to the days when Virginia was a Colony of England. According to records in the library at the University of William and Mary, Bloodhounds were imported extensively to be used for defending the colonists against the Indians, for it was wild country when they settled at Jamestown in 1607. It was not until after breeders had produced the Virginia Foxhound (predecessor of the modern American Foxhound) in the mid-1700's that thought was given to the tailoring of a specialized breed for raccoon and possum hunting. Prior to that, foxhunting had been the big sport, but it was mostly for the landed gentry, not the poor and lower middle class farmer. These men hunted afoot.

The Coonhound: the Bloodhound ancestry can be seen. This is Canadian and American Ch. Melinda of Ten Oaks.

The Black and Tan Coonhound was admitted to registration by the A.K.C. in 1945, but it has not yet caught on with show exhibitors. Few shows in the big eastern seaboard area have any entries of the breed, but it is bigger in the Mid-West and South. However, after more than a quarter century it is only about 90th among 116 breeds, with yearly registrations of 150 to 160.

While many other somewhat similar breeds, like the Redbone, are used in coonhunting, the Black and Tan is considered supreme in treeing his quarry in the fastest and most efficient manner.

The first impression of a Black and Tan is that he is fundamentally a worker. He is capable of withstanding extremes of either cold or heat, and his stride must be powerful, enabling him to cover a lot of ground in a minimum of time. His expression must be alert, friendly, eager and aggressive. His cleanly modeled head has a medium stop; overall the head measures 9″ to 10″ in males, an inch less in females. The skin is devoid of folds or excess dewlap; skull should tend toward oval outline. Eyes should be from hazel to dark brown in color. His low-set ears, well back, should hang in graceful folds, giving him a majestic appearance, and should extend, when stretched forward, well beyond the tip of the nose. Teeth fit evenly – slight scissors-bite.

Ribs should be full, round, and well sprung; back level, powerful and strong with visible slope from withers to rump. Forelegs are straight, elbows well let down, turning neither in nor out; quarters well-boned and muscled. When standing on level ground, the hind feet should be set back from under the body. The coat should be short and dense.

The male stands 25″ to 27″ at the shoulder, the female 23″ to 25″. Dogs that are over-sized should not be penalized if otherwise sound and in good proportion.

Dachsbracke

(Erz Mountains, Westphalian)

In 1896 it was decided that the hunting dogs of the Bavarian-Styrian mountains on the border of East Germany and Czechoslovakia, should be known as Dachsbracke. The breed is described as a transitional conformation between the Dachshund and the long-legged hound, and has been used for decades in the mountains for hunting hare and fox, and occasionally for deer (for which purpose it is restrained on a long lead) and for searching out and setting up other wild game. Its scenting power is considerable. The Swedish Drever is a closely related variety.

The first litter in Britain was bred by the late Miss W. A. Riley in 1949.

There are three types, Westphalian, Erz Mountains and Alpine. The Westphalian is now almost extinct, and is the smallest of the three, 12″ to 14″ in height. The other types have the same physical characteristics, coat and coloration. Height $13\frac{1}{2}$″ to $16\frac{1}{2}$″, straight rather long back, prominent breast bone. The head has strong jaws, pronounced stop, slightly protruding lower lip. The coat of all three is short and dense, with little undercoat. The Westphalian is sometimes called "bright-white", a reference to its hound coloration of white with red and any other color. The colors of the Erz Mountain and the Alpine are black with rust red markings; brown with lighter brown markings; red (chestnut, rust, orange) with markings of lighter shades.

A typical specimen of the Erz Mountains type.

Dachshund

Mrs. R. Gale's Ch. Womack Wrightstarturn, a gloriously sound dog, standing well over the forelegs. Note the deep, well-shaped keel, small eye, long neck, correct shoulder placement, firm top-line and well angulated hindquarters.

history and development

It is certain that by chance, mutation and finally by recognized breeding, the Dachshund, or Teckel as it is known in Germany, has been evolved from the oldest known breeds of dog. In old German documents there is mention of the "Tracking Dog" and of the Bibarhunt or predecessor of the Teckel.

In 16th century documents repeated reference is made to "Little Burrow Dog", "Badger Dog" and "Dacksel", and woodcuts of 1576 to 1582 show cross-bred dogs on lengthy Dachshund bodies. At the end of the 17th century the "Badger Fighter" is described as a "peculiar low crooked legged specie", while in 1848 Teckels became well known to hunting historians of that period and were described as follows:—

> A good looking Dachshund is long and low, the back arched, belly drawn up weasel fashion, chest deep, neck long and strong, canine teeth interlocking closely, the eye expressive and spirited, the tail fine and not carried too gaily. The hind legs more stiff and straight than is usually the case in other dogs. Forelegs strong and muscular, not crooked but only with the broad strong feet turned outwards.

Throughout the centuries our Dachshund was bred as a hunting dog. Definitely to the year 1848, the Smooth-haired variety was the off-spring of the crossing of the Miniature French Pointer, or Bracke, with the Pinscher (Vermin Killer). And the Long-hair was the product of the crossing of the Smooth-haired Dachshund with the Spaniel, and the old German Stoberhund (Gun Dog). To amplify these two varieties further, at the close of the 19th century the Wire-haired Dachshund was created by inter-breeding with the Wire-haired Pinschers, Schnauzers and English Dandie Dinmonts, and Scottish Terriers. And at the beginning of the 20th century the Miniature and Kaninchenteckel were brought into being by crossing the Smooths with Miniature Pinschers, the Longs with Papillons, and the small type Schnauzer in the making of the Miniature wire.

This Miniature Wire-haired bitch, Mrs. Hood Wrights' Ch. Selwood Poinsettia, excels in top-line, length of keel and neck, together with the correct angle of shoulders and hindquarters.

The oldest Dachshund Club in the world, founded in 1881, and at that time for Smooths only, is that of England. The Deutscher Teckelklub was formed in 1888.

In the latter half of the 19th century many breeds were defined and the English, above all, excelled in how to produce new varieties.

Of the smaller breeds, one which continued to increase the number of its breeders and admirers was the Dachshund. But he developed as a house dog, and most unfortunately became a fashionable dog. As by nature he was already of comical and original appearance, he gradually became still lower, still longer and still heavier, being depicted as the sausage dogs of the comics.

From this time Smooth Dachshund breeding improved with the whelping of Jackdaw in 1886, and in 1887 his son Snakes Prince was acknowledged as the best of his breed so far produced in England and probably as good as anything in Germany. In 1903 Racker Von Der Ecke was imported into England, his assets being excellent legs, feet and bone. He was widely used at stud. Following the 1914–18 war the need for new blood was realised in England and two animals were imported who were destined to form the foundation of what was then called the modern type. Remagan Max came to England when the general quality of available breeding stock was rather low. He was much used at stud and had the knack of getting good products from all kinds of bitches. In 1930 a stud force of the first magnitude was imported in Wolf Von Birkenschloss, a small dog, very compactly and strongly built, excellent in soundness, shoulder placement, hindquarters and feet. Again in 1938 another import who was to make a lasting influence for good, not only on the Smooth variety but also (from the recessive long-haired factor) on the Long-

haired variety, was Zeus Von Schwarenburg.

In Long-hairs the earliest imports of note occurred around 1900; the foundation stock came from Austria. Following the war years 1914–18 an important import was Ratzmann Von Habitschof, a dog with a glorious head, enormous length, very heavy bone, sound close feet, and a profuse coat of perfect texture. He was much used at stud and in the absence of any other dogs of note, the results of close and persistent inter-breeding inevitably appeared. In 1928 Elfe Von Fels was imported in whelp, and her son, bred to existing stock, produced a long line of outstanding specimens. In 1931 the famous Otter Von Fels was imported, to found the Von Walder Line; the Habitschof blood again being brought to

Although he has a long neck and good top-line, fore-chest and sweep of keel, this dog stands too high on leg.

Mrs. Fielding's Ch. Delphik Debbret, a Miniature Long-haired bitch of exquisite type, enhanced by the small eye, head carriage and feathering of ears; and Debbret as a ten-week puppy, showing already the correct round, thick feet, bone in legs and good width of fore-chest.

It is difficult to fault this dog, American Ch. Vantbe's Draht Timothy, a Wire-hair. He stands true, has heavy bone and thick, round feet, good length of neck, proud head carriage, good top-line, fore-chest and length of under-line.

England through Ursel Von Der Golderen Pearl as his mate. By the mid 1940's the Long-hairs again needed new blood, this being provided for by the birth in 1954 of Imber Coffee Bean, son of the Long-hair Imber Black Coffee (the great-great-grandson of the imported Smooth Zeus Von Schwarenburg) ex daughter of Suse Von Fuchensohl, again carrying the Von Habitschof blood. This dog was used extensively.

For the Wires, the first known import was of a dog called Woolsack born in 1888. No determined effort being made to bring Wire-hairs to prominence in England till 1927, when several good dogs and bitches were imported from Germany. These being followed by the importation from Sweden of the Sports line just previous to the 1939 war; these representatives firmly establishing a type.

Dachshunds may be found in almost all countries. In Australia, New Zealand, and South Africa the breeders give much credit to the soundness of the imported English stock, while in America breeders have relied upon the German lines, and developed some outstanding specimens in all coats and sizes. The A.K.C. registered its first specimen in 1885, an American-bred named Dash, whelped in 1879. It was a Smooth; the Long-hair and the Wire-hair were not registered in the U.S.A. until 1931.

color

A study of color effects is very important in this breed. Many colors are found in the Dachshund, black and tan, chocolate and tan, red, with the occasional dapple, most frequent at present in the Miniature Wires. The Long-hairs seldom produce the dapple coat, although brindles can be bred for. In the Wires brindle is the most frequent color. No white, other than a small spot on the chest is permissible, but not desirable.

In breeding for color, two basic principles should be borne in mind. The first is that weak pigmentation is often accompanied by constitutional weakness; the second that in breeding whole-colored individuals together there is a tendency for the progeny to be less strongly pigmented than their parents. The original fount of pigmentation in Dachshunds is the red coloration. All the other color varieties – red, brindle, chocolate and dapple – derive from this and represent a weakening, or dilution, of the original pigment factors. If red is bred to red, generation after generation, the color becomes pale and washy. The resulting bad-colored specimens will probably show light eyes, pink or brown noses and white markings on chest or toes, and this faulty coloration will go with diminished vitality, constitutional weakness, and lack of substance. It is not suggested that in this breed the mating of a red dog to a red bitch is always unwise. In the Long-hairs, brindle represents the next step to black and tan, and may also be used to strengthen pigmentation in the reds. Light eyes frequently occur in stock bred from parents showing this fault. Two light-eyed Dachshunds should on no account be mated together. Chocolate represents, it is believed, a deviation from black and tan caused by the loss or repression of a pigment factor. The origin of the color is, however, rather problematic. Chocolate is not a good color to breed to red, as such matings almost invariably produce washy chocolates or chocolate reds with pink noses and light eyes. Chocolate should only be mated to chocolate if both parents are especially dark and rich in color. Mated to black and tan, chocolate usually produces deep-colored chocolates or richly marked black and tans. Chocolate in the ancestry will often crop up as a recessive factor in offspring many generations later.
The brindle coat of the Wire is dominant; to breed a black and tan, a red

Despite his good head, shape of eye and ear feathering, this Long-haired dog is short of body coat and has an incorrect top-line, resulting in too low tail set and faulty hind angulation.

Small eyes, very good fore-chest, weight equally placed on front feet, good top-line; yet this dog has over-built hindquarters, shown by excessive length of bones, from foot to hock and hock to stifle, giving a wide, toed-in stance. In movement this could not be correct.

or a dapple, one parent must be of this color. In the Smooth-hairs two dapples should not be mated together, for the risk of albino characteristics (an almost white coat, and small, pale, near-blind, or blind eyes) is too great. Strangely, it is possible to do this mating in the Wire-hairs, without incurring these defects.

care

Rearing of Dachshund puppies is not difficult providing the owner is prepared to make it impossible for them to scramble up steps, stairs or on to furniture. If this is allowed the shoulder muscles, which at a youthful age are very elastic, will become overstretched, so allowing the points of the elbows to become prominent. This is an ugly fault and one that maturity cannot improve.

Diet is important, the puppies requiring raw meat in small quantities from the third week, with adequate amounts of milk feeds. By the time they are eight weeks the amount of meat should be eight ounces. The Dachshund puppy should have freedom to run around and sleep when tired, and sunshine with the Vitamins C and D is invaluable for speedy growth.

character

The Dachshund character is (provided it is given the opportunity to develop) one of ready intelligence, indomitable spirit, blended with craft and humor. The Smooths and Wires are more demonstrative, with the Long-hairs showing much dignity and independence.

342

A very good Dachshund in miniature, showing long neck, good fore-chest, well laid shoulders, correct top-line, depth of keel and hind angulation. Mrs. Gracey's Miniature Smooth-hair Ch. Runnel Petticoat.

The forward, upright shoulder placement gives a short neck. The keel is too steep and straight, resulting in lack of fore-chest and no nicely sweeping under-line.

The very correct flat coat on this Long-haired Dachshund covers a deep body. The fore-chest is particularly good, with well placed, well laid shoulders. The hind angulation is correct but the neck could be longer, and the ears should be fringed. Mr. and Mrs. Spiers' Ch. Merula of Sarfra.

standards

The Standards require that the height at the shoulder should be half the length of the body from point of breast bone to "set-on" of tail, the girth of the chest being double the height at shoulder. The lowest point of the keel being on a level with the wrist joint. The top-line must not dip behind the shoulders, neither should the hindquarters be higher than the shoulders. The top-line should not be completely flat and should show a very slight rise over the loin falling easily to the tail set. The crook of the forelegs is, in the present day Dachshund, not so pronounced, and no greater turn of the feet must be seen than would show if the dog were standing on a clock face with six o'clock mid centre and its feet at five and seven o'clock, and with the weight evenly spread on all parts of the foot. In America and Canada the Miniature weight is 9 lbs. and under; in the near future this will probably rise to 10 lbs. In England the weight of all varieties is 11 lbs. and under. The Australians do not weight their Miniatures, the responsibility being placed upon the judge.

The sporting instinct is fostered in Germany, and the Dachshund used by the foresters is required to be not too low to ground and a good mover. A dog too low soon becomes wet in rainy weather or in snow, and if working under ground could damage its chest, and if in pain might well be unwilling to continue its track. The German Dachshund is not only used for tracking hares, wounded deer and fox, but also for the sauhatz or boar. The Dachshund being able on account of its stature and nimbleness to avoid the boar's tusks.

The German Dachshund must not weigh more than 20 lbs. and consequently there is no gap between Miniatures and Standards. That is to say that if a dog's chest measures more than 35 cm., it is Standard. But they are not light in bone; they must have good bone whatever the size. The Long-hairs must show feathered ears, tails and legs, and have a flat body coat. In Wires the Deutscher Teckelklub has stopped the crossing of Wire to Smooth-hair. They demand a good, harsh coat, but the dogs at present appear to have a "Smooth type" head. Judges seem to prefer the appearance of a broader muzzle on Wires. Recently the Teckelklub has removed the suggested weight of 4 kilos (8·8 lbs.) for Miniatures, and now only measure at the limit of 35 cm. This chest measurement is taken immediately behind the front legs around the deepest part of the chest. Heads in all varieties are much flatter on top of skull, giving a much bolder appearance. Continental judges do not like "domed heads".

In America the demand is for a larger, more imposing animal (in some cases as much as 28-30 lbs.) who can win a Group. The American Dachshund is required to have a very heavy front with the breast bone even more prominent than is required in England. The heads are bred long and narrow. The Long-hair, Miniature or Standard does not always have the profuse coat of the English dogs. Presentation in America is very important, and the animals are really handled while in the ring. In Germany no animal must be touched by the owner, and must be shown on a completely loose lead.

Young, and very faulty. Incorrect length of leg, short, steep keel, and showing too much daylight.

Deerhound
(Scottish)

Miss A. Linton's Ch. Brandt of Geltsdale, a beautiful hound bearing himself with the dignity and grace which is so characteristic of this ancient breed.

A pair of Geltsdale hounds, Forrester and Jasmine.

history and development

In the *Art of Deerstalking* by William Scrope, published in 1838, there is a description of the Highland Deerhound by Archibald McNeil of Colonsay, "The deerhound is known under the names of Irish Wolfhound, Irish greyhound, Highland deerhound and Scotch greyhound".

Dogs resembling the Greyhound of the present day were known in Britain as early as the third century, and later on in this book Scrope says "Whatever be the origin of the name, there is no doubt as to the antiquity of a species of dog in this country bearing a great resemblance in many points to the Greyhound of the present day, and passing under that name, though evidently a larger, nobler and more courageous animal".

We know that the Deerhound has been a British breed since the ninth century, although we cannot be certain what they looked like before the 18th century.

The early Deerhounds were bred for strength and speed, to be used entirely for sport; they were then as now the aristocrats of the canine world – used for hunting by day, and at night allowed to lie in the baronial halls. In the 19th century however, with the introduction of breech-loading rifles, shooting was preferred to hunting, and hounds were only needed to help find the wounded deer, and at that point the breed

Scottish Deerhound.

declined sadly.

Mr. Archibald McNeil and his brother Lord Colonsay, luckily for the future of the breed, still wanted to breed hounds able to kill without assistance, and in their home-bred dogs Buscar and Bran, they amply maintained this quality.

In 1860 the first dog show to schedule Deerhounds was held in England at Birmingham, when "Col. Inge's Deerhound was a grand winner in a class that was quite unworthy of him, and his fair companion Brinstone had the same honor".

The early winners are nearly all descended from the old working hounds. The Deerhound Club was founded in Britain in 1886 – the description being drawn up by Messrs. Hickman and R. Hood Wright, and approved at a meeting of the Club on November 24th 1892, when Sir Walter Evans became president, and remained president until he died in 1935. Deerhounds have throughout the decades been lucky in that they have always had staunch supporters to help over lean times.

The attitude of breeders towards maintaining the ancient type and the success with which their efforts have been rewarded is shown by a comparison of the present-day Deerhound with those depicted in Weston Bell's famous book *The Scottish Deerhound*, published in 1892, soon after the Standard was established. It is difficult to determine any change.

A few years ago the Scottish Deerhound Club of America was formed. Membership of the Club is increasing and, in view of the distances involved, members show a remarkable enthusiasm in getting together and comparing their Deerhounds at shows all over America.

color

Color can range from cream to very dark gray. There is however no doubt that most breeders would choose a dark blue-gray, with silver gray for second choice. In the years I have had Deerhounds I have only seen one cream hound. Brindle in my experience is the least popular and least pleasing color, so that it is satisfactory when a brindle pup develops into a gray hound, as oftens happens. Yellow and sandy-red or red-fawn are popular colors, especially when the dogs have black points; this is indeed the coloring of the strains having the longest known pedigree, the McNeil and Cheethill Menzies strains. While white is objectionable,

Ch. Mac of Bencombe and Georgina of Ardkinglas coursing the hare, which can just be seen at the right of the photograph.

little objection is raised against a white chest and white toes; but the purists prefer the Deerhound to be a self-colored dog – the less white the better, and certainly no white blaze on the head, or a white collar. Whatever the color of the hound, the ears should be black or dark colored.

care

The Deerhound is a strong, healthy animal with a shaggy coat to resist the weather. It prefers cold to heat, and neither needs nor likes additional warmth in its kennel, except when very young, or old, or ill.

It is however to be remembered that, although it is under two pounds at birth, it can weigh sixty or seventy pounds at six months, and therefore needs careful rearing to remain sound in limb. For showing it needs very little trimming – just the long hairs taken from its ears, from the sides of its neck, and sometimes the long untidy hair from the legs.

Not naturally a showman, it requires careful training to make the most of itself in the ring. Generally only too willing to please, it is apt to regard a dog show as a bore.

Despite its dignified appearance and aristocratic bearing the Deerhound is keenly aware of everything around him – as portrayed to perfection by this picture of Miss Linton's Vivian of Geltsdale.

character

What can one write of character that has not already been written. Once a real Deerhound lover I think one always remains so – they are gentle, loving, affectionate and devoted – always wishing to be with their humans and content to leave it at that. They do not fuss – a reproachful look is their only manner of complaining.

Deerhounds make ideal companions – for their size they eat the minimum – even less than one pound of meat per day plus houndmeal will suffice, provided that they have been well fed as puppies. They will need at least twice as much food at their maximum period of growth.

They are handy to exercise, because they will take as much or as little as one has time and energy to give, and they do not easily put on excess weight.

Having long legs they do not carry much dirt into the house, and their shaggy coat sheds very little over the carpet.

Naturally if one wants to course hounds, they will need a good deal of exercise to get into hard muscular condition, and they will then need more meat to sustain them.

Deerhound puppies.

Ch. Mac of Bencombe and Georgina of Ardkinglas, waiting to be slipped.

standards

Since the original Standard was drawn up in 1892, with dogs at 28″ to 30″ at shoulder, weighing 85 lbs. to 105 lbs., and bitches 26″ to 28″, weighing 65 lbs. to 80 lbs., Deerhounds have altered remarkably little. As a general rule height has increased by a maximum of two or three inches but weight has remained the same as it was, thus the bone is not quite so heavy. The Standards state that "the body and general formation is that of a Greyhound of larger size and bone". He should be a "shaggy dog, but not over-coated". "The proper coat is a thick, close-lying ragged coat, harsh or crisp to the touch."

The distinctive head should be like that of a Greyhound but coated with moderately long hair, softer than the rest of the coat, and it should have a good moustache of rather silky hair and a fair beard. The ears are set-on high, folded back when calm, and raised but still folded when excited.

The shoulders should be well sloped, with straight forelegs, broad and

Miss A. M. Hartley's Ch. Vanda of Rotherwood, a lovely example of a Deerhound bitch, whose grace of conformation and movement are the result of careful selective breeding for many generations.

flat with good broad forearm and elbow. The hindquarters are drooping, broad and powerful, with hips wide apart. Hind legs well bent at the stifle, with great length from hip to hock, which should be broad and flat. The feet are close and compact, with well arranged toes, and strong nails.

The tail is long, thick at the root, tapering and reaching to within around $1\frac{1}{2}''$ of the ground. Well covered with hair, thick and wiry on the inside, longer on the underside; and a slight fringe towards the end is not objected to.

The coat should be harsh and wiry, about three or four inches long, the hair on the head, breast and belly being much softer. The slight hairy fringe on the inside of the legs should not be so definite as the "feather" of a Collie.

While the U.S. Standard is virtually the same as the British, it is true that in America a larger hound is favored. The A.K.C. specifies 30″ to 32″ for dogs; bitches from 28″ upward. Weight 85 to 110 lbs. for dogs; 75 to 95 lbs. for bitches.

Drever

This short-legged hound, very similar to the Dachsbracke, comes from Sweden.

The "Swedish type Beagle" – the Drever – has for many years kept its position as one of the three or four top breeds in Sweden as far as registrations go; usually well over 2,000 Drevers are registered annually. Practically every Drever will be used, to some extent, for hunting while very few breeders seem to bother about anything as futile as a dog show.

Although the Drever is now considered a truly native Swedish breed, it originated in Germany: the first few specimens were imported shortly after 1900. At that time, it was known by the German name, "Dachsbracke", but as time passed and the breed began to differ slightly from its forebears, a Swedish name and an official breed Standard became necessary. The name, Drever, came into use in 1947, being derived from the substantive "drev", meaning to hunt, and not until 1949 was it officially recognized by the Swedish Kennel Club. It has since been one of the country's most numerous breeds although little known outside of Sweden – Denmark in fact breeds its own almost identical type, called the "Strellufsstövare".

The Drever should be a strong, muscular dog, standing just over 12″ at the withers. The color is white with black and/or tan markings, and a white blaze down the forehead and a white collar are considered desirable.

Dunker

The Dunker or Norwegian Hound, dating from about 1820, is a strong but not heavy dog, built more for staying-power than for speed.

The skull is slightly arched and the occiput and stop clearly defined. The rather long muzzle is straight but not snipey. The eyes should be dark, rather large, but not protruding. China eyes are permissible in harlequin dogs. Ears of medium width, soft and slightly rounded at the end are set on moderately low and carried close to the head.

Dew-claws should be removed. The tail should reach to the hocks or a little beyond, thick at the set-on and tapering gradually towards the tip, forming a continuation of the straight back-line. It should be carried slightly curved but not curled.

The coat should be black or harlequin (blue marbled) with fawn and white markings. Deep chestnut is objectionable and predominant white with harlequin markings or liver should be a disqualification. The coat is close, hard and straight.

Height: 18½″ to 22″.

A good quality bitch of this Norwegian hound breed.

Estonian Hound

Before the 1917 revolution there were several excellent hound breeds in Russia, but today only three of them are recognized. The Estonian Hound is one; the others are the Particolored Russian Hound and the Russian Hound. Estonia is now a Republic within the U.S.S.R., but the history of this hound goes back to pre-Revolutionary days, when there was a nobility in the country, and hunting was one of its major pastimes.

The Estonian Hound is a strong, fast-moving hound of medium size, around 20″. The head has clean lines and a roundish skull. The muzzle is fairly long, the nose wide and black. The ears are set-on low; they are long and hang close to the cheeks.

The body is long, twice as long as its height, and the back is broad and straight, with straight, muscular quarters, and a tail, reaching to the hocks, straight and well coated with hair, giving it a thick appearance. The coat is short, dense and rough; black with fawn markings.

The elongated body and long ears of the Estonian Hound.

Fauves de Bretagne

(Basset, Briquet)

A pair of typical Fawn Bassets; note the comparatively smooth ears, the broad, large feet and the coat, long yet flat lying.

Basset: Like the Fawn Briquet, he is descended from the Grand Fauves de Bretagne. Good ones are now almost non-existent and it is a matter of urgency that every effort should be made to resuscitate the breed. It is a small rough-haired Basset, short coupled, red gold in color with a white patch on chest and neck. He is a grand worker and hunts well in dense cover. Although small, he is untiring and will hunt any kind of game.

He is a lively, compact little dog, 13″ to 16″ high, speedy for his size.

Head fairly long, with marked occiput. Ears thin, set-on at eye level and barely reaching the end of the muzzle. Covered in hair finer than that on rest of body. Back long but not exaggeratedly so. Loin broad, tucked up and muscular. Front legs straight, or slightly heavy and crooked. Hocks strong, broad and slightly bent. Sickle tail.

Briquet: There are still one or two specimens to be found and the Club is trying to resuscitate the breed, descended, as is the Basset from the Grand Fauves de Bretagne. He is a more rough-looking dog than the Griffon. Of medium size, muscular, vigorous and rugged. In the field, he is perhaps a little too fiery and impetuous and therefore sometimes gets carried away on to a false scent. He is said to be an excellent and brave hunter of foxes and wild-boar under the most difficult conditions.

Color – Fawn, the best being wheaten gold or bright golden brown.

Of medium height, some 19″ to 22″, he is well-boned and muscular, giving the impression of great vigor and ruggedness rather than of elegance. Skull, fairly long with marked occiput. Ears set-on at eye level, and barely reaching to the muzzle, pointed and covered with hair which is finer and softer than that on the rest of the body. Back short and broad. Loins appearing tucked up, thanks to the strongly muscled hindquarters. Well-made tail, well carried, of medium length. Coat very harsh but not too long.

Finnish Hound

The Finnish Hound, or Suomenajokoira, is the most popular breed in Finland, accounting for over 3,000 out of a total annual registration of 20,000 dogs. In appearance it is not unlike the Harrier. Although the word "ajokoira" means a dog used for hunting the hare or fox, the Finnish Hound is also used to drive moose or even lynx. It is not the Finnish practice to breed dogs especially as Foxhounds, and this breed is allowed to develop into a hare- or fox-hunting dog according to circumstances.

A typical specimen.

The breed was created during the 19th century, largely through the efforts of V. E. Tammelin – a goldsmith, by crossing the old Scandinavian, Russian, German, English and Swiss Hounds, and the Finnish Kennel Club drew up its first Standard in 1893.

The Finnish Hound is a medium-sized, short-haired dog ($21\frac{1}{2}$″ to 24″ for dogs; 20″ to $22\frac{1}{2}$″ for bitches) with an imposing head and beautifully hanging ears. It is a little longer than its height; the tail is long and carried just below the level of the back. It moves with a long, springy gait; when hunting it gallops. The coat is short, with a pronounced sheen, in tricolor combination of tan, black saddle and white markings on throat, breast, head, lower parts of legs, and tail.

Foxhound, American

history and development

The first record of hounds being kept to chase the fox in America dates back to June 1650, when Mr. Robert Brooks landed in what is now the State of Maryland, bringing with him his wife, ten children, twenty-one manservants, seven maidservants, and "his hounds to run fox". These hounds are described as large, racy animals, with heavy coats, flag tails, dark roan saddles, buckskin legs and white points. It is recorded that these are the hounds which form the foundation for the present-day American Foxhound. Court records in Virginia reveal that packs of hounds were

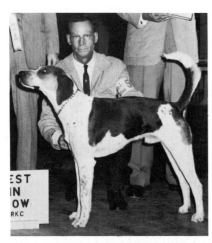

Ch. Kentucky Lake Mike, the first American Foxhound ever to win best in show at an American all-breed show, in 1963. The handler is Bob Waters and the all-breed judge, William Kendrick.

Ch. Kentucky Lake Dandy, handled by John C. Sawyer, wins a Group under well-known all-round judge, Percy Roberts.

kept to chase fox in the year 1691. The editor of the *Virginia Gazette* finds American foxhunting in a rather advanced state in 1736, and describes meeting a pack of hounds. "I heard the cry of Hounds, and my Horse (for want of Exercise) grew Headstrong, and carried me in the midst of them. . . . I must acknowledge I was highly delighted with the Sight, which was quite new to me".

Dr. Thomas Walker established a pack of hounds in Virginia in 1742, and named them "The Castle Hill Hounds" after his estate, and he later moved to Kentucky with his pack to hunt there.

Lord Thomas Fairfax landed in Virginia in 1746. He had a strong passion for foxhunting, which he transmitted to George Washington, then a lad of sixteen, and he, from 1759 onwards, devoted most of his leisure time to the sport. During this period of development there was no Standard for the Foxhound, no standardized type, no organizations, merely a trial and error process, breeding and cross breeding native stock with stock imported from England, Ireland and France, trying to produce a hound suitable for American hunting conditions.

The beginnings of pedigree breeding began with the importation of two hounds from Ireland around 1830, Mountain and Muse. Mountain eventually came into the hands of Dr. Buchanan of Sharpsburg and from him Dr. T. Y. Henry of Virginia received Captain, descended from Mountain and Muse. Dr. Henry bred from Captain and his descendants for several years in Virginia, where they became famous as the Irish Hounds.

Around 1850 the red fox appeared in the South and the breeding of American Foxhounds got under way. There was much competition among the breeders of the time, and such men as T. Y. Henry of Virginia, George Washington Mauphin of Kentucky, George L. F. Birdsong of Georgia, Hayden C. Trigg of Kentucky, Willis C. Goodman of Kentucky, Nimrod Gosnell of Maryland, and many others began to breed for blood, and some of them began to pull away from the average speed and trailing packhound to a hound that had individuality to start, drive, catch and kill a red fox alone.

The first bench show in America was in Chicago in 1874. No Foxhounds were entered, and this was followed by the first combined Field Trial and Bench Show in October 1874 in Memphis, Tennessee. The first time American Foxhounds were entered at a dog show was at the Westminster Kennel Club's show in New York in 1877; six dogs were entered.

The first stud book published in America was in 1878 but it was not until 1883 that the first American Foxhound was registered in a public Stud Book. The American Kennel Club first entered a Foxhound in its Stud Book in 1886, but from around 1875 to 1900 the breed figured in many all-breed shows, winning their share of championships. In 1894 the Brunswick Foxhound Club and the National Foxhunters Association drew up a Standard for the American Foxhound, which was adopted by the American Kennel Club, and remains to this day, with only minor changes.

American Foxhounds figured in more and more shows through the years, and won many hound groups until, in 1963, a Foxhound named Kentucky Lake Mike won best in show at the all-breed American Kennel Club show at Baton Rouge, Louisiana. Since then they have won five best in shows at major shows, and registrations are higher than they have ever been.

color

The Standard of the American Kennel Club allows any hound color.

care

The Foxhound is primarily a kennel or a pack dog, and needs the care only necessary to keep him fit for the chase. Individual grooming, to a point deemed right for the show bench, is rarely given to a pack hound – good food, veterinary attention, dry, warm quarters and frequent exercise, in discipline with the rest of the pack, is all he needs. But he has the capacity, as all dogs have, for forming deep attachments to human beings, and in this respect he is a one-man dog, he does not give his affection twice. It is not easy to train him for activities foreign to his hunting nature, after all he has had deliberately bred into him a deep instinct for hunting, which comes to the surface whenever it is provoked. But with patience, he can be trained to reasonable house dog behavior.

character

He is gregarious, likes the company of other members of the pack, and rarely quarrels with them. He is single minded at the chase; with his nose down, and his tail waving when he sights or scents his quarry, he has no thought for anything else. He is one of the most enduring dogs, going for hours without let-up, and coming into the fray with as much vigor as when he started.

standards

This is a breed confined to America, only a few specimens have found their way elsewhere. The Standard of the American Kennel Club is the one and only Standard. It calls for an animal with all the hound characteristics – a close, hard, hound coat of moderate length; a body with sloping shoulders conveying the idea of freedom of action with activity and strength; deep chest, narrower in proportion to depth than is the English Foxhound, and well-sprung ribs. His back is moderately long, muscular and strong with broad and slightly arched loins. The forelegs straight, the feet fox-like, with full and hard pads, and well-arched toes. The hindlegs have strong propelling power, stifles strong and well let-down, hocks firm, symmetrical and moderately bent. The tail is set moderately high, carried gaily, but not turned forward over the back; it should have a slight curve and a very slight brush.

Dogs should be 22″ to 25″; bitches 21″ to 24″.

Compare this photograph of Ch. Kentucky Lake Big Red with the one heading this chapter, where he was conditioned for show. Here he is conditioned for the field, indeed this photograph, posed by his owner Dr. Braxton B. Sawyer, was taken at the close of four days hard field running at the National Foxhunters Association field trials.

A head study of Kentucky Lake Fireboy, a big winner in 1970.

A group of American Foxhounds in the charge of their kennel master.

Foxhound English

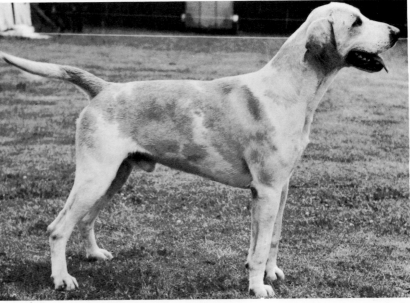

Heythrop Cardinal, supreme Foxhound champion at the 1965 Peterborough Royal Foxhound show. An example of beautiful construction throughout.

It is quite impossible to write fully about this peculiar breed of the canine species in the small place allotted to me here. Selective breeding down through the last 150 years has produced the Foxhound of today, but what was deemed perfection and considered to be the very pattern and unchanging standard set for all time in the hound of fifty years ago has changed beyond all recognition in what is thought, no, known to be the ideal Foxhound of today.

Improvement, both in shape, make and ability is still sought by the would-be perfectionist, while the remaining "die-hards" of the old school cry, "Enough, more than enough, we have gone too far"; let each one, in fact stick like the cobbler, to his last, and retain, regardless of comment, that which suits him the best. It is difficult, with so much change in fashion to put a concise account of "The Foxhound" on record in any encyclopedia, even in one about dogs.

In Britain the stag was still the popular beast of the chase until the middle of the 19th century, and only in the reign of George I were packs being formed to hunt foxes. After Thomas Boothby in Leicestershire in 1750 came Squire Draper in the north filled with the same foxhunting ideals. Hugo Meynell, although only 18 years old when Boothby died in 1753, was one of his best friends and he was bequeathed the whole establishment, including the country over which Boothby had hunted.

Meynell bought Quorndon Hall, and devoted his life to a complete change in the style and method of hunting foxes, and when, almost seventy years old, he handed over his Mastership of his hounds, now called the Quorn – the most famous British pack all down the ages and so it is today – to Lord Sefton, it had become a very fashionable sport indeed. Meynell is often called "the father of foxhunting", and his demand for speed and yet more speed both in hounds and horses revolutionized hunting as it was then enjoyed. Thoroughbred horses replaced the heavy, slow, cart-horse types that had previously sufficed those who only rode so that they could be sufficiently close to their slow patient hounds to see and hear exactly what they were doing.

It was not enough, however, that hounds could gallop. They had also to have such an ability to run on a faint scent, that they could follow a fox at full speed. They had to possess the stamina to last through the longest day; be filled with courage yet docile and obedient enough to obey every command, and they had also to be well put together with coats that shone like satin. An impossibility one might have thought, but Hugo Meynell, by skill, patience and infinite knowledge, produced in all his glory that most magnificent of all animals, the Foxhound. Other great breeders emulated him, and down the ages famous names are on record who attempted to perfect what was considered perfection.

These hounds were black, tan and white, standing 24″ at the shoulder for dogs, rather less for bitches; legs were straight with necks and shoulders in the style of race-horses, deep chested and round and stout over the ribs and with great muscled thighs and backs. Such hounds can still be seen at Belvoir and many other kennels who breed the old type of Foxhound and in Shropshire the Ludlow Hunt have Foxhounds of Meynell's type that are a joy to see and which do all that is expected of them.

However, at the turn of the century came the rebels, or perhaps those stalwarts who held to their own opinions and thought that a standard hound was not what they wanted wherewith to catch foxes in their own particular country.

Sir Edward Curre of Itton in Monmouthshire bred a pack of completely white Foxhounds, very similar to those West Country Harriers which the great Eames family had made so famous at Cotley, and which hunted foxes as did other English West Country packs, with light colored hounds. Sir Edward met with great criticism and opposition, but he did not care, he had bred just what he wanted and very soon indeed packs from all over the country were desperate to obtain "Curre blood" to improve their hounds.

In the mountainous Lake District, the long-legged Fell-Hound, a light hound with the greatest powers of endurance imaginable, was the only hound that could follow and kill foxes in that precipitous country. Sir Alfred Goodson, perhaps the greatest breeder of all time, started a pack during the 1920's which he called the College Valley, using Fell-Hounds and hounds bred from them, establishing thereby and also maintaining, the best pack of fox-catching hounds in the world for over half a century. These are white hounds, and with the automobile making it so much easier for Masters and huntsmen to travel to see other packs of hounds than their own, a slow change gradually overtook most of the hunting establishments. White and light colored hounds predominate today where a few years ago they would have been regarded with horror.

Great breeders of hounds, like His Grace the Duke of Beaufort, Lord Halifax and Captain "Ronnie" Wallace of the Heythrop are among those who have helped tremendously in the modern trend to produce a hound to suit modern conditions. The standard hound is almost with us again. He is however white and lighter of bone, the perfect foxhunting machine at last. An average male stands about 24″ at the withers.

The head of an English Foxhound.

The East Kent hunt set off, at Ealham, near Canterbury, England; twenty couple of hounds were in the pack.

Gascon Saintongeois
(Grand, Petit)

The Gascon-Saintongeois originated as a result of the crossing of two very ancient breeds from which the name derives. Pierre Megnin (1889) wrote that, after the revolution of 1789, only a few specimens of the old breed of Saintonge survived, and these finally became the property of Monsieur de Saint-Legier, who kept the breed going during his long life.

In 1846 the last Chiens de Saintonge were crossed with the beautiful Chiens de Gascogne belonging to Monsieur de Ruble. Both breeds had the same height at the shoulder, a very good nose and a fine voice. There were various differences however between the heavier and coarser Chiens de Gascogne and the finer, more elegant Chiens de Saintonge. Notwithstanding these differences, the mixing of the two breeds resulted in a very beautiful hound.

The Chiens de Virelade (a district of France), as they were first named, were similar to their ancestors, the Saintongeois belonging to Monsieur de Saint-Legier.

In 1889 twenty-two Chiens de Virelade at the show on the terraces of the Tuileries in Paris, won the special prize awarded by the President of the Republic, for the finest pack.

The breed is now rare and only occurs in France.

The coat is very short and thick – white with black patches, more or less black spots in the white, and tan markings.

A characteristic point which obtains frequently is a grayish-brown (the color of dead leaves) patch on the back of the thigh, near the pastern, called Marque de Chevreuil (roe-deer mark).

The shoulder height is 24¾″ to 27¼″ for dogs and 23½″ to 24½″ for bitches. The head is extremely dry, and long, with long, thin, well-curled ears placed far back and low on the head.

A pack of these hounds may occasionally appear at provincial shows in France.

Side and front views of typical Gascon-Saintongeois bitches.

Greyhound

history and development

There is little doubt that the Greyhound is one of the very few breeds which can claim to be true. One of the oldest, if not the oldest, of sporting breeds, it has been recorded as the Gazehound, the hound which runs on the sight of its quarry. This is undoubtedly so; it has very keen eyesight, but this does not mean that the Greyhound is not well equipped to hunt and scent its quarry.

It is a theory held by some that the Greyhound family is nearly as old as civilization. There are wall-paintings in some tombs in the Valley of the Nile which portray dogs of the greyhound type but, of course, one cannot elude the possibility that the Saluki also could be the animal illustrated.

Mention of the breed occurs in the Bible, in the Book of Solomon, Chapter XXX, Verses 29-31: –

> There be three things that go well, yea four that are comely in going,
> a lion which is strongest among beasts and turneth not from any:
> A greyhound, an he goat also, and a king against whom there is no
> rising up.

In this ancient world of the Bible, caravans of the merchants and nobles conveyed these hounds along the valleys of the rivers Tigris and Euphrates and throughout ancient Iraq and Persia to the colder climate of Afghanistan, where in time, a version emerged with a heavier coat adapted to the harsher climatic conditions. The same thing occurred in Russia, but at all times the beautiful lines of its ancestors were preserved.

It is thought that the Celts brought the Greyhound to Britain. It was called the Celtic hound, and was definitely of the Greyhound type. In chronicles of the 9th century, Saxon chiefs are recorded with greyhound-type dogs, and King Edward the Confessor took much pleasure in hunting with a pack of swift hounds.

In England in the 11th and again in the 14th centuries, laws were made to the effect that only persons of Royal blood or noblemen could possess a Greyhound.

In 1486 Dame Juliana Berners wrote a description of the Greyhound: –

Headed lyke a snake, and necked lyke a drake,
Backed lyke a beam, syded lyke a bream,
Footed lyke a catte, Taylled lyke a ratte.

The Greyhound is prominent in many human activities. As a show dog it is amenable, and its showing attracts many adherents. As a competing dog in sport, and in the hunt it excels; for few of its quarry are fleet enough to escape it. During the past years, as a development of coursing, where the Greyhound was put to live quarry, there has developed a major sport in Britain, and in the United States, highly organized and well attended by afficionados – that of Greyhound racing. The animals are released from pens as an artificial hare passes by. So well are these animals used to competing in these conditions that they obviously need the mechanical "hare" only to start them off. After that they appear whole-heartedly to enjoy racing against each other.

Greyhounds were not classified at the first ever dog show, at Newcastle, England, in 1859. A little later, at Islington in London, a few Greyhounds were shown, and from that time the show Greyhound was specified and bred. The "sport" of showing Greyhounds tended to die out and receded to a "stronghold" in Cornwall, England, and the animal was often known as the "Cornish Greyhound".

The first Greyhound to attain the title of champion on the show bench was called Go Bang, to be followed by Rambling Dan and Radnor Prince. Among the bitches in these early days of showing were Bit of Courage, Helen MacGregor and Mullion Fairy – progenitors of many of our Greyhounds of today?

color

Greyhounds come in several colors, ranging from black, blue, brindle and white to particolors, any color is accepted by the British Kennel Club. Up to a few years ago there was a prevalence of self-colors, to be followed by a period when particolors were favored, but today we have the above-mentioned varied range of colors in which white markings are probably in the majority.

Eng. and Amer. Ch. Seagift Parcancady Royal Tan, a best in show winner in both America and Britain, including Blackpool championship in England in 1958.

Showing that blood will out Royal Tan had a litter sister, Eng. and Amer. Ch. Seagift Parcancady Bluebell, who also won best in show on both sides of the Atlantic. Notice particularly her graceful feminine appearance and calm deportment.

A good spectacular colored Greyhound is certainly an eye catcher in the variety ring, with his lovely clean lines. Ch. Rosyer Poner, owned by Mr. R. H. Parsons, is yet another championship best in show winner in the post-war era. He took this award at the West of England Ladies Kennel Club show in 1969. He was later exported to America.

care

Looking after a Greyhound is a simple matter. A warm, dry, clean bed is necessary; for the Greyhound's coat is not one to withstand the cold and damp. Change the bed regularly to ensure the absence of parasites. Exercize does not mean running the dog for miles and miles each day; a long walk, on a leash, finishing up with a free, short gallop in a field or park. Before kennelling, give the dog a short run over with a hound glove, and a wipe down. Give it a routine examination to see that all is well physically, and a good meal, one only per day: the Greyhound carries a great deal of bone, and calcium in the diet is necessary, as are the corresponding vitamins. Meat is most essential, whether it be beef or offal. Bones also for teeth and gums.

Greyhound, typical side head.

Puppies are best reared on an assorted diet. It is better to feed whelps a little, often, than one large meal each day. Here again a large bone, one which will not splinter, is a great aid when the adult teeth are coming through; it helps to dispose of the first (milk) teeth.

character

The Greyhound has a distinctive character all its own. Perhaps its long lineage has given it a certain aloofness, obvious to anyone who has observed it among other breeds. It has a distinct wariness towards strangers but to the owner it gives a love and faithfulness which is not surpassed; in fact in many ways a Greyhound, even the largest, can be really "soft". As in all breeds there is the occasional odd one which is aggressive, and at the other extreme, extremely timid, and on occasions it has received adverse publicity for attacking other dogs, but this is true of almost all breeds, although few of them are named as is the Greyhound whenever he transgresses in this way. Racing Greyhounds, however, always wear muzzles to prevent fighting.

A head study of an outstanding Greyhound, Mrs. D. F. Whitwell's Ch. Seagift Perran Polar Queen.

standards

The Standard as issued by the British Kennel Club requires that the general appearance of the Greyhound should be that of a strongly-built, upstand-

359

In the ownership of Mrs. J. de Casembroot and Mrs. B. Greenish, Ch. Treetops Golden Falcon won best in show at Cruft's in 1956. Here he is with some of his trophies.

ing dog of generous proportions, muscular power and symmetrical formation. The head should be long, moderate width, flat skull, with a slight stop. The jaws should be powerful and well chiselled, with the incisor teeth of the upper jaw clipping those of the lower. The neck should be long and muscular, elegantly arched, well let into the shoulders. The shoulders should be oblique, well set back, and the forelegs should be long and straight, with bone of good substance and quality. The chest deep, with ribs deep and well sprung and carried well back. The back should be rather long, broad and square, and the loin powerful, slightly arched. The hindquarters should show the great propelling power of the Greyhound, thighs and second thighs wide and muscular, with stifles well bent and hocks well let down. Feet of moderate length, with compact, well knuckled toes and strong pads.

The tail should be long, set-on rather low, strong at the root and tapering to a point. The coat should be fine and close. The height of dogs should be 28″ to 30″, bitches 27″ to 28″. The American Kennel Club Standard specifies 65 to 70 lbs. for dogs; 60 to 65 lbs. for bitches.

The British Standard differs from the American on one small point. The latter Standard shows a preference for a "hare" foot whereas the former encourages the breeding of "feet lyke a catte". Which is the more suitable depends on the kind of terrain; where the going is gritty and hard, the hare foot suffers less damage, where it is soft and spongy, the cat foot has the advantage.

Although movement is not mentioned in the Standards it is obvious that it is a major factor. The front legs and feet should move straight and the hind-legs should move in unison but slightly wider. A side view should show the dog appearing to "swim" along, with a smooth rhythm.

This lovely quality, feminine Greyhound bitch, English, American and Canadian Ch. Shalfleet Starlight of Foxden, born in August 1965, has many top successes on both sides of the Atlantic. In Mrs. Barbara Odell's hands she won best in show at Windsor championship show, and in America, where she is owned by Mr. and Mrs. James Farrell Jnr., she is a top winning Greyhound.

Greyhound, Chortay

The Borzoi is the best known Russian breed of the Greyhound type, but there are three others, all pure-bred hunting dogs, unknown elsewhere than their native part of Russia. The Chortay is a hound of the European Russian Steppes.

It is long-coated like the Borzoi, but it is a good deal smaller, being 25″ to 26″ to the shoulder. It is extremely swift, graceful and spirited in its running, and is used for coursing hare, fox, wolf and deer. The typical Greyhound conformation is apparent – long, arched back, loins well tucked-up, long, powerful quarters, and a long, sabre-shaped tail.

The head is wide at the skull, and long, tapering towards the muzzle with powerful jaws. The eyes are large; the ears are rose-shaped.

The coat is long and hard; all colors are accepted.

Greyhound, Hungarian

This Hungarian Greyhound or Magyar Agar has a history going back at least to the 9th century where its likeness on tombstones of that date in Hungary is clearly recognizable.

During the nineteenth century it was infused with imported English Greyhound blood and between the two World Wars it is estimated that this Greyhound blood was present in between 90 per cent and 95 per cent of a sample of some hundreds of dogs. Speed is the essence of its body structure; streamlined and slim, its powerful muscles can clearly be seen beneath the close coat.

The Magyar Agar, one of the most ancient of the Hungarian Greyhounds.

The head is very long and the stop is slighter than that of the Greyhound – somewhat resembling that of the Hungarian Sheepdog. The ears are small and flat, lifted a little when excited but never quite erect.

The long, flat body is deep chested, has practically no withers and the loins are well tucked-up. The long tail is normally curled upwards and is used, when running, to assist in change of direction.

The coat is short; slightly longer in winter, and variously colored – black, sandy streaked, sometimes ashen; rarely white or pied.

It has a friendly disposition, usually devoted to its owner and fitting well into a household as companion and watchdog. Its sense of smell is not at all acute, but it has good eyesight and with its considerable speed (38 to 40 m.p.h.) can outrun the hare or fox which it will catch and kill.

Weight of a male is 60 lbs. to 70 lbs. and a bitch from 50 lbs. to 60 lbs.

Greyhound, South Russian

This is the largest of the Russian Greyhounds, standing some 28″ at the shoulder. It is found chiefly in the regions from Stalingrad down to the Caspian Sea at Astrakhan and Grozny, as far West as Stavropol, and to Orenburg in the East; a vast area, yet the South Russian Greyhound is quite unknown outside Russia, and very little known in other parts of Russia.

It is a very strongly built hound, not unlike the Saluki, but with a close-haired coat, hard to the touch. It has a broad skull, rather long, with ears which hang down on its cheeks.

It is used, as are the other two recognized Russian Greyhounds, for coursing hare, fox, wolf and deer. It is a working dog, whose enthusiasm for the chase knows no bounds.

Greyhound, Tasy

Another of the Greyhounds found only within Russia, in the Central Asian region: it is also known as the Mid-Asiatic Greyhound.

The Tasy is an enthusiastic hunter of hare, fox, wolf and deer.

This breed has a dense, short coat, hard to the touch. It is a large dog, up to 27″ in height, with typically arched back, loins and croup, and the tail, thin and twisted, carries a little feathering.

The head is long and cone-shaped, with large, oval eyes and smallish, drooping ears.

Colors are fawn, gray, black, grayish yellow, or black with fawn markings.

Griffon Nivernais

Descended from the dogs of the Nevers region of Gallic/Roman times, the Griffon Nivernais is still one of the best dogs for hunting wild-boar. He is an excellent hunter, courageous in dense cover. He is an unkempt looking dog of primitive rugged appearance, but is nevertheless distinguished at his own level.

He looks sad, but affectionate. Clean cut with a lean head. He has great staying power but is not very speedy. Unfortunately, there are very few good specimens of the breed to be found today.

Color: Preferably wolf-gray or blue-gray, wild-boar gray, black, black with reddish speckles, tan on cheeks, eyes and legs; or fawn muzzled with white and black hairs.

The Griffon Nivernais is of workmanlike build as if made for long, arduous, rather than fast work. Sad looking, but not fearful. Head, lean, light but not too small; good ears, rather long nose. Small beard on chin. Eyes preferably dark. Ears set-on at eye level. Chest deep, great length of rib cage. Back long, good upright carriage.

The coat is long, bushy and hairy, fairly harsh and rough, neither wooly nor curly.

This is Nellye, a fine specimen of the Nivernais Griffon, with shaggy coat hiding powerful limbs and speedy lines. Owned by M. Huet.

Griffon Vendéen, Briquet

This is a small edition of the Giant Griffon. Everything about the dog has been reduced harmoniously without loss of general appearance and working qualities.

The history of the Briquet can be traced back to 1910, but the two wars seriously disrupted breeding, although the breed is regaining popularity and is increasing. He is very sturdy and exceptionally swift, and does a remarkable job coursing hares as well as flushing out larger game. Found principally in Europe.

Color: Fawn, hare, white-orange, white-hare, white-gray, black and white, or tricolor combinations of these colors.

Of medium height, 20″ to 22″, intelligent and of distinctive appearance, the Briquet is well proportioned, lightly built and strong without heaviness.

Head short with eyes dark, large and lively. Ears narrow, and covered with long, but not overlong, hair; set-on below the level of the eye. Skull rounded, muzzle broad, straight, with deep stop. Lips well covered with moustaches. Back short, strong, straight or, preferably, slightly sloped, with tail short, set-on high and carried scimitar fashion. Coat long, but not too long, rough to the touch, with dense undercoat.

M. Guilleme's Senateur d'Appelvoisin.

Griffon Vendéen, Grand

This is a smooth-coated variety of the Vendéen and from it come the "White Dogs of the King". Originally much used for wolf-hunting, the breed declined considerably with the extinction of its quarry. However, it is now again on the upgrade, being quite extensively used for hunting wild boar. He is a remarkably athletic dog of about 26″, very sturdily built and muscular. His appearance is very distinctive, and he has a highly developed instinct for hunting. He is extremely swift, his staying power is superb and he is remarkably intelligent.

Color: White with orange markings preferred. Admissible colors are fawn, hare, white with hare, white and black, or tricolor.

The Giant Vendéen is well proportioned and sturdy without heaviness. The head is long and not too broad between the ears. Eyes dark, large and alive. Ears narrow and thin, covered with long hair and set-on below the level of the eyes. Lips covered with thick moustaches. Nose black, nostrils wide. Legs straight and well-boned; feet tight but not too heavy. Chest well developed in depth but not too broad. Back, firm, straight with slight rise. Tail set-on high and carried scimitar fashion. The coat should be fairly long, bushy and rough with thick undercoat. Eyebrows very pronounced but not covering the eyes.

Height 24″ to 26″ or more.

The dog in front is Rafale, at a field trial in France. Rafale is of the pack known as "l'equipage du bois roux" – "the russet wood".

Griffon Vendéen, Grand Basset

This is a version of the Giant Vendéen Griffon with shortened legs in the manner of the Basset Hound. This "misfit" results from selective breeding of one of the "Giant" versions of the small game dogs.

Around 1900, after the Count d'Elva had improved them, Monsieur Paul Desamy determined a definite type for one specific end – coursing; and Giant Basset became the "Desamy Type", and he is the leading small-game dog in France. He has far greater speed than any other dog of his size. He is the ideal dog for the small-game hunter on the Continent.

Color: Fawn, hare, grayish white, white and orange, white and black, white and tan or tricolor of any of these colors.

Slightly longer than he is high, 15″ to 16½″, the Giant Basset must not be heavily built. Head somewhat domed with deep stop. Eyes big and dark. Expression friendly and intelligent. Ears, narrow, covered with long hair, and reaching at least to the end of the muzzle, set-on below eye level. Muzzle long and square. Lips covered with moustaches. Back long, broad and straight with tail set-on high and carried scimitar fashion. Coat, coarse but not too long.

Note the long, Basset ears on Pirate de la Levraudière, of the Rallye Bocage, owned by Mr. Desamy.

Griffon Vendéen, Petit Basset

A Basset which is not cumbersome is the aim of many small-game hunters. For years, the attempts to breed large animals with short legs succeeded only in producing a heavy dog which tired very easily. In 1944, the President of the Club, Abel Desamy, drew up a detailed Standard. In the years since, the Miniature Basset has become fairly established. P. Doubigne has described the dog – "it is not a small Vendéen Basset simply by being shorter, but a Miniature Basset reduced in size and proportions while retaining all the qualities of the breed; the passion for hunting, fearlessness in the densest coverts; activity and vigor, which have brought justifiable renown to the Giant Vendéen".

The colors are the same as Giant Basset.

He is a lively, busy little dog, very slightly longer than his height, $13\frac{3}{4}''$ to $15\frac{1}{2}''$, head slightly domed and a little long, with deep stop. Well developed occiput. Eyes rather large and intelligent. Ears, narrow, covered with long hair, set-on at eye level, and not reaching the extremity of the muzzle. Muzzle much shorter than that of the Giant Basset and square at the end. Fairly heavy bone, but in proportion to his size. The coat should be rough, but not too long.

Mlle. Desamy's Petit Prince de la Levraudière.

Hanoverian Schweisshund

The three types of Hannoverscher Schweisshund are differentiated according to the locations in which they are found; the Hanoverian Jaegerhof, the Harz mountain area and the Solling.

This hunting dog is of medium or somewhat smaller size, some 19″ to 24″, strongly built and rather low and long. The head, which is not carried erect, has a solemn expression, with typical Bloodhound ears, very wide, rounded underneath, high-set, drooping smoothly, without folds or creases.

The tail is long and reaches at least to the hocks; thick at the root and gradually thinning to the tip. The hair on the underside of the tail is longer and rougher, but without forming a definite brush.

The coat is thick, full and smooth with a matt, silky gloss. Colors are gray-brown (as with the winter coloring of red wild animals e.g. foxes), burnt black-brown, reddish brown, reddish yellow, yellow ochre, dark fawn or brown, burnt or streaked; generally with darker coloring on the muzzle, around the eys and ears, and with darker stripes on the back.

The Hanoverian Schweisshund is relatively unknown outside Continental Europe.

This German hound has a powerful sense of scent.

Harrier

The Windermere Harriers, Master, John Bulman. The photograph shows the light colored hounds used in the high fells to aid viewing when hunting on a distant mountainside, in this case the Langdale Pikes and other high fells around Langdale, in the English Lake District.

Compare this photograph of Vale of Lune Racer, 1912 champion stallion hound at Peterborough, with Credit '65, one of the latter-day Vale of Lune Harriers. The similarity of type, head and build between these two hounds, separated by fifty-eight years, is quite remarkable.

history and development

The Harrier, a hound bred specifically for hunting the hare, is one of the oldest of the British breeds. Believed to be descended from the long extinct Talbots and St. Hubert hounds, it may also carry the blood of the Brachet and, much later, the French Basset, all blended to make the early Southern Harrier, from which the old-fashioned Harrier descended. The packs hunted on foot or mounted, just as they do today, according to the country. As the hunter became much faster and of better quality, so the gentry who followed the Harriers demanded a faster, better quality hound. This was effected around 1825 by the infusion of Foxhound blood altering the type, which became much more up on the leg, with shorter ears and dead straight fronts.

Undoubtedly the Welsh packs bred-in Welsh Foxhounds, giving a very light, leggy type of Harrier, often with a slightly broken coat.

Owing to the different terrain and methods of hunting a pack of Harriers, there is a greater divergence in size and style than in any other type of hound.

The Harrier, already known as a distinct breed *circa* 1130, is frequently mentioned throughout the succeeding centuries. Several well-known packs in Britain date from the mid-18th century, notably the Holcombe Harriers and the Craven Harriers.

color

Any hound color is permitted, perhaps the most usual being hare or badger-pied. In Wales, the Harrier color is mostly a few palest lemon markings, the hound otherwise being virtually white. In the mounted packs, the colors have a wide range, black-and-tan on a white ground, hare-pied, badger-pied and, rarely, blue-mottled. One Irish pack was entirely black-and-tan without white. These were Harrier type and size, with a look of the Bloodhound in them, the head having a trace of peak, with rather longer ears than in the stud-book Harrier.

Liver-and-white is not a hound color.

care

The Harrier needs only the routine care given by a good kennel huntsman to any breed of hounds. Ears, eyes, coats and condition will be carefully watched, also the anal glands and feet. The right food will be given and the right amount of exercise. This applies to all hounds and there is nothing extra required by the Harrier other than this routine care.

character

The Harrier is a charming, gentle hound, sensible and kindly. Like any other hounds, they can be dangerous if a bad one gets among them, but this seldom happens with Harriers. They are a pack hound and need discipline when young, but there is no vice in them and they become most level-headed and obedient hounds.

This picture of Vale of Lune Credit '65, winner at Peterborough and Rydal Hound Shows, illustrates the head properties perfectly, with the true Harrier expression. The overall impression is of a Hound built for speed and grace, yet with adequate strength for his job.

standards

There is no official Standard in Britain; the various Masters selecting puppies to suit their own purpose. For example the Welsh and West Country hounds are exceptionally light in type and coloring, often virtually all-white with a very faint cream or lemon head-marking, while the mounted Vale packs breed a heavier stronger type, of darker color,

A pack of Harriers, headed by the Master of the Pack, set off to the start of a hunt.

more on the lines of a Foxhound in miniature, often hare-pied or tan-and-white, with much heavier bone than the Welsh Harrier.

The size also differs, ranging from 18½″ at the shoulder to 22″. The A.K.C. Standard specifies 19″ to 21″. In England each pack goes for its own optimum size, keeping the pack level at that particular size and type.

The head is longer and shallower both in stop and muzzle than the Foxhound, and less square and blocky than the Beagle. The expression is gently refined when relaxed; sensible yet alert when aroused. There is a slight stop; the lip also is not overdone. The throat and neck are clean without flews and the head shows no wrinkle. The neck is long, strong, and graceful, running smoothly into well-laid back shoulders. The body deep, with adequately sprung ribs and slight lift over the loin, well ribbed back. Legs straight and sound, elbows free from crook, the line from shoulder to foot vertical without trace of bandiness at elbow or knee. Pasterns strong and straight, though capable of plenty of spring, ending in a neat oval foot; the hare-foot being preferred to the cat-foot in the mountains. Hindquarters very strong and muscular, the stern being carried in a nice sickle and fairly high. The coat is slightly coarser than the Foxhound, and may be broken in some of the Welsh Harriers.

The voice is a high melodious note, very pretty to hear and, when on their proper quarry, the note is that of a mellow tenor bell.

Hellenic Hound

Adaptable to any kind of terrain, this Greek hunting dog, the Ellinikos Ichnilatis, is strong and vigorous, with very keen scenting powers. It is used in a variety of ways according to the ground and the preference of its master; singly or in packs, in flat lands or mountains. The baying of a pack makes a resonant and harmonious sound.

It is of medium build, with full, deep chest, long, straight back, and lightly arched loins. The tail is set-on high, of medium length, reaching to the hock, fairly thick at the set-on. In movement it is carried raised and lightly curved, it is never curled.

The Hound has a long head, with scarcely discernible stop, black nose and wide nostrils. The ears are about half as long as the head, set high, and hanging down without folds. The eyes are brown, with a lively, enquiring expression.

The coat is short-haired and dense, a little rough, and close.

Colors are black and tan; a small white spot on the chest is permitted. Height of a dog 18½″ to 21½″; bitch 17½″ to 21″.

Hungarian Hound

The Erdelyi Kopo is a Foxhound bred and used in the plains of Transylvania. It is of medium size, well made, fearless, steady, has a keen nose and is quick to learn. There are two varieties, one long-legged and the other, short-legged, differing also in color and coat.

The long-legged variety is most frequently black in color and its hair longer and thicker than the short-legged, which is red-colored. The larger dog is used for hunting wild boar, stag, lynx, etc. and the smaller for fox and hare.

The head is not snipey; there is only a very slight stop and the nose is straight with wide nostrils. The dark brown eyes are medium-sized, oval and set somewhat slanting and the ears are set medium high and lie close to the cheek.

The tail, which is not docked, is set-on low and carried with a curve upwards towards the tip.

Height for the larger dog is 22″ to 25½″ and for the smaller 17½″ to 20″.

Hygenhund

A Norwegian breed of comparatively recent origin, bred by F. Hygen in the late 1800's from selected Northern hunting dogs. The Hygenhund is bred for strength and endurance rather than for speed.

It is compact and solidly built, with a short back and strong loins. The tail is set in line with the back and carried gaily, but not curled over the back. Medium-sized head, with distinct stop, and broad, deep muzzle. The ears do not hang close to the head; they are broad and reach only half-way to the tip of the nose.

The coat is straight and close, and a little hard to touch, with a definite sheen. A little feathering is accepted.

The colors are tan or light tan with or without black shading, and black and tan. Both color combinations may occur with white – white with tan patches or spots or black and tan markings.

Height about 22″ for males, bitches less, but very good males up to 24″ or more are accepted.

A well balanced specimen of the Hygenhund from Norway.

Ibizan Hound

Diana Berry's Sol, the Ibizan Hound who attracted many people to the breed with her wins in variety competition.

Anubis, from the tomb of Tutankhamen, about 1344 B.C.

history and development

This is one of the really ancient breeds and it is supposed that all other dogs today have some Ibizan blood in their veins. The breed has been unmistakably depicted by the ancient Egyptians on papyrus records, and in drawing and painting on wood, stone and rock-face from as early as 3,000 B.C., and it is also thought, from the evidence of bones discovered in ancient sites, that the same type of hunting dog was used in the very earliest dawn of Egyptian history, nearly 5,000 years ago. There are carvings on the Beni Hassan tombs which date from 2,200–2,000 B.C., and on the tombs of many of the Egyptian rulers down through the centuries, including the famous tomb of Tutankhamen, 1,344 B.C.

When the Carthaginians invaded the Island of Ibiza, in the Mediterranean Balearic Islands, in the 6th century B.C., it was one of their last strongholds after the destruction of Carthage by the Romans. They held the Island for approximately one hundred years, and it is on this island, only twenty-five miles across, that the hunting dogs they had brought with them were left to breed; and they bred true for 2,500 years. It is from this island that the purest Ibizan Hound may still be obtained, and in fact they are being brought back into Egypt to restock that country.

Ibiza being part of a Spanish province, the dogs were first registered with the Spanish Huntress Association in 1922 (this Association does not now exist), and in 1931 the breed was registered with the Fédération Cyno-

370

logique Internationale (F.C.I.) as the Podènco Ibicenco. In 1928 it was brought to England, and exhibited at Cruft's Dog Show the following year; but as there was no inoculation against distemper the Hounds did not survive long in Britain. It was not until Mrs. I. D. G. Hoult brought in two more in 1957 that the breed was re-established in Britain. It used to be said of them that if you took them from their island in the sun, they would die, and in those days they did.

As a hunter the Ibizan Hound is unequalled, and has the ability to hunt by day or by night, singly or in pairs.

color

The Ibizan Hound can be white; or red, or lion with white markings, or white with either red or lion. The red is a rich chestnut color, and the lion is fawn. The illustrations show how the colors are distributed.

care

This is not a dog which will thrive in kennels. He is a highly developed individual and should never be shut up alone, or tethered for long periods. He needs exercize and should be given the chance to run free every day, even if it is only in the park; he responds readily to easy command and is not prone to run riot when given his freedom. His food needs are fairly standard, one meal a day for adults; and three times a day for puppies, with a main meal containing meat, wheat-meal, and supplemented by two lighter meals with eggs, milk and protein foods. The addition of raw fish and fruit to the diet of an adult dog is an aid to health, and he definitely needs a lot of water.

Two Ibizan Hounds. The dog on the right has a faulty ear.

371

Note how the ears of this Ibizan Hound are moved independently of each other. This is Sol, owned by Mrs. D. Berry.

character

His characteristic manner of hunting is to determine the whereabouts of his quarry by scent, sound and sight, and when hot on the scent gives spasmodic tongue. His large, erect ears catch the smallest sounds and the game is never safe even in the densest cover, while his prodigious agility (he can leap eight feet without a take-off run) enables him quickly to catch up and keep within reach of his quarry, even in dense bush and among rocks. He brings game to hand at a very early age and is so versatile that he has been used with success in Britain as a gun dog and as "herder" to live poultry, bringing the birds to hand without disturbing a feather. He can be used for coursing, and as a family pet he is particularly trustworthy, never attacking other dogs, and possessing a kindly nature.

As a guard dog he uses his strong bark to good effect, deterring intruders, but he is not temperamental, and is slow to anger. One particular point about the Ibizan Hound is that he should be trained and controlled by kindness, and should never be shouted at; his large, sensitive prick ears make him more than usually reactive to loud commands, and his spirit can easily be crushed.

standards

The breed is not yet accepted for championship status by either the American or the British Kennel Clubs. The Standard laid down in Europe is for a dog of hound structure, but with shallow ribs, long and flat, yet he must be short coupled to allow acceleration and rapid changes of direction. His height can vary between 22″ and 28″, bitches somewhat less, weighing 49 to 50 lbs. The head, which is long and narrow, carries very large, mobile, erect ears, the whole head being slightly convex. He is a narrow, slight, light-boned dog with a thin-skinned coat, either rough or smooth, but in both cases hard, and his low-set tail is long and thin; it may be carried high when the Hound is excited, but it should never touch the back or curl within itself.

He moves at a suspended trot, giving him a stilted look on level ground, but he can twist at speed on hilly country; and his front dew-claws also help in this, and must not be removed.

A graceful portrayal which should be compared with Anubis, on the preceding page.

Irish Wolfhound

Mrs. F. Nagle's Ch. Sulhamstead Match, by Ch. Sulhamstead Max ex Ch. Sulhamstead Maria; winner of ten C.C's. He was best of breed and best stud dog at the Irish Wolfhound Club championship held in England in conjunction with the Ladies' Kennel Association in 1970, under the American judge, Miss Mary Jane Ellis.

history and development

The original Irish Hound or Wolfdog was used in Ireland to hunt the wolf, stag, boar and the gigantic Irish elk, which stood six feet at the shoulder.

As far back as 273 B.C. hounds of this type were brought to Greece by the invading Celts and the breed was well known in Roman times. In a letter to his brother Flavianus in A.D. 391, Quintus Aurelius Symmachus refers to them. They were highly prized and were given as presents to kings and potentates. King John of England presented such a Hound, the faithful Gelert, to Llewellyn, Prince of Wales, about the year 1210. It killed a gaunt wolf and thus saved the life of his master's child. From the 12th to the 16th centuries, the Irish Wolfhound flourished; but in the 17th century, owing to the extinction of wolves in Ireland and the excessive exporting of the hounds, they became very rare. An order passed in parliament in Kilkenny in 1652 prohibited their exportation.

By 1840 only about four people owned any of the original strain and it is from these that Capt. G. A. Graham revived the breed by using the Scottish Deerhound as an outcross. He also introduced a single cross of Tibetan Wolf Dog. Later, other breeders introduced a Dane cross. The old strain of Irish Wolfhound must have been very prepotent, since puppies show no sign of reversion to the breeds which were used as an outcross.

Side head view of the Irish Wolfhound.

color

The Irish Wolfhound can be almost any color from pale cream to black,

A charming study of Ch. Sulhamstead Maria with her puppies.

Irish Wolfhound, frontal head view.

An outstanding brood bitch, Ch. Sulhamstead Melba, dam of Ch. S. Marco, American Ch. S. Matador, Ch. S. Merman (best in show at Cruft's 1960), Ch. S. Maria, Ch. S. Marika, American Ch. S. Marta, American Ch. S. Marda. Melba herself is by Ch. Sanctuary Rory of Kihone ex Ch. Sulhamstead Mesa.

but is mostly gray-brindle, red-brindle, red, black, pure white or fawn, or in any other color that appears in the Deerhound.

care

Puppies are not difficult to rear if one remembers the extraordinary growth rate from birth to six months. Weight at birth is usually between $1\frac{1}{2}$ and 2 lbs. At one stage they may gain between half and one pound per day and an inch in height a week. Therefore they need plenty of food, feeding as much as they will eat at each meal. Initially, four meals a day are necessary. Meat and biscuit or wholemeal bread for two meals; the other two meals can be milk and egg and milk. Give a little cod-liver oil twice a week and occasionally change to a meal of tripe and boiled fish. This should be boiled so hard that all, including the bones, will go through a mincer. Added calcium is not necessary provided they get it naturally through the milk and fish.

Earth or grass is necessary for the runs, and wood flooring in the kennel. Do not attempt to rear them on concrete or cement. No exercise should be forced on them. Until six months, let them play until tired and when older, allow them to gallop about to muscle up the hindquarters, but again, no forced exercise. Teach them to the lead at about six weeks.

Contrary to most people's belief, an Irish Wolfhound does not need more exercise than smaller breeds but it needs some every day; being taught to walk and trot on a loose lead. In grooming, the long hairs on the ears and neck and any long hairs on the stomach can be tidied up by using the finger and thumb. Do not forget that it is a hunting hound, so train it to be good with stock and do not let it run loose among sheep.

character

The breed has a wonderful temperament and is very good with children. They live up to the motto "gentle when stroked and fierce when provoked". They do not attack tradesmen coming to the house, but are nevertheless good guard dogs. They should, however, not be kept on a chain as this will make them either shy or savage. They are not pack hounds but faithful companions and prefer to live with master or mistress as a friend. Being so powerful, they cannot be forced; it is their nature to obey because they want to please. Therefore wise and understanding discipline is necessary when training them as puppies.

standards

The Irish Wolfhound should be less massive or heavy than the Great Dane, but more so than the Deerhound, which in general type it should otherwise resemble. Of great size and commanding appearance, the Wolfhound is very muscular, strongly though gracefully built, with movements easy and active; head and neck carried high. Its tail is carried with an upward sweep with a slight curve towards the extremity. Head and skull long, frontal bones of forehead very slightly raised and very little indentation between the eyes. Skull not too broad. Muzzle long and moderately pointed. Eyes dark and small, ears Greyhound-like in carriage. The rather long neck should be very muscular and strong, well arched, without dewlap or loose skin about the throat.

The chest should be very deep and the breast wide. A rather long back, loins arched and belly well drawn up. Shoulders should be muscular and

set sloping. Elbows tucked well under, turned neither inwards nor outwards, with the whole leg being muscular, strong and straight. The
muscular thighs and second thighs should be long and strong as in the
Greyhound. The hocks well let down, turning neither in nor out. The feet
should be moderately large and round toes well arched and closed with
very strong, curved nails. The tail should be long and slightly curved,
moderately thick and well covered with hair. The coat rough and hardy
on body, legs and head; especially long and wiry over the eyes and under
the jaw.

The minimum heights and weights are as follows: dogs, 31″ and 120 lbs.;
bitches, 28″ and 90 lbs. Anything below this should be debarred from
competition. Great size, including height at shoulder and proportionate
length of body, is the desideratum to be aimed at firmly to establish a
breed that shall average from 32″ to 34″ in dogs, showing the requisite
power, activity, courage and symmetry.

The following are faults: too light or heavy a head; too highly arched
frontal bone; large ears; ears hanging flat to face; short neck; full dewlap;
too narrow or too broad a chest; sunken, hollow or quite straight back;
bent forelegs; overbent fetlocks; twisted feet; spreading toes; too curly a
tail; weak hindquarters and general lack of muscle; too short body;
pink or liver-colored eyelids; lips and nose any color than black; very
light eyes.

It should be remembered that the Irish Wolfhound's original role was
to catch and kill wolves. This requires substance with quality, so that
they are fast enough to catch a wolf and strong enough to kill it.

*Ch. Sulhamstead Merman won for
Mrs. Nagle the prize everyone dreams
about but so few achieve: best in show
at Cruft's – in 1960. He is by Ch.
Sulhamstead Sedlestan Rebel ex Ch.
Sulhamstead Melba.*

Illyrian Hound

This medium-sized hound is named for Illyria, that ill-defined region of present-day Yugoslavia which borders the Adriatic approximately West of the Dinaric Alps. It is a strong-looking, sturdy animal, and an enthusiastic hunter of fox and hare, and sometimes wild boar. It is highly regarded for its tracking abilities.

Its compact build gives it a stocky appearance; standing around 18″ to 22″, it weighs between 36 and 50 lbs. The back is long and broad, the loins broad and short, and the tail, set-on not too high, has a slight upward curve.

The head is about 9″ in length, with a fairly broad skull, a well-defined occiput and a muzzle which is square and blunt. The ears are set-on near eye level, long, narrowing towards the tips and hanging, with no folds. The top coat is harsh, a bit stand-offish, with guard hairs of some 4″ in length. There is an undercoat, soft and plentiful, thicker in winter.

Colors are white, pale fawn or biscuit, tones of a reddish color, or gray; with flecks or ticking of the other colors, especially on the ears and on the body. Sometimes white is seen, but only on neck, chest, legs and feet.

Istrian Hound

The Istrian Hound; this is Cico, whelped in Yugoslavia in 1939.

This sporting dog was originally bred in the Istrian region of Yugoslavia. It is used for hunting hare, fox and deer. It has a keen sense of smell and is sometimes used by the police to follow a trail, like a Bloodhound.

It has a large forehead and the occiput is well-formed and often covered with long, soft hair; the stop is not too marked, the muzzle square in shape. The ears are set back a little behind the eyes, not too high on the skull, covered with shorter hair, drooping along the cheeks, straight and rounded off at the tip.

The body is well-knit and powerful and with a deep chest. The tail reaches to the hock or a little below and is carried in a slight upwards curve.

The top-coat is rough, long, harsh, bristly and stand-offish. It should not be wavy or curly. The short, dense under-coat is soft. The basic color is snow-white, and there are rich orange markings on ears and forehead. Tricolor is not permitted. Height: for a male from 18″ to 23″, and bitches slightly less.

Italian Hound

This hound, the Segugio Italiano, is recognized as the only true hound on the Italian mainland. It is of ancient descent, is used either as a pack hound or alone, and has great endurance; its build allows it to move at speed and to remain working for long periods. It is often to be found as a house or companion dog.

It is medium-sized, around 20″ to 22½″ for dogs, and lightly built. The body shows strength; it is clean cut, the back rising slightly to the croup over slightly arched loins. The tail is set-on high, thick at the root, tapering to a point, sabre shaped.

The head is a little long, the skull slightly arched, with a definite occiput, but little stop. The ears are set-on low, long enough to reach the nose, hanging close to the cheeks.

The coat is hard, dense and it should lie close to the body.

Colors are black (not a glossy black, rather dull), chestnut or tricolor.

Otterhound

history and development

The Otterhound is one of the most ancient of British breeds, its origin being known only by tradition, although it is recorded in various documents for many hundreds of years.

Believed to be descended from the long extinct St. Hubert Hound, the Otterhound certainly contains the blood of various Griffons, in particular that of the Griffon Vendéen, as well as those two very old breeds, the Southern Harrier and the English Water Spaniel. The Bloodhound obviously played a big part, and other crosses took place down the centuries. Thus, the modern pure-bred Otterhound descends from much ancient blood, known also to include in the last 150 years that of the Kerry Beagle, Staghound, and Welsh and Dumfriesshire Foxhounds, this latter breed being a smooth black-and-tan hound. These outcrosses were worked in most carefully so as never to lose the peculiar attributes of the old breed, the astounding nose and the ability to swim for hours on end, which combination of qualities no other breed possesses. The first known pack of Otterhounds belonged to King John, who had six couples in 1212. Edward II was the first Master of Otterhounds, having in 1307 six couples kept by a huntsman and two assistants. Since then many of the Kings of England kept their own packs. Elizabeth I was the

The work of the Otterhound is, with the pack, to follow the scent left by the otter in his nocturnal wanderings and, having followed this "drag" to the holt where the otter is bedded down for the day, to "mark", indicating by a single loud baying note that the otter is at home. Once the hounds "mark" they are taken away, the terriers put in and the otter bolted. A group of Otterhounds here wait while the terriers try to bolt their otter, when the hunt proper will begin.

first Lady Master of Otterhounds.

The best period for otterhunting was prior to the First World War, when there were twenty-four packs in existence in Britain, mostly composed of Foxhounds, but many had a few Otterhounds in their packs to provide the nose and the strong swimmers.

Otterhunting continued to thrive between the two wars, but after the Second World War, time and public opinion changed; there was less support, less money, and river pollution so that the fish died and the otters left, and the number of hounds gradually dwindled. At the time of writing there are probably not more than eighty couples of pure rough Otterhounds in existence, the bulk in England being in the hands of the Dumfriesshire and the Kendal and District packs, the only pure-bred packs to remain, and who account for about forty-five couples between them. Many other packs, however, in England and Ireland still have the odd few couples of rough hounds, the rest being scattered over the British Isles and America; those in Britain being the "odd men out" in the various Otterhound packs which are mostly composed of Foxhounds; while in America Otterhounds are mostly in show hands, a few being used for coonhunting. However all these hounds are either of Dumfries or Kendal blood, there being no other blood extant. The future of otterhunting, and the Otterhound itself, is in a parlous state; like the Mastiff, they will hang on the verge of extinction, a sad day indeed for one of the earliest authenticated and recorded English breeds.

color

The Otterhound may be any recognized hound color, the large majority being whole-colored, although at one time white hounds with houndmarkings predominated. The most usual colors today are grizzle, sandy, red or wheaten, or blue-and-tan, black-and-tan, black-and-cream or, occasionally, liver-and-tan. The famous old color of white with either grizzle, lemon, black or badger pied still appears in pure litters, also the blue-mottles, coming no doubt from the Southern Harrier hundreds of years ago. Liver-and-white is not recognized and is never seen in the Otterhound.

care

The Otterhound, being a pack-hound, needs only the routine care given to any hunting hound. Feet and coats, anal glands and ears are all watched by a professional and expert eye, that of the kennel-huntsman, who spots the earliest signs of trouble. Good benches and suitable food, with the correct exercize are given, and apart from watching the skin, pads and ears rather more carefully than in other breeds of hounds, owing to the constant immersion in water, no other special care is required.

character

This is a hound, not a dog, and should always be treated as such. Mild and gentle even with the smallest children at the meet or in kennels, the Otterhound is nevertheless a pack hound, bred to the kill, and however friendly the hound may be, this fact should always be remembered and no liberties should be taken with him. He is not bred as, and neither is he suitable for, a house pet, and I hope he never will be, or his distinctive character will be gone.

standards

There is no official Standard in Britain, although there is a vague one in America, but in both countries the exact type required is known and adhered to. The Otterhound should be a very big, strongly boned and built hound, weighing from 75 lbs. in bitches up to the 90 lbs. mark in dogs, the average probably being about 80 lbs. No official size limits are specified.

The head is massive, yet clean, deep rather than wide, the domed skull having enough width for brain-room, being slightly less narrow and sharply peaked than that of the Bloodhound. The muzzle is deep, with plenty of lip and flews, though not exaggerated. There is a wide nose-bone and huge, wide nostrils, a necessary point of the breed, as this presents an extra large scenting surface. The eyes are deep-set, showing the haw, although this is not exaggerated. The skull is rounded and domed, clean, without wrinkle.

The ears are distinctive, being long and pendulous, hanging in a curious inward fold close to the cheeks, this fold being an important point, as it is lost when a foreign outcross is introduced. The neck is fairly long and very strong, with good shoulders.

The body is very deep, with a fair spring of rib, and well ribbed back. The hindquarters are strong and active with good thighs and stifles, the legs straight and sound, with heavy bone right down into the feet, with good strong pasterns. The feet are unlike those of any other hound, being very big and round with good pads. They must be fairly compact when standing, spreading slightly when swimming or on mud-banks. But not too much, in case they become sore from the constant work on pebbles, stones and rocky river bottoms.

The coat is distinctive, being fairly long and very rough, of a good hard texture, having a dense waterproof undercoat. The voice is a most important feature. It is a very loud, deep, bell-like note, and most melodious with its deep resonant tone.

Otterhound head.

379

Pharoah Hound

Birling Tico, best dog in show on Gozo in 1968. The tail carriage is typical of the breed when its interest is excited.

A beautiful photograph of a Pharaoh Hound in repose, showing the star-shaped white chest marking. This is Kilcroney Senjura.

history and development

The Pharaoh Hound, as it is called in Britain, must be one of the oldest breeds in existence and appears to have altered little over the past 5,000 years. In type it is still the same as those depicted on the tombs of Egypt.

Certainly these dogs were very great favorites of the Pharaohs, and these prick-eared hounds are referred to in a letter of the 19th dynasty, a translation of which says: "The red, long-tailed dog goes out into the hills. He makes no delay in hunting. His face glares like a god who delights in his work". Reliefs of these dogs hunting oryx are found in the tombs of Mereruwka and Senbi, both dating from the Middle Kingdom (*c.*2000 B.C.).

It is thought that these hounds came to Gozo and Malta with the Phoenicians who, as a maritime nation, traded between the North African coast, Malta and Greece. Greek sculpture often depicts hounds with large, upright ears and curled tails. It has been suggested that the word "Greyhound" is a corruption of Greek hound. Once established on an island like Gozo, only four miles by nine miles, they would have remained cut-off from the outside world and have continued to breed pure over a period of probably 2,000 years. These dogs are known on Gozo and Malta as Kelb-tal-Fewek or rabbit dogs. The breed is also found in Sicily and is known to have existed there before the Greeks colonized the island. The very earliest illustration dates from the agricultural settlements of the Stone Age on the banks of the Nile. It is a circular disc showing two hounds chasing a gazelle, and was probably part of a game. It dates from about 4,000 B.C.

Pharaoh Hounds were first imported into Great Britain in the early 1920's, but it was not until 1968 that any serious effort was made to establish them. At that time eight specimens were brought from Gozo and Malta and the breed is now registered with the U.K. Kennel Club and has its own breed club.

Note the extra large ears in this head study of Kilcroney Senjura.

color

Tan; rich tan being preferred but a white tip on the tail is encouraged; white on chest, preferably star-shaped, and white toes is allowed and a slim white snip on the center line of the face is permissible. Other white is undesirable.

care

The silky, smooth coat needs little attention and the Pharaoh Hound seems to adapt itself readily to any climate. Special care must be taken not to let these hounds get too fat. Although they are small eaters, they need a lot of exercise and they are not suitable for town life; they are far too active and restless. On Gozo, they are fed mostly on soup and goat's milk and have little meat in their diet, but they always look hard and fit.

character

A hound of striking appearance. They are great hunters and can run like Greyhounds. They hunt both by sight and scent, and give tongue like hounds. Friendly, affectionate and playful, they make good companions, but do require to be kept active.

standards

The Pharaoh Hound is a medium-sized hound with hard, clean-cut lines. It is graceful, well-balanced and very fast running, with a free, easy

Two Pharaoh Hounds, Birling Zahara and Pingo, hunting on the island of Gozo, where the breed has been established for many centuries.

Best puppy in the annual show on Gozo in 1968, Birling Żahara, at eight months. Zahara is the daughter of Tico.

movement. The general appearance gives a strong impression of grace, power and speed.

It has a long, lean and chiseled skull with the foreface slightly longer than the skull. There is only a slight stop. The top of the skull lies parallel with the foreface thus representing a blunt wedge. The powerful jaws have strong teeth which meet in a scissor bite. The nose is flesh or light fawn colored, blending with the coat.

The eyes convey a keen, intelligent expression, are deep amber in color, oval and moderately deep-set. The ears are erect when alert, but are very flexible, broad at the base, fine and large.

The neck and head carriage disclose a nobility of bearing; the neck is long, lean, slightly arched and well-muscled with a clean throat line. The forequarters have long sloping shoulders which are well laid back; strong, without being excessively muscled. The forelegs are straight, parallel and flat-boned with the elbows well tucked in. Pasterns straight.

The body is lithe with an almost straight topline. There is a slight slope from the croup to the root of the tail; a deep brisket – almost down to the point of the elbow – and the ribs are well sprung. The body length, from breast to haunch bone, is slightly greater than the height of the withers to the ground. Dew-claws are usually removed in puppyhood.

The tail is fine and whip-like and reaches to the point of the hock when the animal is in repose. In excitement, it is gay and waving, being carried high and circular without touching the back. The coat is fine and glossy, short with no feathering at all.

Height: Dogs, 23″ to 25″ and bitches, 21″ to 24″.

Poitevin

Erable at the Rallye Combreux (Duc d'Estissac). He was born at the Rallye Kereol (Dr. Guillet).

The Poitevin originated in the Haut-Poitou in France. It is a first class hunting dog, strong, elegant and swift. Its history goes back to late 18th century. According to Viscount Emile de la Besge, one of the originators of the breed, the dog derived from the orange and white Ceris Montemboeufs, and the tricolored Larrye, both now extinct.

When rabies decimated his Persac pack in 1842, M. de la Besge was left with only one dog and two bitches and, in order to rebuild, he introduced some English Foxhounds. Thus was born the famous "Batard du Haut-Poitou", but early in the 20th century the trend was again towards the French type of the famous Persac pack of 1850.

The wars of 1914 and 1939 nearly finished the packs and, to rebuild, the masters looked for especially well-built dogs of almost any breed capable of running and catching the quarry. Practically the only person to conserve the old type was the master of the Vouzeron-Sologne pack, but it now appears to be returning and some very attractive Poitevin hounds can be seen at the shows in France. The Poitevin has no Standard as yet in America and England, but the French Standard calls for a hound-like animal, with slightly oblong head, flat skulled, with half-length ears. This is traditionally a tricolored dog, in the hound colors of black, orange and white, but he is occasionally white and orange. The coat is short and sleek. Height 60 cm. (24″) to 70 cm. (27½″). Weight around 30 kilos (68 lbs.).

Polish Hound

Large to medium in size, measuring up to 24″, the Polish Hound, or Polski Ogar, has had a fairly long history of hunting in Poland, and is at home in all the extremes of weather to which that country is subject. It is little known elsewhere, for it is only when a breed fortuitously or otherwise, captures the public imagination that it appears in other parts of the world – and the Polish Hound is essentially a hound suitable mainly, if not entirely, for work in its own hunting country in Poland.

The head is medium sized, with a blunt muzzle, a dark, broad nose, dark eyes, and ears, broad at their base and hanging close to the head.

The body is powerful and long, with well-angulated quarters and a long, strong tail.

The coat is smooth and dense, black with some tan markings on its underside.

The Ogar Polski, or Polish Hound, one of the most successful of the Eastern European hounds.

Porcelaine

The Chien de Porcelaine, formerly named Chien de Franche-Comte, a province in the Southeast of France, is nowadays one of the most common, though by no means numerous, French hounds.

With a shoulder height of 21½″ to 22½″ for dogs and 20½″ to 21½″ for bitches the breed belongs to the medium-sized hounds. The very short and full coat should be very white (that is the reason for the name – Porcelaine) with round orange markings. Small spots on the ears are characteristic. The head is fairly long, dry, with medium long ears falling in soft folds, not set-on too low.

At the end of the 18th century these smaller white/orange hounds originated in the West of France. The last abbot of Mixeuil, who had carefully maintained the breed, gave a number of his dogs to his doctor, Dr. Coillot. However, Dr. Coillot's son was no hunting man and, on inheriting his father's hounds, dispersed them. But *his* son *was* a hunting man, as his grandfather had been, and he was able to recover a few of the hounds, regarding it as a worthy aim to build up a new pack of pure Franc-Comtois; although he had now and again to introduce fresh blood into the pack. For this he used the Harrier.

At the show in the Tuileries in 1889, Dr. Coillot's pack was much admired. Occasional hounds of the Porcelaine breed are met with outside France; they are never seen at shows, except in France in the provinces.

White with pale markings, the Chien de Porcelaine.

Portuguese Warren Hound

This is the small version of the Rabbit Dog, which has only one kind of coat, short and smooth.

This is the wire-haired variety. Note the powerful hindquarters and the racy lines apparent through the rough coat.

The Podengo, or Portuguese Warren Hound, seen mainly in North Portugal, is used mainly for rabbiting, sometimes also for hare, but seldom against other game. The Podengo is in three sizes: Grande (large) is used for hare hunting, Medio (medium) and Pequeno (small) are used against rabbits; either alone or in packs.

Considerable intermixing with the Spanish and other Greyhounds has occurred but the breed yet conforms well with the Standards.

The Podengo Medio is of medium build and height; well proportioned, lively and intelligent.

The physical characteristics of all varieties are similar in proportion to their size. The head has a fairly pronounced stop and the nose is moderately long and sharp. The very mobile ears are large, set high and carried erect, slightly inclined forward and open in the front.

The body is moderately long and muscular as are the loins, and the legs are strong-boned. The tail is set-on high, of medium length, thick at the root and carried like a sickle.

The coat is either long or short-haired; silky when short and harsh when long; the short coat is denser than the long. Predominant colors are fawn and yellow.

The Podengo Medio stands between 17″ and 21″. The Podengo Grande is taller, between 21″ and 27″, and the Podengo Pequeno is very similar, except that the skull is flat or slightly rounded and, of course, smaller. It stands 8″ to 10″ in height.

The eager, listening attitude of the smaller variety.

Rhodesian Ridgeback

Ch. Mingo of Manscross, bred by Dr. and Mrs. K. C. Mackenzie, owned by Mrs. R. Bailey. A leading sire of the late sixties and a very typical specimen, showing substance and quality without white markings.

history and development

The origin of the Rhodesian Ridgeback undoubtedly springs from the ridged dogs belonging to the Hottentots mentioned by G. McG. Theal when describing conditions in South Africa before 1505. The infusion of blood from the European dogs belonging to white settlers in the Cape, which were mainly Pointer, Greyhound, Staghound, Bulldog cross Mastiff and the occasional Fox Hound, began to alter the basic appearance but the ridge persisted and so did the outstanding ability to hunt big game and hold it at bay.

Cornelius Van Rooyen bred from a pair acquired from the Rev. Charles Helm, and as he used them for hunting in lion country, they were often called Lion Dogs. By 1920 there were many types of Lion Dog in Rhodesia so in 1922 Mr. F. R. Barnes set about standardizing the breed and getting it recognized by the S.A. Kennel Union. A special meeting was called at Bulawayo and a Standard was drawn up taking the most desirable points from the many dogs which were brought to the meeting. That Standard, with a few amendments and alterations, is still in use today. Because the name "Lion Dog" gave the impression of a savage and ferocious animal, it was renamed Rhodesian Ridgeback. Thus the great dog family which has no peer as lion hunter, was born.

Ch. Ironsay Idol, bred by Mr. R. Irons, owned by Mrs. W. F. Hayes. A typical bitch of the breed, showing the hard, muscular condition stripped of all excess weight.

385

The beautiful head of Mrs. W. F. Haye's Ch. Mentamery Monarch.

Front head view of a Rhodesian Ridgeback.

Ch. Fundu of Footpath, bred by Mrs. R. Bailey, owned by Mrs. A Woodrow. A son of Ch. Mingo of Manscross and, like him, a well balanced substantial hound of character and quality.

In Britain the breed, once introduced, steadily gained popularity. Capt. G. Miller, uncle to the late Cicely Hick of Owlsmoor fame, brought his Viking Leo of Avondale to England where he won the class for foreign dogs at the Kensington show in April 1933. Leo will be found at the back of most pedigrees in Britain today. The Kennel Club granted them championship status in 1954. The honor of first British champion went to Maiduba of Manscross owned and bred by Dr. and Mrs. K. Mackenzie who did so much to promote interest in the breed and help form the Rhodesian Ridgeback Club of Great Britain in 1952. Registrations have steadily increased from a mere 56 in 1954 to 230 in 1969. Great strides have been made during that time, stabilizing type and perfecting the ridge.

color

The Ridgeback is wheaten in color varying from light to rich red. Toes and chest may carry a little white but excessive amounts here or on the belly are undesirable. Dark muzzles are in order but the darker color must not extend to the eyes to form a mask. Ears also may be darker. The nose can be black or brown; black noses with dark brown eyes to tone with the coat color; brown noses with amber eyes, never yellow or pale green.

character

As a working dog for the lion hunter he served his master, if need be at the cost of his life. Today as a family pet and companion he still retains that essential quality, devotion; and for all his size and great strength he is the gentlest of friends. A good guard, quiet about the house with a touch of the clown in his make up.

care

Care is a matter of simple day-to-day grooming, a hound glove is ideal for this. Clean bedding, good food and plenty of exercise all play their part to ensure gleaming condition. He must present a hard muscular appearance with plenty of substance, stripped of all ballast.
One point which must always be watched is the threat of the Dermoid Sinus. Now happily rarely seen, but a serious heredity fault. This is a tube of skin attached to the ligament connecting the upright bony projections of the cervical vertebrae and opening up on to the skin surface like a tiny funnel.

standards

The Standards in Britain and America still follow closely the original Rhodesian established in 1922. A handsome, upstanding animal is visualized with every appearance of being able to carry out a hard day's work in rough country. Good compact feet with well arched and knuckled toes are essential. Pads tough and elastic. The height at shoulder for a dog is 25" to 27", bitches 24" to 26". Desirable weights are 80 lbs. dogs and 70 lbs. bitches, with a permissible variation of 5 lbs. above and below these weights. It will readily be seen that no dog well muscled and heavily boned could afford to carry any surplus fat and still keep within such a weight limit. His intelligence is there for all to see in his bright, sparkling eye.

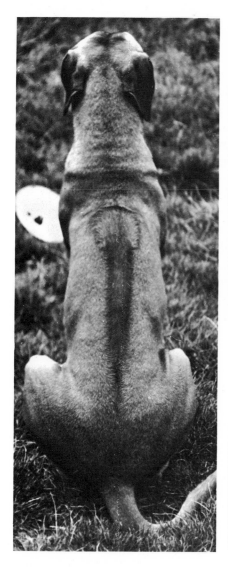
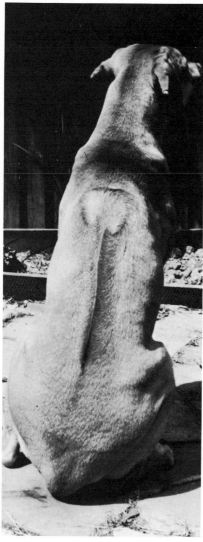
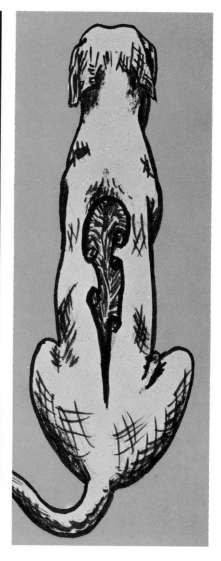

The ridge, which must be regarded as the escutcheon of the breed, is a ridge of hair growing in the reverse direction from the rest of the coat, clearly defined, tapering and symmetrical. Starting immediately behind the shoulders and continuing up to a point between the prominence of the hips. It must contain two identical crowns opposite each other, the lower sides of which must not extend further down the ridge than one third of its entire length. The Ridgeback's coat should be short and dense, sleek and glossy, but neither wooly nor silky.

The head and skull should be of fair length, the skull flat and rather broad between the ears. A reasonably well defined stop and not in one straight line from nose to occiput. Ears should be set up rather high, of medium size rather wide at the base and carried close to the head. The neck fairly long, strong and free from throatiness.

The shoulders sloping, clean and muscular and the forelegs straight, strong and heavy boned; elbows close to the body.

Left to right.
Ch. Mentamery Monarch showing well shaped ridge. The crowns are even and level, the taper is regular and reaches to the haunch bones.
Slightly imperfect ridge. Crowns not exactly opposite, and insufficient taper.
Faulty ridge, showing extra crowns distributed about the ridge. On no account should such an animal be bred from.

387

Russian Hound
(and Particolored)

Russian Hounds.

These two hounds are recognized in Russia as two breeds, and there are sufficient differences between them to justify distinction. They are both used in Russia for hunting hare, fox and occasionally badger.

An indication of their relative popularity is given by the numbers of each breed shown at the Hunting Dog Show of Moscow in 1955 – 258 Russian Hounds, 128 Particolored and, incidentally, only two Estonian Hounds.

Russian Hound: Sturdily built, medium sized (22″ to 25″) with a wedge-shaped head and broad muzzle. It has long ears hanging close to the head. The body is longish, with powerful quarters and a thick, long, tail, narrowing towards the tip.
The coat is short; black with fawn markings.

Russian Particolored Hound: Similar in conformation, except that the ears and tail are shorter and the Particolored is perhaps an inch taller. The coat is dense, short and hard; deep tan or reddish-tan in color, with or without a black saddle, and with white or yellowish markings.

Sabueso Hound

The Sabueso Español is a hound of considerable antiquity, tracing its ancestry back to the Celtic Hound, the *canis segusius,* or coursing dog, of the Celtic tribe inhabiting central France in ancient times. It is of medium size, and there are two types, the De Monte being heavier than the Lebrero – height for the former 20″ to 22″; under 20″ for the latter (one inch less for bitches in both cases).

Although bred and used for centuries as a pack hound, it is used nowadays for a variety of other uses, notably for police work.

Apart from size both types have identical physical characteristics; the head is broad and rounded, with very large ears and brown eyes. Strong neck (with some loose skin allowed), level back with short loin; quarters straight and strong; tail set-on low, tapering and hanging down in repose, slightly curved in movement.

The coat is fine, without feathering; the basic color white with large patches of black or deep orange. On the Lebrero the patches can almost cover the body except for neck, muzzle, chest and feet.

Saluki

Mrs. Hope Waters's Ch. Burydown Freyha, the most beautiful and outstanding bitch the breed has known. She excelled at coursing and was seldom beaten in the show ring winning, among many top awards, sixteen C.C.s. In 1964, in a record entry of 8,279 dogs, she was best bitch all breeds and reserve best in show at Cruft's. She is dam of three champions in Britain, one in America, one in South Africa and one in Australia.

history and development

The word "saluki" in Arabic signifies running hound. It is possibly derived from the ancient town of Saluk in the Yemen, Southern Arabia. Salukis were already an ancient breed in the days of the Pharaohs, and have bred true to type throughout the centuries, thus our hounds of the present generation are identical to the mummified remains buried with the kings, and carved on the rock tombs nearly 9,000 years ago.

The Arabs carried on the tradition, breeding always for perfection, stamina and prowess in the chase.

The first authentic references to Salukis in Europe were of the desert hounds brought back from the East by the Crusaders. A portrait of King Henry the Pious of Saxony in the Dresden Art Gallery shows a Saluki at his heels, wearing a collar decorated with silver scallop shells, the badge of the pilgrims. In 1835, when a litter of "Persian Greyhounds" was bred in the Regent's Park Zoological Gardens in London, they were stated to be the only specimens in the country. In 1897, four Arab hounds were brought to England. Two of them, a white dog and bitch from Kirghis, left no descendants, but the other two imported by Colonel Jennings-Bramly, were presented by him to the Hon. Florence Amherst, and were the foundation of her famous Amherstia kennels.

For some years, in spite of occasional importations, the breed remained more or less in obscurity, then just as the press and public began to take an interest in them, the 1914–18 war broke out. This proved to be an advantage, as several hounds were brought back from the East by the returning army. Conspicuous among these were the beautiful black-and-tans brought to England by Brig. General F. F. Lance, who had owned and bred them in the Middle East.

Miss D. Steed's Ch. Bedouin Caliph has beaten all records for Salukis in the show ring. He has won twenty-one C.C.s, being best of breed on fifteen of these occasions, and many other top awards. A born showman, this beautiful cream dog has everything one looks for in a Saluki.

American Ch. Rasim Ramullah of Pine Paddocks, the first smooth Saluki in the world to gain his championship. Bred and owned by Mrs. E. B. Knapp of Ohio, U.S.A.

The famous Ch. Sarona Kelb, with his daughter Sarona Shawa and granddaughter Sarona Mehrbani. This picture shows clearly how characteristics and a family resemblance are handed down from one generation to another. Even today, fifty years later, a descendant of Kelb is quickly recognized by anyone knowledgeable of Salukis.

In 1922, Salukis were first registered as a breed by the Kennel Club. In July 1923, all dogs previously registered as Persian Greyhounds, Arabian Salukis, Saluki Shami, or slughi, were re-registered as Saluki Hounds, but as Saluki is the general name given in the East to all dogs of the running type, this title was altered in the November to Saluki or Gazelle Hound, under which name they are still known today.

The first Saluki to become a champion was the beautiful white and black particolor bitch, Orchard Shahin, owned by Mrs. L. W. Crouch and bred by Brig. Gen. Lance. She was closely followed by her sire, the famous black and tan Sarona Kelb, bred in Damascus by Gen. Lance in 1919 and brought to England in 1921 to form the nucleus of his Sarona Kennels. The third Saluki champion was the red dog, Zobeid, owned by the Hon. Florence Amherst. Certificates were granted for the first time in 1923 at the Kennel Club Show, and at this first championship event for Salukis, the classes were divided into two sections, four for feathered and four for Smooths. Although the Smooth variety were fairly numerous at that time, it was not until 1963 that Mr. A. V. S. Henderson's grizzle dog, Kumasi Kommandan, became the first Smooth champion.

Interest in the Saluki was not roused in America until 1927, when a few fanciers got together to form the Saluki Club of America, closely followed by official recognition by the American Kennel Club. In the same year, two Salukis were shown at the Westminster Show in a miscellaneous class, where they created so much interest that classes for the breed were scheduled in 1928. By 1945, the American Kennel Club had received 350 registrations, 149 of these owned by Mr. Edward K. Aldrich Jnr., who founded his famous Diamond Hill strain in 1932 with the purchase of

Amherstia Nazarat O'Redledge. Much of the keen interest shown in the breed today has been sponsored by Mrs. Esther B. Knapp, president of The Saluki Club of America.

Salukis are gaining rapidly in popularity in Sweden, where the smooth variety has recently been coming to the fore. On the Continent, where they have maintained a steady balance for some years, they still hold their own, especially in Holland, where several kennels specialize in them.

Saluki puppies at three months old, showing the great variation of colors in one litter, yet all are of the same type.

color

Any color or combination of colors is permissible in Salukis.

care

Contrary to popular opinion, Salukis are not delicate; far from it. Young Salukis require plenty of freedom if they are to grow into strong, healthy adults, and for the first few months of their lives they should be allowed to choose their own exercise and play together happily in a large run. Most Salukis dislike the rain but a brisk rub down with a warm towel, if they do happen to get wet, will soon restore their happy outlook on life. A daily grooming with a soft brush, followed by a rub down with a hound glove, will keep their coats smooth and glossy. Gentle combing of the long fringes on ears and tail of the feathered Salukis will prevent tangling, but care should be taken not to break the hair.

character

Although hunting dogs by instinct, Salukis are valued as much for their companionable qualities as for sport. They are excellent house dogs, entirely without odor, and very clean in their habits. Their bark is deep and melodious, quick to give warning when strangers approach, but not given to unnecessary noise and never aggressive. They are trustworthy

Hama of Homs, one of the early importations into Britain from Syria after the 1914–18 war. She was the dam of Sarona Nurnisha. Note the cropped ears, a custom among the Arab tribes.

391

Three champions out of one litter, bred and owned by Mrs. H. M. Parkhouse. Sara, Selim and Zeki of Shammar traced their pedigrees back to Kelb. Selim was the first post-war champion, in 1947. Sara and Zeki became champions at Cruft's in 1948.

Sheba Mazuri, a great-grand-daughter of Ch. Sarona Kelb, bred from the original Sarona and Amherstia strains. She was the founder of the Mazuri line.

and gentle with children. Though slow to make friends with strangers, their dignity and aloofness to all outside their own family is one of their greatest charms. Their intelligence is exceptionally high, and they are docile, tractable and most affectionate with their owners. But one must never forget that they are still by instinct hunters, and they should never be allowed to roam about unattended.

standards

Salukis vary enormously in size and type, the Standard allowing for dogs to be from 23″–28″ at the shoulder, bitches being proportionately smaller. The Standard thus covers all types, each type being correct.

The Saluki should give the impression of grace, agility and great stamina. The sloping shoulders should be set well back, the hindquarters strong with stifles only moderately bent. The feet should be well feathered, the toes long and flexible, the two middle toes on each foot being noticeably longer than the others. Head should be long but not domed, teeth strong with a scissor bite. The leather of the ears should reach to the corner of the lips when brought forward. Tail should be set-on low, the tip of the bone should reach to the hocks. It is carried naturally in a curve, but should not be ringed. The movement of a Saluki has a characteristic of its own. It differs from a Greyhound, being more springy when walking and more prancing when trotting.

For the Smooth variety, all points should be exactly the same except for the coat, which is finer and shorter and has no feathering.

392

Sicilian Hound

The Cirneco dell'Etna, or Sicilian Hound, is a Greyhound-like animal of medium size. It is of very ancient lineage, being descended from the Roman hounds, *canes sagaces*. It is very lightly built, and can move at considerable speed, and manoeuvre with great agility in its pursuit of rabbits – its usual quarry.

The Sicilian Hound is comparatively tall, 18″ to 19½″ for dogs; bitches 16″ to 18″, and rather light in weight, dogs 23 to 26 lbs; bitches 18 to 22 lbs. Its body is the same height as its length, the back short and straight, the loins short, broad and well-muscled, the croup falling away to an angle of about 45°.

The chest is narrow and deep, the ribs lightly sprung, the belly well tucked up in the manner of all Greyhound varieties. The shoulders sloping, the forelegs vertical and lightly boned, hind-legs clean and straight.

The tail is fairly long, set-on low, and without long hair.

The coat is close-lying on the back, chest and tail, and shorter on the head and limbs; harsh to the touch.

The colors are pure white, or white with markings of tan, or a fawn saddle.

Sloughi

A racy dog of the Greyhound type, believed to be descended from ancient Egyptian gazehounds. Registered with the F.C.I. as a French breed, where it is popular in the South.

This is a fleet, but not heavily muscled, dog, with lines which are not so accentuated as a Greyhound's, and a head somewhat heavier, with a flat skull, distinctively rounded at the back, with very slight stop. The eyes have a soft expression; velvety black eyes with the light coats, brighter-looking yellowish eyes with the darker. The ears must droop and be set close to the head, differing considerably from the Greyhound's.

It has a level back, fairly short, a thin whip-like tail reaching to the hocks. The belly is well tucked-up, but again, not so much as the Greyhound, and the hindquarters are strong and of great propelling power.

The Sloughi is medium to large sized, 22″ to 30″ in height. It has a smooth, close coat, sandy in color, or all shades of fawn, with or without a black mask, and it can have a darker saddle. Other colors are off-white, brindle, black with tan and brindle. Black and white is permissible but not desirable. The darker colors are sometimes marked with some white on the chest.

The graceful, Greyhound-like lines of the Sloughi.

Slovakian Hound

A very handsome hound, of middle size, selectively bred in what is now Czechoslovakia, from the many different types of hound used in the area in the past. It is very hardy and active, with a well proportioned head with fairly long ears. The body is rather long, the back straight, the loins and croup muscular and broad, falling slightly to the tail. The quarters strong, the tail fairly long, carried horizontally, having a stiffish brush, but no fringing.

The coat is medium-long, smooth and close, with abundant undercoat. Colors are black, with markings of tan over the eyes, on cheeks, feet and under the tail.

Stovare, Halden

Another Norwegian hound breed, the Halden.

A Norwegian hunting breed, one of a number commonly used in Scandinavian countries and for Northern conditions, and little known elsewhere. The Halden is built for staying, not so much for speed, and it has considerable stamina.

The head is of medium size, the stop definite but not abrupt. The ears should reach to the middle of the muzzle. The eyes should be dark.

The back is straight, the loins broad, the hindquarters muscular, and the tail is rather thick, medium set-on and carried rather low. The Halden-stövare is not a large dog: the F.C.I. Standard describes it as medium-sized.

It is strong, long bodied, white in color with black patches and brown shadings on head and legs and surrounding the black. Small black or brown spots are not desired, and black must not predominate.

The coat is smooth, very dense but not too close or short.

Styrian Mountain Hound

This breed is about ninety years old, the result of crossbreeding the Istrian Hound with the Hanoverian Schweisshund (having marked Bloodhound characteristics) and the Austrian Hound. Its purpose is roughly the same as the other two Austrian Mountain Hounds, the Austrian and the Tyrolean – to hunt, without direct control, the higher regions of the mountain country. Its keen nose and great powers of endurance fit it admirably for this work. The credit for the original work on the breed goes to Peintinger, whose name the breed originally bore.

This is a rough-coated breed but the coat is not shaggy, rather it is hard, and slightly wavy. On the chest and backs of the lower fore-legs the hair is a little longer. Colors are red and fawn, the only white permitted being a blaze on the chest.

It is a dog of medium height, 16″ to 20″, well muscled, longer than it is high, with the tail carried straight.

Swedish Hounds
(Hamiltonstövare, Schillerstövare, Smalandstövare)

The topography of Sweden calls for somewhat special methods of hunting. There are no large open fields or farmland for coursing, beagling or fox-hunting, but instead there are numerous large forests where the most efficient type of hound for hunting is that long-legged, strong hound called the stövare. They do not hunt in packs and have to be fairly tall and very strong to be able to follow their quarry through deep snow, must possess a very good nose to be able to scent it and a loud, resonant bay to allow the waiting huntsmen to prepare themselves for the shot when the hunt is heading in their direction.

Smalandstovare: The oldest of the three Swedish varieties of stövare is the Smalandstövare (Smaland being a particularly densely forest-covered county in the southern parts of Sweden). Although not officially recognized by the Swedish Kennel Club until around 1920, hounds of this type have been used for hunting for a very long time. The breed has never been really popular – only a few hundred are registered annually – and is hardly ever kept as anything but a hunting dog, (in fact, the hunting instincts of the stövare varieties are so very strong that they should never be kept only as pets and house dogs). The Smalandstövare is around $19\frac{1}{2}''$ tall, always black with slight tan markings. It can be born with either a very short tail or one reaching down to the hocks, but the tail is under no circumstances docked.

This is a naturally short-tailed dog, with the tan markings apparent in this photograph.

The bicolored Schillerstovare.

The Schillerstovare and Hamiltonstövare: both have the names of their respective original breeders. They are much more popular than the Smalandstövare – the Hamiltonstövare is in fact one of the most popular breeds in Sweden with over 1,500 registrations annually. It is slightly taller than the Schillerstövare, which however is of earlier origin, and still remains very popular with the hunters.

The difference in their origins is actually wider than their fairly similar looks would lead one to believe; the ancestors of the Schillerstövare came from the southern parts of Germany, Austria and Switzerland and bred true to type much earlier than the first Hamiltonstövares. These were, to a greater extent, mixed up with the old-fashioned native "stövare" varieties and their popularity is of fairly recent date.

Apart from the size difference – although both breeds measure around $19\frac{1}{2}''$ to 24", the Hamiltonstövare should be slightly stronger and heavier all over – it is easy to tell the two breeds apart, from their different expressions and of course through the color; the Schillerstövare is always tan-colored with black on neck, back and tail, while the Hamiltonstövare should always be tricolored with white on the nose, throat, feet and tip of the tail.

Note the heavier build of the Hamiltonstovare, apparent in this photograph.

Swiss Hunting Dogs
(Bernese, Jura, Lucernese, Swiss)

A typical example of the Lucernese, Cora Catschaidur, whelped in 1950.

The smooth coated Lucerne type.

Not to be confused with the smaller Swiss hunting dogs, there are some four varieties, the common Swiss Hound, Bernese, Lucerne and Bruno de Jura (Bruno type and St. Hubert type). All, except the St. Hubert type, share the same general characteristics, medium height, slightly longer than they are high; strong, enduring, and good-looking. The St. Hubert favors the Bloodhound and is separately classified in the Standard. The hound head is clean with fairly long muzzle, and the ears are large and set-on low. It has strong, straight forelegs, with well muscled hindquarters, and a level, strong, longish back; well muscled loins, long, obliquely placed shoulders and deep chest. Tails are not too long, carried horizontally or with slight upward curve, well covered with hair, and in the smooths tapered to the extremity. The rough tail is hairy, but not heavily feathered. The St. Hubert tail is medium long, carried fairly high, with little curve, never over the back, strong, well-covered with hair, but never feathered.

The hounds all have keen noses, and give tongue continuously when on the scent of their usual quarry, the hare, and they refuse to be shaken off by any manouevre.

Color does differ among the types. Bernese, tricolor, black and tan on white; Lucernese, mottled gray, or blue or with large patches of either color or black, on white, with tan markings on head, body and feet. The Bruno type and the St. Hubert have the same coloration – self-colored yellow-brown or red-brown, or with a black saddle. In some cases entirely black, except for a tan patch over the eyes, on cheeks and under parts. The common Swiss hound has a white coat with largish orange, orange-yellow or reddish-yellow patches. Red colored dogs are accepted and speckling of red spots is not faulty.

Apart from the Lucernese and the St. Hubert type, whose coats are always smooth, the Swiss hound coats can be either smooth or rough, the colors remaining the same, and the rough having a thick undercoat.

The minimum height is 17½″ for all types, including the St. Hubert, but this type has the greatest differences in its head – strong, heavy, broad and well-domed skull, with pronounced stop and a long, broad muzzle, well-developed flews, furrowed forehead, pronounced occiput, and strong, close fitting jaws. A massive head, very like a Bloodhound's, with big, heavy ears set-on low and towards the back of the head, folded and turned inwards. The neck is thick, strong and throaty.

Two photographs demonstrating the differences between the two types of Jura hounds; top – Vedette du Bois Brulé, of the type Bruno; below – Vestale du Bois, of the St Hubert type.

The head of the Bernese, showing the exceptionally long leathers and the pronounced occiput.

This head study of le courant Suisse commun (the common Swiss Hound) shows the typical features of the head, in particular the ears, carried by all Swiss Hunting Dogs.

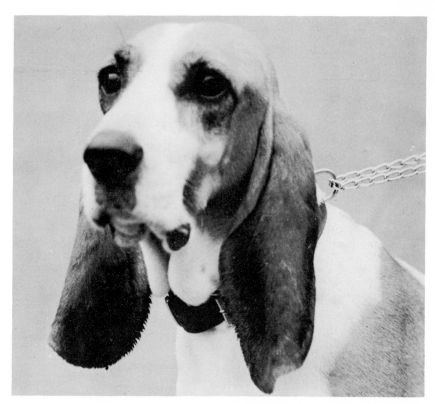

A typical Niederlaufhund of the Jura type.

Swiss Short-legged Hound

This is the smaller Swiss hound, 13½″ to 15″ high, moderately long, strongly built, with a good sized head of noble appearance. The four types are bred for the conditions of the regions of Switzerland where they were developed. It is purely Swiss, first recorded in 1905, and nowadays watched over by the Swiss Niederlaufhund Club which exists to promote the development of a Laufhund (Trans. run-dog), a smaller type of hound, with an ideal height of 14″ to 15″. The Fox Terrier was used in the crosses which followed, but not very successfully, and better results were obtained with the Dachshund. The present types vary mainly in their coloration – the Schweizer is white and red; the Bernese (alone in having smooth and rough coats) is pied or tricolor; the Lucerne blue roan, often with tan; the Jura black and tan.

The head, thin from the front, broadens to the back, with long ears, folded, reaching the tip of the nose or further when drawn forward. Medium length foreface, protruding lips, powerful and regular bite. The back straight with slightly prominent backbone, medium length, broad and well developed. The rump cuts down sharply with tail strongly haired at base, tapered, not flagged, carried hanging when walking. Forelegs and shoulders well developed, straight, paws directed forwards. Coat smooth (except for the Bernese variations) and thick, hard with little undercoat.

Trail Hound

The start of a Hound Trail. The dogs are slipped when the trail is set.

history and development

The Trail Hound is a development of the Fell-foxhound. In Britain it is found almost entirely in the counties of Cumberland, Westmorland and North Lancashire. It is carefully bred, under stringent regulations, for the sole purpose of racing against other Trail Hounds over a nine or ten mile paraffin and aniseed drag laid over the Fells of Lakeland.

At one time the hounds used were the pure-bred Fell-foxhounds, every pack-hound going out to a summer "walk", living in the inns, farms and cottages until hunting was resumed in September, when they returned to kennels. Then, after a hard winter's hunting they needed to be rested during spring and lambing time, one of the busiest times for the fell farmers; but round about mid-April each farmer would want to match his hound against others in speed and durability, and this was the beginning of Hound Trailing. The sport has certainly been practised since 1850, and over the years faster blood, Greyhound, Whippet, Pointer, Saluki, has been worked in, producing the speediest possible hound, with endless stamina. The breed is now fully evolved and the type is absolutely uniform.

For the next sixty years after 1850 the sport was extremely corrupt; large sums of money being wagered on individual hounds, leading to many forms of cheating, such as changing (or ringing) a tired hound with a fresh one half way round a trail; over-feeding a rival hound just before the start, or netting a favorite in a gateway to delay him and spoil his chance. However, in 1907, a move was made to regulate the sport. The Hound Trailing Association was formed and became the ultimate authority. A Register was started and only pure-bred hounds of Fell or Trailing blood were allowed to run, or to be registered. The actual Trail was also strictly

Trail Hound, showing the close shaving all over, except for a strip on the loin, and on the vulnerable tail tip.

controlled, and watchers were posted to prevent ringing, and a system introduced whereby the hound was secretly marked just before the start, so that substitution was further prevented.

color

Any normal hound color is allowed; most hounds being either lemon, black-and-tan or hare-and-badger-pied. White predominates because Trailing is a spectacle to be watched at a distance and a white hound is more easily seen. A few animals are liver-and-tan or black-and-tan, but only liver-and-white is never seen, this combination not being recognized as a hound color.

care

The Trail Hound receives very special methods of care, methods which are a closely guarded secret and are handed down the generations. The hound is fed on a diet of best steak, hare, port and "cock-loaf", this last is a luxury and its recipe is the most closely guarded secret of all. Every hound gets ten or more miles of road work each evening; and it is shaved right out except for its loins and tail tip, where hair is left for protection.

character

The Trail Hound has a true hound temperament, although it lives an unusual life for a hound, never leading the normal pack life. To the uninitiated the hounds appear cruelly emaciated, but actually they are perfectly produced racing machines, trained to run the most arduous Trail

Trail Hounds today are all privately owned and trained. This is Jackpot, the winner of innumerable Trails, both junior and senior, over seven seasons. He is shown with his trainer, Miss Edith Rodgers, after winning a Senior Trail.

Hounds on the trail are not daunted by any kind of obstacle.

over the mountainous slopes of Helvellyn or Skiddaw.

standards
There is no official standard, the Trail Hound being built on the lines of the Fell-foxhound, but smaller, lighter built and racier altogether. The back should be long, with the long arched loin of the Greyhound, very cut up underneath. The head is like that of the Foxhound, though slightly snipier and with longish ears. Legs more lightly boned than the Foxhound, ending in oval feet, the tendency being towards the hare-foot rather than the cat. The body should be long and deep in the brisket, with a moderate spring of rib; every rib, the backbone and the haunch-bones showing under the pelt, there being no flesh, only sinew and muscle. The shoulder should be long and sloping, beautifully laid back, with a long, graceful neck. The pasterns and stifles should have plenty of spring in them. The height is usually around 22″ to 26″ at the shoulder, a big diversity in size though not in type, which is uniform.

Tyrolese Hound

In the mountains of Austria the hounds are bred and trained for work, not only in the high regions but also in places which are inaccessible to man, and where the dog must work without direct control. The Tyrolean Hound (Tyroler Bracke) is such an animal; together with the Austrian Hound and the Styrian Mountain Hound, the breed makes up a trio of special hounds – keen scented, agile and enduring, and deeply loyal and obedient. It is used alone, not in packs; and with the diminishing of the areas previously hunted it has become increasingly necessary to make the sport satisfying from better knowledge of terrain and quarry, from better tactics and expertise – and these hounds are well suited for this.
The Tyrolean Hound is small to medium (16″ to 19″) somewhat longer than its height.
Its coloring is the combination usual in these Austrian Mountain Hounds, basically black or red or rust, with some small white markings; also tricolor, black with tan, brown or red on feet, breast, underside and head, again with some white markings. Exceptional spotting and too definite white are faults.
The coat is smooth or rough, thick, with a good undercoat. The underside well covered, the tail with a brush.

Whippet

Mrs. D. McKay's Ch. Laguna Ligonier, a beautiful dog bred from two champions, who became one of the leading winners and stud dogs of the sixties.

history and development

Deductions can be made from a variety of evidence about the origins of the Whippet as a separate breed, but there is no certainty about any of them. They were exhibited at Cruft's in London for the first time in 1897 and were recognized by the Kennel Club in 1902. Many people have supported the theory that they are a cross between greyhound and terrier, dating from the 19th century, but it would seem more likely that the Whippet's progenitors were the Pharoah Hounds, or Maltese Rabbit Dogs, probably introduced into Britain at the time of the Roman invasion in 55 B.C. The Whippet coat is always of the finest texture, soft, close and silky. This characteristic would seem to oppose the idea of an outcross with a rough-coated breed. No doubt such crossing has been done, but the results are obvious and the pedigree Whippet has bred true to type for so long that the original stock must have possessed the same basic characteristics which we see today.

Whippets, and dogs of various sizes but looking just like them, who hunted by both scent and sight, have been known for thousands of years. The name "whippet", "whappet" or "whippert" first appeared in print in 1610. John Taylor, a prolific versifier, in *A dogge of Warre, or the Travels of a Drunkard,* published around 1628, mentions "The little curre whippet or house dog . . ." and there are other allusions of the same period. There may be minor differences between these "little curres" and the Whippets of today, but when they are mentioned in written work so long ago, there is no reason to doubt the fact of their existence at that time.

The antiquity of the Whippet-type dogs is generously supported in ancient sculptures, bronzes, tapestries, and most commonly of all in

Whippets breaking from the trap at the start of a race.

paintings, great numbers of which portray the Whippet over many years and in many countries. Two of the most striking and typical examples of the Whippet in art are the Paul van Somer portrait of Anne of Denmark (1604), the property of Queen Elizabeth II, and the portrait by Battoni of the Marquis of Northampton, in the Fitzwilliam Museum, Cambridge, England. Both show Whippets which are closely characteristic of the breed today. There is also early painting of the Emperor Maximilian I of Bavaria (1756–1825), one of Napoleon's great adversaries, with his pack of Whippets. It may be no coincidence that the Maximilian family was connected with the porcelain factory at Neudeek, which was transferred to Nymphenburg in 1761, and that this factory produced many lovely models of Whippets. Going farther back; excavations at Corstopitum, a Roman town situated between Hexham and Corbridge, near the ancient Hadrian's Wall, have produced large quantities of bones providing evidence of the domesticated and wild animals of North Britain during the Roman period. Bones of dogs were numerous, and included, among others, animals of the Whippet conformation.

Mr. B. W. Evans's Sapperly Tiptree Pilot, a war baby born in 1942, proved to be a famous sire who had great influence on the breed. He sired six British champions and four in other countries.

The Whippet has always been used for sport, obviously for hunting by reason of its great speed (today's Whippet is capable of around thirty-five miles per hour!) but a sport which is on the increase both in Britain and America and on the Continent is Whippet racing, a sport greatly enjoyed both by dogs and owners. There are clubs all over England, affiliated to the Whippet Racing Association, founded by the Whippet Club of England to standardize Whippet racing in England, in keeping with the practices of the Continent. The dogs racing under the control of the W.R.A. are animals registered with the British Kennel Club, competing on a standardized handicapping system of a yard per pound of weight. There is also a Whippet Coursing Club which holds meetings from September to March, where Whippets can pursue hares in their natural state, as Greyhounds do.

color

The breed has a variety of permissible colors. The most popular in the show-ring are particolors (white with patches of any other color, fawn, brindle, blue or black). Fawns, brindles, blacks and blues are less numerous, although no less elegant, and these solid colors have always been the most popular in the field, blacks and blues reputedly being especially favored by poachers. Another theory claimed that a hare would be more likely to be alerted to the approach of a conspicuous white, or white-marked dog than by one of a solid color which would blend into the landscape.

care

The Whippet, when properly cared for, is not a delicate dog, despite its elegant appearance. When fit, it can endure a long day's coursing in any weather and over difficult terrain. The essential comfort in the house is a warm dry bed well out of draughts. Regular attention to nails and teeth and plenty of exercize are the chief requirements of the healthy Whippet. For the show ring, a little tidying up of the tail is almost all a Whippet needs. Patient training from an early age will pay dividends when your puppy makes his show debut, but Whippets do not need elaborate handling in order to present them at their best. They should be shown as naturally as possible, on a loose lead, and just taught to stand quietly while

One of the many British-bred Whippets who have won top honors in the States. American Ch. Laguna Lucky Lad won the hound group at Westminster in 1958.

the judge looks them over or handles them.

Whippets tend to mature later than many other breeds and do not reach full maturity until eighteen months or two years of age. It is not usually advisable to breed from a bitch at her first season, which can be anything from twelve months to two years. Before it is finally decided to mate a bitch you should study her pedigree and a dog chosen whose blood lines tie in with hers. If she has any outstanding faults, it is advisable to find a stud dog that does not also carry those particular faults. Puppies should not be allowed too much exercize at any early stage but lead training from four/five months will be a great help when at six months you want to start showing your puppy.

character

The Whippet is particularly loving and affectionate and makes an ideal dog for the home. They are very clean in the house and, having short coats and small feet, make very little work. They are also excellent performers in the field with hares, rabbits and rats. Both racing and coursing also come absolutely naturally to the Whippet and it is one of the most exciting and dramatic sensations a Whippet owner can experience to see the dog he has trained and cared for, and perhaps bred, run in competition with other Whippets on equal terms. It is rare to find a breed which makes such an ideal house pet and which, at the same time, fully satisfies all its owner's sporting instincts; but the Whippet achieves all this. Many of the Whippets, which are raced and coursed, are also regular winners in the show ring, so it is the general temperament and correct construction of the Whippet which contributes to its success in all the competitive fields for which it is eligible.

standards

As the Whippet is primarily an English breed, the English Standard is the one which should be the basis of an analysis of the breed. The Continental Standards follow the English one very closely, but the American Standard

Whippets have many color combinations, one of the most attractive being the brindle with flashy white markings as seen on Miss E. M. Hawthorn's Ch. Deepridge Mintmaster, a great winner of the late sixties.

differs from the English on the matter of size, to such an extent that a different type of animal is produced and rather different characteristics tend to be emphasized. The ideal height for the English Whippet is $18\frac{1}{2}''$ for a dog and $17\frac{1}{2}''$ for a bitch, measured at the shoulder, although many specimens in the ring today are considerably larger and more in line with the American Standard which allows a dog to be 22″ and a bitch 21″. The larger animal tends to lose some of the Whippet characteristics and to become more like a small Greyhound, and as far as field work is concerned, the height laid down in Britain has been found to be perfectly satisfactory. The American Standard also requires the eye to be "at least as dark as coat color" whereas the original English version says simply "expression bright and alert" laying down no color definition. Otherwise the Standards are virtually the same, requiring a balanced streamlined animal, built for speed and covering a lot of ground. Shoulders should be flat and sloping, well laid back, not bossy or open at the top. Chest deep with plenty of heart room. Loin strong and slightly arched, legs and feet well boned and straight. Feet well knuckled up and tight, good strong pads, tail long and tapering with no heavy feathering, carried with a slight curve upwards but never higher than the back. Ears should be rose-shaped, small and fine in texture and folded, not pricked, when alert. The head should be long and lean, flat on top, rather wide and with a slight stop. The Continental and Scandinavian Standards are very similar to the British, and their judges are very strict in their interpretation of the Standard when they are judging the breed. The Standard, which has to be followed on the Continent, is the one written by the Fédération Cynologique Internationale in Brussels (to which most of the European Kennel Clubs belong) and their Standard does not include that phrase "Judges should not penalize an otherwise good specimen for size", which is a part of the British Standard for the Whippet. The most important thing, on which Whippet fanciers of all nationalities are agreed is that the overall impression of the Whippet should be a combination of speed, strength and beauty.

A perfect example of a lovely Whippet head with correct ears, long, clean neck, keen, alert and teeming with class and quality – Mrs. D. F. Whitwell's Seagift Sophia.

Int. Ch. Laguna Leader, by Ch. Laguna Ligonier ex Laguna Lunette.

Terriers

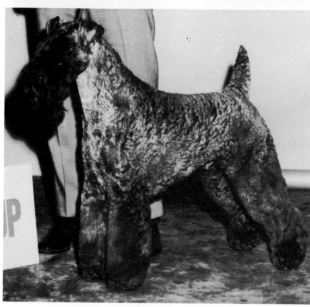

The Terrier group at Cruft's, 1971, was won by this great champion, Blackdale Handful, a Lakeland Terrier.

Supreme in the Terrier group at Westminster, 1971, was this superb Kerry Blue Terrier, Ch. O'Connell of Kerry Oaks.

Airedale Terrier

Ch. Riverina Tweedsbairn, owned by Miss P. McCaughey and Mrs. D. Schuth and bred by Mrs. C. M. Halford, won best in show at Cruft's in 1961. In all he was best in show at eight championship shows in England and Dog of the Year in 1960 and 1961.

history and development

The Airedale Terrier originated in the county of Yorkshire in northern England, in that beautiful part of the English countryside through which run the little rivers of the Aire and the Wharfe. It is not known exactly where and when the breed emerged as an entity, but certainly by the beginning of the First World War it was well established. There is no doubt that the Welsh Harrier, the Otterhound and the Old English Terrier played a prominent part in its development.

The Airedale was bred specifically for the sport of otter hunting, for which there was a great love in the dales of the River Aire and the River Wharfe. It was originally known as the Bingley Terrier (after the town of Bingley in Yorkshire) or Waterside Terrier. Assuming it to have been deliberate, it was a stroke of genius to have crossed the working terriers with the Otterhound, for the Airedale as it emerged was completely suited to the task it had to perform, and large numbers of these large terrier-hounds were distributed over the sporting districts of the North of England. The name Airedale Terrier was accepted in Britain by 1878, and in 1883 Airedales were classified at Birmingham National Show. The Airedale, as it had then developed had no equal as a dog bred to hunt, and to destroy vermin, but now those early breeders turned to the Bull Terrier and the Irish Terrier to breed out the hound formation of big ears, thick skulls and light eyes, for nobody had hitherto regarded these characteristics as faults; only absolute gameness and willingness to hunt and work was desired by the breeders; but the hard, dense coat was

A champion of the 1920's: Ch. Kelowna, bred by the author's father, Mr. F. J. Bridge. Kelowna lived from 1922 to 1932.

409

One of the important sires of the breed immediately after World War II was Ch. Murraysgate Minstrel, owned and bred by Mr. J. Kerr. He became a champion in 1947.

Ch. Kresent Beloved, owned by Mrs. D. Hodgkinson and handled here by her husband for photographer Stig Alberg, a noted Swedish terrier authority. This close up, natural picture of Beloved shows the beauty of an Airedale perfectly presented for show.

An Airedale head

considered desirable, with its oily undercoat so suited for their work in water.

Within fifty years the handsome dog we know today was evolved and it has achieved a fame and popularity which has made it a favorite in America and on the Continent of Europe, and it grew in regard as a sporting dog, trainable to the gun. In Germany, famous for its police dog breeds, the Airedale is much valued for that onerous duty.

Eighty years ago there were large classes of Airedales at the shows in Yorkshire, and at Otley in the West Riding of Yorkshire the Gold Medal for the best Airedale was hotly contested; but after the First World War their popularity began to decline, until the thirties, when the rush of regard for the Boxer was at its height, and probably was a contributory factor in this decline. But the Airedale was throughout unfailingly supported as a show dog, and particularly as a family dog. He was held in great esteem in America where, it is said, he hunted bear in the Rockies. A contrast to its usual hunting role, which is to extinguish vermin of all kinds, rabbits, moles, skunk, in fact wherever there was a job for a sporting terrier the Airedale could do it supremely well. Of course, being so large, it really does not qualify as a true Terrier i.e. able to follow its

Top winning terrier in England in 1970, Mr. A. Lodge's home-bred Ch. Optimist of Mynair.

quarry to ground.

color

The characteristic colors of the Airedale Terrier are a handsome combination of black and tan. Its head, ears and legs up to the thighs and elbows are tan, and the body is black or grizzle, grizzle being a combination of black and dark gray, or rust and black. The ears are a darker shade of tan than the head.

The black saddle, the area along the dog's back, is probably the more attractive part of the Airedale's color scheme because of the marked contrast with the tan, but a saddle of grizzle is not wrong. It is well said that "a good horse cannot be a bad color" for, in a dog sense, this certainly applies to the Airedale.

care

The Airedale is a very hardy breed and requires no special care, beyond the routine of keeping its coat in order.

Twice a year from when it is seven months old, it will cast its coat, and here it should be emphasized that its typical hard coat needs little care, only a daily run over with the comb and brush, in contrast with the dogs with sheep-like coats which need constant attention and clipping. A weekly trim to remove the uncomfortable, shaggy hair should be kept up.

The particular requirements for grooming for showing can be learned

An Airedale in ordinary, everyday trim.

411

A picture taken from an unusual angle to demonstrate the ideal hindquarters, so important in this largest of the terrier breeds.

Full of character, this study of Ch. Riverina Tweedsbairn shows the correct ear carriage, eye set, and the alert terrier expression.

from the nearest breed club, where the novice can meet other Airedale owners, and can share his or her enthusiasm. Considering its size the Airedale needs a comparatively moderate amount of exercise. It adapts itself to town or city life, content with a regular trot around the block, and a romp in the park, but it is happiest in the country, in the fields and woods. But watch it in that lake, it is a water dog, remember.

It needs affection, and enjoys the companionship of its owner. Not a lazy dog, it will be happy to trot around by its owner's side all day long. Although this hardy dog can stand any amount of cold, it does need, as with most dogs, a draughtproof bed. Regular feeding, one meal a day for grown dogs, meat and meal, meat raw or lightly cooked.

standards

The Airedale should be beautifully constructed, with a long brick-shaped head, strong, short, well-ribbed body and great substance. There is nothing weak about this fellow; its straight legs and cat-like feet and strong hindquarters contribute to an ideal, active dog, and its dark eye, and V-shaped ears, with a side carriage, give an expression all its own, keen and alert, even humorously wicked, yet combined with a kindly and knowing look.

The breed Standards give a weight for dogs of 45 lbs., and for bitches slightly less, with a preference for dogs weighing a pound or two over this weight, rather than less. The height should be 23″ or 24″ for dogs, to the top of the shoulder, and bitches should be 22″ or 23″.

Australian Terrier

history and development

The national terrier of Australia. Its origins can be traced to about one hundred years ago, but even just after the Second World War, its acceptance in Australia varied. In South Australia dogs from one litter were being registered as Australian Terriers, Sydney Silky Terriers (now Australian Silky Terriers), or even Yorkshire Terriers, according to the size, coat texture and general characteristics to be expected at adult age. Registration in the early days in Australia was a haphazard affair. In South Australia it cost sixpence (six cents) to register a dog. The malpractice of registering a dog born of Australian Terrier parents as of another breed was not occurring in New South Wales but it was in some of the other States. The registration authorities of the time, with whom re-registration was automatically required, were not the present-day State Controlling bodies forming the Australian National Kennel Control, but were the then recognized authorities. It was necessary to register a dog in each of the States in which its pedigree might be relevant.

I have on occasion described the Australian Terrier as the breeding together of "the best of the smaller British breeds", and even today there are throwbacks to the types of Yorkshire Terrier, Australian Silky Terrier, and even the Cairn Terrier, the Norwich Terrier and the Dandie Dinmont. But adamant culling and intelligent line (or in-breeding) is producing a high-quality breed type, and judges in Australia are careful to assess all the qualities which have been established for this Australian national breed.

The first twenty years are the most important in the formative period of

A famous Australian Terrier in England just after the Second World War was Ch. Dandy of Zellah, owned by Miss Swyer.

any breed and for the Australian Terrier this period has passed. I remember as a boy in Tasmania that my late grandfather, Henry Burnell, was developing the breed. His "Aussies" at that time were similar to those of today. More than fifty years ago, he bred Norwich Terriers to Yorkshire Terriers, and their progeny was bred to dogs owned by friends who were similarly interested in the development of the breed.

The Australian Terrier Club was formed in Victoria in 1890, marking the recognition in that State that here was a true breed, and initiating moves to establish it in other States of the Commonwealth. Similar clubs were indeed formed throughout Australia and today the breed is well catered for in shows, on a specialist and an all-breeds level.

color

Colors run from blue-and-tan, the "blue" being black shading into blue or silver, and the tan a pronounced, rich color, to clear red or sandy.

character

The Australian Terrier is a rugged type of small working dog, sturdy in appearance, and low set. It is affectionate, quiet and willing to please, and its ability as a working dog with sheep has made it a breed which is respected and fostered in the country of its origin.

One of the top winners of the early fifties was Ch. Elvyne Blaze the Trail, owned by Miss Swyer.

standards

It is important that the now well-established individual characteristics of the Australian Terrier should be preserved, and that it in no way resembles the Silky or the Yorkshire Terrier. The Australian Terrier should be approximately 14 lbs. in weight, and about 10″ in height to shoulder. A personal characteristic is that his toenails should be strong and black or dark. The coat should be straight and dense, about 2½″ in length, with a harsh texture. No long hair should be present on muzzle, feet or lower legs. The top-knot in blue-and-tans should be blue or silver, and in sandy or red dogs should be slightly lighter than the other head color, which is permissible in both cases. The head is long, with moderately wide, flat skull, and a slight but definite stop.

Australian Ch. Nukara Nimmitibel is a good example of a sandy, shown in Australia. Owned by Mr. and and Mrs. Neale.

Bedlington Terrier

Mrs. B. Clifton's Ch. Vardene Blue Grenadier shown with the Send Gold Vase he won as the best Terrier at Cruft's in London in 1969. Grenadier also won best in show at the National Terrier Championship show in the same year. A beautiful headed dog with excellent body properties and extremely sound, he also excelled in coat and color, an altogether first rate Bedlington.

history and development

The exact origin of the Bedlington Terrier cannot be definitely ascertained, but it is generally believed that it appeared at about the same time as the Dandie Dinmont. Of similar obscurity is the combination of breeds that went into its making. The body contours of the Bedlington point to a relationship with a hound breed. The Otterhound has been suggested as a possible forebear but this is something that can only be guessed at, and the Greyhound or Whippet seems more likely. In addition to hound blood, the Bedlington probably goes back to some type of now extinct otter terrier; this ancestor is probably shared with the Dandie, as old prints of Dandies and Bedlingtons show a striking similarity, although they are not so alike today.

In the latter part of the 18th century, a breed or strain of terriers existed in Northumberland in and around the Rothbury Forest, which was held in high esteem in the neighborhood for its excellent qualities and especially its gameness. Their matings in the first place were probably arranged entirely with a view to perpetuate these qualities, rather than their outward appearance; to get dogs with strength, courage, endurance, nose and the like. Whatever it was required to do in the animal killing line, which was no doubt its main vocation, it would need a powerful, punishing jaw and strong teeth. It is known that Mr. Edward Donkin had two of these Rothbury Terriers, very celebrated in the district, named Peachem and Pincher, and it is this Peachem we must regard as the great patriarch of the Bedlington world.

In 1820, an important date in Bedlington history, a Mr. J. Howe came to Bedlington and brought with him a bitch, Phoebe. She was subsequently given to Joseph Ainsley, who already had a number of these terriers in his possession. It was this visit which led to the Northumberland village giving its name to the breed. It must be said that, but for this visit, the breed might not have been perpetuated at all, as its continuance in purity seems to have been largely due to Joseph Ainsley himself. In 1825, Ainsley mated Phoebe to Anderson's Old Piper – both descended from Peachem, and obtained Young Piper, said to be the first dog called a Bedlington Terrier, Joseph Ainsley having so named the strain which he founded.

It is known that Bedlingtons were being shown before 1870, and the first Bedlington Terrier Club was formed in 1875. Since then the Bedlington has maintained a steady level of popularity, many being kept purely for their working qualities. A climax came in 1965 when a Bedlington won the Terrier Group at Cruft's for the first time in the breed's long history.

There are now three flourishing clubs in Britain, and many more throughout the world.

The outline of a woodcut of Mr. J. Picket's champion Bedlington Tyneside, born in 1870, shows that in those early days the head and general type were already developing along the lines of the modern dog, only the roach back was missing. Tyneside was the first Bedlington champion to be entered in the Kennel Club stud book.

color

The first named Bedlington was liver in color, but it is known that some of its forebears were blue-and-tan. Other colors are blue, sandy, liver and tan but not many of the bicolored are bred now. Liver is the dominant color. The puppies are born black and dark brown, beginning to change to blue and liver when they are around three months old.

care

The Bedlington is a hardy dog able to stand any amount of cold, but not draughts. It needs a box or basket large enough to move about in and stretch its limbs. This must be raised from the floor. The bedding should never be of straw or wood-wool as this is injurious to both coat and eyes. The best is a bed of newspaper which it can tear up and arrange to suit itself. The Bedlington puppy will soon learn proper habits and, once clean, will never soil its bed.

Grooming plays an important part in keeping a Bedlington healthy and happy. If left untrimmed it will get a very tangled, knotted coat; it never casts its old hair and therefore it is important to groom it daily; always combing the reverse way, from tail to head, and from feet to shoulders. The coat should stand away from the skin. The comb should not be so fine as to remove the soft, linty undercoat, which is peculiar to the breed. It is a good idea to give a good brushing weekly, using a fairly stiff brush.

It is not necessary to give weekly baths as the combing and brushing will keep it clean and too many baths will soften the dog's coat. The ears should have the hair removed from the inside, about once a fortnight. This is easily done, the hair being pulled out with either finger and thumb or round-ended tweezers. The hair between the pads should always be trimmed out so that the feet are closed and not splayed.

Bedlington—head views.

character

The Bedlington Terrier is one of the most strikingly unusual of all the

Mr. and Mrs. B. Reddington's Ch. Berengreave Pink Perry, a liver bitch of similar type to Blue Grenadier. She was one of his contemporaries. Again, a beautiful head and splendid body properties.

Mrs. B. E. Wardman's Ch. Burley-dene Mischief was not only a noted winner at shows in the fifties but would also act as a gundog and retrieve feathered game.

A Bedlington puppy.

*(opposite)
A lovely study of two of Mr. Worrell's champions of the early fifties, Ch. Golden Sun of Manaton and Ch. Blueday of Manaton.*

Ch. Workman of Nonnington, owned by Mrs. O'Brien, who was such a force in the breed in Britain over so many years. This photograph was taken in 1958.

dog breeds. Its lamblike appearance is its special trademark. A dog of great heart and courage, its appearance is very deceptive. It is full of life, and is capable of holding its own as were its forebears. The ideal family dog, adored by children and adults alike, quick to protect its home and family, yet obedient. One well-known obedience-trained Bedlington is Mrs. Ida Sill's Andy Capp of Vistablu which has delighted many with its obedience displays for charities.

standards

The Bedlington is a graceful, lithe, muscular dog with no sign of weakness or coarseness. The whole head should be pear or wedge-shaped and its expression in repose, mild and gentle, though not shy or nervous. When roused, the eyes should sparkle and the dog look full of temper and courage. They are capable of galloping at great speed and should have the appearance of being able to do so. The coat is very distinctive; thick and linty, standing well from the skin but not wiry. There should be a distinct tendency for the coat to twist, particularly on the head and face. The head should be narrow, deep and rounded with a profuse nearly-white, silky topknot. Jaw long and tapering, no stop, close fitting lips. Nostrils large and well defined. Black nose in blue and blue-and-tan dogs; livers and sandies must have brown noses. Teeth large and strong, level or pincer jaws. The eyes small and well sunk and looking triangular, blues have a dark eye; blue-and-tans, lighter with amber lights; livers and sandies a light hazel eye. Ears low-set, moderate filbert-shaped and hanging flat to the cheek, with a fringe of whitish silky hair at the tip. The American Standard gives the greatest width as approximately 3″.

Long, tapering neck, deep at the base with no throatiness, the head carried rather high. The body muscular yet flexible, shoulders flat and sloping, the chest deep and fairly broad, the ribs flat and deep through the brisket. The forelegs should be straight, the hindquarters muscular and graceful. The back roached, loins arched giving the hind legs the appearance of being longer than the forelegs. Long hare feet with thick, closed-up pads. The tail a moderate length, thick at the root and tapering to a point. Set-on low but never carried over the back.

Height in Britain should be about 16″ at the shoulder and weight between 18 and 23 lbs. America asks for $16\frac{1}{2}″$ for dogs, $15\frac{1}{2}″$ for bitches. Dogs under 16″ or over $17\frac{1}{2}″$ and bitches under 15″ or over $16\frac{1}{2}″$ are faulted.

Border Terrier

Ch. Falcliffe Topper, bred and owned by Mr. E. Mawson. Born 1960, winner of seven Challenge Certificates in England and sire of four champions to date.

A very early photograph of Mr. J. T. Dodd's Fury and Flint. Flint was whelped in 1894 by Mr. Jacob Robson's Rock out of Mr. Tom Robson's Rat. Fury was born in 1898, by Flint out of Vene. Flint was a well-known worker and also won more prizes than any other Border had up to that time.

history and development

There is strong evidence that a terrier similar to the Border Terrier has been known in Britain in Northumberland, the borders of Scotland, and possibly Cumberland and Westmorland, for many centuries. There is little doubt that the Border is closely related to the Dandie Dinmont Terrier and the Bedlington Terrier although which breed was the progenitor of which is uncertain.

In the early days Borders were known by several names, such as the Coquetdale Terrier, derived from the various localities from which they came. Finally, in 1870, the name Border Terrier was settled upon, taken from the long association of the breed with the Hunt known as the Border Foxhounds, where the breed was used exclusively for work with the Hunt.

The first Border to be shown, Bacchus, was exhibited in Newcastle, England, with little success around 1870. The breed was first scheduled at Bellingham Show in 1881, which has always been the Mecca of Border exhibitors, who value an award there above all others. The Border Terrier Club of Great Britain was formed in 1920, the year the Kennel Club granted official recognition to the breed, although there were several registrations prior to then.

The breed has a strong following in America and Sweden, and to a lesser degree in Canada, Holland, Germany, Denmark and Italy. The first Border was registered in America in 1930, and the breed arrived in Sweden in the 1930's.

color

The colors of the Standards are red, wheaten, grizzle-and-tan, or blue-and-tan. The clear red usually has a black mask and ears. Grizzle-and-tan

420

Mansergh Biddy's Midge, showing the blue-and-tan coloring, also illustrating a beautifully laid shoulder and good hindquarters. Owned by Mrs. M. Roslin-Williams, bred by Mr. Coburn in 1957. Later exported to America.

Ch. Eignwye Enchantress, a great bitch, owned and bred by Mr. R. A. Williams of Hereford, England. Born 1957. Color, grizzle. The ideal presentation for show, tidy yet workmanlike, and with a wonderful coat texture.

is a mixture on each hair of red, black and white giving the effect of a heather mixture in a tweed. The general effect can be a very rich color with dark hairs predominating, or a washy red and gray mixture. The blue-and-tan should appear blue with plenty of light hairs predominating, not a black with one or two light hairs.

Both grizzle-and-tan and blue-and-tan puppies will be virtually black-backed in the nest. However, on rubbing the coat back the wrong way, if it is to be grizzle, the brown will be seen underneath.

Small patches of white on the chest of a puppy do not matter as they will merge in later. Some judges do not like white toes. White stockings, blazes or collars are definitely frowned upon as indicating alien blood.

care

Border Terriers make excellent house dogs and are soon house trained. They require the normal comfort of a draught-proof bed, slightly raised off the floor, and in a quiet corner of the house.

One small meal per day is required, with the meat chopped very fine to

Border Terrier, typical head and expression.

Ch. Hanleycastle Judy, Hanleycastle Vicky and Hanleycastle Russ with the Croome Foxhounds.

A Border swims after a rat . . .
. . . and gets it.

avoid choking if gulped too quickly, and the dog should be checked for loss of weight, by feeling over its back occasionally, as the coat can be very deceptive.

The coat will need attention twice a year, in the late spring so that the dog is not carrying an enormous coat through the hot weather, and again in the late autumn so that it will carry a tight heavy winter coat. This can be done easily with a blunt penknife, used against the thumb, to pull away the hair in the direction that it grows, once the coat is blown and ready to come off. Test this by pulling one small tuft sharply with fingers from the back, if this comes away easily the coat is ready to strip. The new coat will take eight to twelve weeks to grow in again. There are those with a very harsh coat which never blows but just requires tidying up with finger and thumb.

The sharp tufts in front of the eyes should be removed in the same manner so that they do not grow into the eyes, causing discomfort. Long hairs inside the ears should also be removed. Toenails should be kept short, also dew-claws, and anal glands squeezed, and hairs under the tail kept short. Regular grooming with brush or comb will keep the Border feeling comfortable. For show, there should be eight to twelve weeks growth of coat, with the undercoat left in (combing removes this). It should be tidied with finger and thumb (never cut) around the skull and ears; the long fringe hairs on neck and back of front legs and hocks removed; tidied up under belly and tail, between the thighs and around the feet. The dog should then look workmanlike and presentable for show.

character
The Border Terrier is a most adaptable dog, content to potter around home and garden, or ready for the hardest day's hunting on the hills, or to follow a young boy around as companion. They are very good with children.

It is not desirable for them to fight, as when doing their proper work with hounds and terriers they must mingle freely with both hounds and terriers whom they will not know. Any sign of fighting should be suppressed firmly straight away, before it ever becomes a vice.

Border Terriers are affectionate but undemonstrative, very dignified and a little dour. This is not a breed to take rough punishment as this breaks their trust and even a cross word will be enough to hurt their dignity. They are anxious to do the right thing and keep out of trouble, so can easily be taught what they may or may not do. The problem of private hunting expeditions may arise, as there is a very strong instinct for work in every Border.

It is inborn in every Border to "have a go" at livestock at some stage or other, be it cats, sheep, rabbits or fowls. They are very easy to break of this if they are firmly told "no" early enough, and they will become quite trustworthy. As working terriers, Borders are courageous, sensible and very tough. They are slower to enter the burrow than other breeds, but once entered are steadier terriers, very reliable, and not being so "gassy", they do not get marked-up as much and they also tend to use their wits rather than their teeth. A bitch that I knew worked twice a week for six seasons with hounds without getting a mark on her. The dense coat and thick skin protect them well while working, but a warm, dry bed is required once they are home.

Typical Border puppies, Ravensdowne Twig and Twinkle. Born 1950, bred and owned by Miss E. J. Fair.

standards

Both the English and American Standards describe essentially a working terrier, combining gameness with activity above and below ground. The distinctive head is like that of an otter, moderately broad in skull with a short, strong muzzle; eyes dark with keen expression, ears small and v-shaped, dropping forward close to the cheeks. Moderate length neck; body deep, narrow and fairly long, ribs carried well back but not over-sprung, (a terrier should be capable of being spanned by both hands behind the shoulders). Racy hindquarters, loin strong, undocked tail carried gaily but not curled over the back. Forelegs straight and not too heavy in bone, small feet with thick pads. Coat harsh and dense with close undercoat, the skin must be thick. Weight, dogs between 13 and 15 lbs., bitches between 11½ and 14 lbs. Apart from the fact that ½ lb. more weight is allowed for the dog in America, the only real divergence between the two Standards is over the set-on of the tail. I quote, English Standard "set high", American Standard "not set-on too high". No height is given in either case, but the old working terrier guide of "an inch per pound" is a rough indication.

The correct otter head and expression illustrated by Ch. Fox Lair, born 1934, bred by A. E. Stephenson, owned by D. Mitchell and Mrs. K. Twist. He appears behind most present-day Border pedigrees. And here is the otter head, note the resemblance.

Bull Terrier

The quintessence of type and quality, perfection: Ch. Souperlative Rominten Rhinegold, owned by Mr. R. H. Oppenheimer and Miss E. M. Weatherill.

Frontal view of a Bull Terrier head.

history and development

The Bull Terrier has his beginning in the bloody sport of baiting the bull. Bred in the stews and steeled in the pit the Bull and Terrier, as the breed was originally known, proved himself the finest exponent of this savage sport. Cross and counter cross, with Bulldog for courage and tenacity; with Terrier for speed, agility, fire and intelligence, were tried as the generations passed, with but one end in view, ultimate prowess in the pit. The Boxer in Germany and the Boston Terrier in America both owe their origins to similar crosses between the opposing types, Bulldog and Terrier. The nearest counterpart to the original crosses today is the Staffordshire Bull Terrier, in which type still tends to veer between the two varieties. In America a larger, taller type, again is known as the Staffordshire Terrier. All these crosses were made in the first place to produce a game dog that would fight till the death and yet be agile enough to avoid injury against all kinds of opponent.

In those times the Bull and Terrier was the champion of the pits but by no means a champion in appearance. Bulls, bears, lions, and other dogs themselves were fought, even a monkey achieved fame as a fighter against the champion dogs of his day. However public opinion turned against the sport and baiting was outlawed by Parliament in 1835. But dog fighting, which like cock fighting could be carried on in secret, unlike the baiting of larger animals, continued long after abolition and it is rumored that both these bloody pastimes have continued in some parts of Britain even today. Law abiding Bull Terrier men took to breeding for a better appearance while retaining those qualities which had served the breed so well in the pits. Among these breeders was James Hinks of Birmingham. By using the

White English Terrier and the Dalmatian on the old Bull and Terrier, Hinks produced an all-white strain and called them Bull Terriers. The birth of the new breed coincided with the beginning of dog shows and at a very early show in 1862 Hinks brought out his famous bitch Puss and was immediately challenged to prove her worth against the older, heavier type. Notwithstanding the Act of Parliament, Hinks took up the challenge and returned his unmarked animal to the show-ring in triumph – the other dog did not return.

This was the beginning of a wave of popularity for the breed which has endured to the present day. During World War II the Bull Terrier rose to being one of the most popular breeds in Britain – with so many men away on active service this was proof of the breed's excellence as guard and companion to home and family. A peak was reached in 1947 when registrations in Britain numbered 3,367. Today annual registrations with the Kennel Club in Britain number about 800 – 900.

An outstanding head, showing length, strength, downface, fill-up and Roman finish. Miss B. Bradbury's Ch. Corinthian Silver Queen of Ormandy.

color

Around the turn of the century a number of fanciers had the notion to re-introduce the colored coat into the breed and some crosses with Staffordshire Bull Terriers (then flourishing in the Midlands, but at that time not recognized by the Kennel Club) were made. Progress was slow at first and opposition strong to these colored Bull Terriers and particularly the color-bred white (whites bred from colored parents) and it was not until 1950

Miss D. Montague Johnstone and Miss M. M. Williams' Ch. Romany Robin Goodfellow, an outstanding brindle, a fine example of all-round excellence.

A lovely white Bull Terrier, with color marked head.

Typical puppies of the breed at eight weeks old. The brindle shows a promising head, and the white the great substance and bone required in the breed.

A promising puppy at four months. Some evidence of an upright shoulder and poor feet: but this one became a champion. Mr. Tom Horner's Ch. Tango of Tartary.

that colored and color-bred whites were finally given equal status in the breed. Brindle has always been the preferred color and this has proved a wise choice, for brindle has the power to re-vitalize a fading strain when mated to white, a property the other colors do not appear to possess. Genetically dominant, brindle is lost unless one parent carries it. Other colors are red, fawn, black and tan and black brindle, and all of these with white.

The white Bull Terrier is in fact a colored dog with the color restricted to certain parts by an inhibiting genetical factor. The actual color of most whites can be ascertained if the tiny spots on the back of the ears are examined under a magnifying glass. Some whites have larger marks on the head which are allowed by the British Standard and clearly indicate the color inherent in the dog. In America markings behind the head of a white, or a predominance of white in a colored, is frowned upon. For breeding purposes it is important to know the color characteristics of a dog.

In the early days of the breed when only white was recognized, deafness was a problem and in 1922 the British Bull Terrier Club made history by being the first organization to tackle in a forthright manner a hereditary disease in a dog. From then on all members of the Club have had to sign a declaration of honor that they will not offer for sale, breed from or show a Bull Terrier whose hearing is not perfect. The result is that deafness is now very rare in the breed.

In Britain the Bull Terrier's ears used to be cropped, and still are in some countries. The Bull Terrier Club subscribed to a fund to support the breeders whose test case brought an end to this barbarous practice. Large heavy ears lent themselves better to cropping than thin ones and when the anti-cropping law was passed it was some years before the erect ear became general in the breed. Now it is universal and most puppies get them up before they are six months old.

care

A Bull Terrier will take all the exercise he is able to get and ask for more,

426

but at the same time he loves his comfort. He must be provided with a warm and comfortable bed, as cold and damp soon penetrate his thin coat. So strong and virile a dog needs to work off his energy and he is the perfect country dog. But he is not ideal for a town flat unless there is a park or similar place nearby where he can be exercized off the lead at least once a day. Apart from a weekly check on ears, eyes, teeth and gums, nails and anal gland, and a daily brush or rub down after exercize, a Bull Terrier needs little attention as he is normally extremely healthy.

character

Throughout all its development the breed's character has been kept unchanged, merely adapted to meet the needs of changing ways of life. In the early years of the century Bull Terriers were exported from Britain in their hundreds and adapted successfully to all kinds of conditions, from the tropics to the Arctic. Today a more docile sort which will fit in to the smaller homes of the modern age is in demand but, and this is vitally important, the Bull Terrier is as demanding as ever of his owner's time and affection. If you cannot or are not prepared to give up some part of every day to exercizing your Bull Terrier's body and brain do not have a Bull Terrier. He does everything flat out and if he is bored and decides to wreck the home, wreck it he will. Master him you must or he will master you, but never forfeit his respect. It will not be regained.

In some their murky past rears its head and once allowed to fight they will quickly acquire a taste for fighting, so never encourage a Bull Terrier to fight. The small pup who fiercely guards his bone or your armchair may seem cute and amusing but nevertheless he must be taught that you are the master and have to be obeyed. Once that lesson is learned he will be much happier.

The Bull Terrier is tough yet responsive to affection, a natural clown, intelligent, full of fire but amenable to discipline and faithful unto death. The ideal playmate for children, a Bull Terrier will tolerate any indignity, even pain, but children must learn to respect his needs – especially a young pup's need of rest between bouts of play.

A supreme guard and ideal companion in any outdoor pursuit, yet softly sentimental to those to whom he gives his affection. It is characteristic of the breed that he will fuss and complain about the slightest scratch or discomfort, even a puddle of water! But if seriously hurt his courage is profound and his powers of recovery nothing short of miraculous, indeed he takes a lot of understanding.

standards

The Bull Terrier is the supreme athlete of the canine world, faster and more agile than any other breed of comparable size and weight, yet stronger and tougher than any other capable of comparable speed. Maximum substance for the size of the dog combined with symmetry, agility and balance make up the ideal specimen. The unique down-faced head, packed solid with bone, with its deep, strong jaws and relentless grip is a perfect example of strength with economy and a stumbling block for the inexperienced judge. Legs straight from any angle, powerful sloping shoulders providing a base for a long arched neck flowing into a short strong body with barrel ribs and deep brisket. Powerful short loins and big rugged quarters that would "cut a good ham" with width and depth of

An excellent front, showing the broad chest, clean shoulder and cat feet. Also shows the impish expression of the breed. Mr. R. H. Oppenheimer and Miss E. M. Weatherill's Ch. Ormandy's Archangel.

Miss D. Montague Johnstone and Miss M. M. Williams' Ch. Romany Ruffino has substance with quality and style seldom seen in so compact a specimen.

A head study of a fine white Bull Terrier, Ch. Abraxas Athenia, owned by Miss V. Drummond-Dick.

powerful muscling let down to strongly marked stifles, short hocks and small tight feet, are characteristics of the breed.

The Bull Terrier must be short in back yet stand over plenty of ground by reason of correct angulation of shoulder and hindquarters. And, as he stands over his ground, he must look as if he owns it, poised on tip-toe, ready for anything with a wicked twinkle in his eye which his owner knows for a sense of humor, but the interloper may be forgiven for mistaking it for the Devil himself.

Since the breed began the size of the Bull Terrier has varied widely. In recent times there have been champions of over 70 lbs. in weight and under 30 lbs. The Standard has no size or weight limits.

Bull Terrier, Miniature

There are also Miniature Bull Terriers; some weighing as little as 10 lbs. are recorded early on in the breed's history. In 1939 Miniature Bull Terriers were accorded a separate register by the Kennel Club in Britain. Many feel that this was a premature step since there were so few strains of the breed that over-intense inbreeding was bound to follow, and it is sad to report that the breed has not kept pace with the full-sized dog in the intervening years. These are sporting and companionable little dogs with all the character of the big 'un, and offer enormous scope to the dedicated breeder, being much in need of improvement.

The Standard is measured not by weight but by height. A Miniature Bull Terrier must not be more than 14″ at the shoulder. In every other respect the Standard is the same as that of the Bull Terrier. A good weight is 20 lbs.

A Bull Terrier does not need to be big to have power and substance, masculinity and Bull Terrier character. Mrs. B. Butler's Ch. Willing of Upend, a typical miniature, has exceptional conformation for a little one.

Cairn Terrier

history and development

It says much for the Cairn Terrier's character that, born and bred in the Highlands of Scotland to work among the cairns and crags with otter, fox and badger, he should have become so popular all over the world.

The breed probably originated around the 15th century. There are descriptions of similar dogs in old books and paintings of the period, resembling the Cairn as we know it today.

In 1774 Oliver Goldsmith wrote of a terrier which was a "small kind of hound, with rough hair, made use of to force the fox or the badger out of their holes; to rather give notice by their barking in what part of the kennel the fox or badger resides. When the sportsmen intend to dig them out."

These small terriers, at that time known as short-haired Skyes, had been kept for generations both by the lairds, the owners of the large estates in the Highlands, and the farmers of the small crofts, but it was not until 1909, at Inverness, that they were first shown. In 1910, after a protest by the Skye Terrier enthusiasts, the name of these wiry-haired, hardy little dogs was changed to Cairn Terrier – a name chosen because of the nature of their work. In the Island of Skye, off the North-West Scottish mainland the otters hide in the cairns, piles of stones on the sea-shore and hillsides, and it was from these hide-outs that the Cairn Terrier used to bolt them. When they were first shown the cairn Terriers were much plainer dogs than they are today. Beginning their strenuous life in the Highlands and developing tremendous agility, they were short in bone

Ch. Redletter McMurran, owned by Mr. W. Bradshaw. Note the perfect topline and tail carriage. An example of a perfectly balanced dog who loves showing himself off.

A good bitch spoiled by lack of coat care. With no pride in her appearance, reluctant even to hold up her tail!

American and Canadian Ch. Rossmar's Clanruf O'Cairndania, whose owner, Mrs. Betty Hyslop, demonstrates to perfection the American way of presentation and handling. Clanruf is shown winning best of breed at the Cairn Terrier Club of America specialty in 1961, under the late Col. H. F. Whitehead, who had gone over from Scotland to judge.

(opposite)
The Blencathra's, owned by Mrs. M. Drummond, are particularly noted for their lovely heads, and Blencathra Curlew is an outstanding example. Note the excellent ears, eye-placement, and balance of skull and muzzle, with correct furnishings. A C.C. winner himself, Curlew comes from one of the most important breeding lines in Britain.

and body coat and furnishings, and their fronts were often crooked, resulting no doubt from the manner of their work in the rocky terrain.

The light-colored dog was considered best for hunting, but there were always the grays as well as the wheatens and reds. Whites also cropped up quite often. Colonel Malcolm of Poltalloch played a large part in separating the whites, which later became West Highland White Terriers and, in 1924, the Kennel Club refused to allow inter-breeding, or white dogs to be used with Cairn Terriers. But this did not happen without much difference of opinion. It should be noted here that inter-breeding between Cairns and West Highlands had already been banned in America. Ch. Ross-shire Old Gold, one of the early big winners, was almost certainly white, and it is a fact that a number of whites came down from his line. There is little doubt also that the sire of Ch. Gesto, the breed's first champion, and of whom Baroness Burton wrote "has probably had more influence on the breed than any dog that ever has or ever will exist", was a "white Westie".

Thus although type in the two breeds is different today it will be no surprise that the Cairn and the West Highland White have a great deal in common. But any resemblance to the *Scottish Terrier* has always been frowned upon. The Scottish Terrier is a heavier-bodied and boned dog altogether, and the head is totally different from the Cairn.

color

One of the breed's chief attractions is the wide variation in color. The favorite today is red, varying from a light sandy color to a deep red brindle. All shades of gray down to nearly black are also acceptable.

An unwelcome color which does occasionally occur in litters, even in these days, is black-and-tan. The body is black with shadings of tan down the legs and on the side of the face and above the eyes. This may have come down through an early cross with the Scottish Terrier, or perhaps even the old Black and Tan Terrier which, together with the old White Terrier, is said to be the progenitor of all terrier breeds.

care

Light-colored Cairns are much improved by dark points round the foreface and ears. Puppies are usually born with dark hairs here and they retain them but the soft black hairs on the body come away by twelve weeks when the harder coat comes through. Breeders usually take out this puppy coat with their fingers and thumb. Pull gently but firmly and these outer hairs come out easily.

It is very important to remember that this breed must present a rugged Highland appearance, with a good double coat resistant to cold and wet

weather. This coat should not be spoiled by artificial trimming. On the other hand the Cairn should not look ragged and unkempt. Ears, feet, legs and tail should be tidied by removing loose ends and straggling pieces with finger and thumb or a fine comb. Apart from the feet, which may be shaped with scissors, no cutting instrument should ever be used on any other part of the body. After a litter, and in the case of young dogs losing their puppy coats, a full strip is best; remove all loose hair, again with finger and thumb, leaving only the under coat as a basis for the new coat to grow. If it is intended to show the Cairn it should be accustomed to the show-ring as early as possible. In England a Cairn has to be shown naturally, and may not be assisted by having his tail and head held in position.

character

The Cairn is an ideal family dog – sporting, as befits a dog with such an ancestry, but quite ready to be petted and made much of, and ready to romp and explore with children. It is very inquisitive and lively.

Fully adaptable to family life, the Cairn does not sulk and resent being left out of things and can be left behind without any of those demonstrations of frustration to which many other breeds are prone. And as a companion on any family outing he is adaptable and disciplined in his

Ch. Toptwig Tilden, owned by Mrs. Marsh and Mr. J. Danks. Tilden won a "grand slam" of four best in show awards at consecutive club shows in 1968–69. Even from a photograph one can almost feel his lovely coat texture. A strong, well-made dog with a beautiful, masculine head and dark points (these are typical and attractive, but are not absolutely essential).

behavior, adding much to family enjoyment.

Some Cairn owners still work their dogs, and one breeder has qualified her champions as working dogs – so the show-ring is not just full of pretty show dogs. Many Cairn owners have also competed successfully with their dogs in the obedience ring. It would be a great pity if this sporting breed were to be spoiled by indiscriminate breeding. Today it is one of the most popular of the terrier breeds, both in registrations and show entries in Great Britain and America, and there are never enough Cairn Terriers to supply both the genuine breeders and the good homes all over the world.

Many Cairns are exported from Great Britain. America and Canada are the main buyers, but Australia, New Zealand, France, Germany, Holland, Sweden and Denmark all seem to like the breed, and have made use of top British stock in their own breeding plans.

Cairn puppies of three months bred by Mrs. and Miss Hamilton and Mrs. Temple. Puppies' ears are not completely upright until five months. During teething they may well flop.

One of the stars in the Cairn world in 1969 was Mrs. M. Drummond's Ch. Blencathra Brat. Note his excellent topline, tail set and general balance.

standards

Although the American Standard is slightly fuller than the British there are very few differences between them. Both are very well and considerately written and are of great help to anyone choosing, or owning, a Cairn. The weight clause is perhaps not quite accurate for the breed today. For a dog with enough muscle and bone, strong quarters and build and

depth in ribs, and obviously not thin, the stated 14 lbs. seems inadequate but, at the same time, too heavy a body with too much depth is not to be encouraged. An ideal weight for a dog would be 16 lbs. The show judge must look for a solid dog with enough scope for agile, quick movement so that he can do his work. It will be understood that the Standards of today are firmly based on the original purposes of the breed.

The American Standard gives 13 lbs. for bitches and 14 lbs. for dogs in addition to the following guide to measurements: height at withers – bitches $9\frac{1}{2}''$, dogs $10''$; length of body – from $14\frac{1}{4}''$ to $15''$ from front of chest to back of hindquarters. This is for matured animals of two years old. Older dogs, according to the Standard, may weigh slightly more, and growing dogs less.

One notation which appears in the British Standard but not in the American is, "a general foxy appearance is the chief characteristic of this working terrier". With the excellent head furnishings of the modern Cairn, probably because he is not allowed to rub it all off by digging, the "foxy" aspect of the Cairn is not immediately noticeable. His head is, however, basically foxy in shape but, of course, there should be nothing mean or furtive about him. A point which must always be watched is that, although the Cairn should never be out at elbow he must not be too narrow in front, which would indicate insufficient strength in chest to carry out his work of digging.

Most important of all is that a good Cairn should be perfectly proportioned. Nothing in any Standard requires any point to be exaggerated.

Contrast this dog with Tilden. Although this light-colored Cairn is smart, showy, typical, and a dog to be proud of, he does not have the size and scope to rival Tilden in the show ring.

Cesky Terrier

The typical working terrier build of the Czechoslovakian Cesky Terrier. This specimen has been prepared for the show ring.

The Bohemian or Cesky Terrier from Czechoslovakia is imbued with all the characteristics necessary for a good working terrier. Although somewhat short-legged, it is hardy and tough, with plenty of stamina and is very agile. Not heedlessly aggressive, but with considerable initiative, it makes a good companion in the house and for children.

The ears are medium sized, set quite high and folded close to the cheeks. The tail, $7''$ to $8''$ long, is comparatively strong and not set too high. When quiescent, the tail is low or with the tip bent slightly upwards; when excited it becomes horizontally sabre-shaped.

The pastel coloring of its coat with its silky luster is a characteristic of the breed.

There are two basic colors – gray-blue and light coffee-brown. Yellow, gray and white markings are allowed on the cheeks and underside of muzzle, the neck, breast and belly and, in addition, on the lower parts of the legs and under the tail. A white collar, or tail tip, is also permissible, but the basic color must be prominent. The coat is wavy and is clipped except on the upper part of the head, the legs, rib cage and belly and, of course, the prominent eyebrows. The transition between the clipped and unclipped areas must be gradual. The hair on the back and the neck should be no more than $\frac{1}{2}''$ long.

Skin on the gray-blue dog is fir-gray and on the coffee-brown dog is flesh colored.

Height for a dog $11''$ to $14''$.

Dandie Dinmont Terrier

Miss C. M. Dandison's Ch. Shrimpney Sunstar, a mustard dog of ideal type and conformation, with a large, well furnished head with strong jaw, heavy boned, sound front and weasely body, with good hindquarters and correctly carried tail. The typical pencilled coat can be clearly seen in this picture.

history and development

Dandies were first heard of as an established breed in the late 1700's in the Coquet Water district of Northumberland when they were largely in the hands of the Border "muggers" or tinkers who used them for drawing and killing badgers, otters and foxes. It must have been in those days that the Dandie developed his proverbial courage and tremendous strength of jaw.

Most Dandie breeders know of Piper Allan, a colorful character of those days, and of his two famous Dandies, Charlie and Peachem. But the outstanding figure in the Dandie world of that era was James Davidson of Hindlee, who kept a large number of the Pepper and Mustard terriers as they were known then and had the odd notion of calling them all Pepper and Mustard, varied with adjectives "big, little, young, old" etc. Davidson's Dandies were the true descendants of Piper Allan's breed and they provide a link between the Dandies of the 18th century and now, as records and pedigrees were kept and handed down to the present day.

Sir Walter Scott obtained several Dandie Dinmonts as they now began to be called, from Davidson and there are many references to them and the litters he bred, in his letters and private writings. From now on Dandies came into prominence and began to be widely bred; they also came into the hands of more distinguished owners. The Dukes of Roxburghe and Buccleugh owned Dandies and it was the Duke of Buccleugh's Old Pepper, found in a trap by a keeper, who founded the celebrated Old Ginger line from which almost all the present-day winners descend.

Mr. G. A. B. Leatham's Ch. Border King. This drawing depicts the early type of Dandie and shows how little the breed has changed over the years.

Dandie Dinmont puppies

435

A head study of Miss Dandison's Ch. Shrimpney Sweet Pepper.

color

Dandies are of two colors, pepper and mustard, the peppers ranging from a pale gray to almost black and the mustards from pale fawn to a rich red-gold. Black peppers and "washy" mustards are not liked and black hair on a mustard is frowned on. Peppers generally have tan feet and legs and sometimes tan patches on each side of the muzzle. White feet, now very rare, are a bad fault but puppies often have some white on the chest which usually fades as the Dandie grows. When mating Dandies, it is best, though not absolutely essential, to cross the colors.

care

This is very simple and consists of regular thorough grooming with a stiff brush and fairly fine comb and a coarser comb for the silky topknot on the head. The old dead coat should be removed with finger and thumb when it is loose and ready to come; the undercoat will then grow and the "linty" top-coat will come through and break it up. A trimming knife or scissors spell ruination to a Dandie's coat and should never be used. Rough hair on the ears should be removed with the fingers and the ear trimmed round, leaving a "tassel" on the end.

Mrs. P. Salisbury's Ch. Salismore Mermaid is a very typical mustard, showing great strength of head and limbs and a well shaped body. Eyes in both colors should be rich dark hazel.

character

The Dandie is very much an individual of strong character. Though generally polite and friendly to strangers, all his devotion is reserved for his owner but that owner must win his respect as well as his affection if he is to get the best out of him. He retains much of the courage and shrewdness of his rugged Border forebears and has great commonsense, and a sense of humor. His working qualities are still to the fore and Dandies are still worked to fox in Scotland. The Dandie does not do well bred in large numbers and confined to kennel and run. He is an excellent

house dog and his deep bark gives intruders the impression of a much larger dog.

standards

The Dandie Standard was drawn up in 1875 by men who worked their Dandies and knew what was wanted in a dog bred to go to ground and tackle fox and badger. Except for slight variations in weight, it has never been altered. In almost every way, it differs from the Standards of other terrier breeds and should be carefully studied by anyone aspiring to judge the breed. The short level back of most terriers is quite wrong on a Dandie whose body should be "long, strong and flexible with a decided arch over the loins" enabling him to twist and turn underground. A "digging front" is needed, his strong, slightly crooked forelegs enabling him to throw the earth out to each side of him so that it does not block his egress. At the same time, he sould never be out at elbows or unsound in front. His forelegs are slightly shorter than his hind ones and the paws are unusually large for a small dog. His coat is "linty", not harsh, with pencilled top-coat and soft under-coat making a weather-resisting combination.

The Dandie's great beauty is his large domed head covered with a white silky top-knot and his large, round, lustrous eyes with their expression of great determination, intelligence and dignity. Their color should be a rich dark hazel, a hard black eye being nearly as unpleasing as a light one. His teeth are unusually large for a small dog and he has an incredibly powerful jaw; he is a big dog in miniature. Weight limits are from 16 (18 in U.S.A.) to 24 lbs., about 20 lbs. being considered the best weight for dogs in good working condition.

Height 8″ to 11″, length from top of shoulder to tail-root not more than twice the height, preferably one or two inches less.

Dandies come in two colors, pepper and mustard. Mrs. P. Salisbury's Ch. Salismore Barvae Pepper is one of the darker peppers. All Dandies have light colored top-knots.

The completely honest and wise expression of the Dandie is very individual to the breed. The large, round eyes, neither prominent nor deep-set, are unmatched by any other breed of dog.

Fox Terrier, Smooth

A painting by M. Lucas of Ch. Laurel Wreath, one of the greatest of post-war Smooths. Bred by G. E. Hurrell and owned by the late Leo C. Wilson. A great winner and a prepotent sire, Laurel Wreath figures in the pedigree of most present-day winning Smooths.

A moderate specimen of forty years ago. Heavy ears, a thick skull, shallow brisket and low set tail detract from the quality and symmetry of this dog.

history and development

How the Fox Terrier was first produced we have nothing but supposition to determine. That there have been varieties of terriers of one kind or another for many hundreds of years cannot be doubted. We are fortunate in having a goodly number of sporting writers of the last five hundred years whose works can be drawn upon to give an insight into the terrier of their day. From as far back as the 14th century, terriers were bred for the sole purpose of hunting, and the royal sport of venerie. Until the turn of the 17th century, they were described as Terrars, which rightly means earth or earthdog, then later as terriers. From the middle of the 18th century, when hunting the fox became popular, they were used as supernumeraries to the foxhound packs, their work being to dislodge the fox when he had gone to ground. By this association with foxhunting, they became universally known as Fox Terriers. We can follow the history of the Fox Terrier through writers right back to very early times. Dame Juliana Berners, the Abbess of Sopewell in 1486, wrote about "Terroures", and devoted a chapter in her book on how she worked them. Again, Dr. Caius, a doctor of medicine in the University of Cambridge and physician to Queen Elizabeth I, wrote the first book on *English Dogges* in Latin in 1576, and devoted a long chapter to Terrarius, the Latin for Terrars. One hundred years later, one Andrew Fleming made a translation into English and from this book is quoted the following paragraph. "Another sort there is which hunteth the fox and the badger grey onely, whom we call Terrars".

The first dog shows in England took place in Birmingham, Newcastle and London, round about the years 1859 to 1865, together with the annual show for Foxhounds at the Cleveland Society's great gathering in Yorkshire. Mr. Tom Wotton of Nottingham, Mr. Stevens of Chester, Mr. Gorse also of Nottingham and other breeders from different parts of England set to work to vie with the professional huntsmen and produced Smooth Fox Terriers which were far superior to the hunt Fox terriers in show potential. Many of these show terriers had no doubt never seen a fox. There were very few, however, which were not capable of giving a good acount of themselves if properly trained and entered to ground.

Birmingham National Dog Show must be given the credit for successfully launching the Smooth Fox Terrier on its show career. At their 1862 show, four Smooth Fox Terriers were exhibited and out of a class containing 44 terriers, all the prizes went to this so-called new variety.

Thus did Smooth Fox Terriers first attract public attention. This period of time coincided with the Industrial Revolution then in full spate in England, when towns and cities were growing overnight. The new working and industrial classes became interested in Fox Terriers. Likewise they became known and admired by what was then known in Victorian parlance as the middle and upper classes of society.

The Smooth Fox Terrier is now popular all over the world as a companion, show dog or working terrier and nowhere more popular than in the hot countries of the Middle and Far East. Between the two world wars, this was specially notable in India and large kennels of Smooths were kept, primarily by the Indian princes and potentates.

One of the reasons was the shortness and durability of the coat which protected the dog to a certain extent from the ticks and vermin indigenous to these hot countries. Smooths are also very popular in Europe, the United States of America and Australia where a good number of Fox Terrier specialist clubs cater for and protect the interest and aspirations of Fox Terrier breeders and exhibitors.

color

Color is important. Black and white, tan and white and all-white, with white predominating (in the two particolors) are standard colors. Brindle, red or liver markings are objectionable. Hound markings, i.e. black, tan and white were popular in the early days of the Smooth Fox Terrier, but are rarely seen in the show ring today.

Smooth Fox Terriers

care

The skills needed for the preparation of the dog for exhibition are not too difficult to acquire. The best procedure is to make a careful study of the way Smooths are conditioned, presented and trained for the shows by the top kennels in the breed. When this knowledge has been acquired, a little light trimming on the terrier should be undertaken about three weeks before your dog is due to be shown. With the use of a safety razor, trim the outside and inside of the ears and the two sides of the skull. Cut away the guide hairs which grow out from the dog's upper jaw or muzzle. Then with thinning scissors carefully trim the ruffle or small excess of

Ch. Watteau Snuff Box, a great winner and sire of the early sixties. Particularly notable for his beautiful neck and shoulders and perfectly balanced outline. Owned by Mrs. Anthony Blake whose father, Mr. Calvert Butler, first owned the Watteau prefix. Mrs. Blake's daughter, Antonia Blake, is now a partner with her mother in the Watteau kennel, making three generations.

A moderate specimen. Although of the same type as the other Smooths pictured here this one is too leggy, shelly in bone, light of body and straight in stifle.

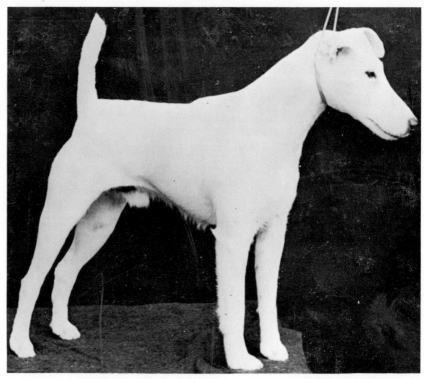

coat which runs from the ears to the base of the neck until the neck and front coat present a level joining. The toe nails should be filed down twice a week with a good file. A cobbler's rasp is the ideal tool for this job. Be very careful not to file too close to the quick. The breechings on the inner side of the hindquarters should also be carefully trimmed using finger and thumb to tidy and level the line of the coat from inside of the thigh to just above the point of the hock.

Grooming should be undertaken daily, with a fine toothed steel comb and a stiff bristled hand-brush. The dog should also be given ring training for about five minutes every day. In this way, when he is exhibited the terrier knows what is expected of him and moves and stands for the judge's examination and appraisal to the best advantage. Correct demeanor in the ring is absolutely vital to the dog's chances of success.

It is imperative that the dog should appear clean with a bright shiny coat on show day. A magnesium chalk block is a wonderful aid and should be rubbed into the coat about three times per day, three days before show day. The magnesium acts as a cleanser and can be patted out of the coat after each application. Wash the Fox Terrier's legs and feet with soap and water the night before the show, and in the ring the following day you will have a bright, clean, alert little Smooth Fox Terrier, full of fire and energy, ready to show his paces to the most critical of judges.

Miss K. Emery's Ch. Hermon Parthings Loyal Lad. Sired by a litter-brother of Ch. Laurel Wreath, Loyal Lad won the C.C. at his first championship show and was early retired to stud. He sired twelve British champions and many other winning Smooths in Britain and elsewhere.

character

The Smooth Fox Terrier has since undergone a great transformation in body shape and has become a show terrier of the very highest standard. He is clean cut in appearance, smart and stylish in design and is at home in both town and country surroundings. He is much sought after by the countryman for sporting field pursuits, by the average Englishman or woman as a companion and by the enthusiastic breeder to further his hobby of exhibiting at the great number of shows held every year all over the world.

standards

The Smooth Fox Terrier Standard demands a high degree of excellence which, although not arbitrary, is absolutely necessary to retain the style, quality and soundness which our present-day Smooth Fox Terriers have inherited from their long ancestry. In symmetry, size and character – the dog must present a general gay, lively and active appearance, bone and strength in a small compass are essentials, but this must not be taken to mean that a Smooth Fox Terrier should be cloddy or in any way coarse. Speed and endurance must be an essential as well as power, and the symmetry of the Foxhound taken as a model. The terrier, like the hound, must on no account be leggy, nor must he be too short in the leg. He should stand like a cleverly-made hunter, covering a lot of ground, yet with a short back. He will then obtain the highest degree of propelling power, together with the greatest length of stride that is compatible with the length of his body. Weight is not a certain criterion of a terrier's fitness for his work – general shape, size and contour are the main points – and if a dog can gallop and stay and follow his fox up a drain, it matters little what his weight is to a pound or so, though roughly speaking, 15 to 17 lbs. for a bitch and 16 to 18 lbs. for a dog in show condition are appropriate weights.

Mr. John Lowe's champion, Ch. Lanneau Jeremy of a type individual to this very successful kennel, which has produced many top winning champions in the post-war period.

The head is the index and denotes the breed of any pedigree animal, therefore great stress is placed on the correct definitions desired in the head of a Smooth Fox Terrier. The skull should be flat and moderately narrow, gradually decreasing in width to the eyes. Not much stop should be apparent, but there should be more dip in the profile between the forehead and the foreface than as seen in the Greyhound.

The eyes, ears, tail set and expression more than anything else denote the character and temperament of the Smooth Fox Terrier. The eyes should

Mr. and Mrs. G. Dallison's Ch. Gosmore Rosemorder Fireaway, an outstanding bitch, photographed as a puppy. Fireaway won her first C.C. at six months old and then won twenty-two out of twenty-four C.C.s offered in one year, twice being reserve C.C.

Ch. Brooklands Lucky Wishbone, owned by the late Mr. Herbert Johnson who, for many years, managed the Watteau Kennel, and later made up several champions under his own Brooklands prefix. Note the initials L.W., given out of respect for Mr. Leo Wilson's breeding.

not be placed too low in the direction of the muzzle. In point of fact, they should bisect the head a little nearer the occiput than the tip of the nose, thus giving a slightly longer foreface with greater scope for jaw power. The eye should be small, circular, dark and penetrating, with a hard venomous expression. In the old days, the ears were preferred to hang more at the side of the head than they do today. The flaps of the ears, the old huntsmen used to say, were to protect the ear from the wind and rain. The present fashion is for the ears to be carried a little higher on the head, with the V-shaped ear tips positioned in a direct line to the corner of the eye. This placement of the ears gives a smarter, more alert effect to the head.

The tail should be upright and pulsating slightly, set-on rather high and it should never flag, particularly in the show ring. No other part of the dog's anatomy is more illuminating as to the correct character and temperament than the positioning of the tail and the way it is held.

Another of Mr. John Lowe's champion Smooths, Ch. Lanneau Jewel.

Fox Terrier, Wire

Mrs. A. Dallison's Ch. Gosmore Kirkmoor Craftsman, who holds the record number of C.C.s in his breed and was dog of the year, all breeds, in Britain in 1969. He was handled by Vincent Mitchell.

history and development

There can be few more widespread and popular dogs than the Wire Fox Terrier. It might even be said to have replaced the Bulldog as England's national breed. Compared with many other breeds, the Wire Fox Terrier has a short history. That it has established itself so quickly is due not only to its looks, but also to its character. The nobility, elegance and beauty of the breed can hardly be surpassed. Its character and temperament is reflected in its appearance and the Wire of today is a living monument to the world's greatest breeder nation. Small wonder, therefore, that when Wires change hands the highest prices are paid.

The origin of the Wire Fox Terrier is obscure. The original short-legged dog was probably a black-and-tan with a patch of white. It would have been a game dog, quick with rats and eager for battle in fox or badger earth. It would have been small but sturdy, tough, with great powers of endurance; able to keep up with the huntsmen and to fight to the death. Such qualities are evident today in the modern Terrier, both working and show strains.

The breed first came to the fore in the middle of the 19th century when the Terriers became an integral part of the foxhound pack, being sent down after the fox when it went to earth. Articles on terriers were comparatively late appearing in the reference books.

The name "Fox Terrier" for a long time covered all types of terrier used to drive the fox from his underground lair (terra (lat.) earth). The breed went first by the name of "English Terrier"; later it was known as "Parson Russell Terrier". The Rev. John Russell was the first to really begin breeding for a purpose; but the Wire must not be confused with the present-day Jack Russell, a hunt terrier, which is not recognized as a pure breed.

The first Wire Fox Terriers to be shown appeared in "any variety classes", and it was ten years before they achieved a class of their own. The breed grew fastest in popularity in the years before World War II. when 6,000 to 7,000 specimens were registered with the Kennel Club, a higher number than for any other breed. Since then the number of registrations has fallen gradually to the present-day figure of about 2,000 annually.

Although ordinary breeding presents no problems, breeding of good Wire Fox Terriers is a very different matter. Competition is strong and without a knowledge both of the breed and pedigree, it is hopeless to try. The breed has generally been protected from the disabling hereditary diseases with the result that Wire Fox Terriers today are a thoroughbred, healthy breed.

color

White should predominate; brindle, red, liver or slaty blue are objectionable. Otherwise, color is of little or no importance.

care

The Wire is a robust dog requiring little special attention apart from daily brushing of his coat. One should not forget, however, to thin the hair inside the ears now and again to avoid the tendency to eczema.

In order to preserve the noble features unspoiled, most breeders do not allow their dogs to chew bones. That the dogs only get finely prepared food to eat can, however, affect the natural cleaning of the teeth, which must, therefore, be inspected once in a while, and cleaned if necessary to prevent decay and infected gums.

If Terriers do not have sufficient exercise on a hard surface their toe-nails become very long and will need attention; the toe-nails should be kept short, otherwise the foot becomes open and spreading, instead of being round and compact.

The Wire needs trimming. His coat consists of two layers, a long-haired layer and a softer undercoat. If one is only keeping the Fox Terrier as a pet, stripping of the outer-coat is necessary four times a year. Everyone can learn to strip his own pet dog so that he always looks neat.

On the other hand, if showing is the aim much experience and many years patient learning will be required. Some of the best hours spent with the Wire can be those preparing him for showing. Others who have really first-class dogs frequently leave preparation for shows to professionals who, especially in England, have much success in keeping their clients' dogs in top form throughout the long showing season. It is particularly in this field of Wires that many professionals are to be found whose skill has without doubt been an important factor in creating the

Another Westminster terrier group winner, again handled by Jimmy Butler, and this time in 1958 – Mrs. Munro W. Lanier's Ch. Emprise Sensational.

445

special interest the general public always has in the breed at shows.

character

A friendly and placid nature is the Wires most outstanding quality. Always good-tempered, he is eager to play and is full of lively pranks. Perhaps a little restless at times, but on the other hand, he loves to be petted in the relaxed atmosphere of the family. He is dependable, quick and willing to learn and comparatively easy to train; good with children, he is gentle but nevertheless on his guard with strangers. He is by no means afraid of a fight, lacking only that prudence to choose an antagonist of his own size; he will tackle anything. In short Wire Fox Terriers have the terrier's "fighting and never-give-up spirit".

Jimmy Butler handled this best-in-show winner at Westminster in 1966, Ch. Zeloy Mooremaides Magic, owned by Mrs. Marion Bunker. Magic was a daughter of Ch. Zeloy Emperor.

The outstanding sire in Britain since the War is Mr. E. Robinson's Ch. Zeloy Emperor. At the beginning of 1970 he had twenty-three champions to his credit. He was also a best-in-show winner at championship shows.

Originally used only for digging, Wires are now primarily kept either as pets or showing dogs. Over the years the modern Wire has increased in size, so that today it is doubtful whether he could get down a fox's earth.

standards

General Appearance: The dog must present a general gay, lively and active appearance; bone and strength in a small compass are essentials, but this must not be taken to mean that a Fox Terrier should be cloddy, or in any way coarse; speed and endurance must be looked to as well as power, and the symmetry of the Foxhound taken as a model.

The Terrier, like the Hound, must on no account be leggy, nor must he be too short in the leg. He should stand like a cleverly made hunter, covering a lot of ground, yet with a short back. He will then attain the highest degree of propelling power, together with the greatest length of stride that is compatible with the length of his body.

Mrs. Dallison's Ch. Gosmore Kirkmoor Tessa, who is the top bitch C.C. winner in the breed in Britain. Winning reserve best-in-show at Cruft's in 1964, she was also a championship best-in-show winner in 1963 amd 1964 – again handled by Vincent Mitchell.

447

Kirkmoor is a prefix which appears often among outstanding Wires. The owner, Mr. Billy Mitchell, was also one of the best professional handlers in Britain, and is Vincent Mitchell's father. This dog, Mrs. Dallison's American and English Ch. Gosmore Kirkmoor Storm, was a top winner on both sides of the Atlantic; Storm is another of Ch. Zeloy Emperor's sons.

This dog, Ch. Crackwyn Cockspur, owned by Bob Barlow, in partnership with Mr. Gill, won best-in-show at Cruft's in 1962. He was later an outstanding winner on the Continent.

Mr. J. Stephenson's Ch. Madam Moonraker, an outstanding bitch of the early fifties.

His head should be long and lean, with much strength in front of his eyes, which should be small and dark, and full of the pride of life.

His ears should be small and like a "V" set high on his head.

His neck should be long and arched, his shoulders should slope back, and should also be long.

His forelegs should be straight, round and thick; the hind legs strong but reachy, the hocks should be near the ground and the feet should be small and round, with thick pads.

His body should have a deep but not broad chest, with ribs making round rather than flat sides; the back should be short and level, and the loins strong and firm.

His tail should spring from the top, rather than the back of the body; it must be docked; neither thin nor curved, but stout, and carried up straight.

Weight and size: A full-sized dog should not exceed $15\frac{1}{2}''$ at the withers – the bitch being proportionately lower. A dog should scale 18 lbs. in show condition – a bitch weighing some 2 lbs. less – with a margin of 1 lb. either way.

Mrs. N. Vasser's Ch. Miss Skylight won her 35th terrier group in the U.S.A. in 1960. Bred in Ireland, Miss Skylight was imported into the U.S.A. by Mr. Anton Rost.

German Hunt Terrier

Sharp and alert, the German Hunt Terrier.

The Deutsche Jagdterrier or German Hunt Terrier is, as the name implies, a sporting dog which will hunt its quarry in the open or follow it to earth and will retrieve small game from land or water. It is a convenient size for town and the automobile but needs plenty of exercise. With an innate sense of danger, it is apprehensive of strangers.

The skull is flat and wide between the ears, rather like that of a Fox Terrier and falls from between the eyes, without any pronounced stop, to the muzzle. The distance between the occiput and the stop is slightly greater than that of the foreface. It has prominent cheeks with strong lower jaw and very strong teeth which meet evenly. The nose is black, but brown is equally acceptable if the principal color of the coat is brown. Ears, not too small, V-shaped and set high.

The well-muscled shoulders are sloping and the legs straight. The back is straight but not too short; chest wide and deep with muscular loins. The docked tail, well set on a long croup, is carried horizontally.

The coat is smooth, close and harsh and is never clipped. Principal color is black. Gray-black mixed or dark brown with lighter tints of brown, red or golden on the eyebrows, muzzle, chest and legs. Either a lighter or darker mask is acceptable. A little white on the chest or between the toes is permissible.

Height to the withers should not exceed 16".

Glen of Imaal Terrier

A typical Glen of Imaal Terrier

This is an Irish breed, officially recognized by the Irish Kennel Club in 1933 and first appearing in the show ring in the following year. It originated in County Wicklow, in the Glen of Imaal, from which comes its name.

Bred and used as a tough, working terrier, it has many of the characteristics of larger breeds. Its courage is proverbial; used against badger and fox (and for fighting other dogs), it is silent when working even when, within the sett, it faces the badger.

The Glen of Imaal is still not so much a show dog as a working terrier, and the Glen of Imaal Terrier Club holds trials over badger in its natural earth, awarding a certificate (the Teastas Misneac) for "dead gameness".

The Glen of Imaal, despite his gameness, has an affectionate nature, is good with children, and becomes closely attached to his owner.

He is a heavily-boned dog, strong and enduring, with a wide chest, powerful loins and hindquarters. He should stand not more than 14" and weigh up to 35 lbs., bitches less in each case.

The skull is strong; drop ears set-on high. The eyes are brown, and well-spaced, and have an intelligent expression.

The legs are rather short, with great bone, the front legs slightly bent and well-developed for digging. The tail is docked and carried gaily.

The coat is harsh, but not wiry; blue, blue and tan, or wheaten.

Irish Terrier

history and development

Records of the Irish Terrier's background are sparse. Early Greek writers mention a terrier of Great Britain which had apparently been cultivated for many generations and which was not found elsewhere in Europe, and there is direct evidence that a breed of "wire-haired" black and tan terriers existed in Britain over 200 years ago and were used for fox and otter hunting and for destroying vermin.

The Welsh Terrier fanciers claim this terrier as the progenitor of their breed. Such terriers were also found in the Westmorland hills, but these were shorter on the leg, and have since been accepted as Lakeland Terriers. This old wire-haired black and tan terrier also was concerned in the origin of the Irish Terrier; and there were around Cork and Ballymena in Ireland, a larger strain of wheaten terrier, which also played a part, a much racier type with longer legs and all one color.

The confirmation of these early breed influences was seen among the early show Irish Terriers, when litters commonly contained some black and tan puppies. At the Dublin show in 1874, there were classes for both large and small Irish Terriers – over 9 lbs. and under 9 lbs. – all pointers to the fact that these terrier ancestors were primary contributors to the breed type of today's Irish Terrier.

A big winner of the early thirties was Ch. Solid Man, bred by Mr. J. Gilmer in 1928 and owned by Mr. F. Calvert Butler. In Britain he won thirteen C.C.s in 1931, '32 and '33.

Mrs. E. M. B. Moore's Ch. Russetone O'Shaunessy, born in 1944. He sired eleven champions and did a tremendous amount for the breed.

This head of Pathfinders Hoopla epitomizes the required points.

The advent of dog shows saw the commencement of the first specialist club for the breed, which was formed in 1879. The following year the members pioneered against the cropping of ears, which campaign we know spread to a number of other breeds, and eventually the practice was banned, but it took ten years before the Kennel Club decreed that there should be no cropping of the ears of any breed in the British Isles. The following years brought the height of the Irish Terrier's popularity, with large show entries, and high prices were paid for the top winning dogs and bitches.

The Irish Terrier is a good breed for a novice owner to take up, whether as a show dog or as a companion. As an exhibition dog there is no other breed of terrier in which competition is so open or where the novice has so good a chance of winning. The established breeders are delighted to welcome all newcomers and give them as much help and advice as possible.

color

Whole colored red, red wheaten or golden; a small patch of white on chest is permissible but not desirable.

care

The Irish Terrier must be trimmed smartly for showing, and even those which are kept as pets need stripping several times a year. However considerable damage can be done to its coat if it is clipped with shears or cut with scissors. This is the cause of the coat losing color and also becoming soft and silky. The wire hair should be trimmed with fingers and thumb or with a trimming tool that is not sharp and which will not cut the hair. Most breeders are prepared to help with advice in this matter. The Terrier needs good grooming regularly and it will then keep clean.

It is a very hardy dog, healthy and easy to feed; an adult requires only one meat and biscuit meal per day, and a dry hard dog biscuit to gnaw at.

An Irish Terrier carrying so much that is not wanted – head lacking quality, short neck, tail not set on top, creating a poor topline, straight hindquarters, and an obvious linty coat.

character

Irish Terriers have outstanding loyalty and very good memories. They are always very willing and responsive to training, and try hard to please. They are great sporting Terriers and quite a number have been trained to the gun and many have taken obedience training with success. They are naturally ideal as pets as they are very good with children, and make excellent guard dogs. They enjoy traveling in cars.

standards

The Irish Terrier should be alert, quick and keen. Character is indicated by the expression of the eyes and by the carriage of ears and tail.

The head should be long, the skull flat and narrow between the ears. Strong punishing foreface, small, keen, dark eyes and small V-shaped ears, set well on the skull, pointing to the eyes. The skull should be the same length as the foreface, with little stop. The neck should be long and set into a well-sloping shoulder. The front narrow with a deep chest and a moderately long body. The loin should be firm and strong with tail set on top. The legs should be moderately long with good round bone and the feet round and compact. The hindquarters should be strong and well developed with good bend of stifle so that the Terrier moves soundly. Teeth should be level, not overshot or undershot. Nose black. The coat is very important. The desired texture on the body is crisp and wiry. On the foreface and legs (furnishings) it should be a little longer, but still coarse and wiry. Any soft or linty hair is undesirable.

The picture required is that of quality, giving a clear impression of a racy Terrier and not that of a red Fox Terrier or small Airedale.

The question of size has always varied, going up and down, but judging by weight alone is, of course, unsatisfactory. What is important is to maintain a clear picture of type and quality with a good, gay temperament showing that spark of fire.

The A.K.C. Standard calls for a dog to be 27 lbs., a bitch 25 lbs. Height at shoulder should be approximately 18″.

A promising Irish Terrier puppy.

Kerry Blue Terrier

Top winning dog in the U.S.A. in 1968, Ch. Melbee's Chances Are, by U.S. and Canadian Ch. Tregoad's Vicky's Victor ex Ch. Kerryglens Nan-c-Lin. The winner of many groups, and sire of champions. Owner Mrs. Melvin Schlesinger.

Ch. Acquire Best Blue, born 1948, by S.A. Ch. Tanjax Red Ticket ex Milady O'Brunner. He won twenty-five C.C.s and sired several champions. Owned by Mr. P. Ledeboer.

history and development

The Kerry Blue comes from the South and West of Ireland, and natives of the region maintain that the Blue has been a pure strain for at least 150 years. In England they were benched at Cruft's for the first time in 1922, when the Kerry Blue Terrier Club was also formed and the official Standard was devised; it was not until 1959 that this same Standard was adopted in America. However the first Kerry was registered by the A.K.C. in 1922 and shown at Westminster that year. The Kerry was a dog for work and for sport – they kept sheep and cattle, drew otter and badger, were indefatigable ratters, and they also retrieved well to hand, and from water! Originally they were rough and unkempt, and trimming was discouraged; except for grooming and bathing they were shown rough.

Introduced into England around 1920, it was Mrs. Casey Hewitt, owner of the Munster prefix, who persuaded show secretaries to put on classes for this rough-looking terrier.

The 1920's was a great decade for Kerries. In 1922 the Misses Henry were showing at Cruft's the litter brother of Ch. Brachill of Bailey. Miss Green had just acquired Martells Sapphire Beauty, the first English Champion.

Captain Watts Williams imported several dogs, including an important sire Ch. Joe of Leysfield, and he also owned Charley's Aunt and Rose, both of Leysfield, also future champions. Also in 1922 a dog called Nofa Jacobin was imported by Mrs. Keane Franks; he became a champion and later, with the entire Franks Kennel, was sold to Miss Paton.

Another import into England from Ireland was Tasha of the Chevin, ancestress of all the wonderful champions bred before the Second World War by Miss Toft in her famous Chevin Kennels. Between 1922 and into the 1930's many excellent kennels were established in England – Ben Edar, Breezehurst, Chevin, Martells, Princeton, Bog, O'Rom, Muircroft, Underbridge, Lisdhu, Overport, Lisnalea, Playfoots, Downsview and Arun, all with winners and champions to their credit up to the beginning of the 1939 war.

Exports from England began around 1924, chiefly to America and these, together with exports from Ireland, formed the basis of the breed in America. These were later supplemented with other well-known Irish and English winners, and the American Kerries have developed to become just as important as the English. The breed is known in almost every country of the world. The chief strongholds, apart from America and Canada, are Germany, Holland and Norway. France made a good start but has fallen away, although one of the two remaining kennels, that of Madame Caranobe, produced the great winner International Ch. Right Blue Black. Australia is a comparative late-comer, imported its first pair in the early 1930's.

Since the second World War, the Kerry has become even more popular; its non-shedding coat and handy size make it an easy breed to keep in small houses. Demand now exceeds supply, and exports from England have doubled. Type has become more even and temperament with it. Since 1945 three Kerries have won best in shows at Championship Shows, Mrs. Littlefield's Ch. Bemel Larrikin, the late Mrs. Dunlop's Ch. Sherwyn Strongbow and Miss Ashworth's Ch. Rownhams Czarina.

color

Kerry pups are born black. The blue color comes later, showing at any time after six or seven months; but many do not turn blue until well over a year old, and not clear in color even then. Sometimes the color grows in under the thick, black coat and is suddenly there when the dog is first trimmed. At other times, there is a rusty transition stage and continual tipping-off brings the blue to the surface.

care

There is a lot of hard work in keeping a Kerry coat in good order, brushing with a stiff brush and a strong, medium toothed metal comb, combing right down to the skin to remove tangles. A monthly bath for the pet, and more often for the show dog, using softened water. Rinsing thoroughly in softened water is essential, followed by a thorough rub down, and drying in warm conditions. When dry, brush and comb well, and you should have a lovely, shiny, silky blue coat. Show dogs should be trimmed, bathed, groomed, and trimmed again to leave a tailored look; and if necessary another bath two days before the show, and a final snipping off of odd hairs. The Kerry has an excellent appetite and is easy to feed, following standard weight-for-age quantities and standard ingredients.

Ch. Overport Liffey of Lisdhu, born 1945, by Arun Beaufighter ex Bemel Blue Buttercup. He is the sire of seven English champions. Owner and breeder Miss B. Parry.

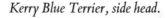

Kerry Blue Terrier, side head.

Kerry Blue, from the front.

455

Kerry Blue Terrier puppy.

Ch. Downsview Double Choice, born 1961. Owned and bred by Miss G. Smith.

A fairly recent creation, and reputedly without the typical terrier hunting instinct – the Kromfohrlander, from Germany.

character

I remember seeing a dog in Tipperary in 1922 which was a "great fighting champion". He beat all opposition yet he ran around loose, behaving like any decent country dog. He would fight only at the right time and place. Kerries have been known to be aggressive to other dogs when on lead, but to ignore them when loose. They respond to firm but kindly training, and develop the usual canine attachment to their owners but, perhaps, their's can be described as a more loving nature than most dogs, and more affectionate.

standards

Size is the one exception to a general international Standard for Kerry Blue Terriers. In those countries where champions are determined by a system of points awards to group winners, that is in Australia, Canada and America, a slightly greater height is allowed than in the English Standard. Against the English standard height of 18″ up to 19″, the countries allowing larger dogs give up to 19½″, with outstanding specimens in other respects being allowed up to 20″ in America or 21″ in other countries.

In America the rule regarding color is more strictly enforced, variations being permitted only up to eighteen months. Closer trimming is allowed in America, more hair is taken off the legs for instance. The late Edwin "Pop" Sayres handled many of the greatest ever shown in the U.S.A. and is credited as the originator of the trim that made the breed popular in the show ring.

Weight in America is 33 to 40 lbs. and in England 33 to 37 lbs.

Kromfohrlander

There are three types of this German dog, which has been created since the First World War; the Short rough-haired, the Rough-haired and the Long rough-haired; used mainly as companion and guard dog.

It is a dog of medium height, between 15″ and 18″ for both dogs and bitches, and somewhat longer in body than the height to the withers. It is an elegant and strongly built dog, and makes a loyal and affectionate companion as well as an excellent watchdog.

The ears are set high and are triangular in shape with the ends rounded. Of medium size, they lie flat to the head, but ears folding down somewhat to the side are also allowable.

The tail, of medium length, is strong at the root and tapers gradually towards the tip. It is carried slightly curved; it may be slightly ringed.

The coat is always rough, varying in length among the three types, and has a dense and impervious undercoat.

The basic color is white with light brown to strong dark-brown markings on the head and ears (these markings should be as uniform as possible) and body markings of various shades of brown in large spots. Saddle markings are preferably broken. Black is not acceptable.

Lakeland Terrier

In the sixties Lakelands scored one success after another in the championship best in show rings in Britain. Most successful handler was undoubtedly Mr. Albert Langley, who handled Mrs. Neal's Ch. Stargazer of Dartvale when winning best in show at the Three Counties show in 1965.

history and development

It is doubtful if anyone knows exactly how the Lakeland Terrier was developed but it is generally thought the Border Terrier, the Bedlington and the Fox Terrier were used in its formation. The breed was originally known by various names, among them Patterdale, Cumberland and Fell Terrier. When the breed was recognized by the Kennel Club in England in 1928 the name Lakeland was adopted instead of the names of the various districts they came from.

The earliest recorded information about the breed appeared in a Cumberland newspaper in the obituary of Tommy Dobson, a famous huntsman of the period. It says: "His favorites were the game little terriers which he bred so successfully and for which he was specially noted. These terriers are most necessary for bolting a fox once it gets to ground in the screes and boulders which cover the Fell sides." Tommy was Master of the Eskdale and Ennerdale Foxhounds for a record fifty-three years and was almost as well known as the famous John Peel. It was thought by many that he evolved these terriers from the Old English Hard-Haired Black and Tan Terrier, now extinct, with a touch of Bedlington for intensifying its gameness.

The old type of Lakeland was much different from those shown today. Leggier and lighter in body, minus the profuse hair furnishings, they looked what they were – real varminty workers. Possessing a bark out of

Compare this picture of Mr. and Mrs. M. B. Jordan's Ch. Susan of Shotover, a winner of the late thirties, with the modern Lakeland and notice the leggier, harder type which was then being shown.

457

Top dog! Top shows! Best in show both at Cruft's in London and Westminster, New York, a record held by Mr. and Mrs. Postlethwaite's Ch. Stingray of Derrybah. In England handled by Mr. Langley and in America by Mr. Peter Green.

all proportion to their size, they would go to earth after their quarry and remain there until the fox or badger was bolted or dug out.

Local shows, which were generally combined with Hound Trails, were held in the Lake District of England, and these little terriers were usually scheduled as "Colored Working Terriers", and were often judged by the local huntsmen.

In 1921 the Lakeland Terrier Association was formed with the Earl of Lonsdale as President, an office he held for many years. His own kennel housed many animals with pedigrees going back nearly seventy years. The Association drew up a Standard and, based on this, breeders began seriously to breed them more to one type. They were first seen outside their native county in 1928, when the Kennel Club included them in their show at the old Crystal Palace in London. Only three appeared, all owned by Mr. Paisley of Keswick, one of the top breeders. The following year saw a better entry and they continued to increase until 1931 when Challenge Certificates were on offer. The first two were won by Mr. Tweedie's Evergreen's Double and Mrs. Graham Spence's Egton Lady of the Lake. Mr. J. J. Crellin, another leading British breeder, owned a dog at that time called Crab of Wastwater, and this dog was a pillar of the breed and his name features in the pedigrees of many of today's famous dogs.

color

The most popular color is red grizzle but there is a wide variation of shadings. Black and tan is another popular color but the tan must be pale, and the rich chestnut color of the Welsh Terrier is frowned upon. Self-red is fairly common and there have been many champions of this attractive color. Blue and tan is a color which, although permissible, is not so well received in the show ring, due probably to the fact that the texture of the coat is not so hard and wiry as in some of the other colors. Liver and tan is permitted but it is genetically virtually impossible to breed a black nose and dark eye in specimens of this color and they are rarely seen in the show ring. In some of the Scandinavian countries self-blacks are exhibited, but I doubt if ever one has been seen in Britain, and serious breeders are at a loss to know how this color came about.

care

The trimming of the Lakeland for the show ring has reached a high peak of perfection, which has enabled him to win best in show awards at several of the larger championship shows. Twice in the last few years representatives of this breed have won the supreme best in show award at the greatest of all dog shows – Cruft's in London. Yet it is fairly easy to keep a Lakeland in tidy condition if the usual care is taken with its daily grooming. Periodically it is advisable to have the dog stripped and trimmed and while, to obtain the best results, it is best to have this done by someone used to the job, a great deal of pleasure can be had by the owner in doing the work himself.

In 1964 in Britain it was Mr. S. Thorne's Ch. Hensington Carefree who was winning best in show awards. The handler was again Mr. Langley.

character

The Lakeland makes an ideal companion and family dog. He is just the size for children, being neither too large to handle nor too small to join in their sometimes boisterous games. He settles down to living in the house and behaves with perfect manners. He is not prone to damaging the furniture if left alone as some breeds do. As a guard he excels, for with his big loud bark and fearless temperament he is a great deterrent to an intruder.

As a show dog he has won great popularity in many countries, particularly in the U.S.A. where top honors have been gained. British-bred stock is eagerly sought after the world over, and there is a wide market for top class Lakelands.

standards

The British Standard is universally adopted, with very minor alterations, and it is worth noting that top winning dogs from Britain are exported all over the world, and so closely do they conform to the other countries' Standards of Points that they continue their successful careers in the countries of their adoption.

In general appearance, the Standards have it that the Lakeland should be "smart and workmanlike, with gay fearless demeanor". As you would expect from an animal which is so well adapted, by temperament and build, for the terrier's real work, the jaws must be powerful and the muzzle broad, but not too long. The teeth should close scissor-fashion, that is, the top teeth should fit closely over the lower – all this making a truly formidable armament against his traditional enemy, vermin.

Strong features are his fore and hindquarters, well adapted for digging – shoulders well laid back, with straight, well-boned forelegs; hindquarters strong and muscular with long and powerful thighs, the straight hocks low to the ground. The feet small, compact, round and well padded. His coat should be dense, harsh and with good undercoat; completely weather resisting. The tail carried "gaily" but not curled over the back. He should weigh around 17 lbs. (bitches 15 lbs.) and should not exceed 14½″ at the shoulder.

If your desire is a dog bred to the Standard, you should not be too happy if his head is too long, his ears are set on the top of his head, or his eyes are slanting, for these are faults.

Lakeland Terrier

Lakeland Terrier – side head.

One of the top terriers in Scandinavia in 1968 was Ch. Chadfield Cockspur, bred by Mr. F. Chadwick and owned by Dr. Johan H. Friderichsen and Mrs. Jeanette Chantelou.

Manchester Terrier

Mrs. R. A. Knight's Ch. Eaglespur Jester, a great dog both in the show ring and at stud. He is one of the many successful offspring of Eaglespur Gwinny Willows Thunderstorm, imported into Britain from America.

history and development

Originally there appear to have been two distinct colorings and coats in the terrier group – white or black-and-tan, smooth or rough coated. As long ago as 1800 the Black-and-Tan Terrier, later known as the Manchester Terrier, appears in an illustration in Sydenham Edwards' book *Cynographia Britannica*.

The Black-and-Tan Terrier seems to have found favor as a dog for killing rats. In due time this became a sport and bets were placed on the time taken to kill a given number of rats. The celebrated terrier, Billy, was matched to kill a hundred rats in eight minutes, a feat he achieved in six minutes thirty-two seconds.

There was a breed, the English White Terrier now extinct, largely because of a tendency to deafness, which very closely resembled the Black-and-Tan Terrier. This appears to have been a white form of the Black-and-Tan Terrier, the build, stance and general appearance being the same.

At the first all-breeds dog show held in Birmingham, England in 1860, the Black-and-Tan Terrier was the only terrier to have a class to itself, which indicates that it was already an established breed. As early as 1862, classes were divided according to weight, 5 lbs., 7 lbs., 9 lbs., and over 11 lbs., so from this date we can pick out the English Toy Terrier (Black-and-Tan) which is the miniature of the breed and which is now classed as a Toy. From 1864, there were classes for dogs with uncut ears but, normally, ears were cropped to make the ear stand erect, no doubt a remnant of the days when, if the ear was allowed to hang naturally, the rat could sink its teeth in and hold on.

In the late 1800's, many dogs were exported from Britain to Canada, and the United States of America and later to Germany. It is probable that those dogs sent to Germany were used in the make up of the Dobermann Pinscher. Among notable British dogs and bitches sent to Canada and the States were Nettle, Salford and almost certainly Champion Vortigern, as his son Lever is the first Black-and-Tan Terrier to be registered in the American Kennel Club Stud Book in 1887.

In 1895 ear cropping was banned in Great Britain and the heavier ears became unfashionable. The thinner, lighter ear which turned over to present an alert terrier became popular. The name of the breed was changed to Manchester Terrier in 1924, possibly because there were a great many fanciers in the Manchester district. In Canada and the U.S.A. the breed seems to have gained popularity and is now better known than in England. In the U.S.A. Toys and Standards may be bred together. The two varieties have a combined total of 920 registrations, but the vast majority were Toys.

After the last World War three American dogs were brought in to infuse British dogs with new blood lines. These dogs were Branley's Scaramouche, Eaglespur Sir Oscar of Chatham Farms and Eaglespur Gwinny Willows Thunderstorm.

Whelped in 1957, Mrs. Knight's Ch. Eaglespur Allspice, by Sorisdale Excalibur ex Jill of Entertane, won his first C.C. as a puppy. He was still winning in 1962, proving himself to be a laster.

color

The only acceptable color for a Manchester Terrier is black-and-tan. The coat must be free of any other colored hairs and markings must conform to the Standards.

care

Manchesters are lively, alert terriers and although they enjoy going for long walks, they can exercise themselves in quite a small space if they have someone or something to play with. Most Manchesters seem to dislike rain but, if they do go out in it, they must be rubbed down afterwards; this is necessary because of their fine, short coat. They keep themselves very clean and, provided the diet is suitable, their coats need little attention. Coat condition is usually the first indication of a dog's health.

Manchesters are very attractive little dogs equally at home in town or country. They seem to live to a good age and are active all their lives.

The Manchester Terrier – front head view.

character

The Manchester is a typical terrier – alert, aloof when it pleases him to be so, very quick on the uptake, sometimes stubborn, especially dogs, who also seem quite distant at times even to their owners, but this may be just a game. They are very good house dogs and are good with children if they have been brought up with them.

They are dogs that respond usually only to one owner or their owner's family, but many will tolerate people of the same sex as their owner to the almost total exclusion of the opposite sex. The Manchester is still a game little dog often tackling rats and other animals such as badgers, cats and hedgehogs. Once they have their quarry they will usually worry

Mrs. Knight's Aprilla is one of the attractive daughters by Ch. Allspice.

it to death even though they may be quite badly cut and torn themselves. Their favorite method of killing rats is to grab the rat's shoulders with their teeth and toss it over their back, breaking the rat's back with a sudden upwards toss.

Manchesters can run very fast and have the ability to change direction, almost like "turning on a sixpence", when in full chase.

standards

The dog should be compact in appearance with good bone and free from any resemblance to the Whippet.

It has a long head, flat in skull and narrow, level and wedge-shaped, without showing cheek muscles; well filled up under the eyes with tapering, tight-lipped jaws.

Its eyes are small, dark and sparkling, almond in shape, set close in the head, not prominent; and the ears are small and V-shaped, carried well above the top line of the head and hanging close to the head above the eyes. Forequarters; The shoulders should be clean and well sloped. The chest narrow and deep. The forelegs must be quite straight, set on well under the body, and of proportionate length to the body, which is short with well-sprung ribs, slightly reached and well cut up behind the ribs.

The hind legs should be neither cow-hocked nor the feet turned in and they should be well bent at the stifle, with feet small, semi-harefooted, and strong with well-arched toes.

The tail is short and set-on where the arch of the back ends, thick where it joins the body and tapering to a point; carried not higher than the level of the back.

The coat is close, smooth, short and glossy, of a firm texture. Coloring on the head; the muzzle to be tanned to the nose, nose and nasal bone jet black. There should be a small tan spot on each cheek and above each eye, the underjaw and throat to be tanned with a distinct tan V. The legs from the knee downwards to be tanned except for the toes which are pencilled with black, and a distinct black mark (thumb mark) immediately above the feet. Inside the hind legs tanned but divided with black at the stifle joint. Under the tail tanned, the vent tanned but as narrow as possible so that it is covered by the tail. A slight tan mark on each side of the chest. Tan outside the hind legs, commonly called breeching, is a defect. In all cases the division between colors shall be clearly defined. Size: desired height at shoulders, 15" to 16" dogs; 14" to 15" bitches.

In the U.S.A. a Standard Manchester is disqualified if he is over 22 lbs. or under 12 lbs.; if classes are divided, 12 to 16 lbs. and 16 to 22 lbs. are suggested. The weights for the Toy variety are 7 lbs. and under, or over 7 lbs. and not over 12 lbs.

Norfolk Terrier

The most successful Norfolk in Britain has undoubtedly been Miss Hazeldine's Ch. Ickworth Ready, who won the Terrier group at the Scottish Kennel Club show in 1969, and reserve best Terrier at Windsor in 1968. A beautiful type dog, having exceptional balance and quality, he is also proving a first class sire.

history and development

The Norfolk Terrier was, until September 1964, the drop-eared Norwich Terrier and its development and early history can be read under this heading in the chapter on the Norwich Terrier. Breeders in the 1930's found that the crossing of the two types of ear carriage led to doubtful ear carriage in the progeny, so they started breeding to one type of ear carriage only. The prick-ears were then numerically stronger and later, during the war, the drop-ears nearly died out, but due to the determination of Miss Macfie of the Colonsays, they were kept going until a few breeders took them up in the mid forties. Every single puppy born in Britain traces back to Colonsay breeding.

The breeding of two separate types of ear carriage almost immediately caused dissention in the breeders. The drop-ears usually registered more each year and gave equal support at most shows, but won fewer of the major awards than the prick-ears.

By the end of the first post-war decade, the prick-ears had made twenty-eight new champions and the drop-ears had only a quarter of that number. In 1957 a referendum of the breed club members found ninety-two in favor of separation and only eleven against. The English Kennel Club was approached and asked to give separate registers for the two types, but this was refused. In 1963, the Norwich Terrier Club submitted separate Standards for each type to the Kennel Club and, in September 1964, the Kennel Club agreed to separate breeds, not separate varieties of the Norwich, and so the Norfolk Terrier was born. Although in the export to most countries the Norfolk Terrier keeps its new name, those which are exported to the U.S.A. revert to the name of Norwich Terrier, since the separation into two breeds is not accepted in America.

The Norfolk Terrier, side and front head views.

A champion Norfolk Terrier, Ch. Nanfan Noctis

color

The Norfolk Terrier comes in many shades of red and black-and-tan. Grizzle is also an accepted color but is rarely seen. In the main, the red ones are a mid-red, although there are quite a number of deep red ones which are much preferred by most breeders. Very light red occasionally occurs. Black-and-tan is not as common as red; in fact, until the late fifties, it was rarely seen. After the introduction of a black-and-tan dog, Hunston Holy Smoke, as a stud dog, that color has slowly taken hold and in 1970, for the first time, a black-and-tan won a Challenge Certificate.

care

The Norfolk is a very hardy little dog and does not need any special care. It can take an unlimited amount of exercise, but can also manage just as well with a run in the park twice a day. Norfolks should not be over-trimmed, but they should have their coats tidied before being shown, particular attention being paid to the top of the head, (which should be short and smooth); by taking long hairs off the elbows and round the feet, and by making the tail and hindquarters neat and tidy looking. In England, Norfolks are shown naturally, on a loose lead; handlers who hold their dog's tail and head in position being frowned upon.

Norfolks are great climbers and it is no use putting them in a run or kennel with low sides, as they will be out as fast as they are put in. I have seen them climb six-foot netting with great ease.

Miss Hazeldine's Ch. Ickworth Prim'n Proper, a daughter of Ch. Ready, had a most successful show career in 1970.

character

The Norfolk has terrific energy; so much that it is nearly impossible to tire it and yet, with its ready-to-please, adaptable nature, it will settle quite happily with you whatever the surroundings. It is a very sporting breed, especially when it comes to rough hedgerow hunting for rats and rabbits. Many have been trained to flush game and they can have surprisingly tender mouths.

As family pets, they are ideal, happy, intelligent little dogs and excellent with children so long as children are good with them. They are not on the whole a noisy breed, but will give warning – day or night – of strange sounds or people. They are generally easy going little terriers, getting on well with people and other dogs, seldom starting a fight but, if pushed into one, will give a good account of themselves.

standards

There are so far only two Standards, one recognized by the English Kennel Club and the other by the American Kennel Club. These vary very little, the American being based on the English Standards. One big difference in the American Standard is that they are still under the name of Norwich Terrier with both prick and drop-ears being allowed. However, the American Kennel Club stamps the registration certificate either P.E. or D.E., showing that two types are allowed. Many breeders in other countries are members of the English Norfolk Terrier Club.

The Norfolk should be a stuffy, stocky little terrier, short in back and leg, broad and slightly rounded in skull with good width between the ears, good stop, muzzle shorter than the overall length of skull (the American Standard pays particular attention to this point, asking that the muzzle should be strong but not long or heavy), with dark eyes. The neck should be short (although the English Standard asks for a slightly greater length), the shoulders well laid back, the stuffy appearance coming from the heavy ruff which a Norfolk in full coat should carry. The ideal height at the withers is 10″. The Standard also asks for good bone and substance.

Ch. Nanfan Noctis comes from one of the leading Norfolk kennels, owned by Mrs. J. A. Taylor. Noctis is a small bitch excelling in breed type. Notice her particularly neat ears.

Norwich Terrier

A thoroughly typical Norwich dog showing excellent conformation without titivating for show. International Ch. Ragus Rain Maker, bred by Mrs. G. B. Marks and Mrs. M. Bunting, had a successful show career in Britain and America.

history and development

In the last century there was a strong trend all over the British Isles to develop local strains of terriers specially suited for work in the particular type of country in which they lived and the East Anglian strain appears to have been small and red or sandy in color.

Landseer painted a picture in 1811 called Two Dogs and one is a short-legged, sandy-colored terrier with prick-ears; a painting by Dyckman (1811–88) which hangs in the Victoria and Albert Museum in London shows an early Victorian group and, in the foreground is a little, red, drop-eared dog; an East Anglian artist named Hepper, painted a group of small, red, drop-eared terriers in 1857.

From these red East Anglian terriers, crossed at intervals with other terrier breeds, sprang the breed which was recognized in 1923 by the English Kennel Club as the Norwich Terrier. Developing through a line of small, red and black-and-tan terriers bred in Trumpington Street, Norwich, England (the early name of the breed was Trumpington Terrier), it was crossed with many other breeds in order to develop a strain suitable for working in the East Anglian countryside.

Both prick and drop-eared breeds were used in its development and, since neither could be termed "original", both were accepted. In 1964, the prick and drop-ears were divided into separate breeds (see Norfolk Terrier). In the early days of this century, a Mr. Frank Jones, Whip to the Norwich Staghounds, began to breed these small red terriers and later his puppies, now in great demand, became known as Jones Terriers and are still known by that name in some parts of the United States. They first were called Norwich Terriers when someone asked Jones the name of his dogs. Having just left the Norwich area, he said they were Norwich

The head of Ragus Robin Hood, bred by Mrs. Bunting.

Terriers.

After the First World War, a Mr. Jack Read, who lived in the Norwich area, started breeding again with his old strain which he had started pre-war, and it was from the many crosses he used that he finally bred a dog called Horstead Mick, who was one of the first Norwich Terriers to be registered with the Kennel Club. He was used extensively at stud and is in the pedigree of the majority of modern winners. Mr. Read with other breeders such as Mrs. Normandy-Rodwell and Mrs. Phyllis Fagan helped persuade the Kennel Club to register the breed and they were first shown at the Richmond Championship Show in July 1932. Challenge Certificates were first awarded in 1935, and from that time, the breed has made slow but steady progress. At Cruft's in 1970 Ch. Withalder Locksley won the Terrier Group, only the second time a Norwich had won a Group. The first to do so was Whinlatter Handsel of Waterrock, who not only won the Group at an Irish Show, but went on to win best in show all breeds.

Side head view of the Norwich Terrier.

color

The official colors of the breed are all shades of red, black-and-tan and grizzle. The red shades vary from a very deep red, which is greatly prized by many breeders, to a light shade of wheaten. One shade occurring in many lines, which trace back to Mrs. Fagan's Ch. Bigger Banger, is an orange red.

Although quite common in the early show days, the black-and-tan color disappeared for about fifteen years, but now it is again quite common. Some breeders, after the breed was first recognized, tried to ban the black-and-tan; in fact it was not allowed in the first official Standard. However, this was altered in 1935 and, from that time, the color has been accepted.

Grizzle is a red coat shot with black hairs. Terriers of this color often have a most attractive ring of black hair round their necks, looking rather like a jet necklace.

care

The Norwich is very hardy and adaptable. It should not be over-trimmed; its coat should be tidied before being shown, paying particular attention to the top of the head (which should be short and smooth); by taking long hairs off the elbows and round the feet, and by making the tail and hindquarters neat and tidy looking. Many have very sensitive skin and it is most essential that they are kept scrupulously clean, and should not be bedded on straw. They do need their dead coats removed twice a year otherwise this also can cause distressing irritation.

Major Bradshaw and Mr. Finney's Ch. Withalder Locksley, who made breed history in Britain by winning the Terrier group at Cruft's in 1970.

character

There is little or no difference in character between the Norwich and the Norfolk.

standards

Although the breed is now resident in many countries there are, so far, only two Standards, those set by the English and the American Kennel Clubs. Many of the Canadian breeders are members of both the English and American Clubs. The breed is now established in many Continental

In recent years some very good black and tans have appeared and Mrs. Marks and Mrs. Bunting's Ch. Ragus Wheatnor Raven, bred by Mrs. E. M. Barney, is an extremely good example.

Mrs. A. L. Howick's Bluecedars Trampus is a notably sound dog who combines small size with great substance. Note his good feet, and the sharp, foxy expression.

countries.

Apart from requiring the ears to be pricked, there is little difference in the English Standard between the Norwich and the Norfolk. Size, conformation, coat characteristics are the same.

Scottish Terrier

history and development

It has been said many times that the origin of the Scottish Terrier dates back several centuries. On this assumption, it is clear that if length of genealogy counts for anything at all, the Scottish Terrier is a real aristocrat in the canine world.

It is, of course, generally accepted that some other breeds of terriers have been described as "Terriers of Scotland". When one considers Scotland with its Highlands and Lowlands and unique variety of terrain, can it be questioned that a number of breeds of terriers were produced for specialized work in certain areas. Without controversy, therefore, it can be claimed that the Scottish Terrier (or Aberdeen Terrier as he was at one time described) as we know him today is descended in a direct line from terriers bred for character, pluck and determination and for a particular purpose. Notwithstanding refinements which, largely for show purposes, have crept into the breed, many Scottish Terriers of today could well do the job their ancestors were bred to do so many years ago.

As already indicated, the Scottie is not a new breed; it has established itself as a firm favorite over a long period.

color

The Standard of the breed allows for black, wheaten or brindle of any color. Many breeders find that the would-be purchasers of puppies as companions have the quite erroneous belief that a Scottish Terrier should be black. It is, in fact, generally accepted that the original color of the Scottie was brindle of various shades. In recent years several exceedingly good dogs have been produced, and reached championship status, which

A head study of a fine representative of the breed, Ch. Gosmore Eilburn Miss Hopeful.

469

An appealing study of a Scottie puppy on the brink of a show career. As the puppy's dam, Miss J. Miller's Ch. Brio Wishbone, was best in show at Chester in 1965, she has a lot to live up to.

Clive and Mabel Pilsbury's Eng. and Amer. Ch. Gosmore Eilburn Admaration, record breaking son of Ch. Kennelgarth Viking, dog of the year all breeds in Britain in 1967 in Mrs. A. Dallison's ownership, and has also had a great winning record in America.

(opposite) Miss B. Penn Bull's Ch. Kennelgarth Viking, leading sire of champions and grandsire of many more. Note the small keen eye and terrier expression. This photograph was taken when he was ten years old, and shows his great lasting qualities.

were wheaten in color. Black is very well established at the present time, although dark brindle may well be still predominant. The texture of the coat is of paramount importance. In general brindles have been considered more likely to possess the all-important double weather-resisting covering. It must be acknowledged however that the black coat has improved in density and texture to such an extent, perhaps, that in texture there is little to choose between the different colors allowed by the Standard.

care

Well reared puppies have every chance of growing into strong, healthy and happy adults. This would hardly need saying but for the fact that so many prospective purchasers often look for the cheapest obtainable. They are tempted to buy a puppy from a dealer who cares little for the vital importance of correct feeding in the early days. Such a puppy can cause much distress to a family as well as untold expenditure on veterinary fees. Established breeders using good breeding stock rear puppies with care and adequate diet. It is from this source that a puppy should be purchased, whether for show purposes or a companion. A well reared Scottish Terrier should under normal circumstances give little trouble regarding health. He is, of course, an outdoor dog, but as long as he has the opportunity of plenty of fresh air he is very adaptable to living indoors.

At about three or four months the puppy coat should be removed with finger and thumb or a suitable "stripping" comb, leaving him with a short new coat. Between six and twelve months he may require the then dead top coat removing – using the same procedure as with the puppy coat. To keep a Scottie tidy, clean and healthy, this procedure usually requires to be carried out about twice a year. For show purposes more expert attention is required and a prospective exhibitor would do well to seek the assistance of someone with experience and also become a member of one of the many Clubs for the breed. In this way much valuable knowledge will be obtained. The importance of regular combing and brushing cannot be over-emphasized – any dog feels better for it. If a Scottie has the right kind of coat it will be found that with regular attention in this way it is quite easy to keep him tidy. The Scottish Terrier is a sturdy, compact little dog looking as though he could do his intended job. For show purposes, he should be in good bloom and by careful trimming made to display his many attributes, but he should certainly not be over-trimmed. Trimming tends to be a little too severe these days. It should be discouraged.

character

Many people have said "once a Scottie owner – always a Scottie owner". This is no surprise, for not only is he a most adaptable fellow in every way but he really makes himself one of the family in a very short time. He can display a stubborn independence which is to be respected. He is easily snubbed when scolded, but just as gay as ever when he knows all is forgiven. Contrary to a fairly common belief, he is not quarrelsome, nor vicious. He will, however, stand no nonsense and will fight if he has to, but he'll fight cleanly and is never treacherous. He is a real character and a gentleman.

Mrs. Dorothy Gabriel, well known in the breed some years ago, and a

great lover of Scottish Terriers, wrote:– "The character of the Scottish Terrier is wonderful. He is essentially a one-man dog, loving his home and his owner and having absolutely no use for outsiders. He is always ready for a long ramble or a day's ratting, but if his master wishes to be quiet at home, then he is content to remain with him, lying peacefully at his feet, the very acme of repose. As a guard it is impossible to better him. He gives his warning and if it passes unheeded, he shows very definitely that he is there and in charge. He is self-centered, deep natured, with a soul both for laughter and tragedy. As a sportsman he is unsurpassed. He will go to earth with the best, and to my knowledge several of the breed have been shot over and have proved to have mouths of velvet. Anything that means 'fur' he will kill, from badger to the lowly house mouse, and woe betide the marauding cat that crosses his path; but his own cat is sacred, a thing set apart from the rest of its kind. There is nothing frothy or shallow in the nature of a Scottie. He never forgets – his heart may break with grief, but he will not yowl about it. He is absolutely honorable, incapable of a mean or petty action, large hearted and loving, with the soul and mind of an honest gentleman".

standards

There does not appear to be any material difference between the Standard of the breed as approved by the Kennel Clubs in England and America and that adopted in other countries.

The head should be long, but without being out of proportion to the size of the dog. The skull should be clean and nearly flat with a drop between skull and foreface just in front of the eye. The nose should be large, the eyes almond shaped, fairly wide apart and set deeply. The ears should be neat, pointed and erect. The neck should be muscular and of moderate length. Long sloping shoulder – the forelegs straight and well boned, the feet of good size and well padded. Chest – fairly broad and hung between the forelegs; the body, well rounded ribs carried well back; the back, proportionately short and very muscular; the hindquarters remarkably powerful for the size of the dog (10″ at the shoulder; 19 to 22 lbs. for males, 18 to 21 lbs. for females). The tail should be of moderate length. Two coats – undercoat, short, dense, and soft; outer coat, harsh, dense and wiry. Movement – agile and active with easy, straightforward and free action. The ideal Scottish Terrier should suggest great power and activity in small compass. Overall balance is of paramount importance.

A frontal view of Gaywyn Top Hat.

Am. Ch. Carmichael's Fanfare, another Westminster B.I.S. winner, in 1965, claims Int. Ch. Walsing Winning Trick in almost every line of her Pedigree. Fanfare is owned by Mr. and Mrs. Charles C. Stalter.

Another to make a name for himself on both sides of the Atlantic was Mr. W. M. Singleton's Eng. and Amer. Ch. Walsing Wild Winter. The trimming style of the fifties left more daylight under the dog than today's heavy furnishing.

Sealyham Terrier

Mr. and Mrs. T. F. Dickinson were the breeders of English and American Ch. Alcide of Axe, one of the outstanding Sealyhams of all time, winner in Britain of twenty C.C.s, a record for the breed. He had an equally impressive record in America. A beautifully balanced dog, combining great substance with intense quality.

history and development

Freeman Lloyd, a great Sealyham authority, traces the breed back to the 15th century when the Tucker family is said to have imported a small, white, long-backed Flemish terrier into Wales. The Tuckers were ancestors of Captain Edwardes, that great sportsman who, in the 1800's, developed the Sealyham to work with his pack of hounds, and for ratting and badger digging, for which the breed became best known in later years. Both the Tuckers and Edwardeses lived at Sealyham House near Haverfordwest, Pembrokeshire, from which the breed takes its name. Their further development is largely due to the efforts of Fred Lewis, known to almost everyone as the father of the breed. Unfortunately, he never wrote a book on the subject of which he had so much knowledge.

He was instrumental in starting classes for the breed at the Kennel Club show of 1903 and he founded, in 1908, the Sealyham Terrier Club of which he was secretary for many years. On the application of Lord Kensington, the president of the club, the breed was recognized by the Kennel Club in 1911. Fred Lewis and others worked hard in those early days for their beloved breed and nearly all present-day Sealyhams can trace their pedigree back to the famous Peer Gynt (Tinker), at one time his property, and to Huntsman. Peer Gynt is reputed to have been unbeaten on the show-bench for five or six years, until the best of his sons, Dandy Bach, came along and he did more than any other dog to perpetuate and establish the breed. Great strides have been made since those early days,

These three champions of the thirties illustrate how little type has changed – Champions Bellona Binks and Baccarat Binks with Ch. Deleglace. Bellona and Baccarat carry the prefix of Captain R. S. de Quincey.

473

to develop what was originally purely a working breed into a lovely show-dog that can hold its own in any company but which is, nevertheless, still a hunter at heart.

The breed became very popular during the mid-twenties and early thirties. The Second World War sadly depleted the ranks and many famous strains faded into oblivion. However, the love and devotion of a dedicated band of breeders put it back on its feet and it now maintains a fairly steady place in the dog fraternity.

color

Sealyhams are a white breed with markings of any color on the head and ears; this can be blue-black, rich tan, lemon, badger (a mixture of tan and gray), or of course all white. In the U.K. a small mark on back or base of the tail is no great handicap and there have been many notable champions with such marking. Black ticking in the body coat is a serious fault which, though prevalent some years ago, is not seen nearly so often today. On the other hand, good pigmentation of the skin is desirable, as lack of it can lead to off-color noses and it may also be connected with deafness, though this is now very rare.

care

No one should own a Sealyham unless he is prepared to look after it

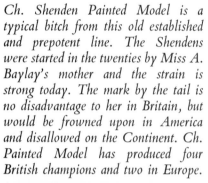

Ch. Shenden Painted Model is a typical bitch from this old established and prepotent line. The Shendens were started in the twenties by Miss A. Baylay's mother and the strain is strong today. The mark by the tail is no disadvantage to her in Britain, but would be frowned upon in America and disallowed on the Continent. Ch. Painted Model has produced four British champions and two in Europe.

Sealyham puppies have an irresistible charm. These youngsters belonged to Mrs. H. A. Cuming and were sired by her Ch. Polrose Plainly Would.

Eastfield is a long established name in the breed and the dogs bred by the owner, Miss F. J. Chenuz, have had a great influence on the Sealyham. Her English and American champion Coon-so-Gay of Eastfield had a great winning career in England, winning best in show at a championship show. Later, in America, he continued his winning career. This is the American style of trimming; the photograph being taken when Coon-so-Gay won the 1957 specialty of the American Sealyham Terrier Club.

Two beautiful pre-war Shenden Sealyhams

properly. The long, profuse, double, weather-resisting coat needs regular combing with a strong coarse wire comb to get right down to the skin; in this way, loose hair is removed and mats in the coat have no chance to form. Puppies should learn to be combed from an early age. Encourage them to stand on a table for this. Eyes and ears should be regularly checked, as many Sealyhams grow a lot of hair in their ears and if this is not kept under control and clean, it is apt to get dirty and matted, and this may cause disease. Nails should be kept short and any matted hair between the toes should be cut away.

They should be stripped at least twice a year and it is worth finding

The lovely head and furnishings of Mrs. H. A. Cuming's Ch. Polrose Plainly Would.

Front head view – Sealyham

someone who can hand-strip and does not clip, as in this way, the coat can be kept really nice. Bathing is not advised unless it is really necessary as it makes the coat soft and silky by killing the natural oil which makes it weather resisting. A good dry shampoo or chalk block is much better. A rub down with white sawdust after a dry shampoo is also good.

character

Sealyhams are most charming and lovable, giving their owners endless love and devotion and, in addition, they are excellent watch dogs. They are, however, self-willed and obstinate and they must learn at an early age who is boss. As adorable cuddly puppies, their new owners are inclined to spoil them; giving in to them on all occasions. This is a mistaken policy. A firm hand in youth will lead to a happy association for many years, for once a Sealyham learns to respect as well as to love you, he will be yours for life. A most biddable and affectionate companion who can be quite wonderful with children. They are strong and sturdy, never giving in and having the most wonderful powers of recuperation.

standards

For many years now the Sealyham has been a superb show dog when really well handled and presented, for he is a great show-off and should enter the ring with great presence, and combining substance with quality and style.

The approved Standard does not give a mental picture of this, and in part is open to misinterpretation. In requiring a back of medium length it means that the dog should be longer from shoulder to tail than from shoulder to ground; he should not in any way be a "square" dog. He should have a good reach of neck, which should be strong and muscular, a really level topline and erect tail, with strong, muscular quarters. There should be a big rib cage with plenty of heart room, sound front as straight as possible, with toes pointing straight forward.

The English Standard height does not exceed 12″ at shoulder, whereas the American, which I believe to be nearer the ideal, is $10\frac{1}{2}″$; the American Standard also indicates size as more important than weight; weights in the Standards are included more as deterrents.

In the Standards, the eye color is that of the eyes themselves; in Britain, dark eye rims are not specified, in fact too much pigmentation here in an all-white dog can give too soft an expression. But in Switzerland and other Continental countries, dark eye rims are specified, and they are preferred in America and Australia. A point to remember is that if a puppy has a few small dark spots on the eye rims it will probably have really dark rims at eighteen months, just as the puppy's pink nose develops into the adult black.

Skye Terrier

Lady Marcia Miles' Ch. Merrymount His Grace, winner of six C.C.s, Skye dog of the year in Great Britain in 1969, also stud dog of the year at that time.

history and development

There can hardly have been a period in history when small earth-dogs were not kept in the Scottish Highlands and commonly used in the work of hunting the fox, the otter, the badger and other mischievous vermin from their lairs in the moorland cairns. These energetic, hardy, little Highland Terriers were not originally differentiated into separate breeds. They all bore a general similarity in size and shape, with their long, flexible bodies, short legs, and rugged raiment of crisp, wiry hair; and they were alike in their characteristic pertinacity, their activity, and their acute senses of sight, hearing and scent. But gradually, in the different glens, clansmen and gamekeepers gave preference to certain family strains and local types which they cultivated for special purposes. On the misty west coast, and the near Islands of Colonsay and Skye, where otters and foxes were numerous, dogs with long, deep, weather-resisting coats were particularly favored for their skill in hunting and their tireless endurance. The best of these were associated with the Isle of Skye, and they received the distinguishing name of Skye Terriers.

Not all the terriers of Skye were long-haired. The closely related Cairn Terrier was formerly known as the short-haired Skye. The Skye Terrier proper was greatly appreciated in the 16th century and noted as peculiar "by reason of the length of heare which makes showe neither of face nor body". It was not, however, until about 1840 that the breed attracted much notice among dog-lovers south of the Scottish border. Queen Victoria's admiration of the Skye, of which she owned many typical specimens, and Landseer's paintings in which these dogs were introduced, drew public attention to the decorative and companionable qualities of the breed, and brought it into request.

color

In the early days of dog shows, the colors of the Skye Terrier varied from

Side and front head views – the Skye Terrier.

477

By Ch. Merrymount Happy Jack ex Ch. Merrymount Sunset, this is lady Marcia Miles' Ch. Merrymount Wot No Sun, Skye dog of the year in 1956 and 1957.

creamy white to fawn and russet, heather brindle, blue-gray and black. The lighter colored ones have black muzzles, ears and tails. Sandy red has become rare, but it is still admired, although steel-gray is the most usual. Liver or chocolate color has never been orthodox, and whatever the color of the coat, the nose must be black. The ears must be either alertly pricked or else pendulous and lying close to the cheeks.

care

The show Skye Terrier's profuse, well groomed coat falling in smooth cascades down its sides, its veil of thick hair shielding fore-face, and the silky feathering of ears and tail, are not attained and maintained without considerable trouble. But inordinate length of coat is not now sought for if it be of the desired harsh consistency, ample enough to hang protectively over the soft, wooly undercoat.

The ideal treatment of young puppies I find is to give them enough exercise by allowing them to run up and down a long passage with plenty of toys such as balls and dumbells to play with, and play about in a fair-sized run, making certain the puppy is free from worms and has the right food.

character

The Skye Terrier has lost none of its inherent gameness. It is still one of the most intrepid and pertinacious of sporting terriers, strong in constitution, wise and resourceful and peculiarly affectionate. An outstanding recommendation is its beauty of character and disposition, its responsive devotion, equable temper and unselfish patience. As a companion it is constant and staunch in its trust. The Skye is a one-man dog with a long memory, distrustful of strangers, but not vicious. Given a chance Skyes are still a very sporting breed. It may be of interest to note that my Ch. Grey Dusk (1924) a drop-eared, was totally untrained as a gundog to the age of three years, when I purchased him, but we soon discovered he had a wonderful nose and retrieved to hand and would hunt a hedgerow as well as any of our field-trained Spaniels, also White Lady of Merrymount, a prick-eared

Winner of eleven championships under as many different judges, Lady Marcia Miles' Ch. Merrymount You'll Do, was best Terrier in show at Blackpool, England, against over 1,000 other entries. Imported into America he won the Terrier group at Westminster.

winner of two Challenge Certificates in the early twenties attacked an otter in a river and in spite of being badly mauled held on to it until human aid came to her.

standards

The weight of a mature dog should be about 25 lbs. But general type and proportions are more important.

The Skye has altered less than most breeds in the last 70 years. The standard in quality is certainly higher, one seldom sees a really bad Skye now-a-days, but that is not to say one does not see many with bad faults. The chief faults seen in the show ring today are bad fronts resulting from bad rearing and which have the disastrous effect of a dip in the back; and some bad tails spoil some otherwise very perfect specimens of the breed. The bad tails are hereditary and in-breeding must be very carefully considered. Good tails are a very valuable asset in a kennel. Light eyes are seldom seen now-a-days, most Skyes have lovely dark, expressive eyes.

A Skye should be long and low to the ground with a perfectly level backline. Head long, not too wide in skull with powerful jaws, black nose, teeth closing level, long neck slightly crested, tail carried down or straight, never curled over the back. Ears can be either prick or drop, when prick they should be fairly small, very upright with graceful featherings, if drop larger and carried close to the side of the head. In 1904 in Britain the two ear varieties were separated and Challenge Certificates given to both until 1922 when the registrations had dropped to 31. Since then the classes have not again been divided. It is seldom now-a-days that one sees a drop-eared Skye, the prick having always been the most

Another Merrymount Skye dog of the year in Britain, in 1964; this time Ch. Merrymount Mid River, winner of eight C.C.s before his retirement.

Drop eared Skyes in the thirties, Bob of Merrymount, Ch. Southerhills Moonglow, Ch. Togo of Merrymount.

popular; personally I have a great admiration for the drops, and it is true that as a rule when one does breed a true drop it is an outstanding specimen. Ch. Merrymount Sunset, the dam of twelve champions, nine prick and three drop, never had a weak-eared puppy in either variety. There are a fair amount of drop-eared Skyes now in America where Skyes are very much larger than in England. British Skyes have been kept very much the same size for the last 70 years.

Soft-coated Wheaten Terrier

The excellent type and build of Ch. Holmenocks Handley, first ever best of breed winner at Cruft's, to be followed by his son, and then by his son also.

It has always been acknowledged that the Soft-coated Wheaten Terrier is the oldest of the native Terrier breeds of Ireland and was the progenitor of several of our better known terrier breeds. No light can be shed on the specific origin of the breed, which is apparently indigenous, especially in the south western counties of Munster.

Evolved originally as a general farm and utility dog it acquired wide popularity as killer of vermin, a characteristic that is still well to the fore today.

Since first making its debut in the show ring and British Kennel Club registers thirty-three years ago, it has not made very much progress. At present in Ireland the breed is at about its lowest ever ebb numerically. Within the last decade in America it has made tremendous strides in popularity; there are over 310 dogs, although it is not as yet registered by the A.K.C.

The mature Wheaten is an attractive, compact, well-built dog, strong and energetic.

His height is up to 18″; weight 35 to 40 lbs.

The coat is soft and silky, wavy or curly, of a warm honey colored hue; most distinctive and unusual. A wooly coat is eschewed altogether.

Every effort has been made to retain the original type and to ensure its continuance by judicious breeding.

The Soft-coated Wheaten Terrier, side head and front.

Staffordshire Bull Terrier

A top Staffordshire Bull Terrier from Scotland, Ch. Sahib of Senkrah, owned by Mr. A. W. Harkness.

history and development

The Staffordshire Bull Terrier, as his name implies, was produced from a Bulldog with one or more of the terrier breeds which abounded in the early 1800's. His main progenitor was the Old English Bulldog of about 1820, when the initial crossings were made. This was a rangier, lighter Bulldog than our modern version – in fact, some students of canine racism aver that the Stafford is actually a fined-down type of pure Bulldog, selectively bred on terrier-like lines with no true terrier infusion. Quite apart from the name "Bull-and-Terrier" used freely in literature for many decades, respected authors like Pierce Egan in *Annals of Sporting* (Vol. I.), 1822, refer to the result of these crossings for the first time as "Bull Terriers". Later in 1829, Captain Thomas Brown in his *Biographical Sketches and Authentic Anecdotes of Dogs,* devoted a special chapter to this "new" breed, the Bull Terrier.

The terrier role in this Bulldog-Terrier alliance is believed to have been performed by the Old English Black-and-Tan Terrier, forerunner of the Manchester Terrier. It is not surprising that size in these old Bull-and-Terriers varied considerably. Some taking after their Bulldog progenitor went 60 lbs. and more at maturity, while others, following more the terrier pattern of their ancestry, would be as light as 20 lbs. Type too seems to have been extremely diverse, but the fact remains that as the breed progressed animals which did not rise to the set standards of courage, and later of type, were weeded out and a better stamp of dog

Rosa, a painting by G. Morley, 1841. Rosa was a Bull-and-Terrier bitch owned by the Baroness Burdett-Coutts. The painting is an important one, for it shows, with the head, the undershot jaw and Bulldog influence, while the feathery tail suggests Terrier blood. The picture was in the Author's collection and was later sold to America.

Padella and Barnard's Butcher, American Pit Bull Terrier, blood cousin of the Staffordshire Bull Terrier. Winner of a historic dog fight in Jaurez, Mexico, in 1939, against the Colorado Dog. The bout lasted two hours nine minutes. His owners are said to have won $1,000.

Ch. Benext Beau, owned by Mr. and Mrs. K. Bailey of Streatham, London. Highly successful brindle dog of current show era. Winner of many C.C.s, and extensively used at stud.

produced with the girth and substance of a smallish Bulldog but speedier and more athletic than that breed by virtue of its terrier inheritance. These dogs were termed Bull Terriers and this name remained with them for over 100 years although in the middle 1850's James Hinks of Birmingham introduced an all-white variety by crossing the old Bull Terrier with the Old English White Terrier (now extinct) and the Dalmatian. This variety developed into a fancier's dog and later, when it was established as a breed, its supporters registered it as "Bull Terrier" with the Kennel Club in Britain. Actually, it was the *original* Bull Terrier (Bulldog-Terrier or Bull-and-Terrier) who as the original of his kind had a right to this name, but later when he assumed show bench status on emerging from a gladiatorial past, he had to be content with the name Staffordshire Bull Terrier. However, today he is proud of the appendage Staffordshire to his name, that English Midlands county where he began and was developed.

Bred in the opening years of the last century to satisfy his sadistic owners' lusts for the savage spectacles of bull-and-bear-baiting the Staffordshire Bull Terrier was later used for badger-drawing and dog-fighting. However, the baiting sports which had become so much out of hand by the end of the third decade in the last century were banned, but dog-fighting went on, some say it exists even today in hole-and-corner places in England and America. For this sport the Stafford was ideally suited, not only by virtue of his physical make-up but because he desired to fight. The Staffordshire Bull Terrier or Pit Bull Terrier, as he was known, "progressed" into the present century still in warlike garb, but with the thirties some lovers of the breed considered his possibilities as a show dog and in 1935 the Kennel Club recognized him as a pure breed. A Standard was evolved and the Staffordshire Bull Terrier Club formed in Cradley

Heath, South Staffordshire, to look after his interests. Today, there are many clubs specializing in the Stafford not only in the United Kingdom but throughout the world where, apart from specialist breed clubs which seem to increase yearly, the Staffordshire Bull Terrier has proved he can thrive in almost any climate from Scandinavia to the tropics. America is developing a lively interest in him now, although the American Kennel Club has yet to "recognize" him. The American Staffordshire Terrier (once the Yankee Terrier) is an offshoot from the English dog formed over 100 years ago. It is a bigger, taller dog and is bred on distinctive lines to suit its fanciers. It is quite popular in the States, as is another variety (more like the English Staffordshire) called the American Pit Bull Terrier, commoner to the Southern States of America, but not registered by the American Kennel Club.

color

The Staffordshire Bull Terrier has always sported the coat colors which mark his Bulldog parentage. In the early days, all-white patched (pied and skewbald) coats were common, followed by fawns and brindles. Today, the preference seems to be more for fawn and brindles, although blue (which color should be well pigmented to be acceptable) was introduced to the breed Standard in 1948. These days black-and-tan (in conjunction with liver colored coats) is strictly taboo in the show ring.

care

The Stafford, being a short-coated dog, needs little attention apart from brief daily grooming and inspection. Like Diogenes, he is capable of living happily in a barrel or if need be adapting himself readily to the comforts of a baronial hall. But make sure he has a comfortable bed, free from draughts and enough fresh, raw meat in his diet. He can take as much exercise as he is given and this is better on hard ground than parkland, to keep his pads hard. He is an impulsive dog – and sees little fear – this is why he should never be free from his lead when traffic is close. He is strongly constituted and is seldom ill, but owners make sure he has a full course of inoculations when a puppy and is thoroughly dried off after a soaking.

character

The present-day Staffordshire Bull Terrier is a fearless, "honest" breed – "game unto death" as they say, and his ferocious aspect hides a surprisingly soft nature. As a house-guard he is good and can be trained to be excellent. As a nursemaid to the very young he is exceptional and is amiable under even the roughest treatment received at their hands. From puppyhood he needs firm treatment, for he inherits from the Bulldog a stubborn streak, which must be mastered immediately it is noted. He makes a wonderful member of any family circle and can offer you great sport in the field, especially where vermin abounds.

standards

The original breed Standard was drawn up in 1935 and revised a little in 1948. An ideal male specimen at present stands 16″ at the shoulder and should weigh no less than 38 lbs., some two pounds more than this contributing perhaps to a better balanced creature. Bitches weigh

Mr. J. Gordon's Ch. Fearless Red of Bandits, one of Ch. Gentleman Jim's most famous sons and outstanding winner of the middle forties, over 500 awards. Believed to be the first Staffordshire to win best in show all breeds, an honor he achieved eleven times.

Mr. and Mrs. E. Williams' Ch. Christopher of Geneva.

Mr. W. P. L. Eagles' Tojen Totem, head studies of a brindle show dog, illustrating in his expression the breed's natural intelligence and loyalty.

Puppies – Staffordshire Bull Terrier.

slightly less, but the important co-ordinating features are type and balance. The Stafford is a wonderful athlete, well endowed with hard, rippling muscle. The head, his prime feature, is very broad in the skull and deep through, with a strong, short foreface and distinct stop. His bite is huge, the mouth opening being capacious, but to conform for show work the upper front teeth should rest over and upon the lower incisors in a conventional terrier mouth. An undershot jaw – the opposite to this, which can be likened to the Bulldog jaw, is quite wrong in the Stafford. His body can be described as a lot packed into a small frame and his broad shoulders, deep chest and barrelled ribs and clipped-in loins and strongly muscled hindquarters proclaim its power. One interesting feature of his forelimbs is the way the feet turn out a little at the pasterns, allowing him greater flexibility in a fighting turn. His eyes should be round and set to look straight ahead and they are better when very dark, although the Standard does permit them to bear some relation to coat color.

Staffordshire Terrier

Staffordshire Terrier – sturdy, independent looking American terrier breed.

When the American Kennel Club registered the breed in August of 1936, the name itself was a compromise. This breed had been called by various names, American Bull Terrier, Yankee Terrier and Pit Bull Terrier.

No one was too happy when the breed was registered as the Staffordshire Terrier, especially since for a time the A.K.C. was permitting this distinct breed to be shown in the same ring with the Staffordshire Bull Terrier, a lighter and smaller boned dog. Cross-breeding of the two was accepted; but there was precedent in the case of the English and American Cocker Spaniels. Actually America's Staffordshire does go back to England's, but added elements have made it truly a product of the U.S.A.

The Standard says: "The Staffordshire Terrier should give the impression of great strength for his size, a well put together dog, muscular but agile and graceful, keenly alive to his surroundings. He should be stocky, not long-legged or racy in outline. His courage is proverbial."

Cropped or uncropped ears are permitted; full drop penalized. In contrast to the 14″ to 16″ height of the Staffordshire Bull Terrier, the American male Staff should stand 18″ to 19″. In either breed any color is permissible, but all white, more than eighty per cent white, black-and-tan, and liver are not to be encouraged. The coat should be short, close, stiff to the touch and glossy.

Welsh Terrier

Ch. Sandstorm Saracen, winner of seven C.C.s, six times best of breed, best in show Birmingham National championship show in 1958, and supreme champion at Cruft's in 1959. Owned by Mrs. D. M. Leach and Mrs. M. M. Thomas, Saracen was sired by Cedewain Clogwyn ex Sandstorm Susan, and handled throughout his career by Mr. Philip Thomas.

Welsh Terrier head, front and side.

history and development

The Welsh Terrier as we know him today is much different from what he was even fifty years ago. Most of the half-legged, rough-coated terriers, i.e. Wire Haired Fox Terrier, Lakeland Terrier etc. are of a similar pattern to the Welsh but each has its own set type. Wires are more racy and refined, Lakies are more cloddy, but the modern Welsh is not so refined as the Wire nor so cloddy as the Lakie.

These half-legged terriers have been bred in Wales for generations and were very popular for hunting vermin – fox, badger, otter etc. Around Amlwch, Caernarvon, Harlech and Pwllheli, there were many devoted and dedicated breeders. Names that readily come to mind are:– "Towyn" Edwards, Arthur E. Harris, Tom Harris, Joe Hitchings and, in more recent years, Harold Snow. Two of the early stud dogs – Ch. Mawddwy Nonsuch and Ch. Bob Bethesda (whelped in 1883 and 1886) – seem to have started an improvement in type and quality. In the 19th century transport difficulties were great and if a desired stud dog was kenneled two hundred miles away, say in 1870, it was almost impossible to get him and the bitch together. Entries at shows in the early years were higher in number than today and competition was keen. By 1900 type and quality had become more pronounced. Although still long backed and light in quarters, they were improving.

One of the more recent stud dogs to stamp type on many bitch lines was Ch. Felstead Futurist.

color

The color of Welsh Terriers is most attractive, especially at outdoor shows

Chamberlain, owned by Mrs. Green, was typical of the Welsh being seen at the turn of the century.

against a green background. He always looks clean as a town dog, as the Black and Tan seems to keep cleaner than white dogs. The darker the tan the more attractive they look. Although grizzle and tan is permissible in the Standard, few are now shown of that color. We come across a black-headed Welsh usually with a very black body coat. This is a color which is not typical in the breed and I hope will not be allowed to become too common. It detracts considerably from the true Welsh type. Most puppies are born almost black, but even at one day old, the black seems to get less and the tan increases so that by three months of age the color is as it should be. The tan on legs and quarters may be paler than we like, but usually with the casting of the puppy coat, the true rich tan breaks through.

The good double coat is weather resistant and, with a dog in good condition and free from worms, glows like satin.

care

Welsh Terriers are trimmed periodically and when one is presented in good order it is most attractive.

Following a litter, the bitch usually moults and it is a good thing to help it along by "stripping", i.e. taking away all loose hair to enable the new hair to come through. Although clipping terriers' coats is frowned upon by professional handlers, I personally think it is by far the best thing to do when one has a pet.

My brood bitches and stud dogs always get the "clipping" treatment twice a year. They are always neat and tidy with no "doggy smell". As far as "spoiling the coat by clipping" is concerned, I have at the present time a twelve year old bitch and a ten year old dog that have been clipped for the past nine years and their coats are lovely.

character

Welsh are good dogs in the kennel or house, being very much quieter than the average terrier. But breeds that are popular encourage people to breed from any bitch or dog whether they are suitable for breeding or not, and dedicated breeders only breed from the best stock, and only animals with stamina, temperament and type should be bred from. More often than not the temperament of Welsh Terriers is good and I always feel that a puppy brought up in the house has a much better start than one brought up in the kennel. If one can bring the puppy into the house at five to six weeks of age so that it gets used to the television, radio, cleaner etc. it goes out into the show ring with its tail up. To take a dog straight from the kennel into the noise and bustle of the show ring is asking too much.

One of the many successful Welsh to cross the Atlantic from Wales to America, American Ch. Cedewain Cynolwyn left several of his progeny in Britain to keep his name alive, including two champions in one litter – Cathy and Cetyn, both owned by Mr. W. A. E. Egerton.

Progressing further towards the modern dog came the type of Kai, in 1930.

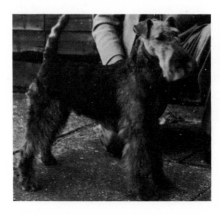

standards

The American Standard is very similar to the British. America prefers a smaller dog than is shown in Britain and I think gives preference to the older type. With careful selection of breeding the British have produced a more elegant Welshman with a rather longer head and classical lines. The Standard says that the height should not exceed $15\frac{1}{2}''$ (in the U.S.A. it is an even $15''$ for a male, bitches less) but $16''$ would not stop a dog winning provided he is balanced and of good type. The ideal weight should be 20 to 21 lbs. The quality Welsh should have a fairly long head and not too narrow between the ears, which should be small and "V" shaped with the fold just above the level of the skull. The tip of the ears should touch the head. Eyes should be small, dark and deep set, giving the desired terrier expression. Foreface should be well filled up under the eyes and not as long as Fox Terriers. Teeth should be of the scissors bite, i.e. top upper teeth just overlapping the lower. Forelegs must be straight with bone down to the feet, which must be small and cat-like. For the show dog, plenty of nice crisp leg hair is most essential. The neck should be long and powerful, running into long sloping shoulders. The back must be level and short with a nicely docked tail set well up. Body must be deep with nice spring of rib. The quarters powerful with good second thigh and nicely moulded stifle which gives a shapely hock.

Many countries now schedule Welsh Terriers and, on the Continent, they are particularly strong. One bred in Wales recently went best-in-show at the all-breeds championship show in Sweden after winning five Challenge Certificates in Britain.

A leading bitch in 1969, Ch. Cedewain Comedy is presented by her handler at the Three Counties championship show in Britain.

487

West Highland White Terrier

Mrs. D. M. Dennis's Ch. Barrister of Branston, born in 1948, by Ch. Hookwood Mentor ex Bloom of Branston, was a great dog and a great showman. He won eleven C.C.s and sired eleven champions.

A typical West Highland White head, side view.

history and development

The West Highland White Terrier has attained a degree of popularity that could never have been imagined when the first clubs were formed in Scotland and England in 1905 when, it would seem, the little white dogs were beginning to be picked out from the small short-legged mixed terriers that had abounded as working dogs in the Scottish Highlands for some three hundred years. According to known records, the breed was first scheduled at the annual show of the Scottish Kennel Club held at Waverley Market, Edinburgh in October 1904, although they had previously been exhibited under their various regional names.

The ancestors of the breed were in the past known under various names such as Poltalloch, Roseneath, White Scottish, Cairn and Little Skye Terriers. (Cairn Terrier was given a separate register and championship status in 1912.)

In *The Dog Owners Annual Canine Literature* 1892 the following article appeared:—

The Poltalloch Terrier

A white variety of the Scottish Terrier existed at one time (and stray specimens may exist) under the cognomen of Poltalloch Terriers, and Captain Mackie, who went expressly to Poltalloch to see this variety, describes it as follows:

The Poltalloch Terrier weighs from 16 to 20 lbs., has a determined, vermin destroying look about it, it is well knit together, is a sort of linty white in color. The hair is hard and bristly, and will be from 1″ to 2½″ in length, excepting on the face and head where it is short, hard and wiry.

The body is medium between cobby and long, but is very deep and stands upon short, bony legs, the fore ones nearly straight. Head very long; nose broad and often flesh colored; teeth extremely large for such a small dog; ears small, prick, and covered with a velvety coat. The tail is slightly bent and carried gaily.

West Highland White – puppies

The Dog Owners Supplement to the *Bazaar*, dated 27th November 1899, included the following article on Roseneath Terriers, from which are drawn the following extracts:—

White Roseneath Terriers

Under the above is classed a sub-variety of the Scottish Terrier distinguished chiefly by the coat color being white instead of that identified with the familiar Die Hard of our shows. These White Scottish Terriers are by no means modern productions, although it is only of recent years that they have come into prominence. The perfecting, however, of the White Scottish Terrier has been left chiefly to Dr. Flaxman.

Strange to say, in the case of Captain Keene's bitch and Dr. Flaxman's finest specimens, they were bred from dark (exceptionally dark in the latter case) parents; many difficulties have had to be encountered by those who undertook to revive the old strain, for that a similar strain existed half-a-century ago there is abundant evidence alike on canvas and in print. One difficulty was, we believe, the pink nose, which frequently was found in the progeny of some of the earliest productions. Dr. Flaxman's dogs, however, boast noses of the blackest jet.

Col. Malcolm of Poltalloch, who was one of the first to help establish the breed. This picture shows him with Westies in their native surroundings, and gives the impression that they were, and are, game, hardy terriers.

After a successful career in Britain in 1965 English and American Ch. Bardel of Branston, by Ch. Billybong of Branston ex Ch. Banner of Branston, owned by Mrs. Dennis and Mrs. R. Mellon, furthered his career in America where he was successful both in the show ring and at stud.

In 1904 all the various regional names were merged to become the West Highland White Terrier. The credit for the development of the modern West Highland White Terrier must be attributed largely to Colonel E. D. Malcolm of Poltalloch.

As previously mentioned, the breed clubs in Scotland and England were formed in 1905, to be quickly followed by the United States of America and Canada in 1909 and 1911 respectively; Australia 1963 and Sweden in 1965. The breed was originally used as a working terrier for the hunting of fox and badger. Even to the present day, one is used by a famous British hunt in preference to any other breed for the bolting of foxes. Their gameness and the tenacious way in which they finish a job must be unsurpassed.

In the west country of England, they are regularly used as working dogs on the farms and sent to fetch up a herd of cows without assistance from anyone. In another instance the Westie has taken over the duties of the old sheep dog who taught him all the tricks of the trade until old age and weary bones made the work too much for him. So, although the majority are probably kept as good companions and show dogs, it is proved that they still retain the instincts for the work for which they were originally bred.

Miss E. E. Wade's Ch. Freshney Fiametta, bred by Mrs. M. McKinney, by Ch. Melbourne Mathias ex Freshney Felicia, was the first post-war champion in the breed in Britain. She was best in show at the all-breeds championship show in Cambridge in 1946.

color

There are no subtleties about the color of a Westie – he is quite simply "pure white". But his nose is black, and so are the underneath of his pads and his toe nails.

care

Feeding and exercise needs of the breed are pretty standard for this kind and size of dog. Grooming, however, is a matter for some extra care. Being a long-coated dog, it is advisable that it should have a daily grooming with brush and comb, which, as well as keeping the double coat free of knots and tangles, will remove any dust or soil and keep its white coat in immaculate condition.

Every Westie should be tidied up by having the surplus coat removed twice yearly, and at the same time shaped to show up a nice neck line; any long hair should be removed from the ears and the tail trimmed to a good carrot-like shape.

Preparing a dog for show is an art that anyone may learn with patience and perseverance. The coat should be about two inches in length on the back and down the sides. The hair on the neck and throat should be considerably shorter and is gradually tapered to the shoulders to run smoothly into the body coat. Any untidy hairs should be removed while yet retaining the rugged appearance. Much can be learned from studying good photographs of show dogs and reading the many excellent chapters in various books on the breed.

Mrs. Dennis's Ch. Bandsman of Branston, by Ch. Banker of Branston ex Ch. Banēssa of Branston, a real aristocrat of the breed who impressed on his progeny many of his own good points. He was whelped in 1958.

character

The Westie has a very equable temperament. It is a good mixer with other canines, and loves the companionship of the family. Fond of sporting life, but enjoying as any its creature comforts and the warmest spot on the hearth.

Most of the present-day terriers retain strongly the instincts of their beginnings, earth dogs, burrow dogs, dogs to seek out the vermin from the runs and tunnels of the earth. Forelegs developed for digging; head and

Am. Ch. Elfinbrook Simon the top-winning Westie of all time. He sired fifty-one American and Canadian champions following his exportation to the U.S.A. as an eleven months puppy by Mr. Len Pearson to Mrs. Barbara Worcester-Keenan of the Wishing Wells kennels.

A frontal head study of Ch. Alpinegay Sonata.

jaws for despatching the quarry at bay.

And a temperament admitting no fear but, at the same time, a latent and now well developed instinct for the companionship of man. The West Highland Terrier has all this, and more. He offers a devotion markedly greater than many breeds; he is teachable, he can be a house dog, or a hunting dog, or a walking companion at will. He can be a town dog, being small, but his heart lies in the country.

standards

The following breed Standard has been adopted in practically all countries in the world, the main exception being a slight difference in size in the United States of America.

As you would expect, the Westie is a small, game, hardy-looking terrier, and the Standard goes on to say that it is "possessed of no small amount of self-esteem". It is strongly built, deep in chest and back ribs, with a level back and powerful quarters on muscular legs. Movement should be free and easy all round, and in particular the movement from behind should be free, easy and forceful. Stiff, stilted movement at the rear is "very objectionable". The skull should be slightly domed, and, when gripped across the forehead, should present a smooth contour. The head is carried more or less at a right angle to the axis of the neck, certainly not in an extended position; and it should be thickly coated with the same kind of hard hair which is required for the outer coat of the rest of the body, where the undercoat is short, soft and close.

The nose should be fairly large and black, and not projecting forward, showing up well against the white of the rest of the animal, and the ears should be small and erect, terminating in sharp points. The hair of the ears should be short and smooth, and should not be cut.

The shoulders should slope backwards, and the forelegs should move freely, like the pendulum of a clock, and they should be covered with short, hard hair. The hindquarters are strong, muscular and wide across the top, with short, muscular and sinewy legs. Thighs very muscular and not too wide apart, and hocks bent and well set-in under the body so as to be close together when standing, or moving. The feet are strong, thickly padded and covered with short, hard hair. The forefeet are larger than the hind feet. The tail is 5″ to 6″ long, covered with hard hair, straight, and carried jauntily, not gay, nor carried over the back. Long tails are a fault, and on no account should tails be docked.

There is no weight Standard. Animals in Britain should be around 11″ at the withers; in America 11″ for dogs, one inch less for bitches.

Mrs. M. Pacey's Ch. Wolvey Patrician, by Ch. Wolvey Guy ex Ch. Wolvey Clover, is a name to be found in almost all of the early pedigrees.

Ch. Wolvey Pintail, an outstandingly beautiful bitch of the thirties, who was twice best in show at famous London shows, owned by Mrs. M. Pacey.

Toy Dogs

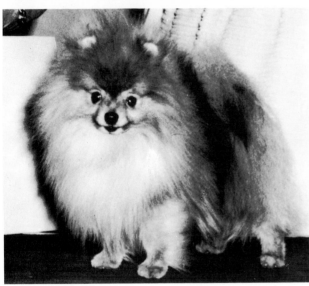

Reserve best in show, Cruft's, 1971, the Chihuahua Long-coat, Ch. Rozavel Tarina Song, a beautiful Toy dog.

Best Toy dog at Westminster, 1971, the Pomeranian, Ch. Duke's Lil Red Baron of O'Kala: outstanding in all points.

493

Affenpinscher

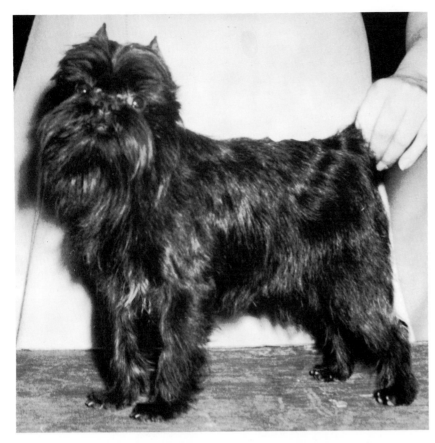

A typical American Affenpinscher champion, a group winner at Westminster.

Afficionados of the Affenpinscher like to claim an ancestry of better than five centuries for their favorite breed; this is based solely on the supposed recognition of it in the work of two famous artists, Albrecht Dürer and Jan van Eyck, the first-named living from 1471 to 1525, the latter from 1390 to 1441. The writer does not remember the specific delineations but, from viewing many similar claims made for other breeds and other artists, would suggest awaiting documented proof.

Certainly the Affenpinscher is not a new breed and it probably goes back far beyond some better-known German breeds. Generally this Toy is grouped with such better-known varieties as the Brussels Griffon, the Miniature Pinscher and the Miniature Schnauzer. In most respects it seems closest to the Griffon, the main difference being in the profuseness of the wiry coat worn by the Affenpinscher; the weight, which is four or five pounds more in the Belgian breed; and in the muzzle. Both are undershot, but the profile of the Belgian is almost flat while the Affenpinscher's muzzle is a trifle longer. You do not notice this unless you push back the long, shaggy hair on its face. Generally speaking, the Belgian breed gives an impression of compact power, but due to its shagginess, the Affenpinscher seems much more fragile.

Some writers claim that this breed, which has been dubbed the "monkey terrier" is related to Germany's rehpinscher, i.e. Miniature Pinscher. Perhaps they would look more alike if the Affenpinscher were trimmed down close to its skin, just as a completely stripped Old English Sheepdog closely resembles an Airedale. However, the Affenpinscher is enough of a Toy dog in its own right to make on its own obvious qualities. Generally, the Affenpinscher is regarded as one of the close-up ancestors of the Belgian breed and its varieties. It was admitted to registration by the A.K.C. in 1936, but its advancement has been slow. Even today, it has only 140 specimens registered a year. However, more of these are exhibited than of breeds that are more numerous. Perhaps this is because it can be taken to shows easily.

The Standard approved by the A.K.C. is one of the shortest on record. Under general appearance it asks for the dog to be small but rather sturdy in build, not delicate in any way. Coat is considered very important. It should be short and dense in certain parts and shaggy and longer in others. It is longer and more loose and shaggy on the legs and around the eyes, nose and chin, giving a typical monkey-like appearance.

The best color is black, but black and tan markings, red, gray and other mixtures are permitted.

The head should be round and not too heavy, with well-domed forehead. Eyes should be good-sized, black and very brilliant. Ears should be rather small, set high, pointed and erect, in the U.S.A. usually clipped to a point; muzzle short and rather pointed with a black nose. The upper jaw is a trifle shorter than the lower; teeth should not show.

The required head points are clearly demonstrated in this Affenpinscher.

(opposite)
A British specimen, the required monkey look accentuated by the comparatively shorter body coat.

The back should be straight and equal to height; chest reasonably deep; only a slight tuck-up at loin; legs straight as possible; hind-legs without much bend at hocks; tail cut short, carried high.

Australian Silky Terrier

Australian Ch. Lylac Playboy joined Mrs. E. R. Naismith's Jernaise Kennels at two and a half years old. Within ten months he was a champion, and was still winning top awards at eight years old.

Originally known as the Sydney Silky Terrier, the breed arose from cross-breeding Yorkshire Terriers with the stronger, more robust, Australian Terrier in which breed Yorkshire Terriers, Cairns, Norwich Terriers and Dandie Dinmonts were all present. As recently as 1945 some dogs were being registered as Sydney Silky Terriers which came from litters of "registered" Australian Terriers and Yorkshire Terriers, the smaller puppies as Yorkies, the coarser coated ones Aussies, the medium sized long coated ones Silky Terriers. But the breed now accords to a definite specification. It is known in America as the Silky Terrier but it is judged in the Toy Group. Clubs have been formed whose objects are to establish and maintain the breed according to definite standards, and these standards are today accepted throughout the world.

Blue-and-tan and gray-blue-and-tan are the Standard colors, with a silver-blue top knot. The colors are very definite. The tips of the hairs are darker than at the roots.

Although a Toy Dog, the breed exhibits many of the qualities of a Terrier – alertness, soundness, agility and a well-developed hunting instinct. A bright, merry, intelligent little dog.

Not recognized in Britain the Silky was accepted in America in 1959.

Fine glossy, silky coat. Head, strong, wedge-shaped with small pricked V-shaped ears. Low-set body about one-fifth longer than height at withers. Tail rather erect, docked, not plumed.

Weight 8 to 10 lbs., height approximately 10″ to shoulder.

Bichon Frise

history and development

We know that the Bichon, like his cousin the Caniche, descended from the Barbet or Water Spaniel, from which came the name "Barbichon", later shortened to "Bichon". The Bichons were divided into four types – the Bichon Maltaise, the Bichon Bolognese, the Bichon Havanese and the Bichon Teneriffe. All originated in the Mediterranean area. Appreciated for their dispositions, the little dogs traveled much through antiquity. The dogs found early success in Spain and it is generally felt that Spanish seamen introduced the breed to the Canary Island of Teneriffe, hence the name Bichon Teneriffe.

In the 14th century, Italian sailors rediscovered our little dogs on their voyages and are credited with returning them to the continent. They soon became great favorites with the Italian nobility and the new middle class of merchants and, as with other dogs of that era, the Bichons were often cut "lion style".

The "Teneriffe" or "Bichon" made his appearance in France under Francis I, the patron of the Renaissance, who reigned from 1515 to 1547. Their great success, however, was during the reign of Henry III from 1547 to 1589. This king so loved the little dogs that he carried them wherever he went in traylike baskets attached around his neck by ribbons, a custom quickly adopted by the ladies of the court.

The breed also enjoyed considerable success in Spain as a favorite of the Infantas; painters of the Spanish school often included them in their works. One finds such a dog in several of the paintings of Goya, (1746–1828). Their success was moderate after this period until a brief renewal of interest under Napoleon III (1808–1873).

But the fate of our aristocratic dog is altered. In the late 1800's, he becomes the "common dog", running the streets, accompanying the organ grinders of Barbary, leading the blind and doing tricks in the circus and fairs.

At the end of the First World War returning soldiers brought a few of these dogs back with them, but no effort was made to breed or keep records. In France, however, four breeders began establishing their lines through controlled breeding programs. On March 5, 1933, the official Standard of the breed as written by Madame Abadie of Steren Vor Kennels was adopted by the Société Centrale Canine of France. As the breed was known by two names, Teneriffe and Bichon, the President of the International Canine Federation, Mme. Nizet de Leemans, proposed a name based on the characteristics that the dogs presented and the name "Bichon a poil Frise" or "Bichon of the curly coat" was adopted. On October 18, 1934, the Bichon was admitted to the Stud Book of the French Kennel Club. The breed is recognized in Belgium, France and Italy, and in 1971 was accepted into the Miscellaneous Class of the American K.C.

The Bichon of today copies no other breed in the style of presentation. He is unique and ready to take his place among the recognized breeds of America.

Mee-Mars Imperial du Chaminade, owned by Melvin and Marvel Brown of Benton Harbor, Michigan, is prepared ready for the show ring.

color

All white, or white with cream, apricot, or gray on ears and/or body.

care

Unfortunately, in the show rings of the Continent, emphasis on meticulous care was lacking. It was the custom to exhibit with little or no grooming. Dogs were unwashed, unbrushed and unscissored, and were generally lacking in the basics of show appearance which are taken for granted in the present-day American show ring.

For effective presentation, the Bichon should be trimmed to show the eyes and to give a full, rounded appearance to the head and body. The hair around the feet should be trimmed to give a rounded look. The effect, when properly brushed, is of a "powder puff". Puppies may be shown in short coat, but the minimum show coat for adults is 2″ long.

standards

The general appearance of this small, gay and playful breed as given in the Standard of the Bichon Frise Club of America is that of a sturdy, lively dog of stable temperament, with a stylish gait and an air of dignity and intelligence.

The head is in proportion with the size of the dog, the skull broad, somewhat round, and covered with a topknot of hair. The ears are drop, covered with long, flowing hair, the leather about half as long as the muzzle. The muzzle is of medium length, not coarse or snipey, with a slight stop. The body is slightly longer than the height, which is not exceeding 12″ and not less than 8″. The back inclines gradually from the withers to a slight rise over the loin, which is large and muscular, and the tail is carried gaily, curved to lie on the back, and covered with long, flowing hair. The coat is profuse, silky in texture, and loosely curled, with a good undercoat.

Bolognese

One of the toy breeds (the Maltese, Havanais and Bichon Frise are others) having many points in common – long coats, heads not too long, broad skulls, pronounced occiputs and well-defined stops. The muzzles short, and blunt; noses black. Eyes large and round; ears drop, well covered with hair and set-on high. The heads carried proudly.

The bodies are longer than they are high, straight backs, broad loins, chests deep and ribs well-sprung. Tails set-on high, plumed, and curled over the backs.

The Bolognese is registered at the F.C.I. as an Italian breed. There is some evidence that the breed was first identified in Italy, in Bologna, in the 14th century and, although these "Bichons" all have a common Mediterranean origin, the Bolognese is thought to have been reintroduced to Italy from the Canary Islands, where its cousin, the Bichon Frise (once named Tenerife Dog), also originated.

The Bolognese should be under 12″ in height, and weigh under 11 lbs. Its coat is long and thick, and the hair short on the muzzle.

It is pure white, but very slight fawn markings are permissible.

Cavalier King Charles Spaniel

Ch. Alansmere McGoogans Maggie May won more C.C.s than any other Cavalier bitch. She represents ideal balance, make and shape, and this photograph shows her perfect set-on of muzzle, flat skull and required ear placement. Maggie May is owned by Messrs. Hall and Evans, and was bred by Mrs. Caroline Kirkpatrick.

history and development

Whatever its origin, the Cavalier King Charles Spaniel is the direct descendant of the small Toy Spaniels depicted in paintings of the 16th, 17th and 18th centuries. Toy Spaniels were quite common as pets among the ladies of the Tudor Court but, in England, it was the Stuarts who showed so much fondness for these little dogs that they were given Royal title of King Charles Spaniels.

Rarely was Charles II seen without several of these dogs at his heels and Samuel Pepys, the diarist, complained bitterly that at council meetings the King would play with his dogs rather than attend to council business. John Evelyn, writing in his diary, said: "He took delight in having a number of little Spaniels follow him and lie in his bedchamber where he suffered the bitches to puppy and give suck, which rendered it very offensive". On the night on which the King died, several of these dogs lay by the fire in the next room, creeping in to their master when the door was left open.

One of the earliest paintings showing a Cavalier type Spaniel is Bacchus and Ariadne by Titian, in the National Gallery in London; it was painted about 1523.

When William of Orange became William III of England, the Pug dog of the House of Orange ousted the toy spaniel from favor and it was not until the 19th century that it made a come-back when a special strain of red and white toy spaniel, with a distinctive lozenge spot, was

Cavaliers are portrayed in this painting by Sir Joshua Reynolds. The painting is at Blenheim Palace and is reproduced by permission of His Grace the Duke of Marlborough.

Ann's Son was the foundation sire of all Cavaliers. He was owned by the late Miss Mostyn Walker.

Ch. Abelard of Ttiweh, a famous blenheim sire, showing extreme quality, lovely expression and fine muzzle. The property of Miss B. Sadler. Note the lozenge spot in the center of the skull.

Ch. Oyster Pattie of Ttiweh, a very feminine bitch with a really lovely expression, and showing the spot on top of the skull, and the correct blaze. Coat not flat enough. The property of Mrs. A. Pitt, Oyster Pattie is by Mars of Ttiweh ex Pearl Blaze of Lochfee.

bred at Blenheim Palace by the Dukes of Marlborough. These little dogs were known for their sporting qualities as well as being favorite companions for the ladies. In those days, there were no dog shows and no recognized Standards, and so both type and size were very varied. With very little transport available, it is likely that breeding was carried out in the most haphazard fashion. It was all a matter of personal taste and probably depended on what stud dogs were available.

During Queen Victoria's reign, breeders began to hold shows and toy spaniel enthusiasts began seriously to breed dogs, and to a desired type. This brought a new fashion; dogs with shorter faces, which gradually evolved into the completely flat face of the modern King Charles Spaniel. At that time, there were a number of very able breeders and they were extremely successful in breeding dogs of the highest quality with flat faces, very high dome and with long, low-set ears. This type is still a popular and lovely breed.

It was at this stage that Mr. Roswell Eldridge, an American, came over to England and was unpleasantly surprised to find that there were none of his favorite little "nosey" Spaniels left. He set about trying to correct this situation by offering prizes over a period of three years (later extended to five years); £25 ($125) for best dog and best bitch, for animals of the Blenheim variety (red and white) as seen in King Charles II's time, exhibited at Cruft's dog shows. The following is a quotation taken from Cruft's Catalog: "As shown in the pictures of King Charles II's time, long face, no stop; flat skull, not inclined to be domed and with the spot in the center of the skull", and the prize to go to the nearest to the desired type.

No one among the breeders took these classes very seriously. After all, they had worked very hard to get rid of the long nose, and to restore it was never a popular move. Gradually, as the prize offer ended, only people who had become interested in reviving the dogs as they had once been were left to carry on breeding experiments. At the end of five years, very little recognition had been achieved; the Kennel Club was of the opinion that not only were there too few dogs, but those that were bred were not sufficiently of a single type to merit separate breed registration.

About this time, Mr. Eldridge died in America and, regrettably, he did not live to see the eventual fruits of his interest and generosity.

In 1928 a Club was formed in England and a title for the breed was chosen – Cavalier King Charles Spaniel. It was very important that association with the King Charles Spaniel should be retained as some of the short-faced stock threw back very quickly and pioneers were often accused of using outcrosses to get the long face. This practice was not recommended by the club. Most reliable breeders realized that the longest way was the quickest, and they persisted in breeding back through experiments, gradually finding those short-faced dogs which threw-back easily to the original type.

At the first meeting of the club held at Cruft's dog show, the Standard of the breed was drawn up and it was practically the same as it is today.

The living dog, Ann's Son, was chosen as a pattern for the Standard along with pictures of dogs of the 16th, 17th and 18th centuries. Since this was a tremendous opportunity to achieve a really worth-while breed, it was agreed that the dog should, as far as possible, be guarded against the dictates of fashion – there was to be no trimming! A perfectly natural dog was desired; not to be spoiled by idiosyncrasy or by being "carved into shape". Twenty years went by until, in 1945, the English Kennel Club granted the breed separate registration, followed in the next year by the first set of Challenge Certificates.

From its very small and unpropitious start, the breed has grown to a registration of over two thousand in the United Kingdom.

The parent body in Britain is the Cavalier King Charles Spaniel Club and there are breed clubs in Australia, New Zealand and in the United States.

Finally, some of the dogs which have played a really big part in the breed: Ann's Son, Ch. Daywell Roger, Ch. Aloysius of Sunninghill (a tricolor), Ch. Abelard of Ttiweh, Ch. Cerdric of Ttiweh and Ch. Pargeter Bob Up.

Ch. Vairire Osiris, all glamor, deep body, well-sprung ribs, long silky coat without curl, well set ears of good length – all male, showing plenty of quality. Not only an impressive show dog, but also a great sire. The property of Mrs. Julia Wilde. By Ch. Cerdric of Ttiweh ex Vairire Isis.

English and Irish Ch. Pargeter Mc-Bounce, a great show dog and sire, excels in the qualities for which the late Mrs. Barbara Keswick's Pargeter Cavaliers were renowned – magnificent heads with gentle expressions, and the richest of blenheim coloring. Following Mrs. Keswick's death McBounce was transferred to Miss Caroline Gatheral's ownership.

503

Ch. Crisdig Celebration, illustrating the desired tapered muzzle, clean cut, with no trace of lippyness. Owned and bred by Mrs. J. Burgess.

color

There are four basic colorations:—

Blenheim: Pearly white with red markings, well broken up, dark eyes, really dense pigment and, if possible, the lozenge spot.

Tricolor: Black-and-white with tan markings inside ears, on brow and down hind legs. These markings should be as clear as in the Blenheim. Over-marking is a blemish rather than a fault.

Black-and-tan: One of the loveliest and, when good, quite one of the best Cavalier colors, but black-and-tans do need a great deal of presentation. At their best they can challenge the blenheims.

Ruby: The most recently bred color and carrying a lot of faults, including thick necks and coarse coats, but it is improving all the time, and we now, at last, have ruby champions.

It is essential that all the colors carry heavy pigment, no excuses being made for the hereditary off-colored nose; a point of defeat for many otherwise good dogs.

care

Reasonable attention to grooming the long silky coat is necessary to avoid tangles; otherwise, normal exercise and feeding are all that is necessary to keep it fit and well.

character

They are extremely adaptable and make excellent companions for both young children and for older people. Sporting in character, absolutely fearless and with a gay, free action.

standards

It must never be forgotten that, although the Cavalier is small, it is a royal breed and thus should possess great presence, quality and glamor. The accompanying photographs are chosen to illustrate this.

Movement is of great importance – the gait should be elegant, light and airy. Temperament must be perfect; the dog should not be nervous or snappy. The breed has attained these qualities and they should be looked for and preserved.

Representatives of the outstanding Pargeter kennel, all now owned by Miss C. L. M. Gatheral. L. to r: Pargeter Pensong; Ch. Pargeter Myrrhis (who was reserve best in show at Belfast and is a litter sister to Int. Ch. McBounce); Ch. Pargeter Melissa (the dam of Ch. Myrrhis and Int. Ch. McBounce); and the C.C. winning Pargeter Hi-Jack, who Mrs. Keswick considered to be an even better dog than McBounce.

The head should be almost flat between the ears and without any dome. The stop is shallow; length from base of stop to tip is about 1½". Nostrils should be well-developed and, as mentioned above, pigmented black. The muzzle should taper well to the point.

Eye placement is very important. They should be set wide apart and be round and dark brown in color, giving that limpid, gentle look which all Cavaliers should have. A narrow head with black eyes, giving a hard "terrier" look is undesirable; so also is a muzzle which is too narrow. The ears should be long and set high, with plenty of feather.

The short-coupled body has plenty of spring of rib, and the back is level. Shoulders should not be too straight; legs are moderately boned and straight. Docking of the tail is optional, but its length should be in balance with the body.

The long, silky coat should be free from curl although a slight wave is permissible. There should be plenty of feather.

Weight has always been a bone of contention, but the Standard calls for a small, well-balanced dog between 12 lbs. and 18 lbs; most of the best have been in the top weights but the breed is still very young, and it is hoped to produce perfection – a medium weight dog with all the virtues.

Ch. Amelia of Laguna, showing the gentle expression, front face. She also has the spot. This bitch won the toy group at Cruft's. The property of Mrs. Frank Cryer.

Ch. Archie McMuck of Eyeworth is the greatest ever representative of a famous Cavalier kennel in Britain – Lady Forwood's Eyeworth kennel.

Chihuahua
(Long-coat, Smooth-coat)

Ch. Rozavel Uvalda Jemima was the greatest winning Chihuahua bitch of either coat Britain has known. She won twenty-one C.C.s and was best bitch, all breeds, at a general championship show. Bred by Mrs. B. Payne, Ch. Jemima was owned by the most successful Chihuahua breeder and exhibitor in Britain, Mrs. Thelma Gray.

history and development

Chihuahuas are the smallest members of the canine family. Contrary to popular belief, they are not Mexican in origin. They have existed, relatively unchanged, for hundreds of years, in the lands of the Mediterranean. Ten years before Columbus made his first voyage one was featured by Boticelli, in a fresco in the Sistine Chapel, Rome, the only dog to receive such recognition. Many modern, cream-colored Smooth Chihuahuas look remarkably like the dog in that painting. However, the show type specimen of today was developed in the U.S.A. They flourish on the island of Malta, where they are known as pocket-dogs (Kelb Ta But), and in England, well before 1850, British fanciers made a number of semi-successful attempts to establish them. Early English breeders stated that these "Maltese" terriers, as they called them, were used to refine several other small breeds before they submerged.

When tourists, soon after 1850, found and purchased specimens from peons in the north Mexican state of Chihuahua, unsuspecting American breeders gave the dog its name and established it as a firm favorite in the U.S.A. They drew up a breed Standard and today it is one of the top popularity breeds, sixth among 116 breeds; most Chihuahuas in Britain and on the Continent stem from American-bred stock. However, it is of special interest to note that one of the most prepotent Smooth-coated stud dogs in England, Rowley Black Mite, resulted from crossing a Smooth red bitch imported from Malta by Lt.-Cmdr. A. J. Egerton-Williams with a Smooth dog brought from the U.S.A. by Mrs. Joan Forster.

A dog similar to the Chihuahua appears to have evolved in Egypt about 3,000 years ago. A detailed description of the mummified remains of one of these little dogs, found in an Egyptian tomb, was recorded by the zoologist, K. Haddon, in 1910. She noted the presence of that curious identification mark of the Chihuahua, the "molera" or "soft" spot which often occurs in their skulls.

The colony of Chihuahuas, or pocket dogs, that thrive on Malta, were taken there from north Africa by Carthaginian colonists around 600 B.C. The Maltese apparently specialized in breeding them and a piece of pottery dated approximately 100 B.C. shows a crude drawing of a man holding two such dogs on a leash.

In the 15th century this dog became the symbol of the drama of Malta. The Maltese on one occasion, finding that they were threatened by an extra large Turkish raiding expedition, fled to the mainland, carrying everything, including their livestock, with them. Although the Boticelli fresco in the Sistine Chapel portrays the life of Moses, this episode is deliberately recorded in it. The boy carrying the tiny smooth-coated dog under his arm, who is included in the group of Israelites being led by Moses from slavery in Egypt, represents the Malta refugees, fleeing from the Turkish menace – and the dog establishes the identity of the group.

In 1530 the Knights of St. John established their base on Malta. After the famous Siege of 1565, Malta and the Order of St. John were much esteemed. The little dogs appeared in England and were mentioned in the Holinshed Chronicles. "The Maltese is little and pretty . . . the smaller they are the better they are liked, and especially if they have a hole (the molera) in the foreparts of their heads," wrote the chronicler.

While Boticelli, using the dog as his symbol, recorded the beginning of the saga, an unnamed Maltese artist appropriately recorded the end. He painted a portrait of Emmanuel de Rohan, when Bailey of the Order, accompanied by one of the pocket-dogs, which hangs in the palace of the Grand Masters at Valetta. Emmanuel de Rohan was the last Grand Master of the Order to rule in the grand manner. In 1800 Malta became British and the little dogs reappeared in Britain. Early records describe some of them as weighing little more than three pounds. The Irish naturalist, Mr. Richardson, published an interesting account of them in 1847, calling them Maltese terriers. His description is unmistakable – smooth coats, black the preferred color, but red or white being acceptable, erect ears and minute size coupled with great courage. His uncle, he stated, had one that weighed four pounds. He mentioned that Sir Edwin Landseer painted one, and this tiny, black, smooth-coated toy-dog, looking startlingly like our modern Chihuahuas, can be seen standing next to the King Charles Spaniel in Landseer's painting, Diogenes. These dogs also exist on Gibraltar, and in Spain and Portugal, but it is difficult to decide whether they were established there by Carthaginian colonists or later by Spanish and Portuguese members of the Order of St. John.

The American tourists who found them near the Villa D'Allende in

Detail showing dog from the Boticelli fresco (1482) in the Sistine Chapel, Rome.

Ch. Rozavel Alfonso Zapangu is typical of the many champions owned by Mrs. Thelma Gray. Bred by Mr. Bryan Mitchell, Ch. Alfonso is the youngest Long-coat Chihuahua ever to have won a C.C. – at seven months.

Chihuahua had no idea that these were the descendants of an ancient Old World breed. Naturally, enthusiasts in the U.S.A. called the dogs "chihuahuas" and searched in the Mexican records for background history. The result was unfortunate. Some believe the Chihuahua became confused with the strange hairless dog, Xoloitzcuintli or Mexican Hairless Dog.

Chihuahua, Long-coated: Chihuahuas on Malta are always Smooth-coated and never throw Longs; this is also true of a number of American lines, and the Chihuahua has been regarded primarily as a Smooth-coated dog. When the breed was re-introduced into England at the end of the 'forties and early 'fifties, Long-coats were rare indeed. Yet, according to the American records, one of the first Chihuahuas to reach the U.S.A. from Mexico was a red Long-coat, Caranza, belonging to Mr. Watson.
Pictures can be found on ancient Greek vases, and Renaissance and later paintings that depict Long-coated dogs very similar in build and type to Smooth-coated Chihuahuas. These were much loved by the Spanish royal family, and were also taken to the Americas by Spanish colonists. At first, Long and Smooth-coated Chihuahuas in both the U.S.A. and

The perfect Chihuahua head is represented by Ch. Jofos Kitty's Little Joe (both pictures). Bred by Mrs. Kitty Culbertson in the U.S.A., Ch. Little Joe was imported into Britain by Mrs. Joan Forster for whom he won eight C.C.s, the first at his first show in the country.

Britain were treated as one breed, but today are classified as separate varieties. Inter-breeding between them will not be permitted by the British Kennel Club after 1976, but it will be many years before the Smooth-coated variety can be depended on to breed only Smooth-coats. Long-coats bred together do not produce Smooths.

There is no difference between the two varieties apart from coat, which vary greatly in quality, some being very thick with heavy undercoats, others being thin, whispy, and lacking the required feathering. Occasionally one turns up with a curly coat. No doubt in time, with careful breeding, this problem of variation will sort itself out, for the Long-coated variety is here to stay.

color

The breed Standard permits any color or combination of colors, and so far, the color inheritance of this breed has not conformed to any recognizable pattern. Optimistic breeders have endeavored to concentrate on one favorite color or another with varying degrees of success. The puppies in a litter seldom resemble either each other, or their parents, color-wise. Even on Malta, where black has been preferred and deliberately in-bred

A bitch showing a number of good and bad points in the breed. To be praised are her excellent neck, level back, good lay-back of shoulder, deep brisket, well sprung ribs and correct proportions of height and length. Against her are her over-long nose, shallow stop and faulty hindquarters (her stifle joints are too straight).

for over 150 years, tans, chocolates, fawns, reds, whites and particolors still turn up.

care

Properly reared and cared for, Chihuahuas are long-lived dogs, sometimes reaching nineteen or twenty years of age. They require a warm, dry bed, well away from draughts, with some heat in winter. The adult should be given one good meat meal every day, but do not over feed with table scraps. They are ideal dogs for the town and will obtain most of the exercise they need following their owners around the house, but naturally, will appreciate a run out of doors, off the lead, if this can be arranged. They can, for the sake of convenience, be carried on buses, trains and in crowded areas in a shopping bag or basket, but should never be treated as invalids.

The normal fondling that a Smooth-coated pet Chihuahua receives is as good as a daily massage, but the Long-coated variety needs regular, gentle brushing and combing. Nails grow fast and must be clipped back regularly. Teeth should be checked frequently, and if milk teeth are still in the gums when a puppy reaches six months of age, the vet should be asked to remove them. New owners and children handling a Chihuahua for the first time must be careful not to let the little dog jump suddenly from their arms. Puppies are especially liable to do this and may hurt themselves badly in consequence.

When breeding, let the vet see the bitch ten days before the puppies are due. Most bitches of reasonable size whelp without trouble, but there are some who will require veterinary attention. But it is unfair both to the bitch and the vet to wait until the last moment should trouble arise. Do not breed from tiny bitches, and remember that a tiny stud dog will not necessarily produce tiny offspring.

A Long-hair puppy of three months old.

character

The Chihuahua, considering its small size, is a surprisingly agile, courageous and fiery dog. In England between 1800 and 1850, the tiny dogs from Malta were tried out in the rat pits. Richardson stated that his uncle's dog, Lion, once killed an enormous rat in a few seconds, but added that they were too small to be really useful and had "degenerated" into "mere lap-dogs". Modern Chihuahuas are equally willing to "have a go", as many present-day owners have discovered.

They are exceptionally intelligent, love to be fussed, but tend to be suspicious and shy with strangers. They live contentedly with other

Ch. Rozavel Mermaid, a very fine Long-coat owned and bred by Mrs. Thelma Gray, displays the typical ear feathering and ruff on the neck.

A promising puppy at three months old.

household pets such as cats, rabbits, and guinea-pigs, but will not tolerate intruders.

standards

The Chihuahua should not weigh more than six pounds, the average weight being about four pounds. It must be compact, fine-boned, with well-sprung ribs and deep brisket. A good Chihuahua moves with a brisk, firm, forceful action that can only be achieved if symmetry and angulation of shoulder and hindquarters is correct. A slightly arched neck of medium length goes with a good lay-back of shoulder and straight front legs. The hindquarters need strong muscles if the dog is to be sound and move correctly. The level back is slightly longer than the height at shoulder, while feet are small and dainty with well-cushioned pads. The skull, with or without molera, should be well-rounded, with erect, large, low-set "fly-away" ears that have plenty of width between them and give the dog an alert, intelligent appearance. The nose must be moderately short and slightly pointed. The stop should be well-defined. The eyes are large and round, but do not protrude. On Smooths the tail should be furry, flattish in appearance, and, after broadening slightly in the center, taper to a point. It should be carried sickle-wise, up or over the back. On Longs it should be well-feathered and carried proudly. The Long-coated Chihuahua should have a large ruff on the neck and feathering on feet and legs. The coat should be long, of soft texture, and never harsh or curly.

Chinese Crested Dog

Winterlea Why-Ho of Crest Haven, imported from America to England by Mrs. Marjorie Mooney. Note the fine, supple skin, spotted on the leg, the profuse crest of hair and the slight feathering on feet and tail. These little dogs are warm to the touch; they have no coat but provide their own central heating.

Now extinct in China the Chinese Crested Dog appears in small numbers in various parts of the world, gaining its firmest foot-hold in Florida. In Great Britain, the Chinese Crested Club was registered with the Kennel Club in 1969. While much of its history is hidden it is certain that the breed has bred true and remained unchanged for well over a century. These little, hairless dogs were once the pets of the Mandarins. It is believed they were brought to Mexico by the Toltecs, who used them as Temple Dogs, and in some countries they are called Chinese Crested Temple Dogs.

Dogs of this kind were known in Central and South America and the West Indies since the 16th century. In 1887 the American Kennel Club registered four specimens as Mexican Hairless. Activity fell after the 1930's. Interest had been dead for a dozen years when the A.K.C. stopped registrations in 1960. There is no connection between this breed and the Chihuahua.

A numbers of colors are allowed; blue, pink, golden, lilac, self-colored or spotted. They frequently change color, being much darker in Summer than in Winter.

Without vice and very affectionate, the Chinese Crested is a clean dog, completely odorless and will not leave hairs on the furniture. Active and graceful, it is the smallest of the hairless breeds. Average weight should be between 6 and 8 lbs. never more than 12 lbs.

The skin is fine and silky. The head carries a crest of flowing hair which is also seen on feet and end of tail.

English Toy Terrier

(Black and Tan) (Toy Manchester)

Mrs. Kitty Voce's home-bred Ch. Bordesley Bow Bells is not only one of the greatest winning English Toy Terrier bitches of all time but also a worthy daughter of the great Ch. Rajah of Ivycourt.

A young English Toy Terrier dog

history and development

The English Toy Terrier, designated by the American Kennel Club as the Toy variety of the Manchester Terrier, was originally used in the destruction of vermin, and in the past no huntsman was without the rough Black and Tan in his pack, to flush the fox "gone to ground". There has always been a great variation in weight, some animals favoring a Terrier type around 8 lbs., others, the tinies, of 3 lbs. upwards. These latter dogs are delightful pets but reflect little credit on the breed, and the variations have resulted in vast differences in size in the show ring. This is caused by haphazard breeding in the past, when the nearest available stud dog was used with little consideration of pedigree. Even today, after many generations of careful breeding, a very large or very small one will turn up in a litter.

Apple heads, large round eyes, tucked up hindquarters and poor thin coats were common up to 1950. Since that time great improvements have been made; true Terrier heads, almond shaped eyes and thick glossy coats

Ch. Lancer of Leospride became a champion as a puppy and went on to become the top winning English Toy Terrier dog of his day with many C.C.s. He is owned by Mrs. Boud and bred by Mrs. Eunice Roberts.

An alert English Toy Terrier.

The only English Toy Terrier to win a Toy group at Cruft's is Ch. Stealaway Golden Girl, whose spectacular show career included two group wins at championship shows. Her owner is Mr. Frank Palmer and her breeder Mrs. Hunt.

predominate today.

The records of the English Toy Terrier date back to the 15th century, from a small rough-haired Black and Tan depicted in an illuminated manuscript dealing with the seasons of the year which also showed Lakeland, Welsh, Irish, Airedale and Manchester Terriers. In the passing of time, Whippets and Italian Greyhounds were bred-in to produce finer bone, and lighter build, and their presence is still evident today, in the hindquarters.

The Black and Tans have always been renowned for their prowess in the rat pits. In 1848, Jimmy Shaw matched his Tiny – the Wonder, a $5\frac{1}{2}$ lbs. miniature Black and Tan, to kill 300 rats in three hours at the Queens Head Tavern, London, where he ran the Toy Dog Club. He won the wager in the unprecedented time of 54 minutes 50 seconds.

Today, dogs reared correctly are just as game. I know cases where for many generations none has ever seen a rat, but at the first sight of one it has killed in seconds.

color

The predominant color is jet black with rich deep tan on muzzle and throat, a spot over each eye, and each cheek, and inside the ears. The color continues on the forelegs to the knee in front, continuing to the top inside. A thin black line (pencilling) on each toe, and pear-shaped marks on pasterns (thumb marks), circular tan marks on chest over each leg (rosettes), hind legs tanned in front and inside and under tail. The colors should be well defined. Tan hairs on the outside of hind legs and white hairs forming a patch (breeching) are serious faults.

care

Although regarded by some as looking frail and delicate, they are in fact very robust. Having a very fine coat, they are naturally housedogs, and enjoy warmth and a comfortable bed. In winter a dog-coat is advisable out of doors, and they hate windy conditions. They are easy whelpers, splendid mothers, with an average litter of three to five.

To keep in condition, give a good brushing each day, and wash the face with a damp cloth. To ensure a sheen on the coat I find nothing better than a teaspoonful of olive oil on their food twice a week, which has a much more lasting effect than anything rubbed on the coat.

Being short-coated they are clean, without smell and a loose hair is hard to find, making them ideal for any kind of house.

character

The English Toy Terrier is one of the most affectionate breeds. He is a "one man dog", who seems to be able to read your thoughts, is suspicious of strangers, and is an excellent house dog, giving warning of any unfamiliar sound before a human being is aware. Go out without him, and he will watch you out of sight and be the first to welcome you on your return. A perfect example of the esteem in which the English Toy Terrier is held in Britain was provided when he won a competition held by a national canine magazine for the ideal dog to take on a world cycling tour, with trailer.

standards

Very few changes have been made from the original Standard, but in the 1960's it was revised in several items. In "general appearance", "unduly" was added to "Nervous specimens cannot rank as wholly typical representatives of the breed". I objected strongly to the "unduly" as it gave the impression that nervous dogs were acceptable providing they were not "unduly" so. This is far from correct, very few are nervous; although they are suspicious of strangers. Ears *must* now be erect from nine months old. Instead of "should not exceed 8 lbs., with no minimum", it is now 6 lbs. to 8 lbs., 10″ to 12″ at shoulders. The A.K.C. Standard permits up to 12 lbs., but many are 7 lbs. or under (the larger variety ranges from 12 lbs. to 22 lbs.). Overall it should be a compact dog, not whippety, with a deep narrow chest, a graceful neck, narrow skull and erect ears to finish the picture. Imagine a racehorse and that is my ideal of an English Toy Terrier. In 1960 the Committee of the Miniature Black and Tan Terriers Club decided to ask the English Kennel Club for a change of name. Many people, when asking what breed they were, were told "Black and Tan Terriers", and then replied "I know that, but what do they call the breed?"

As this was a very old English breed, the name requested was English Toy Terrier (Black and Tan). This was granted and the breed carried that name from April 1960.

The Standards abroad are practically identical with the British, and in U.S.A. and Canada they are known as Toy Manchesters. Registrations in Britain average about 100 to 150 a year.

Ch. All Gold of Lenster will be remembered for all time as the breed's greatest sire. With seventeen offspring he won the progeny class, competing with all breeds at Windsor championship show in 1970, having been second in 1969.

The breed's first international champion, Ch. Stealaway Shula who won her titles in Britain and Australasia. She is a full younger sister to the great sire Ch. All Gold of Lenster (both bred by Mr. Frank Palmer), one of whose daughters is Ch. Stealaway Golden Girl.

English Toy Spaniel
See page 528

515

Griffon
(Brabançon, Bruxellois)

Success in the show ring and also at stud is not always found in the same dog, but Ch. Skibbereen Olliver of Otterbourne can claim an impressive record in both fields. He was bred by Mrs. M. Dixon and owned by Mrs. E. Street.

Black and tan champion Griffons are a rarity, and Ch. Chosendale Penni-candy of Tunlake is the breed's top winning black and tan in the United Kingdom. She was bred by Miss R. Deck and owned by Mr. D. Gregory.

history and development

As their name implies the Griffon Bruxellois (Brussels Griffon) is essentially a Belgian breed.

There are many theories about the ancestry of the Griffon. The most logical explanation would appear to be that the Belgian street dog (now practically, if not entirely, extinct) and the German Affenpinscher formed the basis of the Griffon. Indeed, the Affenpinscher and the rough Griffon do still bear a close resemblance. Toward 1880 the Belgian street dog/ Affenpinscher mixture was crossed with the Pug which, at that time, was popular in neighboring Holland. To this cross is attributed the shortened muzzle of the present-day Griffon, its breadth of skull and jaws and the clean outline of its body. The Affenpinscher and Belgian street dog both had longish coats and the introduction of the Pug is responsible for the smooth or short-coated Griffon. This variety is known as Petit Brabançon. In the early days, the Petit Brabançon was not recognized and all smooth-coated puppies were destroyed. However, soon the practical advantages of a smooth-coated dog became apparent and the Petit Brabançon was permitted. It was originally known as the Griffon Brabançon – "Griffon" signifying thickly coated, no matter what the breed.

The Griffon was first exhibited in 1880 at the Brussels Exhibition. At that time, classes were divided into two – Griffon Bruxellois and Griffons of all colors. The Bruxellois were red. Gradually the breed became popular with the nobility in Belgium and were in great demand as the pets of society. Queen Astrid of the Belgians was a Griffon owner. In 1914 the breed was almost at the height of its popularity in Belgium, but the First World War reduced breeding drastically. One of the few dogs to survive was Bouquet who, after the war, won first prize in a mixed class of 125 Griffons Bruxellois and Petit Brabançons. The first Griffon Bruxellois were imported into Britain in 1894 where, in 1896, the Griffon Bruxellois Club was formed.

There was little uniformity in type and appearance in the early days of the breed and, although this is becoming more regularized, there is still quite a diversity of type today. At the Alexandra Palace Show in London in 1900 Copthorne Pasha and his son, the unbeaten Ch. Copthorne Top-o-the-Tree, made their first appearance and Pasha is credited with being a great influence on the breed, giving the stamp of the correct underjaw and breed type to his many descendants. Registration figures in Great Britain have remained fairly static, currently running at around 550 per year. At present both varieties of Griffons are shown in mixed classes, but it is hoped that if registrations increase the classification may be altered to provide separate classes for smooths and roughs as in other breeds such as Fox Terriers.

The great American Griffon Bruxellois, Am. Ch. Barmere's Mighty Man, eleven times best in show and the first Griffon best in show winner in the U.S.A. Mighty Man was bred and owned by Mrs. Miriam Breed.

Surely one of the great achievements of the breed in Britain occurred when Ch. Skibbereen Victor of Campfield won best in show at Leicester Championship Show while still a puppy. Two of the most significant litters ever bred in Britain must certainly have been those from the mating of Ch. Playboy Simon and Brabjoy Malmsey which produced Ch. Oscar of Otterbourne in the first litter and Ch. Skibbereen Olliver of Otterbourne and Ch. Olive of Otterbourne in the repeat mating.

In America, yearly registrations are now around 200. Undoubtedly, the best known American-bred Griffon must be Ch. Barmere's Mighty Man who was the first Griffon to win best in show at an all-breed show and was eleven times best in show all breeds as well as being top winning toy dog in the U.S.A. in 1962 and 1963.

Ch. Robinvale Spice, owned and bred by Mrs. Madge Sheehan.

Griffons were first imported into Australia just before the 1939 war. The breed died out for lack of new blood and, in 1955, five red rough Camp-field Griffons were brought in and they, with other British exports, form the nucleus of Griffons in Australia today. In 1969 there was an estimated registration, in the whole of Australia of 127 Griffons.

Interest in Griffons is wide-spread, registration occurring also in South Africa, Denmark and Italy. In Sweden, incidentally, registrations are separated between Brabançon and Bruxellois, and there are now around sixty-three Brabançon and 135 Bruxellois registered. In the country of their origin – Belgium – cropping of ears is the showing rule, in America it depends upon the State law and some dogs, both imports and home-bred, are shown uncropped. Sweden does not permit cropping, neither does Australia and it is not allowed in Britain.

color

There are now three varieties of the breed. The Griffon Bruxellois, which

Miss B. M. Gorringe's Ch. Litahni Ninette, born in 1950, provides a particularly lovely subject for a head study.

A head study of Mr. R. Irving-Lowther's Griffon Bruxellois, Ch. Annabelle of Kirkmarland.

we now accept as the rough-haired variety, is either clear red, black or black and rich tan. The red should be a clear, rich color the black a clear black with absence of gray, white or rust hairs and the black and tan a good clear black combined with rich tan markings.

The Griffon or Petit Brabançon is a smooth-haired variety in the same colors as the Bruxellois.

Thirdly, there is the Griffon Belge which would appear only to be recognized on the Continent and has a red and black mixed coat – the colors must not be patches of either color, but every hair must be a mixed color without any shading.

care

Griffons are easy to care for and are better without frequent baths. However, daily grooming is essential. The smooth-coated variety are best brushed with a rubber brush, towelled over with a piece of rough towelling and finished off with a piece of velvet, silk or chamois. Particular care should be taken to clean, with a damp cloth, in between the folds of the muzzle.

The roughs should have a terrier-like coat and it should be treated as such. This means it will require stripping right down about twice a year and periodically trimmed to keep it looking nice. This can be done with the finger and thumb or with a stripping comb – not knife and certainly never scissors. A knife tends only to cut the coat and consequently the new coat does not come in a rich color because all of the old coat has not been properly removed. Routine care for a rough should include daily grooming with a wire glove (except immediately after stripping when a soft hound glove is recommended), whiskers washed off with a damp cloth, eyes gently wiped with damp cotton wool – make sure to take the hair from the corner of the eyes – and ears inspected. The legs and whiskers should be combed with a wire comb. Nails on both varieties should be kept short.

character

One of the most charming attributes of the Griffon is its monkey-like face which has almost a human quality of expression. These dogs possess great intelligence – many have been trained as obedience dogs. Vivacity and intangible charm combine together to produce the unique character of these delightful little dogs with their terrier-like temperament.

A lovely example of a feminine Griffon head, Mrs. M. Dixon's Ch. Olive of Otterbourne, showing the monkey face and quizzical expression of a typical Griffon Bruxellois.

518

The Griffon is not a delicate dog, but hardy and full of fun. More than any other breed, they seem to go through a "teen-ager" stage and it is very difficult at such times to assess their final potential. One can often see the quality there at anything from a few hours to a few days old, and they are forever changing until they reach maturity.

standards
A prominent turned-up chin is now recognized as being one of the most important physical attributes of the breed. Red pinwire coats are in the majority.

The present-day British Standard calls for a dog from 3 lbs. to 10 lbs. Most desirable being 6 to 9 lbs. Size has always varied in winning Griffons and even in the early days some weighed under 3 lbs. while others tipped the scale at 9 lbs. The Standard in the U.S.A. suggests 8 to 10 lbs. but should not exceed 12 lbs.

The Griffon should have a large head, with plenty of width between the ears and a black nose, short and set well back with a deep stop between the nose and skull. To preserve the expression the eyes must be large, round and black or nearly black with black rims. The chin must be prominent and slightly undershot, but the teeth must not show; the muzzle wide and with a good turnup. In the rough variety the beard should be profuse. Griffons are cobby little dogs with short backs, straight fronts and muscular hindquarters.

One of the surprising aspects of breeding Griffons is that you never know what to expect in any one litter because rough and smooth coats frequently occur in the same litter and in any of the accepted colors.

Mrs. M. Dixon's Remosa Relko of Otterbourne represents the Griffon Brabançon, of which breed he is an outstanding example. Both coats compete together and without the advantage of coat the Smooth variety does well to hold its own.

Havanese

This Cuban breed is one of the Bichons, of which the Maltese is the best known, which come from the Western Mediterranean area. Undoubtedly its ancestors travelled to Cuba during the days of the Spanish empire. Like the other Bichons it has been bred as a pet; for its looks and for its charming friendly nature.

The head is wide with a definite stop and a slightly pointed muzzle; the rounded nose is black in color. The large eyes are very dark, preferably black and the pointed ears fall gently in a light fold.

The body is a little longer than it is high and the sides are rounded, with the flanks lifted high. The line of the back terminates in a flat rump. Straight, rather slim legs, with slightly lengthened feet, with slim toes. The beautiful tail is held high, curled over the back and has a plume of long, soft hair.

The coat is rather flat, fairly soft and whispy, with light curls at the ends; varying in color from all white, which is rare, through light and dark beige to a tobacco brown. It may also be gray or white, marked widely with beige or tobacco brown.

The hair on the muzzle may be lightly trimmed but it is preferable to let it grow naturally.

It is a small dog, weighing not more than 13 lbs.

Italian Greyhound

The Marchesa Montecuccoli of Rome owns some of the world's most outstanding Italian Greyhounds. Three are seen here, including, on the right, the dam of Int. Ch. Ulisse di Peltrengo of Winterlea.

history and development

It seems likely that the Italian Greyhound stems from the same source as the dog of the greyhound group depicted in carvings on the tombs of the Pharaohs many thousand years ago. The late Mrs. Thring in her recently published book on the breed says it is thought to have been taken by the Romans from Egypt to the Mediterranean areas in the 6th or 7th centuries B.C. In England the breed was known and obviously popular at the courts of the Stuarts possibly having been brought back from the Continent by gentlemen as gifts for their ladies. Witness to this fact are paintings depicting members of aristocratic families with their dogs, usually Spaniels and Italian Greyhounds. The most famous is that of Anne of Denmark, consort of King James I, painted by Van Somers in 1614, with five of these little hounds, all pied, and one which looks very small, although the others are larger than we see today. Blue or gray, with white markings, they show all the characteristics and postures peculiar to the breed.

Queen Victoria owned Italian Greyhounds while, in Prussia, Frederick the Great was reputed to adore these little dogs who travelled with him everywhere. In the last century it would seem the breed was considerably reduced in size judging by the following description from a writer at the commencement of the 19th century. "A diminutive native breed which seems only calculated to sooth vanity and indulge frivolities: these dogs are so deficient in spirit, sagacity and fortitude . . . as not to be able to officiate in the services of domestic alarm and protection and in consequence are dedicated only to the comforts of the tea-table, the fire-side carpet, the luxurious indulgences of the sofa and the warm lap of the mistress." It may well be that this fashion for breeding smaller and smaller animals was responsible for the near extinction of the breed resulting in the production of unsound, apple-headed and nervous animals. This was about 1860 when most Italian Greyhounds were in the hands of dealers.

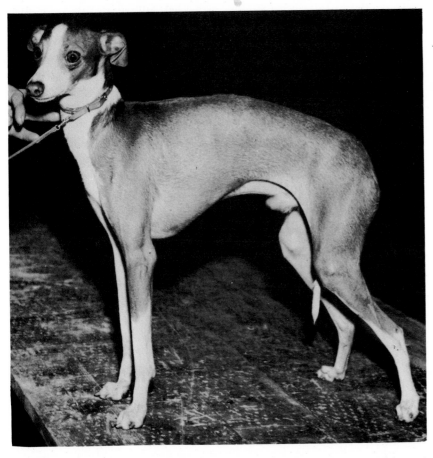

In 1890 a Miss Mackenzie took an interest in them and by sensible and clever breeding built up a remarkably successful kennel. Literally sweeping the board at shows she was largely responsible for keeping up and improving the breed. At a later date Mrs. Scarlett, building her strain on Miss Mackenzie's stock, developed a strong kennel of winners and valuable breeding stock from which many of our present-day dogs descend. In 1900 several Italian Greyhound enthusiasts in England formed the Italian Greyhound Club, the first patrons and presidents included Lord and Lady Waterford, Lady Abinger, Lady Brisco and Baroness Campbell von Laurentz, all owners of well-known dogs. The Club has flourished ever since, with the exception of the war years of 1914 and 1939. At the end of World War II the breed in Britain was revived with the introduction of fresh blood from America, France, Italy and Austria, combined with what was left of the old English blood lines, and it is in a stronger position today than for many years.

color

Favored colors have changed many times over the years, shades of gold, peach or apricot were at one time thought the most desirable although in the 1896 edition of Stonehenge's *Book of the Dog,* he says "the favorite colors are blue and fawn but the latter should be of an auburn hue. At one time cream colored dogs commanded the highest prices, then white with black nose but particolored dogs are not thought much of". At present there are a number of pieds of very good formation being exhibited although this color is not recognized on the Continent (where the breed is also classified as "Windhunds", not Toys) by those countries who take

Illustrating the difference in size between Greyhounds and Italian Greyhounds is Mrs. Molly Garrish's homebred Ch. Fleeting Fleur de Lys, a grand-daughter of Int. Ch. Ulisse. On this occasion the Italian won BOS in show to Mrs. de Casenbrook's Greyhound's best in show.

their Standard from the Italian one which bars animals having more than a tiny white mark on chest or toes. Any color or mixture of colors is acceptable in America and Britain with the exception in Britain of brindle or black and blue with tan markings, the latter being the result of a cross many years ago with the Black and Tan Terrier; and Black and Tan Terrier markings are disallowed in America.

care

Nothing more than an occasional grooming with a duster or silk handkerchief is necessary, except in the case of whites or pieds who require a warm bath before being shown. Care should be taken to see that they are thoroughly dry. Teeth require constant attention as they collect tartar quickly. Cleaning with cotton wool soaked in a mixture of persipticated chalk and peroxide of hydrogen, plus scraping if tartar is present. Nails require cutting back fairly frequently, unless the dog has a lot of road exercise. A warm bed or basket is needed, away from draughts and containing a soft blanket or rug. Most Italian Greyhounds love to wrap themselves up completely in their blanket even in the hottest weather, but though they do not mind cold or even snow, they hate the wind and wet. Good food and sensible exercise while carrying a litter will result in an easy whelping and healthy pups.

character

The best description of the Italian Greyhound is that of Mr. J. H. Walsh (Stonehenge). "The Italian Greyhound is one of the most graceful or perhaps the most graceful and racy looking animal on the face of the earth, being the most beautifully proportioned animal in creation." It is no longer the little, delicate creature who must never be allowed to get wet or go out without a dog-coat, but a vivacious alert little dog, highly intelligent and while sensitive to loud voices or harsh words from its owner, is exceptionally brave and courageous in illness. When kept as companions in the house they are gay and affectionate; loving human

Austrian and British Ch. Odin Springinsfeld, bred by Mrs. Pfleger, was imported into Britain by Mrs. M. B. Garrish and Mrs. M. Barnard. His influence as a sire and his success as a show dog make him one of the breed's great dogs in Britain. He won thirteen C.C.s in 1966 and 1967.

companionship, they do not thrive as kennel dogs. They require plenty of exercise but are accommodating enough to keep well and fit running and playing in a small garden. They are keen hunters and will tackle rabbits or even rats. Being quite free of "doggy" smells, their fine coats, which seldom moult, make them ideal house dogs and pets.

Though small, Italian Greyhounds are easy whelpers and good mothers. As they produce comparatively small litters, three would be the average, there is little danger of them becoming a commercial breed but one valued for its particular attributes and rarity.

standards

Always a matter of controversy the Standard mentions weight only, with nothing to say about height though it is generally accepted in England that 15″ at the shoulder should be the maximum. At one time classes were provided for under 8 lbs. and this is still true in the U.S.A.

The present English Standard with the exception of one or two minor points has been in existence since the formation of the Club in 1900. The Italian Greyhound should have a high stepping and free action. It is a miniature Greyhound, more slender in all proportions and elegant and graceful. Its skull is long, flat and narrow; its muzzle very fine and its nose dark in color. The ears are rose shaped, placed well back and delicate. The neck should be long and gracefully arched and the shoulders long and sloping, with straight legs well set under the shoulders. The pasterns are fine with small, delicate bone. The chest is deep and narrow; the back curved and drooping at the hindquarters, with rather long tail, fine and carried low. The hocks are well let down, thighs are muscular and feet long and hare shaped. The coat is fine and supple, the hair thin and glossy, like satin. The most desirable weight is from 6 to 8 lbs., not exceeding 10 lbs.

A personal opinion is that the Standard is in need of alteration. It is remarkable that the only mention under "faults" is that of color. In America black and tan terrier markings are not allowed.

Typical Italian Greyhound heads.

An illustration of what Italians should not look like. Note the heavy, badly carried ears, coarse heads, heavy, coarse bone, bad fronts and weak pasterns.

Japanese
(Japanese Spaniel)

Perfect type, represented by Ch. Pierre of Kurraba, the greatest C.C.-winning Japanese ever known in Britain. A model of the breed Standard, Ch. Pierre was owned and bred by Mrs. C. J. Batterbury.

The Japanese; a typical head from the side.

history and development

Rare indeed are those breeds of dog which have remained unaltered in appearance during the course of time. One such rarity is what is known in its country of origin, Japan, as the Chin; in Britain as the Japanese; and in the Americas as the Japanese Spaniel. No authoritative guide is available as to when Japanese first left their native country. Although Commodore Perry is generally attributed with initiating trade between Japan and the Occident in 1853, this is an exaggeration. In fact, the Portuguese were resident traders in Japan as early as 1542. From this may be surmised the possibility that Chins found their way to Europe during the 16th century. A Japanese was first exhibited in England in 1862. A similar event in the U.S.A. is recorded as taking place during 1882. In Europe Manet painted a Japanese in 1872, while the Empress of Germany was given two representatives of the breed in 1880; these are said to have come from the Japanese Imperial court.

Little reliable information concerning the breed during the 19th century exists until the Japanese Chin Club was formed in Britain in 1895. The Japanese Spaniel Club of America, in its present form, dates from 1912. Queen Alexandra, as the Princess of Wales, was an early patron of Chins, and her interest caused the breed to become fashionable as pets.

As a result of the First World War, Japanese Chins waned in popularity in Britain and for many years only a small number were registered annually. The Second World War further decimated the breed's numbers.

However, from yearly registration figures of around fifty during the 1950's, Chins recorded registration figures of 175 in 1969, and it has been growing for several years. The corresponding number in the U.S.A. was 251. More than 8,000 members of the breed are registered in Japan every year; a staggering total.

That Japanese share a similar origin to Pekingese there can be little doubt, even though the two breeds are only superficially alike. It is believed that Chins may have arrived in Japan from China some time after A.D. 520 in the hands of Zen Buddhist teachers. Alternatively, a Korean prince might have been responsible for their introduction to Japan in A.D. 732.

Whatever their origin, Chins became favorites of members of the Japanese Imperial family and their immediate circle. An 18th century Emperor of Japan decreed that all dogs, not only Chins, must be worshipped; a decree rescinded after his death, when Chins still retained favor at court. Very small representatives of the breed were kept in hanging cages, in much the same way as birds!

Certainly in the late 19th century, and possibly before, Chins became known outside Imperial precincts and were kept, if not widely, certainly by a greater cross-section of the Japanese people than were Pekingese in China.

color

White is the predominant color on Japanese. One color is splashed with black and the other with red. In both colors the markings should be well broken up over the body while the head, bar the muzzle which is white, should be colored, with a white blaze between the eyes and completely parting the colored parts on both sides of the head. A spot of color in the center of the blaze on top of the head is greatly prized in Japan and desired, though not essential, elsewhere. A rather charming legend exists around this spot, known as "the sacred island of Japan" or "Buddha's thumb mark". It is attributed to Buddha's blessing of the breed when he placed his thumb on top of a Chin's head.

Although the color black needs no explanation, red is not so straightforward. This term embraces every shade from pale lemon to sable and brindle. Tricolor – white with black and red patches – is not permitted. Black and whites must have black pigment – failure in this respect is a disqualification in America – whereas the pigment of red and whites may be black or self-colored. Either is equally correct.

care

Japanese are simplicity itself to maintain in good condition. Though the

Showing obvious Kurraba ancestry in type is Ch. Gorsedene Hirohito of Yevot, a leading sire today. He was bred by Miss Tovey, and owned by Mrs. Lilian Davis.

Riu Gu puppies bred by Mrs. Crau-furd in Britain. They are by Aquilo of Riu Gu, who sired more British champions, post-war, than any other Japanese.

breed's color is predominantly white, kept in normally hygienic conditions they maintain a clean white by a few minutes grooming every day. Fringes should be treated with special care; ear, leg and tail fringes, the bib in front and skirts behind should be brushed thoroughly but gently to ensure that as little hair as possible is destroyed. The best implement for grooming is a pure bristle brush. Bathing must always precede every show, preferably the day before. Coat trimming is normally unnecessary but it is wise to check their pads and trim appropriately, but not the actual feet feathering which is a desideratum of the breed. Japanese bitches are, generally, good whelpers and splendid mothers. Their puppies pose no problems associated only with this breed. Puppies should be acquainted with walking on a lead early in their lives and to standing on a table if they are to be shown.

Probably no dog has had more influence on the breed than Mrs. Craufurd's Ch. Pegasus of Riu Gu. A champion soon after the Second World War, almost every Japanese in Britain, and many elsewhere, can claim him as ancestor.

character

One of the breed's most attractive features is its lively and good tempered personality. Always gay, always happy, always essentially "alive" – that is the Japanese. It cannot be stressed too much how important correct temperament is to Japanese.

standards

British and American Standards for Japanese were originally based on one formulated in the breed's native country and consequently are similar. They describe Japanese as: "A lively, high-bred little dog of dainty appearance, smart compact carriage and profuse coat. These dogs are essentially stylish in movement, lifting the feet high when in action, carrying the tail (which is heavily feathered, proudly curved or plumed) over the back". And this description gives a good idea of how important the correct temperament, previously described, is to Japanese.

526

While the British Standard asks that the neck "should not be too long", the American Standard is more explicit with: "Neck – should be short and moderately thick".

A correct head is of vast importance on Japanese. It should be: "Large for the size of the dog, with broad skull, rounded in front; muzzle very short and wide and well cushioned, i.e. the upper lips rounded on each side of the nostrils".

A weakness in the American Standard is its failure to define the breed's correct expressions; an important feature, unique to Japanese. This involves the eyes' inner corners being white, thus providing the characteristic look of astonishment.

"Ears should be small, set wide apart, and high on the dog's head, and carried slightly forward, V-shaped".

Though the American Standard makes no mention of mouths, the British Standard says they should be "wide, neither undershot nor overshot". Correct mouths, so long as they are not wry, are usually considered less important than other head features but the finish of face is important and, generally, the better the mouth the better the finish of face. A Pekingese-style finish of face is entirely wrong.

A dainty effect is partly achieved by fine boned, straight legs. Feet should be long, hare-shaped and feathered.

Ideally, the body is "Squarely and compactly built, wide in chest, cobby in shape. The length of the dog's body should be about its height". Emphasis is often placed on shortness of body but Japanese which are ultra short frequently have restricted movement, which is a serious failing. When the Standard asks for the length of body to be "about" its height it means precisely that. A balanced Japanese should be aimed for.

"A long, profuse and straight coat, free from curl or wave, and not too flat . . . with profuse feathering on the tail and thighs" all go to achieving the finished effect of a supremely glamorous dog.

Size is a controversial point in Japanese, all breeders having their own ideas on what is correct. The Standard says: "When divided by weight classes should be for under and over 7 lbs. In size, they vary considerably, but the smaller they are the better, provided type and quality are not sacrificed". In this description "provided" is the key word.

Japanese, frontal view.

Ideal balance and daintiness, portrayed by Miss Tovey's home-bred Ch. Chiisa of Yevot who, together with her litter brother, Ch. Aki of Yevot, have had a great influence on the breed.

527

King Charles Spaniel
(English Toy Spaniel)

Mrs. Pennington's tricolor, Ch. Homehurst Merry Monarch, was a well-known winner in Britain in the early sixties.

history and development

For many centuries small, aristocratic spaniels have been known. They have been much loved favorites of ladies at court, who esteemed their decorative qualities and their small size, convenient for carrying them in the deep cuffs of the robes which were fashionable at the time. It is possible that the name King Charles Spaniel derives from the simple fact that they are portrayed in pictures painted of King Charles I by Van Dyck in the 17th century, but dogs of this size and appearance, obviously progenitors of the breed, are mentioned in writings of the 14th century.

In 1903 an attempt was made to give the breed a name which conformed with the fact that it was a spaniel and a toy dog, and the Kennel Club in England offered "Toy Spaniel" as a more suitable name. There had been in England since 1860 a Toy Spaniel Club, and it seemed neat and tidy that the breed name should conform. But King Edward VII, a notable fancier of the King Charles, intimated that he disapproved of the change, and it has remained in Britain with official approval, as it has always been since the days of King Charles – the King Charles Spaniel. In America the King Charles is officially one of the four varieties of the English Toy Spaniel, the others being Prince Charles, Ruby and Blenheim.

This endearing little dog has cropped up throughout recorded history in England. A black and white spaniel was found hiding in the folds of Mary, Queen of Scots' gown after her execution. Macaulay tells in his *History of England* that King Charles II endeared himself to his people when he could be seen in St. James Park in London, before the dew was off the grass, playing with his spaniels. Dr. Caius, the 15th century physician and an early chronicler of dogs, proclaimed the breed as the "gentle comforter, a chamber companion, a pleasant playfellow, a 'pretty worme'".

As with nearly every other breed, there have been many theories about the origin of the King Charles, but these theories are as unsubstantiated as most of the others. It is generally accepted that their origin is Japanese, and that they were introduced into Britain by William and Mary from Spain in the late 17th century. But another view of their origin in Britain is that they were bred from the sporting spaniels of Queen Mary in mid-16th century; she is known to have kept a pack of these spaniels for hunting, and at that time such packs were, for the gentry and nobility, an accepted part of country living.

A blenheim owned by Mrs. Gristwood, Cyprion of St. Lucia.

In appearance, the King Charles has changed little from the references down through the years. The continental dwarf spaniel was described as having long, silky ears, slightly rounded head, with sharp muzzle turned up at the tip, and with a dainty body and plumed tail. Small spaniels were also described as being nicely marked on ears and back, with a pretty little straight face, black, with a tiny nose, also black and much turned up at the tip. The eyes are well-shaped and slanted upwards at the sides (I term this now the "almond eye", as opposed to the bold, round eye, both of which appear in our present day King Charles). The coat of this older small spaniel would be silky, on a longish body, with very short legs. In 16th century works of art, and in the writings of the time, both this short muzzled and a longer muzzled type appeared. Since the 19th century the retroussé nose has become even shorter.

Three generations of King Charles, owned by the Hon. Mrs. Lytton in 1912.

Two of Mrs. Chisholm's well-known British winners of the middle fifties were the tricolors, Ch Wildboy of Sandycuft (bred by Mrs. N. M. Alexander) and Ch. Goldendays Gay Galliard.

A notable name in the development of the breed is Mrs. Raymond Mallock who, when she came to England from Long Island, U.S.A., brought with her a superb tricolor, Ashton Defender, rather larger and flatter headed than the British dogs, and Ashton Rollo, a blenheim with spot, and a sharply turned up jaw, prettily petite, and with clear markings. With these animals, and with the help of Mrs. Florence Mitchell, Miss Ella Brunne, Lady de Gay and Lady Fowler, she did much to further the type and to establish the four colors which are now standard in the breed in America and Britain. In black and tans, the work of Mr. and Mrs. Whiting and their family, with the Minasters prefix, was especially valuable. Lt. Col. and Mrs. Raymond Mallock later changed their prefix to Ashton-more, which was such a force in the breed until the time of Mrs. Mallock's death in 1939.

color

In the paintings of Van Dyck in King Charles' day, the small spaniels were shown as chestnut or liver and white. In 1860 the principal coloration was a tricolor of white background, with even black patches distributed over the body, and tan lining the ears, over the eyes, under the tail and often as ticking on the legs. Attempts to breed out the traces of white resulted in the black-and-tan, and from this the Ruby gradually appeared.

There are now four color variations – the black-and-tan (or King Charles); the tricolor, which is white with black and tan markings (Prince Charles); the ruby (a chestnut red); and the blenheim, which is white with red markings. A few white hairs on the chest of the whole colors are not rejected but anywhere else they are unacceptable. The blenheim is much

The attractive Ch. Zepherine Clement, owned by Mrs. Sciver, was a top winner in 1968.

prized if a spot the size of a sixpence appears on its head, but the absence of the spot does not disqualify.

Puppies – King Charles Spaniel.

care

The King Charles may be a toy dog but it is very hardy. After rain he should be rubbed well on chest, legs, feet and tips of ears before returning to his bed or kennel. The bed should be warm and dry, newspaper is good bedding material, although he may make it look like a paper-chase. He should be bathed monthly, except in cold weather. It is advisable to wipe the eyes every day with cotton dipped in weak saline solution. Grooming is important; the ears should be wiped out twice a week with anti-canker powder, and attention should be paid to the characteristic double toe nail; this can be treated by the veterinary surgeon if it becomes a nuisance to the·dog.

character

As you would expect with a breed which has for centuries been associated in domesticity with human beings, the King Charles has a strong affinity with people, with families, and is rather reticent until he becomes used to you. He is clean, good with children, who nevertheless should not take liberties with him, and he has a most retentive memory. He is meant to be a part of the family, where his personality develops, and he does not respond to kennel life. He is a good house dog, with a built-in "early warning" system – and he appears to love cats!

standards

The Standards in Britain and America are the same.
The average King Charles weighs 6 to 12 lbs., and an experienced judge allows 2 lbs. either way. One should aim at a small compact dog.
The head should be globular, high and broad, with a broad muzzle, black nose in a straight line with the cheeks, and with a slight stop; it must not appear "nosey". The lips should meet exactly, giving a sweet expression. He should be cobby and compact, and his tail should be well flagged, falling as a fan does. Ears and feet that are heavily feathered are desirable on all colors.

An early tricolor champion, Ch. Whirlwind, owned by the Hon. Mrs. Lytton in 1912.

The head of a blenheim champion, Ch. Ashtonmore Lovesong, owned by Mrs. Swan in 1938.

531

Lowchen

The Lowchen, or Little Lion Dog, is a Toy Dog, registered with the F.C.I. as of French origin (Petit Chien Lion), but it would appear certain that it is one of the group of small breeds of Mediterranean beginnings, which include the Maltese, as well as the lesser known Havanese, Bolognese and the Bichon Frise, which is now becoming more widely known.

There is evidence that the Lowchen was known on the Continent in the late 1500's, and it has long been the practise to clip its hair into the semblance of a lion's coat, with a mane and a tuft on the tip of the tail; and this is why it has the name (although other Toy breeds are also referred to as Lion Dogs, the Pekingese among them).

The breed is featured in a number of paintings, dating from the 16th century, in France, and in Spain, where Goya's painting of the Duchess of Alba depicts a dog having a strong likeness to the Lowchen.

The Lowchen has an average weight of around 12 to 15 lbs.

The coat is long, soft, silky and thick, and it may be of any color.

Mrs. E. M. Banks's Lowchen, Cluneen Butzi v. d. 3 Lowen, bred by Dr. Hans Rickert.

Maltese

The top winning Maltese in Britain in 1970, Ch. Vicbrita Sebastian, bred and owned by Mrs. Ronald White, is by Vicbrita Gambore ex Ch. Vicbrita Samantha. Sebastian topped his 1970 career with reserve best in show at the Hove championship show.

history and development

The history of the Maltese, as the oldest European toy dog, can be traced back many centuries to the pre-Christian era. Since they originated in an area which early became civilized, few breeds have had so much written about them at so early a time. Callimachus the Elder (*c* 384–322 B.C.), Strabo (*c* 63 B.C.–A.D. 24), Pliny the Elder (23 B.C.–A.D. 79) and Martial (*c* A.D. 38–A.D. 104) all wrote of the qualities of the Maltese dogs, praising their beauty and intelligence, and they had by this time become "comforters" and pet dogs. It seems probable that they were exported through the ports of Malta and that their widespread dispersal in ancient times can be related to their being exchanged for goods along the trade routes, and also to their having been made as gifts by visiting diplomatic missions. They were quite common in China and the Philippines, between whom there was much trade.

Although it is generally believed that the first Maltese came to England during the early part of the 14th century, their popularity at the time of the Holy Roman Empire makes it likely that they were brought over during the Roman occupation of England, many centuries before William the Conqueror.

Dogs of the Maltese type appear in Italian paintings as early as 1466 and they continued to be included as part of the scene in paintings by such artists as Dürer, Rubens, Hals, Jourdaens, Hogarth, Van Eyck, Goya, Titian, Reynolds and Landseer, who in 1830 painted the portrait called The Lion Dog from Malta – The Last of His Race – indicating their scarcity at that time.

In 1841 the two dogs Psyche and Cupid were brought to England from

Manila as a gift from the East India Trading Company to Queen Victoria. However, their condition after nine months' traveling made them unfit as royal presents and they passed into the hands of Mr. Lukey, a mastiff breeder. In 1859, one of their children, another Psyche, was exhibited at a Newcastle-upon-Tyne dog show. The breed did in fact enjoy royal patronage; the Duchess of Kent's Lambkin, painted by Landseer in 1851, was a great favorite and his "beautiful silky-white hair" was mentioned by the Queen in her letter of condolence to the Duchess when Lambkin died.

However, old as their origins are, it is only during the last hundred years that they have been standardized in type through breeding controls, although those featured by artists and sculptors many centuries previously are very readily recognizable. Indeed, the name "Maltese" is comparatively modern, they were referred to as "shock dogs" and, following the Chinese habit of clipping the hindquarters, as "lion dogs". Although declared by some to be "spaniels", they were classified in the Terrier Group by Richardson in the middle of the 19th century, hence the name Maltese Terrier which was in common use in England until the late 1950's, although they lacked terrier characteristics and were not suitable for the work of an earth dog.

There is not much information available about the first importations of Maltese dogs into the United States. In 1877 we find the record of the first Maltese to appear in the American show ring, and it was entered as a "Maltese Lion Dog" called Leon, owned by Mr. W. Morgan.

Ch. Vicbrita Fidelity, owned by Mrs. White, has had a great career both in the ring and at stud. Among his many wins was best in show at the Three Counties championship show in England in 1963, a success one of his daughters, Ch. Vicbrita Petit Point, repeated in 1966. Fidelity was also group winner in 1963, 1964 and 1965.

The popularity of the Maltese in the show ring is gradually increasing and they are exhibited in most countries of the world.

color

All Maltese seen in the show ring today are pure white in color although lemon or light tan markings, often associated with deep pigmentation, are sometimes seen on the ears and body coat and these do not count against the dog. A previous Standard of the Maltese Club of Britain included the ruling that the breed could be any self-color, and this is borne out by the offering of classes for Maltese "other than white" at several of the major shows between 1908 and 1913.

care

As the mantle of white hair with which the Maltese is covered is such an attractive feature it is obvious that puppies should become accustomed, from an early age, to the daily grooming routine. A suggested procedure is to lay the puppy on its back on one's knee and brush with a bristle brush (never nylon) through the legs and tummy hair. Then the same areas are combed through using a comb with widely spaced teeth. At this stage, a little baby powder can be sprinkled on the leg and tummy hair to keep the dog tidy between baths.

With the dog now standing on a table, the body coat is brushed through in horizontal layers from beneath until it is all lying flat against the body, and the operation is repeated using the comb. The hair on the head is

An eight-weeks-old Maltese puppy, Vicbrita Conquest.

An eight months puppy destined for stardom. For this was Ch. Vicbrita Tobias, winning one C.C. in 1967 while still a puppy and eight C.C.s in 1968 (also being best toy at Birmingham City in 1971) and one C.C. in 1969.

Int. Ch. Vicbrita Pimpernel, by Invicta Stormcock ex Vicbrita Magnolia, bred by Mrs. White and exported by her to Signorina Bianca Tamagnone in Italy, has had an outstanding career. Note the careful grooming, with the head hair finished in two plaits.

In 1962 this Maltese, Ch. Vicbrita Spectacular, had a sensational show career in Britain; her wins included best bitch in show, all breeds, and third in the final line-up at Cruft's. The daughter of a champion, she herself has a champion daughter and grand-daughter, making a remarkable line of champion bitches.

A famous pre-war Maltese was Ch. Nicholas of Fawkham, owned by Miss Worthington.

combed out and tied up with ribbon in either one or two topknots, or in two plaits. The hair is then given a central parting along the back. Finally the "debris" from the hair beneath the inner corner of each eye is removed with a fine comb and that hair is wiped with a piece of damp cottonwool to minimize the staining which can occur on the face of any white dog.

Because of the long hair on their feet, the toe-nails are not kept short by wear and must be regularly clipped back. As with most toy breeds, the teeth require regular cleaning and this can be done with a baby toothbrush and a mild dentifrice. If the care of the coat seems too much for the pressure of family life, it is possible to cut the hair short over the head, legs and body while leaving the ears and tail hair the natural length.

character

The Maltese has, through long association with man, developed great intelligence and sensitivity.

They are sweet-tempered, gentle and extremely good with children, so that they make ideal family companions.

Their intelligence has led to their being worked in obedience classes and circus acts. They are most adaptable about exercise and will equally well manage a two mile walk or five minutes round the block.

Despite their small size, they are vigorous and healthy little dogs, having a long life span, and remaining gay and playful into old age.

standards

The American Standard is considerably more detailed than the English one, but both ask for a sweet-tempered, lively dog which is compact in body and level in topline.

The question of size is met in England by requiring a dog to be not more than 10″ at the shoulder, while in America the criterion is weight, with the ideal being between 4 and 6 lbs.

Both Standards ask for moderate angulation in the hindquarters which helps to give the typical smooth-flowing gait.

The coat is single and has no undercoat so that the dogs do not molt. The hair should be of good length, lying flat, straight and silky over the sides of the body with no suggestion of curl or wooly texture. Both British and American Standards apply here.

Pigmentation, that is the color of the nose, lips, eye rims and pads of the feet, should be black, while the eyes are dark brown.

The length of the neck should be consistent with a fairly high head carriage, adding to the elegance of the dog. The legs should be short and straight with shoulders well-sloped. The English Standard, unlike the American, lists outstanding faults separately as, a bad mouth, over or undershot; a gay tail; curly or wooly coat; brown nose; pink eye rims; unsound in any way.

By the end of 1970 Mrs. Lewin's Ch. Ellwin Leppu Zaza had seven C.C.s, although still under two years old. She also had the distinction of being the only Maltese to beat Ch. Vicbrita Sebastian in 1970, the year he was top winning toy in Britain.

Manchester Terrier (Toy)
See page 513

Mexican Hairless Dog

Although not recognized by the British or the American Kennel Clubs, the Xoloizcuintli (pronounced Shollosquintly) or Mexican Hairless Dog, is one of the oldest breeds, now almost extinct. It is thought that they came from China, where similar dogs are still to be seen, across the land-bridge which is now the Bering Strait, into Alaska.

Clay effigies of these hairless animals found in tombs at Colima, on the Pacific coast of Mexico prove their existence 2,000 or more years ago. The breed has long been domesticated, but in the days before Columbus they were used as food and for medicinal purposes by the natives. The heat of their bodies (mean temperature 104°) was regarded as relief for rheumatism and kidney troubles, and they did not harbor fleas. The dogs became objects of reverence, connected with the god Xoloth, hence the breed's ancient name.

The smooth skin may be a variety of colors, solid or mottled. The Mexican Hairless has an attractive, intelligent, character, affectionate, hardy, easy to train and, being without hair, needs no grooming, apart from a little oiling of the skin.

They are usually 16″ to 20″ at the shoulder and weigh between 25 to 36 lbs. They lack pre-molar teeth; have a tuft of hair on the head, tip of tail and between the toes; and they perspire through the skin, not through the tongue.

Mrs. Olga Frei-Denver's Pequeno Bobby, a typical example of the Mexican Hairless Dog. Notice particularly the hair on the head and tip of the tail.

537

Miniature Pinscher

Ch. Birling Wawican Constellation, winner in Britain of twenty-six C.C.s, three times best of breed at Cruft's and a consistent group winner. A fine example of a Miniature Pinscher dog.

A painting of a Miniature Pinscher dated 1840, very like the early Dutch imports into Britain, and a strong influence on the development of the breed.

history and development

Small dogs of Miniature Pinscher type have existed in Germany and on the Continent for centuries. The German Smooth-haired Pinscher has been known by name since the 16th century and it is from these terrier-like dogs that the smaller type evolved. They are certainly not bred down from Dobermanns which are a very new breed in comparison.

Dr. Reinchenback, writing in 1836, was of the opinion that Italian Greyhounds and small Dachshunds had been used to improve the breed. This is quite possible and would account for the hackney action characteristic of Miniature Pinschers; and the clear, red coloring could be inherited from the Dachshund. In Germany, their native country, they are known as Reh Pinscher because they resemble so closely the roe deer found in such numbers in the forests of Germany.

Dogs very like the Miniature Pinscher frequently appear in early paintings by famous artists. A picture by Le Nain in 1640, now in the Louvre in Paris, called The Peasant Family, shows people grouped round a fire and in the foreground a small, red dog and a cat, both much the same size.

The dog is elegant and fine-boned with prick ears. I have in my possession two paintings of Miniature Pinschers of about 1840 and a sculpture of a bitch by the famous French sculptor P. J. Mene of the same date. They all look much like some of the early Dutch imports into Britain.

The breed was already well-known in Germany by 1870 and was officially recognized and, by 1880, a Standard was included in the German Stud book. The first breed show was held in Stuttgart in 1900 when 93 exhibits were on view. From then on they grew in popularity and have spread all over the world.

Miniature Pinscher head, front.

Miniature Pinschers have a big following in America where many outstanding dogs have been bred. The American Miniature Pinschers tend to be more racy and elegant than those on the Continent. It was not until after the Second World War that the breed became established in England. The Pinscher-Schnauzer Klub of Germany, which wrote the initial Standards for the breed, stimulated interest in Germany, particularly during the first part of this century, up to the beginning of the First World War. Although importations into America occurred soon after the end of the war, only a limited amount of breeding was undertaken and it was not until 1929, when the Miniature Pinscher Club of America Inc. was formed, that the breed's popularity increased. It now continues to grow steadily.

color

Black, blue, chocolate with sharply defined tan markings on the cheeks,

Both prick and drop ears are accepted. This is a first class drop ear, Birling Simian.

Compared with this stockier Continental type of Miniature Pinscher the American type is more elegant, and racier. Dutch champion Ch. Stella Petit Bonheur, a strong-looking bitch.

This bitch, Ch. Birling Blissful, has a beautiful stance, and shows to perfection the graceful, slightly arched neck and straight back-line slightly sloping to the rear.

Ch. Birling Brightstar has been very prominent in the breed in Britain. To the end of 1970 he had won sixteen C.C.s, and many toy groups at championship shows.

lips, lower jaw, throat, twin spots above the eyes and chest, lower half of forelegs, inside of hindlegs and vent region, lower portion of hocks and feet. All the above colors should have black pencilling on toes, with no thumb marks; also whole-colored red of various shades. A little white on chest is permissible but undesirable.

In America the A.K.C. Standard does not recognize blue; and white on chest must be limited to a half inch in its longest dimension. Solid red or stag red are the preferred colors.

care

The smooth coat and the dog's small size make it an ideal house dog. The coat needs little attention. It is a small eater – but tends to get fat if fed too much starchy food. Plenty of exercise is essential, for they are really agile and active little terriers. My own dogs used to go out with me when I exercized my hunter and would keep up with the horse for miles.

character

In character it is proud, fearless, alert and very self-possessed. An excellent guard because of its acute hearing. A great hunter – who loves to chase rabbits or rats. Although unrelated many of the Dobermann's characteristics can be seen in the Miniature Pinscher and it is, by nature, more suggestive of a dog of much larger size than a toy. Its lively temperament and considerable intelligence make it particularly suitable for showing, it is often called the "King of Toys".

standards

In general appearance the Miniature Pinscher is a well-balanced, sturdy, compact, elegant dog. Its close, smooth coat imparts a well-groomed, proud, vigorous and alert appearance and its precise hackney gait, fearless animation, complete self-possession and spirited presence, combine in a most impressive, individual canine personality.

The head and skull are rather more elongated than short and round. The nose should be black only, except for livers and blues which may have a self-colored nose. (The U.S. Standard allows a self-colored nose only in the case of chocolates). The strong graceful neck is slightly arched and free from throatiness.

The body should be square with a straight back-line sloping slightly towards the rear. Belly moderately tucked up, ribs well sprung and deep rather than barrelled. The tail should be a continuation of the topline, carried a little high and docked. A well developed forechest, full and moderately broad with clean, moderately sloping shoulders. The hindquarters should be well developed and muscular with a good sweep of stifle and the hocks should turn neither in nor out. The coat should be smooth, hard and short. Straight and lustrous.

Height range 10″ to 12″. Under 10″ or over 12½″ is disqualified in America.

Papillon
(and Phalene)

history and development

The Papillon has bred true to type for some 700 years or more, as can be verified in the art galleries and museums of the world. It was undoubtedly developed much earlier, and may well have its origin as far back as the 2nd century A.D., or even before then.

A terra cotta statue of a somewhat similar dog has been located in Belgium in a Roman tomb of the 2nd century, by Baron Houtart, but there is then a gap until the appearance of dogs typical of the drop-eared variety of today in paintings and frescoes from the late 13th/early 14th centuries. From that time onwards, they have figured in many famous works of art. A close investigation of old paintings reveals that a number of the Toy Spaniels can be clearly identified as Papillons, and yet others bear distinct earmarks of being ancestors of the present Cavalier. By about the 16th century the Papillon had spread from Central Italy, where it had been first identified, to virtually the whole of Europe, and became a favorite of the Royalty and Courtiers of many lands, including France, Spain, England, Sweden, the Netherlands and Poland.

The breed today exists in two distinct forms. The Papillon has erect – or more correctly – oblique ears. Identical with the Papillon, except that its

This typical Papillon puppy at three months became Ch. Picaroon Urbino, best of breed at Cruft's, 1961/62. Bred and owned by Mr. Russell Roberts.

Mrs. Russell Roberts, owner with her husband of the Picaroon Kennel, with two of her early champions, Ch. Picaroon Ambrose (right) and his daughter, Ch. Picaroon Belita.

The typical ear carriage of the Papillon.

Papillon – side head.

ears are fully dropped, is the Phalene, or Continental Toy Spaniel. In French, the former means "butterfly" and the latter "moth". The Papillon derives its name from the head, in which the oblique ears, which must be heavily furnished with long, abundant, silky "curtain" fringes, resemble the wings of a butterfly. When the dog "uses" its ears, an irresistible effect of a butterfly in flight is produced, heightened by the figure-of-eight blaze on the forehead which resembles the body of a butterfly. In the Phalene, the dropped ears resemble the folded wings of the moth. Unlike many Spaniel breeds, the tail is carried in an arc, loosely, over the back, with the heavy tail plume falling gracefully to one side or other of the spine. In fact, this last feature at one time gave the breed the soubriquet of "chien ecureuil", squirrel dog.

color

This must be predominantly white, but relieved with some other color. Any color, or admixture of colors is permissible in most countries, although certain color combinations entail disqualification in America. These are liver (which also is not an admissible color in Great Britain), coat of solid color or all white or one with no white, and white patches on the ears or around the eyes.

care

This is a breed which is absolutely normal in all respects, with no exaggerations of structure or features. They accustom themselves readily to varying climates and altitudes and are successfully bred from sea level to 9,000 feet, and from the tropics to the frigid winter conditions of the Canadian Plains. Little out of the ordinary care is, therefore, called for. The feeding can vary a little, but is basically meat and cereal, with occasional fish, eggs and lightly cooked vegetables. The quantities should be proportionate to the size of the dog.

The coat and fringes are important features of the breed and regular grooming and coat care is essential to preserve these.

Being free from physical abnormalities, they usually are easy whelpers, and make good mothers. However, as in any breed, there are exceptions to this generalization.

character

They are by nature dainty little creatures in appearance, but are physically extremely resilient and adaptable. Active by nature, they love plenty of

exercise, and when in good physical condition, are well capable of enjoying a ten mile walk. However, exercise is not necessary as they will happily take adequate exercise on their own, if allowed to run free in a garden of reasonable size. As house dogs they are excellent. Passionately attached to their owners, they tend to resent intruders, and will raise the roof with their barks if an unrecognized person enters the premises. Also they lend themselves well to training.

Three generations of Stouravon champions, owned in Britain by Mrs. Harris: Ch. Stouravon Elegant Mink (right); his son, Ch. Stouravon Greenjackets Mariner (left), winner of twelve C.C.s; and Ch. Mariner's son, Ch. Stouravon Beaujolais (back).

standards

There exist substantial differences between the Standards in various parts of the world. The British and American Standards differ little in intent, the main divergence as we have seen being concerned with color. In both the U.S.A. and Britain the Papillon and the Phalene are covered by the same Standard and judged together as one breed. In the U.S.A. a speci-

Ch. Bretta Dawn, multiple C.C. winner and influential sire just after the Second World War.

Mr. Laurence Ratigan's Ch. Wychdale Manxman typifies the many champions in the Laurigan Kennel in Britain.

men over 12″ in height is disqualified. Height limits are 8″ to 11″; weight must be in proportion.

In France, the Standard of the Fédération Cynologique Internationale (F.C.I.) however, separates the Papillon and the Phalene into two separate breeds, judged separately. Both French Standards refer to the breeds as Spaniels, and are, in fact, the only ones to recognize them as such. It also emphasizes the necessity of the dogs resembling miniature Spaniels, and that they should bear no resemblance to the "Spitz" breeds.

Basically, the Standard lists two types, those under 5½ lbs. and those over this weight. The former are required to have a more pronounced "stop" and rather shorter foreface than the latter. The F.C.I. and American Standards are much less forceful on the matter of the blaze on the forehead than the British. It is mentioned, but not as a firm requirement, neither is the color of the blaze specified. In all these Standards, there is absolute agreement on the structure, build and movement of the dog. In short, this calls for a sound, balanced dog, the proportions generally similar to a miniaturized Spaniel, with a free movement and no points exaggerated in any way.

Pekingese

Ch. Acol Ku Anna, one of the great Pekingese bitches, on the show bench. A daughter of Ch. Caversham Ku Ku of Yam, she was probably his best offspring. She won numerous Challenge Certificates and had the distinction of winning best in show at the Pekingese Reform Association championship show three years running. She also won best toy dog at Cruft's in 1959.

history and development

The Pekingese is an oriental breed and consequently much of its history is steeped in the mystery that surrounds the East. An ancient breed, the Pekingese appears in many early Chinese paintings, usually at play. One painting dates back to 1720, but long before this the symbolic Fo Dogs and Kylins were popular as works of art and these greatly resemble the Pekingese. The different breeds from the East must all have a common origin with the Pekingese. Paintings as far back as 900 A.D. show a rather short-haired, pug-faced dog, as well as longer-haired breeds, rather like the Shih Tzu. There was also the spaniel type, which was higher on leg and of lighter build and much more dainty. Probably inter-breeding between all types gave the Chinese the compact little Pekingese which became such a firm favorite at the Chinese Court.

The face of the Pekingese

Succeeding dynasties favored the Pekingese in varying degrees. Out of favor in the Ming Dynasty, they were still bred and cared for by the court but were not granted the high honors of the previous Mongol reign. With the advent of the Manchus in 1644, the dogs again became treasured possessions and were especially favored by the Empress Tsu Hai.

Pekingese were little known in China, except in Peking itself, and were never seen outside the precincts of the Palace. The punishment meted out to anyone removing them from their royal home was usually death. Consequently few ever passed beyond the Palace walls.

In 1860, in retribution for offensive action taken against them by the Emperor, certain western nations, including Great Britain and America, marched on the Imperial Palace causing the Court to flee. Most of the "lion dogs" were taken, but five were inadvertently left behind and fell into the hands of the British officers, and thus found their way back to England. None of the five weighed more than 6 lbs. indicating that the

American and Canadian Ch. St. Aubrey Tinkabelle of Elsdon. In the author's opinion the greatest of the forty-odd champions bred by him in partnership with Nigel Aubrey-Jones. The winner of the best bitch at three consecutive summer specialties of The Pekingese Club of America in the sixties, and the dam of an international champion.

Ch. Caversham Ku Ku of Yam, acknowledged as the greatest Pekingese of all time. Winner of a record number of Challenge Certificates (forty) in England, and many best in show awards at All-Breed Championship Shows. A brilliant sire of champions, an offer of £10,000 ($24.000) was refused by his owner, Miss de Pledge, of Shaftesbury, England.

The ideal type, portraying the short, compact body, heavy bone and the true Pekingese rolling action. Ch. St. Aubrey Carnival Music of Eastfield.

Ch. Ku-Chi of Caversham, the greatest post-war winner until surpassed by his famous son, Ku Ku. He excelled in deportment and arrogance, and was a successful stud dog. The property of Miss de Pledge and Mrs. Lunham of the Caversham Kennels.

Ch. Toydom Ts'Zee, the breed's greatest winning particolor Pekingese. Best of breed at Cruft's. Owned by Mrs. A. C. Williams of the Toydom Kennels, England.

English, American and Canadian Ch. Che Le of Matsons Catawba. Purchased just before the Second World War this little dog was exported to America to become the greatest winner up to that time, winning over thirty best in shows. Owned by Mrs. J. M. Austin of Old Westbury, L.I., N.Y.

547

English, American and Canadian Ch. Goofus Bugatti, one of the most travelled Pekingese in the world. He won best of breed at Cruft's and then went to America where, among other wins, he was best of breed at the Westminster K.C. show in New York. Returning to England he won best in show at the Pekingese Club in London. He is owned by Nigel Aubrey-Jones and R. William Taylor of Montreal, Canada and Wendover, England.

original Pekingese were quite small.

Interest in the breed grew rapidly in England and great pains were taken to import this fascinating new breed from its homeland. In 1893, Mr. Loftus Allen imported Pekin Peter and he was shown at Chester in 1894, the first time a Pekingese was exhibited in the British show ring. Peking Prince and Pekin Princess, both blacks, followed in 1896 and the Pekin strain was created. The Duke of Richmond had earlier started the Goodwood kennel which accounted for some of the best of the early specimens. In 1896, the famous Ah Cum and Mimosa were imported directly from the Imperial Palace by Mrs. T. Douglas Murray and the Palace strain was established.

The Pekingese was at first catered for by the Japanese Spaniel Club and in 1898 the Standard of Points was drawn up. 1904 saw the founding of the Pekingese Club in Britain. Its aim was to breed a small compact dog under 10 lbs., adhering to the type of specimen found in the Imperial Palace. No weight limit was adopted, but the founders of the breakaway Pekin Palace Dog Association stipulated that only dogs of a maximum weight of 10 lbs. could be exhibited at shows run by the Association and many trophies even to this day have a 10 lbs. weight limit. However the Pekin Palace Association had to relinquish the weight limit as the Kennel Club would not allocate Challenge Certificates with weight restrictions. The Pekingese Club of America was founded in 1909. Its Standard is much the same as that adopted in Great Britain save that, at present, there is a weight limit of 14 lbs. This is no doubt due to the fear that the breed would become large, and a copy of the Standard of the breed in America in 1913 showed that anything up to 18 lbs. was acceptable. Few champions made up today in Britain weigh over 10 lbs. In America, size is generally larger, with weight anywhere up to 2 or 3 lbs. more in a number of specimens.

Although now virtually extinct in China, the Pekingese has elsewhere been extremely popular for many years. Much is owed to the ingenuity of the breeders in England that the breed has reached the pinnacle of perfection recognized the world over. While a few Pekingese were imported directly into the U.S.A. from China, it was stock from Great Britain that was the basis of the breed in that country.

The aforementioned Goodwood, Palace and Pekin Kennels established the breed in England. Several kennels were founded on the bloodlines of Goodwood Lo and Goodwood Chum, the first Pekingese champions, which became world famous; the Manchus, the Broadoaks, Sutherland Avenue, Nanking, the Burderops and the most famous of all, the Alderbournes, still in existence today.

color

The prospective owner can choose from red and fawn brindles in varying shades, to pure whites and glistening blacks, the latter often with tan and white markings. There are also particolors, as well as clear reds, creams and fawns. Black masks are desirable although not a necessity while shadings or markings around the eyes, called spectacles, often lend character to the expression and outlook.

care

Despite its flowing coat, the Pekingese is not a difficult dog to care for. A

Ch. Tong Tuo of Alderbourne, one of the famous post-war champions in the celebrated Alderbourne Kennels, Ascot, England. He is the grandsire of Ch. Caversham Ku Ku of Yam.

careful brushing with a wire pin brush, followed by a pure bristle ensures a coat free from mats and tangles. Knots occurring behind the ears, under the elbows and the skirting can be combed out with a steel comb. Naturally, a brushing once a day is advisable, but a weekly "going over" is really a necessity to keep the dog in good condition. A Pekingese seldom needs a bath; only when it begins to shed its hair when, for the interest of removing all dead hair quickly, a bath would be advisable. In between, a good grooming lotion sprayed or brushed into the coat is all that is needed to keep a dog's coat lustrous and sweet-smelling. Occasionally, a fine talc powder should be sprinkled into the coat so that it absorbs any dirt or grime; this is then brushed out. Black Pekingese only require the occasional bath and coat dressing.

The most important features to care for are the face and eyes. The wrinkle should be well wiped so that no dirt accumulates in the folds either below the eyes or on top of the nose. Eyes should be washed with an eye lotion and care should be taken that no hair touches the eyeball itself.

The Pekingese needs no cutting of hair apart possibly from removing it from under the pads of the feet. This, in all probability, will wear down itself if the dog is given sufficient road exercise but, if not, then cutting away will prevent the hair from knotting and causing further discomfort.

character

Stout-hearted, the Pekingese has the courage of a lion with boldness, self-esteem and independence. This latter quality is typical of the breed and should any person desire cloying devotion or servility, then the Pekingese is not for him. It has great determination and should it once think that it can get the better of you, then it will tend always to want its own way, which may lead to crankiness if it cannot get it, and the reputation it occasionally earns of being bad-tempered. But if treated with firmness and understanding, the Pekingese will soon realize who is the master and respect your every wish. Slightly stubborn, it displays almost human qualities of intelligence and is a faithful companion.

Puppies – Pekingese

549

The alert, oriental expression and independent character of Solin of Alderbourne, owned by Misses M. and C. Ashton Cross.

standards

The Standard of the breed requires a massive broad skull, very flat and wide between the ears. These ears are heart-shaped and should be well feathered and set neither too high nor too low. The nose is black with broad open nostrils; the muzzle short and very broad and the jaw undershot, but the teeth should never show. The mouth is level. Eyes should be dark, large, round and lustrous, giving the breed its quaintness and its oriental outlook.

The head is the most important feature of the breed. Shape, firmness of body and sound, well-constructed legs are essential to achieve the typical rolling action that is also such a distinctive characteristic. The body is lion or pear-shaped, very heavy in front with well-sprung ribs tapering away to lighter hindquarters. The front legs are heavily boned and well bowed, tight at shoulders. Pasterns are strong and feet, which are large, should turn outwards. The hindquarters are lighter but firm with well-let-down hocks. It is this build that produces the rolling gait which should be free-flowing and a delight for everybody to see. The tail should be high-set and carried well over the back, the plumage covering the back and falling to one side or the other. The coat is a Pekingese's crowning glory. It is a double coat, a thick soft undercoat beneath a straight, rather coarse-textured, standoffish outer coat. The fringing on tail, ears, legs and skirtings should be long and profuse, softer in texture but never silky. The mane should be profuse over the shoulders, forming a ruff around the front of the neck.

The great beauty and delightful temperament of the Pekingese appeals to pet owners and breeders alike. It is not an easy breed to produce to perfection. It is extraordinarily difficult to combine type with balance and quality, keeping the essential characteristics and combining all this with soundness of limb.

Ch. St. Aubrey Fairy Ku of Craigfoss, owned by Nigel Aubrey-Jones and R. William Taylor. An outstanding winning bitch, noted for her fabulous coat and fringing as well as balance of construction. She is the essence of femininity, an essential in any bitch.

Pomeranian

A good Pom is always an eye-catcher in all-breed competition for, despite their small size, the best specimens are sound, good showmen and have lovely coats which are presented to the best advantage, all this besides the essential breed points. Miss Harper's Ch. Cynpegs Gentle Thoughts displays these points outstandingly – among her many triumphs in 1970, in nine championship shows, were six C.C.s, three reserve C.C.s, two toy groups, two reserve toy groups, and best in show at the City of Birmingham championship show.

history and development

The Pomeranian is a breed of dog which can claim great antiquity. Throughout history it has been used for many purposes, but the type has remained unchanged. Depicted in many relics of the Roman era, the essential points of shape of head, carriage of ear and plume, body and coat differ but slightly from today.

There seems little doubt that the modern Pomeranian is of central European origin and that a few of the early specimens brought into England came from Pomerania, Germany, and for this reason were given the name Pomeranian.

Although there were several imported into Britain from time to time, the breed made little impression until the year 1870.

These early imports were large dogs of up to 30 lbs. in weight but the size was rapidly reduced, until in 1896 Pom classes at shows were divided by weight, 8 lbs. and over and under 8 lbs. In 1915, the Kennel Club withdrew Challenge Certificates for the overweights; that is, dogs over 8 lbs., and today the most popular size is $3\frac{1}{2}$ to $5\frac{1}{2}$ lbs.

The whites were the first to be exhibited with success, and it was not until 1890 that blacks were exhibited. The progress of the breed was at first slow. However, in 1891 the first meeting of the Pomeranian Club was held at Cruft's Show where Mr. Theo Marples was made Hon. Secretary and Miss Hamilton was the President. This same year, the breed was given a boost when Queen Victoria exhibited a dog known as Windsor Marco

A Pom champion of the early thirties, Ch. Shelton Debonair, owned by Mrs. Wetwan.

in the April show of the Kennel Club. From then on progress was steady, until in the Kennel Club Show in October 1905, 125 Poms were exhibited in the 30 classes provided.

In May 1907, the Pomeranian Club held a breed show and has held them annually since, except for the war years. Although the breed lost some of its popularity as a household pet, it has always had its staunch supporters who have kept it prominent in the show ring, and in recent years its popularity is being regained. At the 1970 Pomeranian Club Championship Show there was a post war record of 84 dogs making 211 entries. Pomeranians were established in America by importations from Great Britain and even in recent years many fine specimens have crossed the Atlantic. There can be little doubt that of these, American Ch. Sealand Moneybox (bred by Miss Henshaw) has had the most lasting effect in the number of champions which are descended from him.

color

According to the Standard, the following colors are permissible and recognized: black, chocolate, orange, cream, orange shaded sable, wolf shaded sable, beaver, blue. In Great Britain today the chocolate, beaver, blue, white and particolor seem to have disappeared, certainly from the show ring, although in other countries many of these are still retained.

The orange shaded sable Ch. Dragon Fly and the brilliant orange Ch. Mars set a fashion for these colors which has remained to this day. This may be one of the reasons for the lack of interest in the less frequent colors.

care

Given the freedom of the garden, a Pomeranian will take all the exercise it needs. Daily grooming is desirable to keep the coat and skin in a healthy condition. A good quality stiff bristle brush will give the best results. The coat should be well damped with cold water then the moisture rubbed in with finger tips and finished off by rubbing with a towel.

Working from the head, the coat should be parted and brushed forward from roots to tips. Another parting should then be made and the process repeated until every inch of the dog has been groomed. If this brushing is carried out correctly, there should be little use for a comb unless it is to remove matted or loose hair. The art of trimming is not easy to describe. The novice would be well advised to seek the help of someone of experience to give him a demonstration and then to practice on the dog at home.

character

The Pomeranian is gay, active, amusing and capable of great devotion to

Top Pomeranian in Britain in 1969 and 1970 was Mrs. L. R. Weinert's Ch. Mosey the Menace of Vernlil, another championship best in show winner.

Miss Harper's Ch. Cynpegs Little Extra, another toy group winner at championship shows, displays the foxy head, short back and good coat and plume, so desired in the breed.

its owner. It is a sporty little animal and a tireless companion if its owner wishes, but is adaptable to any situation and will live happily in either a one-roomed apartment or a mansion.

The Pomeranian has a bad reputation for yapping. This is a great pity as most Poms can be taught that yapping, without cause, is not allowed. It is also very quick to learn whom it can take advantage of, but is happiest when well trained. It will rarely fight but on being approached by a bigger dog looking for trouble, it will hold its head high, walk on the tips of its toes in order to make itself look as big as possible and give such a look of indignation and rage that the other dog will usually walk away.

Two attractive Pom puppies owned by Mrs. Holroyd in 1939.

standards

In appearance the Pomeranian is a compact, well balanced dog. The tail is perfectly straight, set high and carried well over the back. This, combined with the unique carriage of the head and the dainty, active, buoyant movement, makes the Pom the eye catcher that it is. The head should be foxy in outline and wedge-shaped. The skull should be slightly flat and large in proportion to the muzzle, which should finish rather fine and be free from lippiness. Ears small, not too far apart nor too low down, but carried perfectly erect like those of a fox. Eyes medium in size, slightly oval in shape, dark in color, bright and showing great intelligence. In white, orange, shaded-sable and cream dogs, the rims round the eyes should be black.

The typical Pom head and expression – Miss Harper's Ch. Cynpegs Guided Missile.

The teeth should be level, neither over nor undershot. The neck should be short and well set-in with a well-ribbed body with the barrel well-rounded. The chest must be fairly deep and not too wide but in proportion. The legs should be fine boned, well feathered, perfectly straight at the front and neither cow-hocked nor wide behind, and must be free in

553

action. The feet should be small and compact in shape.

The coat is profuse and off-standing, the under-coat soft and fluffy while the top-coat is long, straight and harsh in texture, forming a frill round the neck, shoulders and chest. The hair over the tail, which should be turned over the back and carried flat and straight, should fan over the body. The hair on the head and face should be smooth and short-coated.

Weight is 4 to $4\frac{1}{2}$ lbs. for bitches and $4\frac{1}{2}$ to $5\frac{1}{2}$ lbs. for dogs. The A.K.C. Standard says 3 to 7 lbs. for a show specimen, and the ideal size 4 to 5 lbs.

Few kennels in any breed in England have had the consistent success of Mrs. Dyke's Hadleigh. Portrayed is her Ch. Honeybee of Hadleigh who was a championship show group winner in 1966.

This Pom puppy displays a low-set tail, bad legs and feet, straight stifles, is leggy and has no coat – all points to be avoided.

554

Pug

The greatest winning Pug Britain has known was the incomparable Ch. Banchory Lace, who was owned and bred by Lorna, Countess Howe and Miss M. Lang.

history and development

There is considerable uncertainty about which was the country of origin of the Pug Dog. It has been generally called the Dutch Pug, but there is also an obscure but confident tradition that the breed originated in Russia; there is a suggestion, however, that the Pug Dog, small though it is, is related to the Mastiff. Both the Pug and the Mastiff were, from a very early date, known in China, and from what evidence we have, it seems more likely that the Pug originated there, and certainly that it is one of the earliest known toy breeds.

The history of the Pug goes back further than any other breed except the Greyhound. It is believed that its name comes from the Latin *pugnus*, obviously a reference to the resemblance its face has to a closed fist. It is generally accepted that the Pug was introduced into Britain from Holland by William and Mary in 1688, when the little dog was an important member of the Royal Household of Orange; at that time it was usual for the Pug to be decked with an orange ribbon, indicating that it was an honored member of the Household. To the present day the Pug Dog Club in Britain has orange as its color. There is a legend in Holland that a Pug saved the life of William the Silent during the wars with the Spaniards.

In 1736 the Order of Freemasons earned the displeasure of Pope Clement XII, and they were excommunicated and forbidden to meet as members

Miss Hatrick's Ch. Miss Penelope, a pre-war champion, had a vast influence on her breed, and many of today's best Pugs are descended from her.

555

Ch. Banchory Sovereign became the first champion Pug dog for Lorna, Countess Howe and Miss Lang, after a succession of bitch champions. Not only a well-known show dog, Ch. Sovereign had a considerable influence as a sire.

of the Order. Erstwhile members set up a new order, organized in the same manner as the banned Order, and named it the Order of the Pug. The little dog became the symbol of the new order whose members displayed a likeness of the Pug on cravat pins, walking-stick knobs, etc.

The Pug was a feature of many models produced by T. J. Kandler, master modeller in the famous Meissen porcelain factory, around 1775. He produced many such models for members of the new Order. Pugs featured in many paintings by famous artists. Jacopo da Empoli (1554–1640) painted a portrait of Louis XIII's dogs, a Pug being prominent among them. Another, by Carlo Gustav Pilo, in 1749, called The Ramels Family Pug, hangs in the Stockholm National Museum. Hogarth, the English artist and a great lover of the Pug, painted a self-portrait with a Pug seated on his lap and, in his The House of Cards, two black Pugs are seen.

In the early part of the 19th century two strains were dominant – the Morrison and the Willoughby. The former, named for its breeder, an innkeeper, is said to have descended from the Pugs of Queen Charlotte, George III's wife. The Willoughby strain was introduced by Lord Willoughby d'Eresby and, from 1840 onwards, both strains were very important to the establishment of the breed in Britain.

Black Pugs were thought to have been introduced into Britain by Lady Brassey, who returned from China in 1880, with several black specimens. In 1883 the Pug Dog Club was formed in England and a Standard was laid down, and that Standard is little altered to this day. The first breed show for Pugs was held in London, under Kennel Club regulations, in 1885. Many well-known breeders exhibited, including Lady Brassey, Mr. C. Houlker, Miss Holdsworth, Mr. Sheffield and Mrs. Mayhew. Litters of puppies were offered for sale at the show at prices from £5 to £50, say, at the money values of the time, $25 to $250, each.

The Pug has become over the years one of the most firmly established breeds. Famous names of the time of the first show, and from which

Ch. Adoram Cinderfella of Pallas, owned by Mr. M. Quinney, highlighted his outstanding show career with a best in show award at the Ladies Kennel Association in Britain in 1969.

present-day Pugs descend, include Stingo Sniffles, Jack Spratt, Loris, Duchess of Wednesbury, Queen Rose, Grand Duchess, Master Tragedy and Sweet Briar; and these dogs themselves came down from dogs with equally famous names in the breed, Mops and Nell who, in turn, descended from Click, whose parents were Lamb and Moss.

By 1900 the Pug was firmly established, and many became worthy champions. Three Pugs which made a great impression in the show world were Ch. Impi (a black), Ch. Bobbie Burns (another black), and Ch. Turrett Joseph. To the present day, Bobbie Burn's record stands – twenty-eight Challenge Certificates! Owned by Dr. Tulk, he was born in 1899 and shown until 1904. Judging from his little red harness with its brass bells, which I have in my possession, Bobbie Burns must have been smaller than today's Pugs, certainly very few of them could wear it.

There were many other well-known strains up to the thirties, which gained top honors in the ring. The Swarland, Turrett, Baronshalt, Laws, Mostyn, Wandle and Grindley strains were among the foremost. From 1930 until the beginning of the Second World War some magnificent Pugs were bred. The standard was high, and only the best could win the top honors. Among the best were some wonderful black Pugs, the like of which we have seldom seen since. Supremely beautiful animals whose names are too numerous to mention, but without question, the greatest of them all, either black or fawn, was Mrs. Curtis's Ch. My Pretty Jane; she was absolutely perfect.

Mrs. V. A. Graham's Edenderry kennel is the oldest extant in Britain in Pugs, and has embraced many champions, two of them being Ch. Edenderry The O'Donovan and Ch. Edenderry Shauna.

Ch. Lord Tom Noddy of Broadway, a well-known winning Pug of the early twenties.

The war saw the end of many famous strains. Among those whose strains survived, owing entirely to their own devotion and hard work, were Miss S. G. Weall, past-president of the Pug Dog Club, Mrs. S. Bancroft-Wilson, Mrs. S. Goodger and the late Miss G. Atherton. Since the war the Pug has gained further popularity; entries at shows in Britain have soared and many new breeders have entered the scene. New generations of worthy Pug champions have emerged, so many that it would be invidious to single any of them out for mention in this limited space.

color

Silver, apricot, fawn or black. The trace (the line marking running along the back from occiput to tail) should be black, but this is seldom seen to perfection nowadays. The moles, thumb mark and wrinkles also should be black. Pale pigmentation is faulty.

care

The Pug Dog of today is a show dog, and a much loved pet. It should not be submitted to kennel life; its place is in the home as part of the family, where its modest requirements of food, grooming and exercise are combined with affection and companionship.

It is not a delicate dog; no special diets are needed, grooming is minimal – a daily brushing will keep its coat glossy, and although regular exercise should be given it need only be light.

character

You have only to look at a Pug to see that it is different; a unique character, highly intelligent with great sporting instincts and adaptable to any domestic situation. They are excellent with children, tolerant and good-tempered.

standards

I am convinced of the necessity of keeping the size of the Pug within the limits laid down in the Standard. The body should be short, square and cobby, well ribbed up, and wide in the chest.

The head should be large, massive and round, not apple-headed – the Mastiff antecedents should be evident. The skull should have no indentation and the wrinkles should be large and deep on the muzzle, and the muzzle itself short, square and well-filled under the eyes, not up-faced nor pinched. The eyes are bold and dark in color, globular in shape, soft and solicitous in expression – and sparkling in animation. Small eyes or light eyes are not tolerated.

The ears are thin, small and soft, they feel like black velvet, and they can be either rose or button, but the latter is preferred.

The forelegs are strong, straight, well-boned and well-placed under the body, and they should not be too long. The hind legs also are strong, straight, and they must not be cow-hocked. The feet are neither as long as the hare foot nor as round as the cat, with well-separated toes and black nails. Weak or splayed pasterns are wrong.

The tails is very characteristic of the Pug. It is set-on high, curled tightly over the hip – a double curl is ideal.

The coat has a gloss. It is not harsh or wooly, but fine, short and smooth. The desired weight of the Pug Dog is 14 to 18 lbs.

Ch. Hazelbridge Paul was one of Britain's greatest Pug sires ever. He was bred by Miss A. Gretton and owned by Mrs. M. Cuming.

Yorkshire Terrier

Post-war record holder, Ch. Deebees Stirkeans Faustina, who won her twenty-three C.C.s under as many different judges. Bred by Mrs. E. A. Stirk, she was purchased as a puppy by Mrs. Beech who piloted her through her highly successful career. Probably the most successful Yorkie in Britain in all-breed competition, she won many toy groups at championship shows.

history and development

Although the history of the Yorkshire Terrier is somewhat obscure, the breed is not of any great antiquity. In spite of its undoubted relationship to the old Scottish breeds such as the Clydesdale and the old Black and Tan, the Yorkshire Terrier, as its name implies, was developed in the West Riding of Yorkshire, England. Undoubtedly other breeds were introduced, for instance the Maltese and the Dandie Dinmont have been mentioned, but this cannot be authenticated.

The prototype Yorkies varied considerably in size, most being much larger than the present dog and weighing up to 14 or 15 lbs. Of a lighter color and having drop or semi-erect ears which were very often cropped, they were nevertheless identifiable with the modern Yorkie. A show in Leeds in 1861 seems to be the first of which there is record of these dogs being shown. All the exhibits in the class for "Scotch Terriers", a term used loosely in those days, were Yorkshire Terriers of a crude pattern. It was not until 1886 that the breed was recognized as Yorkshire Terrier by the Kennel Club in England. These early Yorkies were used mainly for ratting and it took many years and the considerable skill of the breeders to reduce the size to that of a toy dog, some specimens ranging from $2\frac{1}{2}$ to $5\frac{1}{2}$ lbs. Specimens introduced into the United States around 1880 caused some confusion because of the considerable variation in size which still existed, but by the beginning of this century the characteristics had

Ch. Martynywn's Surprise of Atherleigh, bred by Mr. Hayes and owned by Mr. Coates, born in 1947, was an outstandingly beautiful dog with many wins to his credit in Britain.

(opposite)
Stirkeans Pretty Polly (two C.C.s) demonstrates the use of paper wrappers used to protect the coat from damage before her show. Her companion is an eight-week-old puppy.

become fixed, the toy breed firmly established and breeding true to type. Today the Yorkshire Terrier is one of the most popular breeds of toy dogs, and in Britain the registrations now reach the four thousand mark. It is, however, one of the most difficult dogs to breed for show purposes. Conformation and color being of paramount importance and the production of the long, straight coat with the true coloring, demanding great thought and care in breeding.

color

Originally the color was lighter than it is today and was described as bright blue. The present Standard lays down a dark steel blue (not a silver blue) with the hair on the chest a rich bright tan.

The fall (hair) on the head to be long and of a rich golden-shaded tan, deeper in color at the roots and muzzle, where the hair should be very long, these are called face furnishings. On no account must the tan on the head extend below the occiput, nor must there be any sooty or dark hair intermingled with any of the tan.

The hair on the legs should be of a very rich golden tan, a few shades lighter at the ends than at the roots, the tan not extending higher than the elbow on the forelegs or the stifle on the hind legs. The tail hair should be of a darker blue than the rest of the body, especially at the end.

Puppies are born black with tan markings on the feet and muzzle. Gradually the color clears and shows itself, remaining dark in the early stages. The tan on the head next appears and then the break in body color starts. It commences at the neck and gradually works down the tail and down each side of the body, the steel blue emerging.

care

The care of the Yorkshire Terrier bred for showing presents a number of problems. Firstly, the care of the coat. Frequently this is parted from the center-back downwards and divided into six or eight parts, each of which is wrapped carefully in tissue paper or muslin, folded over and tied. This is done to protect the long, beautiful hair from damage. Very dry or brittle

Mrs. Baynes's Ch. My Sweet Suzanne, a particularly lovely bitch winning in the early sixties. Note her compact body, alert expression and good topline.

hair is gently stroked with fine quality vegetable oil to condition it. Indeed, great care and attention is paid to its care and cultivation. Another problem is temperature. The Yorkie, with its long coat, needs an air-conditioned environment when in hot climates. In cold areas warmth is needed, for ideally the dog needs a temperate climate in which to thrive. If it is being kept only as a pet the coat can be cut to any desired length and, of course, this reduces the amount of time which has to be spent on coat maintenance.

The Yorkie is one of the few dogs which does not shed its coat and it is therefore necessary to brush well each day to remove any loose hair. It can get all the exercise it needs by running about the house or garden, but it enjoys the company of its owner.

It likes the best meat, but in small quantities. Sugar confectionery and candy should not be given, but a good, hard bone will help to strengthen and clean its teeth.

A bitch chosen for breeding must be of a suitable size, about 5 lbs. or more, fully grown.

character

Yorkies are hardy, game and protective. They are versatile and easily trained, and make tough as well as decorative pets.

But this courageous little dog is not just a pet; he is a worker as well. An example of this, where its small size and gameness combined to useful effect, was the Yorkie which was used during the last war to carry communication lines through narrow pipes. And another, a bitch called Tidy Tiddler, weighing 4 lbs who, in between her maternal duties of six litters, went rabbitting with her master, an eighty-one years old poacher, who carried her in his pocket. She would mark to ground, and on one occasion

(opposite)
Mrs. E. Munday's Ch. Luna Star of Yadnum demonstrates the ideal head with beautiful face furnishings, good eye shape and small, well placed ears.

A group of Stirkean Yorkies showing the difference between the mature bitch, with her flowing face furnishings, and the young dog and bitch on the left and the young bitch on the right. The three youngsters, all winners, are between twelve and eighteen months old.

had to be dug out! She is reported to have bolted 129 rabbits in less than three months.

standards

The general appearance of the Yorkshire Terrier should be that of a long-coated toy terrier. The coat hanging quite straight and evenly down each side of the body, a parting extending from the nose to the end of the tail. The animal should be very compact and neat, and the carriage should be very upright, conveying an "important" air. The general outline should convey the impression of vigor and good proportions.

The head should be rather small and flat, not too prominent or round in the skull, nor too long in the muzzle, and with a perfectly black nose. The jaws should be even, without crooked or misplaced teeth. On the Continent the scissor bite is essential. The eyes, placed so as to look directly forward, should be medium, dark and sparkling with a sharp, intelligent expression. They should not be prominent. The edge of the eyelids should be of a dark color.

Ears should be small and V-shaped, and carried erect or semi-erect, not far apart. They should be covered with a very rich tan, short hair. The hair on the body should be moderately long and perfectly straight (not wavy), glossy like silk and of a fine silky texture.

The legs should be quite straight and well covered with hair, and the feet should be round with black toe nails. The tail is cut to a medium length and covered with plenty of hair, carried a little higher than the level of the back – a tail which is too gay is a fault.

The body should be very compact with a good loin and short, level topline.

The Yorkie should weigh up to 7 lbs.

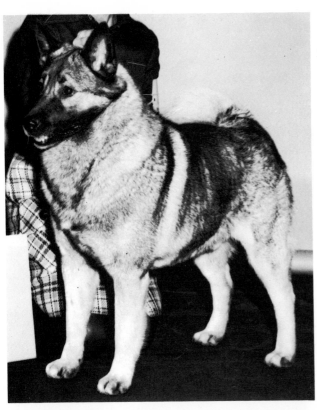

Spitz or Nordic Dogs

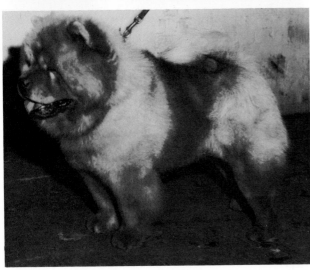

Included in our Spitz section, this outstanding Norwegian Elkhound won his group at Westminster, 1971. He is Ch. Vin Melca's Vagabind.

The Utility group at Cruft's 1971 was won by this lovely Chow Chow, Ch. U-Kwong King Solomon

Alaskan Malamute

A strikingly handsome and important American champion, Ch. Tigara's Togiak Chieftain.

history and development

Comparatively few breeds can lay claim to being the product of evolution, and perhaps the majority of the breeds for whom the claim can be acknowledged belong in the Spitz group. The characteristics which are common to this group are longish, close coats, prick ears and tails curled over the backs. The Spitz dogs have developed in the main in the cold climates, and they are to be found in all areas of the Far North; and not only are they adapted to the climatic conditions but, because of this, also to the work to be done in those regions; sledge hauling is one of the tasks for which the Malamute has been used in Alaska for many, many years, and is still. It is the heavy freighting dog of all the Arctic types. The sledges of Admiral Byrd's expedition to the South Pole in 1933 were drawn by Malamutes.

The Malamute happens to be better researched and documented than many breeds, thanks to the great interest and devoted work done by Mr. and Mrs. (Eva) Milton Seeley who, in the early 1920's, spent some eighteen months in an Eskimo village far inside the Arctic Circle studying the Malamute, compiling pedigrees and information. They returned early in the thirties to check and to establish further pedigrees, and the result is a more scientific definition of the breed, and information which has influenced a more enlightened attitude on the part of the breeders and has

One of the prominent Malamutes of 1970, Ch. Glaciers Burbon King, owned by Lois and James W. Olmen.

established a "natural" Malamute for today's fanciers. The breed was recognized by the American Kennel Club in 1936, and the Standard derives almost entirely from the work of Mr. and Mrs. Seeley.

The breed is seen more and more frequently in the show ring, and is gaining an increasing number of top awards in best in show and group competition. The Malamute is also gaining successes in obedience competition.

color

The colors range from light gray through to black, "wolf gray" is the most common, always white on underbodies, parts of legs, feet and part of face, the so-called mask markings. A white blaze on forehead and a white collar or a spot on the nape of the neck is attractive and acceptable but broken color extending over the body in spots or splashes is undesirable – color and markings should be symmetrical. The only solid color allowed is white.

care

Normal care and feed as for other dogs of this size, except that the Malamute is a light eater.

They keep themselves clean, and are normally free from odor. An occasional brushing is all that is needed, and a bath only when necessary. The Malamute is a hardy breed which can be raised successfully, indoors or outside, in any climate, but it needs, more than most, sufficient exercise to keep it in trim.

character

The age-long association of Malamute and man in the terrible conditions of the frozen North have established a special relationship, one of interdependence and discipline. In popular terms therefore the Malamute, because it is so intelligent and teachable, is a family dog; it is good with children, and in return for its owner's regard and affection, it will offer unbounded affection and faithfulness of its own. It can be dignified, yet playful when invited to be. Control must be established at an early age, as with all dogs, and discipline maintained throughout its life, but the well-trained Malamute is an asset and a pride for any owner.

Another Darlene Martin champion, American Ch. Tigara's Diamond Jim, a male of great beauty and quality.

standards

The Alaskan Malamute is a powerful dog, substantially built with a deep chest and a compact body. His thick, coarse outer coat overlies a dense wooly undercoat, and stands off from it to a length of one to two inches when the dog is in full coat. The depth of the coat varies in summer and winter. The head is broad and powerful, with wedge-shaped ears, placed on the side of the skull and small in proportion to the head, which are erect when alerted, pointing slightly forward. The muzzle is strong, only slightly lessening in width and depth towards the black nose, but not pointed, nor long, nor stubby. The lips close-fitting, broad upper and lower jaws with large teeth, scissor bite in front; never over or under shot. The skull, broad between the ears and moderately rounded, flattening off towards the eyes. There should be a slight furrow between the eyes, which are brown, almond shaped, fairly large, set-in obliquely; wolf-like in position, but conveying an impression of softness.

The face markings are a distinguishing feature – either it has a cap over the head with the rest of the face in a solid color, usually grayish white, or the face is marked like a mask; combinations of cap and mask sometimes occur.

The tail is plumed and carried over the back, but it should not be like a fox brush, nor should it be tightly curled.

The Malamute moves gracefully, energetically, with a proud carriage, head erect, eyes alert. Its feet are large, tight, deep, and with well-cushioned pads. There should be a protective growth of hair between the toes.

The front legs are straight with big bone, and the hind legs are broad and powerful, moderately bent at the stifles. Both fore and hind limbs should be strong for work. The dew-claws are not wanted and should be removed shortly after whelping.

The neck is strong and moderately arched, the back straight and gently sloping to the hips. The loin well muscled and not so short as to interfere with the easy, tireless movement which is so characteristic of the breed.

The Malamute must give an impression of great strength and tremendous propelling power; in fact in America show judges are advised to assess them giving consideration above all else to their function as a sledge dog for heavy freighting.

It is a rule that size considerations should not outweigh type, proportion and factors relating to the function of the Malamute. There is a natural size range in the breed; the desirable sizes for freighting are – males 25″ at the shoulder, weighing 85 lbs., females 23″, weighing 75 lbs. All other considerations being equal these desirable sizes secure the highest regard on the show bench.

One of the best-known Alaskan Malamutes in Britain, Tote-Um's Arctic Hawk, owned by Miss Parkyns and Miss Edmonds.

Basenji

history and development

The Basenji is one of the most fascinating of all breeds, in history, appearance and disposition. Its form is similar to the dogs of Ancient Egypt, and its skull, in proportion and dimensions, so similar to that of the oldest of the Canis Palustris, that it may be taken for a living fossil. From the time of Ancient Egypt until the middle of the 19th century, Basenjis faded into complete obscurity, though undoubtedly they were valued and preserved as hunting dogs by their native owners in Africa. Then, around 1860–70, these unusual dogs began to be commented on by the early explorers of the Dark Continent, and were referred to by various names, either after the tribes who owned them, or the district in which they were found, such as Zande dogs, Nyam-Nyam dogs, Bongo, or Congo terriers. Explorers found the dogs of special interest because they were barkless.

Basenjis came to England in 1895, and again in 1923, but they had no immunity to distemper and all died of it. In 1929, Mrs. Olivia Burn went to the Belgian Congo, and managed to bring back to England one dog and two bitches, plus a litter of puppies. These were a sensation when shown at Cruft's in 1937, and proved to be the foundation of the breed as we know it today, with the addition of various other imports from the Belgian Congo and the Southern Sudan. The British Kennel Club registered them as Basenjis, a name chosen by Mrs. Burn, the literal translation of this native word being "bush thing".

Since 1937 a number of other Basenjis have been imported, just enough to give the essential new blood, but importation is not easy, owing to the inaccessibility of the true Basenji country, the forests of the Congo and the swamps of the Southern Sudan. However, the Basenji is now safely established and British specimens have been exported all over the world; many other countries already having their own Basenji Clubs.

color

Red and white is the most popular color. This should be a bright orange red with white points. Other colors are, black, tan and white, and black and white. Cream Basenjis have been known, but these are not desirable as they have pale noses and eye-rims. Tiger-striped brindle is known and admired in the Southern Sudan, but so far there are few tiger-striped brindles outside Africa. Apart from the essential white feet, white chest and white tail-tip, the extent of the white markings is optional. A fair amount of white makes a more striking looking dog, and the most popular seems to be a narrow white blaze, a white collar of medium width and white stockings on the forelegs.

Three puppies of growingly popular breed; note the pronounced wrinkles.

care

In spite of its tropical origin, the Basenji is a remarkably hardy and healthy dog, but its fine coat and love of warmth and comfort mean that it is not suited to real kennel life. If kept in a kennel, it should be of the large loose-box type, with plenty of bedding. An infra-red lamp is an essential in winter. The ideal place for the Basenji is as a house pet. It can live happily in an apartment provided it gets plenty of walking exercise daily, and if possible, a free run in a park. But it can do with, and loves, any amount of exercise and is particularly good with horses. It dislikes the rain, and should be carefully dried after being out in a storm.

Its short coat is easily kept clean with grooming with a hound glove. Exercise should keep the nails short, otherwise they should be filed with a dog nail-file. A weekly sawn-off shin bone keeps the teeth clean. Its diet should be approximately half-pound fresh meat daily, with wholemeal biscuit to keep the dog slim and muscular, but with no bones showing. Green vegetables can be added, as Basenjis are amazing grass eaters, and really should be allowed access to fresh grass daily.

character

Much of the charm of the Basenji lies in its individuality and extreme intelligence. It is impish in its way and has an uncanny sense of fun. Though affectionate and demonstrative, the Basenji is not slavish in its devotion; there is too much curiosity in its make-up and it is not content to take things for granted. Everything has to be examined and enquired into, which makes it a wonderful companion, but not over-obedient. Some have been most successfully obedience-trained, especially in America, but when it is remembered that they have but recently come from the African jungle, where they do not even wear collars, strict obedience training does not seem natural. We do not want the Basenji to lose its originality, it is still the unspoilt dog whose brains have not been bred out, and it is fascinating with its amazing intelligence and natural reactions.

One of the Basenji's claims to fame is as the "barkless dog". It makes all

Basenji puppies in the Southern Sudan in 1952.

Ch. Fulafuture of the Congo, the breed's greatest sire. He sired twenty-five champions and won the stud dog cup in Britain in 1964, 1965, 1966 and 1967. Miss Tudor-Williams refused a firm offer of £2,000 ($4,800) from America for him.

Fula of the Congo, imported into Britain by Miss Tudor-Williams from the Southern Sudan in 1959.

Mbunga of Laughing Brook of the Congo, who was imported from Central Africa in 1961, provides a lovely subject for a head study.

the usual doggy noises, growling, yelping and whining, but the bark is conspicuous by its absence. Why the Basenji does not bark is open to conjecture. One theory is that for hundreds of years it has been trained for silent hunting, and the habit persists. Another theory is that it has a different formation of the larynx from that of other breeds. Its own particular noise is best described as a mixture between a chortle and a yodel, and is not unlike a young cockerel's first attempts at crowing. It uses this unique gift as a form of speech, different intonations of yodel being used to express different reactions.

Its extreme cleanliness, ease of house-training and total lack of doggy smell makes it hard to beat as a house pet. Most Basenjis are very sensitive, responding to love and kindness; voice being far more effective in shaming them over wrong-doing than physical punishment. But like all dogs of character, it must learn who is master and to obey. This should be done with kindness but firmness.

standards

The Basenji is a small, lightly built dog, high on the leg compared to its length, the legs being fine and dainty, giving the appearance of gazelle-like grace. It should be a finely pointed aristocratic looking animal. The action must be free, with the straight forelegs swinging well forward from the shoulder, and the elbows under the body, so that the utmost length and lightness of stride is obtained. The description "greatly resembling a racehorse trotting full out" cannot be improved upon. Poor movement, short legs and heavy bone being some of the worst faults.

Ideal height is 17″ at the shoulder for a dog, a bitch being about an inch smaller. Dogs weigh 24 lbs. and bitches 21 lbs. (22 lbs. in U.S.A.). The skull should be flat, well-chiselled and of medium width, tapering towards the nose with only a slight stop. Eyes should be dark and almond-shaped. Small, pointed ears, erect and slightly hooded, set well forward. A level mouth with a scissor bite, the upper teeth slightly overlapping. A good length of neck, which should be strong and without thickness, should be well set into laid back shoulders. The hindquarters should be strong with long second thighs and moderately bent stifles. The tail curls tightly over the spine with a single or double curl.

The coat is short, sleek and close and very fine, and the skin is very pliant.

Bear Dog, Karelian

This black Spitz of medium size, extensively used as a hunter for moose and deer, as well as bear, was accepted by the Finnish Kennel Club in 1935 and by the F.C.I. in 1946. About 700 are registered each year.

The Karelian Bear Dog, a near relative of the Russian Laiki, is almost sullen in character, which has prevented it from becoming as popular in its native country as the other breeds domestic to Finland. It has a special aptitude for finding the bear's winter hide-out. The dogs are quarrelsome, and are therefore used in the hunt singly; but they form strong attachments to their masters. This is not a breed for town conditions.

It is a sturdily built dog, with a double coat, the outer being stand-offish and the undercoat soft and wooly. The coat is longer on the back, throat and back of the hindquarters, and it is always black, a matt black with no sheen, and almost a brownish tinge, with white markings on head, throat, stomach and quarters.

The head is wedge-shaped, strong and fairly broad, with erect, pointed ears. Its eyes are small, dark brown, and fierce in expression. The body is slightly longer than its height, very powerful, and the tail is curved over the back in the tightest possible curl.

The size varies between 20″ and 24″ at the shoulder.

Courageous, but difficult to handle, the black and white Karelian Bear Dog.

Bear Dog, Tahl-Tan

A spicy little animal, now nearly extinct, originally used by the Tahl-Tan Indians of Canada. The breed is recognized by the Canadian Kennel Club, but no specimens have been registered or exhibited for a great many years.

It is difficult to breed, as it usually only mates once a year, and has a litter of one to four pups, which the dam will immediately kill in a fox-like fashion if she is in any way molested or threatened.

The breed was used for hunting the bear (this usually with two dogs at a time), lynx and porcupine. The Indians carried the dog on their back in a hide sack until the quarry was sighted, to preserve its strength. It was then let out, and it circled the prey, nipping its hocks, barking in a fox-like yap, and holding it at bay until the hunter came close enough for a kill. Despite various attempts, the breed has not adapted itself to living conditions outside the Northern environment. In temperament, the dog is bold, independent, good-tempered and affectionate to its master.

The Tahl-Tan Bear Dog is 12″ to 16″ high at the shoulder, and has a foxy head with large, erect, bat-like ears.

Its color is black, black and white, or grayish-blue and white.

A special characteristic of the breed is its tail, which is from 5″ to 8″ long, carried erect, and extremely thick from set-on to tip, quite different from the tail of any other breed of dog.

Note the large ears and alert expression of this fierce little Canadian dog.

Chow Chow

Mrs. V. A. M. Mawnooch's incomparable Ch. Choonam Hung Kwong, winner of forty-four Challenge Certificates, and best in show at Cruft's in 1936. He was valued at £5,250 ($12,600).

The superb quality of the Choonam and Rochow dogs is still remembered in the seventies. This is Ch. Rochow Dragoon, owned by Mr. C. D. Rotch, seen standing naturally without collar or lead. Dragoon won thirty-six C.C.s in the early thirties. He measured 21½" to the shoulder.

history and development

A basic relic of a Miocene canine intermediate between dog and bear the Chow Chow is generally believed to be the only breed to possess the blue-black tongue, a characteristic shared with certain small bears which have their origin in the same area. Although the Chow Chow has an anatomy and general biology resembling other breeds, it differs in a number of details and in the 10th century B.C. was referred to as "the peculiar dog of a kind found with the barbarians". When the Tartars invaded China around the 11th century B.C. legend has it they brought with them a vast number of enormous lion-like dogs with black tongues. This is the dog mentioned in the earliest Chinese chronicles and referred to as "the Tartar dog" or man kou (dog of the barbarians).

There are many references to sporting dogs in early Chinese literature. The definition of this particular group being "all dogs used in the capture of game, including the foreign Chow Chow". The breed deteriorated when selective breeding of dogs ceased with the ending of the Imperial Hunts, and only in isolated monasteries and in the households of wealthy merchants and noblemen were the original pure-bred Chow Chows carefully preserved.

The name "Chow Chow" appears to have originated either from the naturist "Chaou" meaning "dog of great strength", or from the word

"Tchau", at one period the name by which important Chinese traders were known. Their various commodities became "Chow Chow" in pidgin English, and this was later applied to the dog commonly found in Canton, meaning a Chinese dog. The smooth coated variety originated in Central and Southern China about 200 B.C.

The Chow Chow is one of the basic ancestors of the Spitz family. The first Chow Chows imported into England in 1760 were inmates of the zoo, and Gilbert White gives us the first detailed description of the breed. For twenty years after the institution of dog shows in 1859 Chows remained comparatively unknown to the general public, until the Chow Chow Club was formed in 1895. A scale of points was unanimously adopted, primarily based on Miss E. Bagshaw's recently imported red dog, Chow VIII, later to become the breed's celebrated Premier Champion and great advertising agent. Chow VIII has been described as the "first of the great ones" and considered by many authorities the supreme model of the true type. Many of the best Chows of today own him as their ancestor.

Another early great one to make a tremendous impact on the breed was Ch. Pusa of Amwell, and between the wars Ch. Akbar, the sensational Ch. Choonam Brilliantine, sold to America in 1925 for the record price of £1,800 ($4,320), Ch. Choonam Hung Kwong and Ch. Rochow Dragoon were supreme. Just before the Second World War the well-known Continental Chowist, the Countess R. de Changy, purchased the superlative little sire, Ch. Rochow Adjutant, who probably has had more influence on the breed than any other dog. British bred Chow Chows are exported all over the world, and as far as can be ascertained, Mrs. Garnett Botfield's Chinese Chum was the first Chow to be exported from England to America, where in 1905, he became the first American Chow Champion of record.

Dr. Wilton R. Earle's American Ch. Red Agate of Water's Gift was a top winner in the U.S.A. in the early sixties. A group winner, this self-red was 21" at the shoulder and weighed 85 lbs.

color

Whole colored black, red, blue, fawn, or cream, frequently shaded but not in patches, or particolored (the underpart of tail and back of thighs frequently of a light color). Red is the most popular color and this may vary from deep chestnut, self red, shaded red to light red. Black is second favorite, and the correct shade of "pigeon-blue" greatly desired. Fawn (or cinnamon) is unwelcome although acceptable, and cream with the desired pigmentation and dark eyes a rarity.

care

Five minutes' daily grooming with extra care and attention once a week is all that is necessary to keep the coat clean and looking well. Unsightly tufts of hair under and around the feet and between the toes should be trimmed away. Unduly long featherings, straggling ends around the ears and neck and between the front legs should also receive attention, but artificial shortening of the coat, which alters the natural outline or expression of the dog, is not allowed. Good brushes are essential, and the comb used to loosen and lift the dense undercoat which acts as a cushioning to the harsher hair, and to increase the general effect. All dead coat must be removed with finger and thumb, vigorous brushing and judicious use of the comb.

With the Chow Chow's slightly different biology correct feeding is advantageous to general well-being. The generous daily allowance of red

Miss E. M. Buckley's beautiful little Ch. Tai Kong of Adel clearly demonstrates the present-day type of Chow in Britain. He was many times best of breed.

Ch. Tiko Ling of Hanoi owned by Mrs. D. L. Smith started his show career early. At eleven months, at Leeds, England, championship show, he won best of breed, the A.V. puppy stakes and was in the last five for best in show. His subsequent career produced many top awards, and he proved an outstanding sire, with champions in Britain, South America, U.S.A. and Rhodesia.

After gaining his title, Mr. J. Egerton's International Ch. Emperor of Junggwaw whelped February 11th, 1953, was taken to Brussels where, in the hands of Comtesse de Changy, he was exhibited six times in four different countries, and was unbeaten by any Chow. Apart from two British supreme best in show awards he won many top awards during his career, and as sire started a line which, in 1970, produced the British "dog of the year" all breeds, Ch. U-Kwong King Solomon.

meat so beneficial to every other breed frequently has an adverse effect on the Chow. Young puppies, in-whelp bitches and nursing dams need a high percentage of good, lean, raw or lightly cooked beef, however, but for general feeding fifty per cent lean beef and lamb and fifty per cent mixed offal, cooked and served with wholemeal biscuits moistened with the gravy is an excellent mixture with a portion of raw beef or lamb suet the size of an egg, chopped up and added to the main meal. Milk, eggs, rice, fish and vegetables can be added to the diet.

character

Centuries of fighting for existence on the outskirts of civilization have helped to produce a temperament possessed by no other dog. So silent, so aloof, so avid for affection, so ruthless in attack. No other canine has a will so strong, a mind so resolute, or such a fixity of purpose which defies coercion. Unswerving fidelity to his owner and home which can and often does induce him to perform feats of endurance and ingenuity quite beyond the ordinary powers of canine reasoning. Scrupulously clean in his habits and free from any objectionable "doggy" smell. Quiet and unbelievably gentle unless roused to safeguard his "rights" and property; suspicious of any unusual happenings, and with a primitive fear of being seized and forcibly handled by people he does not know, and if subjected to captivity, will silently wait with uncanny patience until he has planned and made his getaway. One of the breed's distinctive characteristics is its complete naturalness.

He will die for you but not readily obey you. He will walk with you but not abjectly to heel, and his inquisitiveness and hunting instincts make it advisable to keep him on a lead in towns and wide open spaces. Harsh tones and shouted commands leave him unmoved, but he will respond in his own good time to the quiet voice and gentle handling of authority.

standards

According to the earliest Chinese records, the Chow Chow was in possession of all its distinctive characteristics some 4,000 years ago and has changed little since. The original Standard, based on the breed's premier champion, Chow VIII, is in force today with certain clarifications. It requires an active, compact, short-coupled and well-balanced dog, leonine in appearance with proud, dignified bearing. Unique in its stilted gait and and its bluish-black tongue.

The magnificent head proudly poised on a strong neck arched at an angle of about 60°. A broad, flat skull free from massive wrinkles but with sufficient "play" of skin to allow for the characteristic scowling expression. A muzzle that is broad and moderate in length, with the peculiar upward curving of the lips that gives the distinctive oriental grin. Small, thick, erect ears set well apart and tilted slightly forward over eyes that are small, dark and almond-shaped. The actual shape is a narrow "triangle" with a short side next to the muzzle. Gums, lips and roof of mouth should be black.

The shoulders should slope downwards and very slightly forward and outwards, with the forelegs straight and parallel at least a hand's breadth apart, presenting a perfectly straight front with a square arch. The back short, straight and strong. The tail set high and well forward, resting on the back in such a way that a constant depression on the coat is visible. The thigh-bone in the Chow falls almost perpendicularly to the stifle-joint, and it is this absence of angulation from the hip-joint, coupled with a modification of the stifle-joint, that gives the straight hind-leg and peculiar stilted gait. The Chow moves from the hip-joint with a stiff, somewhat jerky movement, and the pads of the hind feet should be only partly visible when in action. The feet small, round and cat-like, standing well on the toes.

The original Chow is a profusely coated animal and both color and climate have influence on coat, which the Standard describes as abundant, dense, straight and stand-off. Outer coat rather coarse in texture and with a soft wooly undercoat. Puppies, particularly reds, are usually born with a black mask which gradually disappears as the adult coat grows through.

Many of today's Chows are far too heavy and low to ground with exaggerated bone and insufficient arch of neck, giving an unbalanced squat appearance, and there is a tendency to pay more attention to general appearance than to important features. The Standard of the smooth variety is the same except that the coat is smooth.

With an English–American pedigree, Mr. N. K. Bloor's black Chow Chow Firehill Black Dakota.

Mr. and Mrs. Antrobus's Ch. Sarah Jane of Subortna at fourteen months old. Notice her good bone, legs, feet and balance, with unexaggerated head.

Elkhound
(Norwegian Elkhound)

Mr. A. Heward and Mr. H. Wreschner's Brann of Eskamere, an outstanding young dog showing beautiful balance and strength with quality.

Elkhound, side head view.

history and development

Since the days of primitive men Elkhounds have been staunch companions, guards and hunters for their masters. In the famous Viste Cave at Jaeren, West Norway, archaelogical investigations found a number of stone implements and bones dating from 5,000 to 4,000 B.C. Two dog skeletons were identified by Prof. Brinchmann of the Bergen Museum as of definite Elkhound type. Dog skeletons were also found in the famous Gokstad ship; and a clay bowl in the grave at Valloby bore in bas relief a hunting scene depicting Elkhounds.

In a rugged country of mountains and forests, rocks and marshes, and with temperatures down to 40° below zero, doing an outdoor job as watchdogs, guardians of home and flocks and trackers of big game such as elk (moose), reindeer, bear and wolves, the dogs had to be hardy and courageous.

In the elkhunting season dogs are used in two ways, the "loshund" which goes ahead to find the elk, then harassing it, and warning the hunter that it has the elk at bay so that he may come up for the kill; the "bandhund" on the other hand is attached by a twenty-foot leash to the hunter's belt, and trails the elk till close, when the hunter ties him to a tree and goes forward to shoot. The dogs must have plenty of courage and stamina, and in getting the elk to stand at bay, his action must be like a steel spring, or bouncing ball, to keep out of the way of antlers and

hooves. Only dogs which have proved their worth in the Norwegian Hunting Trials may be awarded the coveted title of champion.

Though they have been known for so long, pedigrees in Norway date only from 1865, from a dog called Gamle Bamse Gram. The first benched show in Norway in 1877 had 124 hunting dogs, including 15 "Bear and Elk Dogs". The first British imports were recorded in 1878, and in 1923 when some 90 Elkhounds had been registered at the Kennel Club, the British Elkhound Society was formed.

About seven years later, the Norwegian Elkhound Association of America was admitted to the American Kennel Club.

In 1948 owners and exhibitors in Holland formed the Scandia Club which caters not only for Elkhounds but for all other Scandinavian Spitz breeds. In Britain three clubs now cater for the breed, and have formed a Breed Council, while Ireland, also, has a thriving Elkhound Association.

In Britain the vast open spaces and big game of Norway are absent, but Elkhounds do well with the gun on both fur and feather, and are excellent vermin dogs, accounting for rats, mice, rabbits and foxes. The late Mrs. Cameron Head used her Elkhounds to track wounded deer in the deer forests of Scotland, and Elkhounds have been included in packs of beagles. Some have been trained for mountain rescue work, where their outstanding scenting ability and great good sense have won great praise. During the War some were used in Civil Defence, and at least one had a Certificate for Loyal and Devoted Service as Police Patrol Dog with the Royal Air Force.

color

Part of the attraction of the Elkhound is its gray color of varying shades, with the unusual harness markings of lighter color. The coat consists of a soft, wooly, light-colored undercoat, topped with longer, coarse hair, light colored at the roots but with dark tips, the overall dark or light color of the dog being determined by the length of the dark tips. Chest, legs and underside of the tail are lighter colored, the longer hair round the neck giving the appearance of a ruff.

care

One of the easiest of dogs to care for, the Elkhound needs only a brushing and combing daily to keep his coat in peak condition, and when in the show ring no extra care is required save to see that the coat is clean and well groomed, legs and feet perhaps washed with a little soapy water, dried and brushed down. For the show ring the dogs require no trimming or cutting of hair, nor powdering, while, in Britain, stringing up, placing

579

Elkhound puppies

legs and feet, and holding head or tail in position are all frowned upon. When moulting, the undercoat comes out in tufts, and the sooner this is combed out, the quicker the new coat will grow. Some males never seem to do a thorough moult, but bitches, especially after a litter, shed the whole coat, then quickly grow a lovely new one. Adult Elkhounds need comparatively small quantities of food for their size and those not taking strenuous exercise need care to see they do not grow too fat. Puppies, however, grow quickly, and they need plenty of good food to cope with their needs. Elkhounds are not fully developed until they are about three years old, but are great lasters, and those which are shown go on winning till ten years old or more.

A great advantage of the breed is the total lack of doggy smell, even when wet, and the clean legs and feet do not carry mud indoors.

character

One of the great attractions of the Elkhound is his fund of common sense, which makes him the ideal dog for a household pet. He knows instinctively when to guard, and the sturdy four-square appearance and deep bark make unwanted callers hesitate. With children they are wonderfully patient.

Their independent spirit means that from puppyhood they must learn what is permitted and what is taboo. The puppy allowed its own sweet way grows into an adult which dominates the household, and no breed can more quickly take advantage of an owner who allows commands to be disobeyed. With an understanding owner, however, there is no limit to what they will do to please him, and quite a few do well in obedience work and in tracking, which they love, and which is, after all, part of their heritage.

standards

Both Britain and America keep closely to the Norwegian Standard, though both countries find it difficult to prevent the dogs putting on weight, especially those kept as pets. At a recent conference of Elkhound judges in Norway it was agreed that, as a matter of guidance in interpreting the Standard, "within the outline formed by the body and legs of the Elkhound, at least one half should be air" meaning that roughly the height from withers to chest line should be less than the height from chest to ground. In Britain the height for males is around $20\frac{1}{2}''$, bitches about an inch less, but the A.K.C. makes it 18".

The expression in the dark brown eyes is frank, fearless and friendly, with a clear considering gaze of great wisdom. Ears are very flexible and one can almost read the Elkhound's thoughts by watching the ears carefully.

The feet, oval in shape, are compact, with tightly closed toes. Points which require watching are that ears must not get too large, and that feet should not be turned outwards. Most important of all is that care be taken not to produce silly, noisy, excitable dogs, sometimes aggressive towards others. Part of the fascination of the Elkhound is his handsome appearance, and his sensible, wise and kindly nature.

Mrs. Griffiths' Ch. Mona of Tortawe, a lovely bitch from South Wales, where the breed is very strong. Mona has a great winning record and has also proved a successful brood.

Eskimo Dog

The Spitz or Northern Dog is widely distributed over something like a third of the earth's surface, and embraces some sixty or more breeds and varieties. The Spitz of North Eastern Europe and Asia, the Laiki, although used for haulage, have been used more for hunting and herding than for pulling sledges. Those of North Western Europe and North America, the Eskimo, are the dogs most people think of when the word Husky is used.

It was at one time the ubiquitous sled dog of North America, but is now declining to such an extent that the A.K.C. has withdrawn recognition and it is currently only recognized by the Canadian K.C., where its numbers are steadily diminishing. The Eskimo Dog was at one time a dual-purpose breed; primarily used for freighting, but raced on the side. However, with the decline in dog-drawn transport; once so vital to the Arctic, this breed was no longer a necessity and, unlike the Malamute and Siberian, which have eye-catching appearance and speed respectively to attract to them the show-bench or sled-racing fraternities, the Eskimo Dog has only the appeal of its usefulness. There are, of course, still breeders determined to perpetuate the breed and it is to be hoped that it never becomes extinct.

This Eskimo Dog is one of the team owned by the British Antarctic Survey.

Both the Eskimo Dog and the Laiki of Asia have deteriorated, from the infusion of "white" blood introduced by the slow but relentless creep northwards of civilization, and below a latitude of 55° North, the Huskies are mostly mongrels. The Indians and Eskimos have, to a great extent, managed to keep their traditional breeds relatively pure; mainly because of their nomadic life where one tribe is seldom in contact with another, or with the "invading" white races.

An Eskimo Dog can reasonably be expected to be around 25″ at the shoulder and weigh from about 90 lbs. The breed is heavily boned, sturdy, with a good spring of rib and a deep chest. The coat and tail-carriage are like those associated with all the sled-dog breeds, the former consisting of wooly, oily undercoat with an outer coat of longer, stiff guard hairs, the latter being curled over the back, though not tightly. Although Eskimo Dogs are seen with very long coats it should always be remembered that such coats are considered a liability in bad weather as they ice up and add considerably to the weights the dogs are pulling. The breed will have oblique eyes which are neither large nor small, a good, strong muzzle, and the small ears will be well-furred inside.

Indeed, the Eskimo Dog has many of the physical characteristics associated with Malamutes, but with two main differences: there are no restrictions as to color and markings, which have made the Malamute such a striking breed, and the ear-set is higher on the head. The Eskimo Dog should have a good temperament, but the eye often belies this and the expression sometimes conveys a "meanness" which is not, in fact, part of the dog's nature.

The feet of the Eskimo Dog are of the type described as "snow-shoe"; that is large, webbed and well-furred between the pads, so that when the feet are splayed out on an icy surface, there is the maximum friction with the ice to prevent slipping, and on soft snow the broad surface presented to the snow minimizes the extent to which the dog sinks.

In Britain, all sled-dogs were originally known as "Esquimaux" dogs, and were referred to as that until after the Second World War, when the term "Husky" was substituted. Since the sled-dogs in Britain, other than Malamutes and Siberians, are of very mixed origins, it should be assumed that both words are synonymous; the British "Husky" is neither a pure-bred Eskimo Dog nor should it be confused with the Siberian Husky; rather it is a true sled-dog whose ancestors came from many different regions of the Arctic and Antarctic.

Finnish Spitz

history and development

The national dog of Finland is called Suomenpystykorva, which means Finnish-Cock-eared dog. When first introduced into Great Britain in the 1920's, it was called Finsk Spets but later became Finnish Spitz. The late Lady Kitty Ritson, a pioneer of the breed in Britain, invented the name "Finkie". The breed belongs to the family of Northern Spitz known as the Laika, derived from a Russian verb, to bark. The origin of these dogs goes back to antiquity when they were the companions of the early hunters wandering over ancient Lapland and Finland. They differed from the majority of the Laika in the coloring of their bright red-gold coats – most of the Laika were gray. With the development of civilization, these dogs became crossed with other breeds or strains until the only pure-bred examples to be found were scattered in the remote northern regions of Finland.

Towards the end of the 19th century a group of Finnish sportsmen recognized the danger of losing this exceptionally intelligent and beautiful breed. They sought out specimens from the north with the aim of producing a good hunting dog which was also a beautiful watch dog. In the early days the dogs were larger; and rather long, low bodies were most admired; the square type soon became the ideal. By the 1920's the

Ch. Siro of Boydon, born September 1933, was the first ever Finnish Spitz champion in England, and the winner of ten C.C.s. By Hello Aaro Ukinpoika, an imported dog, ex Finsk Minca, he was a handsome, typically masculine dog with a perfect temperament.

A more recent champion in Britain, and winner of the hound group at Bath championship show in 1970, Mrs. E. King's Ch. Kopari Brett, by Cullabine Toni ex Kopari Adella.

Mr. and Mrs. D. Cavill's bitch, Cullabine Greta, a double grand-daughter of Tommi, showing the alert, intelligent expression which is so characteristic of the breed.

influence was effective of the three well-known stud dogs, Ch. Natti, Topi Nattinpoika, and Onni. In the 1930's a certain amount of in-breeding was carried on in Finland to establish the type required. Gradually breeders of hunting dogs all over Finland took up the breed, using it in the field chiefly for flushing birds, but also for other game. Many strains specialize in elk-hunting, and the brave little Spitz has even on occasions attacked wolves and bears.

color

A Finkie must be a clear red but it may be a pale red-gold or a dark chestnut red. The cheeks, underparts, tail and shadings on the shoulder are always paler and may be deep cream, but never white; the undercoat is also paler. Some black-tipped hairs are permissible, even desirable, but most clear as the dog gets older. A narrow white strip, or spot, not exceeding a centimeter in width is allowed on the chest, and white marks on the feet, but none elsewhere.

Dirty color and distinctly defined differences between the colors are faults – shading should merge with the coat color. Eyes must be brown, preferably dark, and nose must be pitch black; the Finnish nick-name for the breed is piki-nokka (pitch nose). Puppies are whelped gray, usually with a good deal of black, but sometimes fawn.

care

The Finnish Spitz is a natural dog with no exaggerated features. Provided reasonable care is taken in wet weather to see that the dog is dried before bedtime all weathers are the same for a Finkie and he likes to be out-of-

doors and free as long as possible. In the evenings he likes to come into the house and will rest quietly in his corner.

A daily brush is good for his coat and essential when the coat is casting. Bath only occasionally – once a year is usually sufficient. In the show ring the Finnish Spitz must stand and move naturally, on a loose lead. He must be taught to do this early in life and also to learn to stay quietly on the bench. Unless he is taken out among people he can quickly become shy and resent handling.

Puppies are exceptionally independent and need firm but gentle handling. At the same time they are very sensitive and easily hurt. It is important that puppies are given plenty of rest time as they grow, otherwise they are inclined to become over sensitive and over excited.

Bitches are usually easy, natural whelpers, so little interference is the best plan at whelping time; unless a bitch obviously needs the quiet re-assurance of her owner she prefers to be alone.

Finnish Spitz puppies Sarumcote Chekko and Sarumcote Coff, born in 1935, owned by Mrs. and Miss Pink.

character

The Finkie is always lively and alert. Though inclined to be suspicious, and therefore cautious of anything unusual, he quickly accepts his owner's friends as his own and loves to play with children. He makes an excellent guard, barking furiously, with raised hackles at any intruder. He has an exceptionally strong homing instinct. He is almost cat-like in the way he cleans himself, and therefore makes an excellent house-dog.

standards

The Finnish Standard is used in every country where the breed is shown. Though it is natural and desirable that our show dogs should look better than hunting dogs yet it would be a pity if this led to another type entirely. In Britain there is a tendency to get show dogs over-weight and over-sized, and dogs which are only medium sized are often criticized as being too small.

The British Standard calls for an almost square body and bold bearing. No weight limits are given but for dogs the height to withers should be $17\frac{1}{2}''$ and length of body $20''$; bitches should be $15\frac{1}{2}''$ and $18''$. The coat on head and legs is short and close; on neck and back it should be stiffer.

In Finland color is judged to be of great importance and any white is often penalized, though the Standard allows a little. In Britain most judges are too lenient and often allow large patches of white in contrast to deep red on chests and even white stockings.

The Finnish Spitz, full face.

In Sweden the Finnish Spitz is becoming very popular as a hunting dog and in the show ring. It is not well-known in any other part of Europe although it is gaining some popularity in France, and a few exhibits are seen now at all the important international shows. In Spain very few are shown but interest there is growing, while in Australia, though only introduced a few years ago, the breed is making good progress. In the U.S.A., though there are several breeders, it is difficult for them because the Finnish Spitz is not yet registered by the A.K.C.

Husky, Siberian

Ch. Kronprinz of Kazan winner of the S.H.C.A. National Specialty Show in 1965, best of breed at Westminster 1966 and a member of the team which won the Siberian Husky Club of America Racing Trophy in 1964. Owned, bred and handled by Paul J. Koehler.

history and development

Centuries ago, the nomadic Chukchi people of north eastern Asia lived a wide-ranging hunting existence and by careful breeding from the several types of dog indigenous to that area, gradually developed a unique breed, tailored to their special requirements. This superb Chukchi sled dog, with a body designed to provide speed, strength and stamina is the ancestor of today's Siberian Husky.

At the turn of the century when the discovery of gold lured men to Alaska, dog teams, composed then of native huskies and mixed breeds, were the only means of transportation in winter. Much skill was required in their training and great rivalry grew up among the dog team drivers. In 1908 an All-Alaska Sweepstakes race was run between Nome and Candle and return, a distance of 408 miles, covering some of the roughest and most desolate terrain in western Alaska. This event proved so popular with the entertainment-starved inhabitants of Nome that it became an annual affair. A Russian fur trader named Goosak competed in the 1909 race with a team of huskies that he had brought over from Siberia. The

Alaskan drivers laughed at these small, docile dogs, never expecting them to stand up to the rigorous challenge of a Sweepstakes race.

The performance of these little huskies from Siberia greatly impressed Fox Maule Ramsay, a young Scotsman who was in Alaska to supervise his family's interests in the gold fields. He went to Siberia, located a Chukchi village, and was able to return to Nome with seventy Chukchi dogs. From them he formed and trained three teams for the 1910 Sweepstakes race. One of Ramsay's teams, driven by the legendary Swede, John "Iron Man" Johnson, won the race, with the others placing second and fourth. It was in the 1914 race, won again by "Iron Man" Johnson and his Siberians, that Leonhard Seppala, a young Norwegian who had emigrated to Alaska, first tried his skill as a racing driver. He had acquired his Siberians in 1913 from his friend, Jafet Lindeberg, who had selected the finest dogs available from the original Ramsay stock, with the intention of presenting them to Roald Amundsen when the latter stopped in Nome en route to the North Pole. However, the outbreak of World War I cancelled Amundsen's Arctic expedition, and the dogs were turned over to Seppala to train and race. For three consecutive years, 1915–1917, Seppala and his Siberians won the All-Alaska Sweepstakes. He set records still unbroken today and was widely acclaimed as the top racing driver in Alaska.

In 1925 an epidemic of diphtheria broke out in Nome and supplies of antitoxin were urgently needed. Seppala left Nome with a twenty-dog

A head study of Ch. Belka of Monadnock, leader of the Monadnock Kennels' racing team in the late 1940's.

The matched racing team of Siberians which was bred, owned, trained and raced by Mrs. Daniel Rice of Shrewsbury, Massachusetts. This team won the S.H.C.A. Racing Trophy in 1970.

Ch. Bonzo of Anadyr, C.D.X., owned by Mrs. Earl Norris of Willow, Alaska. Bonzo, besides being a bench champion and holder of an obedience title, is the first Siberian to win best in show in America, and to top off, is the leader of the Norris racing team, a winner of the S.H.C.A. trophy.

team, led by Togo, to meet the serum sent by railroad to Nenana and deliver it to the stricken city, travelling a total of three hundred and forty miles. The bronze statue of a sled dog that stands in Central Park in New York City today serves as a symbol of a tribute to all the dogs who toiled so valiantly in the serum run.

Seppala later parted with some of his dogs to Mrs. Elizabeth Ricker in Poland Springs, and others went to Mr. Harry Wheeler in Ste. Jovite, Quebec. With stock from the latter Mrs. Marie Frothingham and her daughter Millie Turner began their Gold River Kennel. Leonard Chapman sent for a male, named Duke, from the Cooney-Johnson kennel in Alaska where descendants of the original Ramsay stock were still being bred. Moseley Taylor purchased an entire team, including a male named Tuck, from Frank Dufresne, the Fish and Game Commissioner of Alaska. Largely through the efforts of Mrs. Ricker, the American Kennel Club recognized the breed in 1930, and that year twenty-four Siberian Huskies were registered.

The selective breeding done by some of the pioneer breeders is of special interest since it laid the foundation upon which the breed rests today. One notable mating was of a bitch named Toto, a daughter of Seppala's Togo, to Mr. Taylor's Tuck, resulting in the female puppy Tanta of Alyeska. In 1932 Tanta of Alyeska was bred to Mr. Chapman's Duke, producing a litter of pleasing type and uniformity. Among these was Tosca of Alyeska, owned by Mrs. Taylor (now Mrs. Nicholas Demidoff) and the foundation bitch of her Monadnock Kennels. Another was Cheeak of Alyeska, retained by the breeders, Mr. & Mrs. Milton Seeley, and the foundation bitch of their Chinook Kennels, where many of the teams for the Byrd Antarctic expeditions were trained.

While performance on the trail still remained the primary goal, some of the New England breeders also saw the merit of proving the worth of their stock in the show ring, and consequently strove to improve type and appearance while maintaining the original conformation and soundness. Some of the early bench show champions, many of which were also leaders or great team dogs, were: Ch. Togo of Alyeska, Ch. Cheenah of Alyeska (the first bitch champion of the breed). Ch. Laddy of Wonalancet, Ch. Vanka of Seppala II, Ch. Panda of Monadnock, Ch. Wonalancet's Baldy of Alyeska (the first Siberian Husky to win a Working Group competition), Ch. Turu of Alyeska, Ch. Vanya of Monadnock III, Ch. Belka of Monadnock, Ch. Chornyi of Kabkol, UDT (the first top obedience dog of the breed), Ch. Kira of Monadnock, Ch. Helen of Cold River, and Ch. Otchki of Monadnock, CD (the first leader to earn both a championship title and an obedience degree).

After World War II, during which many Siberian Huskies performed nobly in the U.S. Army's Search and Rescue teams, interest in the breed grew. Through the sale of stock from both Chinook and Monadnock Kennels, Siberian Huskies were introduced to other areas: Kabkol Kennels in Washington, D.C., Stony River and Long's Peak Kennels in Colorado, Dichoda Kennels in California, and Anadyr Kennels in Alaska.

Through the 1950's the reputation of the breed grew considerably, not only as fine racing and show dogs, but as endearing family companions, and many more kennels were established. Some of the dogs finishing their championships during this decade proved to have a profound influence upon the breed: Ch. U-Chee of Anadyr, Ch. Aleka of Monadnock,

Ch. Kiev of Gap Mountain, Ch. Kara's Idyl, Ch. Bonzo of Anadyr, CD, Ch. Alyeska's Suggen of Chinook, Ch. Monadnock's Pando, Ch. Kenai Kittee of Beauchien, CDX, Ch. Sieksuh's Cissie, and Ch. Stony River's Rinda.

The Siberian Husky Club of America, founded in 1932, has consistently encouraged the perpetuation of the dual capabilities of the breed. Since 1960 a trophy has been awarded annually to the member's team which best exemplifies, through its racing and show record, its ability to conform to this basic ideal.

The greatest upsurge of breed popularity occurred during the 1960's, with annual registration at the American Kennel Club for the first time topping 1,000 in 1963. In 1969 the number of Siberian Huskies whelped and registered totaled a staggering 4,880. It was also during the 1960's that exportation of the breed to several European countries took place. There are now active groups of Siberian owners, drivers and exhibitors in Switzerland, Finland and the Netherlands. They may be found in smaller numbers in Norway, Germany, Belgium, and also in England, where the larger Greenland Husky is better known.

A head study, taken in 1940, of Zoe of Kolyma, owned by Mrs. Samuel D. Post.

color

All colors and white, and all markings are allowed but shades of wolf, silver grays, tan and black with white points are the most usual. The cap-like mask and spectacles are typical.

care

This highly adaptable dog requires no special care but, having been bred for hard work, requires plenty of exercise.

character

The delightful temperament found in the breed today is also a heritage from the past. Since the Chukchis depended upon their dogs for survival, it is logical that they held them in high esteem and treated them humanely. They were often housed in the family shelters, played with the children,

Typical Siberian Husky puppies sired by Ch. Monadnock's Pando ex Ch. Kara, bred by Mr. C. A. Posey of Alexandria, Virginia.

Ch. Dichoda's Yukon Red winning the S.H.C.A. Specialty at the Kennel Club of Beverly Hills, Santa Monica, California in 1969. Yukon Red also took a second in the working group under Maxwell Riddle. He is owned and bred by Mr. and Mrs. Frank S. Brayton at their Dichoda Kennels in California.

and were well schooled in team conduct. Today the Siberian Husky is a loyal family companion, but also has no suspicion of strangers and will greet guests cordially. So, contrary to popular opinion, he is not an aggressive guard dog, although he may unwittingly act as a deterrent to those ignorant of his true nature. The typical Siberian Husky is strikingly beautiful, gentle and affectionate, and readily amenable to training.

standards

The Siberian Husky is a medium-sized working dog of powerful but graceful build. Its general appearance and body proportions reflect a basic balance of power, speed and endurance. A moderately compact frame, erect ears and brush tail suggest its northern heritage. Its free effortless gait is characteristic and its remarkable pulling power and amenable disposition make it the ideal sledge dog.

It has a medium-sized head, slightly rounded on top. Skull and muzzle are finely chiseled and the jaws strong with close fitting dark lips. The medium sized ears, carried erect, are moderately rounded at the tip and well furred on the inner side. The strong, arched neck is fairly short. It has a compact body with deep strong chest; powerful shoulders, well laid back; strong level back and lean, taut loins.

The hindquarters are powerful with good angulation; well bent stifles. The straight, well-muscled legs have substantial bone, but not heavy, and the oval feet are compact and well furred between the toes, forming a typical showshoe foot. The double coat is dense, soft and downy on the undercoat and thick and smooth textured on the outer coat.

Dogs measure 21″ to 23″ at the shoulder and bitches 20″ to 22½″.

Husky, Greenland

Angagssuak I, who was lead dog of the Oxford N. Greenland Expedition of 1935. He had wins at Cruft's from 1936 for three years.

The American explorer, Peary, expressed the opinion that there was only one breed of sled-dog, and that any variations were of a purely regional origin. He was writing before sled-dogs appeared on the show-benches under different breed names, and when one tries to distinguish between some of the unrecognized varieties that are regarded as different breeds, one cannot help wondering whether he might not have been right!

Greenland has its own type of Husky, and it is a Spitz breed which is probably purer than any other, since the Danish government has, for many years, prohibited the importation of "white" breeds of dog, realizing that the outcrossing of sled-dogs with other breeds has led to the degeneracy of most North American huskies.

It is difficult to define the characteristics of the Greenland Husky; those unquestionably Greenland Huskies used by the trans-Arctic walk differ considerably from the Greenland Huskies recognized as such by the F.C.I., which differ again from those in Britain, said to have predominantly Greenland breeding behind them.

Those dogs that are unquestionably of Greenland origin appear to be 24″ to 25″ with a body weight slightly lower than that of Malamutes and Eskimo dogs. There is a greater length of loin and less bone than one is accustomed to in dogs of this size. The ear-set is high and the eye small and dark, obliquely set; the predominant colors appear to be black and white and there is no restriction on markings.

Icelandic Sheepdog

Although the Icelandic Sheepdog is mentioned in most comprehensive dog books from the late 19th century to the present-day, the information given tends to be contradictory. Some say there are two Iceland dogs, one being the size of a wolf; some say Iceland Dogs are white, others that they are white with black or brown patches; indeed the only point on which they seem to agree is that the Iceland Sheepdog *is* a sheepdog.

A few examples have appeared in the show-ring in Britain and these have been charming animals about 19″ high and, in appearance, somewhere between a Norwegian Buhund and a Finnish Spitz. They are slightly taller and heavier than the Buhund and have a denser coat than the Finnish Spitz. The eyes are larger than is usual in Arctic breeds, round rather than oblique. The erect ears are fairly large in proportion to the skull, though not large enough to be termed "bat-ears".

In many ways, the Iceland Dog could be described as a miniature Husky, since it shares the general physical characteristics of the Spitz group, but this would give an incorrect impression of temperament – the Iceland Dog is a sheepdog and should not have the hunting propensities displayed by the sled-dogs. The breed is recognized by the British Kennel Club, but is certainly one of the rarest breeds in Britain. Since 1960, only two appear to have been exhibited, and since 1965, there have been only nine registrations.

Konni of Wensom, owned by Mr. Mark Watson, competed in the any other variety section at Cruft's in 1959.

Japanese Breeds
(Akita, Sanshu, Shiba, Shika, Ainu)

The Akita, the commonest of the Japanese Spitz breeds (right and below).

The dog plays an important part in Japanese social life. His place in the home as a pet, as guard dog, working or sporting dog corresponds to his circumstances in these respects in the West, and a number of breeds have emerged as a consequence of selective breeding for purpose. These breeds specific to Japan, are comparatively little known in the West and, indeed, many of the dogs to be seen in Japan today are Western breeds and types. The Japanese system of registration and competition is highly organized under the auspices of the Japanese Dog Federation, and the government breed award, "National Treasure" is highly coveted. 1970 was in fact "The Year of the Dog" in Japan, coinciding with the famous Expo '70 in Osaka, and great attention was directed to the canine species during that year, even to the extent of commemorating the dog on a series of postage stamps.

The breeds domestic to Japan are the Akita, Sanshu, Shiba, Shika, Ainu and the Tosa, which is included in the section on Working Dogs.

Akita: This is the largest and the best known of the Japanese breeds. It is sometimes known as the Large or Shishi Inu. Originating in the Polar regions the breed has a recorded history dating back for over 300 years. Bred for hunting deer and wild boar, it was also used occasionally for the Japanese black bear. It could formerly be owned only by royalty and nobility.

Great attention is currently being paid in Japan to improving the breed, and it is gaining favor in the U.S.A., where there are several specialist Akita breeders.

The Akita is swift and, with its fully webbed feet, is a powerful swimmer. Its double coat and soft mouth enable it to retrieve even in the coldest waters. It is large, compact, requires little exercise, and comparatively little food. The head is broad, flat across the skull, with moderate stop. Muscular, fairly short neck, straight back, with well-boned, straight legs. The tail is curled and carried over the back. The top coat is medium to soft and straight; the undercoat thick and furry. Colors are fawn, wheaten, gray, brindle, russet, tan or black-and-tan, and all-white.
Height: 21″ to 24″ for dogs; 19″ to 21″ for bitches.

The Ainu, or Hokkaido Dog

Sanshu: This medium-sized Japanese Spitz comes from the Aichi region where, after the Meiji period ended in 1912, it was bred by the introduction of Chow Chow blood into the old Aichi breed. This was done to give more substance and to impart characteristics designed to make it more suitable as a family pet. Robustly built, of good shape (when seen in profile its body is very nearly square), the Sanshu is intelligent, and excellent as a guard dog.

The skull is relatively large, somewhat flat on top, with the front gently rounded. The muzzle is strong, short, and wedge-shaped. The dark eyes are almond-shaped; the ears are small, triangular, set rather close together, erect, and inclined gently forward.

The withers are well-developed, the back short and straight, loins strong, chest deep. The tail is tightly curled. The coat is hard, dense, of moderate length. Colors are rust-red, black-and-tan, tan, fawn, salt and pepper, and white with patches.
Height: 20″ to 22″ for dogs; 18″ to 20″ for bitches.

The Shika

Shiba: The smallest of the Japanese Spitz. The Shiba is one of those breeds in which cunning is more highly developed than in many others. It is used for hunting small game, particularly in the areas where it originated – the prefectures of Gifu, Nagano, and Toyama in Central Japan.

It is well-built, well-muscled and has an elegant attractive appearance. It is very agile, and its friendly nature makes it a favorite family pet. The back is rather long and the chest deep. The tail is long, and is carried curled over the back or sickle-like.

A Shiba

The ears are smallish, triangular, erect and face slightly forward. The eyes are small, almond-shaped, dark brown in color. The coat is hard and straight, without any fine hair, and the colors are red, salt and pepper, red pepper, black pepper, black, black-and-tan, spotted or white.
Height: 15″ to 16″ for dogs; 14″ to 15″ for bitches.

Shika: The Medium Nippon Inu, or Shika Inu was, in earlier times, used to hunt deer in the mountainous regions of Japan. The breed was often referred to as a deerhound, and also was known by the districts in which it could be found – Hokkaido, Kyushu and Ochi.

The Shika is very like a larger version of the Shiba, but the withers are higher and more developed, and the loins are stronger.

It is used today as a guard dog, and a companion, and also as a sporting dog. Intelligent and lively, the Shika becomes strongly attached to its master.

Colors are pepper and salt, red pepper, black pepper, red, black, or white. Height: 19″ to 21″ for dogs; 16½″ to 19″ for bitches.

Ainu: This is one of the ancient breeds of Japan, bred by the Ainu, who originally inhabited the Island of Hokkaido. It was used for hunting and as a guard dog. It has a reputation for strength and courage, as well as for obedience and its intelligent response to training. The Japanese authorities, in 1937, took special measures to protect the breed, and at that time gave it the name Hokkaido Dog, although it is still better known as the Ainu Dog; indeed it is registered with the F.C.I. under that name. The Ainu is not a large dog, it stands around 16″ to 19½″ but its thick coat gives the impression of a greater size.

The colors are red, white, black, pepper and salt, pepper and salt red or black, and black/brown.

The Sanshu

Italian Spitz

The Italian Spitz, or Volpino Italiano, is a small dog, used for many useful purposes – the breed is found on many an Italian farm performing the duties of guard to property and stock, and it is commonly seen in vineyards where it protects the vines and, on the carts, guards the produce on its way to the market. The breed also figures as a companion and domestic dog in many Italian families.

The breed has long been known in Italy, and there is evidence that it was known to the Romans, who depicted a dog of similar type on decorated drinking vessels.

It is an all-white dog, with a long, silky coat and a thick undercoat. The general conformation is that of a typical Spitz, but it is rather smaller than most – around 11″ high, and weighing about 9 lbs.

It resembles mainly the Small German Spitz but it has a somewhat longer muzzle, and the ears are longer, and the tips more pointed.

Jamthund

The Jämthund bears a strong resemblance to the internationally better known Norwegian Elkhound, and it has been officially recognized as a separate breed since 1946. In its native Sweden, it is almost twice as popular as the Elkhound – around 1,000 are registered yearly.

The breed history, however, is closely linked to that of the Elkhound. Spitz-type dogs have for many centuries been used for hunting elk in the middle and northern forests of Sweden and Norway and, while what is now known as the Norwegian Elkhound was the most commonly used, huntsmen in the county of Jämtland stubbornly refused to recognize any other type than their own. Argument raged as to which breed was the best elkhound – rather a tenuous argument it may seem as, apart from their physical resemblance, the two breeds share the same historical background, but it is a fact that the Norwegian type was the one to gain international recognition as a popular show-dog, while the Jämthund is hardly known outside Sweden.

The Jamthund, a Swedish Spitz, used for hunting elk and other game.

The most important difference between Jämthund and Norwegian Elkhound is the greater size of the former – it sometimes stands four impressive inches taller at the withers than its Norwegian cousin. Head type and expression also differ slightly, and the Jamthund usually has light markings on the nose.

Keeshond

Ch. Evenlode Monarch of Merrybelle, by Ch. Randalone of Rhinevale ex Ch. Rondina of Rhinevale, was bred in 1958 by Mr. T. Merry and owned by Miss O. M. Hastings. He won seventeen C.C.s and best in show, all breeds, at the important West of England Ladies' Kennel Association's championship show and the Ladies' Kennel Society's championship show in 1962. He sired Ch. Merry Christmas of Ven and Ch. Saskia of Ven.

history and development

Keeshonden were the dogs of the peasantry – living in villages and on farms as well as on the barges. Whilst not appearing in any major masterpieces of Flemish or Dutch art they can be seen in some of the homely scenes painted by Jan Steen (1626–79). There are two explanations offered for the name Keeshond (plural Keeshonden). According to Miss van de Blom, who did much for the breed in Holland, Cornelis de Witt – brother of the Grand Pensionary, Johan de Witt – was always known as Kees and was the owner of a spitz dog. In 1672 the brothers were massacred by the rabble and, in contradiction to the increasing popularity of Pugs, the traditional favorites of the House of Orange, the people favored the dog of Kees – the Keeshond.

Alternatively, the name may have come into use some hundred years later at the time of the widespread unrest that preceded the French Revolution when Cornelis – or Kees – de Gyzelaar led the rebellious Patriot party. His spitz dog became its symbol or mascot. Many cartoons, lampoons and badges depicting Kees dogs can be seen in Dutch museums and galleries and some claim that it is from de Gyzelaar's dog that the Keeshond dog got its name. In America this is the accepted basis of the title.

One of the great trade routes of Europe has always been the Rhine. The watch dogs of the Rhineland and Westphalian farms and homesteads were valuable assistants to the bargees who made the long, slow journeys along the waterways and into the Netherlands. Since this traffic continued over a long period the spitz dogs became as much a part of the Dutch rural

Keeshond puppies

scene as they were of the German. Whether it would be quite correct to call these dogs the national breed of Holland is doubtful, nor was the title Keeshond (pronounced Kayzhond) brought into use until comparatively recently, but they were certainly ubiquitous around Dutch farms and hamlets, while others of their kind lived the main part of their lives on board the barges, tucking themselves away when they were not needed but always ready and alert at the first sound of an intruding foot on their territory. The 19th century brought speedier methods of transport and less demand for the barge dogs but it was also the time of increased interest in systematic dog breeding and organized dog shows.

In 1905 Miss Hamilton-Fletcher – soon to become Mrs. Wingfield Digby – visited Holland and was fascinated by the barge dogs she saw. On her return to England she imported two puppies, Zaandam and Barkles, who were followed by Schie, Dirk and Edam. It was 1923 before Mrs. Wingfield Digby's two "Dutch Barge Dogs" appeared at Birmingham National Show. In 1925 a specialist club was formed and first called "The Dutch Barge Dog Club" but later became "The Keeshond Club". From 1925 onwards things moved fast – in 1928 Challenge Certificates were awarded for the first time. In 1929 Dochfour Hendrik, owned by Baroness Burton and bred by Colonel and Mrs. Wingfield Digby became the breed's first champion.

The head of an English and American champion, Ch. Tom Tit of Evenlode.

There were many importations into Britain at this time, among them Ch. Bartel van Zaandam, Hendrik van Zaandam and Alli von der Sternwarte, all imported by Mrs. Wingfield Digby, but the former owned by Mrs. Moore, who also imported Black Bock, later owned by myself. Mrs. Morton also imported Cely v. Jura de Witt. Some importations were from Holland and others from Germany. The result was a variation in type that is still apparent, the German legacy being a longer and more crested neck and greater profusion of coat.

While English breeders were working to establish the Keeshond, dog lovers in America began to take notice of the breed. Their first importations came from Germany in 1930 but were soon followed by a number of dogs from England. The most prominent exhibitors in the next few years were Mr. Irving Florsheim and Mrs. Fitzpatrick; their kennels contained dogs with the van Zaandam affix as well as the Guelder prefix of Mrs. Gatacre. Mrs. R. Fort, well known to English breeders today as Mrs. J. R. Collins (of Ven), had taken her dogs with her to America, including Prestbury Sister, the first American champion bitch who, with her Black Peter, Herzog of Evenlode and Annie van Sandar were pillars of the breed in the States. The majority of American Keeshonden can trace their pedigrees back to dogs exported from England.

In England the outbreak of war reduced all dog breeding to a minimum. By 1946 things were getting under way again and Mrs. I. Tucker's well established Vorden kennel, Mrs. Emerson (Rhinevale) and Miss Glover (Welford) increased in strength while Mr. and Mrs. Greenwood's Wistonias came to the fore. An amalgamation of Evenlode and Vorden blood produced Eng. and Amer. Ch. Tom Tit of Evenlode who, in Mrs. Fitzpatrick's hands, did an enormous amount for Keeshonden in America, while in England Ch. Big Bang of Evenlode became winner of eight Challenge Certificates and sire of twelve champions. A great triumph for the breed came in 1957 when Mrs. Tucker's home-bred Ch. Volkrijk of Vorden was best in show all breeds at Cruft's.

British, American and Canadian Ch. Wrocky of Wistonia, the greatest winning Keeshond in America, owned by Mrs. Porter Washington of California and bred in England by Mr. and Mrs. Greenwood.

Ch. Volkrijk of Vorden, bred and owned by Mrs. I. Tucker, won twenty-four C.C.s at twenty-five successive shows, best bitch and best non-sporting group at Cruft's 1956, and best in show, all breeds, at Cruft's and Ayr in 1957. She also proved her worth as a brood, being the dam of Ch. Volkrad of Vorden and American Ch. Vangabang of Vorden.

In 1962 my own Ch. Evenlode Monarch of Merrybelle won top awards in England and in 1965 English, American and Canadian Ch. Wrocky of Wistonia was 35 times best of breed, won 33 groups and was 18 times best in show in America.

color

The body color should be wolf or silver gray. The undercoat should be pale cream – not yellow. The longer hairs of the outer coat have black tips, giving the characteristic shading. The plume of the tail is white with black tip. The legs and feet should be cream with black toe nails. Black marks below the knees are a fault. The shorter hair of the head is shaded with lighter colored "spectacles" pencilled from eye to corner of each dark ear. Eyes dark.

care

The Keeshond's long coat requires special attention once a week with a stiff brush, working from tail to head. Since the coat should be offstanding, care should be taken not to take out all the supporting undercoat, and use of the comb should be confined to the moulting period. Choke chains should never be used on a Keeshond since they ruin the ruff.

character

Although the Keeshond is a "one man dog", he accepts the family of the person he owns! He is sensitive, even-tempered and, although somewhat independent in outlook, accepts discipline in order to please those he loves. The Keeshond's keen hearing makes him an excellent watch dog.

standards

The Standards adopted in 1935 have not been altered. The American Standard is much fuller but does not differ in any important respect. A Keeshond, well groomed and trained for the ring, is a beautiful sight, standing with his ears pricked, his tail carried over his back, alert, ready to respond to his handler.

The worst faults are yellow coloring, light eyes, low-set tail and nervous demeanor.

Size has long been controversial, both the Standards give 18″ at the shoulder for males (bitches 17″) as the ideal height, "but size should not unduly prejudice type" and most of the best dogs measure more than 18″. Many breeders feel that the smaller types may revert to Pomeranian size if efforts are not made to keep good bone and strong, handsome dogs.

Ch. Vivandiere of Ven, born in 1963, is owned by Mrs. J. R. Collins. She won eleven C.C.s and was one of the top winning bitches in the sixties.

Ch. Big Bang of Evenlode, bred by Miss O. M. Hastings, won eight C.C.s, and was a great sire. He sired twelve champions and was the holder of the breed stud dog cup in Britain in 1957, '58, '60, '62, '63, '64 and '65.

Laiki

(Russo-Finnish, East Siberian European-Russian, North Russian Samoyed, West Siberian)

Russo-Finnish Laika

Laiki are seen all over Northern Russia. They are strongly built, medium-sized animals with erect ears, curly tails, dense, heavy coats and lively, active characters.

The name derives from the Russian word "layat", which means "to bark". When a Laika, out hunting, sees a bird in a tree or bush, it barks ceaselessly, thus indicating to the sportsman with his gun the position of the bird. If the bird flies off before the hunter arrives, the Laika follows it noiselessly until the bird alights, and the dog again indicates its presence by barking.

The four breeds of Laika which are the most common of the working dogs in Russia today are the Russo-Finnish Laika, the Russo-European Laika, the Siberian Laika and the North-Russian Samoyed Laika. Again, these breeds are named for the regions in which they are bred and used. They are mainly bird dogs but they are also used for a variety of small wild animals – ermine, squirrel, wild-cat and even otter.

In addition to hunting the Laiki are commonly used as sledge dogs, and even for herding.

There are a number of other local varieties of Laiki none of which are recognized.

An indication of the comparative popularities of the different breeds is

Siberian Laika

given in the statistics of the Hunting Dog Show in Moscow in 1955, when of 199 Laiki exhibited, 119 were Siberian, 66 Russo-European, only two Russo-Finnish and no Samoyed at all.

Russo-Finnish: This breed is on the wane and can be found mainly in the Karelian region, south of Murmansk and bordering on to Finland. It has a resemblance to the Finnish Spitz and is the smallest of the Laiki.
Squarely built, from 16″ to 19″ in height, the body is stocky and the tail is curled tightly over the back.
The head is wedge-shaped, with a short muzzle; the eyes are oblique and dark in color, and the ears small and erect.
The coat is dense and rough to the touch; fawn in color, in various shades.

Russo-European: Found mainly in the forest areas of North European Russia, the Russo-European Laika is similar to the previously mentioned type, but somewhat larger in size, 20″ to 25″ at the shoulder. The head is a little shorter and the muzzle more blunt, the eyes dark and slanting, the

600

ears widely separated on the skull, small and erect.
The coat is thick and rough; fawn, gray or a combination of black and reddish-gray.

Siberian Laika: The largest of the four types. The Siberian Laika is found in a large area of this vast continent, spreading from the Ural Mountains, across Siberia to the coasts on the East. It is also used as a sledge dog.
This is a strong, active breed with a long body and standing up to 26″ at the shoulder. The head is longish and not so clearly wedge-shaped as in the previous two breeds; the ears are triangular, erect, and set-on high, and the eyes are slanting.
The coat is thick and harsh to the touch, varying in color.

North Russian Samoyed: This is the cold-climate Laika, found in the Arctic regions of North Russia, where it lives a nomadic life in company with the reindeer herdsmen. The herds and their masters wander ceaselessly in search of food, and the Laika are used as herd dogs; in other areas it is also used as a sheep herding dog, as well as in its gundog role. It is not a large dog, measuring up to 21″ at the shoulder.
The head is broad with a short muzzle, the eyes small and round, the ears triangular and erect.
The body is long and powerful, with strong, straight quarters.
The coat is either long or shortish, varying in color.

A Russo-European Laika

Built for work, the Siberian Laika.

Lapphund

The Lapphund, or Lapponian Herder, was for a long time used exclusively for a very specialized type of work; that of herding reindeer belonging to the Laplanders in the far north of Scandinavia. Originally it was probably wild, hunting more or less by itself, but when the reindeer was made a "farm" animal, the Laplanders soon managed to train the Lapphund into an unsurpassed "cattle" dog. With civilization moving north into the wilderness, reindeer became more difficult to keep and the Lapphund would probably have been extinct as a breed had it not been for the interest it created in visitors to the north.
Many of the Lapphunds went south to be kept as pets, and some of the best strains now are to be found around the Stockholm area, while the dogs in the north frequently have been mixed with other breeds, and in many cases have been made unsuitable for herding. The transplanted Lapphund, perhaps surprisingly, thrived well in its new surroundings and, during the last ten years or so, has increased in popularity as a pet and show-dog: around 250 were registered in 1969 as against 47 in 1962.
The most desirable color is described as "bear-brown", but black is very common and white is also acceptable.
The Lapphund is slightly more rectangular in build than most Spitz breeds and should be fairly long in back. It measures around $17\frac{3}{4}$″ at the withers (2″ more is accepted for a male; 2″ less for a bitch) and its most typical feature an abundant, harsh coat of an almost oily texture.

The Lapphund has a striking head, of typical Spitz type.

Lundehund

This is a small Norwegian Spitz dog with characteristic erect ears, tail carried curled over the back and double coat. It comes from the little island of Vaerög, where it was developed from the miniature Elkhound. On the coasts of Northern Norway it is used mainly in searching out sea birds and their eggs in inaccessible places on rocks and cliffs. The head is wedge-shaped and clean in line with a pronounced stop. The skull should not be domed, neither should the brown-colored eyes protrude. The ears are rather broad at the base and carried erect with the opening facing forward, but may be folded backwards, like rose-ears. The strong, clean-cut neck is of medium length and is set on a strong, rather long body. The back is straight and the chest long and spacious. The forelegs are straight and strong and the hindlegs are well angled and strong. There are double dew-claws on all legs.

The coat consists of a relatively long and harsh outercoat which has dark tips to the hair, and a light-colored, soft, dense undercoat. The hair on the head and front of the legs is short and smooth.

Colors are black, gray, brown in various shades combined with white.

Dogs measure $12\frac{1}{2}''$ to $14''$ and bitches from $11\frac{1}{2}''$ to $13\frac{1}{2}''$.

Used particularly for searching out sea birds, the Norwegian Lundehund.

Norrbottenspets

This elegant Swedish Spitz is a white dog with markings.

The elegant little Norrbottenspets ("Norrbotten" is the inclusive name for the whole northern region of Sweden, and "spets" of course means spitz) is, at the moment, one of the most noted breeds in Sweden.

It is the Swedish counterpart of the Finnish Spitz and the Norwegian Buhund, and if it has hitherto failed to attract the international attention of these two, this has been for natural reasons.

In 1948 the Swedish Kennel Club declared it "extinct", and it was not until the 1960's that a sufficient number of typical representatives of the breed were produced to make a fresh start possible. A few hundred Norrbottenspets have already been registered and there seems to be no risk that the breed will have to suffer the same fate once again.

The Norrbottenspets is slightly smaller and lighter in build than its Finnish and Norwegian relatives: it should not measure over $15\frac{3}{4}''$. Also it differs from them in color – preferably the Norrbottenspets should be white with black, cream or red markings.

Norwegian Buhund

Mrs. J. H. Stanley's Ryfjelds Snorre, imported into England from Toralf Raanaas of Norway, sired the first two British champion Buhunds and many other winners.

history and development

The Icelandic Sagas (900 to 1300 A.D.) tell of dogs brought to Iceland by settlers from Norway in 874 A.D. The Iceland Dog resembles the Norwegian Buhund in many ways, and is also used for herding, rounding up ponies and in warning of strangers, indicating that the first Iceland dogs were descended from the Buhund. Travellers to Norway may see these little dogs lying outside the remote mountain huts or farms, where they act as watchdog, and as general purpose farm dog. Bu in Norwegian means booth, or stall. The breed was first brought to England in 1946 when a bitch in whelp and an unrelated stud dog were imported. The bitch produced seven puppies, and most of the present-day Buhunds in Britain stem from her. In 1953 another stud dog was brought over, and between 1965 and 1968 three more dogs and three bitches came. In 1968 the Norwegian Buhund Club was recognized by the British Kennel Club, while in 1970 the first sets of certificates were granted. By June 1970 the breed could boast of its first dog and first bitch champions, both sired by one of the latest imported stud dogs.

Three dogs were exported to Australia, where they not only became Australian champions, but worked the sheep on their owner's large sheep

Messrs. M. Quinney and T. McHaffie's Ch. Fossfell Cora was the first British bitch champion.

Ch. Renbank Storm was the first dog champion in Britain. Bred by Mr. J. H. Stanley, he is owned by Mrs. S. Gray.

The bright, enquiring gaze of a typical Buhund of good quality, Friochan Glenguard Cora.

Mrs. S. Gray's Munter, imported into England from Norway, is in the pedigrees of many of today's dogs.

Norwegian Elkhound
See page 578

ranch. Recently one has gone to France, and is attracting much publicity there.

color

A large range of colors is permissible, all shades of wheaten, from biscuit to ripe wheat, red (if not too dark), wolf-sable, black. Self-color is preferred, but small symmetric markings – white on chest, blaze on head, narrow ring on neck, white on legs – are permissible. In Norway the lighter shades of wheaten are preferred, as being easier to see against trees and rocks.

Color in newborn puppies varies from very dark gray, almost black, to light biscuit. The coat turns later on to varying shades of wheaten, wolf-sable and biscuit. So far no black has been born in England, and very few wolf-sables.

care

Many puppies are born with double dew claws on the hind legs, which should be removed at four days old. The Norwegian dogs use these for climbing or holding on to the rocks but elsewhere, where they are not required, they give an ugly look to the clean legs. Regular brushing and combing keeps the coat in immaculate order, and the dogs themselves keep their legs, feet and undercarriage clean, licking themselves like cats.

No other attention than routine grooming is needed to present the Buhund in show condition. Though they are working dogs some judges seem to like them placed on a table to examine, so it is well for the dogs to get used to this, when being groomed.

character

Gay and lively, the Buhund makes an ideal family dog, and its keen sense of hearing gives quick warning of intruders, but they are very friendly with bona fide visitors. The coat is trouble-free and lacking in doggy odor. They are natural herders, rounding up anything from cattle to poultry. With children they are excellent companions, playmates and guards.

standards

The Standard in Britain is that worked out by the Norsk Buhundklub and Norsk Kennelklub in 1943. It calls for dogs fearless, brave and energetic; typical Spitz dogs of under middle size, lightly built, with short compact body, erect pointed ears, tail carried curled over the back.

The coat is close and harsh with soft wool undercoat, smooth on front legs and head, longer on chest, neck, shoulder, back of legs and inside of tail curl.

The ears (height greater than the base) are very mobile. Eyes are dark brown, lively, with a fearless expression. Feet are rather small, slightly oval shaped, with tightly closed toes.

Height of dogs – not more than 45 centimetres ($17\frac{3}{4}''$); bitches smaller.

It is of prime importance that the Buhund should be a well balanced dog, free from all exaggeration and should be capable of the arduous work for which it is bred.

Samoyed

Ch. Demetrio of Kobe, a famous Samoyed renowned for his affectionate nature, who achieved championship status in England, Canada and America, and whose progeny includes many top winners on both sides of the Atlantic.

history and development

The Samoyed has the characteristic pricked ears, the tail curved over the back, and the off-standing coat of the Spitz family, but its development was localized for centuries, resulting in distinctiveness of temperament and appearance.

It emerged as the domesticated dog belonging to a primitive, nomadic group of people who themselves were called Samoyeds (the pronunciation is virtually Sam-yeds). These once inhabited the former great forests of Central Asia, but later were driven northwards to wander in the tundra bordering the Arctic Circle, particularly the area between the Ural Mountains and the River Ob, extending northwards into the Yamal peninsular. The Samoyed people came to depend upon their herds of reindeer which grazed upon mosses and lichens, and which therefore had to be continually moved to find adequate food. The dogs were used almost entirely for herding and guarding the reindeer, mainly against bears – not with the rigid precision of the modern sheepdog, but with considerable freedom which developed their independence and resourcefulness, which characteristics are easily seen in the modern Samoyed dog. The dogs lived in the hide tents ("chooms") of the Samoyed people, eating and sleeping as members of the family.

In 1889, Mr. Kilburn-Scott returned to England from the northern coast of Russia with a puppy, obtained from a settlement of people, thought to be Samoyeds, on the mainland near the Island of Waigatz. Subsequently he obtained a bitch from a sailor whom he met by chance in London. This bitch was Whitey Pechora, who was mated to a dog named Musti

Samoyed, front and side head.

605

A slightly different type of bitch, with a shorter but very dense coat and more "Mongolian" shape of eye. Compare this bitch, Ch. Crownie Cor Caroli of Equinox with Ch. Whitewisp Snow Rose; the two bitches well illustrate the slight differences in type allowed within the breed Standard.

Samoyed puppies have a unique appeal which many people find irresistible. However, difficulty is sometimes experienced in foreseeing the type of adult into which the puppy will develop. This one, White-wisp Snow Tansy, is the litter sister of Ch. Whitewisp Snow Rose, and grew to look very like her.

which had been imported by Lady Sitwell. Many present-day Samoyeds can be traced directly to this pair.

In 1894 the explorer Nansen collected a mixture of dogs from an agent who had assembled and driven them from the vicinity of Salekhard across the northern slopes of the Urals to the coast. He records that some of these were white, others a mixture of colors. In his subsequent journey in *The Fram*, and on his sledge journey attempt to reach the North Pole, these dogs were used for hauling.

In the same year, Major F. G. Jackson set out to explore Franz Josef Land, using dogs collected from the same area. When he returned, he brought the surviving dogs and bitches home presenting one, Jacko, to Queen Alexandra. These, together with a few other imports, were used to develop the breed in England.

The survivors of nine white Samoyeds used by Borchgrevink in an expedition to Antarctica and, in 1907, also by Shackleton, were probably landed in New Zealand and Australia, for a few years later Mr. and Mrs. Kilburn-Scott found a Samoyed, Antarctic Buck, in Sydney Zoo, and brought him back to England where he sired two litters. The Kilburn-Scotts were largely responsible for the development of the breed, and they drew up the Standard incorporating the points which they considered most typical from eight discernible strains which had appeared in their kennels. This Standard is little changed apart from clarification; the Samoyed is essentially a natural dog, unaltered by the whims of man – and modern breeding skill lies in keeping it so. Stock from England has been used to develop the breed in most countries where it is known today.

color

In the early days, black, deep biscuit, light biscuit with dark patches, cream and white all appeared, but the lighter colors, particularly white, predominated. Now, white, cream and biscuit are permitted; the large majority being white, occasionally with delicate patches of biscuit. The biscuit is often seen on the ears, and tiny patches – engagingly called "tea stains" – sometimes appear on the foreface.

care

About ten minutes thorough brushing and combing two or three times a week will maintain a good appearance. It is important that the comb reaches the roots of the hairs – particularly behind the ears, on the tail, and on the rear of both hind legs. When a dog gets wet and dirty, a quick rub down with an old towel is important. Then, when the coat is dry, normal combing and brushing will restore a remarkably clean appearance. A proprietary cleansing powder patted into the coat and *thoroughly brushed out* may sometimes assist general appearance. Pristine whiteness, however, can only be achieved by bathing, but this should not be necessary often under normal circumstances.

Usually once a year, the soft undercoat will be shed. When this occurs, comb out as much as possible, then bathe and dry the dog – which loosens the dead coat – and comb thoroughly again. In this way, all the shedding coat is taken out at once, rather than allowed to fall out gradually. When the new coat is growing, it is difficult to loosen any hairs in the coat of a Samoyed in good physical condition.

character

Because many generations of Samoyeds have shared the homes of the Samoyed people, they are happiest still when in human company. A dog will share a family relationship as an equal, retaining a slight degree of independence which it is unwise to attempt to quell entirely. The puppies are gay and inquisitive, and being intelligent can easily be trained in matters of household routine, responding best to kind but firm handling. The adult dogs are entirely safe with children, provided, of course, that they are not deliberately maltreated. The breed Standard specifies that Samoyeds should display a "marked affection for all mankind". They love a romp, particularly in snow, which they adore, and many become adept at ball play.

standards

The British Standard was the basis for those of all countries, but the American Standard is more explicit in detail, and contains a slightly increased height limit – A.K.C., males 21″ to 23½″; British K.C., 20″ to 22″. Both measure to the same point, which the British refers to as the shoulder, and in America is called the withers.

The essential requirement is a dog of medium build with good but not over-heavy bone. Bitches should be slightly finer in appearance, and may be slightly longer in back, but neither dogs nor bitches should be either unduly long or, conversely, cobby in back. They should have a double, off-standing coat with the longer hairs carrying the unique glistening silver tips. Again, the bitches' coats may be slightly finer in texture than that of the dogs'.

Ch. Whitewisp Snow Rose, a recent champion bitch with a full double coat, good bone and broad head, which is nevertheless unmistakably feminine. Note the very slightly longer back required in a bitch.

The head should be reasonably broad between the ears and, viewed from above, should show a distinct wedge shape when the fringes at the side of the face are pushed back. This wedge should not finish in too sharp a point at the nose, neither should there be any bulge in the cheek below the eyes When the mouth is open the characteristic "smiling" or "laughing" expression is seen which is another unique feature of the Samoyed, emphasized by the long, dangling, pink tongue. Eye rims should be black, and black noses and lips are preferred although flesh-color in the lips and nose is not listed as a fault in the British Standard.

Gait, important in both British and American Standards, should be free and graceful, but with a powerful thrust from the hind legs. The Samoyed's natural walking pace is equivalent to a man's slow trot or very brisk walking pace. Viewed from the rear the hind legs should move parallel to one another at the walking pace without deviation from the vertical. It is a fallacy to assume that, where Samoyeds are used for sledge work, they must be very large; experience shows that usually these are inferior in staying power to those of medium build, which are required in the Standards.

Vastgotaspets

The Vastgotaspets shows a remarkable likeness in type to the Pembroke Welsh Corgi, but it is in fact higher on the leg, and shorter backed.

Dogs of practically the same type as the Västgötaspets have existed in the middle and southern parts of Sweden for over 1,000 years, and the dramatic circumstances of its near-extinction only twenty years ago brought it much publicity.

Before 1950 there were few typical specimens to be found (the Västgötaspets was then not officially recognized by any kennel club but had been used as a very efficient cattle dog), and it was due to the energetic work of one or two dedicated persons that the breed was saved. It is now steadily increasing in popularity as a pet and show-dog – at least 300 are registered yearly.

The similarities in general type between the Welsh Corgis and the Västgötaspets are great; the breeds are obviously closely related. It is still to be debated, however, whether the Vikings brought their own cattle-dogs to England and these later developed into one of the modern Welsh Corgis, or whether they took back with them an old Celtic dog which eventually produced the Västgötaspets in Sweden.

The breed's name means the "Spitz of the West Goths". Compared to the Pembroke Welsh Corgi, the Västgötaspets appears slightly higher on the leg and shorter in back. Its color may vary from bright red to wolf sable, but the majority seen in the ring are various shades of gray. White markings are allowed but not considered desirable and should under no circumstances cover the greater part of the dog.

Nutrition

The role of the dog in our society has changed appreciably over the years from that of a natural hunter and provider of food to a companion which relies almost entirely on being fed by man. Many methods and products for feeding are available and they range from natural ones such as a meat and milk diet to various proprietary lines available in cans and plastic packets; biscuits, crumbles or kibbles etc.

Although the basic nutritional requirements for dogs have been worked out on a scientific basis, the actual feeding of dogs is still largely an individual matter. All manner of things influence the canine diet. Growth rate, activity, climate, size, age – all have some bearing on the amounts and the quality of food offered; so does the taste, liking and appetite of the individual animal.

Regardless of the food offered, it should always be fed under the most hygienic conditions possible to prevent bacterial infection and subsequent gastro-intestinal upsets.

Basic Requirements

Food is made up of carbohydrates, fats, protein, minerals and vitamins, each of these ingredients serving a particular purpose.

(1) *Carbohydrates:* These substances provide the bulk of energy for daily activity. Such energy is measured in calories. As a rough guide a dog weighing 5 kg. (about $10\frac{1}{4}$ lbs.) requires approximately 91 calories per kg. (or 45 per lb.) body weight in each daily ration. A 10 kg. (22 lbs. plus) dog needs about 75 calories per kg. (or 35 per lb.) body weight and larger animals approximately 49 calories per kg. (21 per lb.). In other words smaller breeds of dogs need more food per weight than do the larger varieties. Apart from providing energy, carbohydrates are essential in that they supply the bulk necessary to satisfy the feeling of hunger and ensure normal faecal consistency. Dietary ingredients rich in carbohydrate include cereals, grains, potatoes, biscuits, bread etc.

(2) *Fats:* Like carbohydrates, fats are necessary to the canine diet for the calories they provide; also they carry the flavors of the food and help to govern its texture. Dogs can tolerate quite large amounts of fat in their diet (estimates go as high as 40%) and there appears to be little or no significant difference in the various types of fats available. Deficiency of fats tends to cause dry scaly skin and also lowers general resistance to disease. Care should be taken not to feed rancid fats as these destroy the fat soluble vitamins contained in the food.

(3) *Proteins:* All proteins, on digestion, are broken down in the gastro-intestinal tract into amino acids and are absorbed and utilized as such for normal growth and daily body metabolism. Although some twenty-two amino acids are regarded as essential, dogs are able to manufacture all but nine of these from other dietary ingredients. The nine essential amino acids *must* be provided in the diet, else symptoms of deficiency will appear. For this reason not only is the amount of protein offered of importance, but so also is its quality. Some foods rich in protein are meat, eggs, some

611

cereal grains etc. and the average diet should include at least 12% of high quality proteins. In young growing animals or those required to undergo severe strains or stresses, for example, racing Greyhounds, the proportion of proteins should be even greater; this applies also to pregnancy and lactation.

(4) *Minerals and Vitamins:* Dogs require minerals in small but essential amounts to regulate the body's activities. The major elements necessary include calcium and phosphorous, iron, copper, potassium, magnesium, sodium, chloride, iodine, manganese, cobalt and zinc. The calcium/phosphorous ratio in the ration should be at 1·2 to 1 to ensure full utilization and good bone growth. Certain vitamins are also essential for normal growth and these have been called the "spark of life". There are many bio-chemical reactions in which these vitamins play an essential part. Vitamins essential to the canine diet include Vitamin A, Vitamin D, Vitamin E, Vitamin B.12, Folic Acid. Thiamine, Riboflavin, Pyrodoxine, Pantothenic acid, Niacin and Choline. Most reasonably varied rations contain adequate amounts of vitamins and a deficiency of this substance is fairly rare. Again, as was the case with the protein, the requirements of minerals and vitamins are higher in young growing puppies, pregnant and lactating bitches as well as animals required to perform strenuous exercise and/or work.

nutrition of puppies

The feeding of puppies is of special significance, as an animal fed incorrectly during puppyhood and/or early life may suffer the after effects of malnutrition for the rest of his life. Adequate amounts of calcium/phosphorous/Vitamin D, in correct proportions, are of particular importance as these ingredients have great bearing on bone growth and general development later on. Although the actual diet offered to young dogs is similar in many respects to that of adults, it is advisable to feed smaller portions, but more often. High quality protein ingredients are essential for ready utilization. For this reason eggs and dairy products are recommended.

nutrition of aged dogs

Basically, as an animal becomes older its activity decreases and various organs such as heart, kidney and liver begin to degenerate. For these reasons the ration offered should be of good quality food, particularly with respect to protein which should be low in comparison to carbohydrates.

Vitamin and Mineral intake should be increased in an endeavor to prevent a rapid deterioration.

Diseases

Like their human counterparts dogs may contract and suffer from innumerable diseases and ailments, some contagious, others not. Each system of the body may be affected individually or a number may become involved together.

It would not be possible, even if permitted by space, to transform laymen into semi-qualified Veterinary Surgeons by way of a simple essay. The study of Veterinary Science takes many years and some considerable practical experience is necessary post graduation to develop the skills of accurate diagnosis and sound principles of therapy.

It is of more importance therefore to acquaint the reader with the *general symptoms of disease and abnormality* in the dog, rather than with those of specific disease entities. Once suspicion of an altered state of health has been confirmed by simple examination, a temporary diagnosis may be established and home treatment instituted. However, it must be stressed that, in the opinion of most of the members of the veterinary profession, it is most unwise to prescribe for and/or treat one's pet without first seeking veterinary advice. In other words, except in the case of the simplest ailments, it is far better to consult a Veterinary Surgeon once some deviation from the norm has been discovered. Remember that the disease process usually has been in progress for some time before any abnormality is noticed.

For the reasons outlined above, this article will deal with the general symptoms of sickness in dogs, rather than with the specific signs of any one particular illness.

These symptoms may be listed under the following headings:

(1) **Abnormal Appetite.** It is usual for dogs which are ill to show some variation in appetite. At first, the appetite tends to wane and the patient either will not eat the full amount of food offered or show little interest in the normal ration, demanding more delicious morsels. Eventually there may be total rejection of food.

In some disease conditions the appetite increases. This is so with most parasitic infestations and with some specific diseases also e.g. Diabetes mellitus. Therefore any distinct variations in appetite, in one form or another, are to be considered as significant, particularly so when viewed in relationship to general appearance and physical condition.

Quite often the drinking habits are affected also, but usually not to the same degree as appetite. At first sick dogs tend to drink somewhat less; later on as high fever develops, the thirst usually increases.

(2) **Abnormal Behavior Pattern.** Ailing dogs frequently show some obvious deviations from normal routine. They may exhibit signs of restlessness, be unable to relax and/or settle down; on the other hand there may be reluctance to move about, with a tendency to sleep and rest more. Any noticeable variation from general trends or habits, both from a physical as well as from a mental aspect must be considered as suspicious. Skilled advice should be called for, particularly if the altered behavior

patterns persist for any length of time.

All the symptoms which can be fitted under the heading of abnormal or unusual behavior pattern such as, for example, vomition, diarrhoea, constipation, violent head shaking, changes in the habits of urination and/or defaecation, persistent signs of irritation in any one body region etc. are to be taken as significant. Alterations in coat qualities and general signs of unthriftyness also should be taken into account.

Whenever any one or any combination of symptoms of abnormality, either physical or mental, is noted, professional aid should be obtained to assist in establishing a diagnosis and to recommend subsequent treatment. This applies particularly to cases in which such symptoms either occur suddenly or have persisted for some time.

(3) **Physical Abnormalities.** This includes a multitude of conditions. Unusual discharge from any orifice, the appearance of lumps, bumps and swellings in any part of the body, alterations in coat quality and texture, excessive hair shedding etc. can be grouped under this heading, with the many others too numerous to mention.

At what time then or at what stage of a disease syndrome should a Veterinary Surgeon be consulted? This question is asked often and is impossible to answer – so much depends, inter alia, on the type and the severity of the symptoms exhibited, the patient's demonstrative type of nature, the owner's powers of observation etc. In the opinion of most Veterinarians it is far better to call for expert advice early, perhaps at times unnecessarily, rather than to allow a disease to develop to such a degree as to make subsequent therapy difficult and expensive. Premature veterinary advice can only be reassuring, never harmful, and the attendant consultation fee undoubtedly will be far less than the cost, at a later stage, of a prolonged course of expensive antibiotic therapy.

Most Veterinary Surgeons, on consultation, will enquire to hear the owner's version of the case history, as a possible aid to diagnosis. After such interrogation it is common practice to examine the so-called Cardinal Signs in an attempt to establish a diagnosis and prescribe treatment.

The cardinal signs referred to are (1) Pulse rate, (2) Heart rate, (3) Respiratory rate, (4) Temperature. Examination and evaluation of the first three items listed requires not only veterinary skills, but also the use of specialized and sophisticated equipment. However, this is not the case with regard to the taking of body temperature. Indeed, this is probably the most important single item in the owner's armament when deciding whether or not to seek veterinary assistance.

The normal body temperature of dogs is appreciably higher than that of man. It ranges roughly from about 100 degrees F. to 102 degrees F. Larger breeds tend to have lower body temperatures, down even as low as 99 degrees F., while smaller, more excitable dogs, often go up to 102 degrees F. plus. The age of the patient also has some bearing on temperature. Puppies often show a one degree F. – 1·5 degrees F. rise above the normal adult level. Excitement also may have some influence and the greater it is, the higher will be the temperature recorded. This is of some practical significance, as most dogs exhibit some signs of nervousness when their temperature is being recorded.

It is not difficult to take a dog's temperature. A short bulbed clinical thermometer is all that is needed. The most satisfactory recording is obtained rectally. Oral temperature readings are not as reliable and tend to be expensive on thermometers. Taking a dog's temperature is done best with the patient standing on all four legs, restrained by the tail – allowing him/her to sit may cause the thermometer to break and result in injury. Lubricating of the thermometer prior to insertion, with Paraffin oil etc. will assist. The illustration shows the correct method of taking a dog's temperature.

Although any increase of the body temperature should be taken as significant when considering the request for veterinary advice, it must be kept in mind that there are a number of diseases and conditions of a serious nature in which the temperature remains within normal limits – therefore a normal temperature reading does not necessarily mean a healthy patient.

Brief mention must be made here about the popular belief that "a cold nose means a healthy dog". Unfortunately this statement does not hold true entirely. In many instances very sick dogs are found to have moist cold noses, while some healthy animals may exhibit dry ones. There is a large number of ailments which may affect dogs. Some of these are specific to canines only, others are transferable to other species of animals, including man. A great number of excellent textbooks are published in this field from the layman's level to that of the professional. References to some of the major works appear in the Bibliography.

Due to restrictions on space, the only diseases discussed in this article are – (A) Distemper, (B) Contagious Canine Hepatitis, (C) Leptospirosis, (D) Rabies, (E) Infestation with internal parasites.

(A) Distemper: This is a virus disease commonly seen in dogs until the introduction of safe and effective vaccination methods in the late 1940's. Since then its incidence has declined.

Infection takes place usually via mucous membrane penetration and most of the body systems may become involved singly or together. Fits, resulting from brain damage caused by the Distemper virus may become a serious aftermath in some cases, even after apparent earlier recovery.

Frequently, during a course of Distemper infection a lowering develops in the body's resistance to bacterial invasion. Therefore, in most cases the disease becomes complicated by bacterial infection in one form or another. Such secondary bacterial invasion will produce one or more of the following symptoms, depending on the system involved:

(1) Respiratory tract (*Fever, cough, ocular/nasal discharge, noisy and rapid respiration etc.*).
(2) Gastro intestinal tract (*Fever, vomition, diarrhoea, bloody stools, etc.*).
(3) Cutaneous form (*Pustules, particularly on the belly and abdominal axillae*).

The incubation period (i.e. the time taken from exposure to infection to the development of clinical symptoms) is from seven–fourteen days. However, the symptoms of nervous tissue involvement may take up to twenty-eight days to appear.

While it is usually possible these days to treat successfully the symptoms of secondary bacterial infection to Distemper by the employ of modern antibiotics, no specific therapy is available against the viral encephalitis form. Once symptoms of brain involvement such as uncontrollable twitching, champing of the jaws, staggering, inco-ordination, epileptiform episodes etc. are observed the prognosis is poor. That is not to say that none of the dogs exhibiting neurological signs ever recover – some do, but the percentage of recovery is relatively low.

The treatment of Distemper falls entirely within the realms of Veterinary Science and is entirely outside the scope of this text. Vaccination against Distemper is possible from an early age onwards and is recommended strongly. Various factors, such as the immune state of the dam, possible parasitic infestation of puppies, likelihood of exposure to infection etc. all have influence on the time of vaccination. Different types of vaccines are available, each with different usage recommendations. Some Veterinarians advise vaccination of puppies from as early as three weeks onwards, others will not carry out immunization until ten–twelve weeks of puppy age. It is suggested that veterinary advice be obtained for each individual case as early as possible and be followed explicitly.

Annual revaccination of dogs is recommended, at least up to five–six years of age.

(B) Contagious Canine Hepatitis: Another virus disease, with symptoms similar in a number of respects to Distemper; in fact it is only over the last twenty years that accurate differential diagnosis between the two diseases has become possible.

Three distinct phases of Contagious Canine Hepatitis exist. These are: (a) *Peracute* – seen usually in very young animals; little or no symptoms are evident and death ensues rapidly. (b) *Acute* – characterized by high fever, profuse clear ocular discharge, bilateral tonsilitis with associated difficulty in swallowing food and dribbling at the mouth, symptoms of acute abdominal pain, diarrhoea etc. Most, but not all, patients recover with intensive therapy, if commenced sufficiently early in the course of the disease. (c) *Mild* – little or no clinical evidence is observed, other than perhaps one or two days "off color". Recovery follows within a short space of time without treatment.

As with Distemper, the treatment of Contagious Canine Hepatitis is a matter entirely for the attending Veterinary Surgeon. Successful vaccination against this disease is possible from eight weeks of age onward and is recommended.

(C) Leptospirosis: Primarily a disease of the kidneys, Leptospirosis is caused by bacterial infection. Two basic types occur, one spread directly from dog to dog (Leptospira Canicola), the other transmitted via the urine of rats (Leptospira ictero-haemorrhagica). In both instances the infection occurs through the licking and/or ingestion of contaminated urine containing the infective bacteria. The incubation period varies from three–fifteen days. Although the symptoms of both forms of Leptospirosis are similar, the rat-transmitted type is of relatively greater importance as it is infectious to man.

Symptoms of Leptospirosis include high fever, lack of appetite, abdominal pain, highly colored and strongly smelling urine followed later by symptoms of jaundice; these manifest by way of yellow coloring of the mucous membranes of the eyes, lips etc. As the disease progresses the skin itself may develop a yellowish tinge.

Accurate diagnosis is based on the symptoms described, together with laboratory investigations; this, of course, requires veterinary knowledge, as does the subsequent treatment. Vaccination against Leptospirosis is recommended and is carried out usually together with Distemper/Hepatitis immunization.

(D) Rabies: This disease, although not uncommon in other parts of the world, has not been reported often in Great Britain. However, two cases occurred in dogs imported from Europe during 1969 and for this reason it deserves mention here.

Rabies is a most important disease, able to affect man as well as most other classes of livestock.

The causative agent is a virus which is present in the saliva of infected animals. It is transmitted from patient to patient by contamination of wounds or breaks in the skin. Once deposited near a nerve ending, the virus is carried to the spinal cord and finally lodges in the brain, where it causes serious damage. The symptoms of rabies vary widely and may be divided into four distinct clinical entities:

(i) Prodromal – characterized by an abnormal behavior pattern. (ii) Dumb Rabies – symptoms exhibited include partial facial paralysis, inability to eat, swallow and drink. (iii) Furious Rabies – the most serious form: this is the syndrome which presents the typical "mad dog" picture. (iv) Mongrel Rabies – a mixture of the symptoms of types (ii) and (iii).

Treatment of affected dogs is unsatisfactory and animals suffering from the disease must be destroyed, particularly so because of the human risk factors involved.

One other point worth mentioning is the extremely variable incubation period of Rabies. While this is usually somewhere between fifteen and twenty-one days, incubation periods of up to nine months and even more have been reported. This makes the laying down of quarantine rules and regulations a difficult task. Although treatment of infected patients is not possible, satisfactory vaccination programs are available and are enforced by law in most countries where the disease exists.

(E) Internal Parasites: Dogs may harbor a variety of parasites, both internal as well as external ones. Some are common, others are not. Some infestations are serious, others are not. Some are simple to treat, others are most difficult.

The most commonly found internal parasites are the intestinal worms belonging to the Roundworm, Hookworm, Whipworm and Tapeworm families.

Although each species of worm produces some more or less specific symptoms, accurate diagnosis is difficult, if not impossible, without laboratory assistance.

The general symptoms associated with worm infestation include: (i) Unthriftyness. (ii) Dull and harsh coat texture. (iii) Voracious appetite, coupled with loss of body weight. (iv) Abnormal stools, particularly loose motions tinged with blood. (v) Foetid breath. (vi) Irritation around the area of the flanks as indicated by biting or nibbling at that region. (vii) Irritation around the anus, as evidenced by sliding on the hindquarters etc.

The signs of parasitic infestation are most noticeable in puppies and young dogs; however they may occur also in adults. Once an owner's suspicion is aroused, it is advisable to collect a sample of faecal material and take both it, as well as the patient, to a Veterinary Surgeon for consultation.

Microscopic examination of faeces, after some prior laboratory preparation, will not only confirm or deny the diagnostic suspicion, but will enable the veterinarian to identify the worm species present. This is essential so that specific remedial measures can be employed. Although the range of medicaments available for the treatment of internal parasites is being added to constantly, there is still not any one single remedy on the market, at the time of publication of this book, which is equally effective against all the commonly found worms – therefore the importance of accurate diagnosis and species identification.

FIRST AID

Many of the older textbooks dealing with dogs and their ailments feature quite extensive sections on First Aid. This advice must have been most valuable in the days when veterinary assistance either took a long time to arrive (i.e. the horse and carriage days) or was difficult to get due to shortage of trained personnel.

Today, skilled attention and advice can be obtained readily and quickly, either by telephone or personal visit and fast transport to Veterinary Hospitals presents no problems. Therefore the field of first aid has become more limited.

These days the only cases which call for immediate aid are automobile accidents (the most common), severe accidental and/or fight injuries, drowning, poisonous stings or bites, ingestion of poisons, plus a few other instances. No specific advice can be given which covers all of these conditions, other than to stress the use of commonsense at all times.

Some advice as to First Aid is offered in the following paragraphs.

(1) Automobile Accidents: Do not move the patient unless absolutely necessary. If transport from site of accident is absolutely essential, try to place the injured animal on a flat surface, e.g. board, and cover up during transport to keep warm so as to prevent shock.

Arrest all bleeding by the application of pressure pads and bandages if available; if not, then by simple digital pressure. If possible cover all external wounds with a temporary dressing. Transport injured animal to a Veterinary Hospital as soon as convenient, taking care not to aggravate any fractures or injuries during transit.

N.B. Most Veterinarians employ the use of an ambulance for emergency cases. This mode of transport is preferable in cases where major damage is suspected.

(2) Electric Shock: Switch off current, then remove patient from electrical appliance and/or wiring. If necessary apply artificial respiration by way of mouth to mouth resuscitation. Keep warm and offer fluids if patient is able to drink. Call for veterinary assistance unless full recovery occurs within a short time.

(3) Accidental or Fight Injuries: Apply gauze pads and bandage to stop bleeding as well as to prevent further contamination of the injured areas. Seek skilled help to limit infection and encourage healing.

(4) Drowning: Hold patient up by hind-legs with the head pointing downwards to drain water from lungs. Swing round in a circular motion if necessary for more effective drainage. Keep mouth open and apply artificial respiration. Once normal voluntary breathing has recommenced, dry patient and wrap up to keep him warm. Call for veterinary attendance to stop possible development of aspiration pneumonia.

(5) Poisonous Bites and/or Stings: If observed, apply tourniquet at most suitable point to slow down absorption of toxin into blood stream. RUSH to Veterinary Hospital for immediate attention. If possible show attending Veterinarian the location of bite, or injury, and assist in identifying the toxic animal.

(6) Poisoning: Most cases of poisoning in dogs are accidental. Ingestion of or contact with insecticides, rodenticides, plant sprays, disinfectants and drugs kept for human usage are the most common causes. However malicious administration of poisons cannot be ruled out entirely. Even if the poison is identified and the antidote known, it is most unlikely that this will be available readily in the average household under normal circumstances. Therefore, First Aid, in cases of suspected poisoning, should consist only of the immediate administration of an emetic. The rest of the treatment should be left in the hands of a Veterinary Surgeon. Needless to say, the sooner such skilled attention is obtained, the more rapid and the more certain will be the recovery. One of the simplest and most readily available household emetics is common table salt. Dissolve about two teaspoons of salt in a cup of water, force open the patient's jaws and administer in the form of a drench.

In conclusion, it cannot be stressed too forcibly that in all cases in which first aid has been made use of, a Veterinary Surgeon's examination and subsequent treatment should be called for as soon as possible as a matter of course.

Showing and Championship Systems

The following articles are presented as typical examples of different national systems; systems differing slightly in some respects do occur in some other countries.

Great Britain: The first dog show was held in England in 1859, for sporting dogs only, but within a few years dog shows for all breeds were firmly established. Naturally, the early shows attracted many of the ex-dog-fighting and bull-baiting fraternity. The foundation of the Kennel Club in 1873 brought unexpected respectability to dog-showing and dog-breeding. The sport has now spread to such an extent that there is a Kennel Club in practically every civilized country in the world.

Registration: registration of a pedigree dog at the Kennel Club is a simple matter; it is usually completed by the breeder, the fee of 5s. (60 cents) registers the dog for life and ensures that a record of its pedigree will be kept for at least twenty-five years after its death. If a dog is not registered by the breeder, the owner must do this but the fee for the registration is then £1 ($2.40). A change of ownership of a registered dog must be recorded, the transfer costs 50p. ($1.20). Forms of registration or transfer can be obtained from the Kennel Club on request. Once registered, a dog's name cannot be changed, except that once in its lifetime a new owner can add his kennel name to the existing name.

Exemption Show: in Great Britain, 2,000 dog shows are held each year catering for every kind of pedigree dog interest. At some stage the proud owner of a dog is tempted to show it but unless he is prepared to wait until the puppy is six months of age, he must start at an "Exemption Show" – that is, a show exempt from nearly all the Kennel Club Show Rules and Regulations. These shows are the casual affairs held on village greens and in vicarage gardens and the proceeds go to charity. Often a dog without a pedigree can be shown, but most exemption shows provide a few classes for pedigree dogs only. In these classes dogs of many breeds are entered and the judge has a difficult task to find the best, and the results must not be taken too seriously.

Match: the smallest event for the show dog is called a Match and these are the successors of the bad old days when owners matched their fighting dogs together for heavy stakes. The Match today provides for a maximum of thirty-two dogs with two in the ring at the same time, and the method of judging is the knock-out system of matching winners together until the judge finds the best of all in the last brace. The loser in the last round is not necessarily the second best, the luck of the draw could have matched him with the final winner in the first round, in which case a different dog would have met the winner in the last round. The owner of a dog at a Match must be a Member of the promoting Society, in fact, this same rule applies to all Shows other than Open and Championship.

Sanction Show: after the Match the next step in the career of the average exhibitor is the Sanction Show, where up to twenty-five classes can be provided for Members' dogs. Unlike the Match there can be a number of dogs in the ring at the same time but in some classes the dogs will all be of the same breed and these are called Breed Classes. In other classes there will be dogs of many different kinds and these are called Variety Classes. Classes can be divided in many ways and considerable ingenuity is shown by some Show Committees in devising different kinds of Variety Classes. For example, there are Any Variety Sporting and Any Variety Non-Sporting Classes and these can be sub-divided for the different Groups – Hounds, Gundogs, Terriers, Utility, Working and Toy dogs. But the exhibitor must exercise care to see that his dog is eligible for the classes in which it is entered, otherwise disqualification will follow. Cases of flagrant carelessness are fined.

Limited Show: the next show in size and importance is the Limited Show – limited as regards both the exhibitors' and exhibits' qualifications. Almost without exception the exhibitors at Limited Shows are Members of the Show Society and the exhibits are restricted to dogs which have not won a Challenge Certificate, or more than a specified number of prizes of a specified value. Information regarding eligibility for entry is published in the schedule of a Show, the Kennel Club describes the schedule as the "contract" between the Show and the exhibitor and all the information necessary to the exhibitor must be stated in the schedule. The Kennel Club enforces the letter of the law as regards the contract and insists that both parties, the Show and the exhibitor, observe the details.

Open Show: so on to the Open Show – open to all who wish to enter, except the few who are black-listed, having transgressed Kennel Club Rules and Regulations. At an Open Show the competition is fierce and a dog which wins a first prize at such a Show is on the road to fame. For example, a first prize at an Open Show when the dog is under eighteen months of age counts as one of the twenty-five points a dog needs for the much sought-after Junior Warrant. At a Championship Show a similar win counts as three points.

Championship Shows: a Championship Show can be described as an Open Show with Kennel Club Challenge Certificates for the top winners. Each year the Kennel Club allots to each breed a quota of Challenge Certificates and these are offered at Championship Shows, some at the Club Specialist Shows but most at the twenty-six General Championship Shows distributed geographically throughout the country. An exhibitor can achieve his ambition and make his dog a Champion by winning three Challenge Certificates under three different Judges, provided one of the Certificates is won when the dog is more than twelve months of age. But a

Gundog is described as a Show Champion until he wins a Qualifying Certificate in the field. A dog which wins a first or second prize in a Breed Class at a Championship Show qualifies for entry at Cruft's Show in the following year, but a dog which wins a Challenge Certificate has a "season ticket" for entry in Cruft's for the rest of his life.

Obedience: there are similar shows for Obedience, where dogs must win on performance rather than appearance and in the same way a dog with an outstanding performance can win his way to entry at Cruft's Show in the following year. The competition is even fiercer than in Breed Classes and many dogs arrive at Cruft's Show having lost less than one point out of a possible 300 in the Obedience ring! The winner of three Obedience Certificates or the Obedience Championship at Cruft's is entitled to be called Obedience Champion.

Best in Show: there are few shows that do not end with Best in Show, when the exhibits that have not been beaten in their Classes are brought together so that the Judge or Judges can decide the best of all. At the major Championship Shows this can mean an outstanding exhibit of every breed in the ring, as many as 120 exhibits at the same time and since this would be too difficult a task for any Judge, the breeds are broken down into groups, each of twenty to thirty dogs, and the Judges choose the best of each group so there are six best of groups, Hound, Gundog, Terrier, Utility, Working and Toy dogs. The final Best in Show is then chosen and, in the case of Cruft's, the name of the Best in Show winner is broadcast nationwide.

United States of America: Dog breeding, both as a hobby and a utility, began in what is now the United States shortly after Jamestown became the first permanent settlement in America in 1607. Dog shows did not emerge until about 1874. Their rules were made by the person or persons promoting the show. There was such laxity and so many contradictions that the serious-minded breeder-exhibitors saw that something had to be done. What they did, on September 17, 1884, was to organize the American Kennel Club, a non-profit organization that would make rules and enforce them. From a dozen or so shows held each year in those early times there are now more than 1,100 champion events taking place every twelve months, and more than 6,000 dogs earning their championship a year.

The process of gaining a championship title in the United States is quite different from that employed by the Kennel Club in England but it must be said that both ways seem to come up with the great majority of titleholders evincing true quality. Both systems have had their detractors, which is normal for the course, but both also have their advantages. One of the obvious good things about England's way is that less clerical help should be necessary; it being comparatively simple to check when a dog has won the three Challenge Certificates needed for the title. Of course, these C.C.'s are not available at all shows in all breeds. They are assigned only for specific breeds depending on the entry. But you will have learned more about England's way of determining titular status in the previous section.

In the first thirty-nine years of its existence the American Kennel Club had tried various schemes for determining show quality and especially for finding those specimens that were of true championship quality. It also had been experimenting with various procedures that would determine a so-called "best dog" in each show. This was something that both the exhibitors (a majority, in any case) seemed to want, despite those purists who always have contended that you cannot judge a dog of one breed against a dog of another breed. The fact is that even in the earliest days of dog shows in the United States prizes were offered for B.I.S. Anyone can check this out through the A.K.C.'s invaluable collection of show catalogs dating back to 1877. There was only one drawback to such honors – many of them were not deserved, since often the winner had been defeated in a class "that did not really count" on his way to the top.

Great changes were on the horizon when in late 1922 the Executive Committee of the A.K.C., backed by the remainder of the Directors and voted by the Delegates, announced that for the year 1923 no "best in show" award could be offered at any show held under the rules of the A.K.C. This was to give sufficient time to a special committee appointed by President John E. de Mund, M.D. to draft, and possibly revise many times, workable rules that would result in an undisputed "best" in any all-breed or multiple-breed dog show. Naturally there were howls of dismay from long-established clubs in many parts of the United States. They thought it would cause a drop in entries. Curiously, it did not. For instance, the great Westminster K.C. which carefully preserves its record of all past shows, carries a laconic line for 1923 "there was no best in show award this year" but on another page in each yearly catalog the figures indicate that 1923 had thirty-one more dogs entered than 1922, which had been only thirty-two better than 1921.

The new system went into effect in 1924 and, with minor changes and adjustments, it is the same one that is operating today, nearly half a century later. Under this system a dog once beaten is no longer eligible to go up to the top award at a show. At the same time the point system was devised. To become an American champion a dog must win fifteen championship points but this total must include "two majors" i.e. a major is a show rated three points or better, and these must be won under two different judges. No show offers more than five points in any breed. One of the changes made in the system about two and a half decades ago was intended to benefit breeds that seldom are able to produce "majors" at any show. It was decided that a dog capable of winning a Variety Group was entitled to similar points awarded to any breed winner that he defeated. In most cases an outstanding Group winner was thus able to pick up the "majors" not available in its own breed.

Presently under the A.K.C. system there are five regular classes in each sex: Puppy, Novice, Bred-by-Exhibitor, American-bred, and Open. Most of these are self-explanatory. Without going into confusing details, it might be said only that to be American-bred the dog must have been whelped (born) in the United States and his dam (mother) must have been mated in the U.S. The Open class is the only one in which an imported dog may compete. No Puppy shall be less than six months old at a multiple-breed show, and a Puppy that is already a champion may not compete. Such a contingency is rare, indeed.

Championship points are gained only in the Winners' class and, as stated, the points range from one to five, according to the official Point Scale for his breed in the particular part of the country where the competition takes place. There are currently some six such Divisions, and the points for any given breed are seldom the same in all. These point scales are based on the average number of dogs and bitches competing the previous year in each section of the country. The minimum, one point, is often the same in both dogs and bitches, but it changes on the way up so that from three to five points might vary greatly from male to female. Since the A.K.C. registers 116 breeds at the time this is written, so this number must be doubled to include both sexes and then multiplied by the number of divisions – a matter of nearly 1,400 calculations to be made. This work is done usually by specialists who have been doing it for years at headquarters of the A.K.C. Then, of course, when the marked catalog gets to the Show Records Department of the A.K.C. it must be checked against its proper scale of points. Usually the Point Scale used at a particular show is published in the catalog of the show.

The winner of each regular class is eligible to compete in the Winners' Class. There is a Winners' Class for Dogs and another for Bitches. After the Point winner is determined the remainder of the class winners compete for the Reserve Winners' award. Also eligible for this is the dog or bitch, in whichever division, that finished second to the one that gets the points. There are no points for Reserve, usually just a ribbon.

When each sex has been judged the male and female compete for Best of Winners. As now judged – to save time – both the dog and bitch go into the Best of Breed Class where they are pitted against the Champions entered only for that class. This answers one of the criticisms of the A.K.C. system in the past that a dog or bitch could become a champion without ever meeting an established champion.

Any specimen that takes best of breed is eligible to compete in the Variety Group competition to which its breed is assigned. There are six such groups: Sporting, Hound, Working, Terrier, Toy and Non-Sporting. At one time the hounds and gun dogs competed in the same Group, but it became too unwieldy. Currently the largest of all Groups is the Working, and there are some who advocate breaking this down some day into Large and Small Working Dogs.

Best in Show is decided by choosing one dog from the six winners of the Variety Groups.

Australia: Although the rules and regulations governing the registration of dogs and their progeny in the various states comprising the Commonwealth of Australia are at least similar, if not identical, the methods of conduct of dog shows and the attainment of the title of Australian Champion vary appreciably from state to state. Unfortunate though this situation may appear at first, it is brought about mainly by a combination of geographical factors and environmental considerations. For these reasons it is justifiable.

Seven individual states make up the Australian Commonwealth. These are New South Wales, Victoria, Queensland, South Australia, Western Australia, Northern Territory and Tasmania. Each one of these states has its own Kennel Control organization, charged with the administration of the dog fancy. On two or three annual occasions delegates from each state meet at conferences called by the Australian National Kennel Club (A.N.K.C.). This body is merely an advisory one and the resolutions passed at such meetings are in the form of recommendations only. Thus they are not binding on the individual state members, which may or may not adopt them, as they see fit. All in all this is a most unhappy set of circumstances, preventing international recognition of the A.N.K.C. In the opinion of most top level administrators the formation of a governing National Kennel Club is a dire future necessity and work is proceeding towards the establishment of such a goal. When and how soon it can be achieved is anyone's guess.

The registration figures for dogs are not available on a national level. Each state collects and publishes its own statistics.

The following table gives the registration figures for the year 1961–1970 at state level:

New South Wales	25,000
Queensland	9,200
Victoria	8,500
South Australia	5,000
Western Australia	4,820
Tasmania	1,000
Total	53,520

The number of dog shows conducted annually in each state including Open Parades, Field Trials and Obedience Tests varies in direct relationship to the numerical strength of pedigreed dogs within the area. In N.S.W. the approximate number of exhibitions held during the course of a year is around 500, in Victoria about 230, in Queensland 190, in South Australia 125, in Tasmania around 125, in Western Australia 90, and in the Northern Territory fifteen.

Apart from the shows staged by actual dog clubs there are numerous agricultural societies in each state which conduct "fair" type exhibitions at a general level, including dog sections. Obviously this sphere of activity increases appreciably the effective number of annual dog shows. As may be seen from the statistics New South Wales, Victoria, Queensland and South Australia are the most active states in the field of dog showing and breeding. It is accepted generally that the quality of show dogs is at its highest in those locales. Some excellent animals do, of course, also reside in the other states, however their numbers are relatively small.

The Australian system of classification of dogs into groups is somewhat different to that employed in England. It is made up of six groups, designated as Toys, Terriers, Gundogs, Hounds, Working and Non-Sporting. An actual break-up of breeds within each group may be obtained by writing to the Kennel Control Council, Royal Showgrounds, Ascot Vale, Melbourne W.2. 3032., Australia.

The methods used to make up dogs into Australian Champions differ quite drastically from those which apply in the United Kingdom. All class winners of each sex and over the age of six months (in Australia baby puppies may be shown from three months of age onwards) are brought back into the ring to be judged for the so-called Challenge Certificate (C.C.) Award. The eventual winner is allotted points at the rate of five points for the C.C., plus one point for each competing dog of its own sex over the age of six months. For example, a dog of any one breed, the entry for which in its sex was, say fifteen, of six months old or over, would receive a total of twenty points for its C.C. win. The maximum number of points which may be awarded in breed competition is twenty-five irrespective of the size of the entry.

At the end of breed judging the dog and bitch Challenge winners compete for the best of breed award. The eventual winner goes forward on to Group competition, along similar lines to those employed in England.

All best of breed winners, in turn, line up for best of group judging. The dog or bitch winning this award is credited with twenty-five points towards the title of Australian Champion, regardless of the number of points it had attained during breed judging provided, of course, that the total group entry exceeded twenty (N.B. this is *not* always the case in each group at some smaller country shows). In this manner it is possible for a dog of a numerically unpopular breed to gain twenty-five points towards its title of Australian Champion by winning the group award, even though the breed entry may have been relatively small. Once again, twenty-five points is the maximum number to be gained in Group Competition.

The six Best of Group Winners ultimately are called in to compete for the award of Best in Show. The winner of this class attains twenty-five points towards his/her champion title regardless of breed or group entry, even in those most unusual circumstances in which this number had not been allotted already in previous competition.

Once an animal has accumulated 100 points or more it qualifies for the title of Australian Champion. A record of its wins and points gained is sent to the Control of the respective state in which the animal resides. This is checked out and if found correct an Australian Championship Certificate is issued.

Certain restrictive qualifications do apply to the attainment of Challenge Certificates. For example, no more than two Challenge Certificates, out of whatever the eventual necessary total, may be issued by any one judge; in Queensland at least fifty per cent of all Challenge Certificate points must have been won in competition within the metropolitan area of Brisbane, irrespective of the owner's abode, which on occasions may be some 500 miles or more from the capital.

In some respects it may appear as though it is a relatively easy task for a dog to gain the title of Australian Champion. In actual practice though this does not hold true in most instances, due to the relatively high quality of competition in most breeds. Furthermore judges are instructed specifically not to award Challenge Certificates to exhibits which they do not consider to be of sufficiently high standard. Certainly, it is possible to qualify an exhibit for Australian Championship status by travelling literally hundreds of miles so as to avoid serious competition, gaining perhaps no more than six or seven Challenge points on each occasion. Very few exhibitors only will go to such extremes and therefore it does not seem justified to enact legislation preventing this situation, even if such regulations were feasible. After all, cheap Champions can be made up occasionally in all parts of the world and Australia is no exception to this rule.

Scandinavia: The Classification at Scandinavian dog shows is a combination of the Anglo-Saxon and the Continental systems. There is a junior class for dogs from eight to fifteen months of age and an open class for dogs over fifteen months (champions may not be entered in the open class; they enter in a special class for champions only). In these two classes (junior and open) a dog can be awarded a first prize, a second, a third or a 0 (nil, or no prize). A first prize should be awarded if the dog in question is a typical, correctly constructed dog with obvious merit and outstanding quality, and whose faults are not so grave as to prevent it from being a very good specimen. A second prize should be awarded if the dog is considered of good type and structure which, notwithstanding its faults, still can be regarded as a moderately good representative of the breed. A third prize to a dog which, though lacking the quality and perfection of construction, cannot be called a really poor representative of its breed. Finally, a 0 is for a really untypical dog; a dog which shows bad mentality in the ring, or one which is extremely difficult to judge, should be given 0, regardless of exterior qualities.

Every dog is judged on its merits regardless of the merits of the other dogs in the same class. Thus, if all the exhibits in such a class are of really high quality, then every dog can be awarded a first prize. On the other hand, if none of them is of high quality, then none should get a first.

All dogs which have won a first prize in junior are entitled to take part in the "junior competitive class", where the best four are placed respectively. Likewise all dogs with a first in the open class go forward to the "winners" class, and exactly the same pattern is followed as in the "junior competitive class".

The definition of a dog worthy of the Challenge Certificate is: *A dog which is typical in all respects, correctly constructed and possessing such distinctive merits and so trifling faults that it can be classified as a worthy representative of its breed for the purposes of breeding.*

The champion class is open to all dogs which previously (not at the present show) have obtained the title of champion – International, Swedish, Danish, Finnish or Norwegian.

At the international championship shows held in Scandinavian countries (approved by the F.C.I.) the international certificates C.A.C.I.B. (Certificat d'Aptitude au Championat International de Beauté) and C.A.C.I.T. (Certificat d'Aptitude au Championat International de Travail) are awarded. To become an international champion, four C.A.C.I.B.'s in three countries under three different judges are required. The dog must be fifteen months of age to compete for his first C.A.C.I.B., and between the first and the last (fourth) C.A.C.I.B. there must be a time lapse of one year. Also the dog's pedigree must contain registered ancestors for at least three generations.

Chow Chows, Schnauzers (Miniature, Standard and Giant), Great Danes, and all sizes of Poodles have C.A.C.I.B.'s awarded in their various colors, but the native Challenge Certificates, as in the U.S.A. and Britain, are awarded only to the best dog and bitch.

Some breeds are not allowed to compete in the winners class unless they have proved themselves in the work for which they were originally bred. The following breeds have to be placed highly in field trials, working and mental tests respectively to gain the title of show champion: Pointers, English, Irish and Gordon Setters, German Short-haired Pointers, Weimaraners, Munsterlanders, Brittany Spaniels, all types of Retrievers and Spaniels, Dachshunds, Stövare, Beagles, Drever, Elkhounds, Jamthunds, Karelian Bear Dogs, Finnish Spitz, Norrbottenspets, Alaskan

Malamutes, Bouvier des Flandres, Boxers, Briards, Collies, Dobermanns, Groenendaels, Greenland dogs, Hovawart, Giant Schnauzers, Rottweilers, Alsatians (German Shepherd Dogs), Siberian Huskies, Tervuerens, and Bavarian and Hanoverian Schweisshunds.

Other minor differences that come to mind are that if a dog is entered for a show (entries usually close approximately one month before the actual show) and there is a change of judge, the entry money will be refunded if so required. If the dog is taken ill or dies before the show (veterinary surgeon's certificate has to be produced) the money will also be returned. Veterinary examinations immediately before a show still take place in Scandinavian countries; all exhibits must be inoculated against distemper, and all males must be entire.

The Dog in Use and in Sport

With so much emphasis placed today on the dog as a pet, companion and show dog, it is sometimes forgotten that, although man no longer needs the dog as a food provider, he is still useful to man in numerous ways. The dog has adjusted remarkably well to modern conditions – we find him working alongside the police in their fight against crime, and in the detection of drugs. We find him helping watchmen to guard property; or acting as "eyes" for blind people; or acting with film stars in delighting film fans; or appearing in advertisements to promote the sale of anything from dog food to automobiles.

Of course not all breeds are equally good at all kinds of work, and the many breeds have evolved to be adaptable not only to the various contingencies but, as in the case of hounds for example, to meet the demands of terrain, climate and quarry.

Since time immemorial humans have delighted in competitive sports; dogs have been included in a vast number of them, and it is possible to see dogs demonstrate their work as a form of competition. The farmer, or shepherd, is proud of the prowess of his sheepdog, and rightly so, for a good dog eases considerably the arduous labour of his work. Indeed, without a dog the shepherd's work in some places would be impossible. The interested public can see exactly what this work entails when they attend any of the sheepdog trials held throughout the country under the auspices of the International Sheepdog Society. The dogs competing are mostly Border and Welsh Collies, which are as carefully bred as any breed recognized by the Kennel Club.

Alsatians (German Shepherd Dogs) and Dobermanns are the breeds usually connected with police work, but other breeds like the Bullmastiff and the Rottweiler have proved their worth, while Labrador Retrievers seem to have found a niche in detecting drugs and explosives.

The police and the armed forces take every opportunity to display the intelligence of their dogs and give frequent demonstrations at agricultural shows and other functions. Also some societies registered with the Kennel Club, notably obedience, Bloodhound, Alsatian and Gundog clubs, hold working trials where the competing dogs demonstrate their skill at various exercises. At championship working trials in England, the work is separated into different grades – Companion Dog, Utility Dog, Working Dog, Tracking Dog and Police Dog. If the dog reaches a set standard he gains the official qualification CD, UD, WD, TD or PD respectively, and if he is particularly successful, these letters are followed by Ex (Excellent). The Bloodhound people also hold working trials to encourage breeders to remember the breed's original work, which lay in the ability to track. The breed is still called upon to aid the police in searching for missing persons.

Obedience competitions are immensely popular in every part of Britain today, and many shows featuring only obedience contests are held throughout the year. If a dog gains three obedience certificates at Kennel Club

A French police dog, a Labrador, demonstrates its drug detection technique.

A tense moment in a Greyhound race

registered shows, under three different judges, he becomes an obedience champion. The exception to this is at Cruft's where dogs have to win during the year previous at least one certificate at an ordinary championship show in order to qualify to compete. However, if a dog with one certificate should win at Cruft's, he automatically becomes a full champion with just the two certificates, because of the supreme height of the competition. These awards are all subject to Kennel Club rules.

Few of the Greyhounds which compete on the track (under the auspices of the National Greyhound Racing Association) will be seen in show ring competition, or vice-versa, but there are notable exceptions and some shows today have a special class for racing Greyhounds. Here it must be mentioned that dogs taking part in both activities must be registered, both with the N.G.R.A. and the Kennel Club. On the other hand, there are several Whippet clubs which have racing sections, and the same dogs compete in races and in the ring.

In similar manner, the Deerhound, Saluki and Borzoi people organize coursing meetings; and Afghan Hound exhibitors also like to give their exhibition hounds a chance to show their paces.

For those people who are interested in hunting on horseback, there are packs of Foxhounds, Buck and Staghounds and sometimes Harriers; and on foot Beagles, Basset Hounds, Harriers and Otterhounds.

These hounds all hunt live quarry, and are followed as close as may be by the Masters, hunt servants and the field, but the Trail Hounds, hound trailing being a traditional and highly popular north country sport in England, with a seasonal championship, run free, following a pre-laid trail, and are under the supervision of stewards dotted round the course to check that there is no deviation, short cutting or interference, for large wagers are laid on the local favorites. The handlers and the spectators remain at the starting and finishing points. Junior and Senior trails are regulated by distance.

All the hounds contribute in variety towards man's pleasure in his sport, and mixed up with these are the hunt terriers who fulfil the meaning of their name – terrier means earth dog – and prove themselves indispensable to those who hunt vermin. The various hunts have always been inordinately proud of their own strains of terrier, which today follow the hunt in a motor vehicle, in charge of the terrier man.

Before automobiles came to complicate hunting, the terriers actually ran with the pack and thus were on the spot when quarry went to ground. One famous strain was created by a Devonshire Parson named Jack Russell: they stood 14 inches in height and were 14 lbs in weight. The smaller hunt terriers of modern times have been sold to the public as Jack Russell terriers, a definite misnomer, for the strain has run out, but they are none-the-less highly popular, and although not eligible for registration with the Kennel Club as pure-bred dogs, they are freely exhibited at hunt terrier shows and various exemption shows, the West Midland Working Terrier Society (not registered with the Kennel Club) caters especially for them. A brisk export trade in hunt terriers has been established with America.

Of the twenty-two terrier breeds registered with the Kennel Club, the most freely in use for work with hounds are the Borders and Lakelands. The Border Clubs issuing certificates for dogs which achieve a certain standard. In the Eastern Counties of England, the Norfolk and Norwich terriers rendered yeoman service in wartime in the destruction of rats around the corn ricks at threshing time.

Badgers and various types of vermin provide work for the terriers, but in Britain, the dogs used on badgers are generally the terrifically game, small, modern hunt terriers, and not the Dachshund (the Badger hound) of the Continent.

Popular although Foxhounds are in America and England, not even the English Foxhound is shown at Kennel Club shows in London, but every year four hound shows are held – at Peterborough, the Great Yorkshire Show, Honiton (Devonshire) and the South of England Show at Ardingly in Sussex, where the best looking of the hounds can be seen. Individual hunts also hold their own puppy shows.

Certain breeds have to prove that they retain the instinct for the work for which they were originally bred, before gaining the title of champion. These are the gundog breeds, which have to demonstrate briefly that they are not gun-shy (steadiness is not essential – only in field trials proper), and for Pointers and Setters that they hunt and point; for German Short-haired Pointers, Weimaraners and Hungarian Vizslas that they hunt, point and retrieve tenderly; for Spaniels or Retrievers that they hunt, face covert and retrieve tenderly, the two latter varying only in method. These quick tests cannot be compared with field trials proper which are exacting competitions. Very few dual champions are made, and in some breeds the dogs being shown in the ring and those appearing at trials are so different that they hardly appear to be the same breed. However, there are societies which have worked hard to bridge the gap and there is great interest in the working showdog, particularly in Spaniels and Retrievers.

There is a big demand throughout the world for a reliable gundog from landowners, shooting syndicates and wildfowlers, and here the important word is, reliable. In the past the different breeds of gundog were used almost exclusively for the work for which they were bred. Today, the accent is on all-round usefulness, and breeds like the Labrador and English Springer Spaniel, and the just developing German Short-haired Pointer, which can combine several purposes, are particularly popular.

Some countries insist that show dogs must also be able to work and, for example, in Scandinavia and in Europe, a high standard of work is demanded. Some countries also require working certificates for other breeds, outside the gundog group – Eire still tests its terriers with the badger, while Germany has trials for Dachshunds. The most important breed characteristics, says the German Dachshund Club, are – "work under ground, ranging and flushing, quality of the nose, baying on the scent, track keen-ness and steadiness. Dogs may also be examined for their achievements learned from training, such as walking on the leash, drop to command, gun shyness and behavior during the hunt. Retrieving from water is not compulsory".

Although so many breeds now appear in show-rings all over the world, it should never be forgotten that they were bred for a purpose, and that the type of coat, the size of the dog, the color, often the very shape of the feet, and so on, did not just happen fortuitously – these characteristics are there because they are those best suited for the terrain, or the animals on which the dogs had to work.

Thus Australia has its Kelpies for sheep, and Cattle Dogs; Africa its Ridgebacks for use against lion; Russia its Borzois to hunt wolf; the Arctic

A Retriever retrieves to hand during trials in Oxfordshire, England.

631

A sheepdog penning sheep at the behest of its master, at a sheepdog trial held in London.

regions their sledge dogs, the Huskies, Malamutes and Samoyeds; France and Switzerland their mountain dogs, not only for rescue work but also to guard the flocks of sheep in these difficult regions. And, of course, throughout the world, each area has its own special sheepdog or hound breed, often with only small differences between them.

It is remarkable how well the dog adapts to changing conditions. At war they have acted as messengers, and have even been used for mine detection. When horse-drawn carriages went out of fashion, the Dalmatian did not just disappear from the scene, but became the guardian of the modern automobile, and he has even been known to act as a gundog. The versatile German Shepherd Dog (Alsatian) was originally a mobile fence, a barrier, and his task of keeping the sheep within certain areas was almost as important as keeping other marauding animals out. And so it is with many breeds, as man's conditions change, so the dog keeps pace.

Books on Dogs

A Selected Bibliography of Books on Breeds with an Introduction on Early and General Works

Having in mind the overall aim of this work to help the reader identify and study specific breeds of dogs I have in the pages that follow this article presented a list of breed books recommended for further reading. This list is a very selected one indeed, for almost thirty classes of canine literature have been purposely omitted: the appearance of the dog in art, literature, poetry, fiction and so on would have taken up half the present work; and as the reader is presumed to be more interested in breed researches it was felt that a workable list of books concentrating on breed origin, history and show points would be of greater use and more appreciated. I was reluctant to omit stud books as such, and breed periodicals, but with limited space even in such a generous volume as this the barrier had to be lowered on all entries other than those which substantially contributed to serious breed researches, yet withal being available through public library borrowing arrangements or purchase from antiquarian booksellers, and (what is most important) not involving the housing of hundreds of volumes as would, say, the Kennel Club Stud Book series.

Moreover, even among the breed books many recent monographs have been deliberately left out – for their production has it seems been governed more by the shovel than the sieve, and I do so want every line in my list to be of value. Mind you there are a few exceptions where the contents of a book however slim or little known approximate the yardstick in breeds which suffer a lack of print. Conversely there are several dozens of books on specific breeds which are unlisted because they are of the utmost rarity despite my having them in my private collection – there is little point in teasing a cynological student with titles which are unobtainable in the general sense! Therefore the reader is asked to regard the list as a working library of books on breeds and remember that a full catalog of dog books would run up to about 20,000 items.

As an additional guide to research material a similarly selective list is given of books on groups of breeds, where more often than not information on an uncommon breed may be found or additional references supplementary to the main catalog.

However, before wielding the sieve to these two ends I feel a good few words should be said on the importance of our general dog books. Many of the breed books published today quote or misquote the earliest of our authors with great reverence yet reveal little knowledge of whether the extracts concerned are of any real value out of context, and in too many instances reveal a lamentable ignorance of the original authors and their works. (Poor old Caius of 1570 has had more piffle attributed to him at the wrong time and wrong place than even dear old "Stonehenge", who so many people seem to think wrote a book called "Stonehenge on the Dog" in 18-something-or-other). So let us briefly run over the last four centuries of British dog books and see for ourselves which have stood the acid test of time through the painstaking diligence and comprehension of their authors – giants in their class whose like we shall never enjoy again.

Although dog appeared in even the very first printed books (see Dame Juliana Berners of 1486) they were first given an entire treatise to themselves in English in 1576 when Abraham Fleming was responsible for a very free translation of the Caius work (*De Canibus Britannicis,* 1570) as *Of Englishe Dogges.* In this little book (now of the utmost rarity) Fleming deals with "the diversities, the names, the natures, and the properties" of the then known breeds – and although it is an interpretation rather than a literal translation of Caius, is a work in strong demand. Usually a reader has to do with the excellent 1880 facsimile edition, when a copy can be found at all!

Skipping past a number of 16th century hunting treatises which embrace both the fast and the slow Hounds of the time the next work in English well worth searching for is John Manwood's *Laws of the Forest,* 1598 (in each case here I give the date of the first edition). This work has a long chapter on dogs with particular reference to Mastiffs and Greyhounds, and for this reason alone any edition is valuable. During the next two centuries much was published which dealt with dogs but it was rather an embarrassment of riches for the huntsmen than a library of useful knowledge for the dog breeder. Turberville, Markham, Cox, Blome and others of the time wrote so much that indeed one of them (Gervase Markham) was even bribed by the booksellers to please not write any more! Still, we at least owe it to Nicholas Cox for having advocated the use of a different breed of Hound for each hunt – and a close study of the many Hounds in this book indicate how well his advice was taken.

But in 1800 appeared at last a work of the first magnitude, Sydenham Teak Edwards' *Cynographia Britannica.* Here we had a superb labor and the first dog book to be illustrated with colored plates. The plates are, of course, the most vital feature of the book – and being a rare book anyway it is almost impossible today to find a complete copy with all the plates intact. A folio work, it was first issued in parts in blue wrappers. It was never completed as it proved too costly a venture – it had planned to cover all breeds, but even so twenty-three breeds appear in its twelve very fine plates. Odd plates appear occasionally in the salerooms and as these are to the cynologist what Gould's or Audubon's exquisite pictures are to the naturalist the prices are high. However, many have been reproduced in the general works of Shaw, Watson, Ash (in particular) and Hutchinson. About this time several large works appeared which are still of great value to the fancier: Bewick's *History of British Quadrupeds,* 1790, with his exquisite woodcuts of Bulldogs, Mastiffs and others; Taplin's *The Sportsman's Cabinet,* 1803–1804, a two-volume folio work of immense importance with fifty plates by Reinagle, Rysbrack, Pugin and Bewick; Daniel's *Rural Sports,* 1801–1802, an even larger but less virile book; and a whole heap of companions, repositories, directories and guides for sportsmen of rather less value. But of the serious productions of the time Church's *Cabinet of Quadrupeds,* 1805, a two-volume folio work should be studied for its eighty-four excellent engravings. And we must not forget the two little volumes on dogs in Jardine's Naturalist's Library, of 1839–1840, although too many of the hand-colored plates have been filched by the print dealers. Yet another book not to be overlooked is Youatt's *The Dog,* 1845, which ran to many editions and is now in demand again.

Now that we have reached the middle of the 19th century it behoves us to sieve even more carefully, and by enlarging the mesh rescue only the really outstanding tomes of yesteryear. They are not really numerous and I know a number of private collectors who are able to fill the gaps in their libraries even now as and when copies appear on the market. Each of the following items is of considerable importance and is worth every bit as much for its real information as for its investment value.

Firstly G. R. Jesse's *History of the British Dog*, 1866, a two-volume pioneer study of all native and some foreign breeds, and E. Jesse's *Anecdotes of Dogs*, 1846, so much sought after for its large-paper fine engravings – together these books give us a considerable insight into breed histories and formation. Then in 1867 came the best general book by J. H. Walsh ("Stonehenge"), *The Dogs of the British Islands*, which ran to five editions all of which are very scarce and much in demand. This work is far superior to his other books and should be studied again and again. Mind you, his *The Dog in Health and Disease*, 1859, and *The Dog: Its Varieties and Management*, 1874, each ran to many editions and are useful reading indeed yet *Dogs of the British Islands* stands head and shoulders above them.

Walsh's best work I believe to be *The Greyhound*, 1853, which with Ash's classic monograph of 1933 make the two finest works in the English language on the Greyhound. But then I must not allow myself to think of the sumptuous breed books as such for these are listed at the tail of this article; although it is unthinkable not to mention in the same breath that books like Arkwright's *The Pointer*, Laverack's *The Setter*, Farman's *The Bulldog*, Cook's *The Dandie Dinmont*, Scott and Middleton's *The Labrador*, Gatacre's *The Keeshond* and Buchanan-Jardine's *Hounds of the World* – mere lines in the catalog, are in fact each and all superb treasures deserving of the closest study by the most assiduous of scholars.

But to return to the general picture; it should be mentioned that T. Pearce ("Idstone") wrote a quite useful little book in 1872 called *The Dog*, which still turns up from time to time. Then in 1879–1881 Vero Shaw's magnum opus appeared, and with its excellent colored plates caught on at once. It began in parts and was later issued as bound volumes – a heavy quarto which has often had to suffer repair at the binders. It won a number of literary awards in its time, and still commands a good price today – *when* its twenty-eight colored plates are intact!

In the meantime quite comprehensive works by Dalziel, Drury, Lee and Stables burst forth, following the immense interest in dogs after the First Great International Dog Show of 1863 and the later series of world-famous Cruft's Dog Shows. Dalziel was undoubtedly the giant of the four with his excellent *British Dogs*, 1880, and several valuable breed monographs. *British Dogs* poured out in over a score of issues yet not even the Druryfied addenda lack vitality. Hugh Dalziel was closely rivaled by Lee, whose *Modern Dogs*, 1894, proved so popular, and whose beautiful work on the Fox Terrier will ever be praised. Even while in the middle of a work in progress I was recently able to add to my forty variant issues of *Modern Dogs* the personal copies of all Lee's books, each graingerized with relevant extra prints and cuttings, and carrying his manuscript notes in the margins ready for the final editions which never were – for he died before seeing them through to the printers. I believe even J. T. Marvin and John Best, two of the greatest authorities on Terrier literature will agree with me that Rawdon Briggs Lee was ever an indefatigable worker – his Sporting, Non-Sporting and Terrier divisions of his major work are in constant demand the world over.

Now the fourth writer, Gordon Stables, was a funny chap: not only because he wrote at least two boys' adventure stories and half a cat book to every dog volume he produced, but because his hearty style made the reading so much easier. His *Our Friend the Dog* is in any edition considered a good and reliable book still. A similar wag was R. L. Price, the man who held the first Sheepdog Trials on his estate at Bala, Wales, in 1893; and whose *Dogs: Ancient and Modern* is a delightful little work.

Mention of this Welshman reminds me of Thompson Gray the author of *Dogs of Scotland*, 1891, a book now extremely scarce; and of H. D. Richardson whose *Dogs*, 1847, was the first important Irish general work. A Scot whose truly magnificent work was first published in New York (and later, 1906, in London) was James Watson, whose *The Dog Book* eventually appeared in two quarto volumes, copiously illustrated and full of first-class material – in fact it was the forerunner of Ash's supreme monument *Dogs: Their History and Development*, 1927.

Of other major works two early American books were G. O. Shields' *The American Book of the Dog*, Chicago, 1891, a classic of over 700 pages, and F. J. Perry's *Kennel Secrets*, Boston, 1893, both of which are invaluable to fanciers of the principal breeds. The little book of W. E. Mason, *Dogs of All Nations*, 1915, was but a potted extract of the tremendous work by Count H. de Bylandt, of which the best edition is the third of 1905. Further afield appeared the very solid work of W. Beilby on *Dogs of Australasia*, 1897, an invaluable reference work on the early importations into Australia of British-bred stock.

By this time the first dog books carrying photographic illustrations had been produced; the generally accepted "first" in this departure from woodcuts and engravings was Henry Webb's *Dogs: Their Points, Whims, Instincts and Peculiarities*, 1872, which ran to many issues, and is today a most important reference for Mastiff and Bulldog researchers. (In passing, however, I should mention that several dog books had already appeared during the preceding decade carrying actual photographs – though certainly not as important works as the Webb volume).

C. H. Lane wrote two very important dog books of which the major is his *Dog Shows – and Doggy People*, 1902. This is extremely useful not only for referring to the canine celebrities of the last century and their dogs but to check their actual wins at the first shows held; the book reporting quite fully on every major exhibition from 1859 to the turn of the century; as Vol. I of the Kennel Club Stud Book is a rarity it can be readily appreciated how useful this record is to researchers. Another publication relating to leading fanciers and dog show politics is E. W. Jaquet's *The Kennel Club*, 1905.

Then followed the multi-volume works which without exception have become absolute "musts" for research purposes. Following the Watson and the de Bylandt two-volume publications came Herbert Compton's *The Twentieth Century Dog*, also in two volumes, in 1904. The year 1906 introduced Harding Cox's most excellent folio issues of *Dogs by Well-Known Authorities*, a series which was never completed owing to the very high cost of production. Very few sets exist today. Then Robert Leighton (husband of a writer and father of a writer, and like Stables, the author of rattling good boys' yarns) produced his *The New Book of the Dog* in 1907. It was variously issued in one, two and four volumes the last being a special subscribers' edition carrying a folding anatomical plate extra to its score of exquisite colored plates by Lilian Cheviot, Maud Earl and five other fine artists. In 1911 J. Sidney Turner and Nicholas Vale's very important work *The Kennel Encyclopedia* appeared in four volumes – though as often as not it is found in three.

Also in 1911 came the classic *Toy Dogs and Their Ancestors* by Judith Lytton, a superb example of fine book production, rich in colored plates and extremely scarce today – without any doubt the best work on small breeds. Related in a sense was another fine production, usually known as Collier's *Dogs of China and Japan in Nature and Art,* 1921, but actually written by W. F. Collins. This also has colored plates and much of value on Toy Dogs – altogether a very beautiful book.

The year 1927 brought what proved to be the all-important and most comprehensive dog book ever published: E. C. Ash's *Dogs: Their History and Development.* It was of two very thick volumes with 160 plates in its ordinary edition, while the de luxe edition was limited to only fifty copies and carried an extra colored frontispiece in each volume, which, being bound in full pigskin is understandably almost unobtainable today. Its many hundreds of illustrations include reproductions of early paintings and engravings relating to most breeds; whilst the text reveals at once Ash's unwillingness to accept as gospel all the tall tales told by some earlier writers, preferring to dig deeply into the past, and the racks of the British Museum Library, and do his own research.

A single volume by C. C. Sanderson, *Pedigree Dogs,* 1927, is to be recommended for the criticisms on each breed by carefully selected breeders. A slightly thicker book of 1928 is F. T. Barton's *The Kennel Encyclopedia,* which has slimmed with the times, yet it is still a very useful work indeed. Barton was a veterinary surgeon who was a prolific writer on dogs and farm animals.

Of all the encyclopedias the most copious is still the Hutchinson's *Dog Encyclopedia* of 1935. First issued in fifty-six parts at 7d. each, it was later issued in three thick quarto volumes in red cloth, green rexine, and a few in half leather. Having fifty-eight plates (thirty-four in color) and covering almost every then known breed it has been in wide demand (R. C. Bayldon, A. Croxton Smith and I were busy many years ago at revising it but after several years of work Capt. Bayldon died and the work was abandoned). Its main value lies in its articles on the lesser breeds and those of eastern Europe and Asia.

Ultimately appeared in 1948 the last of the great works, *The Book of the Dog,* edited by Brian Vesey-FitzGerald, and carrying excellent articles on all major breeds, with superb sections on the dog in art and literature by Hesketh Hubbard and A. Croxton Smith, respectively. It was also the first general dog book to give an extensive bibliography. With its superb colored plates its several issues are much sought after (its full pigskin de luxe edition is already rare) for, as Herm David, the collector, so rightly says, it is an indispensable work indeed.

Recommended Books for further reading on Breeds and Groups of Breeds

In this list, broken into breeds and groups for convenience; authors are given by their best-known names and where the real author of a work is generally unknown the book is included under the attribution of the supposed author as on the title page of the work concerned – for example, while Prince Julius de Vismes wrote Laverack's *The Settler*, 1872, I have listed Laverack to avoid confusion. Similarly *Dogs of China and Japan in Nature and Art*, although written by W. F. Collins has been listed in the usual way as by Collier. Joint authors are given without their initials, and where three or more authors have created a book they are listed under the first author of those on their title-page.

The dates given are in all cases those of the first editions unless there has arisen a special reason: for example the third edition of Farman's *The Bulldog* is the first to carry a chapter on the French Bulldog, while Jessop's *The Yorkshire Terrier* was not illustrated until its fifth edition ... in such cases I have selected the editions most useful to each breed.

As already mentioned in the introduction to this bibliography some thirty classes of dog books have been purposely excluded yet a few exceptions appear to have been made: again there is a special reason; for example Dawson's *Finn* and *Jan* are not only rattling good yarns but reveal much of Irish Wolf hound character, as does Stables' *Sable and White* tell us a good deal of the true Collie; again Dame Ethel Smyth's *Inordinate (?) Affection* is a "must" for Bobtail fanciers (inordinate indeed), and even Mrs. Montgomery-Campbell discloses valuable knowledge of Yorkshire Terrier temperament in her *Chronicles*. Finally although obliged to omit Sir Percy Fitzpatrick's *Jock* and Count Cronstedt's *Grip* (two capital Bull Terrier stories) I am glad to acknowledge that Lyde's *Golden Lady* and Ironsides' *Lung Chung* claim inclusion through unexpected merits.

Afghan Hound
Hubbard, C. L. B. *The Afghan Handbook*, 1951
Miller and Gilbert
The Complete Afghan Hound, 1965

Airedale
Aspinall, J. L. E. *The Airedale Terrier*, 1948
Bowen, A. *Airedales*, 1950
Buckley, H. *The Airedale Terrier*, n.d.
Haynes, W. *The Airedale*, 1916
Jowett, F. M. *The Airedale Terrier*, n.d.
Saunders, J. *The Modern Airedale*, 1929

Alsatian (German Shepherd Dog)
Ash, E. C. *The Alsatian*, 1936
Brockwell, D. *The Alsatian*, n.d.
Elliott, N. *The Complete Alsatian*, 1961
Horowitz, G. *The Alsatian Wolf-Dog*, 1923
Humphrey and Warner *Working Dogs*, 1934
Leonard, L. *Alsatians*, 1956
Pickett, F. N. *The Book of The Alsatian Dog*, 1950
Pickup, M. *The Alsatian Owner's Encyclopedia*, 1964
Schwabacher, J. *The Popular Alsatian*, 1922
Von Stephanitz, M. *The German Shepherd Dog*, 1923

Australian Terrier
C., A. F. *The Show Australian Terrier*, 1935
Ireland, J. L. M.
The Book of the Australian Terrier, 1965

Basenji
Tudor-Williams, V. *Basenjis*, 1946

Basset Hound
Appleton, D. *The Basset Hound Handbook*, 1960
Johnston, G. *The Basset Hound*, 1968
Millais, Sir E. *Bassets*, 1885

Beagle
Appleton, D. *The Beagle Handbook*, 1959
Colville, A. R.
Beagling, 1940

By Permission of the Master, 1947
Free, R. *Beagle and Terrier,* 1946
Lloyd, J. I. *Beagling,* 1954
Paget, J. O. *The Art of Beagling,* 1931
Shepherd, et al *Beagling,* 1938
Williams, A. C. *Beagles,* 1955
Wood, P. *Thoughts on Beagling,* 1938

Bedlington Terrier
Redmarshall et al
A List of Leading Bedlington Terriers, 1932

Bloodhound
Appleton, D. *The Bloodhound Handbook,* 1960
Brough, E. *The Bloodhound,* n.d.
Whitney, L. F.
Bloodhounds and How to Train Them, 1947

Border Terrier
Horn, M. H. *The Border Terrier,* n.d.
Jackson and Irving *Border Terriers,* 1969
Lazonby, T. *Border Lines,* 1948

Borzoi
Chadwick, W. E. *The Borzoi Handbook,* 1952
Craven, A. *The Borzoi as I Know It,* n.d.
Guy, E. H. *Mythe Borzois,* n.d.
Thomas, J. B. *Observations on Borzoi,* 1912
Walzoff, Count D. *The Perchino Hunt,* 1952

Boston Terrier
Axtell, E. *The Boston Terrier and all About It,* 1910
Craven, A. *The Boston Terrier as I Know It,* n.d.
Penn, P. *The Boston Terrier in England,* n.d.
Perry, V. G. *The Boston Terrier,* 1941
Rine, J. Z. *The Ideal Boston Terrier,* 1932
Rousuck, E. J. *The Boston Terrier,* 1926

Boxer
Daly, M. *The British Boxer,* 1955
Dunkels, J. *The Boxer Handbook,* 1951
Gordon, D. *The Boxer,* 1948
Hemery, M. E. *Boxers,* 1957
Meyer, E. *Judging the Boxer,* 1946
Somerfield, E. *The Popular Boxer,* 1955
Stockman, F. *My Life With Boxers,* 1968
Wagner, J. P. *The Boxer,* 1948

Bullmastiff
Craven, A. *The Bull-Mastiff as I Know It,* n.d.
Hubbard, C. L. B. *The Bullmastiff Handbook,* 1959
Makins, E. *The Bullmastiff,* n.d.

Bull Terrier
Adlam, G. M. *Forty Years of Bull Terriers,* 1952
Davis, R. H. *The Bar Sinister,* 1903

Dighton, A. *The Bull Terrier and all About It,* n.d.
Glynn, R. H. *Bull Terriers and How to Breed Them,* 1936
Gordon, J. F. *The Bull Terrier Handbook,* 1957
Hogarth, T. W.
The Bull-Terrier, 1931
A Bull-Terrier Notebook, 1936
The Colored and Color Breeding, 1932
Hollender, V. C.
The Bull Terrier and All About It, n.d.
Bull Terriers, 1951

Bulldog
Cooper, H. St. J. *Bulldogs and Bulldog Men,* 1908
   and Browne *Bulldogs and All About Them,* 1914
   and Clarke
      Bulldog Kennel Book and Toy Bulldog Breeder, 1901
      Bulldogs and Bulldog Breeding, 1905
   and Fowler *Bulldogs,* 1925
Crowther, F. W. *Pedigrees of Bulldogs,* 1897
Deacon, S. H. *Show Bulldogs,* 1908
Farman, E. *The Bulldog. A Monograph,* 1899
Fulton, R. *The Bulldog,* 1895
Gordon, J. F. *The Bulldog Handbook,* 1958
Hutchison, J. H. *The Perfect Bulldog,* 1908
Meyer, E. *The Bulldog,* 1960
Nugent, J. R. *The Gorgeous Sourmug,* 1933
Sturgeon, A. G. *Bulldogdom,* 1919
Thomas, M. E. *British Bulldogs,* 1910

Cairn
Ash, E. C. *The Cairn Terrier,* 1936
Beynon, J. W. H. *The Popular Cairn Terrier,* 1929
Caspersz, T. W. L.
The Cairn Terrier Handbook, 1957
Cairn Terrier Records, 1932
Rogers, Mrs. B. *Cairn and Sealyham Terriers,* 1922
Ross, F. M. *The Cairn Terrier,* 1925
Woodward, J. *The Cairn Terrier,* n.d.

Cavalier
Forwood, M. *The Cavalier King Charles Spaniel,* 1967
Stopford, R. R.
The Cavalier Spaniel and its Derivations, 1951

Chesapeake Bay Retriever
Bliss, A. A. *The Chesapeake Bay Retriever,* 1933

Chihuahua
Gray, T. *The Popular Chihuahua,* 1961
Harmar, H. *The Chihuahua,* 1966

Chow Chow
Collett, C. E. *The Chow Chow,* 1953
Dietrich and Davies *The Chow Chow,* 1926
Dunbar, Lady *The Chow-Chow,* 1914

Ingleton and Rybot *The Popular Chow Chow*, 1954
Leighton and Baer *The Popular Chow Chow*, 1927

Clumber Spaniel
Farrow, J. *The Clumber Spaniel*, 1912
Phillips and Cane *The Sporting Spaniel*, 1906

Cocker Spaniel
Ash, E. C. *The Cocker Spaniel*, 1935
Broughall, N. M. B. *The Cocker Spaniel Handbook*, 1951
Daly, M. *The Cocker Spaniel*, 1947
De Casembroot, J. *The Merry Cocker*, 1956
Harman, I. *Cocker Spaniel*, 1950
Lloyd, H. S.
    The Popular Cocker Spaniel, 1924
    How to Tell a Good Cocker Spaniel, 1949
Lucas-Lucas, V. *The Popular Cocker Spaniel*, 1953
Mathews, V. A. H. *The Cocker Spaniel*, 1948
Moffit, E. B. *The Cocker Spaniel*, 1935
Woodward, J. *The Cocker Spaniel*, 1938

Collies
Arnsonian *Training the Working Collie*, 1958
Baker, T. *The Collie and its Show Points*, 1899
Baskerville, W. *Show Collies*, 1923
Dalziel, H. *The Collie: Its History*, 1888
Lee, R. B. *The Collie or Sheep Dog*, 1890
Osborne, M. *The Popular Collie*, 1957
Packwood, H. E. *Show Collies*, 1906
Puxley, W. L. *Collies and Sheep-Dogs*, 1948
Stables, W. G. *Sable and White*, 1893

Dachsbrack
Henderson, Sir N. *Hippy*, 1943
Hubbard, C. L. B. *The Dachshund Handbook*, 1950

Dachshund
Biss, A. *Dachshunds*, 1960
Daglish, E. F. *The Book of the Dachshund*, n.d.
Hubbard, C. L. B. *The Dachshund Handbook*, 1950
Lister-Kaye, C. *Dachshunds*, 1952
Naylor, L. E. *Dachshunds*, 1937
Riley, W. A.
    Wisdom of the Simple, 1948
    With a Tithe-Pig's Tail, 1949
Sanborn, H. *The Dachshund or Teckel*, 1937
Sawyer, M. J.
    The Dachshund Reference Book, 1949
    Modern Dachshund Breeding, n.d.
Sayer, J. *Illustrated Standard of Points*, 1939
Woodiwiss and Allen *Dachshund Pedigrees*, 1898

Dalmatian
Frankling, E. *The Popular Dalmatian*, 1964
Hubbard, C. L. B. *The Dalmatian Handbook*, 1957

Saunders, J. *The Dalmatian and All About It*, 1932

Dandie Dinmont
Cook, C. *The Dandie Dinmont Terrier*, 1885
Gordon, J. F.
    The Dandie Dinmont Terrier Handbook, 1959
Williams, R. P. *The Dandie Dinmont Terrier*, n.d.

Deerhound
Bell, E. W. *The Scottish Deerhound*, 1892
Cupples, G. *Scotch Deer-Hounds and Their Masters*, 1894
Graham, G. A. *Scottish Deerhound Pedigrees*, n.d.
Hartley, A. N. *The Deerhound*, 1955

Dobermann Pinscher
Curnow, F. *The Dobermann Pinscher*, 1958
Gruenig, P. *The Dobermann Pinscher*, 1939

Elkhound
Crafts, G. C.
    How to Raise and Train a Norwegian Elkhound, 1964
Ritson, Lady K. *Elkhounds and Finsk Spets*, 1933

English Setter
Bepler, M. I. *Setters*, 1930
Hubbard, C. L. B. *The English Setter Handbook*, 1958
Laverack, E. *The Setter*, 1872
Tuck, D. H. *The Complete English Setter*, 1951

English Springer
Goodall, C. S.
    The Complete English Springer Spaniel, 1958
Hooper, D. M. *The Popular Springer Spaniel*, 1963

Field Spaniel
Phillips and Cane *The Sporting Spaniel*, 1906

Finnish Spitz
Ritson, Lady K. *Elkhounds and Finsk Spets*, 1933

Fox Terriers
Ackerman, I. C. *The Wire-Haired Fox Terrier*, 1928
Astley, L. P. C. *The Perfect Fox Terrier*, 1910
Bruce, R. *Fox Terrier Breeding*, 1923
Bruce, R.
    Fox Terrier Breeding, 1923
    The Popular Fox Terrier, 1950
Castle, S.
    Breeding Fox-Terriers, 1927
    A Monograph on the Fox Terrier, 1910
Daly, M.
    Fox Terriers, 1954
    The Wire Fox Terrier, 1947
Dalziel, H. *The Fox Terrier*, 1889
Dangerfield, S.
    The Wire-haired Fox Terrier Handbook, 1958

Harrison, T. H. *The Breeding of Show Fox Terriers*, 1897
Lee, R. B. *The Fox Terrier*, 1889
Naylor, L. E. *The Modern Fox Terrier*, 1933
Northen, C. F. *Wire Fox Terrierdom*, 1933
Pardoe, J. H. *Fox Terriers*, 1949
Skelly, G. F. *All About Fox Terriers (Wire)*, 1948
Skinner, A. J. *The Popular Fox Terrier*, 1924
Vernon, S. R. *Breeding and Rearing Fox Terriers*, 1943
Woodward, J. *The Fox Terrier*, 1938

Foxhound
Acton, C. R.
    The Breeding . . . of the Foxhound, 1935
    The Foxhound of the Future, 1953
    The Modern Foxhound, 1935
Bathurst, Earl *The Breeding of Foxhounds*, 1926
Bentinck, Lord C.
    The Foxhound, 1925
    Foxhounds, 1923
Lord Bentinck, H. *Foxhounds*, 1922
Bradley, C.
    The Foxhound of the Twentieth Century, 1914
Corbett, R. *Notes on Managing Foxhounds*, 1928
De Trafford, Sir H. *The Foxhound*, 1906

French Bulldog
Farman, E. *The Bulldog*, 1903 (3rd ed.)
Stubbs, W. J. *The History of the French Bulldog*, 1903

Golden Retriever
Charlesworth, W. M.
    The Book of the Golden Retriever, 1933
    Golden Retrievers, 1952
Stonex, E. *The Golden Retriever Handbook*, 1953

Gordon Setter
Adams, M. K. *The Storey of the Gordon Setter*, 1968
Bepler, M. I. *Setters*, 1930
Gompertz, G. *The Gordon Setter*, 1971
Schillbréd, C. *The Gordon Setter*, 1939

Great Dane
Becker, F. *The "Great Dane"*, n.d.
Booker, B. L. *Great Danes of To-day*, 1938
Keckler, V. *The Great Dane*, 1949
Mackenzie, M. *Great Danes Past and Present*, 1912

Greyhound
Ash, E. C.
    The Book of the Greyhound, 1933
    The Chart of the Greyhound, 1933
    The Greyhound, 1935
Clarke, C. F. C. *Greyhounds and Greyhound Racing*, 1934
Clarke, H. E.
    A Complete Study of the Modern Greyhound, 1963

    The Greyhound, 1965
    The Greyhound: Breeding, Rearing and Training, 1954
    The Modern Greyhound, 1947
Dalziel, H. *The Greyhound*, 1886
Dighton, C. A. *The Greyhound and Coursing*, 1921
Ellis, W. *Pedigrees of the Winners*, 1897
Ellis and Dunn: *A Complete List of Greyhounds*, 1902
Genders, R. *Modern Greyhound . . . Coursing*, 1949
Goodlake, T.
    The Courser's Manual, 1828
    Continuation of the Courser's Manual, 1932
Henderson, A. A.
    Practical Remarks on . . . Greyhounds, 1860
Hurndall, J. S.
    Dogs in Health . . . as Typified by the Greyhound, 1886
Matheson, J. *The Greyhound*, 1929
Stanley, E. A. V. *Successful Greyhound Breeding*, 1938
Walsh, J. H. *The Greyhound*, 1853

Griffon Bruxellois
Cousens, M. *Griffons Bruxellois*, 1960
Deck and Tyler,
    Lines and Families of Griffons Bruxellois, n.d.
Rhodes, M. P. *The Cult of the Griffon Bruxellois*, 1926
Spicer, M. H. *Toy Dogs*, 1902

Harriers
Bryden, H. A. *Hare-Hunting and Harriers*, 1903

Husky
Dovers, R. *Huskies*, 1957
Machetanz, S. *Seegoo: Dog of Alaska*, 1962

Irish Setter
Bepler, M. I. *Setters, Irish, English and Gordon*, 1930
Millner, J. K. *The Irish Setter*, 1924
Naylor, L. E. *The Irish Setter*, 1932

Irish Terrier
Jones, E. H. *Irish Terriers*, 1959
Jowett, F. M. *The Irish Terrier*, 1907

Irish Water Spaniel
Phillips and Cane *The Sporting Spaniel*, 1906

Irish Wolfhound
Dawson, A. J.
    Finn the Wolfhound, 1908
    Jan. Son of Finn, 1917
Gardner, P. *The Irish Wolfhound*, 1931
Graham, G. A.
    The Irish Wolfhound, 1885
    Irish Wolfhound Pedigrees, 1893
Hogan, E. *The History of the Irish Wolfdog*, 1897
Starbuck, A. J. *The Complete Irish Wolfhound*, 1963

Keeshond
Digby, G. W. *My Life With Keeshonden*, 1969
Gatacre, A. *The Keeshond*, 1938
Johns, R (ed.) *The Samoyed and Keeshond*, 1936

Kelpie
Hamilton-Wilkes, M. *The Kelpie and Cattle Dog*, 1967

Kerry Blue Terrier
Clarke, E. *The Popular Kerry Blue Terrier*, 1927
Handy, V. *The Modern Kerry Blue Terrier*, 1933
Montgomery, E. S.
   The Complete Kerry Blue Terrier, 1950
White, H. *Kerry Blue*, 1932

King Charles Spaniel
Birchall, M. J. *King Charles Spaniels*, 1960
Lytton, J. *Toy Dogs and Their Ancestors*, 1911

Labrador Retriever
Beck, Baroness E. *Train Your Own Labrador*, 1965
Henry, C. *Training Your Labrador*, 1947
Howe, Lady L. *The Popular Labrador Retriever*, 1957
Naylor, L. E. *Labradors*, 1952
Roslin-Williams, M. *The Dual-Purpose Labrador*, 1969
Scot and Middleton *The Labrador Dog*, 1936
Sprake, L. *The Labrador Retriever*, 1933
Whitworth, J. *The Labrador Retriever*, n.d.

Lakeland Terrier
Johns, C. (ed.) *The Lakeland and Border Terriers*, 1936
Kirk, A. P. *The Lakeland Terrier*, 1964
Morris, I. *Line Breeding With Lakeland Terriers*, 1946
Spence, A. *The Lakeland Terrier*, n.d.

Mastiff
Kingdon, H. D. *The Old English Mastiff*, n.d.
Savigny, A. G. *Lion the Mastiff*, 1896
Turner and Vale *The Kennel Encyclopedia*, 1907–11
Webb, H. *Dogs*, 1872
Wynn, M. B. *The History of the Mastiff*, 1886

Norwich Terrier
Anguish, P. G. *The Norwich Terrier*, n.d.
Monckton, S. *The Norwich Terrier*, n.d.

Old English Sheepdog
Hopwood, A. *The Old English Sheepdog*, 1905
Keeling, J. A. *The Old English Sheepdog*, 1961
Smyth, E. M. *Inordinate(?) Affection*, 1936
Tilley, H. A. *The Old English Sheepdog*, 1933

Papillon
Roberts, P. and B. R. *The Papillon Handbook*, 1959

Pekingese
Allen, M. L. *Show Pekingese*, 1923
   and Astley *The Perfect Pekingese*, 1912

Ash, E. C. *The Pekingese*, 1936
Ayscough, F. *The Autobiography of a Chinese Dog*, 1926
Carter, W. G. *Pekingese Genealogy*, 1934
Cross, C. A. *The Pekingese*, 1932
Daniel, M. N. *Some Pekingese Pets*, 1914
Dixey, A. C. *The Lion Dog of Peking*, 1931
Godbold, B. *Pekingese in Australia*, 1962
Godden, R. *Chinese Puzzle*, 1936
Harman, I. *Pekingese*, 1949
Hopkins, et al *The Pekingese*, 1924
Howe, E. and E. *Pekingese Scrapbook*, 1954
Hubbard, C. L. B. *The Pekingese Handbook*, 1951
Ironside, M. *Lung Chung*, 1946
Lyde, L. W. *The Golden Lady*, 1937
Nicholas, A. K. *The Pekingese*, 1939
Soutar, A. *A Chinaman in Sussex*, 1931
Taylor, W. H. *Success in Pekingese*, 1961
Verity-Steele (and later Slater)
   Book of the Pekingese, 1914
Vlasto, J. A. *The Popular Pekingese*, 1923
Waring, J. *The Fluffy Lions*, 1955
Younghusband, E. *The Surroundings of Fu Hi*, 1951

Pointer
Arkwright, W. *The Pointer and his Predecessors*, 1902
Bruette, W. A.
   Modern Breaking . . . Setters and Pointers, 1906
Daly, L. M. *The Pointer as a Show Dog*, 1939
Dobson, W. *Kunopaedia*, 1814
Hochwalt, A. F. *The Modern Pointer*, 1923
Thornhill, R. B. *The Shooting Directory*, 1804
Watson, J. *The Dog Book*, 1906

Pomeranian
Harmar, H. *The Pomeranian*, 1967
Hicks, G. M. *The Pomeranian*, 1906
Ives, I. *Show Pomeranians*, 1911
Parker, E. *The Popular Pomeranian*, 1928

Poodles
Bowring, C. *Poodles*, 1960
   and Munro *The Popular Poodle*, 1953
Daly, W. M. *Our Pal the Poodle*, 1955
Dangerfield, S. *Your Poodle and Mine*, 1954
Hopkins, L. *The Complete Poodle*, 1951
Hoyt, H. B. *Your Poodle*, 1952
Naylor, L. E. *Poodles*, 1949
Price, P. H. *The Miniature Poodle Handbook*, 1960
Sheldon and Lockwood
   Breeding From Your Poodle, 1963
   Poodles, 1957
Tracy, T. H. *The Book of the Poodle*, 1951
Walne, S. *A to Z of Poodles*, 1960
Hints on Clipping the Poodle, 1948

Pug

Featherstone, G.
  The Pug Dog, 1952
  The Pug Dog Roll of Honour, n.d.
Goodger, W. S.
  The Pug Handbook, 1959
  The Pug, its History and Origin, 1930
  The Truth about the Pug Dog, 1947
Pughe, L. J. E. *Black Pugs,* 1905
Weall, S. G. *The Pug,* 1965

Pyrenean Mountain Dog

Prince, C. R.
  Introduction to the Pyrenean Mountain Dog, n.d.
  The Pyrenean Mountain Dog, n.d.
Trois-Fontaines, J. H.
  My Travelling and My Dogs, 1949
  Pyrenean Mountain Dogs, 1937

St. Bernard

Barazetti, W. F. *The Saint Bernard Book,* 1955
Dalziel, H. *The St. Bernard,* 1888
Denlinger, M. G. *The Complete Saint Bernard,* 1952
Dickin, N. *The St. Bernard and English Mastiff,* 1936
Fleischli, J. A. *The Saint Bernard,* 1954
Grey, F. D. *The Dogs of St. Bernard,* 1903

Saluki

Amherst, F. M. *The Gazelle Hound,* 1912
Waters, H. and D. *The Saluki,* 1969

Samoyed

Baillie and Auckram *The Samoyed (N.Z.),* 1961
Johns, R. (ed.) *The Samoyed and Keeshond,* 1936
Keyte-Perry, M. *The Samoyed,* 1962
Puxley, W. L. *Samoyeds,* 1934

Schipperke

Freeman, C. D. *The Schipperke,* 1907
Holmes, E. H. *The Schipperke,* 1934
Root, V. M. *Official Book of the Schipperke,* 1965
Williams, M. L. *Darling Dogs,* 1912

Schnauzers

Daly, W. M. *Odd Dogs,* 1955
FitzGerald, A. *The Miniature Schnauzer,* 1935
Nash, C. *Yours Faithfully,* 1938
Paramoure, A. F.
  The Complete Miniature Schnauzer, 1959

Scottish Terrier

Ash, E. C. *The Scottish Terrier,* 1936
Bruette, W. A. *The Scottish Terrier,* 1934
Buckley, H. *The Scottish Terrier,* 1913

Caspersz, D.
  The Scottish Terrier, 1938
  The Scottish Terrier Handbook, 1951
  Scottish Terrier Pedigrees, 1930 (and Supplement)
Daly, W. M. *The Scottish Terrier,* n.d.
Davies, C. J. *The Scottish Terrier,* 1906
Ewing, F. C. *The Book of the Scottish Terrier,* 1932
Gabriel, D. *The Scottish Terrier,* 1928
McCandlish, W. L. *The Scottish Terrier,* 1909
Robertson, J.
  Historical Sketches of the Scottish Terrier, 1900
Woodward, J. *The Scottish Terrier,* 1938

Sealyham

Barber, W. *The Sealyham Terrier,* 1938
Bilney, N. H. *The Sealyham Terrier (Coat),* 1966
Chenuz, F. J. *Sealyhams,* 1956
Lucas, J.
  Hunt and Working Terriers, 1930
  The New Book of the Sealyham, 1929
  The Sealyham Terrier, 1922
Marples, T. *The Sealyham Terrier,* 1922
Rogers, Mrs. B. *Cairn and Sealyham Terriers,* 1922

Shetland Sheepdog

Baskerville, W.
  Show Collies . . . and Shetland Sheepdogs, 1923
Gwynne-Jones, O.
  The Shetland Sheepdog Handbook, 1958
Osborne, M. *The Popular Shetland Sheepdog,* 1959

Skye Terrier

Miles, Lady M. *The Skye Terrier,* 1951
Montgomery, E. S. *The Complete Skye Terrier,* 1962
Wilmer, A. *The Skye-Terrier,* 1907

Staffordshire Bull Terrier

Barnard, J. W. *The Staffordshire Bull Terrier,* n.d.
Beilby, H. N. *The Staffordshire Bull Terrier,* 1943
Dunn, J. *The Staffordshire Bull Terrier,* 1947
Gordon, J. F.
  The Staffordshire Bull Terrier Handbook, 1951
Hollender, V. C. *Staffordshire Bull Terriers,* 1952
Ormsby, C. A. *The Staffordshire Terrier,* 1956

Sussex Spaniel

Phillips and Cane *The Sporting Spaniel,* 1906

Weimaraner

Denlinger, M. G. *The Complete Weimaraner,* 1954

West Highland White Terrier

Buckley, H. *The West Highland White Terrier,* 1911
McCandlish, W. L. *The Scottish Terrier,* (1st ed. only)

Marvin, J. T.

   The Complete West Highland White Terrier, 1961

Pacey, M. *West Highland White Terriers*, 1963

Welsh Corgi

Albin, D. *The Family Welsh Corgi*, 1970

Evans, T. *The Welsh Corgi*, 1934

Forsythe-Forrest, E. *Welsh Corgis*, 1955

Hubbard, C. L. B.

   The Cardiganshire Corgi Handbook, 1952

   The Pembrokeshire Corgi Handbook, 1952

Lister-Kaye, C. *The Popular Welsh Corgi*, 1954

Perrins, L. *Keeping a Corgi*, 1958

Welsh Terrier

Thomas, I. M. *The Welsh Terrier Handbook*, 1959

Whippet

Daglish, E. F. *Whippets*, 1964

Fitter, B. S.

   Forty Years of Whippetdom, n.d.

   The Show Whippet, 1954

Lloyd, F. *The Whippet and Race-Dog*, 1894

Renwick, W. L. *The Whippet Handbook*, 1957

Todd, C. H. D. *The Popular Whippet*, 1961

Yorkshire Terriers

Jessop, S. *The Yorkshire Terrier* (5th ed. onwards)

Montgomery-Campbell, M.

   The Chronicles of Baba, n.d.

Munday, E. *The Popular Yorkshire Terrier*, 1958

Swan, A. *The Yorkshire Terrier Handbook*, 1958

Gundogs

Barton, F. T. *Gun Dogs*, 1913

Chalmers, P. R. *Gun Dogs*, 1931

Clark, A. *Gun Dogs and their Training*, 1935

Hardy, H. F. H. *Good Gun Dogs*, 1930

Moxon, P. R. A. *Gundogs*, 1947

Smith, A. C. *Gun Dogs*, 1932

Hounds

Acton, C. R. *Hounds*, 1939

Buchanan-Jardine, Sir J. *Hounds of the World*, 1937

Hore, J. P. *History of the Royal Buckhounds*, 1893

Kuechler, O. *'Cooning with 'Cooners*, 1924

Lloyd, T. I. *Hounds*, 1934

Thomas, J. B. *Hounds . . . Through the Ages*, 1934

Non-Sporting

Barton, F. T. *Non-Sporting Dogs*, 1905

Compton, H. E.

   The Twentieth Century Dog, 1904 (Vol. I)

Deeson, A. F. L. *Large Dogs*, 1963

Lee, R. B. *Modern Dogs (Non-Sporting Div.)*, 1894

MacInnes, J. W. *Guard Dogs*, 1949

Retrievers

Barton, F. T. *The Retriever*, 1907

Bevan, F. R. *Observations on Breaking Retrievers*, 1879

Cooke, H. R.

   Short Notes on . . . Retriever, 1908

   A Few More Short Notes, 1930

   Short Suggestions for Judging, n.d.

Eley, C. C. *The History of Retrievers*, 1921

Eley, W. G. *Retrievers and Retrieving*, 1905

Rivière, B. B. *Retrievers*, 1947

Smith, Sir H. *Retrievers*, 1898

Smith, S. *Retrievers*, 1910

Sprake, et al. *The Popular Retriever*, n.d.

Warwick, T. S. *Retrievers and Spaniels*, 1901

Setters

Bruette, W. A.

   Modern Breaking . . . Setters and Pointers, 1902

Dobson, W. *Kunopaedia*, 1814

Hochwalt, A. F. *The Modern Setter*, 1935

Lloyd, F. *All Setters*, 1931

Lyttle, H. *Breaking a Bird Dog*, 1924

Shelley, E. M.

   Twentieth Century Bird Dog Training, 1921

Thornhill, R. B. *The Shooting Directory*, 1804

Watson, J. *The Dog Book*, 1906

Sheepdogs

Capstick, T. *Sheep Dog Training*, n.d.

Gosset, A. L. T. *Shepherds of Britain*, 1911

Greig, J. R. *The Sheep-dog*, 1956

Holmes, J. *The Farmer's Dog*, 1960

Hubbard, C. L. B. *Working Dogs*, 1947

Humphrey and Warner *Working Dogs*, 1934

Longton and Hart *Your Sheep Dog*, 1969

McCulloch, J. H. *Sheep Dogs and their Masters*, 1938

Moorhouse, S. *The British Sheepdog*, 1950

Spaniels

Carlton, H. W. *Spaniels*, 1915

Phillips and Cane *The Sporting Spaniel*, 1906

Watson, J. *The Dog Book*, 1906

Sporting

Barton, F. T. *Sporting Dogs*, 1905

Compton, H. E.

   The Twentieth Century Dog, 1904 (Vol. II)

Deeson, A. F. L. *Large Dogs*, 1963

Lee, R. B. *Modern Dogs (Sporting Div.)*, 1893

Terriers

Barton, F. T.
   Terriers, Their Points and Management, 1907
Bristow-Noble, J. C. *Working Terriers,* n.d.
Davies, E. W. L. *Memoirs of the Rev. John Russell,* 1878
Free, R. *Beagle and Terrier,* 1946
King, H. H. *Working Terriers,* 1931
Lee, R. B. *Modern Dogs (The Terriers),* 1894
Lucas, J. *Hunt and Working Terriers,* 1931
Matheson, D. *Terriers,* 1922
Maxtee, J.
   English and Welsh Terriers, 1908
   Scotch and Irish Terriers, 1909
O'Conor, P.
   Sporting Terriers, 1926
   Terriers for Sport, 1922
Russell, D. *Working Terriers,* 1948
Smith, A. C. *Terriers,* 1931
Smith, B. *The Jack Russell . . . Terrier,* 1962
Sparrow, G. *The Terrier's Vocation,* 1949

Toy Dogs

Barton, F. T. *Toy Dogs,* 1904
Lytton, J. *Toy Dogs and Their Ancestors,* 1911
Raymond-Mallock, L. C. *Toy Dogs,* 1908
Spicer, M. H. *Toy Dogs,* 1902
Williams, M. L. *A Manual of Toy Dogs,* n.d.
Wimhurst, C. G. E. *The Book of Toy Dogs,* 1965

Basic Canine Anatomy

Bradley, O. C. and Grahame, T.
   Typographical Anatomy of the Dog, 1959
Miller, M. E., Christenson, G. C. and Evans, H. E.
   Anatomy of the Dog, 1965
Sisson, S. *Anatomy of the Domestic Animals,* 1956

Canine Medicine

American Veterinary Publications, Inc.
   Canine Medicine, 1959
Kirk, Hamilton, MRCVS, *Index of Diagnosis,* 1948
Kirk, Hamilton, MRCVS, *Index of Treatment,* 1948

National Canine Authorities

Argentina	Kennel Club Argentino, Florida, 671, Buenos Aires.	*Finland*	Suomen Kennelliitto – Finska Kennelklubben, Bulevardi 14a, Helsinki 12.
Australia	Australian National Kennel Council, Royal Show Grounds, Ascot Vale, Victoria	*France*	Société Centrale Canine pour l'Amelioration des Races de Chiens en France, Rue de Choiseul 3F - 75, Paris - 2e.
Austria	Osterreichischer Kynologenverband, Karl-Schweighofer-Gasse, 3, A-1070, Vienna.	*Germany West*	Verband für das Deutsche Hundewesen Schwanenstrasse 30, D-46, Dortmund.
Barbados	Barbados Kennel Club, Avondale Bank Hall, St. Michael, Barbados, W.1.	*Greece*	Ellinikos Kynologikos Organismos, Rue Irodotou 24A, Athens.
Belgium	Union Cynologique Saint-Hubert, Avenue de l'Armee, 25, B-1040, Brussels.	*Guernsey*	Guernsey Dog Club, Myrtle Grove, St. Jacques, Guernsey, C.I.
Bermuda	Bermuda Kennel Club, P.O. 1455 Hamilton, Bermuda.	*Holland*	Raad van Beheer op Kynologisch Gebied in Nederland. Emmalaan 16, NL, Amsterdam 2.
Brazil	Brazil Kennel Club, Caixa Postal 1468, Rio de Janeiro.	*Hong Kong*	Hong Kong Kennel Club, Room 623, 9 Icehouse Street, Hong Kong.
Burma	Burma Kennel Club, Room 10, 342 Maha, Bandoola Street, Rangoon, Burma.	*Hungary*	Magyar Ebtenyesztök Orszagos Egyesülete Wallenberg u.2, Budapest XIII.
Canada	Canadian Kennel Club, 111 Eglinton Avenue, Toronto 12, Ontario, Canada.	*India*	Kennel Club of India, Vilayet Manzil, Begampet, Deccan, Andhra Pradesh.
Caribbean	Caribbean Kennel Club, P.O. 737, Port of Spain, Trinidad.	*Indonesia*	Perkumpulan Kynologi Indonesia Dj. Dompo 1/83; Blok E-2, Kobajoran Baru, Djakarta.
Chile	Kennel Club de Chile, Casilla 1704 Valparaiso.	*Ireland*	Irish Kennel Club, 4 Harcourt Street, Dublin 2, Ireland.
Colombia	Club Canino Colombiano, Carrera 7a 84-61, Apartamento 101, Bogota.	*Israel*	Israel Kennel Club, P.O. Box 33055, Tel Aviv.
Czechoslovakia	Federalni Vybor Mysliveckych, Svazu v. CSSR, Husova 7, Prague 1.	*Italy*	Ente Nazionale della Cinofilia Italiana Viale Premuda 21, 1 - 20129, Milan.
Denmark	Dansk Kennelklub, Norrebrogade 40, DK 2200, Copenhagen N.		

Japan	Japan Dog Federation, 9-8, 3-chome, Uchi-Kanda, Chiyodaku, Tokyo.	Peru	Kennel Club Peruano, Las Magnolias 889, Of. 209, San Isidro, Lima.
Jersey	Jersey Dog Club, La Huppe, Birches Avenue, St. Saviour, Jersey, C.I.	Poland	Zwiazek Kynologiczny W Polsce Nowy-Swiat 35, Warsaw.
Kenya	Kenya Kennel Club, P.O. Box 511, Nairobi, Kenya.	Portugal	Clube Portugues de Canicultura, Praca D. Joao Da Camara 4, Lisbon 2.
Luxembourg	Union Cynologique du Grand-Duché de Luxembourg, Rue J. P. Huberty, 42, Luxembourg.	South Africa	Kennel Union of Southern Africa, P.O. Box 562, Cape Town.
Malaysia	Malaysian Kennel Association, P.O. Box 559, Kuala Lumpur, Malaya.	Spain	Real Sociedad Central de Fomento de las Razas Caninas en Espana, Los Madrazo 20, Madrid 14.
Malta	Malta Kennel Club, 12 Our Saviour Street, Sliema, Malta, G.C.	Sweden	Svenska Kennelklubben, Box 1121, S-11181, Stockholm.
Mexico	Asociacion Canofila Mexicana Zacatecas 229 - Desp. 318, Mexico 7, D.F.	Switzerland	Société Cynologique Suisse Case Postale 2307, Ch-3001, Berne 1 Facher.
Monaco	Société Canine de Monaco, Palais des Congrès, Avenue d'Ostende, Monte Carlo.	United Kingdom	The Kennel Club, 1-4 Clarges Street, Piccadilly, London, W1Y 8AB.
Morocco	Société Centrale Canine Marocaine, Boite Postale 78, Rabat.	United States of America	American Kennel Club, 51 Madison Avenue, New York, N.Y. 10010.
New Zealand	New Zealand Kennel Club, P.O. Box 523, Wellington 1, New Zealand.	Uruguay	Federacion Canina de Venezuela, 1064 Apartado, Caracas D.F.
Norway	Norsk Kennel Klub, Bjorn Farmannsgate 16, N. Oslo 2.	Yugoslavia	Federation Cynologique de la Republique Federative Socialiste de Yugoslavia, Rue Alekse Nenadovica, 19-23, Belgrade.
Pakistan	The Kennel Club of Pakistan, Fortress Stadium, Lahore, West Pakistan.		
Paraguay	Paraguay Kennel Club, Calle Oliva 560, Asuncion.		

Notes on Contributors

The greater part of this book consists of articles and information contributed by some of the world's leading authorities on the individual breeds and supplementary canine matters. The following (necessarily brief) particulars indicate the extent of their connections with the breeds or other subjects. The contributors themselves are, in the main, internationally known, particularly in the United Kingdom and America. The kennel names given, and the names of specific dogs, are those which are likely to be found in the relevant pedigrees of thorough-bred dogs on both sides of the Atlantic.

In the majority of cases there are a great many more famous champion dogs attributable to each kennel than space permits us to mention.

Editor

Ferelith Hamilton; Editor of *Dog World* (England); breeder, exhibitor and international judge at championship shows.

Associate Editor in America

Mr. Arthur F. Jones; for many years Editor and Editor in Chief of *Pure-Bred Dogs, American Kennel Gazette*; author and editor of many books on dogs; well-known television and radio commentator on dogs.

The Contributors

Evolution of the Dog, Books on Dogs – Mr. Clifford Hubbard, author of many books on canine matters, including *Working Dogs of the World, The Complete Dog Breeder's Manual, Dogs in Britain;* owner of the world's largest library of dog books; lecturer, broadcaster, bibliographer and antiquarian bookseller.

Basic Canine Anatomy, Diseases of Dogs – Mr. Harold R. Spira, B.V.Sc., M.R.C.V.S., H.D.A.; eminent Australian veterinarian; well-known in canine circles in the U.K. and America.

Canine Nutrition – Mr. R. M. Kibble, B.V.Sc., H.D.A.; eminent Australian veterinarian; specialist in canine diet.

The Dog in the Home – Mr. Joe Cartledge; inherited dog interest from uncle, Arthur Cartledge, professional terrier handler; kennel manager to Mr. J. R. Barlow, owner world famous Crackley Wire Fox Terrier kennel; became professional handler, handling the Airedale, Ch. Riverina Tweedsbairn, to best in show at Cruft's, 1961; international championship show judge and all-round judge; columnist *Dog World* (England); owner large boarding kennel.

Showing and Championship Systems –
United Kingdom – Mr. C. A. Binney, Secretary of the Kennel Club (Great Britain).
America – Mr. Arthur F. Jones.
Australia – Mr. Harold R. Spira.
Scandinavia – Mr. Bo Bengtson, owner of the Bohem Whippets and Afghans in Sweden; reporter for *Hundsport* (Sweden) and *Dog World* (England); a young man who is all set for a brilliant career in the world of dogs.

The Dog in Use and in Sport – Mr. F. Warner Hill; international all-round judge of high repute, also a field trial judge. Before the war bred English Springers under the Beauchief prefix.

Working Dogs (Sheep, Cattle, etc.)

Alsatian (German Shepherd Dog) – Mrs. M. Pickup; life-long breeder and international judge; owner of the Druidswood Kennels; breeder of Ch. Edana of Combehill (Cruft's, best Non-Sporting, 1951), Metpol Argus (top winner, London Metropolitan Police Dog, 1970); author *Alsatian Owner's Encyclopaedia, Complete German Shepherd Guide.*

Anatolian Sheepdog (Karabash) – Charmian Steele, first importer of breed into United Kingdom; studied the breed in its natural habitat while living in Turkey for two years.

Australian Cattle Dog, Kelpie, Australian Terrier, Australian Silky Terrier – Mr. Roy B. Burnell; member of Australian family long associated with dogs; breeder, writer and judge.

Belgian Sheepdogs (Groenendael, Laekenois, Malinois, Tervueren) – Information provided by Mme. Nizet de Leemans, noted all-round judge in U.K., U.S.A. and Continent; President of the Standards Committee of the F.C.I. Information also provided by the Royal Berger Belge Club and the Société Royale Saint Hubert, Brussels.

Bouvier de Flandres – M. F. E. Verbanck; has worked for many years for this breed and is noted authority on them. Secretary, Club National Belge du Bouvier de Flandres.

Collie, Bearded – Mrs. G. O. Willison; championship show judge and life-long breeder; owner of the Bothkennar Kennels (now no longer existing); breeder of Ch. Bravo of Bothkennar (B.O.B., Cruft's), Ch. Bracken Boy of Bothkennar; author of breed handbook.

Collie, Rough and Smooth; French Sheepdogs (Beauceron, Briard, Picardy, Pyrenees) – Miss M. Osborne; owner of the Shiel Kennels; international championship judge; author of *The Popular Collie*; breeder of several champions.

Kelpie – Mr. Roy B. Burnell (See page 648): Also information provided by The Working Kelpie Council of New South Wales.

Komondor – Mr. John J. Kincel; officer (with his wife) of the Komondor Club of America; editor of Club newsletter; researcher; breeder of American champions.

Kuvasz – Information provided by Mrs. Dana I. Alvi, owner (with her husband, Dr. Z. M. Alvi) of the Hamralvi Kennels, Beverly Hills, U.S.A.; breeder of the top winning Hamralvi strains of Kuvaszok.

Maremma - Mr. G. E. Spears; owner of the Ammeram Kennels; breeder of Ch. Ammeram Pietro Rossano (B.O.B., Birmingham, Eng., 1969).

Old English Sheepdog – Miss Florence Tilley; championship show judge; owner and breeder of many champions; daughter of Mr. H. A. Tilley, whose Shepton Kennel has been located at Shepton Mallet, Somerset, England since the 1880's. Now world famous, the Shepton strain has been the backbone of the great rise in popularity of the Bobtail in modern times.

Puli – Mrs. Sylvia Owen; owner of the Skysyl Puli Kennels, the first to be established for the breed in America; breeder of Ch. Skysyl Apeter-Pan, Ch. Skysyl Barna Szem, CD, CDX, Ch. Skysyl November Leaf; author *Juli the Puli*.

Pyrenean Mountain Dog (Great Pyrenees) – Mrs. F. S. Prince; breeder and owner of many champions, including Ch. Bergerie Knur (best in show, Cruft's, 1970); owner (with her husband) of the Bergerie Kennel; she and her husband are championship show judges, Mr. Prince judged at Trenton, U.S.A. in May 1971.

Schapendoes – Mrs. Backx-Bennink; noted Dutch breeder; owner of the Reeuwijk affix for Old English Sheepdogs, Schapendoes, Briards, and Shih Tzus; well-known Continental judge.

Saint Bernard – Mr. A. K. Gaunt; with his wife, breeder and championship show judge; owners of the Corna-Garth Kennels which has produced over sixty full champions.

Shetland Sheepdog – Miss Felicity Rogers; co-owner, with her sister, Miss Patience Rogers, of the famous Riverhill Kennel whose champions have a definite type, noted for their soundness and good movement; recognized as having unrivalled knowledge of history and pedigrees of the breed.

Swiss Mountain Dogs (Appenzell, Bernese, Entlebuch, Great Swiss) – Information provided by Mr. J. Leumann, Secretary of the Schweizerischer Club fur Appenzeller-Sennenhunde; Mr. A. Kobelt, Secretary of the Klub fur Grosse Schweizer Sennenhunde; Miss Irene Creigh, breeder and owner of the Kisumu Kennel (for the Bernese).

Welsh Corgi, Cardigan and Pembroke – Mrs. Thelma Gray; noted breeder and author; it could almost be said that Mrs. Gray "made" the Pembroke Corgi in its present form. Being attracted to the little heeler from the hills of her native Wales, she set out to improve and popularize the breed. Her Rozavel Red Dragon set the type for countless generations to follow. The Cardigans joined the Rozavels at a later date but are no less esteemed by their owner for that.

Other Working and Utility Dogs

Boston Terrier – Mrs. Charles D. Cline; began in California, owning, breeding and showing dogs; A.K.C. judge for Dachshunds 1941; adopted her husband's (Mr. Charles D. Cline) breed, Boston Terriers; Associate Editor on *The American Dachshund*; columnist *Kennel Review*, and *American Kennel Gazette* since 1952; author *Pet Boston Terrier*, a handbook; now a judge of a number of breeds.

Boxer – Mr. Arthur F. Jones (See page 648).

Bulldog – The late Mrs. E. E. Smith, a lifelong devotee of the Bulldog, who very sadly died before this book was completed. Hers is one of the most famous names in Bulldogs and her efforts over many years have influenced the establishment of the desired sounder points in the breed. Mrs. Smith owned the Leodride Kennel which produced a stream of handsome champions whose names figure prominently in Bulldog pedigrees all over the world.

Bullmastiff – Mrs. R. E. Short; together with her husband, a fancier for over twenty-five years; owners of the small but influential Bulstaff Kennel; breeder of Ch. Bulstaff Achilles, winner of twenty-four C.C.s.

Dalmatian – Miss Betty Clay; bred her first champion over forty years ago; owner of the Tantivvey Kennel; breeder of Ch. Tantivvey Naomi (sister of three other champions from the same litter), Ch. Tantivvey Fanhill Filomel.

Dobermann (Doberman Pinscher) – Mr. A. T. A. Curnow; with his wife one of the first importers of Dobermanns into Britain after the Second World War; both are international championship show judges; owner of the Tavey Kennel; breeder of Ch. Iceberg of Tavey (Dog of the Year, U.K., 1966).

Dogue de Bordeaux – M. Maurice Van Cappel, President de la Société des Amateurs du Dogue de Bordeaux.

French Bulldog – Mrs. Vivien Watkins; breeder and championship show judge; owner of the Bomlitz Kennel; owner of Bomlitz Mix von Schubinsdorf (first post-War import into Britain), Ch. Bomlitz Edwardbear; President, French Bulldog Club of England; regular contributor *Dog World* (England).

Great Dane – Mr. Alan Stockwell; owner, with his wife, of the Bandarilla Kennel, discontinued when they left for five years in America; owners of Bandarilla Momma of Merrowlea; breeders of Bandarilla Bala Perdida, Bandarilla Lucir Nina; show judge England and America; contributor to club journals England, America, Australia.

Mastiff, Tibetan Mastiff, Neapolitan Mastiff – Mr. Douglas B. Oliff; owner of Bullmastiffs for twenty years; owner of the Wyaston prefix; breeder of Ch. Wyaston Tudor Prince; devoted student of the Mastiff family as a whole; championship show judge; columnist *Dog World* (England).

Newfoundland – Mrs. May Roberts; breeder and international judge; family connection with the breed began in 1886, when her father was a founder of the Newfoundland Club of England – and she is now President; owner of the Harlingen Kennel; breeder of many champions, including Ch. Harlingen Ace, Ch. Harlingen Sand Piper; contributor *Dog World* and *Our Dogs* (England); active also in Maltese.

Poodle – Mr. Philippe Howard Price; owner and breeder; commenced breeding Miniature Poodles in 1940; owner, with his wife, of the Montfleuri affix, named after family house in France international show judge; breeder of Ch. Toomai of Montfleuri, an influential sire in the development of black Toy Poodles.

Rottweiler – Mrs. Mary M. Macphail; trained in Germany as specialist judge, now international judge; owner of the Blackforest Kennel; particularly interested in working side of the breed; trains own dogs, concentrating on dual-purpose Rottweilers of German blood; owned Rintelna the Bombardier, C Dex, U Dex, and Ch. Horst from Blackforest.

Schipperke – Mr. Lawrance Ludford; with his wife, owner of the Schippland prefix; championship show judge, including Cruft's; Secretary, the British Schipperke Association; breeder of eighteen champions, including Ch. Cracker of Schippland (Best of Breed, Cruft's 1971 and, in 1970, the first Schipperke to win a group at a championship show).

Schnauzer, Griffon Brabancon and Bruxellois – Mrs. Pamela Cross-Stern; the third generation of her family to breed, exhibit and judge dogs; owner of the Sternroc Kennel; lived America, where founded

St. Louis Poodle Club; licensed A. K. C. handler; made Cruft's documentary film, *Best in Britain* (1968); owned Am. Ch. Sternroc Nicomur Chasseur, Am. Ch. Sternroc Sticky Wicket (both Min. Schnauzers); active also in Chihuahuas, Japanese, Lhasa Apsos.

Shih Tzu – Mrs. L. G. Widdrington; owner of the Lhakang Kennel; specialist judge; owner and breeder of Shih Tzus since 1939, when obtained her first from Lady Brownrigg (Mee Na of Taishan); breeder of Ch. Shebo of Lhakang, Ch. Jen-kai-ko of Lhakang (Cruft's, B.O.B., 1970) and many other British and overseas champions; contributor to numerous breed journals and dog publications.

Tibetan Breeds – Lady Freda Valentine; member of the committee which produced rules for Kennel Club registration of the four breeds – Lhasa Apso, Tibetan Terrier, Tibetan Spaniel, Tibetan Mastiff; owned Apsos since 1932; prominent dogs owned include Changtru (1932) and Wamo, both were winners.

Gundogs

Pointer – Mr. F. Duke; became interested first in black Cocker Spaniels (English), in 1939; added English Setters with some successes during 1960; introduced Pointers to his Dalric Kennel in 1960, breeding the famous Sh. Ch. Dalric Fern, and his present champion, Sh. Ch. Dalric Crookrise Rosemary; championship show judge since 1952.

Pointer, Old Danish – Mme. Jeanette Chantelou; well-known journalist in Denmark; breeder and owner of Wire Fox Terriers and Lakelands; owner of top winning Lakeland on the Continent.

Retriever, Chesapeake Bay – Mr. Arthur F. Jones (See page 648).

Retriever, Curly-coated – Mrs. Audrey Nicholls; daughter of Mr. and Mrs. Frank Till, owners of the Darelyn prefix; showing in her own right since 1962; owned Sh. Ch. Darelyn Dandini and Sh. Ch. Darelyn Darren, both descended from Ch. Darelyn Dellah (record nineteen C.C.s).

Retriever, Flat-coated – Mr. Read Flowers; a gamekeeper with a deep knowledge and experience of gundog work; has long been a successful breeder and exhibitor of Flat-coats, under the Fenrivers prefix; owner Ch. Fenrivers Golden Rod.

Retriever, Golden – Mrs. Joan Tudor; championship show judge, including Cruft's; owner of the Camrose Kennel; owned or bred a record thirteen champions including Ch. Camrose Nicholas of Westley (twenty C.C.s), Ch. Camrose Fantango (B.O.B., Cruft's, seven times stud dog of the year).

Retriever, Labrador, Harrier, Otterhound, Trail Hound – Mrs. Mary Roslin-Williams; owned Labradors since 1939; championship show and field trial judge;

owner of the Mansergh Kennel; breeder of Ch. Midnight of Mansergh (four C.C.s, B.O.B. each time), Ch. Damson of Mansergh (six C.C.s, and still working at the time of writing); author of *The Dual-Purpose Labrador;* active also in Cocker Spaniels (English) and Border Terriers.

Setter, English – Miss Margaret Barnes; championship show judge; owner of the Suntop prefix since 1950; owner, among many, of Ch. Suntop Suzette of Sowerby, Sh. Ch. Suntop Royalbird and Suntop Songbird; first handled her mother's English Cocker Spaniels in the ring in 1936.

Setter, Gordon – Mrs. M. M. C. Rowe; owner of the Cairlie Kennel; owner and breeder of several champions and show champions; contributor to *Dog World* (England); for many years one of the main supporters of Gordons in Britain.

Setter, Irish – Mr. Lee Schoen; international championship show judge; owner of the Kinvarra Kennel, Connecticut, U.S.A.; breeder of Kinvarra Kermit; co-author of the official breed Standard in the U.S.A.; Mr. Schoen is internationally known and respected for his deep knowledge of the development of his favourite breed.

Spaniel, Cocker (American) – Mrs. Ruth Kraeuchi; representative of the American Spaniel Club, deputed by the Executive Committee to write this contribution; has been a regular contributor to *American Kennel Gazette*.

Spaniel, American Water – Mr. Arthur F. Jones (See page 648).

Spaniel, Clumber, Field, Irish Water, Sussex, Welsh Springer – Dr. Esther Rickards, O.B.E., M.S., F.R.C.S.; retired surgeon; breeder, and gundog and all-round judge; owner of the Tarbay Kennel; breeder of Sh. Ch. Hornshill Elizabeth (Sussex), Sh. Ch. Tarbay Florian of Broomleaf (Welsh Springer), Sh. Ch. Jakes of Tarbay (Irish Water), Titian of Tarbay (Cocker).

Spaniel, Cocker (English) – Miss P. Neilson; carried on and expanded her mother's interest in the Cocker, their Noslien Kennel specializing in blacks, reds and goldens; breeders of numerous champions.

Spaniel, English Springer – Mrs. Olga Hampton; associated with Spaniels for thirty-odd years; owner of the Larkstoke prefix; breeder of many winners in England, the best known being Ch. Larkstoke Ptarmigan; interested in working qualities as well as good looks; international gundog championship show judge; Secretary of the English Springer Spaniel Club in England for some eighteen years.

Spaniel, Picardy – Comte de Catalan, President of the Club de l'Espagneul Picard.

Stabyhoun, Wetterhoun – Dr. J. P. Otto; Secretary of the Nederlandsche Vereniging Voor Stabij-en Wetterhounen, Sneek Holland.

Weimaraner – Mrs. Diana Oldershaw; an economist; owned her first Weimaraner in 1963 (Gunmetal Guy, CD Ex, UD Ex); owner of the Gunmetal prefix; contributor to breed journals and breed correspondent *Dog World* (England); owner, breeder, and trainer.

Spanish and Portuguese Breeds – Information provided by Dr. Antonio Cabral, past president of the Fédération Cynologique Internationale (F.C.I.), President of the Clube Portugues de Canicultura; leading veterinarian in Portugal.

Northern Breeds (Russian, Finnish, Polish, etc.) – Mr. E. Pellikka; one-time Secretary of the Finnish Kennel Club; wide knowledge of the Northern breeds rare in America and Britain; main interest is in the sight hound breeds (also contributed the article on the Borzoi).

French, German and European Gundogs – M. Jean Servier; President of the Club du Braque Francais; noted authority and writer.

Dutch Gundogs and French Hounds – Mrs. A. Gondrexon-Ives Browne; noted authority on Continental sporting breeds, in particular hounds; well-known European judge.

Hounds

Afghan Hound – Mr. Donald A. Smith in collaboration with Mrs. Gordon Miller and Dr. William Waskow. Mr. Smith served as President of the Afghan Hound Club of America for the greater part of 1955 to 1967 and since 1953 has written the Club column in *Pure-Bred Dogs – American Kennel Gazette.* Mrs. Miller is co-author of the *Complete Afghan Hound* (New York 1965). Dr. Waskow is a renowned championship show judge in America and since 1954 has served as the parent club Delegate to the A.K.C.

Ariegeois, Poitevin – M. P. Willekens; well-known authority on the breeds on the Continent.

Basset Hound – Mr. George I. Johnston; founded his Basset Hound Kennel in 1939, with the prefix Sykemoor; four generations of his family have kept hounds; international championship show judge; founder member of The Basset Hound Club in Britain and member of the Club Griffon-Vendéen; author *The Basset Hound* and articles and breed notes in canine magazines; owner of Ch. Rossingham Amber; breeder of Ch. Sykemoor Aimwell, Int. Ch. Sykemoor Blossom, among others.

Basset, Artesian Normand – M. L. Soutoul; well-known on the Continent as an authority on the breed.

Beagle – Mrs. G. M. Clayton; started breeding in 1926 with Chow Chows; then Wire Fox Terriers, West Highland Whites, Pembroke Welsh Corgis, Great

Danes, Beagles and many other breeds, Beagles holding pride of place; breeder of many international champions with the Barvae affix; breeder, among others, of Ch. Barvae Paigan, a top winning Beagle of the 1950's; championship show judge since 1948.

Billy – M. Anthony Hublot du Rivault, a descendant of the creator of the breed, M. Gaston Hublot du Rivault. Highly respected hound judge.

Bloodhound – Mrs. Y. Oldman; owner of the Barsheen Bloodhounds and one of the leading Bloodhound breeders in the world; Barsheen champions have won innumerable honors in Britain and abroad; breeder of the famous black and tan stallion hound, Int. Ch. Barsheen Nicholas.

Borzoi – Mr. E. Pellikka, (See page 651).

Coonhound, Black and Tan – Mr. Arthur F. Jones (See page 648).

Dachshund – Miss Katharine Raine; owner of the Imber Kennel, founded in 1938 with Standard Smooths; Wires came later and, in 1954, a recessive Long-coat appeared in a Smooth-bred litter; from this dog the famous Ch. Imber Coffee Bean was bred, who became the sire of fifteen champion progeny; Vice President of the Dachshund Club in Britain and known in the breed world-wide.

Deerhound (Scottish) – Miss Agnes H. P. Linton; owner of the Geltsdale prefix, primarily as a private interest; owned or bred Ch. Dramatic of Ross, Ch. Jock of Geltsdale, Ch. Meg of Geltsdale.

Drever – Mr. Bo Bengtson (See page 648).

Brittany Hounds – M. Hubert Desamy, President of the Club du Griffon Vendéen, President of the Société Canine Bas Poitou, and a noted authority on hounds in France.

Foxhound, American – Dr. Braxton B. Sawyer; a noted figure in the breed in America; leading show judge; owner of the Kentucky Lake Kennels.

Foxhound, English – Mr. R. de Courcy Parry; famous writer on hunting under the pseudonym of "Dalesman".

Greyhound – Mr. R. H. Parsons; has bred Greyhounds (and Whippets) since he was ten years old; his hounds all have names bearing his own initials, R.P.; breeder of Ch. Rosyer Poner (B.I.S. W.E.L.K.S. 1969); Chairman of the Greyhound Club in Britain.

Harrier – Mrs. Mary Roslin-Williams (See page 650).

Ibizan Hound – Mrs. Diana Berry; owner of the Ivicen affix (also the Sin affix for Basenjis); one of the first to import the breed to Britain when it was known by the Spanish name of Podenco Ibicenco; owner of the famous bitch Sol.

Irish Wolfhound – Mrs. Florence Nagle; owner and breeder since 1913; owner and breeder of thirty-one champions in England, fifteen in the U.S.A., and

several on the Continent; owner of the Sulhamstead Kennel, famous also for Irish Setters (see article on the breed); breeder of Ch. Sulhamstead Merman (best in show, all breeds, Cruft's 1960).

Otterhound – Mrs. Mary Roslin-Williams (See page 650.)

Pharaoh Hound, Miniature Pinscher – Mr. L. Hamilton Renwick; pioneer of Dobermann, Miniature Pinscher and Pharaoh Hounds in Great Britain; owner of the Birling prefix; owned the two record-holding Min Pins, Ch. Birling Wawocan Constellation and Ch. Birling Painted Lady.

Poitevin – M. P. Willekens (See page 651).

Rhodesian Ridgeback – Mrs. W. F. Hayes; breeder and championship show judge; owned first Ridgeback in 1953; regular contributor *Dog World* (England); owner of the Mentamery prefix; breeder of Ch. Mentamery Maradella (dam of brother and sister champions), Ch. Mentamery Malomba and Ch. Mentamery Monarch.

Saluki – Mrs. Gwendoline M. Angel; championship show judge; breeder and owner of the Mazuri affix; owned Salukis since 1934 (Sheba Mazuri); breeder of Int. Ch. Mazuri Orno, Mazuri Erizada (three champions from one litter); writer and contributor to *Dog World* (England).

Swedish Hounds (Hamiltonstövare, Schillerstövare, Smalandstövare) – Mr. Bo Bengtson (See page 648).

Swiss Hunting Dogs (Bernese, Jura, Lucernese, Swiss) – Information provided by Dr. G. Riat, President of the Club Suisse du Chien Courant (Schweizer Laufhund-Club), and a noted authority on Swiss Hounds.

Swiss Short-legged Hound – Information provided by Mr. Peter Jud, Secretary of the Schweizerischer Niederlaufhund-Club, of Zurich.

Trail Hound – Mrs. Mary Roslin-Williams (See page 650.)

Whippet – Mrs. D. M. McKay; breeder of show dogs, and coursing and racing dogs; owned first Whippet in 1939; breeder of American Ch. Laguna Lucky Lad (Hound Group, Westminster 1958), American Ch. Laguna Lucky Ligonier; English Ch. Laguna Ligonier, leading sire in Britain in the Sixties.

Terriers

Airedale – Mrs. Dorothy Hodgkinson; breeder and championship show judge; owner of the Kresent affix; associated with Airedales all her life; breeder of Kresent Model Maid (dam of ten British, one American and one Swedish champions), and Ch. Kresent Bonny Boy (B.O.B., Cruft's 1962).

Australian Terrier – Mr. Roy B. Burnell (See page 648).

Bedlington Terrier – Mrs. Barbara Clifton; breeder and championship show judge; owner of the Vardene Kennel; breeder of Ch. Vardene Blue Grenadier (ten C.C.s, ten B.O.B.s, etc.) and Vardene Blue

Guardsman; active also in Boxers and Kerry Blue Terriers.

Border Terrier – Miss Anne Roslin-Williams; daughter of Mrs. Mary Roslin-Williams (see Labrador); breeder (kennel name Mansergh); has worked Border Terriers with Foxhounds, Otterhounds, and also to badger; made her first champion at age of eighteen; championship show judge; well-known professional photographer of dogs; breeder of Int. Ch. Mansergh Dandyhow Bracken and Ch. Mansergh April Mist.

Bull Terrier – Mr. Tom Horner; owner, breeder and international show judge; manager of the Ormandy Kennel of Mr. R. H. Oppenheimer, whelped and reared the famous Mr. McGuffin; owner of the Tartary affix; breeder of champions; contributor to *Dog World* and *The Field* (England).

Cairn Terrier – Mrs. Diana Hamilton; breeder and international championship show judge; owner of the Oudenarde affix; has bred and shown Cairns for about thirty-five years; breeder of Ch. Oudenarde Special Edition (B.O.B., Cruft's 1963); and owner of Ch. Oudenarde Midnight Chimes, another of the breed's famous sires; there are Oudenarde champions in America, Canada, Ceylon, South Africa, Sweden, Holland, France and Britain.

Dandie Dinmont Terrier – Miss Christine Dandison; breeder of Dandies since 1927; registered her prefix Shrimpney that year; championship show judge, including Cruft's; breeder of Ch. Shrimpney Sweet Pepper and American and Canadian Ch. Shrimpney Scarlet Star, and many others.

Fox Terrier, Smooth – Mr. John Lowe; breeder of a long line of champions from his Lanneau Kennel, many being exported to America; championship show judge, as also is Mrs. Lowe.

Fox Terrier, Wire – Dr. A. N. Krasilnikoff; son of Dr. A. Krasilnikoff, famous international judge and breeder; a Dane, he has judged the breed on the Continent and in Britain.

Irish Terrier – Miss Norah Woodifield; breeder and international show judge; owner of the Pathfinders Kennel; has handled over seventy champions in the breed, owning or breeding the most outstanding sires over twenty years, including Ch. Pathfinders Dragonfly and Int. Ch. Pathfinders Hopscotch.

Kerry Blue Terrier – Miss Phyllis Parry; breeder and owner of the Lisdhu affix; owned her first Kerry Blue in 1925; breeder of Ch. Lisdhu Caubeen and Ch. Lisdhu Gossoon.

Lakeland Terrier – Mr. L. Atkinson; breeder and owner of the Beldon Kennels; professional handler for twenty-five years; championship show judge.

Manchester Terrier – Miss Catherine Ince; keeps Manchesters as a personal interest; interested in breed history; owner of Ch. Eaglespur French Pippin, whose sire was the American import to Britain, Eaglespur Sir Oscar of Chatham Farms.

Norfolk Terrier, Norwich Terrier – Mrs. Marjorie Bunting; breeder and owner; championship show judge; owner of the Ragus affix; Int. Ch. Ragus Rain Maker (B.O.B., Cruft's twice, top stud dog U.S.A.) and Int. Ch. Ragus Goodfellow (also, previously, top stud dog U.S.A., averaging a champion per litter) writer and contributor *Dog World* (England).

Scottish Terrier – Mr. W. Max Singleton; breeder and exhibitor of Scottish Terriers since 1930; international show judge; owner of the Walsing affix; breeder of Int. Ch. Walsing Winning Trick and Walsing Warrant; President of the Scottish Terrier Club (England); life member Scottish Terrier Club of America and the Danish Terrier Club.

Sealyham Terrier – Miss A. G. Baylay; breeder and owner of the Shenden Kennel, a Sealyham kennel established by her mother over fifty years ago; international judge of a number of breeds; breeder of Ch. Shenden Probity (1964 and 1965) also active in Griffons.

Skye Terrier – Lady Marcia Miles; international judge and authority on the breed; brought up with Skye Terriers and a life-long breeder; owner of the Merrymount Kennel, which has housed a large number of champions, both prick and drop-eared; President of the Skye Terrier Club in Britain.

Soft-coated Wheaten Terrier – Mrs. Maureen Holmes; owner of the Holmenocks Kennel, Co. Kildare, Ireland; breeder of Ch. Holmenocks Handley (B.O.B., Cruft's, twice).

Staffordshire Bull Terrier – Mr. John F. Gordon; breeder and owner for over thirty years; Cruft's and international championship show judge; owner of the Bandits Kennel, mainly as a private interest; author of *Staffordshire Bull Terrier Handbook, The Staffordshire Bull Terrier,* and other books on Staffordshires and other breeds.

Staffordshire Terrier – Mr. Arthur F. Jones (See page 648).

Welsh Terrier – Mr. W. A. E. Egerton; owner and breeder; owner of the Cedewain Kennel in Wales; breeder of B.I.S. winners Ch. Cedewain Cymro and Ch. Cedewain Cynnes.

West Highland White Terrier – Mrs. D. M. Dennis; breeder, owner and championship show judge, including Cruft's; owner of the Branston affix; made her first Westie champion in 1947; breeder of Ch. Barrister of Branston (1950), a great sire of champions; author of *The West Highland White Terrier.*

Toy Dogs

Affenpinscher – Mr. Arthur F. Jones (See page 648).

Australian Silky Terrier – Mr. Roy B. Burnell (See page 648).

653

Bichon Frise – Mrs. Melvin (Marvel) Brown; owner of the Mel-Mar Kennel; breeder and exhibitor of Bichons since 1967; past President of the Mid-States Bichon Frise Club; currently corresponding secretary for the Bichon Frise Club of America; contributor to *Kennel Review* and *Popular Dog* magazines (America).

Cavalier King Charles Spaniel – Mrs. A. Hewitt Pitt; started breeding Cavaliers in 1924; owner of the Ttiweh affix, probably the most influential in the breed; daughter of Sir Everett Millais, pioneer of Basset Hounds in Britain; breeder or owner, among many others, of Ch. Harmony of Ttiweh and Ch. Daywell Roger.

Chihuahua – Mrs. Eileen Goodchild; owner, breeder and championship show judge; owner of the Talaloc affix; breeder of Ch. Lansdahlia Talaloc Twinkle (B.O.B., Cruft's 1966) and Jnt. Ch. Talaloc Tane-Atan; contributor *Dog World* (England); author British Chihuahua Club handbook.

Chinese Crested Dog – Mrs. M. Mooney; breeder of great experience, with successes in Italian Greyhounds and Chihuahuas; has done much to promote the Chinese Crested in Britain.

English Toy Terrier (Black and Tan) (Toy Manchester) – Mr. E. Speight; has spent a lifetime among dogs; owner and breeder; owner of the Whiterails affix; breeder of Ch. Black Magic of Whiterails (bitch, seventeen C.C.s, winner Cruft's C.C. three years running) and Ch. Falcon of Whiterails.

Griffon, Brabancon and Bruxellois – Mrs. Pamela Cross-Stern (See page 650).

Italian Greyhound – Mrs. Mollie Garrish; owner and breeder and international championship show judge of many breeds; owner of the Fleeting affix whose Italians head the list of winners in Britain almost every year; active also in Whippets.

Japanese (Japanese Spaniel) – Mr. Bryan Mitchell; though young in years has a deep knowledge of many of the Toy breeds, the theory and practice of breeding and an understanding of the value of pedigree, all of which have helped him to breed and own champions as a very young man.

King Charles Spaniel (English Toy Spaniel) – Mrs. M. E. Gristwood; owner of the St. Lucia prefix; well-known show judge; breeder and owner of many champions including Ch. Goldendays Gay Galliard of St. Lucia and Ch. Goldendays Penn Rose of St. Lucia.

Maltese – Miss Gilean White; an artist at presentation, Miss White has piloted many of her mother's and her own Vicbrita Maltese to high honors in Britain, including best in show, all breeds, at championship shows.

Mexican Hairless Dog – Mrs. Olga Frei-Denver; a trainer of animals before taking up breeding Chihuahuas, in which she bred champions; has great experience and understanding of canine psychology; owner of the Pequeno affix.

Miniature Pinscher – Mr. L. Hamilton Renwick (See page 652).

Papillon (and Phalene) – Mrs. E. Russell Roberts; specialized in Papillons in the early fifties when, with her husband, she started the Picaroon Kennel; championship show judge (including Cruft's); breeder of Ch. Picaroon Ambrose (1958); joint author of *The Papillon* and contributor to *Dog World* (England) and other publications.

Pekingese – Mr. R. William Taylor; breeder, exhibitor and international show judge; owner of the Elsdon affix and, with Nigel Aubrey-Jones, of the St. Aubrey affix; Mr. Taylor is Canadian and has made many champions in Canada, America and Britain.

Pomeranian – Miss Cynthia Harper; owner and breeder; owner of the Cynpegs Kennel; owner of Ch. Cynpegs Zardi of Zanow and breeder of Ch. Cynpegs Gentle Thoughts (B.I.S., Birmingham, England 1970).

Pug – Mrs. V. A. Graham; breeder and championship show judge; owner of the Edenderry affix, known to generations of Pug breeders; owner and breeder of many champions including Ch. Edenderry the O'Donovan; Mrs. Graham is Irish.

Yorkshire Terrier – Mrs. Edith Stirk; owner and breeder of champions under the Stirkean affix; long experience in the Yorkshire Terrier, and a source of great help to the novice.

Spitz or Nordic Dogs

Alaskan Malamute – Information provided by the Alaskan Malamute Club of America by courtesy of the Secretary, Mrs. Jane Fulton.

Basenji – Miss Veronica Tudor-Williams; few people can have gone to greater lengths to further the interest of their breed. Has twice traveled under rigorous conditions to the Congo and Southern Sudan in successful search of fresh blood for the Basenji breed in Britain; author of *The Basenji, the Barkless Dog*; kennel name "of the Congo"; imported and owned Fula of the Congo, a bitch who has had a profound influence on the breed, world-wide.

Chow Chow – Miss C. E. Collett; owner, breeder and international specialist judge; four years in the U.S.A., breeding, exhibiting and judging the breed; owner of the Barwick Kennel; breeder of Ch. Anthea of Barwick (B.O.B., Cruft's; and B.O.B., Chow Chow Club Jubilee Show, with C.C. each time) and Ch. Viking of Barwick; author of *The Chow Chow* (1953, revised 1959).

Elkhound (Norwegian Elkhound), Norwegian Buhund – Mrs. Kitty Heffer; owner, breeder and international judge; breeder of Friochan Rinta (top brood bitch U.S.A., thirteen champions to date) and Friochan Erla (both Buhunds); contributor *Dog World* (England) and *Our Dogs,* and author of *The Elkhound;* President of the British Elkhound Society and Vice President Norwegian Buhund Club (British).

Eskimo Dog, Greenland Husky, Icelandic Sheepdog – Mrs. Janet Edmonds; owner, breeder and exhibitor; owns the Highnoons Kennel of Alaskan Malamutes in Britain; free-lance writer on animal topics.

Finnish Spitz – Mrs. Griselda Price; three times winner of the award for the outstanding breeder of the year, her Cullabine Kennel has had a marked effect on the Finnish Spitz in Britain.

Siberian Husky – Mrs. Lorna Demidoff and Mrs. Margaret A. Koehler; Mrs. Koehler, with her husband Paul A. Koehler, has bred and exhibited Siberian Huskies since the mid-fifties; Board member Siberian Husky Club of America and Chairman of Standards Committee; columnist *Popular Dogs* and *American Kennel Gazette.* Mrs. Demidoff has bred, exhibited and trained Siberians since early thirties; drove top racing team for twenty-five years; one of the organizers of S.H.C.A., and officer and Board member ever since; A.K.C. judge all working breeds; author *How to Raise and Train a Siberian Husky;* owner of the Monadnock Kennel.

Jamthund – Mr. Bo Bengtson (See page 648).

Keeshond – Miss Osmonda M. Hastings; breeder of Keeshonden since before the War, her Evenlode Kennel has housed many champions and important winners; her Ch. Big Bang of Evenlode is a pillar of the Stud Book; international judge and authority on the breed.

Laiki – Mr. E. Pellikka (See page 651).

Lapphund – Mr. Bo Bengtson (See page 648).

Norrbottenspets – Mr. Bo Bengtson (See page 648).

Norwegian Buhund – Mrs. Kitty Heffer (See page 654).

Samoyed – Mr. Geoff W. Grounds; owner and breeder; owner of the Whitewisp affix; breeder of Ch. Whitewisp Sleigh Lad (B.O.B., Cruft's 1971); editor and part writer of *The Samoyed,* published by the Samoyed Association (England); researcher into breed history at Scott Polar Research Institute, Cambridge, England; Secretary Samoyed Breed Council; executive council Samoyed Association.

Vastgotaspets – Mr. Bo Bengtson (See page 648).

Glossary of Words and Terms

Affix: The kennel name of the breeder

Albino: A dog born without pigmentation

Almond eye: The tissue surrounding the eye is almond shaped

Anal Gland: Gland sited at the anus

Angulation: The angles formed where bones meet

Apple-headed: Pronouncedly domed skull

Apron: Frill of longer hair on chest and below neck

Babbler: Hound which gives voice when not on scent

Badger: Hair of mixed gray, brown and white coloring

Balanced: Symmetrically proportioned as a whole

Bandy: Bow-legged

Barrelled: Rounded rib section

Bat ears: Broad at base, rounded at top, erect and with opening in front, as in French Bulldog.

Bay: Voice of a hunting hound

Beaver: Mixture of brown and gray hair

Belton: Colored and white hairs intermingled, as in English Setter

Benched: A Bench is allotted to each dog at all large shows

Bent: Angled at a joint

Bite: Position of upper and lower teeth when mouth closed

Blaireau: Sable markings on Pyrenean Mountain Dogs

Blaze: A prominent white mark down the head of a dog with a colored head

Blood line: A pedigree showing consecutive generations of breeding to the same family

Bloom: The sheen on a coat in good condition

Blown: A coat which is molting or casting hair

Blue: Usually gray or blue gray coloring

Blue Merle: Silvery blue, splashed and dappled with black, seen in Collies, Shetland Sheepdogs and Cardigan Corgis, also with tan and white markings

Bobtail: Very short-docked tail. Name for Old English Sheepdog

Bolt: To drive an animal out of hiding

Bossy: Over-developed shoulder muscle

Breeching: Tan-colored hair on the outside of the thighs of a black-and-tan dog

Brindle: (a) Definite black stripes on a red or yellow background, as in the Great Dane (b) Black hair mixed with other colors, as in Cairns and Pekingese

Brisket: Part below chest and between forelegs

Broken Color: Whole color broken by white or other color

Broken-up face: Face showing correct stop, chiseling and in some cases wrinkle

Brood bitch: Bitch used for breeding

Brush: Tail well covered with hair; bushy

Burr: The irregular formation visible inside the ear

Butterfly nose: Dark nose spotted with flesh-color

Button ear: Ear with flap folding forwards covering orifice and tip pointing towards eye

Canker: Gross inflammation of the external ear due to infection

Cape: The hair behind the shoulders on the Schipperke

Cat foot: Short, round, compact, cat-like foot

Cheeky: Having thick, protruding, prominently rounded cheeks

China eye: Clear blue eye

Chops: The thick, pendulous upper lips or flews

Cloddy: Thickset, low and heavy

Cobby: Compact in body

Collar: Markings, usually white, around neck

Colors: The predominating hair color of a dog e.g. liver, brindle, white with black markings etc.

Conformation: The assembly of the parts of the body taken as a whole

Corky: Alert, lively and active

Couplings: That part of the body between the last rib and the croup

Coursing: A sport which pits, for example, the Greyhound or Whippet against the hare or other game

Cow hocks: Hocks turned inwards towards each other

Crank tail: Crooked tail

Crest: The arched portion of the upper neck

Crooked front: With the forelegs bent inwards or outwards

Crook tail: Crank tail: malformed tail

Cropped ears: Trimmed in puppyhood to stand erect, forbidden in some countries

Crossbred: Offspring of dam and sire of differing breeds

Croup: That part of the back lying above the hindlegs

Cryptorchid: An adult male with testicle(s) undescended into the scrotum

Cull: To weed out from litters the weak and undesirable puppies

Culotte: The longer hair on back of hindlegs

Cushion: The thick part of the upper lips

Cynologist: One who studies dogs

Dam: The female parent, bitch

Dappled: Mottled markings of different colors

Dew-claw: An extra rudimentary claw found on inside of lower portion of fore legs, sometimes on hindlegs

Dewlap: Loose, pendulous skin under the throat

Dished: Concavity of line of head, dish-shaped as in the Pointer

Distemper teeth: Teeth discolored or pitted by distemper

Dock: To remove at puppyhood part of the tail – only in some breeds; colloquial name for the tail

Dome: Convexity of skull

Dominant: A marked parental characteristic transmitted to a hybrid descendant

Down-faced: Nasal bone sloping downwards to the nostrils

Drench: Liquid dose given by mouth

Drop-ear: Ears hanging flat and close to cheeks

Dual-purpose: Equally suited for working or showing

Dudley nose: Brown or flesh-colored nose

Elbow: Joint at top of foreleg above forearm

Fall: Fringe of long hair on top of head overhanging the face

Fancier: One especially interested in dogs

Feather: The long fringe of hair on ears, legs and tail of some breeds

Fiddle front: Forelegs out at elbows, in at pasterns and with feet turned outwards

Field: The terrain of working trials, hunting (as opposed to showing)

Field trial: A competition for sporting dogs

Filled up face: Having the bone of the foreface close to the surface, giving a smooth contour to the profile

Flag: The long tail of Setters

Flat sided: Insufficiently rounded ribs, chest too narrow

Flecked: Coat lightly ticked with other colors and not spotted or roan

Flews: Pendulous inner corners of upper lips

Flying ears: Unsettled ears, not assuming correct position

Foreface: That part of the face between the eyes and the nose

Foxy: Head or expression like a fox, pointed, sharp and alert

Frill: An apron of fine hair projecting from the throat and chest

Furnihings: The desirable hair, featherings and whiskers of a dog

Gaily: Tails that wave as a flag does, as hounds when trotting

Gait: Manner of walking, or running

Gassy: Full of aggressive spirit

Gay tail: A tail carried too far over the back

Grizzle: Iron or bluish gray color; black and white hairs mixed

Gundog: Accompanies the sportsman who shoots game e.g. Pointer, Setter, Retriever or Spaniel

Handler: One who handles dogs at field trials or shows

Hare foot: An elongated oval foot

Harlequin: A white dog with usually black or blue irregular markings

Haunch: Buttock or rump

Haw: An inner eyelid or membrane at inside corner.

Heat: Oestrum or season

Heeler: A cattle herding dog; from their method of snapping at the heels of cattle

Height: Perpendicular measurements from withers to ground

Hock: Joint between rear pastern and upper part of hindlegs

Hound: A hunting dog; a group term recognized by most authorities

Hound coloration: Tricolor or tan-and-white, lemon-and-white, blue mottle, pieds and occasionally liver-and-white

In-breeding: Breeding from closely related dogs

Isabella: A light straw or fawn color

Jabot: Longer hair between the front legs of a Schipperke

Keel: The sternum

Kennel: Outdoor accommodation for a dog; or a pack of dogs or hounds. The establishment of a breeder

Kink tail: Sharply bent tail

Layback: (a) Angle of shoulder blade to the vertical (b) Receding nose of a Bulldog

Leathers: The loose part of the ears hanging from the set-on

Leggy: Too high in the leg

Level bite: Teeth meeting evenly, edge to edge

Liam: Leash

Lippy: Excessively pendulous lips which do not meet

Litter: A family of puppies born at one whelping

Liver: Deep reddish-brown color

Lobular: Applying to the ears

Loin: Part of the vertebral column between the last ribs and the hindquarters

Lumber: Heavy and clumsy build

Mane: Long hair growing from top and sides of neck

Mantle: The darker portion of the coat on shoulders, back and sides

Mask: Shading of darker color on foreface

Master: Leader or controller of a hunt

Molera: The "hole" or soft spot in the top-skull of a Chihuahua

Mongrel: Dog with parents of mixed breed

Molting: The seasonal casting of the outer coat

Music: The baying of hounds

Mute: Without baying or barking

Muzzle: The head in front of the eyes, from eyes to nose

Non-slip A Spaniel or Retriever so trained as to be capable of working loose, not kept on a lead

Nose: The power in a dog to scent out game

Occiput: The back point of the skull

Orange: Color of an orange or light tan, used of coat color in some breeds

Ottertail: Thick, tapering tail, hair very thick and short

Out at elbows: Elbows turning out from body

Out at shoulders: Jutting out shoulder blades loosely attached to body

Out of coat: Lacking quantity of coat, coat out of condition during molt.

Over-shot jaw: Upper front teeth projecting beyond lower

Pack: A group of hounds bred for and used in hunting

Pads: Soles of the feet

Particolors: Two clear and distinct colors

Pastern: Lowest part of leg, below knee or hock

Peak: Occiput (q.v.)

Pedigree: The ancestry of a dog

Pencilling: Dark lines divided by strips of tan on feet of Manchester Terrier

Pied: Unequally proportioned patches of white and one other color

Pig-jaw: Overshot jaw (q.v.)

Pigment: Coloration of nose, lips and eye rims

Plait: Manner of walking or running, in which the legs cross

Pointer: A gundog which indicates the position of the bird by rigidly pointing with his whole body, nose extended

Points: Color on ears, face, legs and tail

Plume: Long hair on the tail

Prepotent: Influential in breed development, used of both dog and bitch

Prick ears: Ears that stand up naturally

Proud: Held high

Puppy: A dog less than one year old

Pure-bred: Having all ancestors of the same breed

Quarantine: Period of isolation of a dog before entry into a country, to ensure freedom from infectious diseases

Racy: Slightly built but long legged

Rat tail: Thick-rooted tail covered with curly hair except at the tip which is bare or sparsely covered

Recessive: (Hereditary) opposite of dominant. Heritable factor passed on to progeny, but which may not show in the offspring

Recognition: Acceptance of a breed on the register of a national or regional canine authority

Registration: Names and pedigrees registered at national or regional canine authority

Reserve: Dog placed fourth in a show class, or field trial or in second place to a winner where only one award is made

Retinal atrophy: A disease of the eyes

Retriever: Dog bred to retrieve game from where it falls when shot

Ribbed-up: Ribs carried well to the rear, compact and tightly knit together

Ring: Show ring; the arena where dogs are presented for judging at a dog show

Ring tail: Tail which curves in a circle

Roach back: Rising over the loin and curving down to the tail

Roan: A mixture of white and any other colored hairs

Roman nose: High-bridged nose, slightly convex

Rose-shaped ears: Ears which are small, thin and folded inwards at the back

Ruby: Color of the gem-stone, as in King Charles Spaniel

Ruff: Larger hair round the neck

Runner: (a) Participant in a race or field trial (b) A bird wounded in the wing and unable to fly but still able to run

Sable: Intermingling of black hairs in a coat of lighter basic color

Saddle: (a) Saddle-shaped black marking on the back (b) Region of the back of an Afghan Hound where only short hair grows

Scent: Odor left by an animal on the trail

Scheduled: Listed in the program of a dog show

Scissor bite: Top teeth just overlapping the lower

Screw tail: A short malformed tail

Season: Oestrum, period or heat

Second thighs: Portion of hindleg between stifle and hock

Self-colored: All one color (also whole-colored or solid)

Septum: Nose bone between nostrils

Service: Copulation by a dog

Set-on: Point of joining on to head or body of ears or tail

Setter: A breed which indicates the location of the quarry by pointing in line with it

Shelly: A weakly formed, narrow body, lacking substance

Short-coupled: Short distance between ribs and hips

Shoulders: Scapula; top part of forelegs adjoining the body

Sickle: (a) The form of tail-carriage of some breeds, over the back but not tightly curled (b) Hocks which cause hind feet to be placed under the body

Sire: Male parent

Snip(e)y: Weak, pointed muzzle

Soft mouth: A gundog which retrieves without damage to the quarry

Solid: All one color (also self-colored or whole-colored)

Spaniel: All purpose medium-sized gundog which hunts game and retrieves it when shot

Spayed: Surgically sterilized bitch

Spitz: Group of Northern dogs characterized by prick ears, stand-off hair and tail curled over back

Spot: Spot of colored hair on top skull surrounded by white blaze, in Spaniels

Spring of ribs: Curvature of rib cage

Standard: The specification of a breed laid down by national or regional canine authority. The standard by which dogs are judged in the show-ring

Staring: Coat dry and lacking sheen; out of condition

Sternum: Breast bone; the structure to which the ribs are joined at their extremities

Stifle: Knee joint between thighs and second thigh on hindlegs

Stop: Step between nose and skull

Stripping: Thinning out the coat of some breeds, using a special comb

Stud: A male dog used for breeding

Stud book: Record of breeding

Substance: Thickness and weight of bone and body

Swayback: Concavity of line between hips and withers

Terrier: A dog bred to follow vermin into the earth (terre)

Thumb-marks: Black marks on the pastern area

Thriftyness: Making good use of the food provided, a "good-doer"

Throaty: Excessive loose skin at the throat

Ticking: Small areas of color or black on a basically white coat

Timber: Leg bone

Tongue: Voice of a hound on the scent

Topline: The line along the dog's back and loin in profile

Toy dog: Very small-sized dog; a group term recognized by most authorities

Top-knot: Long hair on the top of the head

Trace: Dark mark down the back of a Pug

Tricolor: Used of a breed whose Standard allows three distinct colors in its coat, usually black, tan and white

Tucked up: Light of loin

Tulip ear: Erect open ear, tulip shaped

Type: Essential characteristics distinguishing a breed

Undercoat: The soft, wooly hair lying below the hair of double-coated breeds

Undershot jaw: The lower jaw protruding further than the upper

Unthriftyness: Making poor use of food provided, a "bad-doer"

Utility: Useful or decorative dogs; group term used by most authorities to describe companion dogs which do not fit readily into the other groups

Varminty: Keen, bright and piercing in expression

Venerie: Hunting and field craft in all its forms

Vent: Opening at the anus

Vermin: Objectionable animals, those which prey on game e.g. rats

Weaving: Crossing the forefeet or hindfeet when in motion

Weedy: Too lightly boned

Wheaten: Fawn or pale yellow color

Wheel-backed: Roached; markedly arched over the loin

Whip tail: One carried out straight and stiffly pointed

Wire-haired: Harsh, crisp, wiry coat

Wrinkle: Loosely folded skin on sides of face or forehead

Working: A group term used by authorities to describe such breeds as Sheepdogs, Boxers and Dobermanns

Index

This index does not contain references to breeds made within the relevant breed articles, and neither does it include the names of breeders, owners or individual dogs mentioned in the captions, since these references are only relevant within the context of the article.

A

B

C

D

E

F

G

H

N

O

P

Q

R

T